Praise for ALICE ADAMS

A *New York Times Book Review* Editors' Choice

"Carol Sklenicka is a lucid, scrupulous writer . . . [who] is prudent and appreciative in her assessment of Adams's work."
—*The New York Times Book Review*

"If you're the sort who delights in the account of the midcentury artistic life . . . *Portrait of a Writer* does deliver."
—Rumaan Alam, *The New Republic*

"In her empathetic, revealing, and brisk new biography, Carol Sklenicka frames Adams's life and work within themes of escape, redemption, and persistence. . . . [She] deftly deploys quoted bits to illustrate how the life and work are so intricately intertwined. The art of literary biography—Sklenicka previously explored Raymond Carver—thus resembles an enormous, three-dimensional jigsaw puzzle. . . . Sklenicka's portrait may well encourage new readers and justifiably revive [Adams's] reputation."
—*Minneapolis Star Tribune*

"Drawing on extensive original sources, Carol Sklenicka gives us the first full-length popular biography of brilliant novelist and short-story writer Alice Adams. For decades, Adams rendered believably three-dimensional female characters in beautiful, cut-glass prose in venues like *The New Yorker*."
—*The Christian Science Monitor*,
Best Books of December

"*Alice Adams* is a perceptive, elegantly written biography that will broaden her renown and readership."
—*San Francisco Chronicle*

"Sklenicka is clearly a skilled biographer. Her writing is engaging yet simple and lacks the pretense and gentility Adams seemingly would have hated. No detail, story, or analysis feels unnecessary, an accomplishment for a work totaling more than five hundred pages."
—*Chicago Review of Books*

"Sklenicka celebrates Adams's work and persuasively situates it in an era characterized both by drastic cultural changes and by the persistence of old expectations, conventions, and biases."

—*The New Yorker*

"Those who love the novels and short stories, which trace women's lives beginning in 1930s America as they celebrate, grieve, and grow with the century, will be startled and delighted to see where the life and the fiction converge. [This] biography often reads like an Adams novel blessedly slowed down to allow the reader to soak for a moment in the atmospheres of a Chapel Hill childhood, Radcliffe College, Paris, and 1960s San Francisco."

—*Booklist*

"Pervasive, deep research informs this inspiring story of a writer who demonstrably earned such a sturdy, illuminating biography."

—*Kirkus Reviews* (starred review)

"After a long apprenticeship, hampered by supporting her husband's own writing career before their 1958 divorce, Adams found an audience in the 1970s that was newly avid for her core concern: female-centric depictions of love and sex. . . . Sklenicka's well-researched biography . . . easily evokes the spirit of Adams's life, times, and works."

—*Publishers Weekly*

ALSO BY CAROL SKLENICKA

Raymond Carver: A Writer's Life

D. H. Lawrence and the Child

ALICE ADAMS

Portrait of a Writer

————————

Carol Sklenicka

SCRIBNER

New York London Toronto Sydney New Delhi

Scribner
An Imprint of Simon & Schuster, Inc.
1230 Avenue of the Americas
New York, NY 10020

First Scribner trade paperback edition December 2020

SCRIBNER and design are registered trademarks of The Gale Group, Inc.,
used under license by Simon & Schuster, Inc., the publisher of this work.

For information about special discounts for bulk purchases,
please contact Simon & Schuster Special Sales at 1-866-506-1949
or business@simonandschuster.com.

The Simon & Schuster Speakers Bureau can bring authors to
your live event. For more information or to book an event
contact the Simon & Schuster Speakers Bureau at 1-866-248-3049
or visit our website at www.simonspeakers.com.

Interior design by Kyle Kabel

Manufactured in the United States of America

1   3   5   7   9   10   8   6   4   2

Library of Congress Control Number: 2019024836

ISBN 978-1-4516-2131-0
ISBN 978-1-4516-2133-4 (pbk)
ISBN 978-1-4516-2134-1 (ebook)

For my family, with love

Lisen Caroline Ma
Kai-Ling Eric Ma
Robert Lewellin Ryan
Katherine Snoda Ryan
Hongshen Ma
Richard Matthew Ryan

A GRATITUDE

Oh, grateful heart,
this is the treasure:
to wander starry-eyed
in a world without measure.

—R. M. Ryan

Contents

Prologue

In the United States in 1950, many people felt there was something presumptuous about women who wanted more than twenty-three-year-old Alice Adams already had. She was a beautiful, dark-haired, long-legged woman with an hourglass figure, a Radcliffe graduate married to a World War II veteran with a Harvard degree. They lived in California, where Alice worked a clerical job to pay the bills while her husband finished graduate school. They'd both intended to be writers until he found his calling as a literature teacher. Alice still wrote. But she was bitterly unhappy, unfaithful to her husband, estranged from her parents. She developed chronic digestive problems—"much vomiting . . . obviously psychosomatic," she said.[1] Her psychiatrist advised her to "Stay married and stop writing."[2]

Alice took half of the doctor's advice. She stayed married to Mark Linenthal—but she kept writing. Then she got pregnant—and she kept writing. A couple months before the birth of her son, hoping that she'd soon have everything she needed to feel happy, Alice submitted the manuscript of a novel to a New York editor she'd met through her famous friend Norman Mailer. She and Mark moved to a three-bedroom house in Menlo Park with a study for Mark and a room they painted lemon yellow for the baby. Alice liked the pleasant neighborhood with live oaks and flowering acacias, the huge kitchen, and the nook with a washing machine. "I could happily stay here for years," she believed.

A rejection of the novel arrived before the baby.

Alice continued to think of herself as a writer, but her writing became haphazard. Most of the pages she wrote in her notebook during this period are gone, roughly torn out, destroyed.

By the spring of 1958 Alice Adams's inner life was again a turmoil of hopes and memories and confusions. Her mother, with whom she had a frustratingly distant relationship, had died and her father had remarried. She felt profoundly alone. On a cold, windy spring day, in a dressing room at Joseph Magnin's department store, she decided to buy some very short white shorts and a full-skirted, bare-shouldered dress with large pink polka dots—summer clothes that were useless in chilly San Francisco.

This time, instead of heeding the psychiatrist's advice, Alice took Peter and left California for the house where she'd grown up in Chapel Hill, North Carolina. She planned to write another novel there, believing that doing so would bring her the money and courage she needed to divorce Mark. She'd avoided that house since before her mother's death, so this was an odd choice, but her motivations were deeper than common sense. She knew her father and his wife would be departing for Maine. Her new clothes made her dream of the smell of jasmine, and the swimming hole in her father's backyard, "of sunshine and warmth. Of not being with my husband. Of, maybe, going to some Southern beach. Of possibly meeting someone. Falling in love."[3]

When he picked up Alice and Peter from the airport, Nic Adams jokingly offered his daughter and grandson slugs of bourbon from a silver flask and talked so rapidly with his pipe in his mouth that Alice couldn't understand a word. The apartment she was borrowing for the summer, a wing of her childhood home, was a shambles—"holes in the walls, pieces of floorboard missing." The first evenings with Nic and his wife, Dotsie, were "alcoholic, boring, quarrelsome." Already the trip felt like a huge mistake.

Yet in every room "stood bowls of the most beautiful, fragrant roses," a welcoming gift for Alice from her father's neighbor, Lucie Jessner. After Nic and Dotsie drove off toward Maine, Lucie introduced Alice to her friend Max Steele. Max was a writer—published and award-winning, though currently at loose ends—with "pale, wide, wise blue eyes, a high forehead, high cheekbones, and a small witty mouth—about to laugh."[4] He invited Alice to a party: "I wore my polka-dotted dress, and we danced a lot in a mildly outrageous way, very sexy and close but at the same time laughing at ourselves."[5]

Alice felt young and desired again. With Max around, she "glided through the summer, happily sure that things would work out." She revised a short story about a love affair she'd had in Europe after the war—a subtle admission that her marriage was doomed even then—and submitted it to a magazine for women with jobs called *Charm*.

The summer of 1958 became the endless summer of Alice Adams's life, the interlude that changed her forever. She and Max avoided declaring love for each other, knowing that writers "can talk a perfectly good love affair to shreds and tatters."[6] Alice's paradoxical and complicated needs were all met in those brief weeks when she had a lover who admired her and encouraged her to write, a mother-figure who praised her ambitions and desire for happiness, and a respite from a marriage she regretted. This uncanny convergence of relationships allowed her to recover her passion for writing. By reoccupying her childhood home, she allowed herself to imagine a new future.

A week after Alice and Max parted with vague plans to meet in Mexico the following winter, *Charm* purchased "Winter Rain." The magazine paid her a then-respectable $350 for that story, enough to allow her to hope that she would easily sell everything she wrote. She made up her mind to divorce her husband.

It would take more than the sale of one story for Alice to get what she needed. Like most women who divorced in the 1950s, she risked poverty; by not staying in the marriage for her child's sake, she also risked being seen as a loose, oversexed woman and a bad mother. Nor was Alice really foolish enough to believe that all her work would sell. She understood that an attractive woman might not be taken seriously in the male-dominated publishing world.

Adams explained what happened that summer in an image: One night while she and Max were walking in Chapel Hill, "a pair of twin black cats came toward us out of the darkness, the country night—two cats thin and sleek and moving as one, long legs interwoven with each other, sometimes almost tripping. At that we laughed and stopped walking and laughed and laughed, both wondering (I suppose) if that was how we looked, although we were so upright. Then we walked on, hurrying, like people with a destination. . . ."[7] The way Alice Adams understood those two black cats in the hot Carolina night as a picture of herself and a man tells us something about the way she saw her destination—the delights and difficulties it entailed.

"I can't imagine anyone without a very intense inner life . . . full of memories and strange confusions," Adams said after she'd published half a dozen books. "I was never interested in relationships that weren't complicated. I never had a simple relationship in my life. I even have a very complicated relationship with my cat."[8]

She admired the dense novels of Henry James, especially *The Portrait of a Lady* with its young American heroine named Isabel Archer who wants to choose her own destiny. But James's treacherous prose and archaic vocabulary would not serve to describe Adams's characters with their modern ambitions and language. Adams wanted to write beautifully and clearly about the heart's entanglements.

To do that she filled her characters' minds with questions, parenthetical thoughts, and feelings that connect with her readers' own complex lives. She interrupts her narratives with wise observations like this one from her most celebrated story, "Roses, Rhododendron": "Perhaps too little attention is paid to the necessary preconditions of 'falling in love'—I mean the state of mind or place that precedes one's first sight of the loved person (or house or land). In my own case, I remember the dark Boston afternoons as a precondition of love. Later on, for another important time, I recognized boredom in a job. And once the fear of growing old." Or she jumps about in time and among characters to reveal the workings of desire in two people: Here are Tom (married to Jessica) and Babs, who will marry each other many years later: "But they are not, that night, lying hotly together on the cold beach, furiously kissing, wildly touching everywhere. That happens only in Tom's mind as he lies next to Jessica and hears her soft sad snores. In her cot, in the tent, Babs sleeps very soundly, as she always does, and she dreams of the first boy she ever kissed, whose name was not Tom."[9]

Adams's subject, which appeared in hundreds of guises, was love—or, more accurately, the value women assign to love and what happens to them as a result. Her characters' journeys through contemporary life are strenuously sexual and emotional, and yet always mediated by intelligent thought as she uses her lyrical, astute prose to tell her stories of women and men living on the edge of their emotions, embracing the complications of their modern lives.

It's no accident that Alice Adams's notebook from the 1990s holds a list of thirty-four men who'd been her lovers followed by a list of thirty-nine magazines that published 115 of her stories and essays. She lived for love and for stories. Her courage and vulnerability, tenderness and tenacity allowed her to break the strictures of her upbringing and transform her intense emotional sensibility into enduring fiction that illuminates women's lives in the twentieth century.

PART I

ORIGINS

CHAPTER ONE

Saved by Her Dolls

*If writers can go to hell and come back, it's because part of them
does not go. Is watching.*

—Alice Adams, notebook,
November 9, 1959

The only daughter of parents who sometimes found her a puzzling
intrusion in their busy adult lives, Alice Adams entertained herself
by making up stories about her dolls. Adams treated her dolls as if they
were characters in a novel. She "deduced and accepted their own intrinsic
natures," she said of her favorites. She "could see that some dolls were
older and wiser than others were, that certain dolls were simply vain and
silly, that others were friendly and kind, that still others would (probably) laugh and have fun." She much disliked dolls "that came already
equipped with names and ready-made stories," like Raggedy Ann and
Shirley Temple. When Alice used a curling iron on the luxuriant red
hair of a "sweet-faced" favorite named Madeline, the doll suffered an
"unhealable blister" on her pink plaster cheek and was left with scraps
of hair too damaged to style. "Shabby, pantalooned and nearly bald,"
Madeline remained Alice's favorite.[1]

On long drives from North Carolina to Sebago Lake, Maine, where
the Adamses spent summer vacations, Alice arranged the dolls she had
chosen for the trip on the backseat of the family Chevy while she
crouched on the floor to attend to them. When the car slid off a slick,
poorly banked curve of the DuPont Highway into a ditch, Alice was
"said to have been saved by the dolls."[2]

Alice was four, already practicing the art that would supply her
vocation as a woman, when the car went into that ditch. The child
who was saved by her dolls became a celebrated short-story artist and

novelist. Her work, her editor Victoria Wilson said seven decades after the accident, was about "the long pull towards clarity of desire and the ways in which people discover (or keep themselves from discovering) what they really want, can have, can become."[3] The people in her fiction grew from Adams's own desire for clarity. She made up stories "to make sense of what seemed and sounded senseless, all around us."[4]

Alice made "friends and familiars" of her dolls in a house and family where she seldom felt at home. Born August 14, 1926, she was the first child of Agatha Erskine Boyd Adams and Nicholson Barney Adams. Her parents, whose weighty names, of which more later, indicated pride in lineage and expectations about the future, were Virginians by birth. They'd both lived in New York City and studied at Columbia University, where Nicholson—Nic—received his doctorate in Spanish literature. When Alice was born they were newly settled in an old farmhouse overlooking woods at the southern edge of Chapel Hill, North Carolina. As an assistant professor at the University of North Carolina, twenty-nine-year-old Nic Adams was entering the town's elite. Agatha, with a master's degree in Spanish, was not only a faculty wife but her husband's partner in academic projects. She also had writerly ambitions of her own.

With such literary parents and a charming rural seat, Alice Adams might have enjoyed a happy and uneventful childhood, reminiscent of those in the English girls' novels she loved to read. But such was not the case. Loneliness pervades her descriptions of life within that old farmhouse and within her psyche. Of an early picture, Alice wrote that she and her parents "look rather frightened of each other, and with good reason, as things turned out."[5]

Alice's parents' legend—"I was said to have been saved by the dolls"— became the true and subversive metaphor of her life. The authorial voice in Adams's fiction first emerged during her reign over her dolls. "If writers can go to hell and come back, it's because part of them does not go. Is watching," she speculated in a notebook.[6] Watching and writing saved her, over and over, first from her parents, then from the thrills and treacheries of her own romantic adventures and the entanglements that ensued.

Alice's loneliness began in infancy. Thirty-three-year-old Agatha gave birth to her daughter by cesarean section, on a Saturday, at Mary Washington Hospital in Fredericksburg, Virginia, near her husband's family home. The hospital birth may have been routine for Agatha's age—by the day's standards, she was old to be a first-time mother—but later medical records for Agatha mention her "contracted pelvis," so it's likely that a traumatic labor was followed by a long recovery from surgery.[7] To help, both Agatha's mother and her brother Thomas Munford (Munny) Boyd, blinded by scarlet fever as a child, stayed in Fredericksburg for a month after Alice's birth.[8]

In her notebook sixty-one years later during a time she was seeing a psychoanalyst, Alice wrote: "10-20-87: Tears: Not for now but for a hungry baby, in 1926, cold, afraid, who counted on her father to feed her."

That complicated trace of memory is a painful picture of oneself to carry through adulthood: Why cold? Why afraid? Was Alice a welcomed or an (unspeakably) unwanted child? We don't know why Agatha did not breastfeed her firstborn or whether her father managed to be a good substitute. Alice's lifelong friend Judith Clark Adams (her married name, no relation) speculated, "I don't think that Nic and Agatha adored Alice. They were older and didn't know what in the world to do with this baby."

The name Nic and Agatha Adams chose for their daughter, Alice Boyd Adams, curiously combined the first name of a deaf, old cousin with the tradition of bringing forward the mother's maiden name as a middle name. But the resulting "Alice Adams" seems to borrow from Booth Tarkington's novel *Alice Adams*, winner of the Pulitzer Prize in 1922.* Thus her name offers a microcosm of the complex jostling of tradition and modernity that marked Alice's entire life and career, a jostling that was well under way before she was born.

Both Nic Adams and Agatha Boyd were white Anglo-Saxon Protestants and well-educated Southerners. Their ancestors on both sides came to North America from the British Isles, but differences of background set them apart to the extent that Adams portrays her mother as "an Episcopalian who secretly believes that she has married beneath her."[9] Indeed, Agatha Boyd's ancestors had been in Virginia longer than Nic's, for at least eleven generations: a William Taylor who came to America in 1638 changed his name and founded the wealthy, politically

---

* Tarkington was both prolific and admired, and the Alice Adams in his novel is a strong, smart, poor Midwestern girl who bravely enrolls in secretarial school after losing her bid to marry a rich society man. If Alice's parents thought the book would be forgotten, they were wrong, because Katharine Hepburn made *Alice Adams* even more famous in George Stevens's 1935 movie. What fun it surely was for Alice to see her name on movie marquees during the summer of her ninth birthday.

influential Tayloe line, to which Agatha was connected through her
own mother, whose maiden name was Emma Tayloe Munford. John
Tayloe II, a fourth-generation tobacco planter, began building Mount
Airy plantation house near the Rappahannock River in the Northern
Neck of Virginia in 1758. With twenty thousand acres and more than
five hundred slaves (during the revolutionary era he was the third-largest
slaveholder in the South), Tayloe built a business empire in Maryland
and Virginia.* He protected himself from fluctuations in the tobacco
market by building ironworks, then cut forests to make the charcoal
needed to operate his smelters. He built ships and annually sent fourteen
shiploads of tobacco and iron to England, using the iron as ballast for
vessels loaded with tobacco. In 1769, when his daughter Rebecca married
Francis Lightfoot Lee, later a signer of the Declaration of Independence,
he built the couple the mansion called Menokin, which, like Mount
Airy, still stands near Warsaw, Virginia.

In the next century, Eton- and Oxford-educated John Tayloe III
saw opportunity in the District of Columbia, then a wooded tract
with just a handful of houses. He expanded the Tayloe enterprises with
postal services and inns along the route to the new capital and purchased lots in the most promising neighborhoods. At the urging of his
friend President George Washington, Tayloe built his Octagon House
on Lafayette Square; President James and Mrs. Dolly Madison made
Octagon House their official residence after British forces burned the
White House in 1814.[10]

When forests were depleted in Virginia, Tayloe III founded new
ironworks all over the South and established cotton plantations in the
Deep South, keeping one thousand slaves, many of whom became
skilled workers. One of his six sons, Harvard-graduate Benjamin Ogle
Tayloe, was one of the few slaveholders on record to condemn the rape
of female slaves by male slaveowners. Through Benjamin, the Tayloes
exerted a defining influence on Whig politics. With stunning hypoc-
risy, Benjamin opposed abolition and received his income from slave-
operated plantations in Alabama after the secession of the Confederate
states, all the while residing directly across from the White House and

---

* The Tayloes were an elite minority. The US Census of 1860 reported that 104 Virginians owned as many as a hundred slaves each, while half of the state's fifty-two thousand
slaveholders owned fewer than four slaves.

hosting American and European political and cultural figures.[11] During the winter of 1861–62, visiting English novelist Anthony Trollope, whose novels would become favorites and models for Alice Adams, spent much of his leisure time at the Tayloe house. Despite his own antislavery views, Trollope felt "more at home" in the genial Tayloe household than at any other place in the muddy, melancholy, corrupt, and war-straitened capital.[12] In his book *North America*, Trollope explained his moral compromise: Southerners had "much to endure on account of that slavery from which it was all but impossible that they should disentangle themselves." Their great sorrow, he said, was "the necessary result of their position."[13]

Alice Adams's direct ancestor was George Plater Tayloe (1804–97), who graduated from Princeton and took over the family ironworks in central Virginia. In 1833, he built his Buena Vista Mansion near the railroad hub of Big Lick in the Blue Ridge Mountains (now Roanoke) and helped found St. John's Episcopal Church and a seminary there. As a representative to the Virginia General Assembly, he was "a strong Union man who voted against secession." But when the secession resolution passed, he hung a copy of it on his wall. Like other slaveholders who opposed secession, he reasoned, as Benjamin Ogle wrote, that dissolving the Union "would touch the pocket book too acutely," and that New York abolitionists posed less threat to the Union than did South Carolina, which was "proud & poor—having been rich."[14] William Henry worried with arrogant, deeply racist sentimentality, "What will become of the Human Beings under us? Owned by us. Humanity demands their care. I have done my duty as Man sees, but not in the eyes of God."[15]

The end of the Civil War marked the end of wealth for many of the Tayloes and their class. No longer a slaveowner, George Plater Tayloe sold his ironworks but retained some property in Roanoke; William Henry, who valued his former slaves at $250,000, hoped to get these freedmen and freedwomen—"poor deluded creatures, I feel sorry for them"—to continue working his lands. At sixty-six, this man who had overseen and profited from the brutal enslavement of hundreds of people felt himself to be "whipped and ruined." He consoled himself by insisting that he had promoted "cleanliness, domestic comforts and religious tendencies on his plantations."

From these new-world aristocratic forebears, Agatha inherited a baroque silver teapot and some antique furniture but little money. Nonetheless, a sinister heritage of pride, gentility, and guilt affected

descendants of the wealthy Southern gentry who owned larger plantations worked by black slaves. Robert Hughes, touring Mount Airy in
the PBS program *American Visions*, summarized the cultural and moral
contradictions of those who built the Southern dynasties as a "defiant
illusory desire . . . to imagine themselves as a full extension of English
culture" whose "genteel surface of hierarchy was stretched over a fabric
of brutality supported by slave labor." Such was the monstrous history
that shadowed people like Alice Adams's mother.

Born in Roanoke in 1893, less than three decades after the Confederate surrender at Appomattox, Agatha Erskine Boyd disapproved of
Southern women who "scramble about frantically in the moldering leaf-
age of family trees" but was not immune to family pride.[16] Her mother,
the Tayloe descendant, was daughter to Brigadier General Thomas T.
Munford, who, after notable service in the Confederate Army, lived on
until 1918 as a grand commander of the Grand Camp of Confederate
Veterans and operator of ironworks in Lynchburg, Virginia.[17]

Agatha's father's antecedents engaged in a more typical moral and
economic struggle.* Her grandfather William Watson Boyd, an Episcopal clergyman and a representative to the February 1861 Virginia
Convention, which sought peace with the Union, received a postwar
pardon from US president Andrew Johnson, along with exemption
from the rule that would have stripped him of property valued at more
than $20,000. Her father, James William Boyd, became an ordained
Episcopal deacon in midlife, after a first career as a lawyer, but never
became a priest or took his own parish because his "health broke" in
1905, when Agatha was barely twelve. He died nine years later, likely
of a heart condition, at age fifty-six.

Agatha completed her degree at Randolph-Macon Woman's College
in Lynchburg, Virginia, the first college in the South to offer a four-

---

* A portrait of Agatha's great grandmother, Margaret Erskine, hung above the fireplace
in Chapel Hill and later in Alice's own homes. While migrating to Kentucky in 1779,
Margaret had been captured by Shawnees who killed her baby and her first husband.
Ransomed a few years later, she returned to Virginia and married Henry Erskine. Alice
preferred a subversive version of the episode: she told people that the woman in the
portrait refused rescue by whites and lived out her "scandalously happy life" with the
Indians. (Virgil Anson Lewis, *History of West Virginia* vol. 2 [Philadelphia: Hubbard
Brothers, 1889], 600; Ruthe Stein, "A Southern Belle Who Grew Up Smart," *San Francisco Chronicle*, February 12, 1975.)

year college education for women. "We were soundly taught and the curriculum carried no hint that we were young women and not young men," remembered Pearl Sydenstricker, who was in the class ahead of Agatha's and became Pearl Buck, the Nobel Prize–winning author of *The Good Earth*. Even though "no girl thought it possible that she might not marry" and students repeatedly petitioned for courses in home economics, the faculty maintained that "any educated woman can read a cookbook or follow a dress pattern. It is the brain that needs education and can teach the hands."[18]

Like her classmates, Agatha wore "flouncy frocks over boned corsets, and bouffant hairstyles bulked out with artificial curls and pads," and submitted to a strict daily regimen of study and worship. Gentlemen approved by the college could visit on two Saturday evenings each month. Still, college was liberating for Agatha. She "made the acquaintance of Horace as a living personality, a wit, a gentleman, and a poet" and chose Latin as her major. As a sophomore, she published an uncanny and naturalistic short story, "The Haunted Deacon," in the campus annual, *Helianthus*. She joined Am Sam, the college's oldest, most prestigious secret honor society (Sydenstricker was also a member) and the Zeta Tau Alpha sorority.[19]

At meetings of the Current Events Club, Randolph-Macon women heard speakers for women's suffrage who stirred their ambitions and planted doubts about the patriarchal hierarchy that shaped their lives. One of Alice Adams's finest stories includes this yearning thought attributed to her barely fictionalized mother: "those distant happy years, among friends. Her successes of that time. The two years when she directed the Greek Play, on May Day weekend . . ."[20] From her classical studies, Agatha said, she had "received a standard of taste in literature and in human conduct which would make her distrust the shoddy, and turn toward the best."[21]

Agatha's picture in the Randolph-Macon annual shows a dark-haired, heavy-jawed profile with thick eyebrows and full lips; her large, dark brown eyes, lovely in a hand-colored childhood portrait, are hidden here by her downcast, pensive pose.[22] She found the strength to be different in her Latin studies and in her friendships with other intellectual girls. Surrounded by women she considered frivolous, Agatha defined herself by her intellect. No doubt her Roman ideals were difficult to abide in ordinary life.

World War I had been under way in Europe for a year when Agatha graduated from college in 1915. But President Woodrow Wilson wanted to keep the US out of Europe's conflict, so there was little reason for Agatha Boyd to believe that this war would much affect her. Instead of returning to her widowed mother and brother Munny in Roanoke, she stayed near her beloved college to teach science and history (her Latin helped with both subjects) at Lynchburg High School.

That year, when she was twenty-two, her happiness irrevocably changed.

CHAPTER TWO

Agatha and Nic

Even then not beautiful, and curious, she had wondered why he loved and wanted her; she decided that it must have been that shyness made her appear aloof and difficult of attainment.

—Alice Adams,
"The Green Creek"

Blue-eyed and dark-haired with a ruddy complexion and Grecian profile, Nicholson Barney Adams, a nineteen-year-old teacher of French and Spanish in his first year at Lynchburg High School, was precocious and hardworking. Tall for the era, he drew attention with his quick gestures and speech. He'd become fascinated with languages when his first sweetheart, who'd lived in Brazil with her missionary parents, taught him some Portuguese. He learned phrases in French, German, and Italian from neighborhood immigrants, studied Latin at school, and read the Bible in Hebrew and Greek with his father.[1] By the time Nic came to Lynchburg, he possessed two bachelor's degrees—one from Fredericksburg College, a Presbyterian institution in his hometown, and a second from more prestigious Washington and Lee University, where he'd been elected to Phi Beta Kappa. When he was not quite eighteen, in a gap between his two college enrollments, Nic saved up tuition for his year at Washington and Lee by lying about his age and serving as principal, drama coach, athletic director, and Sunday Bible-class instructor of a school in Ottoman, Virginia.[2]

Even if some exaggeration has slipped into Nic's résumé over the years, he seems to have dazzled Agatha Boyd, so recently bereft of her father and separated from college friends who had moved to Richmond. Nic and Agatha were about as different in background and temperament as two WASP, native-Virginian schoolteachers living in the early twentieth century could be.

Nic Adams descended from a line of English Puritans who emigrated from Somersetshire to Braintree, just south of Boston, early in the seventeenth century. Five generations of his male Adams ancestors were born in Massachusetts before the Revolutionary War. One of these, Henry Adams II, and his wife, Edith Squires, had eighty-nine grandchildren, including the progenitors of Presidents John Adams and John Quincy Adams, and of historian and autobiographer Henry Adams. Their fifth son, Peter Adams, moved west to Medway, Massachusetts, where he became grandsire to a line of Adams men that included several stern-looking Presbyterian preachers.

Five generations later, a musician named Joel Willard Adams, born 1823, came to give a concert in Fredericksburg, Virginia, stayed to court and marry a Southerner, and found himself in the midst of the Civil War. After serving as a Confederate soldier, he became proprietor of Adams Book Store on Main Street. His son, Joel Willard Adams Jr., born in 1864, succeeded his father at the store and expanded the stock to include musical instruments, art supplies, and picture postcards of local views. The woman he married, Belle Barney, devoted herself to memorializing the Confederacy. The couple had two children, Nic and his younger sister, Virginia. Belle's family tree boasted two naval heroes: Commodore Joshua Barney, whose warship defended Philadelphia during the American Revolution, and Commander Joseph Nicholson Barney, Nic's grandfather and namesake, who graduated first in his class at the US Naval Academy but joined the Confederate naval forces and defended Richmond, Virginia, against the federal fleet. Pardoned by President Johnson after the Civil War, he eventually settled in Fredericksburg with his wife, Anne Dornin Barney, who became a founder of the United Daughters of the Confederacy.

And yet—to illustrate the complexity of the loyalties within this family—Anne Barney's parents (Nic's great-grandparents) took opposite sides during the Civil War. Her father, Commodore Thomas A. Dornin, who was born in Ireland, captured two slave ships on the coast of Africa in 1855 and released the fourteen hundred Africans aboard in Liberia, then continued to fight on the Union side during the Civil War. His wife, Anne Moore Dornin, remained in Norfolk, Virginia, throughout that war, and his two sons fought for the Confederacy.[3]

*   *   *

The Nic Adams that Agatha Boyd met in Lynchburg in 1915 was thoroughly Southern, "much more of a Barney than an Adams," according to his sister.[4] His abundant charm won the day. Agatha's intellectual superiority was twined with a strong desire for romantic purpose. As Alice Adams imagined it later in an unpublished story (with faulty chronology but emotional conviction), her parents

> had spoken a rather literary language of love to each other in the parlors and boxwood walks of Sweetbriar College where he had come to see her in his lieutenant's uniform, back from Europe. Even their situation had been literary and abstract. But she had loved his blue eyes, and their furtively prolonged kisses had seemed real. Even then not beautiful, and curious, she had wondered why he loved and wanted her; she decided that it must have been that shyness made her appear aloof and difficult of attainment.[5]

Whether Nic and Agatha fell passionately and secretly into love at first sight or had a long, chaste, decorous Victorian courtship, they could not have dated openly during this era when female teachers were not supposed to keep company with men. The next fall, Agatha took a position at the newly founded Collegiate School for Girls in Richmond's Fan District, leaving Nic a romantic train ride away in Lynchburg. As America's entry into World War I loomed, Nic enrolled in an interpreter's course at Columbia University with intentions of passing the army's language exam. Agatha told her colleagues and students at Collegiate that she planned to leave her job to join (and marry?) him.[6] It was difficult for Agatha and Nic to make any personal decisions as the stalemated conflict and unabated suffering in Europe clouded their future.

Nic passed the exam and returned south to enlist in Richmond, Virginia, at the end of August 1917. Underweight for officer's training, he became a private, assigned first to shovel cement, then sent north to train at Camp Mills on Long Island.[7] That same summer, Agatha and other Richmond teachers escorted a group of girls to Camp Owaissa in Maine by overnight train. First established early in the century, summer camps offered self-reliant post-Victorian girls the rustic outdoor experience and nature studies that boys had long enjoyed. Despite her earlier announcement, Agatha returned to Collegiate School, where she continued to teach Latin for three more years. She shared a house on Grove Avenue with her mother, an aging housekeeper, and three boarders.[8]

Nic trained with the Forty-Second ("Rainbow") Infantry Division for only about a month before embarking for France on October 18, 1917. In a journal begun that fall, he writes with frustrating brevity that he's been to New York, "where [he saw] Agatha, and late in September [will] get leave home." As a translator-interpreter, Nic saw little combat but was "tickled with first sample of French cooking." He met the poet Alfred Joyce Kilmer, who was to be killed in the Second Battle of the Marne. Unwounded himself, Nic witnessed horrifying scenes: in Troche, he noted that he didn't "care to lie down for fear of lying on dead man or horse. Men of 26th Div. are lying all over fields"; in Bois de Montfaucon, he recorded, "The abomination of desolation. Trees are all cut off or scarred by shells. We cannot find space enough to pitch tent because of old shell holes."

When peace arrived on November 11, 1918, just after Nic's twenty-third birthday, he wrote: "Not much celebration of armistice. We learn that we are to be part of Army of Occupation." Now a commissioned second lieutenant in the Corps of Interpreters, Nic served out the winter as a translator in a sanitarium for nervous cases in Ahrweiler. Happily discharged in the spring, he spent two weeks going to museums, plays, and operas in Paris. He had perfected his French but longed to escape war-stricken France for Spain, the country that held his imagination.

Presbyterian Nic was fascinated by Catholic Spain. His most enduring book, *The Heritage of Spain*, praised that country's contrasts—a desert for "ascetic and idealistic Don Quixotes" and "a lush land in which the lurid passion of Carmen and Don José reaches ecstasy and tragedy." A man of fierce internal conflicts, Nic was drawn to both "the emaciated saints of El Greco" and "the rich-fleshed *majas* of Goya."[9] In spring 1919, he toured Spain for two months, from San Sebastian to Madrid to Seville, before sailing home to enroll as a graduate student in Spanish at Columbia University.

*   *   *

After a five-year, mostly long-distance courtship, Nic Adams and Agatha Boyd married on June 12, 1920, at Christ Church in Roanoke, where her late father had served as deacon.[10] Agatha accompanied her husband back to Columbia University. She traded in her beloved Latin studies to begin work on a master's degree in Spanish and become an assistant to Nic's academic work. He completed his PhD with a dissertation on the nineteenth-century playwright García Gutiérrez,[11] whose plays provide the Romantic story lines for Verdi's operas *Il Trovatore* and *Simon Boccanegra*. Approaching their thirties, Nic and Agatha still cherished dreams of a bohemian life as writers. They ventured downtown to Greenwich Village and made plans for Europe. With Nic's dissertation in press as a book, Agatha spent part of the summer codirecting Camp Pukwana, which she now owned and operated with her friend Fanny Graves Crenshaw on Lake Sebago in Maine. The newlyweds sailed together from Hoboken to Cherbourg in September of 1922.

This would be the mythical year of their marriage, one to look back at with longing. Nic's sister, Virginia, then in college, admired Nic and Agatha so extremely that her roommate would ask her if she'd heard from the PBs (Perfect Beings).[12] Imagining the life her parents had before her own birth, Alice Adams gives this thought to a character like her mother: "It's wonderful . . . to have known, to have been sure."[13]

Alice, decades later, understanding that her mother's enthusiasm for Nic had collapsed, asks what drew her parents together: In "Are You in Love?"—one of Adams's Chapel Hill stories in which Jessica and Tom Todd stand in for Agatha and Nic—the narrator wonders if Jessica married Tom because he was "writing a book on Shelley." Then the narrator adds: "(Not true: she married him because of passionate kisses—then.)" Agatha and Nic's sojourn in Europe was a romantic *and* intellectual adventure. The couple kept a single diary, taking turns recording their days. Agatha's lush descriptions—"I discover unearthly shade of emerald in crest of black waves"—alternate with Nic's notes about people they've met—"a Jew, son of immigrants, brilliant, no manners." They cross France by train, stopping without reservations to find delight in one hotel room after another. This joint diary, as well as concern for comfortable, quiet hotel rooms and good food, suggests a congenial marriage. In Madrid husband and wife enroll in classes at Universidad Central and live with "loathsome" (Nic writes) other boarders who have no manners; but they enjoy a busy routine of study, tennis, and plays. They do not keep house.

Life in Spain was infectiously provocative for both Nic and Agatha. In Andalusia for Christmas, they attend an "oppressively limp and lifeless" (Agatha) English church, but offset that with a "wild mixture of the comic and the mystic" in a Spanish nativity play with wise men who bring girls to do a seductive dance before the Savior and offer Him a lottery ticket for good luck. They take tea in the Moorish courtyard of the famed Pasaje de Orient restaurant, where the "wealth and fashion of Seville stares at us as if we wore bathing suits."

One evening Agatha wrote, "Nic and I, alone for once, spend the morning happily in the beautiful Parque de Maria Luisa . . . a hospitable Andalusian turns on the fountain for us—a delicate jet of sparkling drops. How imaginative and poetic are Spanish parks." Between the lines, Agatha seems to be longing for more time alone with her young husband.

University classes finished, in spring Agatha and Nic depart on a bicycle and train trip through Italy and Switzerland and France. They stop in villages, such as Rolampont, where Nic was during the war, sometimes locating people he stayed with before. But others are dead, and Agatha writes, "One cannot feel in France that the war is over— soldiers everywhere—a nation armed to the teeth." A French couple accommodates them in a low-ceilinged room with a feather bed "too narrow for one person—a somewhat restless night," Agatha notes. "Inevitable scorching plum brandy" is "forced down our throats," accompanied by "talk about its remarkable purity and quality, it being made at home." Happily, there is one exception: "a magical yellow liqueur made of quince." Near Reims they visit the farm where Nic slept under an apple tree during a night of shelling. Everywhere they encounter "trees split and tortured by shells, a grey bleakness . . . Drab blighted forests ruined by the stupidity of fighting." Nic no longer writes in the little quadrille-lined notebooks with black covers. It has become Agatha's work to keep this bleak record. Perhaps the bleakness began to seep into their marriage.

While Nic and Agatha were at Columbia and in Europe, Agatha's next younger brother, Beverley Munford Boyd, served in the Army Air Corps and became an Episcopal priest, fulfilling the dream that had eluded their father. Ambition ran deep in Agatha's family. Her youngest brother, blind Munny, became a lawyer with help from their mother, who read his casebooks to him. Nic's parents kept their bookstore in Fredericksburg and sustained a secondary household made up, reportedly, of their two mothers and *five* maiden aunts.[14]

Passing over opportunities to live near relatives after their wander year, Agatha and Nic returned to the place where they'd met, Lynchburg High School in Virginia, and resumed teaching. In 1924, the University of North Carolina, in the town of Chapel Hill, offered Nic a position as assistant professor in the Department of Romance Languages.

Nic and Agatha arrived in North Carolina during a time of cultural renovation and excitement. H. L. Mencken, in his famous 1917 screed "Sahara of the Bozart," had called the American South a "stupendous region of worn-out farms, shoddy cities and paralyzed cerebrums . . . as sterile, artistically, intellectually, culturally, as the Sahara Desert." Mencken regretted the destruction of the gentry whose "civilization of manifold excellences" thrived in old Virginia before the Civil War. That war "left the land to the harsh mercies of the poor white trash, now its masters," as cultured Southerners moved north, leaving behind "a vast plain of mediocrity, stupidity, lethargy, almost dead silence." The remnants of the old aristocracy, Mencken argued, needed to reestablish their influence; thus he initiated a Southern literary renaissance and prompted white Southern writers to explore their identity.

From earliest colonial days, North Carolina, settled by small farmers and never a large slaveholding state, languished economically between Virginia and South Carolina—"a vale of humility between two mountains of conceit," as a popular epithet has it. Chapel Hill in 1924 was a village of about two thousand people situated at the eastern edge of the state's Piedmont region, which had, Agatha wrote, "no spectacular beauty, but a subdued loveliness which grows with familiarity."[15] The town's heart and reason for being was the University of North Carolina, considered the oldest public university in the United States (1789), whose salmon-pink brick buildings didn't yet fill its five hundred acres on a low granite hill. A block of shops on Franklin Street, a few dozen fine houses, and the Episcopal and Baptist churches flanked the college; beyond that were many unpaved roads.

In returning to the South—and perhaps especially to North

Carolina—Nic and Agatha were taking on the challenge of reviving Southern culture. The university offered almost tuition-free admission to white boys who had graduated from high school in North Carolina and was "crowded with country youth whose parents were unbelievably proud of them for being in college." One of those youths, Thomas Wolfe, had recently departed Chapel Hill and gone to Harvard to study playwriting, which he would later abandon to write *Look Homeward, Angel*, part of which reprises his days as a UNC undergrad. Another Tar Heel State native, playwright Paul Green, upon whose biography Alice Adams drew for a character in her Southern novels, had just built himself a new house southeast of town. That house became a gathering place for those who wanted to write or talk about books, including Green's wife, Elizabeth; his brother-in-law, biographer Phillips Russell; and such visitors as poet Allen Tate and novelist Caroline Gordon.

When Nic and Agatha Adams moved to Chapel Hill, the village was becoming the "bookish" town that Alice Adams described when interviewers asked her about her youth there: "Being a writer was the best possible thing. Writers were our folk heroes. So I was always serious about being a writer, or to put it negatively, nothing else occurred to me to be."[16] At UNC Agatha completed the master's degree she had begun at Columbia with a thesis on a legendary Romantic character in the nineteenth-century Spanish drama *El pastelero de Madrigal*.[17] With a degree in her husband's chosen field, Agatha had to face the fact that the university had not a single female faculty member. She wanted to teach, but she later told her fellow Randolph-Macon alumnae, "My lot was thrown in with the University of North Carolina [which] has been for one hundred and fifty years a man's university, has admitted women students lately and grudgingly, and still regards women faculty members as somewhat irritating phenomena. . . . It is part of the folklore of the state that young North Carolina males are so robustious, so incredibly rambunctious, that no mere woman could possibly keep their attention on the niceties of English prose composition."[18]

While UNC squelched Agatha's ambition to be a teacher, she continued to collaborate with Nic on his projects, including a coauthored guide to Spanish literature in English translation. Soon motherhood and domestic responsibilities absorbed more of her time. It was difficult to find rental housing in Chapel Hill and too costly to purchase a house in town. Instead she and Nic bought adjoining parcels of land (.85 acre altogether) including an old farmhouse, barn, and stable, a mile south of town on the road that led to Pittsboro. Alice wrote later,

> [Nic and Agatha] must have been drawn to all that space, a couple of acres; they may have already been planning the gardens, the tennis court and the grape arbors they were to put in later. And they must have fallen in love with the most beautiful view of farther gentle hills and fields, and a border of creek. They would have placed these aesthetic advantages above the convenience of a smaller lot, a tidier house in town. And along with the space and the view, they chose an unfashionable direction (which would have been characteristic; my parents—especially my mother, a snobbish Virginian—were always above such considerations).

Because the Southern rural economy had collapsed at the end of World War I, the Adamses acquired their little acre for a total of $200. The arrival of Alice prompted Nic and Agatha to add a wing: an upstairs master bedroom with a living room below. Additions that continued over the years gave the house "some strangeness . . . some awkwardness as to proportion and transition from one room to another. Upstairs, there was even a dead-end hall."[19]

CHAPTER THREE

The Family Romance

*I do remember a not-quite conscious feeling that my parents were
too far away from where I slept; that they were also far from each
other did not strike me as strange until some time later.*

—Alice Adams, "My First and
Only House," *Return Trips*

In the fall of 1926, after Alice's birth and Agatha's long convalescence in
Fredericksburg, baby Alice and her parents returned to the farmhouse in
Chapel Hill. Verlie Jones, a black woman about Agatha's age, came to work
for the family and stayed for twenty-four years, an ever-present maternal
figure for Alice. Mrs. Jones—always Verlie to her employers—walked two
miles up old state highway 75 to the Adamses' house from the dirt-floored
shack with leaning walls where she lived with her husband, Horace; three
daughters; and a son named Bontue Jones. Almost every day she arrived
in time to make breakfast for the Adams family and stayed until she'd
finished preparing dinner. Verlie appears repeatedly in Adams's fiction,
most memorably in her 1974 story called "Verlie I Say Unto You," which
takes its title from Verlie's reply to Mr. Todd's question about her name:

"You know, it's like in the Bible. Verlie I say unto you."
    Tom felt that he successfully concealed his amusement at that,
and later it makes a marvelous story, especially in academic circles,
in those days when funny-maid stories are standard social fare. In
fact people (white people) are somewhat competitive as to who has
heard or known the most comical colored person, comical meaning
outrageously childishly ignorant.[1]

As US Census reports show, Verlie (short for Beverly) was a common name in North Carolina early in the twentieth century. Maybe the Adams family didn't know that, or maybe Verlie was quietly making fun of her employer as he was of her. In another story by Adams, a North Carolina girl explains bitterly to a visitor from Cambridge: "I think Southerners are afraid if the talk gets abstract they'll end up on the Negro problem, and as close as they can get to that is these boring stories about funny maids or complaining about the help situation."[2]

Indeed, racial segregation and an assumption of white supremacy reigned in virtually every aspect of social and economic life in pre-civil-rights-era North Carolina, from housing to schools and hospitals and movie theaters; very few black citizens were allowed to vote, and none were enrolled at the University of North Carolina. In 1925, fiery speakers for and against the active, contemporary Ku Klux Klan filled Memorial Hall on campus.[3] Not much later the *Tar Heel* published a photo of five "darkies" who had served Carolina students for periods ranging from 15 to 50 years as janitors after these "old boys" (aged thirty-nine to seventy-three) led a cheer at a football game.[4]

One of many episodes revealing the racial attitudes that surrounded Alice as she grew up during the Jim Crow era unfolded when novelist Richard Wright came to Chapel Hill in 1940 to collaborate with playwright Paul Green on a play based on Wright's novel *Native Son*. Wright could not stay at the university-owned Carolina Inn or dine in any restaurant in Chapel Hill, so Green found him a room and board in the black neighborhood between the university town and the white, working-class town of Carrboro. It was, in fact, the neighborhood where Verlie Jones then lived with some of her children. University president Frank Porter Graham (a liberal who'd been chided for hosting James Weldon Johnson and Zora Neale Hurston in Chapel Hill and would later be accused of communist affiliations by HUAC) granted Green a room in Bynum Hall where he and his Negro guest could work. It was summer, so Graham hoped no one would notice the collegial relations of Wright and Green. That was not to be. As Wright's biographer Hazel Rowley reports: "Curious faces would look in at the window. Never had the South seen such a sight. A white man and a black man were sitting across from each other at a long table."

The collaboration resulted in a successful Broadway play directed by Orson Welles, even though, as Green later regretted, he addressed

Wright as "Dick" while the younger man called him "Mr. Green." For all his good intentions, Green was typical of the sort of Southern liberal Alice would come to dislike. Like Alice's parents, who knew him well, Green was "a Southern gentleman" prone to saying things like the following, which Rowley quotes with bitter irony: "We are just full of the drip of human tears. . . . The love between the Negro and the white is something wonderful to behold in the South."

But before Wright and Green finished their work in Chapel Hill, Ouida Campbell, who was Green's secretary, invited both writers to a party at her family's home in Carrboro. The next day several men with pistols, upset by reports that a Negro had visited Campbell, threatened to run "that boy" Wright out of town. Green claimed he spent the night in a cotton patch next to Wright's room in case the white mob showed up. They didn't, and Wright returned to New York by train.[5]

According to the 1940 book *North Carolina: The WPA Guide to the Old North State*, about 30 percent of the state's population were Negroes, but the "average white person never ha[d] any dealings with Negro professors, lawyers, doctors, insurance men, merchants, or restaurant operators, though he ha[d] many contacts with Negro laborers." Certainly Verlie Jones was an essential presence in the Adams household during Alice's girlhood. Critical of the ironic distance with which her intellectually liberal parents protected themselves from thinking about race in segregated North Carolina, Adams confronted the subject repeatedly throughout her long writing career.

Adams began writing with about black characters in her unpublished early stories. In one of these, a girl named Maude is warned not to drink water from Green Creek by her family's maid, Odessa: "White ladies call it nigger water, say their children get black if they drink it . . ." Maude, whose own mother is unhappy and disagreeable, would rather be black and have Odessa for her mother. Soon after Odessa sends word that she is stricken with "misery in the leg," Maude runs away to the creek, drinks the water, and waits for her skin to change. She tries to find Odessa. Sent home again, Maude is lovingly greeted by her father but feels lost: "She would sit here for the rest of her life, and nothing would be any different."[6]

The reality of Verlie's situation was stark. The 1940 census reports that Verlie worked forty-five hours a week, fifty-two weeks a year, and earned $520 a year (equivalent to about $9,000 in 2019).* With what seems to be flawed memory, "Verlie I Say Unto You" reports that Verlie is paid "more money than most maids, thirteen dollars a week (most get along on ten or eleven). And she gets to go home before dinner, around six (she first leaves the meal all fixed for them)" because Mr. Todd "likes to have a lot of drinks and then eat late." Verlie also got one Sunday a month off so she could go to church.

Nic Adams's career at the university advanced rapidly, in tandem with the university's improving national reputation during the post–World War I years. Named associate professor in 1927, Nic left Agatha and Alice home in the summer of 1929 while he traveled to Spain to research Spanish folktales and Spanish literature for American publishers.[7] *Contemporary Spanish Literature in English Translation*, coauthored with Agatha, also appeared in 1929, as did an edition of *Don Juan Tenorio* by José Zorrilla that was closely related to the topic of Agatha's master's thesis. Shortly after Borzoi Knopf published the Zorrilla book, Nic was invited to lunch at the Carolina Inn by Blanche Knopf and then entertained both Blanche and Alfred Knopf, who was a wine connoisseur, at home, where Nic served him "the worst sort of raw corn liquor imaginable" (it was Prohibition).[8]

In 1930, Nic celebrated his promotion to full professor by damming the creek to make a swimming pool in the ravine north of their house. The big, deep hole roughly cemented over figured largely in the Adamses' expanding social life and in their daughter's imagination. In his thirties, slender, vibrant Nic Adams cultivated the jazz-age look of F. Scott Fitzgerald. Likewise, he and Agatha were part of a circle of literature professors who partied together often with bootleg liquor in little kegs from nearby Fearrington Farm, meat grilled on a poolside pit, and other drinks and food (much of it prepared by Verlie) carried down the stone steps from the house.

Soon after Nic was promoted, the already almost-bankrupt state of North Carolina was hit by further revenue reductions due to the Great Depression. Faculty salaries were cut by 10 percent, but being part of the university community buffered the Adams family from the worst

* I could not identify Verlie Jones in 1930 Census records.

effects of the Depression. Nonetheless, times were bad enough that Nic
Adams's younger colleague and friend Thomas J. Wilson abandoned
teaching in the French Department to become an editor at Henry
Holt & Co. in New York City. Soon the two men were corresponding
about textbook projects, including Nic's long-gestating *The Heritage of
Spain*.[9] Nic's letters to Wilson during the winter of 1930–31 mention
illnesses as often as they mention salary cuts and books.

Agatha in particular spent much of the season in bed with "vicious"
colds. Alice later remembered a fantasy she'd had when she was "extremely
young": "My mother being sick and my taking care of her, I think I
even talked her into acting it out with me—I brought her pretend-tea in
bed. I think that must have been a way to make her less terrifying—and
of course to put myself in charge."[10] In the spring, Agatha seemed "a
little better" and everyone understood that her indispositions during
the previous winter had been complicated by pregnancy. Her baby was
due in August.

Meanwhile, Agatha and Nic coped with their rambunctious four-
year-old by considering Alice difficult. The little girl who looked adorable in little white smocks and slippers became known as a "fabulous
crawler" who happily knocked over a neighbor boy who was just learning to walk. Her parents let her know that as a baby she "had been
hyper-aggressive in a very unfeminine (un-Southern) way."[11] Adams's
story "The Visit"—written many decades later with Hortense, Buck,
and Grace standing in for Agatha, Nic, and Alice—proposes that the
child's difficultness is a projection by uneasy parents:

> Her father, a classic *beau* of his time, was handsome, and drank too
> much, and chased girls. Her mother . . . was smart and snobbish . . .
> tended to say exactly what she thought, and she wasn't one bit pretty.
> Neither of them seemed like ordinary parents, a fact they made a point
> of—of being above and beyond most normal parental concerns, of not
> acting like "parents." "We appreciate Grace as a person, and not just
> because she's our daughter," Hortense, the mother, was fairly often
> heard to say, which may have accounted for the fact that Grace was
> a rather unchildlike child: precocious, impertinent, too smart for her
> own good. Rebellious, always.

*   *   *

As her parents adjusted to an expanding family and a constricting economy, Alice began kindergarten early and opened the imaginary world she shared with her dolls to encompass other people. In a letter she dictated to her mother for her grandmother Boyd, she said, "I love you so well. You come to help me take care of dolls. We will both be happy if you do come. Verlie cooks beautifully."[12]

Another kindergartner, Josephine MacMillan, became Alice's best friend, as she remembered in her story "Child's Play," wherein she becomes Prudence, opposite to Josephine's Laura Lee: "A long time ago, in the thirties, two little girls found almost perfect complements in each other. Theirs was a balanced, exceptionally happy friendship: skinny, scared, precocious Prudence Jamieson and pretty, placid, trustful Laura Lee Matthews." Though the friendship had been arranged by the girls' parents for their own convenience, "Prudence and Laura Lee really took to each other, as their grateful hard-drinking parents remarked." During long summer twilights,

> the small girls used to play in the sprawling, bountiful Matthews garden, and one of their favorite pastimes involved making a series of precariously fragile, momentarily lovely dolls out of flower petals. Pansy faces with hollyhock skirts, like dancers' tutus, for example, or petunia skirts and tiny rosebud faces . . . This occupation entirely absorbed both children, and it formed an idyllic part of their childhood, something they lightly, laughingly mentioned to each other as they became more complex but still firm adult friends.[13]

There were other kinds of play, too. Neighborhood twins Robert Macmillan and Dougald Macmillan IV (unrelated to Josephine) were the first boys to hold Alice's attention, and she remembered one scene all her life. As she and Robert walked through the woods by their houses, he asked her if it was okay if he peed. "I had never seen a penis before, and I truly thought it was marvelous, so pink and pretty. Emitting an arc of pee off into the leaves," Adams wrote, he "went on to explain that his thing was indeed marvelous. He could make it stand up just by thinking about it, he said to me. And he showed me."[14]

The Adams house was filled with books. Agatha read poems to Alice from *The Sugar-Plum Tree and Other Verses* or from the tissue-thin pages of *The Home Book of Verse*, where they preferred "long, sad Scottish

ballads." Young Alice made elaborate, expressive crayon illustrations of
smiling cats or groups of children that her parents preserved, and she
read Victorian books about dolls that Agatha had saved from her own
childhood. After those came "trash novels" (as she later called them,
probably echoing her mother's opinion) about large, happy families,
like Margaret Sidney's *Five Little Peppers*, and a series of novels about
the exemplary Grace Harlowe (generous, kind, and always ladylike,
but also smart and independent) and her friends at school and college
by Josephine Chase (pseudonym Jessie Graham Flower). She received
books in the mail from a children's book club and eventually chose
whatever she wanted from her parents' shelves; the Bull's Head Book-
shop, which her mother helped found in the basement of the new
University Library; and that library's three hundred thousand books,
one of the largest collections in the South. Other entertainment came
from movies at two picture houses downtown and plays at the Playmakers Theatre.

In the last year of her life, Adams thought about her tendency to
relocate the literature she read to her own "known, familiar sites," so
that her favorite fairy tales took place in the woods near Chapel Hill or
a boathouse in Maine. She also mentally rewrote the endings of stories
she read, turning them into wishful enactments like the stories she'd
invented for her dolls. On the ending of "Goldilocks and the Three
Bears," for instance, she wrote, "The intruding little girl, Goldilocks, is
somehow ejected from the home of the bears, sometimes thrown from
an upstairs window . . . [or] peaceably leaving through the front door
. . . But I seem to have found or invented still a third version of my
own, in which having at last come upon such a warm and congenial
family, Goldilocks is adopted by that family, with the Littlest Bear for
her brother (something I very much wished I had)."[15]

As the end of her pregnancy approached, thirty-eight-year-old Agatha
was scheduled for surgery at Duke University Hospital.* Alice was sent
to spend a month with her grandmother and other relatives in White

---

* Endowed by American Tobacco Company founder James Buchanan Duke in 1930,
the new hospital in Durham was deemed the best medical institution between Baltimore
and New Orleans. North Carolina had long lacked adequate medical facilities.

Plains, New York.[16] Contemporary practice dictated that a woman who'd once had a cesarean section could not afterward have a vaginal delivery. At five, perceptive Alice certainly knew her mother was pregnant and probably sensed the apprehensions and expectations that were circulating within the family while she was away. Alice made herself "difficult" and, probably, "fell in love" with her aunt Virginia's husband, Edgar Dare.[17] Those circumstances appeared in her novel *Rich Rewards*, where she portrayed a five-year-old girl who clamored for attention from an uncle, "a perfectly nice, rather ordinary young man in his middle twenties," who never suspected that the child "who behaved with such consistent brattiness" was filled with "wild emotion" about him. Adams attributed her character's "nutty obsessiveness with love and men" to being in love with an uncle when she was five. That hilarious account masks a different loss that Adams rarely spoke of and never wrote about.

Midmorning on August 30, 1931, Agatha gave birth to a son by C-section. While she was under anesthetic, her surgeon repaired a hernia and performed a tubal ligation to sterilize her. Before Agatha can have been much recovered from these procedures, the baby died. He had lived just six and a half hours. According to his death certificate, signed by G. E. Harrison at Duke hospital, the cause of death was status thymo-lymphaticus. Autopsy notes in the obstetrical logbook translate the condition as "hypertrophy of thymus gland." The baby weighed five and a half pounds.

Joel Willard Adams was small, but the condition to which his death was attributed by the staff at Duke was by that time no longer regarded as unusual, diseased, or dangerous by medical researchers.

The history of the diagnosis status thymo-lymphaticus provides a sad footnote to the death of the Adams baby. As a favored explanation for the sudden death of an infant, the term entered medical literature in the 1880s. Many doctors and much of the public came to believe that an enlarged thymus gland, because of its location near the heart, aorta, and lungs, could cause internal suffocation. The condition was often diagnosed in babies who died under or immediately after anesthesia with chloroform, and yet the anesthesia was seldom considered the primary culprit.

In the early twentieth century, pathologists began to question the diagnosis while "a growing number of anesthetists took the existence of *status lymphaticus* for granted and stressed diagnosing the condition in

advance of surgeries" on young patients. In 1926, though, the Medical
Research Council and the Pathological Society of Great Britain and
Ireland organized an investigative committee that found the diagnosis
has "no more value than affirmative evidence in cases of witchcraft"
and "ought to be abandoned." In 1931 the *Lancet* declared the end of
the diagnosis in an article titled "The End of Status Lymphaticus." The
British Medical Research Council committee excused the long mistake
with the following observation: "It is simple humanity to search for
some explanation which will satisfy the modern mind where 'the visitation of God' would once have been enough. Hence the doctrine of
'*status lymphaticus*' which, owing to our ignorance of the anatomy of
the normal healthy human body, has survived longer than it should."
American medical texts still included status lymphaticus in the 1940s,
and American doctors were using radiation to shrink infants' thymuses
until in the 1950s they realized that the radiation was causing cancer.
Historian of medicine Ann Dally's fascinating chronicle of the diagnosis argues that doctors had unintentionally created a mythology of
disease because there was a "need" for it: status lymphaticus offered a
desperately wanted explanation for deaths that could not otherwise
be explained, especially in light of a desire *not* to blame anesthesia for
deaths in surgery.[18]

In fact, Duke University Hospital used a complicated anesthesia
protocol for cesarean sections in the 1930s. Operating under the belief
that narcotics did not cross the placenta (disproved by Dr. Virginia
Apgar in 1952), Duke anesthesiologists sedated obstetric patients using
a dangerous method that administered ether as needed without accurate
measurement of the amount inhaled. Next they often used "layered"
anesthesia, a protocol that did not become common elsewhere until
the 1940s. In addition to ether they "administered a spinal or caudal,
local procaine, *and* nitrous oxide plus halothane and/or cyclopropane,"
reports historian of medicine Jacqueline Wolf, who has studied obstetric records from that era at Duke and other hospitals. "It's not hard to
imagine killing an infant with all those drugs," Wolf commented. "It's
harder to imagine so many surviving such a birth."[19]

Yet many did survive. There is no clear reason why Alice's baby
brother did not. Perhaps the "simple humanity" of the diagnosis spared
Nic and Agatha the trauma of asking how much Agatha's age and need
for a cesarean-section birth and anesthesia contributed to their loss.

Joel Willard Adams, named for Nic's father and grandfather, was buried in the Old Chapel Hill Cemetery at the edge of the University of North Carolina campus. The grave marker, if there ever was one, has not survived.[20]

At the end of October, two months after Joel's death and Agatha's surgery, Nic wrote Tom Wilson: "It will certainly be fine to see you Thanksgiving. Don't fail to come. We miss you badly. Agatha is still improving, though not so very strong yet. She had a rough time of it." Before the end of the year, Agatha wrote a poem she titled "To a Caller":

> My eyes you say are very calm and quiet
> You praise my strange tranquility of mien;
> You do not know that far behind this stillness
> There dwells a woman you have never seen,
> Who screams and runs forever through the mazes
> The dark and secret alleys of my brain;
> A woman weeping for her only son,
> Rebellious to inexorable pain.

The effects of Joel's death on Agatha's health and sexuality, on her and Nic's marriage, and on little Alice were incalculable and incontrovertible.[21] When Alice's grandmother brought her back to Chapel Hill to enter first grade, the family universe was entirely changed, full of sadness and repressed anger. "Alice took this all upon herself as her fault," her friend Judith Clark Adams believed. "And I think that was her first broken heart. The first broken love affair. Alice never talked about it."

Nic Adams continued to expand the house, but it seems that no one slept in the new master bedroom. Agatha slept in the guest room and Nic slept on the sleeping porch, while Alice remained upstairs with her own bathroom in the old section of the house above rooms that were rented to a bachelor professor named Bill. Alice remembered "a not-quite conscious feeling that my parents were too far away from where I slept; that they were also far from each other did not strike me as strange until some time later."[22]

By the time Alice was old enough to realize such things, a severe, unspoken emotional distance separated her mother and father. The contrast that attracted them to each other—Agatha's seriousness and maturity, Nic's extroversion, high spirits, and flirtatiousness—was exacerbated by Nic's heavy drinking. The usual constraints of marriage, motherhood, and a lack of her own intellectual work became a stranglehold for Agatha. "They were at odds temperamentally," Judith Clark Adams thought. "Their Southern manners did not allow for overt conflict. I cannot imagine Agatha and Nic screaming at each other. I cannot imagine Agatha ever raising her voice. She had a beautiful, modulated Southern accent. But what took place was actually more vicious than that because of the ironic, sarcastic distancing of Nic. And Agatha was just too inhibited and too rigidly polite. Certainly there was tremendous unhappiness there. And I think losing the baby had a really profound effect."

Tellingly, in story after story that mirrors Alice's girlhood in Chapel Hill, the couple who resemble Nic and Agatha—usually Tom and Jessica Todd, or sometimes Taylor—have two children: a girl named Avery and a boy named Devlin. The characters with A names are ciphers for Alice, while Devlin represents the lost baby, Joel. Such a longed-for unit of loving parents and children haunts much of the fiction Adams wrote about her growing-up years.

In a photograph of the Adams family from late 1931, Agatha, wearing a sad, private smile, stands with an older woman while little Alice, grasping a bunch of flowers and her mother's hand, eyes the camera from under her bangs and recedes behind the fur cuff of her mother's coat. Nic, lanky, handsome, biting his pipe stem (just as Alice often described him), occupies the left half of the picture. He seems both self-involved and distracted, focused on a wide-brimmed hat and black cat that he holds. One can't infer too much from one photograph, but Nic's standing apart from the three females in that picture seems to confirm Alice's recollections of him as more a performer rather than a participant.

In a world and a family mired in depression, Alice needed new companions—books, friends, and nature—to help her grow into herself.

CHAPTER FOUR

Depressions

— 1931–1937 —

And I felt the most passionate envy of that condition, that bodily family warmth. As I imagined it, they would all lie cuddled like puppies, with the mother and father on the outside edges, protectively.

—Alice Adams, "My First and
Only House," *Return Trips*

Nic Adams became more attractive and sociable as he aged, while Agatha lost her youthful complexion and figure. In "Roses, Rhododendron," Adams's iconic story of adolescent friendship and the silent undercurrent of unhappiness within her parents' home, she describes her mother as Emily Farr: "a small plump woman, very erect," who "sat down very stiffly" because of "some terrible, never diagnosed trouble with her back; generally she wore a brace." Her dark brown hair had turned beautifully and uniformly white, though it was "badly cut in that butchered nineteen-thirties way." It would be frivolous to impute Agatha's rage to loss of sexual appeal. Since graduating from college and meeting Nic Adams twenty years earlier, she had suffered the loss of her health, her husband's companionship and devotion, and her intellectual vocation. She was hurt and she was angry.

If it's true that Agatha never raised her voice, her restraint only increased the weight of her criticisms of both her husband and her daughter. Near the end of her life, Adams wrote in a notebook: "My mother was given to unkind truths which she expressed at considerable length. Complex, intelligent insights into the deficiencies of my character. I think she must at times have done the same thing to my father—but maybe not, she both loved & feared him more, in fact some of the rage I got may have been deflected."[1]

Adams tried repeatedly to fathom her mother by portraying her in her fiction. As Jessica Taylor in an early unpublished story called "The Wake," she is a Tidewater Virginian for whom "the personal was infinitely difficult." In her first published novel, *Careless Love*, Daisy Duke's mother's suicide—prompted by her husband's philandering—devastates ten-year-old Daisy. As Jessica Todd in stories in *Beautiful Girl*, she has a "mournful, exacerbated and extreme intelligence" that "is not compelling" to her husband, Tom. When a young man talks to her about poetry and recommends books to her, Jessica feels respected and desired: "A woman desired is a woman not seen as herself, is a woman re-created—she is remembering Tom's brief blind passion for her."

The deepening economic depression closed Agatha's and Fanny Crenshaw's Camp Pukwana, but the two women continued to own property on the southwest shore of Lake Sebago, where the family spent summers throughout Alice's childhood. As millions suffered unemployment, homelessness, and hunger, Nic kept his salaried job as a professor; he complained only that the university was building a bell tower instead of purchasing books for the new library. The low cost of labor allowed him to continue renovations on their house. Agatha worked as a volunteer at the bookshop. With other faculty couples such as the twins' parents, Laura and Dougald Macmillan (a Restoration drama expert), Margaret and Urban Holmes (a medieval scholar), and Dollie and Wiley Sanders (a sociologist who did pioneering work in criminology) living nearby, the Adamses' neighborhood became a circle within precincts of "the Athens of the South," as Chapel Hill was happy to call itself. When writer Daphne Athas came to Chapel Hill as a sixteen-year-old in 1939, she observed that "most of the highfalutin" lived in the Adamses' neighborhood, including "three families with three beautiful daughters, the Holmeses with Mollie, the Adamses with Alice . . . and the Sanderses with Harriett."[2] Highfalutin or not, the message Alice remembered from those depression years was "Take what you are given and be grateful."[3] They had a big vegetable garden near the creek, a tennis court, and a lush flower garden. There was a treehouse for Alice and a separate study where Nic worked. Curiously, Alice never saw her father read a book for pleasure.[4]

Nic Adams's mental health was severely strained as he approached his thirty-fifth birthday. It's hard to say how much he was affected by the dreadful news that bombarded the nation in 1932. That year unemployment of male workers reached 24 percent (for black men the number was 50 percent) and suicide rates rose; and, perhaps most poignantly for Nic, the "Bonus Expeditionary Force" of forty-three thousand ragged, hungry World War I veterans and their and supporters encamped in Washington, DC, to demand early payment of promised bonuses was brutally evicted from the city by cavalry and foot soldiers using bayonets and tear gas grenades. On November 8, 1932, voters overwhelmingly elected New York governor Franklin D. Roosevelt, who promised a new deal. He would be president during the next twelve years, virtually all of Alice Adams's youth.

Within days of Roosevelt's election, Nic Adams mailed his overdue manuscript of *Brief Spanish Review Grammar and Composition* to Tom Wilson at Holt. Then he collapsed. He'd been working at a dead heat since leaving home at the age of seventeen. On December 11 Agatha wrote Wilson to explain that Nic had been in the hospital at Duke for "overtired nerves." Alice was sent to her grandparents in Fredericksburg for Christmas while Agatha took Nic to an inexpensive resort in Palm Beach, Florida. Ominously, his condition was still so serious in February 1933 that Agatha had to proofread and complete a preface for the Spanish textbook. The banking system had failed and the nation remained in perilous disarray. Many cheered Roosevelt as a savior when he gave his famous "the only thing we have to fear is fear itself" speech and took office on March 4, but more circumspect people understood what First Lady Eleanor Roosevelt meant when she said, "One has the feeling of going it blindly, because we're in a tremendous stream, and none of us know where we're going to land."[5]

Nic Adams probably favored FDR, just as he favored the elected Republican government in the Spanish Civil War. Agatha, whether due to patrician noblesse oblige or genuine empathy for the poor, was enthusiastic about FDR. When Prohibition was repealed in December 1933, much of North Carolina, including Chapel Hill and Orange County, remained officially dry. Nonetheless, Nic Adams continued to drink more and more heavily. "It was hard for Nic to be an alcoholic, but he managed," Tom Wilson's son recalled.

Nic had recovered from his breakdown when Gertrude Stein and

Alice B. Toklas stopped in Chapel Hill in February 1935 during Stein's lecture tour. They stayed at the Carolina Inn, visited the Intimate Book-shop (where leftist and rumored communist Ab Abernathy edited a magazine called *Contempo*),[6] and saw "the best collection of Spanish books anywhere in the world and lots of students from everywhere in the world and a nice town and a pleasant spring," Stein wrote.[7] Alice was under the very credible impression that her mother arranged the Toklas-Stein visit; certainly the couple came for cocktails at the Adams house,[8] but Alice, confined by the chicken pox, had to settle for Stein's get-well note addressed to "Alice asleep upstairs" instead of meeting her.[9]

Nic lost both of his parents in 1935. Belle, who had enrolled young Alice in an organization called Children of the Confederacy, died in June of 1935, aged sixty-six, followed in August of that year by her husband. During that same grief-ridden summer, another distressful event challenged Nic and Agatha's marriage when the Adams and Wilson families spent a vacation together at Lake Sebago. It was there, according to Tom Wilson Jr. ("Tombo"), that Nic Adams fell in love with Dorothy Stearns Wilson, a vivacious brunette ten years younger than he. The attraction between Nic and Dotsie, as she was called, was evident to all and discussed later by their grown-up children. It became the subject of several of Adams's stories. In "Alternatives," Jessica "feels the currents between Babs and Tom but she accepts what she senses with melancholy resignation. . . . Nothing more will happen with Babs. It is only mildly depressing for Jessica, a further reminder that she is an aging, not physically attractive woman, that her excellent mind is not compelling to Tom. But she is used to all that." Nonetheless, Agatha watched Nic with a feeling Adams describes in "Roses, Rhododendron": "that pained watchfulness of a woman who has been hurt, and by a man who could always hurt her again."

Tombo learned to swim in the Maine lake and begged impatiently to return there, but the visits ceased after 1935. After his parents divorced in the late 1940s, he recalled: "My father told me, 'Your mother will probably get married again, but don't let her marry that Nic Adams.' He had no room to be jealous nor had he kept his part of the marriage vows, but he resented Dotsie's attraction to Nic."

The strong feelings that stopped the Wilsons from vacationing in Maine with the Adamses did not interfere with their more distant cordiality. In the wake of falling in love with Dotsie, Nic had another mental breakdown early in 1936. This time he was an inpatient under the care of Dr. Malcolm Kemp, a psychiatrist who had returned to his native state to establish Pinebluff Sanitarium in Pinebluff, North Carolina. What embarrassment it probably cost Agatha to write the following letter to Tom Wilson:

Chapel Hill, May 4, 1936

Dear Tommie,

I'm sorry to bother you about this, but I wonder if it would be possible for Nic to receive the balance of his royalties now instead of later. It would be a great convenience to me since of course all the expenses of his illness have to be met with cash. But if it will upset the system too much or embarrass you in any way, just forget it.

Nic continues to improve, but is not yet well enough to leave—and I try not to think too far ahead. . . .

Tell Dotsie I want to write to her, but I've been very busy lately. I hope she is keeping well. My love to her and Tombo—and many many thanks to you.

Most cordially,
Agatha[10]

Two days later, Wilson sent Agatha a check for just over $100, the unpaid royalties on Nic's Holt books for 1935. He wrote, "[It is] a real pleasure to accommodate you and we shall be very glad to co-operate similarly in the future." Nic Adams's Spanish textbooks continued in print for several more decades.

Two novels that Alice Adams admired, *The Death of the Heart* by Elizabeth Bowen and *What Maisie Knew* by Henry James, investigated the effect of parental affairs on a child's consciousness. In her own fiction Adams turned similar themes every which way—experimenting with the figures in her life as she'd once played with her dolls. In the short story "At First Sight," for instance, a young boy named Walker Conway falls in love with a small, blond woman named Posey whose flirtatious femininity and light blue dress—a contrast to his large, somber mother—entrances him just as Dotsie probably once entranced Alice. The couples in the story, like the Adamses and Wilsons, maintain a lively friendship, "animated, of course, by the strong attraction between

Posey and John." In the end both Posey's husband and Walker's mother commit suicide, leaving Walker to feel punished when Posey becomes his stepmother. By then he is an adult and openly gay. With Walker, we are left to feel that women are emotionally threatening.[11]

Nic's depressions—Alice considered him a manic-depressive, though a stress disorder rooted in his war experiences, marital unhappiness, or grief for his son, all of it exacerbated by alcohol, also seems possible— recurred through much of his life. In the early summer of 1937, he was too ill to leave his doctors to go to Lake Sebago, so Agatha stayed with him in Chapel Hill and wrote Tom Wilson to request an extension of the due date of the history of Spanish literature for which Nic was contracted. Wilson's reply indicates that she was doing "spade work" for the book, and he encouraged her to go beyond that: "We ourselves will be just as glad and proud to publish a book by Adams and Adams as we would be to handle a work by only one Adams." Understanding that Agatha might need to support herself, Wilson also agreed to send her occasional freelance editorial work.[12]

Even during this awkward time, as Agatha faced reversals of love and fortune, Nic Adams pursued Tom Wilson's wife until, upon receiving a gift from him late in 1937, Dotsie replied, "Thank you so much for the powder—I like it—but getting a present from you has caused me a considerable amount of worry—the point is this—you absolutely must not write me or send me anything again. . . . The only thing to do is to completely forget me and all of us. . . ."[13]

Alice escaped the emotional uncertainties of home at the "formidable brick square" public school on Franklin Street that housed all eleven grades of Chapel Hill's white student body. Even the youngest pupils were conscious of the town's "three, and only three, distinct social classes. (Negroes could possibly make four, but they were so separate, even from the poorest whites, as not to seem part of the social system at all; they were in effect invisible.)"[14] As a professor's child, Alice was part of the top stratum, above the children of townspeople and far above those who rode in from the country on yellow trucks. She excelled at school, where she had skipped a grade, and looked the part of a good, normal Southern girl. Nonetheless, she saw herself as an outsider: "I was a dark[-haired] little girl and the two girls across the street who were very beautiful were blonde, so I think of blondness as a kind of impossible, forbidden condition."[15] Feeling herself to be different, Alice was intrigued by the uncouth, often overaged "truck children" who represent "forces that [are] dark and strange" in her story "Truth or Consequences." Her narrator describes Carstairs Jones: "Helplessly I turned around to stare at the back of the room, where the tallest boys sprawled in their too small desks. . . . There was Car, the tallest of all, the most bored, the least contained. Our eyes met, and even at that distance I saw that his were not black, as I had thought, but a dark slate blue; stormy eyes, even when, as he rarely did, Car smiled."*

For Alice Adams, as for Emily in the story, this "different" and "abnormal" male outsider becomes a violent sexual force. Given a choice of "being covered with honey and eaten alive by ants" or kissing Carstairs Jones, Emily, who has a literal mind, chooses kissing. When word gets out to Car, he tells her she is "the prettiest one of the girls" and summons her to meet him alone: "He stared at me, stormily, with what looked like infinite scorn . . . was I less pretty, seen close up? . . . Car reached for my hair and pulled me toward him; he bent down to my face and for an instant our mouths were mashed together. (Christ, my first kiss!) Then, so suddenly that I almost fell backward, Car let go of me. With a last look of pure rage he was out of the trellis and striding across the field, toward town, away from the school."[16] Unclear about what this boy-man wants of her, the girl is gripped by confusion. "Car was mad, no doubt about that, but did he really hate me? In that case, why a kiss?"

Agatha Adams called her daughter "my obstreperous one" and noted that she could be "extremely sweet at times!"[17] Alice was probably thinking of herself with approval when she described SallyJane in *A Southern Exposure* as a "rude, aggressive, assertive little girl. Never 'sweet' like all the other daughters of their friends." When Alice's six-months-younger cousin, Mary Elizabeth Jervey, who stayed with the Adams family in Maine one summer, had had enough of Alice's bossiness, she threatened to write her mother. Alice retorted, "You can't

---

* Adams based Jones on Walter Carroll, a rural Chapel Hill classmate who first married Mary Smith, daughter of *A Tree Grows in Brooklyn* author Betty Smith, who lived in Chapel Hill. Carroll became a playwright. In 1977, Adams was prompted to write her story by news that Carroll had become the third husband of actress Julie Harris.

because I control the mail!" which was true in that Alice usually went to the post office. Mary got the last word by telling Alice, "I'll write it in my heart and my mother will know." Years later, Mary heard that Alice had told the incident to her psychiatrist: "It bugged her that my mother was so close with me that she would know if I was upset. Alice didn't get along with her mother because Agatha didn't understand Alice's artistic bent. She was more literal and bookish. Alice adored Nic. They were all very bright, but Nic was charming. He was my mother's favorite cousin."

Another episode Alice never forgot occurred when she stayed with the Jerveys in Washington, DC. Tired of what he considered Alice's overproud intelligence, Mary's father (once a football star at Clemson University, then a disabled World War I veteran who worked for the Pentagon) set up a rigged spelling bee. He asked his daughter to spell "cat" but demanded "Constantinople" of Alice. In the story she wrote about the incident forty years later, Adams describes herself as "a dark sharply skinny child, with large melancholy eyes and a staggering vocabulary," who envies a "plump and pretty and blond" cousin who "could just smile to get love and not have to spell Constantinople." Associating her uncle's nonvaluation of her intelligence with his Southernness, Adams called the story "A Southern Spelling Bee."[18] Ironically, it was published by the *Virginia Quarterly Review*.

"They all drank like fish," Avery Russell, daughter of Phillips Russell and playwright Paul Green's sister, Caro Mae Green Russell, said of her parents' generation in Chapel Hill. "Their parties began at five and ended at three in the morning." To Russell, Agatha and Nic were a striking couple: "She wore her prematurely gray hair cut short, kind of butch style. She was a handsome woman and Nic was a powerfully attractive man, a great entertainer. He played classical guitar and sang at the parties. When he recited Garcia Lorca's poetry in Spanish in a deep sonorous voice, everybody just swooned. My mother adored Nic."

At one of those parties, Alice pushed her classmate Sandy McClamroch, later a mayor of Chapel Hill, into the swimming pool: "I was wearing all my clothes," he recalled. "She was aggressive." After that incident, as Adams tells it in "Are You in Love?," everyone at the party screams except the girl who did the pushing. Her "face is terrified, appalled." The girl's mother then shouts at her, "loudly, terribly, 'What's the matter with you, are you in love with Harry McGinnis? *Are you in love?*' "*

Love and terror, it would seem, were thoroughly entwined in Agatha's mind. Because of the criticism inflicted by her mother, Alice, like SallyJane in *A Southern Exposure*, found that "thinking of her parents . . . literally *fill[ed]* her, with a heavy, familiar, hard-to-name, and quite intolerable emotion. 'Terror' and 'guilt' are the words that come closest . . ." In Avery Russell's opinion, "those women who had come of age in the 1920s, the flapper era, were just terrible mothers. They were feminists and rebels, and Chapel Hill was very much a matriarchal society—the women ruled—the men kind of sat back and were quite passive. Agatha fit right in there."

And yet, because her parents were both busy, and because Chapel Hill was a small, safe town, Alice was quite free in her personal movements, though required to be in bed by eight-thirty on school nights. Given a lockable diary at Christmastime 1936, she kept up daily entries for three months of her eleventh year.[19] The range of references gives a tender, prescient sketch of a girl poised to leap from childhood to adolescence: she calls her father "Daddy" or "Pop" and complains (often) when he arrives late to pick her up after school or Girl Scouts; she makes clothes for her doll and tries to write a poem every night; she meets her father's friends and renders quick judgments on them: "Met Mr. Crofts. Like him a lot." She prides herself on winning at Monopoly and memorizing 207 new words and has "loads of fun" making colors with Craig, who has a chemistry set. For a Scout project, the troop leader made a Negro puppet; at choir practice, "Mr. Lawrence told [them] about slaves. When he talked about breaking up family's [*sic*] tears were rolling down Margaret Neal's cheeks." Alice doesn't say if she then saw any connection between historic slavery and Verlie Jones, who's mentioned as having provided a "swell supper" or "being very mean."

Names of both boy and girl classmates populate the diary, but Alice's best friend is still Josephine MacMillan, who often spends the night. As

* To critic Richard Poirier in 1974, Adams explained that "Are You in Love?" was "about a woman at some extreme of very specifically sexual frustration, so that any hint of sexuality, especially of course from her daughter, would be unbearable."

spring approaches, Alice writes less often in her diary. Her social life is busy with chapel, dancing lessons, choir practice, a Girl Scout flower hike, and a game of Truth or Consequences played with boys—"that wasn't as much fun but it was okay." There are boys who like her that she can't stand and a favorite, Craig, with whom she's building a double tee-pee in the woods; but, she says, "Craig is lazy so I did most of the work." A few days later, teepee finished, she and Craig "played on the other side of the creek," "had a whole lot of fun," and found "good hiking places in the honeysuckle vines." The children acted out comic strips, and Alice would later tell her own son how she'd hated being assigned the role of an Amazonian "Alice the Goon" from *Popeye*—understandably, because that Alice is a bald bruiser whose nose resembles a flaccid penis. When her cousin Sally Boyd visits from Richmond, the two girls organize an Easter egg hunt for "little children," including "Tombo" Wilson, who is visiting from New York with his mother, Dotsie. Behind the busy girl's days lap the tides of her parents' lives, increasingly distant as she peoples her world with her own friends.

Nic's psychiatrist, Malcolm Kemp, was a frequent visitor to the Adams home during the months Alice kept her diary. Slightly younger than Nic Adams, Kemp was a tall, slender, handsome, gray-eyed man. He probably noticed that Alice needed a companion. In late February, as Alice was recovering from the flu, Kemp brought a particular gift for Alice: "Mother said I would get a grand surprise [*sic*] that would fully make up for [the flu]. I guessed and guessed. At about 8:40 P.M. a car drove up holding [two doctors] and a darling Scotty [*sic*]. He is for me from Dr. Kemp. I love him (I mean the Scotty)." By the next morning, Alice had decided to name her little black dog "Malcome" [*sic*] after Dr. Kemp. "I can call him Mac. I took care of him most of the morning. He really is a great something to care for."

Scottie dogs, by the way, were popular during the FDR era, when several of them, including the president's favorite, Fala, occupied the White House. History tells us that the nation and Nic Adams were still in a depression, but you wouldn't know it from the photograph of Alice with Mac in front of the hearth in the late 1930s. The fire blazes, the andirons are big and brassy, there's a sizable pile of logs ready to burn. Alice is achingly preadolescent in a plaid cotton dress from which extend her long, white, slender arms, long legs, and large feet in white socks and patent leather shoes (chosen with her father, as noted in her diary). Her legs are awkwardly splayed under her low footstool; her soft, uncurled brown hair is drawn back from her pretty face by a headband; and her sweet smile is all for the dog, which returns her adoring gaze.

Like many children, especially only children who feel outnumbered by adults, Alice suspected her family was unlike others. In an unpublished story a girl named Jane asks, "Was this the way other people were together? She had been wondering that all her life, since early and appalling scenes with her parents, and she had never found an answer. . . . In the books of Jane's childhood, parents and children went on excursions that turned out well, and lived sunnily ever after. How was one to know what was possible?"[20]

Alice's mother meant to recognize deficits in Alice's upbringing when she wrote a Wordsworthian poem called "Legacy" for her. In it she confided that she'd been unable to give her daughter "beauty / Or the glow of charm" and instead offered her the "subtler weapons" of nature's "loveliness remembered" as "a sanctuary from all hurts and fears."[21] In this Agatha misjudged herself and maligned Alice. The "subtler weapons" she would bequeath to her daughter were courage in the face of disappointment, along with dignity, ambition, and a not-always-endearing pride. Agatha could see that Alice already trembled on the edge of her own beauty and charm and that the freedom she enjoyed outdoors was teaching her not escape but rather a direct and vital sensuality. Arriving in Maine in time for a "flamboyant Sebago sunset" one August, Agatha wrote, "Though I was too tired to express rapture as vigorously as Alice did, by leaps and shouts and hugging trees, I felt it just as much."[22]

Alice's joy in nature also appeared in the poems she wrote. A sapphire-blue notebook labeled "Scriblings" [sic] in one place and "The Poems of Alice Adams by Alice Adams" in another—a contrast that reveals uncertainty about how seriously to take what is obviously quite serious for her—holds dozens of them composed between 1934 and 1939. Most of her verses are about the peace of the woods, sun, and trees. They surpass Agatha's in their close sensory observations of nature. They're seldom didactic and abstract, and the images are often striking: "Mortal's ghosts are white and dull / . . . the ghost of the sun is the radiant sky / . . . It glows in lakes and human hearts and harmonizes perfectly."

Nic and Agatha enjoyed their daughter's literary precocity—"writing sonnets at all was considered both virtuous and unusual, by everyone, including myself"—but as an adult and a fiction writer, Adams dismissed her poems as "an exceptionally pleasant pastime, all those nice words tidily arranged." She'd relished the attention that her poems garnered but came to believe that such praise as "Oh, what a darling little poem, and Alice is only six. Isn't she just the smartest little thing?" from her parents' friends was patronizing. Well-brought-up Southern women were expected to be pretty, charming, and agreeable. If they were smart, as of course many were, they were not to display it: "To be smart, in Polite Southern Conversation, meant to be out of line, somehow; if you were a woman, it meant that you were being most unwomanly."[23]

Poems and good spelling marks weren't enough to offset Agatha's melancholy and criticism or Nic's emotional absence. No matter how beautifully Alice dressed her dolls, how many words she memorized, or how many sonnets she wrote, she felt alone in her family's house. With a curious inversion of importance and description, her essay "My First and Only House" devotes pages to describing the surrounding gardens and woods. There, life abounded: "What I most remember is flowers—everywhere. Roses, pink and white ones, climbed up a trellis and over the roof of the porch, entangled there with thick wisteria vines, rose petals and heavy lavender blossoms brushed the roof's green shingles and the ground."*

Adams flinches from describing daily life inside of the house: "[It] was splendid for parties, for bringing people home to. Everyone admired its impressive size and the splendid view. And we three difficult, isolated people got along much better when there were others around. Even Verlie . . . liked cooking for parties more than for just us three. So my parents entertained a lot." But other people were not enough to fill the void. Summer parties that stretched into the night terrified Alice as she lay alone in her room: "They sang a lot, her parents and their friends, as the night wore on . . . they sounded like the cannibals in Tarzan movies."[24]

The house on the hilltop south of Chapel Hill where Alice felt that she'd slept too far away from her parents held iconic power in Alice's

---

* Although it's collected with short stories, the piece first appeared as nonfiction in *Geo* magazine in 1984.

imagination, a symbol of something missing from her childhood. She was, she said, haunted by "the irretrievableness" of her past and a longing to "revise that past and make it different."[25] Alice never named the missing thing in her childhood. But her essay about the house tells us: "Below us, in a small house down the hill . . . lived a family of six: two parents, four small children. Very likely they were truly needy people. I somehow learned, or heard, that they all slept together in one bed. And I felt the most passionate envy of that condition, that bodily family warmth. As I imagined it, they would all lie, cuddled like puppies, with the mother and father on the outside edges, protectively."[26]

To find "bodily family warmth" would be one of Alice Adams's quests for the rest of her life. In 1937, she found some comfort in her little Scottie: "Mac sleeps on my bed. He is nice and warm," she told her diary. As she approached her eleventh birthday, as her breasts first developed, Adams recalled, Robert Macmillan (he of the marvelous penis) suddenly took new interest in her. While they did "nothing significant like holding hands" (certainly nothing involving the erogenous zones), they "somehow arrived at a point of writing intense love letters" when Alice went to camp in Maine. She "loved writing to him" and getting letters in return, though she later quipped, "What I did not know then was that I simply loved to write."[27]

CHAPTER FIVE

Girls

— 1937–1940 —

*There in the heavy scent of roses on the scratchy shingles, Harriet
and I talked about sex.*

—Alice Adams, "Roses, Rhododendron,"
Beautiful Girl

At Camp Wabunaki in Cumberland County, Maine, for a month
before her family's annual sojourn at Sebago Lake, Alice shared
a "tenthouse" with six girls her age and a counselor. She acquired a
nickname—Timmie—and learned to sail, ride horseback, and hike—
activities that distanced her from her sedentary parents. The camp had
vague lesbian overtones. " 'Crushes' on counselors . . . were openly
acknowledged, teased about, and thus encouraged, as 'romances' with
boys were not," Alice wrote later. She was made to feel "somewhat
aberrant, if not downright sleazy," for maintaining her crush on Robert
Macmillan.[1] Experiencing the quick loyalties and jealousies, giggly secrets
and confessions of girldom as well as the joy of feeling connected to
the deep lake and mountains, Alice began to know and enjoy herself as
an independent being outside of Nic and Agatha's sphere of influence.

When she came back from Maine to begin seventh grade, eleven-
year-old Alice's high forehead, finely arched brows, straight nose, hazel
eyes, and full lips were framed by thick brunette hair cut shoulder length
and softly waved. She returned to the same brick school on Franklin
Street where she'd attended the elementary grades, but her changing
body and emotions transformed her perception of this world.

Adolescence is nothing if not desperately self-conscious. It was especially so for Alice.

At camp Alice had dropped her Southern accent for a "very Bostonian manner of speech, with an emphasis on broad A's," symbolically rejecting Southernness: "I thought anyone who talked like that, with that accent, was stupid and ignorant, and unkind and unfair to Negroes. I disliked southern girls especially, and generally did not feel liked by them."[2] Her North Carolina girlfriends with their cute double names and nicknames—Betty Sue, Snooky, and the like—their belle-in-training talk and flouncy dresses, now bothered Alice. She saw her mother's unhappiness in her role as a Southern wife and sensed few alternatives for herself. If Agatha, whom everyone conceded was brilliant, could not find her way out of the morass, how could Alice? Like feminist mothers in later eras, Agatha probably wanted to teach her daughter to rely on her mind more than on her beauty. As parental good intentions are wont to do, this one misfired. Years later, Adams put a bit of dialogue in her notebook about a mother whose daughter (Cary) has been praised for being pretty: " 'You mustn't take things people say too seriously—it's what's inside that counts,' from which Cary concluded that she was not pretty, inside or out."[3]

While sitting on the window seat in her living room on a bright fall day in 1937, Alice saw an unfamiliar girl with long blond braids striding along Old Pittsboro Road. The girl moved along the red-clay road like a Yankee, Alice thought. The next day Alice saw the girl again, riding toward town on a blue bicycle. When the girl returned, Alice was standing by the road with her own bike, which happened to be identical. "We exclaimed at the coincidence of bikes, and I pointed up at my house. 'That's where I live,' I told her." The other girl declared, "God, what a wonderful house!" in a voice Alice found serious and emphatic. More pleasing to Alice than the girl's opinion of the house were her Northern accent and manner. "Nice southern girls . . . did not say 'God' in that way." Moved more to action than talk, Alice told the girl she knew a really good bike ride, and off they rode.[4]

So began six decades of friendship between Alice and Judith Walker Clark. At least that's one way Alice wrote the story of a meeting that changed her youth, and possibly the rest of her life. Judith later recalled that their parents met first and brought the girls together, which sounds accurate but less true to Alice's desire for this crucial friendship to begin

outside of Agatha and Nic's realm. Judith saw in Alice "this astonish-
ingly beautiful, brilliant, difficult, sensual girl."[5] The two girls liked to
read "the same odd mix of children's and 'grownup' books"; no one
restricted their reading and they could get all the books they wanted
from the Bull's Head, where Agatha "presided over genteel teas" for
guests and authors.[6] They both read *Look Homeward, Angel* and *The
Grapes of Wrath*. Steinbeck's novel about the Dust Bowl thrilled Alice
with its forbidden words and allusions to sex—"the freedom to say
exactly what you wanted to say"—and disturbed her because "he was
writing about appalling conditions that existed even at the moment of
my reading about them."[7]

Many decades later, Judith asked Alice, "You were totally un-
Southern. How do you suppose you managed to escape that, Alice? You
were absolutely unlike Kitty, Snooky, Betsy, and the rest of them—how
come? Brains alone? I think we became such good friends because we
were both pretty damn direct and had such passions for words and
woods!"[8]

Judith Clark came to North Carolina from Wisconsin by way of
Connecticut with her parents, James G. and Dorothy Funk Clark, and
older sister, Jane, so that her father, an engineer in his forties, could
pursue his dream of getting a PhD in Civil War history. Living on
income from Iowa farmland and the sale of a family business to the
OshKosh B'gosh overalls company, the Clarks took advantage of North
Carolina's low cost of living and an introduction to Chapel Hill by their
friend Johnsie Burnham, who had been the first female violinist in the
Metropolitan Opera Orchestra, to sit out the Depression in Chapel
Hill. If this was a sensible and frugal plan, the Clarks carried it out with
style. They arrived in a café-au-lait Cadillac convertible bought from a
friend in distress and, like the Baird family in Adams's novel *A Southern
Exposure*, moved into a suite in a local inn.

Even before she met Judith, Alice had free run of her surroundings.
Though her mother or Verlie sometimes scolded her for mussing her
clothes, for Alice the outdoors was a realm of contentment and beauty.
Citing novelists, including Emily Brontë and Colette, who wrote boldly
about female experience, Simone de Beauvoir notes that they turned
to nature when they felt trapped between the restrictions of childhood
and the limitations of adult womanhood: "In the paternal house reign
mother, laws, custom, and routine . . . in the midst of plants and animals

she is a human being . . . freed both from her family and from males. She finds an image of the solitude of her soul in the secrecy of forests." When such a girl "takes possession of [nature], she also proudly takes possession of herself," de Beauvoir concludes.[9]

Alice asserts just such possession in her 1936 poem "When I Was Queen." Placing herself among honeysuckle-covered trees, she declares, "My blood seemed made of joy and love . . . The wind in the trees seemed mine / The brook sang only for me." With a moss-cushioned stone for a throne, she "was queen for the day."

The more athletic and adventurous Judith introduced Alice to all-day vagabonding by foot or by bicycle. "Nobody worried about us. It was a great gift. We could have hurt ourselves but we didn't," Judith said of their wanderings along Morgan Creek and through the woods with her black English setter named Cinder. "The great thing about the woods from a child's point of view," Adams wrote decades later, "was that parents almost never came along; the woods were quite safe then, and there was a lot to do."[10]

These "woods as dense and as alien as a jungle would have been—thick pines with low sweeping branches, young leafed-out maples, peeling tall poplars, elms, brambles, green masses of honeysuckle," twine throughout Adams's fiction. Judith remembers, "We discovered that waterfall together that Alice writes about over and over—she was really crazy about that waterfall." Another place was Laurel Hill. Judith's long, vivid memory corroborates what Adams wrote in stories: "We came to a small beach, next to a place where the creek widened and ran over some shallow rapids. On the other side, large gray rocks rose steeply. Among the stones grew isolated, twisted trees, and huge bushes with thick green leaves. The laurel of Laurel Hill."[11] In Adams's psychic geography the woods take on a symbolism that's familiar in American literature—in Washington Irving and Nathaniel Hawthorne, for instance—opposite the domesticated and gardened world, a place of privacy and intimacy and fecundity that's also dangerous.

But Adams's woods lack the dark forces that torment Hawthorne's Puritans. When Judith and Alice bragged about going to Laurel Hill, boys told them the area was full of snakes. But, Judith said, "We never thought about it! In those years we spent wandering around those woods, we never saw a tramp, we never saw anybody. We saw one cottonmouth snake which scared us to death but we'd been wading in the creek and we decided, well, we'd better not do that anymore. I think we had the grace of innocence. It was just gorgeous, really beautiful."

The girls' ramblings allowed Alice to stop being the "skinny and nervous" version of herself who expresses her frustrations in "Child's Play" with a "long-worded, show-off way of talking." In the woods no one else heard what she and Judith said or cared if they sat like ladies or dirtied their dresses. Outdoors, de Beauvoir exclaims, "having a body no longer seems like a shameful failing . . . flesh is no longer filth: it is joy and beauty."[12] In a short story called "An Unscheduled Stop," Adams's protagonist, a writer named Claire who is flying across the South, "bursts into violent tears" at the sight of the lush pinewoods where she spent "her true childhood. . . . Claire's excess of feeling is like a secret life exposed."

In her friendship with Judith, Alice enjoyed a specifically female intermission between her solitary childhood spent in an adult society and the adolescence that even then bore down upon her. Her fiction shows that freedom to wander the woods and creeks of the Carolina Piedmont was a counterpoint to the confusion and shame that girls usually feel about the new protuberances and discharges of their bodies. The fullness of Alice and Judith's friendship affirms Mary McCarthy's belief that friendship is "the growth hormone the mind requires as it begins its activity of producing and exchanging ideas. You can date the evolving mind, like the age of a tree, by the rings friendship formed by the expanding central trunk. In the course of my history, not love or marriage so much as friendship has promoted growth."[13]

Judith's parents may have been as much a revelation to Alice as their daughter was. During their first year in Chapel Hill, Jimmy Clark bought a lot near the Adamses' enclave. He designed a modern house and hired two black laborers who were both named Charlie to build it. Influenced by Frank Lloyd Wright's Jacobs I house in Madison, Wisconsin, the Clarks' multilevel house was set into a hollowed-out hillside. Dorothy Clark collected art and antiques and painted bright murals in all the rooms. A game room—something no one else had in Chapel Hill—on the coolest, lowest level, opened out to a flagstone terrace. That room, equipped with a couch and record player, became a perfect place for parties as the girls got older. Unlike Agatha and Nic,

Judith's parents were affectionate with each other when they were happy and openly hostile when they fought. Both of them adored Alice and engaged in conversations with her when she visited. Dorothy Clark drew twin charcoal portraits of Alice and Judith, and Jimmy Clark played guitar and sang, often performing with Nic Adams at parties.

Alice Adams and Judith Clark, by Judith's mother.

On the other hand, the elegance and gentility of the Adams household was "terribly important" to Judith. The living room, with Agatha's desk on one side, was full of beautiful old furniture. There was polished silver in the dining room. Most of all, Judith remembered the scents that lingered in the hot summer air: roses baking in the sun beneath open windows, the furniture and silver polishes, Nic's pipe smoke, something from Agatha—lavender perhaps?—and Verlie's lemon cake. Alice's room had wood floors and rag rugs, a rocking chair, and low bookshelves beneath the windows. Often Judith spent the night on a cot beside Alice's walnut four-poster bed. On sweltering summer nights, the two girls would climb out the sewing room window to sit on a slanted roof facing the woods.

Sitting on that roof would become a scene in "Roses, Rhododendron": "There was a country smell, invaded at intervals by summer country sounds—the strangled croak of tree frogs from down in the glen, the crazy baying of a distant hound. There in the heavy scent of roses on the scratchy shingles, Harriet and I talked about sex." Most of their talk was hearsay, but the freedom Alice felt in her friendship with

Judith is remarkable. In "Roses, Rhododendron" a girl who has moved to North Carolina from Boston narrates how she "fell permanently in love with a house, with a family of three people and with an area of countryside." That family comprises Harriett, Emily, and Lawrence Farr, who live in what is essentially the Adams house and carry on the lonely motions of Adams's family story. The story's perspective exemplifies how becoming intimate friends with Judith allowed Alice to expand her sense of possibilities for her own future.

Agatha Adams also began a dramatic change in her life in 1937. That autumn she persuaded a skeptical committee to admit her as an undergraduate in UNC's Library School, even though she was ten years past the upper age limit for admissions and already possessed degrees in other subjects. It helped that her husband had "permitted" her to "work on vocabularies of Spanish texts and do a little proofreading and editing," she wrote. "The distrust with which they finally admitted me was only surpassed by my own distrust of my ability to make the grade," she added. But she felt she had no choice. At forty-four, still observing the decorum of the patrician-class and Southern womanhood to which she was born, Agatha could not decide to divorce Nic Adams—nor could she rely on him to support the family. Her fellow Randolph-Macon alumna Pearl Buck had just won the Nobel Prize in Literature, while Agatha's literary aspirations had come to naught.

In her Library School classes, Agatha considered herself "an old woman in a class of college youngsters," but she finished her ten necessary courses in five trimesters, receiving her bachelor's degree in library science in April 1939. Immediately she took a position with the Extension Library at UNC, where she provided reference services to people all over the US. "Whether the requests are stimulating, or amusing, or merely annoying," she told the alumnae at her alma mater, "they guarantee that no day's work will be monotonous." She also wrote study guide booklets for extension courses with titles ranging from "Nature Writers in the United States" to "Contemporary Negro Arts." Agatha found her new profession more satisfying than her previous one, which she described as "learning to keep house . . . and helping a child along from cod liver oil to dancing school."[14]

Though Alice Adams's childhood sounds middle class to some readers today, it was truly privileged compared to that of many of her Southern neighbors. In the nearby towns of Carrboro and Pittsboro, poverty was severe. The 1940 census reports that Agatha earned a salary of $1,300, a significant addition to Nic's professorial salary of $3,700 and book royalties of $300. Whether there was also some inherited money is unclear, but a school application Agatha filled out for Alice that year lists bank accounts in both Chapel Hill and Fredericksburg, Virginia. The census values the Adamses' house, which had not just indoor plumbing but an extra toilet for Verlie, at $15,000. That was probably an overestimate for those times when the South was "the Nation's #1 economic problem," as President Roosevelt wrote in 1938. FDR based his statement on a study that showed that half the families of the South had an annual income of less than $300. Statistics don't always give a vivid picture: consider that one-third of urban Southern homes lacked indoor plumbing, while fewer than 1 percent of farm families had an indoor water supply. Though they were getting along comfortably, Nic and Agatha had again voted for Roosevelt in 1936 as the politician most likely to bring the United States out of the Depression.

During the summer of 1938, Alice went first to visit relatives in Ocean City, Maryland, and then to several sessions at Camp Wabunaki, while Nic and Agatha traveled for two months in Cuba and Mexico. Their trip to Spanish-speaking America was motivated by the impossibility of visiting their beloved Spain since the outbreak of the Spanish Civil War in July 1936. That year, Nic had canceled a trip to Spain he'd planned with his favorite cousin, Anne Jervey, and her daughter, Mary Elizabeth.[15]

"Even after all these years," Nic Adams wrote in *The Heritage of Spain* (1943), "it is difficult to write of the Spanish Civil War with proper objectivity." He takes pains to explain that the Spanish Republicans were socialists rather than communists, and that Roosevelt and 76 percent of Americans favored the Loyalists but opted for nonintervention. He's bitterly clear about his opinion that the democratic nations that now deplore fascist Spain "shilly-shallied and permitted the triumph of Franco, ally of Hitler and Mussolini."[16] The Adamses would have

approved of Mexico's official support to the Spanish Republic. Furthermore, since the end of the Mexican Revolution in the early 1920s,
Mexico had become a popular destination for foreigners, especially
the "American leftists who had come down to enjoy the revolt of the
masses," as D. H. Lawrence biographer Brenda Maddox puts it.[17] Lawrence, himself part of the band of literary tourists who passed through
Mexico in those years, made scornful fun of those who were "Bolshevist
by conviction but capitalist by practice."[18]

As an adult, Adams claimed that her complicated feelings about her
father interfered with her efforts to learn Spanish or read *Don Quixote*.
And yet, in what seems another sort of inheritance, she loved Mexico.
Perhaps Agatha influenced that. While Nic didn't write about Latin
America until the 1960s, Agatha used her notes and memories of the
summer of 1938 for her extension course guide called *A Journey to Mexico*.
"No one can fully understand Mexico who takes Europe with him or
who goes hoping to find there a transplanted Spain," she warns in that
pamphlet.[19] Her personal travel diary of Cuba and Mexico is a subtly
different document from the one she and Nic kept in Europe in 1922
during a brighter year of her marriage. Her Mexican journal rarely mentions Nic by name ("Aug. 10: Nic went to guitar factory").[20] Nonetheless
her notes reveal an inquisitive, responsive woman rarely disturbed by
the inconveniences and dangers of travel. Stopping first in Havana, the
woman whose daughter saw her as a snobbish Virginian-Episcopalian
notices "a synthesis of races—all over the city impossible to tell Cuban
from Spaniard from negro. Some very black African types, e.g. the big
male rumba dancer—more mulattos—and all the intervening creamy
golden shades." She wonders, "Is our cult of sunburn of the past few
years a tacit admission that brown skin is more attractive than white?"
She is taken with a Negro orchestra "with jungle rhythms in its beat"
as well as with "the wriggling flexible brown hips of the golden-skinned
dancer, her strong pliant waist, her frank sexuality."

In Mexico City the Adamses called upon a fellow North Carolinian, US ambassador Josephus Daniels, whose son they knew at
home.[21] While they were at the embassy, on August 16, Agatha notes,
"A messenger came in to say that the entire Spanish cabinet in Barcelona resigned today. . . ." A distraught Ambassador Daniels exclaimed
that this was "the worst thing that ever happened" and predicted that
Spain would henceforth belong to Hitler and Mussolini. Despite his

pro-democracy views, the elder Daniels had been a key player in a successful turn-of-the-century campaign to disenfranchise Negroes in North Carolina. A generation later, men like Jonathan Daniels, the son the Adamses knew at home and editor of the Raleigh *News and Observer*, were considered "liberals" on race in the 1930s because they "desired to see more justice and opportunity for blacks within the segregated system," writes historian Jennifer Ritterhouse.[22] It's likely Nic Adams shared that position.

Agatha Adams was politically more progressive. Her views probably moved further left as she corresponded with a variety of people through her work at the extension library, from a soldier who requested the Kinsey report to help him with his homosexuality to a man imprisoned in the North. Agatha owned and studied *The Intelligent Woman's Guide to Socialism, Capitalism, Sovietism, and Fascism* by George Bernard Shaw; more practically, as Adams's short story "Child's Play" indicates, Agatha volunteered to drive sick Negro women to see doctors and, against considerable resistance, recruited other faculty wives to do the same.

Visiting Mexico thrilled Agatha. "The traveller to Mexico crosses psychological boundaries far deeper and wider than the torpid stretch of mud and silt which we call the Rio Grande," she writes. "He must be ready to go very far back into unwritten history."[23] Now the streets are "an endless variety show. Heaps of fruit, spread out on sidewalks or on small tables often artistically decorated with leaves and piled in rich mounds of color—grapes, big wine-red plums, frosty green cactus pears, pineapple, watermelon, pears, peaches, mangoes, avocadoes . . . glass barrels full of violently colored fruit drinks—magenta and yellow and green and watermelon pink. Everywhere color—clashing."

Agatha's sense of humor shows too. About an advertisement for Acapulco—"the fisherman's Paradise, where beautiful women bathe in the sea all the year"—she editorializes, "At last the truth about fishing trips!" Observing that modern Mexico is Indian rather than Spanish, she writes: "the Cathedral on the Zocalo is a tawdry bedizened old grande dame, who has taken to dope, and drags her tarnished velvets in the dust . . . Here the Catholic church is moribund—the cathedral smells of death."

Some people considered Agatha Adams a difficult woman. But, as her daughter writes in "The Wake," with Jessica standing in for Agatha, "there was another truth, another Jessica who lurked, unbidden and misunderstood . . ." Her Mexico journal gives glimpses of that freer, more receptive woman. One night in the silversmithing town of Taxco, she (and Nic, presumably) drank *tequila almendrado* (almond-flavored tequila) with a couple of acquaintances: "Vicento and Tito took us out on a serenata, & played their guitars on the hilltop shrine and the milky way swung up over the mountain behind Taxco."

The woman who wrote those words is truly the literary mother of Alice Adams.

While the beautiful woods of Maine and North Carolina and Judith's friendship were the first forces that liberated Alice from the complicated emotions of her home, the male sex soon became the more urgent. Puberty came upon Alice early and hard. She was crazy about boys, or rather about falling in love with such beings, but her quest to grow up was greatly complicated by the charm of her face, the early maturity of her breasts, the sensitivity of her intelligence, and her painful perceptions of her parents' marriage.

Adams later said that she "remembered everything that ever happened to her," and that almost seems to be true of what she called her "strenuous" adolescence. In becoming an adolescent she was also—unknowingly at that time—entering the great subject of her life and fiction. Adams "threw a different kind of light on women and what they want, or think they want," the Canadian novelist Mavis Gallant wrote. "They were women whose beauty was part of their dilemma, almost a handicap."[24] If that's so, Alice's dilemmas began early. If her father was too self-involved to notice her, there was no shortage of suitors and lovers who did, and she in turn fell in love with many men in her life.

The first stage of dating, at least for Alice's set in Chapel Hill, was the afternoon movie date. "Sex among the barely adolescent was extremely limited in scope; we actually did very little, certainly none of the advanced goings-on that I have since heard and read about," Adams recalled in 1991. But in the middle of Laurence Olivier and Merle Oberon's 1939 film of *Wuthering Heights*, a boy named Kurt reached for and held on to her hand, and she later wrote, "It is hard, now, to describe the extreme sensuality of those two warm adolescent hands, closely gripped. I can only say that it was just that, extremely sensual, totally involving. Thrilling is possibly the word." There's nothing unusual about that scene. But for Adams, and apparently for that boy, a recent refugee from Germany, holding hands led to an "engagement," which was necessarily brief because Kurt's parents soon took him with them to New York. When he broke the news, adding that he'd write but she should feel free to see movies with other boys, Alice was relieved. And excited: because now there would be "other hands to hold."[25]

Some of those hands belonged to boys who walked her the mile and a half home from downtown Chapel Hill. These walks "sometimes came to include a chaste but passionate kiss" on the secluded dirt road. Such a kiss in *Families and Survivors* tells Louisa she is in love: "Waking on Monday to a thick silent world of snow, and waking in love with Richard (since she loves to kiss him, she must be in love with him, mustn't she? Of course she is) . . ." And so it will continue perhaps throughout Alice Adams's life.

"I don't think Alice had a stronger sex drive than the rest of us," Judith Clark said. "But she loved the narrative of a love affair." Her experience and her theory of love were modern, somehow bridging Victorian and postsixties moral codes. The Jazz Age was over, of course, but it had loosened the rules. Still, the kind of unattached sexual desire and freedom men are said to enjoy was not allowed to girls when Alice was growing up. To enjoy passion, young Alice wanted to feel emotional attachment—love. And that feeling of love often ran ahead of any reasonable attempt to decide if a particular male, a particular relationship, was what she needed or wanted. Inexorably, her mental agility turned the experiments and misadventures of her love life into remarkable fictional explorations of the subject of love.

Eighth graders in 1938, Alice and Judith, then twelve, were considered freshmen at Chapel Hill High School because CHHS, like most Southern public schools then, did not offer twelfth grade. "We were all *very* anxious to grow up and get out of our parents' way," Judith recalled. There were about 120 students in their class, and Alice had known most of them since she was five. She played flute in the band and was vice president of Junior Hi-Y, a coed social and service club. With Judith, she attended Episcopal confirmation classes at the Chapel of the Cross, mainly because the Macmillan twins and other boys of interest were there. During the summer of 1939, Judith ordered instructions from a magazine for starting a sub-deb club, the purpose of which was to exchange gossip and beauty tips and plan small dance parties. That was probably as trivial as it sounds, but it offset the galloping pace of world events that reached them through newsreels, radio programs, and adult discussion. The Munich Agreement, signed by England, France, Germany, and Italy, had led to the takeover of Czechoslovakia by Germany; the mayhem of Kristallnacht made clear to anyone paying attention that Hitler's intentions toward the Jews were deadly. Judith's father, James Clark, began raising money for a British war relief organization, something he did so successfully that he soon set aside his doctoral studies and began a new career.

Agatha's full-time return to school and work further urged Alice toward adulthood. Agatha owned the book *Life Begins at Forty*, in which self-improvement promoter Walter Pitkin urged his readers to plan for productive middle years, and Alice sensed that her mother's work was at least partly motivated by the knowledge that she and Nic might separate. According to Agatha's unmarried friend Willie T. Weathers, Agatha "stuck things out" for Alice's sake and felt "loyalty" rather than "duty" toward Nic. Strangely enough, Nic's problems with severe depression, which were at least partly related to his unconsummated attractions to other women, served to bind Agatha to him.[26]

Alice's discontent with her family intensified her adolescence: "I was eleven, and both my parents were in their early forties, and almost everything that went so darkly and irretrievably wrong among the three of us was implicit in our ages," she writes in "Return Trips." In that story a narrator who is "eager for initiation into romantic sensual mysteries" explains: "For my mother the five years from forty-two or forty-three onward were a desolate march into middle-age. My father, about ten months younger than my mother—and looking, always, ten years younger—saw his early forties as prime time; he had never felt better in his life." (This was true of Nic, who was actually three years younger than Agatha and looked it—at least when he was happy. But there were the depressions.)

Agatha, for so long an earnest and frustrated woman, naturally worried that Alice would fall in love unwisely or go too far with boys. In "Return Trips" the mother "wept and raged, despairing and helpless as she recognized the beginning of [her daughter's] life as a sensual woman, coinciding as it probably did with the end of her own." In jottings toward a story in Adams's 1954 notebook, pale young men who are practice teachers at the high school intrigue her mother with talk of modern poetry, while she, aged thirteen, follows the same men on her bike and longs to tell them that she too writes poetry. With a final Freudian touch, Adams writes that her father "might once have been such a pale, young man."[27] Since Alice was involved with psychoanalysis in 1954, it seems plausible that she had come to believe that she and her mother had been sparring over Nic Adams all along.

Alice and Judith stayed friends for their two years together at CHHS, even as boys held center stage: "Sometimes we were rivals, though never for the same boy at the same time . . . each of us was highly aware of how big a 'rush' the other got at a dance . . ." At the same time, Alice and Judith were confederates who said "mean things to each other about the sweet surround of southern girls" and confided the times they'd kissed and been kissed, measured their waists and chests and hips with tape measures, and even snuck into the school files to compare their IQ scores. Alice's was higher, but neither of them "put much stock in IQ tests."[28]

In their talks on the roof outside Alice's window, the girlfriends discussed the great mystery of their young lives: "The word sex was rarely used. The act was 'doing it,'" Judith remembered. "Alice told me a boy had told her it made you strong! I think it was one of the Macmillan twins who told her." They heard other theories too: doing it a lot makes your hips get wide; it hurts women a lot, but Filipinos can do it without hurting; colored people do it more than whites, as do Catholics in Boston. On another hot, humid night they stripped off their clothes and practiced "sex appeal" poses from magazine ads at the edge of the Adams swimming pool. The episode became the first chapter of Adams's 1974 novel, *Families and Survivors*.

Adams wrote candidly and often about breasts. In the voice of Melanctha in *A Southern Exposure*, Adams complains about how she suffered from them: "Why do I have to get them? They're sore, and the boys all tease me." Melanctha's mother thinks but doesn't say, as Agatha probably didn't either: "Because you're my daughter . . . having always disliked her own breasts, she can hardly bear to imagine Melanctha's life, in a body very much like hers." No doubt Alice's menstrual periods also commenced early. In the 1930s girls who could afford them relied on disposable napkins attached to ribbon or elastic belts. (Disposable tampons were on the market but deemed unsafe for virgins.) The belts were bulky and showed through clothing, and the lumpy pads made of wood fiber or cotton fit poorly, especially on thin girls, and often leaked. "We called our periods the curse," Judith remembered. "What an unholy mess that was, awful. Lots of accidents and horrible embarrassment."

A girl becoming a woman in modern decades prior to television and formal sex education was beset by confusion. This sudden bleeding that occurred for no apparent reason seemed like a wound. Adolescence threatens a girl, de Beauvoir realized, with a change that is psychic as well as physical, a displacement and limitation of her identity; she "foresees in these changes a finality that rips her from her self; thus hurled into a vital cycle that goes beyond the moment of her own existence, she senses a dependence that dooms her to man, child, and tomb."[29] If Alice could not fight physiology, she nonetheless fought hard against the psychic disruptions that came with it. This meant, for the time being, that her parents, who represented that foreseen doom, were the enemy and her contemporaries were her allies.

Coming to the letters written by Alice Adams when she's away from home in the summers of 1938 and 1939 is a shock after reading her fiction set in the same era. Whatever may have been in the author's mind about puberty and breasts and doing it, whatever rage and confusion she had about her parents, these are the words of a very proper and slightly naughty child with careful grammar. And yet, they show a difference in her feelings about her parents. To Agatha, Alice gave minimal information—"I am having a nice time . . ." To Nic, on the same date, she is complimentary, almost flirtatious: "I like your letter . . . the paper is lovely. Thank you for going back to mother." She doesn't say why he's been away—at Malcolm Kemp's sanatorium again?—but he's apparently been taking care of her "livestock" and one can surmise that the wry term for pets was first used by Nic. In another letter she apologizes for not writing any poetry despite days of rain at camp but says, "Everything is so exquisite here that I feel as though I could not sleep for the weight of unwritten poetry."[30] Or maybe she was just having too much fun with people who did not try to write a poem every day.

Of course Alice is more direct with Judith. Alone on the train to New York, she sits across from a blond boy who gets off before Alice "could do much more than wiggle [her] eyebrows" and buys a ham sandwich, hot chocolate, and apple pie for eighty cents. Lost briefly in Penn Station, she gets help from a "sweet Red Cap" and is soon "slowly suffocating" from the stiffness and formality of her relatives' home in White Plains. At camp, she found the other kids "peachy" and "swell" but disliked her counselor as "an awful, sloppy, fat, horsy, drip." She has "sort of a crush" on a tall girl who has a "ritzy" figure and "the friendliest grin you ever saw." Her unabashed admission of a "crush" on another girl shows an innocence that would be less possible for several succeeding decades. But the high point of camp, as intended, was a "perfectly perfect" overnight expedition to Emerald Pool and South Baldface Mountain with so much climbing that she was "terribly stiff." (Even then Adams favored adverbs.)

Alice asks Judith for gossip about Chapel Hill, especially about one Sammy Andrews: "[He's] still tops with me but he's slightly icy or shy or something like that. You didn't tell him what I said in my last letter, did you? I wouldn't really mind if you did, if you also told him what I said in this one." That intricate message to Judith illustrates how a restriction like the one that says a girl must not pursue a boy outright becomes, in de Beauvoir's view, a defining female characteristic, perhaps an asset: "her interior life develops more deeply . . . she is more attentive to her heart's desires that thus become more subtle, more varied; she has more psychological sense than boys turned toward external goals . . . She tests her situation's ambiguity on a daily basis."[31]

When she was thirteen, Alice was a young woman with a style that distinguished her from most of the other Southern girls in the CHHS *Hillife* class picture. Both she and Judith Clark wore simple figure-flattering flared skirts and sweaters, while the others wore cotton dresses. And yet, there's something vulnerable about Alice: she stands as Judith does with one hip cocked, but her pose looks a bit knock-kneed and uncertain. Alice remained a serious and romantic child, not yet the alluring woman she imagined. Novelist Daphne Athas, then editor of the school's literary magazine, recalled that Alice brought her a poem in the mimeograph room. "She was beautiful, but kind of shy. And the poem was very good. But to me Alice was a snob because she was a professor's daughter."*

During most of her thirteenth year, Alice's boyfriend was James Baugham McMullan. At fifteen, tall, dark-haired Jim McMullan lived in a boardinghouse because his parents had moved to another town where his attorney father had a job. He was the youngest child in his family. Maybe he was the boy in *Families and Survivors* who had "a fantastic collection of records, but not the ordinary ones—Jimmy Lunceford, the Goodman Quintet, Bobby Hackett; Louis Armstrong"—the kind of swing music Alice would favor for years to come. McMullan also, people who knew him later said, loved words, so he and Alice had an affinity there too. "Her first affair or real relationship" was with McMullan, Judith remembered. In love, the woods took on new meaning too, offering her "romantic shelter and privacy for kissing, touching—whatever forms early love took."[32]

If Alice's budding sexuality led her away from home, there was, of course, a short circuit in that path that pulled her back into her confusion about her parents' marriage. Repeatedly Adams writes a version of this scene that evokes "burning rage, a painful, seething shame" in a girl who's out in the night with a boy. In "Return Trips" it goes like this:

> We saw a car stopped, its headlights on. Guiltily we dropped hands . . . In [the car] was my father, kissing someone; their bodies were blotted into one silhouette. If he saw and recognized us, there was no sign . . . I would guess it's more likely he did see us but pretended to himself that he did not, as he pretended not to see that my mother was miserably unhappy, and that I was growing up given to emotional extremes, and to loneliness.

Teenage Jim and Alice spoke of plans to marry on December 20, 1949, ten years to the day after their first date. He wrote it in her yearbook and mentioned it again later. Judith believed that Jim and Alice loved each

* Athas's father, an eccentric Greek intellectual, brought his family south from Gloucester, Massachusetts, to survive the Depression. Athas tells that story in her extraordinary novel *Entering Ephesus*, published by Viking in 1971.

other "dearly." Jim still spoke fondly of Alice to his late-in-life second wife.[33] Genuine as her feeling for Jim was, Alice in love was also enjoying a new form of play with dolls, as does Louisa in *Families and Survivors*: "And Louisa is well embarked on what is to be a lifetime occupation, or preoccupation: the enshrouding of any man at all in veils and layers of her own complexity, so that the love object himself is nearly lost . . . By the time he comes to her door, blond and smiling and happy to see her, he is also innumerable other people, with whom she has imaginatively acted out a hundred passionate episodes."

In the meantime, Jim was going to boarding school at Porter Military Academy in Charleston, South Carolina. They made a date for Christmas vacation, December 20, 1940.

By then Alice would be a thousand miles away in Madison, Wisconsin—where her father went as a visiting professor at the university for the academic year of 1940–41. Alice's wish not to be a Southerner was coming true. Her father thought spending the year at the University of Wisconsin would better his position at UNC: "One is more appreciated at home if it is seen that outsiders are interested." Wisconsin considered Nic "one of the leading Hispanic scholars in the United States" and "an authority on Romanticism" and offered him $4,750 for ten months, a thousand more than his UNC salary. The invitation was less welcome to Agatha, who was just embarking on her paid career with the library in Chapel Hill. She gave up more salary than Nic gained.[34]

Alice would never spend another full year in Chapel Hill but the South was part of her. When she and Judith Clark met, they were thrilled to discover that they both cherished the same line from North Carolinian Thomas Wolfe's *Look Homeward, Angel*:

Oh Lost, and by the wind grieved, ghost, come back again!

Ghosts of Chapel Hill and its people would return to Alice in story after story, year after year, for the rest of her life.

PART II

PREPARATION

CHAPTER SIX

North and South

— 1940–1943 —

Hitler must be stopped. The urgency of it possessed her, what Hitler was doing to the Jews, the horror of it always in her mind. . . . There in the isolationist Midwest she was excoriated as a warmonger.

—Alice Adams, "1940: Fall,"
After You've Gone

"Madison that year burst glamorously upon her," Adams wrote of her arrival in Wisconsin late in the summer of 1940. In an unpublished sketch, she describes her first impressions of the place through the eyes of a classmate who observes her, the new girl from the South: "The color of the urban college crowds, dash of convertibles and football sweaters and chrysanthemums worn on fur—even we, the high school crowd, struck her as vivid, daring—we wore lipstick and high heels to parties, the boys drove cars; violent romances were felt in the sunlit air."[1]

Alice was invited into a popular crowd at Wisconsin High School. They found her bright and self-confident and barely noticed that she had just turned fourteen while most of them were sixteen. In "The Nice Girl"—written some thirty years later—Adams describes a girl like herself who has just moved to Madison from the South: "She observed the complex patterns of the admired, the sought-after, the loved, the popular—the shunned, the derided. She watched couples who went steady . . . watched the prettiest girls flock across the street to Rennebohm's for Cokes after school. All heightened and intensified it came through to her romantic mind."

Terrible news came from the war in Europe that summer when the Adams family moved north. The Nazi army occupied Paris in June. Two million French soldiers and eleven thousand British soldiers became prisoners of war. The port cities of southern France were crowded with Spanish Civil War veterans and Jews from every nation who were now desperate to escape the occupied continent. Just twenty-three years after American troops—Nic Adams among them—had fought the first world war to liberate France from Germany, all had been lost again. Americans were anxiously uncertain about joining another European war. The economy at home was still depressed, the extent of the Nazi genocide was yet unrevealed, and many simply did not want to sacrifice American lives in a foreign war. In July 1940, after newly elected British prime minister Winston Churchill refused to negotiate with Hitler, the German bombing of Britain—the Battle of Britain—commenced. It had taken the Nazis only two and a half months to conquer western Europe. It appeared that Britain stood alone to prevent an invasion of North America.

At first the possibility of America's entry into the war had little effect on Alice. Like Shelley Carter in "The Nice Girl," in "the exhilarating alien air" of Madison she was wondering, "What will the boys here be like?" If Alice had discovered boys in Chapel Hill, in Madison she encountered the complicated landscape of teenage dating and sex. September in her Southern hometown, Shelley remembers, is a "bleached-out, wilted time," but in the new town streets are lined with "monumental poplars, elms already yellow, almost gold. The sky is a brighter, more intense blue than the tranquil Southern skies." Like Shelley, on her first day of high school Alice wore no lipstick but carried a tube of a modest pink shade in her pocketbook "just in case." Seeing that her peers' lips were colored blood red or plum, she applied the pink to her pretty, full lips at the first recess. After school, she bought a darker shade.

Alice's best friend that year would be Jean Salter, a leader in student government. Jean's mother, Katharine Shepard Hayden, was a well-known poet and political activist in Madison, and her father, John T. (Jack) Salter, was a professor of political science. Jean recalled that Alice was "very bright, but most of all she was fun—one of the best friends I ever had. We two really loved each other. It was delightful."

Madison had a town-and-gown social structure like Chapel Hill's, but its differences from that Southern village were critical for Alice in

1940. When the Adamses moved there Madison was a thriving city and state capital of 67,000 that had suffered little in the Depression. The town boasted seven movie theaters and two radio stations. With 11,400 students, the University of Wisconsin was about three times the size of UNC. The Adams family rented a one-story bungalow at 301 Highland Avenue, southwest of the university campus where Nic worked and Alice went to school.

Wisconsin High School, operated by the university for teacher training, was small and selective, with moderate fees. Students who couldn't compete there were diverted to the city's public high schools. On a California Test of Mental Maturity early in the fall, Alice achieved an IQ score of 131, which broke down into 141 for language factors and 116 for nonlanguage factors. She earned A's in most of her classes, which included English, geometry, third-year Latin, and first-year French.

Alice's Carolina accent, which she'd tried to shed at camp, was immediately apparent to her fellow students in Madison, who teased her in their flat Midwestern voices about her difficulty in pronouncing a Northern *R*. Every weekend Alice had dates for movies or dances, followed by pie or French fries and malts at a diner. On December 13, 1940, she began dating Bobby Walker, a tall senior with blue eyes and brown wavy hair, "one of the three smoothest guys in school." Bobby owned a black Ford coupe of which, according to Alice, he was a "marvelous driver" who "usually [went] about 70 . . ." To Judith, she excused his driving—"It's all very gay"—but came closer to truth later when she noted that "Bobby was known to drive wildly."[2]

"The Nice Girl" condenses much of what Adams learned about love during her heady romantic year in Madison. Driving through snowy hills under a full moon that made "patterns of brightness and shade on the smooth, inviolate and endless snow," with a boy named Frank Matthiessen (a stand-in for Bobby), Shelley "wishes that they could drive all night, forever into the white enchanted silence." In Wisconsin, going steady meant an exclusive relationship with ill-defined sexual privileges. The aching anticipations of "All the Things You Are," sung by Helen Forrest with Artie Shaw's band, became *their* song: "I'll know that moment divine / When all the things you are, are mine."

Thus holding hands and kissing in honeysuckle caves in the Southern pine woods was replaced by necking in a car "in the marvelous privacy of deep snowbanks," with "curious pink light on all the surrounding miles of white, reflected in all the lakes." Again, for Adams, the landscape is eroticized by her strong emotions. While naïve characters in the stories notice clichéd romantic symbols like the full moon, the authentic, intelligent characters notice wind, clouds, water, trees, or patterns of light.

Adams toggles often between these two kinds of imagery, just as she alternates between simple romantic fantasies and more detached analysis. Amid the excitement and the kissing, the girl (in the story) wonders what her steady boyfriend is really like: "They still don't talk much, and so his existence is largely in her imagination—and her senses. They are absorbed in kissing, gentle and prolonged." After a formal Christmas dance the girl is in love with her boyfriend and "also in love with the dance, that scene, chiffon and silk and black ties . . . the fragrance of pine and perfume." That night in their parking spot, with the branches around the car laden with fresh snow, "not quite aware that their mouths have opened," the boy "reaches inside her coat, he touches her smooth bare shoulder, but then pulls his hand back. (He 'respects' her.) He says, 'God, some times I wish—' And then he says, 'Are you hungry? Want to go out to O'Connell's?'" The carnal possession promised in "their" song having been postponed, the couple continue to spend most of their time kissing—French kissing, in the black coupe.

The words her boyfriend has spoken about a friend (Steve) who is "just out for what he can get" with his girl echo in Shelley's mind. She decides something must change. On New Year's Eve, under a slender moon, she determinedly tells her boyfriend, "I don't think we should do that any more." Respecting her, he agrees. She playfully asks, "You'll love me anyway?" The boy agrees that he loves her anyway. Stating the lesson Alice would learn—and unlearn—in Madison, Adams explains: "For he believes in her premise, believes he should love her anyway, kissing or not. Love is more important than sex: love is not the same thing."

Despite this belief, the Shelley and Frank in "The Nice Girl" soon break up. They are "wretched and inarticulate" and the girl wishes she could say, "I've changed my mind—let's go off in your car. I love you." She doesn't say that. Instead she spends most of January 1941 "suffering in a classic way." To Judith, Alice explained, "I didn't know what was expected of one when going steady. When Bobby and I broke up I thought life was over."

Alice's letters to Judith tend to confirm that she, like her heroine Shelley in "The Nice Girl," dated several boys from West Madison High

School who drank too much and took her to ballrooms with names like the Top Hat and the Hollywood. Shelley "worries a little that she is becoming fast, but there are so many girls who are a lot faster than she is." Thus Alice's adventures in the backseats of Madison brought her full circle from a doomed attempt at love without sex to seemingly easier and ultimately far more confusing versions of sex without love. One wonders how far Alice went that spring of her debut as a popular and sought-after girl. The evidence of Adams's letters, fiction, and later notebooks suggests that Alice probably did not go "all the way" with any of those Madison boys. Some things could not go in letters: "I'd give *anything* to talk to you for about five hours," Alice complained to Judith. "I've got so *awfully* much to tell you about. You have no idea."

As Alice's school year closed in June, Jim McMullan from North Carolina came to visit her in Madison, staying two days and writing in her yearbook that he intended to win her back from "Mac" when she returned to Chapel Hill. Mac, whose last name Alice didn't record, may have been the fast, older boy "just out for what he can get" in "The Nice Girl." Whoever he was, Alice didn't tell him about Jim McMullan's visit—"Tricky, aren't I?" After McMullan's visit, Alice confided to Judith that her "love life [was] still so damn muddled," and said, "I think I'd like to start going steady again. That would certainly simplify matters but there's no one on the horizon whom I'd want to go with. Mac asked me to, but that would not be at all a good idea."

Oddly enough, just days before her final departure from Madison, Alice accepted Mac's offer to go steady. She explained to Judith, "I think it's a poor idea in general but I thought under the circumstances, it's best," and said that Mac was "not too handsome but very smart. Perfect personality . . . has much higher ideals than most guys. He never drinks."

The boys of Madison so affected fourteen-year-old Alice that she had no qualms about giving advice to Judith when she was severely hurt by a breakup with Robert Macmillan in Chapel Hill: "My advice is to get as many other men as you can and in doing that you'll either forget Rob, get interested in some one else, or get him back, and any one of those things would be ideal from your view point." Has the romantic Alice been subsumed in a worldly femme fatale? Has she ceased to believe in true love? Not quite. The advice to Judith continues: "Don't say you can't get anyone else, because I know damn well you can. As long as I've been in Madison, I have only met about four girls who have as much on the ball as you . . . I'm trying to say something that will help you but even then it's hard for you. I finally got over Bobby but even now there's a funny feeling when I see him."[3]

Adams's year in Madison became the basis for a revision of her thinking about the problematic relation of love and sex. Shelley of her uncollected story "The Nice Girl" reflects on the problem twenty years later. Her current husband tells her that she was taken in by "the whole myth . . . the sex-love thing. The division. In a way you were acting like a boy." This interpretation offered from a man's point of view stirs resentment in the woman. She doesn't want to admit that she separated sex from love and prefers "her own version, which is vague as to outline, but vivid as to details: the pink mist above the city, the snow, Frank's sharp shoulder blades."

Sensual details are Adams's answer to the conventional rules that hemmed and twisted her youthful sexual curiosity. Despite its appearance in mainstream *McCall's*, "The Nice Girl" complicates its "love story" genre. Shelley's persistent longing for the boy who "respected" her but also broke her teenage heart because he too wanted sex leads her to ask herself, "But why couldn't I have gone on with Frank, and done all those things with him that spring? I really cared about Frank." She has turned the love-sex equation on its head: "by some curious (unconscious) contemporary logic, because she is not 'in love,' these sexy explorations do not count."

"The Nice Girl" takes self-awareness one step further by questioning the premise of the "heartbreak story" in which the man does wrong to the woman. In telling the story long after its main events take place, Adams asks, did Shelley actually want "the pain of breaking up? Practicing heartbreak?" She gives her story two codas. First, a meeting with Jean five years later reveals that Frank married one of the popular girls who was both beautiful and fast. Second, twenty years later, there's the conversation with her husband about the sex-love divide. And then there's one more layer to this Russian doll of a story: Adams's remembering of the episode and transformation of it to fiction thirty-some years after it occurred.*

---

* Women's magazines that paid well for fiction in the mid–twentieth century are rarely preserved by libraries. Researchers often turn to eBay to seek the critical stories of women's told in *Redbook*, *McCall's*, *Good Housekeeping*, and the other so-called "ladies."

*   *   *

While it might seem that Alice cared about nothing except kissing and going steady during her pivotal year in Madison, some of the vividness the year held in her memory was due to the national political debate and the disturbing news from Europe.

Since 1938, the US had been building up armaments in what President Roosevelt called "measures short of war, but stronger and more effective than mere words." But events continued to outflank American hopes of avoiding war. In September Japan officially allied with Germany and Italy and continued attacking China and other Asian countries. FDR maneuvered to aid Britain without inflaming isolationists, who now called themselves the Committee to Defend America First and drew support from such influential figures as Henry Ford, Joseph P. Kennedy, and Charles Lindbergh. Nonetheless, Congress enacted universal conscription. In October more than sixteen million men aged twenty-one to thirty-five registered, though many also married in hopes of winning deferments. Photographs of London in flames under an onslaught of Nazi bombers made the case for war more strongly than the president could. Roosevelt, with Henry Wallace as his vice president, defeated Republican Wendell Willkie in a campaign season dominated by debate between isolationists and interventionists. In November Americans were divided 50-50 about helping England. By December, the balance had shifted: 60 percent of Americans polled by Gallup favored assisting England. With Willkie's endorsement, FDR expanded military contracts.

Isolationists remained vocal among Wisconsin's fundamentalist Lutheran and German-American populations, and Alice's friendship with Jean Salter brought her close to the debate. Confined to bed with a pregnancy in her forties, Jean's mother had become obsessed with the war news. "She went off the charts in a way," her daughter recalled. She wrote pro-war letters to the *Capital Times* in Madison and other papers, and promoted the settlement of displaced European families in cities across the United States. Her idea was that every sizable town could sponsor a refugee family. A German family resettled in Madison lived across the street from the Salters. Friedrich Roetter, a lawyer, left Germany for England after unsuccessfully defending German Communist Party leader Ernst Thälmann, who was arrested by the Gestapo in

1933 and killed at Buchenwald in 1944. In Wisconsin, Roetter earned a PhD in political science and became a teacher while his wife, Ada, gave lectures across the Midwest about conditions in Germany. Their son, Jurgen Roetter, attended Wisconsin High School.

In her story "Fall: 1940," Adams invokes the Salter and Roetter family connection and revisits Alice's tender feelings about her days in Madison, and how she absorbed the political context of that year. For Caroline Coffin Gerhardt, who is based on Jean Salter's mother, the coming war is a worry that prevents her from thinking about anything else beyond routine care of her children: "Hitler must be stopped. The urgency of it possessed her, what Hitler was doing to the Jews, the horror of it always in her mind. . . . There in the isolationist Midwest she was excoriated as a warmonger." Because of their work with the resettlement committee and friendship with refugees, the Salters were apprised of persecutions, medical experiments, and killings at concentration camps (Adams names Dachau and Buchenwald in her story) before news of the camps and proof of extermination programs appeared in mainstream media.*

In June 1941, as the Adams family was packing to leave Madison, Hitler's troops attacked the Soviet Union, ending the Nazi-Soviet pact, forcing the Russians to join the Allies, and at least postponing a Nazi invasion of England. To some the Nazi turnabout seemed like a reprieve that would allow the United States to stay out of the war. For Nic and Agatha Adams, leaving Madison also came as a reprieve. In February, Agatha published a poem in the Chapel Hill newspaper complaining that she was tired of reading in that paper about daffodils and roses while she faced three more months of winter in the frigid north: "Consider us in exile and in gloom, / And spare us these long columns filled with bloom."

Alice and her steady, Mac, said goodbye at the end of June. Because Alice declined to spend a fifth summer at camp even though Judith Clark

---

* Jean Salter married Jurgen Roetter in 1946. On a book tour in 1984, Adams noted in her journal, she tried to locate the Roetters in Madison but by then Jean and Jurgen had long been settled in Massachusetts. It seems unlikely that Adams had a source outside of her own imagination for the encounter with "Egon Heller" that occurs in "Fall: 1940." And yet, while Jean told me in 2013 that she hadn't seen Alice since the summer of 1942, an address book from the latter decades in Adams's life lists Jean Salter Roetter with an Amherst, Massachusetts, address and phone number.

was returning for another session, the Adamses invited Jean Salter to spend the summer with them at Lake Sebago. As usual, they broke up the long drive with a stay at the home of relatives in White Plains. In Manhattan they saw two plays, Emlyn Williams's *The Corn Is Green* with Ethel Barrymore in the lead, and Lillian Hellman's *Watch on the Rhine*, about the struggle against Nazism in the United States. Once Jean and Alice were allowed to take the train into the city alone for what Alice described to Judith as "one of the best days of my life."

Mac wrote Alice every other day as promised but said he couldn't visit her in Maine because he'd taken a job at "a big national defense factory . . . Damn Hitler anyway!!!" Thinking over her love life, Alice realized—as she also wrote Judith—"It's funny—every year [starting at age eleven!] I say goodbye to someone and then wait for their letters in White Plains; Robert, Sammy, Jim & now Mac." Curiosity about her feelings matches her desire for romance: "I don't think I miss Mac as much as I did his three preceders [*sic*], though he's by far the most wonderful & sweet & smooth . . ."[4]

At Lake Sebago Alice and Jean slept in a screened cabin away from the main house. "We would get into our cabin at night and just crack jokes and make comments that struck us as being brilliant," Jean remembered. "There was no other kid out there to say we were not. It was a lovely friendship." Jean and Alice canoed, walked into the nearest town for the mail, and tried to meet boys from Camp Pokomoke. They succeeded. Alice became "awfully crazy about" two of them, Tom with an "adorable smile" and a portable record player and Eddy, winner of a national Gene Krupa drumming contest. She'd returned Mac's pin to him by then, having decided that she "really didn't like him and had no desire to string him along." Jim McMullan, whom she'd see again in Chapel Hill, had fallen from favor too: "I'm so afraid of going home to all those kids. They'll all hate me. Especially I don't want to see Jim and I know I don't like him and kissing him would make me violently sick."[5]

For a girl just turned fifteen, for a girl who saw herself—and was seen by others—as bright but reserved in school and nervous around boys, Alice had racked up a long list of discarded boyfriends. Remembering that Alice's chest was well developed, Jean Salter laughed, "Alice was more savvy than I, and she knew what to do with breasts." Nonetheless, Alice's knowing talk and frequent falls for "perfect" boys who turned out to be only human and horny suggest she was navigating rough interior territory as she tried to prove herself different from Agatha or sought the affection that she didn't feel from Nic.

Because Alice needed another year of high school beyond what Chapel Hill offered before she could apply to colleges, her parents planned to send her to a boarding school where she'd be protected from the predations of college men and prepared for a good women's college. By midsummer Alice was looking forward to enrolling at St. Catherine's Episcopal school in Richmond, Virginia, and ordering uniforms and working through Latin exercises and reading lists: "We have to take notes on all the stuff we read, which is hell. They're all swell books but I've read most of them before and taking notes as I go along ruins them anyway."

As her summer in Maine ended, Alice's cousin Mary Elizabeth Jervey was visiting. While Alice reread *The Forsyte Saga* ("decidedly my favorite book"), Mary Liz read "a rather spicy little one and [Alice was] continually having to explain to her about 'adultery,' 'bastards,' and 'rape,'" Alice semicomplained in a long letter to Judith. Her cousin would be "lucky if [Alice didn't] murder her brutally" for being "so infernally and eternally sweet" and "as dumb and childish as humanly possible." Poor Mary Liz found herself in the path of Alice's rebellion against all things Southern—in particular Southern belles.

With three years of Latin behind her, Alice was well prepared for the curriculum at her new school; in addition, two of her mother's friends in Richmond private school circles, Miss Fanny Crenshaw and Miss Katherine Cory, had added their "social" endorsements to Alice's application. But the excitement Alice professed during the summer quickly evaporated. "Alice had a feeling about St. Catherine's that it wasn't teaching us the right things," her first roommate, Barbara Bates Guinee, remembered. "It was teaching us honesty, integrity, being a complete person, being your own self. I don't know why she didn't like that."

One reason, plainly, was that St. Catherine's was an all-girls school. Boys were nearby at St. Christopher's School but the girls rarely saw them. To Alice, who'd always attended coed schools and lived close to a university, the chaste compound on the edge of Richmond was a prison. She felt further restricted by the deeply Virginian qualities of St.

Catherine's, which she described in *Careless Love* (keeping the school's name but moving its location to Charleston): the girls came from "good Southern families, lesser fortunes . . . famous antebellum names" and received a "surprisingly good education" because "what else was there to do but study?"

Founded by Miss Virginia Ellett in 1890 and operated by the Episcopal Diocese of Virginia since 1920, St. Catherine's prepared its white day students and boarders for competitive national colleges on a classy Georgian campus in the West End of Richmond. Its formidable headmistress during Alice's years was Mrs. Jeffrey Richardson Brackett (née Louisa deBernière Bacot) of Charleston, South Carolina, and Goucher College. As Miss Jefferson in *Careless Love*, the headmistress marries, at sixty, a Mr. Howe, who is eighty-two. "Was Mrs. Howe a virgin? This was much discussed."

In the fall of 1941 Alice joined a junior class divided between "boarders" and "day girls" from Richmond, the latter of whom were in the majority. Boarders wore uniform dresses made by the Doncaster Collar and Shirt Co. Day girls wore "their own" clothes. Pages of rules governed boarders' attire. One struggles, for instance, to grasp the logic of this one: "*Plain* brown belts, no thicker than one inch are the only belts other than regular cloth belts which may be worn with *any* uniform." If that sounds manageable, consider this: "jacket sleeves *never* rolled or pushed up . . . riding jackets worn *only* for riding." Round-the-clock, seven days a week, boarders lived by the school's strict regimen. They awoke to a clanging bell at seven a.m. and were scheduled to the minute for classes, meals, and activities except for two free hours in the late afternoon before mandatory vesper services. Boarders were forbidden to wear makeup or to shampoo their hair more than once a week. Study hall began after dinner and lasted until bedtime at ten. Sundays offered moderate excitement when girls were escorted to the same church service that the St. Christopher's boys attended. One boarder recalled, "You could not go any place except one nearby drugstore without a teacher to chaperone you. They had us on a $5 a month allowance, and you had to pay for your chaperone to go out with you if you wanted to go to a movie or a play. So $5 didn't go very far."

The intent was to squeeze frivolity out of these young women and teach them discipline. "The complexity and general restlessness of society today," Mrs. Brackett stated in a school catalog, "make it necessary to

limit the students' outside interests in order to secure that atmosphere
necessary for sound scholarship." Nonetheless, popularity with boys
determined prestige among the boarders: "Since dates or visitors were
not allowed, this was measured by the stories one had to tell after
vacations, and concretely, by the number of letters visibly stuffed into
a mailbox," *Careless Love* says. But maybe Adams exaggerated the monas-
tic nature of St. Catherine's in her fiction. In winter 1943 an ice storm
forced cancellation of an alumnae-senior dance: "The rush to notify dates
from as far away as Connecticut blocked school lines," the *Arcadian*
(St. Catherine's news sheet) reported. "Some Chapel Hill boys arrived
after the dance was postponed." One imagines Alice knew those boys.

Despite her dislike of the school's atmosphere and restrictions, Alice
held editorial positions on the literary magazine *Inklings* and the annual
Quair, sang in the choir, worked for the Free French committee, portrayed a fairy in Gilbert and Sullivan's musical *Iolanthe* in 1942, and
played her flute for *The Pied Piper of Hamelin* in 1943. She went to
Sunday dinners at the home of Elizabeth Robinson, a day girl who
sat next to her in English: "We read standard books like *Tess of the
D'Urbervilles*. We practiced the kind of essay that was on the college
boards in those days, and were graded on ten things from Grammar to
Diction. That came easily to me. I'm sure Alice was good at that too."
The school had "funny old teachers," one alumna thought, including
a lesbian who had been there for years: "I didn't know what a lesbian
was but the girls told me. Everyone just understood that and laughed
at times. She wore tweed jackets and straight skirts and men's-type
shoes and was a very good teacher." The French teacher, believed to be
a relative of Charles de Gaulle, taught poorly but had a good accent.
During the Depression some teachers had worked in exchange for room
and board, but now, with better times, they received salaries "below
anything you could imagine," as history teacher Evelyn Kelley wrote
to a friend in Massachusetts.

Headmistress Brackett objected to weekend trips home by boarders
because the girls returned tired or sick and unprepared for class. When
wartime travel restrictions began in 1942, she lengthened Christmas
vacation and canceled weekend passes. Like any highly motivated girl
her age (the word "teenager" wasn't yet in common use), Alice got
around the rule. She made a convenient appointment for her precollege
physical with the family doctor in Chapel Hill, where she apparently

had a boyfriend at the time, and got permission for Barbara Bates to accompany her. "Alice asked me to have a date with her date's friend, who must have been in his first year at UNC," Barbara recounted. "That to me was WOW—I didn't know what to wear or what to say. It was a fraternity party. Luckily I was careful about what I drank. My date was not careful about what he drank and was probably bored with me. Alice was mature and socially at ease—after all she was raised in Chapel Hill." One conversation from that evening stands out in Barbara's memory: "They were talking about this gal, and they said, 'She's a nymphomaniac.' And I'm so naïve I wasn't sure what that was. Then the girl came in, and I said to myself, she certainly looks like a normal person. This is the kind of thing that fascinates you at that age!"

"The throbbing issue at the school was that of virginity," Adams wrote in *Careless Love*. "The patron saint had dreamed that she was mystically married to Christ, had awakened wearing a ring." Alice probably lost her virginity to a man named Hank—that's the first name on a list of lovers she made decades later. She also mentioned "feeling rather glum about Hank" in a letter she wrote to Judith from Madison.[6] Whenever and wherever the deed occurred, Adams brought the details of her deflowering to life in her novel *Careless Love* and placed it in Chapel Hill.* The Hank who appears there could be an amalgam of boys Alice knew. He's certainly *not* a nice Southern boy she's known forever: a stranger is more erotic. Daisy "abandons" nice, Southern prelaw Hugh at a fraternity party to go off with Hank Cassidy from New York: "black hair, pale skin, and a jutting cleft chin. His eyes were narrow and dark and bored." Kissing Daisy beneath the columns of the University Baptist Church, Hank says, "You may find this romantic . . . but I'd give ten years of my life to have you in bed." She takes the bait but "there was no time, no place: the classic dilemma of adolescent love." Hank sends a Billie Holiday album to Daisy at school, and "she crie[s] over those

---

* "Never trust the teller, trust the tale," D. H. Lawrence warned. "The proper function of a critic is to save the tale from the artist who created it." By trying to reconstruct Alice Adams's sexual history from a combination of letters and stories, I wish to emphasize that her fiction offers imaginative truths that no amount of factual accuracy would improve upon. I believe Hank existed but cannot be sure whether she met him in Chapel Hill in 1940, later in Madison, or later again in Chapel Hill.

songs for the rest of the spring." The following summer in Chapel Hill
Hank finally takes Daisy "to bed—or rather, in a cave of honeysuckle
near Laurel Hill. An embarrassing non-success: he told her that she was
too conditioned to merely necking . . . The wilting pink rhododendrons
all around them seemed to her symbolic."

What does Adams mean by "a non-success"? The elided scene par-
takes of every cliché of the era regarding female sexual experience. Daisy
(a flower) was "taken" and symbolically "deflowered" (those wilting
rhododendrons) by a supposedly more experienced man who then "told"
her why she had not felt what he intended her to feel. De Beauvoir
writes that because "both anatomy and customs confer the role of initi-
ator on the man . . . a young girl needs a man to make her discover her
own body."[7] Unsatisfactorily initiated by Hank, Daisy feels she made a
mistake: "Hank represented to her the adolescent stricture: if you like
a boy, don't let him know; play hard to get."

As eager as a precocious girl like Alice might have been to shed her
virginity, in the 1940s her expectations for that event could not have
been realistic, whether they came from gossip, novels, or clandestine
study of sex manuals.* For young women of the early twentieth century, as de Beauvoir writes, "the feminine sex organ is mysterious to
the woman herself, hidden, tormented, mucous, and humid; it bleeds
each month, it is sometimes soiled with body fluids, it has a secret and
dangerous life."[8] Mary McCarthy, another writer of the generation
just ahead of Adams's, described her first experience of intercourse at
age fourteen: "I was wildly excited but not sexually excited . . . I was
unaware of there being a difference between mental arousal and specific
arousal of the genital organs. This led to many misunderstandings. In
my observation, girls tend to mature as sexual performers considerably
after puberty . . . and this is confusing for young men and for the girls
themselves, especially when mental development, with its own excitement, has far outdistanced the other."[†9]

---

* In *Entering Ephesus*, Daphne Athas tells about requesting a book about sexuality by
Krafft-Ebing from a locked vault of the University of North Carolina library.

† McCarthy continues: "The act did not lead to anything and was not repeated for two
years. But at least it dampened my curiosity about sex and so left my mind free to think
about other things." After describing the man, McCarthy continues, "Of the actual
penetration, I remember nothing; it was as if I had been given chloroform."

Like McCarthy, Adams insists on describing the event as she felt it—even including Hank's disappointment and criticism. Labeling Daisy's experience with Hank as a "non-success" is a refusal to romanticize sexual initiation that at the same time blames the myth of love for the confusion. Hank's appeal as Adams portrayed him in *Careless Love* is mental. He is exotic (perhaps Jewish, since Adams "disguised" several Jewish men she knew by making them Irish or Italian in her fiction). By associating Hank with Billie Holiday, Adams also connects him with another thread in the history of her love life: "When I was young and foolish I wanted to be Billie Holiday."[10]

St. Catherine's students and teachers alike were enthusiastic Anglophiles during the bombardment of Britain by Germany. "During our daily chapel services, a teacher went to a big world map and talked about the news, especially about the war, for maybe twenty minutes," Lib Buttenheim recalled. "I was aware of the battles and where the troops were." The *Arcadian* published pleas from alumnae who lived in England, and the girls raised money for mobile canteens to feed soldiers. After Pearl Harbor and the United States' entry into the war, St. Catherine's contributed to both British and Chinese war relief projects. In Chapel Hill, James Clark, the father of Alice's friend Judith, had worked for the British War Relief Society so successfully in North Carolina that he took a job doing similar work in New York. That's when Judith spent a revelatory year at a small girls' school on the Upper East Side with "marvelous bright girls" including the future Balanchine dancer Diana Adams. Then a navy friend asked Clark to work for him as an inspector of shipyards in Houston. Except for a visit in New York during the summer of 1942, this move separated Judith and Alice for the next few years.

That same summer, Jean Salter rode the train from Wisconsin to New York and again stayed with the Adams family in Maine. They lived simply there, Jean said, "having wonderful meals that Agatha cooked, sitting on the porch, going in the canoe, laughing in our cabin, reading books." Alice and Jean corresponded until college and the war distracted them. Across the ocean, on a single night in mid-July, the horrors Jean's mother had foreseen were happening: thirteen thousand Jews, including four thousand children, were seized by French police in an operation planned by Adolf Eichmann and delivered to the occupying Nazis in Paris. Almost all would perish in Auschwitz.

By the time Alice was a senior at St. Catherine's, Russian and French relief committees had been added to the roster of the girls' charities. To free laborers for defense work, Student Aid Squads assumed much of the daily cleaning and yardwork on campus. Alice, as literary editor of the class of 1943 *Quair*, contributed to the book's foreword: "In planning what we wanted to do after we graduate, we felt that we must consider that we were entering an entirely new world, and that we must subordinate our desires to its needs." Idealistic jargon, perhaps, but during their last two years of school Alice and her classmates had seen almost every young man they knew along with many of their fathers become soldiers, sailors, or marines. Most of the girls thought about joining the WAVES (Women Accepted for Volunteer Emergency Service) or WAC (Women's Army Corps). When Alice went home to Chapel Hill, she saw half of the men on campus wearing navy uniforms and participating in drills on Emerson Field, next to the university library where Agatha worked. Agatha now served as assistant supervisor of the Information Center for Civilian Morale, providing "up-to-the-minute information on all phases of World War II." Photographed with stacks of file folders and books in January 1942, Agatha and her colleagues look eager to serve, but the news was overwhelming.[11] On December 20, as the first year of American military participation in the war came to a close, the Allied governments told the world that Germany had "transformed Poland into one vast center for murdering Jews, not only those of Polish nationality but those of other European nationalities also." Five million people were in danger of extermination by "methods utterly foreign to any known standards of human behavior."[12]

The "Senior Statistics" section of the yearbook reveals the following about Alice: Favorite Pastime: Changing colleges. Pet Peeve: Sweetness and light. Ambition: To be a Mata Hari. Admired for: Literary ability. The stats also listed Alice's ideal man—French actor Jean Gabin, the star of Jean Renoir's classic World War I film *La grande illusion*.

Alice's first college application was to Swarthmore College, then as now a Quaker-influenced, coed liberal arts college near Philadelphia. St. Catherine's academic dean Hope Fisher observed in her accompanying letter that Alice was "still young and a little immature, in that her critical ability is sometimes ahead of her constructive ability." This unevenness, Fisher felt, accounted for Alice's ranking of ninth in the 1943 graduating class of seventy-nine girls. Nonetheless, Alice was "a superior girl with a very quick mind and fine interests." What did it mean—if Alice read that letter—to hear herself called "superior" at the vulnerable and stubborn age of sixteen? Certainly the word was lodged in her mind in later years.

Alice roomed with another superior girl for her senior year. Strikingly pretty, tall, and fair-haired, Rosalyn Marchant Landon from Ruxton, Maryland, "had boyfriends and was more mature" than most of the girls, a classmate said. Ros was named the "St. Catherine" of her class because she typified the school's ideals. Alice and Ros decided to go to Radcliffe after a former St. Catherine's teacher, Miss Phoebe Gordon, then secretary of admissions at Radcliffe, lectured Upper School students on "women's part in the war." Barbara Guinee, who studied art history at Barnard, said, "My mother said I couldn't go to Radcliffe because they only graduated teachers and secretaries, but Alice and Ros thought Radcliffe was more modern." On her application to Radcliffe, Alice declared, "I want ultimately to write but I had thought of some sort of foreign diplomatic work first. I have also considered being a newspaper reporter."[13]

Commencement at St. Catherine's retained a late-Victorian quaintness. After gatherings that included communion service, breakfasts and teas with parents and alumnae, sermons and speeches by Episcopal priests, and a debriefing by Mrs. Brackett, seniors donned long white afternoon dresses for the actual ceremony. Alice received her diploma and never returned or sent a dollar to the place she would later call "an appalling school, such totally rotten values."

"School Spirit," an unpublished story Adams wrote in 1958, reveals the values that bothered her. In the story, a lonely sophomore at a girls' school passes a secret note to a popular senior declaring her admiration of the senior. The senior's obsequious (and jealous) sidekick intercepts the note and takes it to the headmistress, who exerts "awesome" power over the girls. The headmistress, sitting "strained and erect, as though she had been arrested in flight," plans to expel the sophomore so as to defend the school from rumors of "unnatural activities" (lesbianism).

A visiting teacher named Anne Moore represents Adams's latter-day views of the incident. She points out that "it was characteristic of the emotional tone of the school" that no one questioned the "motives or good sense" of the snitch. Furthermore, she accuses the senior girl, a "perfect girl" who "had everything," of lacking humanity—a condition she finds more dangerous than homosexuality.

"School Spirit" encapsulates Adams's feeling about the school she attended: "Women should not live together; they created intricate trouble for each other with their needs and indirections and complexities. She did not imagine that men were simpler, but at least they were more direct, and trouble between them more open." Those, of course, would not be Adams's last words on the subject. But her sense that women without men were incomplete never fully abated.

Adams's criticism about what she considered hypocritical and privileged attitudes at St. Catherine's certainly drew some of its venom from her mother, who had her own complex relationship with Virginia society and history. Thus Alice failed to acknowledge what she'd gained there. But Bryant Mangum, a professor of literature at Virginia Commonwealth University who met Alice several times in the 1980s and had known St. Catherine's women over many decades, saw "something distinctly 'St. Catherine's' in Alice's demeanor. She had a Daisy Buchanan–ish charm accompanied by a depth and intelligence and sensitivity that don't typically accompany Daisy's charm. *Poise* is the word that I associate with the St. Catherine's influence, and Alice had that."*

Radcliffe admitted Alice. Buoyed by the Henry Clay Jackson scholarship of $300, her parents took out a loan against their house to pay for the rest. One evening Alice, Agatha, and Nic sat together by their pool in Chapel Hill and talked about her plans for college—later one of only two happy moments she could remember spending with the two of them.[14] Soon she moved to Cambridge to take her place in the accelerated wartime program. The decision transformed her. She would always feel in herself an opposition of the warm South and the colder North, of her demanding body and her strong mind, of love and work.

---

* When Mangum drove Adams to deliver a lecture in Charlottesville in 1984, they circled St. Catherine's but couldn't see much because it was dark. "She was not upbeat about St. Catherine's," Mangum recalled, "but she was very interested."

Along with the emotional curiosity that would feed her fiction, the South had given Adams many advantages. But that South, for her so flawed by its hypocrisies about race and class and by the failures of love in her family, was now behind her.

This superior girl was on the road to womanhood, smart and beautiful, a wide and dangerous world all before her.

CHAPTER SEVEN

Rumors of War

— 1943–1945 —

I remember coming out of Harvard Hall, from a course with F. O. Matthiessen in the criticism of poetry, and being almost unable to breathe, in that heady Cambridge spring air; I was so bedazzled by the brilliance of his lecture, and by sudden contact with poets I had not read before: Donne, Yeats, Eliot and Auden—to name only a few.

—Alice Adams, "Why I Write"

"I really thought I'd died and gone to heaven," Alice said of her arrival in Cambridge in the summer of 1943. Only sixteen, she was thrilled "to be as far from St. Catherine's as possible and to be where the boys were."[1] Going to Radcliffe College was one of the "best and wisest choices of [her] life," she said when she looked back after fifty years, amazed that she'd had the sense to come to a place that suited her so well.[2]

The eight hundred women at Radcliffe encountered Harvard men every day of the week. 'Cliffies had always, since the days of famous alums including Gertrude Stein (1897) and Helen Keller (1904), been taught by the all-male Harvard faculty, who, for extra pay, crossed Massachusetts Avenue to repeat their usual lectures for "the girls." That tradition continued for the freshman class in 1943.

Nonetheless, a landmark change was under way when Alice entered Radcliffe. So many Harvard faculty had taken government jobs or entered the military that there was no spare professorial energy for Radcliffe. After their first year, "girls were allowed to hear the remaining faculty on its home ground," writes social historian Elaine Kendall. "They filled the empty chairs until the veterans returned, and by then they were too firmly entrenched ever to be dislodged."[3] Some professors remained ambivalent or outright hostile to having females sully the pure virility of their classrooms and kept them out by such dodges as limiting enrollment to students invited by the professor. To Alice's classmate Alison Lurie, their position was like that of "poor relatives living just outside the walls of some great estate," where they were "patronized by some of our grand relatives, tolerated by others and snubbed or avoided by the rest."[4]

During the war, both Radcliffe and Harvard ran three semesters annually, shortening the usual four-year course by a year. When Alice arrived, the civilian student population at Harvard was a mere 1,082 men—25 percent of its prewar enrollment—but more than 6,000 men in twelve on-campus Army and Navy Schools filled the residence halls. They studied everything from indoctrination and communication to medicine. Among those Alice dated was Leon Harris, a "cute blond sailor" in the V-12 navy program who was also the scion of a Dallas department store family. "I was too high-minded at the time and refused to marry anyone rich," Alice later said of Harris.[5] At Radcliffe the military's presence included one hundred WAVES ensigns quartered in Briggs Hall, where they evoked "pity and awe" for their "tight, unflattering uniforms and evident discomfort as they drilled on our snowy quad," writes Lurie.

For the nonmilitary women of Radcliffe, the war produced more inconvenience than fear, but it infiltrated their lives and heightened every mood. Students had to stay indoors, pull down window shades, and turn out lights during air-raid drills because Eastern Seaboard cities feared a German air attack. They wore shorter skirts to save fabric and schemed to get scarce items such as silk stockings and shoes. Butter, meat, eggs, gasoline, tires, and new automobiles were rationed. Students handed over their ration books for restricted food items to their housemothers at the beginning of term. Mary Bachhuber, a friend of Alice's from Wisconsin, received gifts of butter from home and turned them over to the kitchen so her hallmates could have a reprieve from the detested colorless oleo.

Despite those annoyances, much of life around Harvard Square went on as usual, with beers at the Oxford Grille, coffee and muffins at Hood's, browsing for books in the co-op, and dinners and dances at the various Harvard houses. Some of Alice's Radcliffe contemporaries came from wealthy or famous families, including Eva Marie Bendix, who was rumored to keep drawers full of money from her family's manufacturing corporation; a daughter of the Steinway & Sons family who kept a harp in the drawing room; and the famous but then-impoverished Sophie Freud Loewenstein, granddaughter to Sigmund. Alice would have lacked status among her classmates, both because she came from distant North Carolina and because she needed a scholarship to offset her tuition and expenses. From their combined income of between $6,000 and $7,000, her parents, who still helped support Nic Adams's aunts in Fredericksburg, contributed about a thousand dollars a year to support Alice.

That first summer, Alice shared a dormitory room in Bertram Hall with Rosalyn Landon, but they soon made new friends in Barnard Hall and moved there. Here they formed the group that became the core of Adams's most lasting college memories: "stray people, an accidental group who'd become intimates." Among these friends were Virginia Berry, Ruth Jenkins, Mary Bachhuber (later Simmons), Anne Fabbri, and Elizabeth White (later Love). By the time she graduated, Alice was closest to Ginny Berry (who was Catholic) and sometimes stayed with her family in New York. Several of these friends glimpsed one another in Adams's novel *Superior Women* but insisted the portraits are not true to life. These women's friendships ebbed and flowed according to "their somewhat conflicting, erroneous but convenient ideas of each other," which were often dictated by unspoken considerations of social class. Megan is deeply hurt when she realizes she is not to be invited to Lavinia's wedding even though "Lavy" has confided every detail of her marriage plans to her handily "admiring, non-censorious" friend. In these pre-feminist days, the situation did not seem unusual to anyone, and Megan learns to see her hurt as a "ludicrous fantasy."

Except for Ros Landon, most of Alice's college friends were Northerners with left-leaning political views. Alice herself by this time had nearly shed her Southern accent and identity. "She thought Southern women had too much of a prescribed role to be ladylike," Anne Fabbri remembered. "She seemed very aware of those cultural restrictions, and said she would never go back to live there." Though Landon remained part of the group, Alice distanced herself from her St. Catherine's friend when Ros warned her against going out with Jewish boys because "if [she] did all their friends would take [her] out." That sounded "swell" to Alice, "though it turned out not to be true."[6]

"Everyone knows that Jewish boys are smarter; they have to be if they get into Harvard, what with quotas," Megan asserts in *Superior Women*. "And often they like music, even poetry." During college, Alice said later, she "envied all Jews for being Jewish."[7] Her feeling probably dated back to her coming of age in Madison, when friendship with Jurgen Roetter and his American sponsors, the Salter family, heightened her awareness of European culture and political concerns. If it now seems incomprehensible that someone would envy victims of genocide, bear in mind that Alice was then an impressionable and sympathetic girl in rebellion against the values of her Southern, Protestant childhood. As she rejected identification with slaveholders and Christian oppressors, she sympathized with Negroes and Jews. Her feelings were enhanced by the domestic breed of anti-Jewish sentiment that thrived before and throughout the war, even as Americans were united in fighting Nazis. In Boston, beatings of Jews and defilement of synagogues were almost daily occurrences; polls showed that nationally only a third of the population would back antidiscriminatory laws.

The sixty or so women in Barnard Hall, Mary Bachhuber Simmons thought, had been assigned there according to numbers of Jews, Catholics, and Protestants: "I am a Catholic so I kind of enjoyed figuring this out—it was maybe 20, 20, and 60 percent. There were quotas, and it seemed that the admissions office was being very careful about what to do with people." One of the Jewish girls in Barnard Hall was Barbara Mailer, younger sister of future novelist Norman Mailer, who was then in the army in the Philippines. Alice would later explain she and Barbara hadn't known each other well then because "in those days Radcliffe girls tended to range themselves along a spectrum with *Pretty* at one extreme, *Intellectual* at the other. Barbara, though pretty, tended toward the intellectual. [Alice], though intellectual, preferred to be pretty." Nonetheless, Alice was drawn to Barbara: "Once I borrowed her copy of *Ulysses*—perhaps to impress her, but I did read it." In addition, Alice was intrigued by Barbara because she knew her Jewish family objected to her non-Jewish fiancé, Jack Maher, and because her brother intended to be a writer. In fact, Alice noted, "Irish Jack and Brooklyn-Jewish Norman looked somewhat alike."[8]

At Radcliffe Alice also met future editor Adeline Lubell (later Lubell-Naiman), future bon vivant and mystic Phyllis Silverman (sister of Norman Mailer's first wife, Beatrice), future poet Maxine Winokur (later Kumin), and future novelist Alison Lurie. As Megan in *Superior Women* reveals, Alice had quotidian college friendships with other gentile girls but was fascinated by the unconventional Barbara Mailer (who, along with Bea Silverman, whom she knew later, was the basis for the novel's Janet Cohen) and by several Jewish men, who were simply more solitary, intellectual, and appealing to her than clubbish, hail-fellow-well-met WASP men. Thus Radcliffe gave Alice a rich canvas for her extended consideration of privileged lives in the mid-twentieth century in her novels and stories.

Alice was "extremely attractive, very voluptuous. Dark hair. Full breasts, full lips," Fabbri remembered. When men were invited in, rugs rolled up, and furniture pushed against the walls in the Barnard Hall living room for "Jolly-Up" parties, both Alice and Anne were popular dance partners. Fabbri later heard that "the reason Alice and I were cut in on so often was that the boys liked to feel our breasts against them during the slow dances." Back then, Fabbri claimed, she and Alice didn't realize that their generous endowments were such a draw. And yet, she thought, "Alice was always very observant of people, always seem[ed] to be listening and studying everyone."

"Don't you know there's a war on?" was a common conversational refrain in Cambridge then, verbal insulation against the knowledge that millions of their peers were in active service while they were enjoying civilian life. From the trains she took south from Boston, Alice remembered seeing "vistas of sea and seashore, lined here and there with clusters of gray battleships," and the "industrial cities, all revved up for war." Indeed the war was closer to home than many people realized. Not until June 1942, after dozens of merchant and military ships had been sunk along the Atlantic coast by German U-boats, were Boston and other cities "blacked out" to prevent silhouetting of the ships against city lights. The year Alice arrived at Radcliffe was the turning point of the war. By mid-1943, after a year and a half of brutal battles and horrific losses in the Pacific, the American forces had taken Guadalcanal and begun breaching the Japanese hold on the Central Pacific. The Americans and the British had defeated Germany in North Africa, the Russians had stopped its eastern assault, and the British and Americans had begun the slow, costly conquest of Italy. But victory was not in sight. If the Allies lost the war, Lurie wrote in her journal, "Cambridge and especially Radcliffe might be doomed, especially considering the Nazi attitude toward educating women."[9]

War anxiety drove many women toward courses in political science and psychology, but Alice, who was already telling friends about her "compulsion to write," signed up for first-year classes in English, French, philosophy, astronomy, and Spanish. She made the dean's list for the second semester of her first year and thereafter kept up a respectable record of B's and C's. By March of 1944, as a seventeen-year-old sophomore on the accelerated calendar, Alice could take classes on the Harvard campus. Officially these were coed, but because so many men were away at war, males were rare in humanities classrooms. Adeline Naiman recalled that the undergraduate men who remained on campus were those who were classified 4-F because of physical problems or declared homosexuality. "It was routine in Cambridge to be tolerant of homosexuality," Naiman recalled. "There were many more acknowledged homosexuals than was the norm before that. Because they weren't drafted. And we also knew many immigrants from Europe, teachers as well as students."

After two semesters of English composition with Theodore Morrison, Alice began her English major in 1944 with two courses from F. O. Matthiessen: "American Literature: Emerson to the Present" and "Criticism of Poetry." FOM, or "Matty," founder of Harvard's American Literature and History program, was known for his passionate leftist Christian political commitment and his enthusiasm for Henry James. His book *American Renaissance: Art and Expression in the Age of Emerson and Whitman* (1941) laid a foundation for the academic field of American literature. When Alice studied under him, Matthiessen was working on his group biography *The James Family*, which attends to Alice James and her journals along with her more famous brothers, William and Henry. It was an "open secret" in Cambridge that Matthiessen and the painter Russell Cheney resided together in Boston and Maine. Some of his correspondence with Cheney was later published, and Harvard named a professorship in gender and sexuality for him in 1986.[10]

For Alice, as for her protagonist in *Superior Women*, obsession with Henry James's novels had "the magnitude of an actual move to another culture . . . a move to the climate of Henry James. Her mind . . . filled with vistas of perfectly smooth green lawns, large houses." Likewise, Alice admired the Jamesian exaltation of personality, the infinitude of human possibilities, the personal capacity for grandeur." Under the influence of James, Alice observed her wealthy friend Ros Landon with a detached curiosity that led her, years later, to use her as a model for

Lavinia in *Superior Women*: "Into the mouth of poor Lavinia, I put the words of every anti-Semite I met while at Radcliffe," Adams said. Another influence was F. Scott Fitzgerald, who was then in vogue. "We used to say anything we really admired was 'very Fitzgerald,'" Adams recalled. "I would hate for you to know how many times I have read both *Gatsby* and *Tender*."[11]

Even if Harvard professors considered the 'Cliffies "poor relations," they had a lifelong impact on women like Adams, who aspired to attain for themselves the intellectual clout they'd witnessed at Harvard. These "larger-than-life" teachers were, Lurie writes, "heroic figures who provided not only interpretations of books and events, but dramatic examples of different world views and intellectual styles."[12] The difference between the parental, Southern academic world of Chapel Hill and the cosmopolitan one of Cambridge was critical for Alice.

The sophistication of Cambridge validated her intelligence. "It seemed okay to be bright. In the South, girls are not supposed to be," she reflected on the occasion of her fifty-year reunion. In college, Alice continued to write poems, but new themes and a looser form replace the nature imagery and rhymes of her childhood verse. "Shake the rum and lemon, not too sweet," she implores in a 1944 poem addressed to a man who speaks of penicillin and Miller-Abbott tubes. His "stethoscope is nearer flesh than love," she writes of this man for whom the "straining awful tenderness" of lovemaking is like "cold and leaden grief." This med student may be part of the nation's effort to mass-produce penicillin, but for Adams he is the precursor of the money-and-status-minded medical student who betrays Megan Greene in *Superior Women*.

Away from her mother's disapproval, Alice discovered it was okay to be sexy as well as bright. Emotional involvement with men drives the poems and short stories that Alice carefully saved from her college years, and she apparently saw no conflict between that involvement and her ambition to write. She refused to regard herself as a bluestocking intellectual like Agatha, who had—at least in Alice's view—renounced sensuality in favor of mental accomplishment.

As Alice made her way at Radcliffe, Agatha Adams, then fifty, also flourished. Finally she could put her work on a par with homemaking or assisting Nic. She relished her job at UNC as a researcher for library patrons, authored study guides and brief biographies of local luminaries such as Paul Green and Thomas Wolfe, and renewed college friendships. Letters from the spring of 1946 reveal a woman on the move, happy that new automobile tires are finally available for purchase and full of news about a trip to Virginia, where she's become a member of the board of trustees for Randolph-Macon Woman's College. Yet, when she compared herself to the women of her generation who had achieved distinction, Agatha sometimes saw herself as a martyr. Even as Agatha achieved professional respect, so-called womanly contentment eluded her. Her bitterness shows in a speech she gave to the small group of female undergraduates entering UNC in 1949. They were allowed at the university, she said, because "some of [their] unglamorous but sturdy forerunners were willing to be laughed at" and "cared more about great literature than organdy ruffles, preferred chemistry to camisoles, and history to hosiery."[13]

Agatha's attack on her daughter's generation seems vindictive. It hadn't been long since Agatha helped Alice with party dresses, at least sometimes proud of her daughter's loveliness. Maybe Alice's blooming sexual appeal and queue of suitors had raised her mother's defenses. Trying to turn her back on the traditions of Southern womanhood had sharpened Agatha's temper along with her mind, something Alice didn't understand until later: "She was both a feminist and a socialist—a highly rebellious, intellectual woman . . . when most of her local contemporaries were perfecting their bridge game and comparing cookie recipes. (There was, of course, considerable anger in all that nonconformity. She was in no way an easy person to live with.) But I am now embarrassed by my own early conformist fever, my lack of imaginative sympathy for my mother . . ."[14]

From the distance of Massachusetts, Alice maintained a politely cool relationship with her parents, and wartime travel restrictions prevented her from seeing them more than once or twice a year. In the summer of 1944, after Alice had attended three consecutive semesters, an assistant dean at Radcliffe advised her parents against letting her attend summer school. Agatha's reply leaves the decision to her daughter, mentioning that Alice has "always been quite strong." Alice loved school, loved Harvard life, and saw no reason to spend time hanging about in Chapel Hill for an undesired rest. Whenever Alice went home she remained distant. "Anne must be in love again," thinks the mother in a story Alice wrote about a visit home. "She wondered for a minute what he was like, what any of the boys Anne knew at college were like. But then, she thought, a little sadly, I'll probably never know."[15]

Agatha Adams had other things to wonder about. Dotsie Wilson, for whom Nic Adams still carried a torch, had returned to Chapel Hill with her husband when he came to work at the University of North Carolina Press. While Tom had been in the navy during the war, Dotsie had worked in an aircraft factory near Baltimore with the much-joked-about task of inspecting pilots' relief tubes. Meanwhile Nic Adams's recurrent depressions had become so intractable that Dr. Kemp recommended electroshock therapy.

The twisted skein of Alice's feelings about her father and his mental problems became more complicated when his psychiatrist seduced her. Less than a decade earlier, Dr. Kemp had been a substitute father who gave Alice a puppy when Nic was ill. She cited him as a personal reference on her college applications. But when Alice was about eighteen, she turned to Kemp for psychological counsel, and the restraints of age and professionalism crumbled. Adams mentioned the episode to at least one friend and in her notebook.[16] She elaborated in the story of Louisa Callaway in *Families and Survivors*, with Malcolm Kemp's initials reversed in the name of Dr. Kenneth Mills:

> One night (also at Virginia Beach) Louisa went swimming alone with the psychiatrist. (Who on earth allowed that? A nubile eighteen-year-old girl and a forty-one-year-old thickening man.) And in the hot black night, on the hard sand, she revealed to him (since he was a psychiatrist) what was ruining her with guilt and confusion: she had been making love (is that the word she used?—no matter) with a young doctor in Boston, an intern at Mass. General, whom she thinks does not really like her very much, certainly is not in love with her. With that confession she and the doctor fell upon each other wildly. Their passion was not consummated, so to speak, that night—in fact, not until much later (during, in fact, her love affair with Norm Goldman), when he (the psychiatrist) came to Boston and in his room at the Ritz there was a violent hurried collision of their flesh . . .

After that "collision" with her father's psychiatrist, Louisa telephones him "weeping with despair and what she calls love, across all those miles, and he tries to explain to her what electric shock is. Electrodes are placed. Convulsions. Her father asks for this?" Dr. Mills violated professional ethics in sleeping with his patient's daughter, but Louisa, and presumably Alice, suspects her own motives as well: "Much later, in San Francisco, she tries to tell her own doctor about all this, but it becomes literary. 'It's all so Southern, right out of Faulkner, all this incest stuff. Screwing my father's psychiatrist instead of him.' "

That sort of flippant, literary obfuscation touches upon an essential mystery about Alice Adams. When she turns a critical episode in her life into a wry, multilayered story, one can't be sure how she feels or wants her readers to feel. So with Louisa and Dr. Mills. Is Adams shocked that her parents allowed their "nubile eighteen-year-old" daughter to swim at night with the psychiatrist? She'd been living away from home for several years—is it likely anyone was even paying attention? Perhaps the scene contains anger about emotional neglect throughout her childhood. That she asked her father's psychiatrist for advice about her sexuality—specifically the guilt she felt about sleeping with a man who didn't love her—suggests that she wanted someone's approval.

The coupling between Louisa and Dr. Mills is also necessarily ambiguous, its violence both passionate and repellent for Louisa. As we've already seen, the stories Adams wrote about adolescent courtship describe uncertainty about the connection of love and sex. Finding love unreliable, Adams sought relief and satisfaction in sex without love. Both Louisa and Megan Greene, Adams's college-aged heroines, are sexual adventurers whose escapades often end in heartbreak. They are motivated by anger as well as by desire. Likewise when Alice had sex with Kemp she was making a bid for love and understanding. As adult Louisa in *Families and Survivors* begins analysis in San Francisco, she thinks, "If [her father's doctor] loved her, all her problems would be solved; that would prove that she is not crazy."

Alice took off the winter term of 1944, spending some of the time in Chapel Hill, where she reluctantly audited a creative writing course with UNC professor Phillips Russell. She was reluctant because Russell was a friend of her parents' *and* because she thought that he, at sixty-one, was too old to know anything. Paradoxically, he knew just what Alice then needed. Like most writers at eighteen, Alice felt overwhelmed by impressions that seemed meaningful to her. As she later explained, "I can't imagine anyone without a very intense inner life."[17] Until then, Alice had tried to arrange her "over-reactions" to life in lyric poems. Phillips introduced her to short stories, which proved to be the perfect genre for her.

Furthermore, Phillips, who had worked as a journalist in London during the 1920s and taught at the Black Mountain Institute for textile workers before joining the faculty at UNC, gave Alice a fresh view of writing and writers' lives. As a prolific biographer, novelist, and poet, Phillips understood that writing was as much a performance for others as an expression of self. His brother-in-law, Paul Green, was a successful playwright, so perhaps he'd learned from him too. Short stories, Phillips believed, had either three acts or five acts. For five-act stories he promoted a formula he labeled ABDCE: Action, Background, Development, Climax, Ending.

A related formula of Russell's, his daughter Avery said, was "Bring on the Bears": "It meant, if you are going to start a story, *start* it. Don't shillyshally around. When he was telling me about Goldilocks and the Three Bears, he kept hemming and hawing and I got very impatient sitting on his lap and said 'Bring on the Bears!'" Most of the 120 short stories Alice would publish in her lifetime began, as Phillips had taught her, in medias res (and some of the unpublished attempts do not). The concept was as old as Homer. But for Alice the practical advice from a popular writer was just the "tranquilizer" she needed.

Back in Cambridge in the spring of 1945, as the Russians and western Allies conquered Germany and revealed Nazi concentration camps to the world, Alice joined another short-story class with less satisfactory results. The Harvard class was taught by Kenneth Payson Kempton, who wrote stories for popular magazines like the *Saturday Evening Post* and novels set in his native Maine. He required one thousand words a week from each student and a longer piece at the end of the term. Kempton gave Alice a C in his course, and earned her undying resentment by telling her "Miss Adams, you're an awfully nice girl. Why don't you stop this writing and get married?" "I think he meant too nice to be a writer," Alice later explained, "but it may have been a more general idea about women."[18] Nonetheless, during this time Alice began to read contemporary stories by John Cheever (already a *New Yorker* regular; his collection *The Way Some People Live* came out in 1943) and Mark Schorer (later her friend), and two women she hadn't read before, Katherine Anne Porter and Elizabeth Bowen.[19]

While the names of the men Alice knew during her first two years at Radcliffe are lost, certain types stand out in her fiction. For example, in *Families and Survivors*, "Norm is the first of a series of those very intelligent, affectionate, and mildly but interestingly evasive Jewish boys who imagine that being gentile makes Louisa stronger than their mothers." But that was hindsight. At the time, Alice had no objections to filling the role of desirable and forbidden shiksa. Like Megan Greene in *Superior Women*, Alice knew the rules and often broke them: "You are not supposed to 'kiss' more than one boy at a time, as it were; certainly you are not supposed to spend Thursday afternoons in bed with one boy, and Saturday nights necking with another." Megan has afternoon trysts with Simon, the Jewish teaching assistant in her philosophy class (whose family-approved Jewish fiancée is in New York), and weekend dates with Stanley Green, who sits next to her in a nineteenth-century-novel course.

Simon tells Megan that she is "a living sexual fantasy" or "a sex witch." She embraces the compliment intellectually, seeing her coupling with Simon as the fulfillment of a phrase used by Professor Matthiessen about John Donne: "the breaking through of virginity to wholeness." But she takes Simon's comment literally too. Despite the secrecy involved, she can summon little guilt about her sexual enjoyment of Simon and her less fulfilling weekend dalliance with naive Stanley. She doesn't love either one, but she "has never felt so well, nor has she ever looked better," as she thrives on the attention of these two men. She decides that "in a sexual way she is indeed different, not quite like other girls." Later another man puts it more bluntly to Megan: "You aren't silly about [sex], the way most girls are. You don't take it too seriously." Actually both Adams and Megan do take sex seriously, with a confidence in their own bodies and needs that sidesteps conventional morality. Nonetheless, racial and religious prejudices held sway in the 1940s. Several of Adams's unpublished college short stories involve Jewish boys who won't marry gentile girls because of their mothers' objections; in *Superior Women*, Janet Cohen suffers because her Irish fiancé's mother will not acknowledge her.*

From Cambridge, Alice went to New York whenever she could. For her, as for Megan Green in *Superior Women*, home-front New York is dizzying, glamorous, and erotic. She is "headily aware of possibilities, as on the verge of love." The city of eight million is dramatically focused on wartime production—and pleasure; certain goods are scarce, but the city energetically makes the best of that. Thousands of men in uniform fill the streets, train stations, and restaurants. When Megan comes down from Cambridge for a secret weekend with Simon (who's hiding from that Upper West Side fiancée), she cannot wait to walk on Fifth Avenue. From her shabby room at the Marlton Hotel on Eighth Street, Simon takes her to the sidewalk café at the Brevoort Hotel on Fifth Avenue, a gathering place popular with Village radicals who can afford the check. The Brevoort is "crowded with uniforms, ribbons and decorations, braid; and with women both beautiful and chic beyond the dreams of San Francisco, the capacities of Boston." Simon orders lobster salad, a delicacy exempt from wartime rationing. Electrified by the energy of the city, Megan thinks "she would have said yes . . . to anything at all."

Megan's opportunity to say yes arrives—as we imagine Alice's did—in one of the shoebox-shaped basement clubs that lined a block of Fifty-Second Street west of Fifth Avenue. On "Swing Street" or "Dream Street," as that block was known, black and white musicians played together in clubs such as the Onyx, Jimmy Ryan's, the Yacht Club, and the Famous Door. These clubs were favorites of the musicians themselves, who came to jam after their regular gigs. "Color was no hang-up" on Fifty-Second Street, pianist Billy Taylor said.[20] Here distinctions of race and class lost their power. "Every sort of raffish and eccentric character mixed with the swells in those smoky brownstone

* Barbara Mailer faced a similar situation in her engagement to Jack Maher, an Irish Catholic from Minnesota. Her mother feigned a heart attack to induce Barbara to break with Maher. Barbara resented that for years, until she realized that "all [she'd] ever had to do was present her with a *fait accompli*. Norman of course had always known that." (Peter Manso transcripts, Norman Mailer Papers, Harry Ransom Center.)

premises," writes Jan Morris. ". . . [T]hey offered the best night out of all—you paid no entrance fee, you were charged no Broadway prices, and over a single beer you could spend half the night listening to some of the best popular music in the world played live before your eyes."[21] In *Superior Women*, Adams describes an "entirely packed room, what looks to be a hundred people, all crammed around tiny tables, in the din, the smoke, and the wild hot crazy sound of a trombone solo." She is dramatizing the night she first saw a musician who became an icon in her life and memory. He's playing out front, in the spotlight: "tall and lithe, swaying, dancing as he plays, thrusting out his long silver horn into the black smoky air—air smelling of gardenias and bad Scotch and mingled perfumes and sweat."

The man with "brownish-yellow skin and wide-apart dark slightly drooping eyes" who was "blasting out his passionate sounds" was James Osborne Young, known as "Trummy" from the days when he played with Booker Coleman and the Hot Chocolates in Washington, DC. Born in Savannah in 1912, Trummy Young was fourteen years Alice's senior. That weekend or not much later, she became his lover for a night, probably for many nights.[22]

When Alice first knew Young, he was leading his own sextet, hosting Sunday concerts at Lincoln Square Center, and playing with well-known musicians including Dizzy Gillespie and Charlie Parker and Billie Holiday. His musical experience bridged generations. Since the 1930s, he'd been in big bands led by Earl Hines, Jimmie Lunceford, Benny Goodman, Charlie Barnet, and Boyd Raeburn, but for a brief, frantic period near the end of the war, as big bands were breaking up, he was on his own. "Sometimes I wouldn't go to bed for three or four days. There was so much to do," Young told an interviewer. "Once when I was married to my first wife I was living up on St. Nicholas Avenue [in Harlem] and my bedroom window was right beside the sidewalk. This woman was jealous—she didn't want me to go out and play. So, Billie Holiday and Lester Young would throw a little pebble on the window from the taxi outside and I would put my horn out the window to them while the chick was in the bathroom and sneak out the door."

That marriage had ended when Alice encountered Young, but it wouldn't have mattered, for she asked few questions. As Adams relived the story in *Superior Women*, Megan believes the trombonist is playing just for her and she responds with a seizure of sexual desire. Pretending to look for the restroom, she follows him backstage and tells him she thinks he's wonderful:

> Jackson Clay's dark look takes her all in, his white smile dazzles her, as he reaches for her arm. They start up the stairs together, he guiding, propelling her, until he turns her toward a door, which he opens. An empty room—lockers, chests, suitcases. He closes the door. Pulls her body to his, their entire lengths touching, merging, melting. His mouth and his tongue incredible—all new. Jackson Clay.
>
> When at last they break apart he is out of breath too; he can barely say to her, "You are some beautiful girl, you know that? Say, when can I see you, you ever free?"
>
> "Well—" Megan gets out. "Tomorrow—" He grins; in that darkness she can see the white shine of his teeth, just tasted. "Well, tomorrow, that is the greatest. Tomorrow is my night off, Sunday night. How about you meet me here? Out front, say, nine o'clock?" They kiss again. Prolonged. At the head of the stairs at last they separate, touching hands. They both whisper, "I'll see you tomorrow." And Megan sees that there is indeed a ladies' room, where she goes to rearrange her disordered face. She is quite oblivious of anyone else who might be in the room.

Whether Alice really followed Young into the hallway of that club where she first saw him or somehow met him later is less important than the fact that she did meet him and become his lover. The encounter that ensues in *Superior Women* is surely the sexiest scene Adams ever wrote, among many scenes that were increasingly explicit over the years: "The most unusual feature of their actually making love, to Megan, is the way Jackson uses his tongue, his tongue all over her, beginning with her hands. He kisses the sensitive palms and in between her fingers. At some point, when she has cried out over a 'kiss,' in a gentle way he says to her, 'And I'd really like it if you'd kiss me too.' But surely that is what she has been doing?"

Jackson Clay is a mentor in love to Megan. The image of a tall, brown man playing the 'bone—indeed, being nicknamed for that most phallic and difficult instrument—makes him a shockingly obvious sexual symbol. Young had fourteen years' more experience than she did, which probably added to his appeal for her. Despite every obvious difference of race, age, class, and experience, Trummy Young and Alice Adams had things in common. With an ethnic background that was a mixture of Geechee (the Gullah people of the South Carolina low country, who preserved many African traditions), Irish, and Cherokee, Young grew up hearing jazz played by the local and traveling musicians, including the famed Jenkins Orphanage Band. His schoolteacher mother and railroad-brakeman father sent him to the St. Emma Industrial and Agricultural Institute, a boarding school for Negro boys located on a former slave plantation near Richmond, Virginia. He excelled in his vocational classes but gravitated to the school band: "They had a military part and I hated the rifles and marching under the hot sun, but the band would sit underneath a tree and play. I had a tendency to be lazy so I dug what that band was doing." He took up the trumpet, then switched to trombone when John Nick of the Jenkins band, "one of the best trombone players [Young] ever met in [his] life," showed him a few things. Nick "never made it," but nothing stopped the boy he inspired. As class valedictorian at St. Emma's, he performed at commencement and then headed straight to Washington, DC, to begin a musical career that lasted more than fifty years.

For most of those years, Young was a sideman. He was tall, elegant of movement and expression, with an easy smile, almond-shaped eyes, an intimate tenor singing voice, and a moderate Southern accent. He's best known as cowriter with Sy Oliver of the song "'T'ain't What You Do (It's the Way That You Do It)." Photographs show Young with a wide, easy smile when he's not blowing into the mouthpiece of his trombone. Young was "well-spoken, friendly and popular, talkative and articulate," with a mischievous look, remembered music producer George Avakian. "My money would be on Trummy as a ladies' man," Avakian continued. He remembered seeing Young with a dark-haired caucasian girl in the 1940s but couldn't be sure that her name was Alice Adams.[23]

But witnesses aren't needed to see the importance of Adams's relationship with Young for her evolution as a woman and writer. Trummy Young's music, charm, and sensual appeal reconciled many dichotomies in her life. With him she crossed the boundary between black and white that dominated her Southern childhood. Half a generation older than she, he gave her the fatherly approval and support she needed without the complications she'd met in Dr. Kemp; as the relationship plays out in *Superior Women*, for instance, Jackson Clay pays taxi fares for Megan and tries to give her money for better clothes and housing: "This small cheap room simply does not coincide with Jackson's view of her. To Jackson she is a superior woman, who should therefore live in grand surroundings. And while Megan does not necessarily agree, she is touched by his concern. Jackson is one of the nicest men she has ever known, if not the nicest."

Part of what makes Jackson nicer than other men in *Superior Women* and other men Adams knew is his capacity to appreciate an intelligent and beautiful (i.e., "superior") woman without envy or jealous possessiveness. With Young, Alice broke through what had become for her a frustrating opposition of love and sex. After they make love for the first time in *Superior Women*, Jackson tells Megan that he was "real careful" not to impregnate her but would gladly marry her if his care has failed. His offer represents a lack of defensiveness that Adams's alter ego Megan has never encountered before. Thus Megan thinks about "the mysteries of their connection" that escape usual definitions: "Certainly none of the current concepts of 'in love' quite apply, although in their ways Megan and Jackson do love each other. But they are not jealous or even curious about other people in each other's lives, as people in love are supposed to be."*

American, Canadian, British, and Free French soldiers were fighting their way across western France in July 1944 when Adams enrolled in a pair of popular courses at Harvard called "Fundamental Issues of the War" and "Philosophical Problems of the Postwar World" with an optimistic red-haired professor named Donald Cary Williams. "He had a sort of bantam self-assurance and he was of great good cheer about the world," Adams recalled. "Democracy and Communism, Russian Communism, had much more in common than either had with fascism, was one of the points he made, with an incisive, affirmative gesture of his small square hands. And, therefore, the postwar world would bring

---

* In two of Adams's stories, her character Avery has an annulled marriage with a black horn player: the magazine version of "Alternatives" reads, "Her first marriage to black trumpet player Paul Blue was annulled: Paul was already married and his wife had lied about the divorce"; "A Southern Spelling Bee" says, "In Avery's case there was a rumor of a very early annulled marriage to a colored trombone player . . ." I've been unable to find any record of such a marriage or annulment.

a new era of harmony, the USA and the USSR joining hands in celebration of their joint defeat of fascism. No trouble at all. No problem."[24]

Allied troops liberated Paris just after Alice's eighteenth birthday in August; when her classes ended in October, the troops' advance into Germany was stalled at Aachen. The following April 12, Franklin Roosevelt, who had been president for almost as long as Alice Adams could remember, died at his retreat in Georgia. Then on April 30, 1945, Adolf Hitler committed suicide in Berlin. The next day, Russian soldiers began liberating POW camps in Germany, and some 7,500 other American survivors flew home. After Hitler's defeated generals surrendered to General Eisenhower, V-E Day, May 8, was celebrated across Europe and North America. Though the war continued in the Pacific, the national mood of emergency was passing. Rationing had ceased months before. Shiploads of soldiers returned to the United States. Many were reassigned to the Pacific, while others returned to their jobs, farms, or families. Some, supported by the GI Bill, made plans for college.

As the spring term at Radcliffe and Harvard ended in June 1945, Americans were still worried that it might take another year and another million American lives to defeat Japan. Nonetheless, the Eastern Seaboard of the United States felt safe and triumphant. Alice took the summer off to contemplate her future. Her college scholarship had not been renewed because of increasing competition from returning soldiers, nor did the downward trend of her grades help her case. She stayed with friends in New York and applied for a job with Bell Telephone in New York City, but the Radcliffe dean's office took weeks to reply to the phone company's request for a recommendation. By the time they declared Alice "a quiet, attractive, and well-mannered girl of dependable character," her New York dream had to be put on hold.

American atomic bombs dropped on two Japanese cities ended World War II in early August. When Alice celebrated her nineteenth birthday on August 14, 1945, the postwar era and the nuclear age had begun. Profound changes were in store for the American survivors of that war, especially for a generation of women who had glimpsed independence and opportunity for themselves during the pressurized years of war.

CHAPTER EIGHT

Cocktail of Dreams

— 1946–1947 —

With a wonderful gesture Billie throws her coat down on the stage,
and for a moment she stands there in the spotlight, mouthing the
words that are coming from the jukebox—"Will the one I love,
be coming back to me?"—as everyone laughs and screams and
applauds.

—Alice Adams, *Listening to Billie*

Ignoring Kempton's advice to quit writing, in her final college year Alice applied for a fiction seminar taught by Albert J. Guerard, who had just returned from service in the army's Psychological Warfare Division. Guerard admitted just two women—Alice Adams and Alison Lurie— and a dozen men from among more than fifty applicants to his class.

Lurie, later a successful novelist, scholar, and critic, recalled: "Alice was dark-haired at that time with a very lush figure. She was extremely beautiful, like a not-quite full-blown rose. She was striking looking." Lurie and Adams didn't become friends until years later: "When we were in class and before and after and at the break it was impossible to speak to her," Lurie said, "because she was such a beauty and so popular and so much pursued by men." For her part, Alice was intimidated by Lurie, who seemed "so New York, so caustic and knowing."[1]

Most of the men in the seminar had just returned from the war and held an advantage of age and experience over both Adams and Lurie. No doubt their values fulfilled Virginia Woolf's ironic observation in *A Room of One's Own*: "This is an important book, the critic assumes, because it deals with war. This is an insignificant book because it deals with the feelings of women in a drawing room." Several of the seminar men, including Stephen Becker, Robert Crichton, and John Hawkes, became professional writers. For Adams, Guerard proved a "sophisticated and sympathetic and extraordinarily intelligent" teacher. After the war and his work in psy-ops, he considered his three earlier novels "realistic and conventional" with "too much on the surface." His later novels, such as *Night Journey*, show greater interest in hidden motivations, while his critical work considered psychological dimensions of Dostoyevsky, Hardy, Conrad, and Gide. Guerard believed that creative writing could be taught only if the teacher "doesn't think of it as a matter of techniques to be passed on, tricks of the trade, formulas for success . . . Every genuine writer has a voice of his own . . . The experienced teacher listens to that voice, helps bring it out."[2]

Adams wrote stories about quibbling couples for Guerard's seminar that were remarkably self-aware and observant from someone not yet twenty. Often they are about a college girl named Anne who smokes cigarettes, drinks sweet cocktails at the Ritz Bar, and unhappily dates men named Mark or Mike or Don or Dan. In one story she takes her boyfriend to Sebago Lake, hoping that the "surge of confidence that being there always gave her" will spread to their "far from ideal" relationship. In "The Cruelest Month," a Jewish man drinks alone, distraught because his blond, gentile girlfriend has refused to marry him.

Guerard was tough. He wrote on the typescript of "Curtains," early in 1946, "Can't you find some more 'serious' subject matter . . . some interesting and genuine human situation? This is literary." Adams's literariness was in the style of Hemingway's abortion story, "Hills Like White Elephants," with a laconic couple struggling to believe they are in love when they probably aren't. But her couple have nothing at stake except plans for the evening. More often Guerard's notes praise the simple structure of Adams's stories (usually single scenes), suggest psychological angles that could be clarified, and propose magazines—*Mademoiselle*, *Story*, *Woman's Home Companion*—where a story might be submitted.

Guerard gave Alice an A on her story about a mother and daughter titled "Wonderful" and called it "cool, firm and sensitive."[3] It opens with a picture of Mrs. Turner (standing in for Agatha Adams) at her desk, trying to write but distracted by her daughter, Anne, who plays love songs on the phonograph in the next room. Then Anne, lounging in a chair with a cigarette, tells her mother that after college she'd "like to live in the Village for a year and try writing." Anne asks her mother what she wanted to do after college but barely waits for a reply.* The question prompts Mrs. Turner to remember when she and her husband dreamed as Anne does: " 'We'll have a small apartment near Washington Square and know lots of wonderful people and buy all the books and records we want and we'll both write and be better and happier than anyone else,' they had said, and it was almost a song."

There's little evidence beyond this story that Alice and her mother talked about their dreams, but here Adams empathizes with her mother. Anne has a boyfriend named Jack who "wants to write too." The indirect way she tells her plans reveals much about an ambitious nineteen-year-old college girl in 1946. All of her words are about Jack, but she seems to have chosen him because he can move her toward her own dream of writing: "He's swell; you'll love him. His stuff is marvelous. I know he'll be good someday." Mrs. Turner, strikingly afraid of intruding in her daughter's life, barely reacts to Anne's news. Instead she says she'll have to talk to Anne's father about her wish to live alone in New York and asks if she should also tell him about Jack: "Oh, no, it really doesn't have anything to do with my wanting to write. I know I'll do that anyway."

Adams's later style was richer, less constrained and minimalist than that of her college stories, even when she was published in the *New Yorker*. Her restrained style here may derive from her fear of becoming her mother. Adams recognized that her mother once held the same shaky, unexamined confidence that she could have a writer's life by marrying a man who cared about writing. Agatha did write, more than Alice gave her credit for, but her marriage failed to sustain her emotionally.

At nineteen Alice was trying to find a way to shake up this cocktail of new and inherited dreams while resisting the postwar marriage mania that surrounded her at Radcliffe. "We had a thing when we were seniors," Mary Bachhuber Simmons said. "The girls who were engaged got little flower rings—it was terrible!"

During the semester she attended Guerard's workshop, Alice was "unhappily in love with" a fine arts student named Myron J. (Mike)

---

* In a related early story, Anne's mother tells her that she lived in an apartment in New York just before she met her father, while Anne listens, "afraid and not sure why." What she fears is becoming her mother. ("A Room Alone.")

Gladstone.* She spent her 1946 spring break in New York, away from him, staying first with Ginny Berry's family and then with her parents' friends Ralph and Eve Bates. On the train down she encountered a Harvard acquaintance, Philip Mayer (himself in love with Alice, he later told her), who took her to a cocktail party given by the Padraic Colums. She found the Irish poet and his wife so "violently Catholic" that it was hard to talk to them, but they discovered a mutual acquaintance in Alice's Wisconsin friend Jean Salter's mother, Katherine Shephard Hayden. At the Colums' she also saw Rosalind Wilson, who took them all to meet her father. The renowned critic Edmund Wilson came down, Alice recalled, "in a very flashy pair of pajamas and striped bathrobe. He's funny. He sat twiddling a pack of cards until Padraic asked him what their purpose was and then he started doing the most amazing card tricks." Later in a memorable night, Mayer took Alice to the 181 Club on Second Avenue, a gay bar renowned for its drag king and drag queen performances.[4]

With graduation from Radcliffe three months away, Alice was seeing herself as an adult among people of her parents' generation during that week in New York. Novelist Ralph Bates, her parents' friend who'd been an organizer of the International Brigade in Spain and later taught creative writing at New York University, criticized one of her stories, advising her to "take away the soft edges and try to get to the core of her characters."[5] And she met a "boy" who gave her a preview of the devastating review he'd written for the Sunday *Times* of Chapel Hill writer Noel Houston's novel *The Great Promise*. In fact, Houston had sent Alice galleys and she declared the book "awful" in her letter to her parents: "I also heard from that boy that the movies have rejected it. I don't see why, except that it is pretty much of the *GWTW* [*Gone with the Wind*] pattern. How does Noel feel about it now?"[6]

Alice carried this insider confidence when she visited with Gus Jennings and Archibald Shields, editors her parents knew at Henry

---

* Gladstone would be Adams's model for Norm Goldman in *Families and Survivors*: "Norm's touch is soft. He is a thin, dark boy, in khaki pants and a crisp seersucker coat. He is 4-F because of a bad ear. . . . He is studying architecture at the School of Design." Gladstone later directed publications at the Museum of Modern Art. Adeline Lubell Naiman described him as "part of the nongay, every-bit-as-good-as-gay, would-be-Oxford-missing-lost-generation, though just a little too late." (Peter Manso, *Norman Mailer: His Life and Times*, 72.)

Holt & Co. They assured her that they'd like to hire her when they
opened a new trade department. With a recommendation from Guerard, she also applied for a job at Alfred A. Knopf, but nothing came
of that. On the strength of Guerard's and Holt's encouragement Alice
set her course for New York City. "My big problem now is getting an
apartment, and it doesn't look too good," she said.[7]

Certainly Alice looked good, as her photo in the Radcliffe *Forty
and Six* yearbook attests. Like half the women in the annual, she wore
dark red lipstick that, in the black-and-white portrait, made her full
lips match her shoulder-length brunette hair and eyebrows. By any
standard, her oval face is one of the prettiest in the book, but what does
her expression tell us? A hint of a smile—a Mona Lisa mystery if you
will—plays at the corner of those carefully bowed lips. Her submissive
wide-eyed gaze is alluring, but her sharply angled Lauren Bacall eyebrows
suggest she's nobody's fool.

Back in Cambridge, on a double date with Gladstone, Alice met Gladstone's friend Mark Linenthal Jr. Mark was recently back from the war in
Europe, and his date for the evening was his cousin. Before the evening
was over Mark and Alice had turned their attentions toward one another.

Tall, thin, and Jewish, the Boston native and Harvard graduate was
now a returning war hero with a recently found devotion to literature.
Second Lieutenant Linenthal had been the navigator in an army air
force B-24 bomber that was disabled by antiaircraft fire on a bombing
run over the Focke-Wulf aircraft factory in Munich on September 22,
1944. Untrained in the use of his parachute, Linenthal "just jumped
and pulled it and the blessed thing opened with a terrific hit in the
groin." For six weeks, Linenthal's parents in Cambridge knew only that
he was missing in action and presumed dead. The letter they received
from the commanding general's office stated that their son's "bomber
dropped out of the formation with one motor disabled. No parachutes
were sighted."

Mark Linenthal had landed in a field near the German-Austrian
border, where a farmer wielding a hammer escorted him to his tractor
and asked if he was Jewish. "*Nein*," Linenthal told the farmer, who took
him to an internee camp in Salzburg. There his interrogators understood
that the H on his dog tags stood for "Hebrew."[8] Eventually Linenthal

was taken to Stalag Luft I, a camp for officers on the Baltic Sea, and segregated with other Jewish prisoners. The Red Cross told his parents he was alive. For the next three months, despite rumors that the US was winning the war, Linenthal and his fellow Jewish prisoners expected to be killed. Indeed, the Nuremberg trials revealed that Nazis had plans to execute forty thousand Allied airmen in reprisal for the deaths of Germans in the firebombing of Hamburg and Dresden.

Stalag Luft I was liberated by the Russians on May 1, 1945. Linenthal was flown into England and back to the States to rejoin his parents, who then lived in a large rented house at 6 Gerry's Landing in Cambridge. Seven months behind barbed wire, living on brown bread (which he liked) and rutabagas and care packages had changed Linenthal. He'd lost weight and become intolerant of "that yiddisher-mama stuff—'love me and all the things I do for you'—I thought it was a crock of shit when I got back," he said.

Otherwise, it seems that Linenthal returned home without bitterness. He had realized he could survive anything as part of a community. As an undergraduate at Harvard, Linenthal had planned to become a journalist. His POW experience turned him toward more personal goals. From the camp library he acquired a novel that met his needs: *Howards End* by E. M. Forster, whom he described as a "social progressive and nature mystic." That book "determined my life," he said. He began writing; he would study literature and become a teacher. A humanist. But first, of course, like most men who had spent eight months in a prison camp, he was looking to meet beautiful women.

Linenthal felt he had a "guardian angel" who had allowed him to survive the war. The yearbook for his 1939 class at Roxbury Latin School, where he was the only Jew in his class, notes that Mark's "inborn imperturbability will carry him through this troubled world." As an undergraduate at Harvard (class of 1941) he'd "majored in Radcliffe"; supported the pro-British, interventionist Liberal Union; and written a column about improvisational jazz for the *Advocate*, where his fellow staff members included an engineering major with literary ambitions named Norman Mailer. Linenthal was also an instigator of a "Tieless Tuesday Tea" group that met for casual literary talk. Their group included Mailer, Jacob Levenson, and a few Radcliffe women; they scrupulously drank tea until five o'clock, when they switched to martinis. As Levenson looked back on all that, what struck him was Mailer "as the cheerful, unpretentious student, who looked very Harvard in his starched shirt despite the open collar—in contrast with the image he later cultivated"—and the way that Linenthal "loved literature socially." Another friend, Louis Pollak, vividly remembered Linenthal as "constantly happy and funny" with a "marvelous quality of sustaining those around him." Despite the "tieless" rule, Linenthal sometimes sported a gleaming white shirt and a necktie when he came to tea.

When twenty-four-year-old Mark Linenthal met Alice Adams, he "thought she was spectacularly attractive." Photographs show that he was attractive as well, with wavy brown hair, prominent dark eyes, and full, serious lips just on the verge of a laugh. Alice saw him as "a very skinny, wonderful-looking returned prisoner-of-war."[9] His good humor and love of jazz and literature attracted her too—she'd had her fill of anxious intellectuals. Enrolled in the master's program in English literature at Harvard, Mark was then making a diligent, undistinguished progress through undergraduate surveys in English literature. Tuition ran $200 a semester. He lived at home but owned his own car.

Verifiable details of their early meetings are scarce, erased by later acrimony. Mark turned the memories he had into quips. Of Alice's attractions, he would say, "She had very large breasts. When she first took off her shirt, I thought, That's too much!" Too much or not, Mark brought Alice to stay overnight at his parents' house, where she was offered a third-floor room above his own on the second floor. "In the night, she just came and slept with me. And my mother was horrified." Mark retold the story decades hence: "My father came to me and said, 'Mother said that Alice spent the night with you'—he didn't ask me if it was true, which was nice! And then my father said, 'I don't want my house turned into a place of assignation.'"*

Mark's mother was Anna Davidson Linenthal, daughter of Kalman Davidson, the first Jewish doctor in Boston who had German medical training, though he was born in Lithuania. Mark's father, Mark Linenthal Sr., the American-born son of Russian Jews who became US citi-

---

* Adams gives a different version of these meetings in *Families and Survivors*, where she also describes Louisa's fascination with Michael's language: "Michael says 'fuck' a lot (as though he were very sexy) and this, too, seems exotic; it is not a word that Norm would use, and God knows not any of the nice Southern boys at home."

zens in 1895, was a Harvard-trained structural engineer whose projects included Suffolk Downs racetrack, the Boston Garden sports and entertainment arena, and buildings at Brandeis University. Though not religious, the Linenthals were sensitive about receiving respect as Jews in quota-era Boston, a city that lacked a long-established Jewish community. During their early marriage, the senior Linenthals had shared a house with Anna's parents. Mark Senior's sons saw him as a puritanical man who nonetheless enjoyed his associations with racetrack owners. His own father, called Michael, was remembered as a charming alcoholic married to Yetta, a "capable and modern" woman who smoked and wore rouge. That, the family speculated, caused the straitlaced tendencies in Mark Sr. Anna was also considered stern, critical of others, and impervious to criticism of herself. Though she was anti-Catholic, she hired Irish maids. She used a foot buzzer to call them from the kitchen and refused to speak of anything personal while they were in the room.

The last-born of three children, easygoing Mark especially admired his older brother, Michael, a Harvard law graduate who practiced with the prestigious firm of Ropes & Gray while involving himself in theater. Levenson, who knew Mark in Roxbury, said that Mark prized Michael's "brightness and sweetness, his living in the kind of cultivated world that we all hoped to grow into." After the war, Michael confided to Mark that he was gay (the slang then coming into general usage) and eventually moved away from law toward theater. "It certainly didn't matter to Mark or me that Michael was homosexual," Levenson added. But when Michael came out to his father, Mark Sr. told him that he expected him to "remain continent." Mark also had a married older sister, Margaret, who to him represented the kind of confinement by family ties that he hoped to avoid—she phoned her mother every day.

The changes Mark Linenthal and his family might bring to Alice Adams's life don't sound foremost in her mind as she writes her mother just before her graduation from Radcliffe and move to New York. She's preparing for general exams, sure she will pass but resenting the time required. Ralph and Eve Bates have offered her their Upper West Side apartment during their summer vacation, and she plans to be in Chapel

Hill for Anne Holmes's wedding on June 12. She's so evidently writing a vacuously informative letter to her mother that one suspects something is left out.[10]

In fact, Alice's father was again staying at Dr. Kemp's sanitarium while Agatha managed her large, empty house, worked at the library, and traveled to Randolph-Macon for a meeting. Letters from Agatha to Nic indicate that she's learned to cope with his absence, though she never falters in her tone of old-fashioned courtesy toward her "dearest" husband. And yet, she has established what one might now call boundaries: "I can come for you with much joy but it would be better for me to come in the afternoon, so I wouldn't have to take much time out of the office."

How to calculate the effect of Agatha Adams's quietly furious stoicism and desperate loneliness on her daughter? Like any happy twenty-year-old, Alice is most excited about the possibilities for her own life. In the midst of setting out for New York, she worries that the people she'll know there will be too similar to the ones she knows in Cambridge. She'd rather be going to Paris, but she says, "I'm too young and I really don't speak French very well at all."

During her college years, Alice lost touch with Judith Clark, who attended Sophie Newcombe Memorial College in New Orleans after she finished high school in Texas, but heard news of her through mutual friends in Chapel Hill. Alice did correspond with her North Carolina beau Jim McMullan, now a naval officer. He was supposed to be part of the D-Day invasion at Normandy but instead spent five days at sea on a landing craft that hadn't made it to the shore. He and Alice met in New York City after her Radcliffe graduation, when he made his third and last entry in Alice's Chapel Hill yearbook: "6 June 1946— Still going strong—3½ years to go. I hope we still want to get married then, Darling." McMullan's second wife, Doris, recalled a story Jim told her. He took Alice to dine at the Waldorf-Astoria, which they soon realized was "too sophisticated and expensive. Jim signaled the waiter, who winked and allowed them to leave without fuss." After law school in North Carolina, Jim married a debutante and made a career as a city attorney.

* * *

During the summer of 1946, Alice began working in the advertising department at Henry Holt & Co. near Gramercy Park. In those days, the so-called Publishers' Row ran from Union Square to Thirty-Fourth Street, housing dozens of independent publishing companies. "The city crawled with writers, Heaven knows," Jan Morris writes, "but it was richer still in editors, and richest of all in advertising managers." The area around Union Square was also rich in bookstores of every variety, from the neat and scholarly to the cluttered and musty. It was an ideal neighborhood for an aspiring writer.[11]

Alice moved into a one-room walk-up apartment on the north edge of Greenwich Village—21 West Twelfth Street. Her room had a bed, desk, chair, typewriter, and hot plate—no air-conditioning, of course; she could smoke a cigarette whenever she liked, as many as three packs a day, she later reported.[12] Her rent of $15 a week came out of her salary of $45. She wrote a story about that room, calling it simply "A Room Alone." Walking home at the end of an August day at the office, her alter ego, Anne, dreams of going home to that room in the fall, "arranging leaves to float in a bowl on the table beside her typewriter" and playing Mozart "on the record-player she was going to buy." She's been imagining such a room of her own, the story tells us, through years of living in college dormitories and vacationing with her parents. Anne looks forward to sleeping "with the sound of rain on the roof." But first, she tells herself, she'll get "a lot of writing done . . . and finish *Howards End*."

Perhaps Mark Linenthal had urged Alice to read the novel that changed his career plan when he was a prisoner of war, or perhaps she put it in her story to please him. Yet, however important Linenthal was to Alice in the fall of 1946, he still competed with an older desire of Alice's: to differentiate herself from her mother. "A Room Alone" dramatizes Alice's coldness toward Agatha.

When Anne opens the door to her room, she's appalled to find that her mother has talked her way past the landlady and commenced making tea on her hot plate. Is it a Freudian slip that Adams typed, "Anne felt herself automatically closing against the affection in her daughter's voice"? Surely she meant "mother's voice"? Over drinks on the Brevoort Hotel's terrace, Anne discovers that her mother once lived in the Village and wanted to write, "just before [she] met [Anne's] father." Ambitious, self-involved Anne is appalled by this similarity to her mother. She imagines herself years hence, with a life more successful than her mother's, when she'll "have known all the people [she] want[s] to know and have walked along all the streets and have written it all."*

And have written it all. Writing was the way out, seemingly a strange rebellion for a girl who didn't want to be like her mother—who also wanted to be a writer. Her feeling seems mean, but a theory Carolyn Heilbrun states in *Writing a Woman's Life* may apply: women in the decades before the 1970s resented their mothers because their "mission was to prepare the daughter to take her place in patriarchal succession, that is, to marry, to bear children . . . and to encourage her husband to succeed in the world"—in other words, to squash her dreams of personal accomplishment.[13] Identifying with Agatha's accomplishments, which were remarkable for her place and time, would have required Alice to shoulder her disappointments as well. Anne can but react with horror when her mother says, "I wanted to write too, you see. So I hope very much that you will, dear." Anne's polite, cold reply is ironic, dismissive: "No more than I do."

Alice's life in Manhattan took a blow in late October when Holt invited her to resign, noting that she did not seem to like her job and did not justify her expense. "I thought all that was required was my presence," she later said of her "minuscule publishing career."[14] Typically, she told her parents she was happy about this news: the "mustering out pay" she'd received would allow her to live "sans job" for a couple of months and "write like mad."[15] Allen Tate, the Southern poet who'd been editor of belles lettres at Holt, was fired the very next week. Tate promised to recommend Alice for other jobs. He offered to read her poems too, but she got cold feet about that and sent him short stories instead, explaining, "I'm more and more convinced of the tremendous amount of time and work that it takes to be good at all."[16]

---

* The room appears again as Megan's in *Superior Women*: "In her narrow room there is a single bed, and a table which holds alternately her typewriter and a hot plate. . . . Her window opens onto a fire escape where she sometimes sits and smokes, on those chokingly hot New York summer nights. From that perch she can peer into what must be a dance studio, on Fifth Avenue (she finds later that it is indeed a dance studio, Martha Graham's). What she sees are portions of marvelously leaping, prancing bodies, long brown arms and legs, in black tank suits or tights." Graham's studio was a block west, but other details were probably exactly as Adams remembered.

At first glance, it's surprising that Alice curried favor with Tate, an influential figure in the Southern Renaissance whose defense of white supremacy clashed with her own progressive outlook and behavior. The simplest explanation is probably that literary ambition makes strange bedfellows, but of course Alice also recognized that every Southern writer wrestles with the topic of race.

Which is certainly one reason why snippets of Alice's New York life that survive in her fiction derive from nights spent at Fifty-Second Street jazz clubs. That's where she'd met Trummy Young, and she continued to see him from time to time. She also "hung around with" Norman Granz, an impresario from Los Angeles who was then producing his Jazz at the Philharmonic national concert tours and making himself known as a pioneer in the racial integration of both bands and audiences. This connection of love and race extends to include Adams's lifelong fascination with Billie Holiday, whom she was thrilled to hear in person at a Fifty-Second Street club on a date with Mark Linenthal. He recalled, "Holiday was disappointing. She didn't sing many songs and her attitude towards the audience was kind of snotty." Alice cherished a different memory, which she wrote into *Listening to Billie*:

> And then suddenly she is there, and everybody knows, and they crane their heads backward to see her, since she has come in by the street entrance like anyone else. Or, not like anyone else at all: she is more beautiful, more shining, holding her face forward like a flower, bright-eyed and smiling, high yellow cheekbones, white teeth and cream-white gardenia at her ear. She is wearing a big fur coat, and behind her is a slouch-hatted man with a huge dog, a Dane, that is straining on a leash. The man has a bandage on his hand: he is Billie's manager, and the dog, Billie's dog, bit him on the hand on the way to the show, and that is why they are late.

The girl remembering Billie is Eliza, a "very young and pretty small girl" who is terribly worried that she might be pregnant. Should she— could she—find an abortionist, or should she marry the young man at her side? She "knows that she is more in love than he is, but it is he who urges marriage." Given the uncertain birth control methods available in 1946, it's likely that Alice did suffer monthly anxieties about pregnancy.

*   *   *

But that's probably not why she decided to marry Mark Linenthal.

Alice had known Linenthal for a year when Holt asked her to resign that Friday in late October. Theirs was meant to be a sophisticated relationship. They were devoted to literary modernism and distrustful of sentiment. They liked jazz. She gave him newly published books from the mailroom at Holt, and they talked about the avant-garde and "bright young Left Bank men," according to a poem she dedicated to him called "Stork Club."* She pledged not to love him "in pulpy words." On the day after Holt let her go, Alice and Mark hitchhiked together to Woodstock, New York, where Mark's brother, Michael, owned and managed the Woodstock Players Theater. They went hunting (but saw nothing to shoot), Alice wrote her parents afterward. Still, it was "wonderful" to be out in the country, "misty with all the colors hazed into purple."[17]

By November 16 Alice has found that she "really does write most of the time" and dreads searching for or *having* a new job.[18] Little more than speculation and flawed memories bridge our story from that determined young writer's declaration to this fact: two weeks later, on November 30, 1946, Alice Adams and Mark Linenthal were married.

As Linenthal told it, Alice grasped him as a "haven in a storm" after she lost her job. But an undated fiction manuscript by Linenthal suggests how eager he was to have a girl like Alice. In his story, a prisoner of war dreams of making love to a "long and smooth and firm" girl named Anne. She says she likes him "a hell of a lot" but doesn't want to limit her freedom. If losing her job made Alice question the benefits of "freedom," then Mark quickly stepped forward with an alternative. Alice announced her plan to marry by phone to Eve and Ralph Bates at midnight. Bates warned her against being impetuous. Apparently she did not listen.

Trummy Young was waiting with Alice when Mark came to pick her up for a plane flight to Chapel Hill. She "had lipstick all over her face" but Mark didn't say anything because he "didn't want to embarrass her, or come on as a big moralist." Alice later commented in a story, "I

---

* Books Linenthal saved included a Holt-published collection of George Herriman's *Krazy Kat* cartoons with an introduction by E. E. Cummings inscribed "Mark from Alice" on September 26, 1946.

knew the marriage was wrong, but while it was taking place I could not admit such a gross mistake. An unhappily familiar story."[19]

Hasty as the wedding appeared, it was not an elopement. Nic Adams met Alice and Mark at their plane in Chapel Hill with, as Mark recalled, "a pipe in one hand and a glass of whiskey in the other." They were married at the Adamses' house with Ginny Berry as maid of honor and Mark's brother, Michael, as best man. Ginny had to comfort Mark in the face of Alice's "curious ambivalent behavior." Presbyterian minister Charles M. Jones, who was known for his opposition to racial segregation and for inviting black citizens to his church for meetings, performed the ceremony. Verlie Jones, the cook and maid who helped raise Alice, attended as a guest.[20]

The senior Linenthals also made the trip south, though Anna Linenthal tried to frighten her son from marriage to the woman who'd had the nerve to sleep with her son under her own roof. For the rest of his life, Mark explained it this way: "My mother said, 'If you marry that girl, I'll commit suicide!' So what choice did I have? But did she keep her promise?"

Mark understood the Freudian interpretation his joke permitted— marrying a beautiful and sexy and intelligent gentile like Alice was a slap in the face to his mother. In Adams's novel *Families and Survivors*, Mark's stand-in, Michael Wasserman, is "thrilled" when his future wife challenges his mother because, "mistaking [her] hysteria for strength, he imagines that she will ultimately protect him from his mother." Alice was poorly equipped to do that, but she did store up her dislike for Anna Linenthal for years. She found Mrs. Linenthal "incredibly stupid . . . and selfish in that it never once occurred to her not to say something that came into her mind, no matter what the effect was. And monstrously ugly, I've never seen such an ugly woman," and defended her own outspokenness by adding, "It's not good for people's character to be that ugly."[21]

The reasons Alice gave for marrying Mark Linenthal changed over the years. From a long perspective, it seems she wanted a safe harbor not just because her job had ended but because her youth had been emotionally strenuous.[22] But at the time, there was a near-mania for marriage among her friends, and Mark had literary ambition, intelligence, and affluent parents. With him Alice expected to have fun and enjoy a kind of freedom as a married woman in the late 1940s that eluded most working single women. Later Linenthal put forth a "wild"—and insightful—theory of his own, adding a caution against taking it "literally": "When we got married I think that Alice thought she was marrying Nic, but she married Agatha." In other words, Alice craved Mark's approval and thought attachment to him would be romantic. She underestimated the difficulties that her independent spirit would feel within a social institution that declares that a man and woman must, as de Beauvoir writes, "meet each other's needs in all respects, at once, for their whole life."

The wedding at the Adams home in Chapel Hill looks like a happy occasion in the black-and-white snapshots that Mark saved. Alice chose sophistication over bridal white. Her gold lamé dress clings to her large, conical breasts, wasp waist, and slim hips. Her dark lipstick matches her fingernails and her dark hair is pulled back from her face and topped with a small, black-feathered hat. Alice's dress was "tight across the ass," Mark recalled late in his life. "It jiggled because she was nervous. I liked it. Agatha and my mother disapproved—not the kind of dress to wear for a wedding, they said. Alice was daring, provocative and a little scary." Mark looks equally sophisticated in a three-piece suit. If they were not a couple in love and lust, they were doing a brilliant imitation of one. Though the gaze they exchange over champagne glasses also carries a note of complicity—somehow, against all the odds, they have reached this moment. Maybe they think they are fooling the adults, forgetting that now they must be adults too.

These wedding pictures offer other insights. Agatha's white hair is elegantly coiffed and she looks older than Nic, but in photos of them together they smile and gaze with some shared emotion—parental pride, perhaps old affection. Dangerous as it is to read a whole marriage into a few snapshots, one wants to say that Alice's parents were not always as unhappy as Alice chose to believe, or that, at least, Southern gentility had its merits. As for the senior Linenthals, if Anna objected to this marriage she surely didn't boycott it. Her dark wool dress, stout figure, and tiny wire-rimmed glasses project an old-world European aspect. She's clearly taking in every detail of the day, even pointing a finger toward the wedding cake to show her daughter-in-law where to make the first cut. Other wedding guests seem to be directly from the casts of the many stories Alice Adams would later write about her hometown.

Verlie Jones poses serenely between a uniformed maid who could be her daughter and a harried but lovely Ginny Berry, who's looking for something in the next room.

Alice and Mark returned to New York, where a professional photographer caught them at a table in the Stork Club in formal dress with cigarettes and martinis and a look of stunned youth on their faces. Then they settled into a small apartment at 60 Brattle Street in Cambridge, where Mark continued his studies at Harvard. He took Matthiessen's graduate seminar in lyric poetry along with courses in American and Irish literature. What Alice did for the next six months is unclear. She may have worked in a bookshop. Her St. Catherine's friend Barbara Bates visited their "very modern" one-bedroom Cambridge apartment: "I met Mark. He was very intelligent, very personable, very attractive. He was obviously very much in love with Alice. I think she was in love with him too. They were cute together." Adams gives a darker view of that half-year in Cambridge in *Families and Survivors*: Louisa and Michael Wasserman live in a dim, dirty, messy attic room on Brattle Street where books and papers are "piled in small stacks, like the droppings of an animal." Louisa suffers from colitis, and Michael makes "laboriously unfunny" remarks to cover his panic and eagerness to please.

Mark passed his written exam for his master's in English in May 1947 and received his degree at Harvard's June commencement ceremony, along with more than two thousand other men (three times the number of graduates during war years) and luminaries such as T. S. Eliot, Robert Oppenheimer, and Secretary of State George C. Marshall, who accepted honorary doctorates. Also on that June day, Secretary Marshall announced his proposal for massive American economic assistance to combat "hunger, poverty, desperation and chaos" in Europe, where the population had just endured the coldest winter of the century without adequate fuel or food. The Marshall Plan, as it became known, intended to prevent the economic collapse and communist takeover of western Europe but it had to appear to be managed by the Europeans. Rebuilding a wrecked, stagnant economy in the fractious and rivalrous political environment would be delicate.

Harvard rejected Linenthal's bid to finish a PhD in literature there.

He'd worked hard to fill gaps in his undergraduate training with courses that "could not have been fun," Levenson said, so this was a setback. Competition from returning veterans on the GI Bill was limiting the privileges usually awarded to Ivy League alumni.

Happily, an immediate opportunity was on the horizon. Three Harvard students had a plan to share American intellectual capital with European students. They wished to "offer the methods and opportunities of an American graduate school to Europe," where there was "an acute shortage of qualified European teachers in the various fields of American Civilization." The resulting Salzburg Seminars were the brainchild of Clemens Heller, a doctoral candidate in history at Harvard who was the son of Freud's publisher in Vienna and a 1938 émigré to the United States. University officials brushed off his proposals, but Heller was resourceful. He persuaded the widow of Austrian theater and film director Max Reinhardt to offer them Schloss Leopoldskron, her rococo castle near Salzburg, which had recently served as a reception facility for Hitler's Berchtesgaden house. He and two other students raised $25,000, invited prominent professors to teach, and got clearances from the State and War Departments. Linenthal, Kenneth Lynn, Jack Levenson, Carl Kaysen, and other grad students joined the ambitious project as assistants. Both professors and assistants paid their own expenses, which Mark's parents were happy to do. Alice helped by coordinating orders for English-language books that were not available in Europe.

On June 21, Alice and Mark sailed to France on the *Marine Tiger*, a refurbished troop ship that charged Mark $127 for a bed in a dormitory with 111 other men; Alice had to pay more but bunked with a mere 30 other female passengers.[23] In Paris they instantly fell in love with the food, wine, and culture. Money was not an issue for the Linenthals during the few weeks preceding the seminar. "The dollar was incredibly strong as against the franc—and stronger still, by eight or ten times, if you traded with any of the Arab boys who were so good at spotting young Americans on the street," remembered Levenson, who arrived shortly after the Linenthals with his wife, Charlotte. "The windfall was so great that, guided by Mark, the most knowledgeable among us in matters of our Paris utopia, the four of us could go one evening to dinner at Maxim's. He knew to steer us for a first course to their remarkable cold artichoke filled with hollandaise. He also knew that it was lowbrow to ask for house wine, and he knew that Graves was a respectable white wine for us to order."

By the time Alice and Mark departed on the Augsburg Express for Salzburg in July, they had already canceled their reservation to sail home by troopship in September. After the stint in Salzburg, they would spend a year in Paris with Mark enrolled at the Sorbonne to keep his GI Bill checks coming in.

In Salzburg the experts from Harvard found themselves in the middle of the hopes, troubles, and chaos of postwar Europe. The seminar students at Schloss Leopoldskron were some one hundred English-speaking students from sixteen European countries, including Czechoslovakia, Hungary, and Greece, as well as two exiles from Republican Spain, Enrique Cruz-Salido and Angel Rizo; seven other displaced persons; and a handful of European professors. Among them were combatants, resistance fighters, concentration camp survivors, and prisoners of war. They paid no tuition. Europeans, after eight years of austerity, were thrilled by the abundance of food and comfort the Americans were able to bring in from Swiss sources, while some Americans complained about the poor quality and variety of food, which was heavy on cucumbers and onions. But that was the least of the differences to be bridged.

Since the Allied victory two years earlier, the political futures of the western and central European countries had been increasingly contested, with communist parties gaining support in the west, and the Soviet Union refusing to give up Poland and the Baltic countries in the east. Many people on both sides of the Atlantic feared that the defeat of fascists had created an opportunity for Stalinists to take over, a theory memorably argued by diplomat George Kennan in *Foreign Affairs* in July 1947, the month Alice and Mark arrived in Salzburg. Most of the seminar faculty were liberal Americans, some more inclined toward socialism than others, but all distinctly in favor of democratic government. For many, it was their first opportunity in more than eight years to enjoy discussion with scholars from other countries. The Euro-Americans who joined this well-intentioned project played a "new and unfamiliar role" as conquerors of their parent cultures in Europe. Among them were anthropologist Margaret Mead (who brought her seven-year-old daughter, Mary Catherine Bateson); actor, dancer, and writer Vida Ginsberg; economists Wassily Leontief and Walt Rostow (then briefly at Oxford, before beginning his long career as an architect of anticommunist and

Vietnam War policies under Kennedy and Johnson); and literary critics
Alfred Kazin and F. O. Matthiessen.

Mark Linenthal, who aspired to be a writer, gave the first lecture of
his life (on Hemingway and Fitzgerald) at Schloss Leopoldskron with
Mead, Kazin, and Matthiessen in the audience. "I was scared shitless,
so nervous I could hardly bring the cup of water to my mouth," he said.
"I became a teacher in that hour. I read and read in this beautiful room,
and then I looked up and saw everybody was listening. I had them."[24]
Alice participated strictly as a wife—Mrs. Mark Linenthal on the roster.
Like Charlotte Levenson, she probably listened to lectures and helped
with clerical work and with finding quarters for the constant flow of
distinguished visitors. There were musical evenings and dances and
trips to the countryside. Being married gave Mark and Alice the benefit
of a private bedroom in the castle while most of the seminarians were
housed in dormitories. What it did not give Alice was autonomy; she
viewed and remembered the proceedings with the slightly jaundiced
attitude of a critical outsider.

The seminar was an exclusive island in a land of "Austrians and
migrants walking up and down in the August heat, the dust stirred up
by the wheels of American military cars blowing in their faces."[25] A short
distance on foot from Schloss Leopoldskron was a displaced persons
camp housing Jews. "We were walking with Mark when we first came
upon it," Levenson recalled. "Mark turned frighteningly pale." This camp
was the exact artillery casern where Linenthal had been held after he was
shot down in 1944. "We were in territory that had scarcely changed from
the war years and the Nazi years. With shocking frequency we encountered the Bavarian-Alpine Hitler mustache. For Mark, this was visceral."
Several American Jews from the seminar staff who came to visit the
camp were rebuffed by a guard who said, "Sightseers we don't need." But
Linenthal, Vida Ginsberg, Carl Kaysen, Alfred Kazin, and others were
eventually given a tour by the camp's chief of police. Linenthal found
his old room, "now inhabited by a woman and a baby—diapers hanging
up—it seemed much smaller." The Americans brought chocolate and
razor blades but could do little to relieve the conditions of these fourteen
hundred homeless people. "It was like a Passover seder," Kazin wrote,
"one after another reading from the Haggadah, but the tale was not of
the escape from Egypt but of the many varieties of hell the Germans
devised for anyone marked in face or body or by name Jew Jew Jew."[26]

Most of the people remaining in DP camps wanted to emigrate to Palestine. In 1945 President Truman's representative Earl G. Harrison had inspected refugee camps and reported, "We appear to be treating the Jews as the Nazis treated them except that we do not exterminate them. They are in concentration camps in large numbers under our military guard instead of S.S. troops. One is led to wonder whether the German people, seeing this, are not supposing that we are following or at least condoning Nazi policy." General Eisenhower had responded to Harrison's criticisms, but two hundred thousand people were still encamped near Salzburg two years later. "The point is that they shouldn't be in any camps at all, but in houses," Harrison said. "Shifting them from one camp to another can hardly be said to be liberation."[27]

For someone coming from postwar America, Salzburg was disconcerting. Kazin's journal mentions visiting the DP camp in the afternoon and hearing Yehudi Menuhin perform with Hitler's favorite conductor, Wilhelm Furtwängler, at the Salzburg Festival in the evening. (Afterward, people from the camp stormed Menuhin's hotel to protest.) "Austria today," Kazin concluded, "is like a W[ater] C[loset]—'frei' yet 'besetzed' [occupied]." Ironies and clashes occurred within the seminar too. A German was asked to leave when Danish students recognized him as a man whom Nazis brought to teach at the University of Copenhagen during the occupation. Everyone at the seminar studied everyone else, while Margaret Mead "introduced her students to the methods of cultural anthropology by assigning them to investigate the community of the Seminar itself, just as though it were a South Sea island," Matthiessen recalled. Adams overheard Mead describe the seminar as "a bizarre but predictable group situation" to one of the organizers, who "scowled as the anthropologist tried to explain." In Adams's iteration, "groups acted within their assigned national characters. The Danes were noble, high-minded, the Austrians untrustworthy, the Spaniards dark and mysterious. The Italians were sexually active, the Americans foolishly ignorant and the Germans pigs."[28]

"Related Histories," a story Adams first published in the *Atlantic Monthly* in 1978, states the seminar's ideals in an opening speech by Professor Harold Stein, who seems to be a composite of Matthiessen and Kazin: "They had all come to this place . . . from widely divergent histories, geographies, in some cases opposing ideologies, but they were all now united in staunch and sober anti-Fascism, were all opposed to the forces of darkness recently defeated."[29]

But Adams's history diverges from Matthiessen's written memoir, *From the Heart of Europe*. According to her, it was, "simply and horribly, *not true*" that there were no fascists at the seminar. A case in point was Adam Wandruszka, an Austrian who had welcomed the Anschluss and fought in the Wehrmacht before he was captured in Africa and imprisoned in several stateside POW camps. He worked in the furnace room of a Negro servicemen's club, where, Matthiessen reported, he read American history and replaced his Nazi ideology with admiration for Jeffersonian democracy. He discussed his reading with black soldiers, who gave him cigarettes and warned him not to tell his white captors.

In her story, Adams gave this episode an ending that revealed problems in the seminar: "a supposedly 'reconstructed' Austrian, who had spent time in a POW camp in Texas and had been horrified at the Southern treatment of Negroes, announced, when asked, that he saw no relationship between that treatment of a 'race' and what had gone on in Germany."

In debunking the official idealism of the seminar, Adams emphasizes the personal interplay of political ideals. At least some of her story is based on what she regarded as a life-changing encounter with the youngest European student there, a twenty-one-year-old Italian law student from Padua named Bruno Trentin. On the last night of the seminar, after Mark went to bed early with a headache, Alice stayed up to talk, dance, and drink watery white wine.

Trentin had the build of a football player and was curious and vigorous, and really interested in politics, Matthiessen wrote. The son of Silvio Trentin, an Italian antifascist leader whose bookstore in Toulouse was an international resistance meeting center, Trentin spent his fifteenth birthday in a Vichy concentration camp and his sixteenth in a similar camp in Italy. Earlier in 1947 he had been in New York inspecting American schools. Now he studied law and worked to organize southern Italian peasants. At the seminar Trentin studied American government, spoke of his admiration for Henry Wallace, and wrote a paper about the possibility of a third party in the United States. Like his father, he was committed to political life.

For the rest, we must refer to Adams's story of seduction and its long afterglow in "Related Histories." Linked by their enthusiasm for Stein's lectures, a young American wife, Diana McBride, and a young Italian she calls Vittorio Garibaldi tell each other about their plans. His "high seriousness" of intention to find work that will serve his country moves her to declare that she too is thinking of going to law school. In fact, her only plan is to support her husband through graduate school and then have babies. Diana and Vittorio move naturally from the dance floor to the terrace, past the clearing to a "cave" formed by small pine trees where they make love. He tells her she is thin and "suddenly, for Diana who had always felt scrawny, inadequate, 'thin' was the most beautiful word in the world."

They never see each other again, this fictional Diana and Vittorio, whose divergent histories crossed in Salzburg, but she knows that he became "a hero of his times" as a socialist leader and judge. Diana puts her husband through grad school but feels "rebuked" by the loss of her ideals. Eventually she divorces her husband, goes to law school, marries a civil rights activist (a cousin of Stein's, in fact), and is elected a district judge. "And she, like Vittorio some five or six thousand miles away, acquired a reputation for fairness, for honesty and kindness—a coincidence all around, which neither of them could possibly have known about, and assuredly, no one could account for."

The conclusion of that story calls for a comment on the Adams coincidence, which is never really a coincidence but rather a fulfillment of an emotional outcome in which Adams deeply believes. The pleasure she took in this brief romance warned her that her marriage to Mark Linenthal was already in danger. Both these men had been imprisoned during the war and both had strong political beliefs, but Linenthal had already become familiar, perhaps tiresome, to her. Trentin awakened her need for autonomy, her need to exist outside of marriage. Alice's pleasure also translated into enduring curiosity about Trentin.

At the end of the seminar, the Linenthals and Kenneth Lynn traveled together to visit new European friends. Despite reluctant partings, the Americans were happy to leave Salzburg, where a cold rain drenched the bombed-out, roofless train station. They stopped in Venice, where Bruno Trentin then resided. Then, according to several letters Lynn wrote to his parents, the two men continued to Rome without Alice: "Alice hasn't come down, she just couldn't bear to leave Venice," he offered. Later, Lynn explained to his wife that the reason Alice couldn't bear to leave was because she was having a hot affair with one of the

Italians from the seminar. "Ken had become Alice's confidant," Valerie Lynn said. "He knew about that affair, and I can't swear to it, but I think that Mark was oblivious to it!"[30]

Alice finally did part from Venice—and Trentin—and catch up with her husband in Rome. As her story "A Week in Venice" suggests, Trentin showed her "the Venice of the poor," emphasizing that "most people in Venice do not live near the Piazza San Marco." But Alice's lover probably declined to follow her to Rome because he was expected at political meetings in Paris. Trentin was a member of a small group of former partisans called Action Party (Partito d'Azione, Giustizia e Libertà), which he expected would soon be absorbed by either socialists or communists. It was, in fact, a time of intense consultations and negotiations among independent groups who felt the crosswinds of efforts by both the United States and Russia to influence the future of Europe.

Once in Rome, Mark and Alice and Lynn met up with Americans, including Alfred and Caroline Kazin and Stanley and Eileen Geist, along with distinguished Italians such as Gaetano Salvemini and Mario Praz. Of arriving in Rome Kazin wrote, "It is as if we had crossed the border into another world—so different in weather, in the faces of the people, in the odor of the streets, in the flowers, the wine, the food, that I find myself breathing deeper, rejoicing in every footstep." Here too, of course, the reconstruction of Europe occupied everyone's mind. For these Americans, the heroes of the Italian resistance were writers and intellectuals. Kazin listed his heroes: Ignazio Silone in Switzerland; Primo Levi in Auschwitz; Salvemini at Harvard; Carlo Levi exiled in Lucania, then imprisoned in Florence. In Rome, postwar, those who survived celebrated "at the *Il Re degli Amici* . . . the café of all good Roman artists, Socialists . . . The beautiful Italian bedlam and intellectual merriment, people calling and flirting from table to table: all one great family party."[31]

Such scenes probably made Alice long for her Action Party lover and ensured her lifelong fondness for Italy. She and Mark stayed in an Italian friend's home, probably Salvemini's. "Alice was rather pretty," Eileen Geist (later Finletter) recalled, "and this Italian writer's father watched her having breakfast on the sofa, kind of stretched out a little having her coffee. Then the old man said, "Aren't those wonderful legs?""

Since her precocious adolescence in Madison, Wisconsin, in 1940, Alice's sensual beauty had been noticed by men and women alike.

Beguiled and confused by her own desire for romance and the male's pressure for sex, she probably hoped that marriage to Mark would be that salve to loneliness that she'd craved while growing up as an only child. Still recovering from his wartime experiences and at odds with his own parents, Mark could not possibly have satisfied all of Alice's contradictory desires.

They had, nonetheless, Paris to look forward to. They shared the romantic idea of being writers in Paris.

CHAPTER NINE

Impersonators

— 1947–1948 —

*Unkindly, Bruno reminded me that if I lived in the Quarter, in
a cheap room, I could now be making hot chocolate and serving
it in privacy. There was always a sort of European practicality
about him—even in love, I thought—and in the phrase betrayed
how American was my own romanticism.*

—Alice Adams, "Winter Rain,"
Beautiful Girl

Three years after the liberation, France still suffered the poverty that
had gripped the country during the war. Severe shortages of coal,
wheat, fabric, leather, and other goods were exacerbated by political
turmoil and strikes as socialists, communists, and Gaullists struggled
to gain a majority in the government. Adams remembered the Paris
of 1947–48 in her story "Winter Rain," where her narrator tells of
being "colder than ever in [her] life." It was a "winter of strikes: GRÈVE
GÉNÉRALE, in large strange headlines. And everyone struck: Métro,
garbage, water, electricity, mail—all these daily necessities were at one
time or another with difficulty forgone."

Parisians were "suffocating and pitiful, taking pleasure in their own
sulkiness," according to Stanley Geist, an acquaintance of the Linenthals
who wrote "Memoires d'un touriste: Paris, 1947" for Simone de Beauvoir
and Jean-Paul Sartre's journal *Les temps modernes*.[1] To cope with shortages, the French government reduced bread rations, adding insult to the
fact that most of the available bread had a high corn content. Parisians
blamed this terrible yellow bread on the United States, believing that
some foreign aid director, following British usage, had mistranslated a

French request for wheat. The black market controlled prices and sup-
plies of desirable goods. Apartments were scarce too. At first, Alice and
Mark lived with Robert Bocquet, a French painter they'd met at the Bal
Nègre nightclub, in a working-class neighborhood near Place d'Italie.
They exchanged "swear word lessons" with Bocquet, and Alice devel-
oped "a minor crush" on him but remained friendly with his girlfriend,
Odette. Next they rented a bedroom in a Haussmann block at 179 rue de
Courcelles beyond Parc Monceau in the Seventeenth Arrondisement.*[2]
Their landlady, a widow called Madame Boissaye, who could no longer
afford her flat in the haute-bourgeois neighborhood once inhabited by
Colette and Marcel Proust, was most likely "*une dame comme il faut*"
described by Stanley Geist: "She had subleased the larger part of her flat
to Americans and she was amassing goods from their Care packages in
anticipation of the revolution of 1948."[3]

Mark stood behind a thoughtful, slender Alice to photograph her
in the mirror above the landlady's elegant marble mantel. Alice wears a
tailored suit and fashionable turban, looking as French as possible and
clearly distinguishing herself from American girls abroad who dressed
in big sweaters and rolled-up jeans. In the next snapshot pasted in the
Linenthal album, their French hostess regards her American guests with
composure, with the "heavy gold-blonde hair" Alice remembered coiled
atop her head, clearly the mistress of her domain.[4]

This landlady became Madame Frenaye in "Winter Rain." In this
knowing look at cultural collision, Alice portrayed herself as Patience,
a naïve, over-romantic, and inappropriately dressed American student
who pays an "enormous amount of money for permission to live at the
cold end of the long drafty hall" of Madame Frenaye's flat. Patience sticks
out the winter "to prove that [she] could do better than yellow coats and
summer dresses in a cold September rain." Mme. Frenaye greedily accepts
Patience's rent dollars and her mother's food packages, giving back a soft
bed in a cold room and French conversation over exquisite dinners.†

---

* Colette had lived at 93 and 177 bis rue de Courcelles from 1901 until she left her first
husband (Willy) in 1909; Proust was at 45 rue de Courcelles from 1900 until 1906.

† Monsieur Frenaye had been a cotton merchant, and "the only Americans he met were
Jewish or from Texas. The Texans, according to Madame, were appalling: they ordered
the most expensive champagne or cognac and then got drunk on it. The Jewish families
whom she met were quite another story. '*Tellement cultivées, tellement sensibles.*'"

Patience sees that she and her landlady are joined by "dubious motives
. . . to live and eat and talk together throughout those difficult historic
months from September until February, until [their] private war became
visible and manifest, and [she] left."

Alice and Mark both lived in the room on rue de Courcelles, but
one would never know that from "Winter Rain," wherein Adams again
describes an affair with an Italian named Bruno in such detail that one
feels sure that Bruno Trentin made at least one visit to Paris that year.[5] In
the story the lovers part with the realization that Patience is "hopelessly
domestic and bourgeois." Patience tells the reader, "He said, finally, that
I would not be a suitable companion for an Italian statesman, and of
course he was perfectly right." Like it or not, Alice was in Paris as the
wife of Mark Linenthal.

Post–World War II Paris was a bargain for Americans, much as it had
been in the twenties. Living in an afterglow of the more celebrated era,
Adams called the novel she began in France "The Impersonators"—
meaning that these Americans are imitating the twenties generation
in Paris. Adams is unfair to herself. Her book echoes Hemingway and
Fitzgerald, but the postwar situation in Paris she describes is particular
to the forties, its people deeply demoralized by four years of German
occupation. Nineteen forty-seven was, French historians have said,
l'année terrible and *l'année de tous les dangers*. The shadow of the concentration camps darkened everything. In "The Impersonators," Ralph
Levin goes to a Buchenwald survivor to purchase black-market francs
with his dollars: "The middle ages in 1947, he thought. Only I'm an
American so I go to money-changers like any rich goy. Hitler, Buchenwald, Auschwitz—they had only translated the old business into
twentieth-century terms, a new kind of barbarism. A few minutes ago
[Levin] had actually detested the man, hated him for the haggling he
was forced to do."

At this time a dawning American empire competed with the Soviet
Union to determine Europe's future. "People talk only of the imminence
of war!" wrote Roger Martin du Gard to André Gide. Some French
feared a Russian invasion of France, while others thought the United
States would attack Russia. The Communist Party exploited the real
grievances of the French working class and labor unions to undermine

the economy before the Marshall Plan could shore it up. Anticommunists denounced Stalin's crimes, which were becoming widely known through the French translation of Arthur Koestler's *Darkness at Noon*. Leading intellectuals like de Beauvoir, Sartre, and Camus, who were anti-American but not communist, hoped for a socialist France.

Few people in the bars and cafés of the Left Bank realized how soon Europe would be divided by the Iron Curtain. "St.-Germain-des-Prés was unlike anywhere else in postwar Europe," write historians Antony Beevor and Artemis Cooper. After four years of German occupation and a virtual news blackout, Paris after the liberation was a place where intellectuals believed that "ideas would triumph over 'filthy money.' "[6] Sartre and de Beauvoir (she just home from a cultural tour of the United States and a torrid affair with the American writer Nelson Algren) published *Les temps moderne* and held court in the smoky basement bar of the Hotel Pont-Royal. Communist and Gaullist politicians and newspapers fought to influence French elections. Young idealists thought their discussions would shape a peaceful, prosperous world.*

Such cultural exchange had been the impulse behind the Salzburg Seminar. Similarly, the Sorbonne offered a *cours de la civilisation française*, which proved to be a savvy means to collect American tuition dollars. Young women from Smith College and other prestigious schools took a year abroad in Paris, and former GIs like Mark Linenthal enrolled to make themselves eligible for GI Bill benefits. As a married man, Mark received $120 a month, while single veterans got $90. "Curious arithmetic, that," Adams noted drily.

One early-November morning, Mark ran into friends from home as he picked up his check at the Veterans Administration office. Norman and Bea Mailer had just arrived in Paris to await publication of his first novel, *The Naked and the Dead*. What Alice noticed first about Norman was the "hot, hot blue of his eyes . . . literally burning eyes."[7] That night the two couples enjoyed a "nice congenial drunk together." Norman wrote his sister, Barbara, that he thought Alice was "an awfully nice dame," adding that Alice recalled Barbara fondly from Radcliffe and regarded her with awe. The Linenthals and Mailers were delighted to

---

* Ironically, while Sartre's philosophical writing seemed more influential at the time (de Beauvoir called herself a midwife to Sartre's existentialism), her critique of patriarchy has shaped the lives and thinking of millions of women and men.

have found each other; they'd felt lonely in a foreign, cold, grayed-out city, even if it was Paris.[8]

"Of all the people I've ever known," Mark told Alice after she'd met the Mailers, "the two who most wanted to be writers were you and Norman Mailer."[9] Alice proved her determination by writing every morning while Mark attended his classes. At first she worked on stories about relationships among Jews and gentiles, whites and blacks in North Carolina—themes that occupied her all her life. Mailer, with a first novel already sold, inspired her to think about her writing *career* in addition to *being* a writer, and she began a novel about a young American woman in Paris. Even though Alice was not published, Mark reflected, "she was certainly a writer and she talked to Norman as a fellow writer."

In other ways, Alice was inspired by the worldliness and candor of Mailer's wife. Beatrice Silverman Mailer had been an officer in the WAVES and received GI benefits in her own right. She was a raven-haired, fast-talking girl from Chelsea in South Boston who had put herself through Boston University by waitressing and giving piano lessons. In some photos she looks like a young Elizabeth Taylor, and she was "a feminist, born that way," her sister Phyllis recalled, undaunted by men because "she went to a camp where men and women used the same latrine." Alice had met her when she visited the Linenthal home to welcome Mark back from the war while Norman was still overseas. On that occasion, Bea annoyed the senior Linenthals with her informal manners and free use of words like "shit" and "fuck"—which only increased Alice and Mark's enjoyment of her.

Though Mark and Alice came from educated, comfortable backgrounds, they got no financial help from their parents. With their two GI stipends and Norman's $1,200 advance from the sale of his novel to Rinehart, the Mailers were comparatively rich. They sailed to Europe on the *Queen Elizabeth* and rented a room at the Hotel de l'Avenir (Hotel of the Future) around the corner from Gertrude Stein and Alice B. Toklas's former apartment in Montparnasse. Then they rented an apartment, a middle-class luxury managed by few other ex-GI students in 1947. Their dusty, mouse-infested three-room apartment with red walls and an orange rug at 11 rue Bréa cost them less than a dollar a day. It came with a piano for Bea, and they poached a maid from l'Avenir, though Norman made a point of saying he would not have "allowed" Bea to have a maid unless he knew she was competent to do the work herself. She was, as it turned out, competent at many things, but her main occupation that year, Alice recalled, was "being Norman's wife." In fact, she was also trying to sell a novel she'd written about her experience with the WAVES, but publishers called it dull and she gave up writing.[10] After the Mailer marriage ended in 1952, some people said she had been shrill, nagging, or envious of Norman's success. Alice called that "bullshit," or at least a "revisionary" view colored by Mailer's prejudices. "This was the middle Forties," Alice declared. Jealousy of a husband's success "would not have been considered a reasonable gripe even by Bea who was a fairly 'liberated' woman."[11]

During that year, before American tourists descended on Europe, St.-Germain-des-Prés was a neighborhood. "We knew almost everyone we saw on the streets," Adams wrote, "or at least we knew who they were. I remember standing in front of Brasserie Lipp one day when someone pointed and said, 'Look, there's Picasso!' And it was, those incredible eyes unmistakable, even at that distance." At nightclubs they saw Irish novelist Liam O'Flaherty and French singer Juliette Gréco. Once, Adams recalled, they listened dumbstruck as Truman Capote spun improbable stories about the American South for Cyril Connolly and a gullible companion.

The Linenthals and Mailers saw each other almost daily, though social life was very unstructured. They met for coffee at places like Café de Flore. Once the Linenthals had a party in their landlady's apartment on rue de Courcelles, and the Mailers often entertained on rue Bréa. Mark Linenthal thought Bea retained the charms she'd had when he met her at Harvard as Norman's fiancée: "Her sexiness was camp. She was like a little girl, wide-eyed and playful at the same time . . . she would make a sexually explicit remark, and Norman would act mock-shocked but was really delighted . . . her debunking Harvard stiffness appealed to Norman . . . One felt she was his companion in *épater le bourgeoisie*."[12]

By the time they re-met in Paris all the Americans were swearing equally, according to Kenneth Lynn: "The sexuality and the frank talk was sort of the style of all of us, men and women alike, as opposed to the way we talked in Cambridge."[13]

Even though almost every American in Paris that year, including Bea Mailer and Mark Linenthal, wanted to be a writer, Norman took note of Alice's determination and talent. In December he sent two of her stories to his editor, William Raney at Rinehart, writing that he thought "The Hills" (a story about a Jewish family in Chapel Hill who are pressured by their white Southern friends to hire a black maid, then criticized for treating her too well) was just about a perfect short story. Raney agreed and asked his "magazine expert" to send it to the *New Yorker*. "But please, please—tell sweet Alice that these things take time." All too soon the *New Yorker* rejected both of Adams's stories, adding that the author had submitted "The Hills" to them twice before. Mailer apologized, awaiting Alice's "*horror*" when she learns how he "screwed up." Raney persevered with submissions to *Harper's* and the *Atlantic*.[14]

The Mailers struck both Alice and Mark as being happy together in those months before Norman became famous. "I thought that marriage was made in heaven," Mark told Peter Manso, while Alice said they seemed "tremendously, enormously fond of each other," but also issued a caution: "I was already beginning not to be happy, so I may very well—this would be typical—I may quite easily have overestimated their happiness."[15] Phyllis Silverman Ott also believed Norman was happy with her sister until the fame of *The Naked and the Dead* upended him. Despite appearances, Norman was restless in his three-year-old marriage. In a letter written aboard ship en route to Europe, he speculated that no couple could live together very long without boring each other, adding that he no longer found Bea exciting in bed.[16]

Alice felt similarly about her marriage. In the Left Bank's Bar Montana she met unmarried couples who lived together and she later speculated (without giving her reasons) that this seemed to her "an interesting and possibly ideal state." Given that both Alice Adams and Norman Mailer later wrote openly about sexual freedom, rumors have suggested that Alice and Norman might have had an affair in Paris. If so, they left no evidence. According to her, except for the mornings when Mark went to the Sorbonne and she wrote, she and Mark were "almost always together . . . as though separate activities might lead to trouble, which was very likely true—in my case it was. Mark was young too, but he seemed to like being married."[17]

There are reasons to think the two writers consummated their friendship in bed. Alice's friend Blair Fuller claimed certain knowledge that Alice had an affair with Mailer: "I think she was unfaithful to Linenthal with Norman Mailer in Paris in that winter. I feel sure because of things that she said, I can't quote any but she would do it with an expression, sort of winkingly." Likewise, Doubleday editor Gerald Howard noted that "a certain tone came into Alice's voice" when she mentioned Mailer and others who had been her lovers. And San Francisco novelist Ella Leffland, in whom Alice later confided freely, said Alice several times mentioned Mailer as one of her lovers, "but the only thing I remember specifically is that she said he was not very well equipped." His name, however, is not on the list of lovers Alice kept at the back of her notebook in the 1990s.[18] Alice and Mailer remained friends until the 1970s, and he held an important place in Adams's literary imagination. She sent him a fan note for every book he published before 1973 and portrayed him in *Superior Women*. Megan Greene (her double) and Adam Marr (her Irish Mailer) are friends who love to argue with each other. Megan becomes the reluctant confidante to whom Marr confesses that he's been sleeping with a French girl named Odette, but history remains mum about any connection between that character and women the Mailers and Linenthals knew in France.

As winter closed in, weak and intermittent electrical service darkened Paris and made New Yorker Mailer long for "the ballsy kind of noise and size and excitement of America." Arthur Miller, who also came to Paris in 1947, found a city "finished" by the war: "The sun never seemed to rise over Paris, the winter sky like a lid of iron graying the skin of one's hands and making faces wan. A doomed and listless silence, few cars on the streets, occasional trucks running on wood-burning engines, old women on ancient bicycles."[19]

For Alice the meals were a compensation. Madame Boissaye cooked for them or they ate in "marvelous cheap local student restaurants" like Chez Benoît ("excellent food, with a carafe of red wine, for about a dollar for the two of us") or Le Bouillon, where Nicolette in "The Impersonators" eats an omelette, bread, salad, cheese, and "*un quart de rouge*" for about fifty cents. Adams's description of that restaurant is one of many passages that show her delight in Paris:

The restaurant was a low narrow room, with a combination cashier's desk and bar on one side of the door and the great wood stove on the other. The owner, Maria, stood at the stove. . . . Her red-brown hair was pushed back from her forehead, black eyes bright in her perspiring face. Her body, one arm settled against her hip was massive, seeming an expression of all potential energy, all violence unexplored. With one huge sweep of her arm she could extinguish the flames that sucked at the rim of the stove.

"My little girl," in a deep and gentle voice. "Where have you been, Nickie? You're getting much too thin. You should eat here, with me." Above her head the row of over-sized copper pots gleamed in the flame light, and she turned back to the crackling meat in the pan.

In Paris, Alice and Mark encountered Enrique Cruz-Salido, one of the Spanish exiles they'd met at Salzburg. Cruz-Salido, who spent his childhood safely in Mexico during the civil war and came to Paris for his education, was a dedicated Spanish Republican who worked to smuggle propaganda into and political prisoners out of Spain. Alice found him "small, dark, incredibly intense." Through him they met Paco Benet-Goitia, whose passport allowed him to cross the officially closed border between France and Spain. These Spanish Republicans (in opposition to Franco's fascist government) drew their American friends into efforts to assist Spanish political prisoners and antifascist organizers. Americans with cars were particularly useful to their project.

In January 1948, the Linenthals and Kenneth Lynn purchased an American car—a Nash—from George Ritter, another person they'd met in Salzburg. Ritter assured them they'd make a big profit selling the car in Spain. "We were extremely broke and we got really greedy," Alice recalled. They were also "wildly sympathetic" with the plight of the Spaniards and determined to see the inside of a fascist country even though many liberals then boycotted Spain.

The threesome drove south carrying names and addresses of resistance contacts and a cache of extra *pesetas* hidden in shaving-cream tubes to deliver to them. They handed over their contraband but were unable to sell the car. "George Ritter was a crook. He was well informed that selling the car was absolutely out of the question," Adams fumed later. "We were stuck with this fucking sky blue Nash."[20]

As their money ran out, the three Americans raced back to the French border with a sense of having escaped from jail. Hidden in their car seat was a manila envelope filled with forbidden poems and reports from resistance organizers that Cruz-Salido, Benet-Goitia, and

their Parisian supporters planned to publish, including the poems of
Pueblo cautivo by Eugenio de Nora with its preface by Pablo Neruda
("Treacherous generals: / see my dead house, / look at broken Spain:
from every house burning metal flows / instead of flowers").[21] Norman
Mailer recalled that when the Linenthals returned from Spain they
were "indignant about the economic conditions, they fulminated at
the atmosphere of police oppression, and they spoke with enthusiasm
of the Spanish people."[22]

Skeptical about an impression their friends had formed so quickly,
the Mailers made their own trip to Spain a few months later with
the intention of helping some imprisoned resistance fighters escape to
France. That failed. But Norman Mailer concurred with the Linenthals
that there was "not another nation in the world where oppression [was]
so palpable as in Spain." He observed that the barren terrain and the
open layout of the cities made it easy for the police to conduct sur-
veillance and impossible for the resistance to act covertly. Nonetheless,
Mailer wrote hopefully, "Every day spawns new revolutionaries, and
there are youths in the Spanish underground who were children when
Madrid was under siege."[23] Franco remained in power until his death
in 1975.

Another trip took Alice and Mark and Kenneth Lynn to a village on
the Côte d'Azur called Cagnes-sur-Mer. In this "really mad place," as
Alice called it, they stayed in a house in upper Cagnes near a château
where Auguste Renoir had spent his last years. Their hostess was artist
Mary de Anders Diederich, the first wife of a sculptor named Hunt
Diederich. Diederich had installed Mary (Marushka) and their two
children in Cagnes when he divorced her in 1922, married Countess
Wanda van Goetzen, and purchased a castle near Nuremberg. Though
Diederich spent World War II in New York, he remained pro-German.
In 1946 the National Institute of Arts and Letters expelled him for using
its letterhead to mail out anti-Semitic propaganda.[24]

Alice and Mark came upon some of these "terrifying tracts" in
Cagnes. Also in Cagnes, Alice "became somehow involved with a leather
fetishist who predicted that [her] marriage wouldn't last," as she wrote
much later to a rediscovered Harvard friend, adding, "Well, that can't
have taken terrific insight."[25] Cagnes-sur-Mer captivated Alice Adams as

a writer and became the setting for part of "The Impersonators." Hunt Diederich became the model for Carl Weller, the father of her protagonist, Nicolette—called Nic—who brings her friends to this bohemian enclave in the hilltop town for an encounter with their own identities. Two American men accompany Nic to Cagnes when she asks her father for money. They are Ralph Levin, a Jewish ex-GI from Boston who is postponing his return home by studying in Paris, and Henry Potter, an *International Herald Tribune* reporter. Ralph Levin and Nic Weller resemble Mark and Alice. Through their courtship, Adams seems to be analyzing her relationship with her husband, being hard on both him and herself. For instance, Ralph "was beginning to be annoyed by the way she managed to keep him on the defensive. She had, it seemed, a series of poses to which he was supposed to suitably respond: the lost child; the brave gay bohemian; now the somewhat nervous cynic."

Ralph has the very limitations that Alice was beginning to find in Mark. Realizing that most of his friends are leaving Paris, Ralph thinks, "he could get a lot of work done during the winter, and then—and then he stopped, his imagination never able to go further, to go beyond the immediate, the arranged." Nic Weller's imagination, on the other hand, "always fled from the immediate, the possible, and her dreams included nothing of the present in their golden aura." Differing styles of imagination can seem like an unbridgeable chasm to a young woman who is just realizing the degree to which marriage has elevated her husband's ambitions in relation to her own.

The way sexual attraction between Nic and Ralph emerges—and falters—may offer another clue to the workings of the Linenthal's new marriage. Nic believes that with Ralph, she "would be completely protected and safe and loved." She wants to marry Ralph and "live always with him somewhere away from everyone that she had ever known." He answers that he must return to Paris. She cries, thinking he does not love her. He wipes her face and tries to kiss her, but she objects that he only kisses her when she cries: "You think I'm four years old and that if you kiss me it will be all right."

It is impossible to say that Mark did not love Alice in 1947. But chances are good that he did not love her in the way she wanted. Age difference, cultural difference, gender difference—as well as Alice's sense of unrequited love for her father and her longing to be swept off her feet—played their roles. As she writes of Nicolette Weller, "she could only conceive of her affair . . . having for its locale a place of impossible and unknown romance." For Alice, the man she'd already married would not seem right. And for him? He'd gone against his mother's wishes to bring a sexy, smart, Southern shiksa into his domestic life. He simply had not considered that she would be a complicated human being with problems of her own.

In "The Impersonators" the concerns of these privileged Americans contrast with stories about people in Cagnes-sur-Mer who are recovering from the calamities of the war. In Paris, Nicolette (like Alice) had been surrounded by Americans like herself, and her acquaintance with real French life was limited by the scrim of language and street life. In the bars and cafés and homes of upper Cagnes she found an intimate microcosm of recent European history. Here were Jojo, who had a pizzeria on the Piazza di Spagna in Rome before he was run out by fascists;* an elderly Polish-born lady known as la Contesse who tells Ralph with marvelous aplomb that she "spent the season in Auschwitz"; and an old soldier who pretends to be la Contesse's suitor as he looks after her in her decline. He calls himself the Duke of Gamberini and speaks of going to fight in Palestine. For them, Cagnes was a place where "the past was left to take care of itself. There were to be no questions as to what one had been or done before."

Ralph Levin notes "the process of expatriation" in Nicolette Weller. He sees her become less innocent, more wary, less romantic. For Adams, this year of partial expatriation meant giving up the notion that Europe's problems could be solved by an Allied victory. American innocence was appalled by revelations about death camps, the risk of nuclear warfare, and the intentions of the Soviet Union toward central and eastern Europe. Even Norman Mailer, who was then intensely interested in politics, struck Kenneth Lynn as naïve—"not self-deluding, but ignorant." When Lynn stated that millions of Soviet citizens had died in a forced collectivization in the Ukraine, Mailer asked how he knew that: "He had never heard this idea before, he was staggered by it. I had known about it half my life."[26]

---

* Mark Linenthal relished a quip about Jojo in years to come. Asked if it was true that he did not speak English, Jojo would reply, "Yes, boss."

The so-called Prague Coup on February 20, 1948, made Soviet intentions clear. On that date Communists forcibly replaced the multiparty government of Czechoslovakia, reprising Hitler's takeover in 1939. Less than a month later, Jan Masaryk, the non-Communist foreign minister who wished Czechoslovakia to participate in the Marshall Plan, was found dead on the stone courtyard below his bathroom window. The Communists claimed he was a suicide. Later investigations concluded he was murdered by defenestration. The loss of hope for democracy and civilized discourse in central Europe was deeply disappointing to the Salzburg conference idealists, especially Matthiessen, who had taught in Prague after he left Salzburg. Thus intellectuals and artists of the 1940s generation were disabused of their American idealism.

"Here her life would find its form," Nicolette thinks at the beginning of "The Impersonators." This making of self is as much personal as political despite the intensely political environment that Europe offered Alice in 1948. Of Isabel Archer, heroine of Henry James's *The Portrait of a Lady*, a book Adams knew well, Michael Gorra writes: "What she now learns is simply what the Old World has always had to teach us. She learns that her own life has been determined by things that happened before she was thought of, by a past of which she was ignorant and that she only understands when it's already too late . . . [that] America itself has had no separate or special creation." The theme of lost American innocence was familiar to Matthiessen's students from their reading of American literature, but the late 1940s made it as current as the news.[27]

Perhaps her own loss of innocence drove Adams to give "The Impersonators" an unsatisfying, nonromantic ending. She considered having Nic and Ralph meet up again in America, but in the end she separated them.[28] After Nic's father dies in a car accident, she casts Ralph aside for a cynical marriage to Potter. Though Alice would stay married to Mark Linenthal for another decade, author Adams had already divorced herself from him. But she was far from giving up her belief in romance. That would take new forms for the rest of her life.

In late January 1948, devaluation of the franc nearly doubled the official value of American dollars, giving them 215 per dollar. Alice and Mark rented "a large, oddly trapezoidal room" in a hotel called Le Welcome that still operates on rue de Seine in the Sixth Arrondissement. Barbara

Probst, a young woman from New York who took the room after they left, complained that it had bedbugs. From their upper floor, Alice could hear and see the street market where "fat silver bellies in the fish stall were arranged in opulent piles, while the vegetable stall next door was still a jumble of crates and sprawling heads of lettuce." Living in a hotel in Paris that year, bedbugs included, was considered bohemian, while having an apartment as the Mailers did was bourgeois. Alice and Mark were unable to cook or set up housekeeping on their own terms in any of the places they lived in Paris, so the year as a whole had a transitional, free-floating feeling about it.

During that winter Mailer negotiated with his editor, William Raney, over editorial changes, cover art, and other details regarding *The Naked and the Dead*. The word "fuck" became "fug," later prompting Dorothy Parker to address Mailer as "the young man who can't spell fuck." Nobody knew, during that long winter in Paris, that the novel would be a bestseller. "Norman's energy and charm and humor was wonderful," Mark Linenthal said. The combativeness and machismo for which Mailer was known later were then "always colored with a real sweetness." Not only that, but there was something fortifying about Mailer's audacity. People felt they were smarter when they were around him. He "ennobled" people and "that was very appealing, especially if you were the one being ennobled," Adams reflected.[29]

By spring *The Naked and the Dead* and its author were on the verge of celebrity. Alice and Mark read the book in galleys and thought it was "a great book." Mark, who was reading Stendhal at the time, told Mailer his book was better than *The Red and the Black*, a remark that Mark thought Norman "hugged to himself." In advance of the publication, Norman's parents arrived in Paris, along with his sister, Barbara, and Barbara Probst, whom they'd met on the ship. At Radcliffe Alice and Barbara Mailer had run in different crowds but in Paris they formed a lasting friendship. In fact, Alice explained to Barbara now, she hadn't really liked her apparent best friend, Rosalyn Landon, whom she considered anti-Semitic, and sometimes she wished to *be* Jewish herself. When the Mailer clan gathered, Alice was the only gentile in the room. "People would say things in Yiddish, and Mrs. Mailer would translate for me," she recalled fondly.[30]

Soon Norman and Bea Mailer purchased a Peugeot for $1,095 and began skipping their Sorbonne classes in favor of travel. For a weekend trip to Normandy, Alice and Mark squeezed into the backseat of the Peugeot with Barbara. Mont Saint-Michel floated beautifully above the fog as they approached it on a causeway connecting the mainland to the ancient fortified abbey on a tidal island. "Hardly anybody was going there then," Barbara Mailer Wasserman recalled. "Restaurants lined the streets and we were accosted by people who wanted us to come in and eat."[31] On a beach they enacted scenes from *The Naked and the Dead*, each playing a character. They didn't ask Mailer if any of the things in the book had happened to him. "It's a question I would never have asked," Adams insisted vehemently when Mailer biographer Peter Manso interviewed her. "No! Still wouldn't. As a writer, I think it's none of one's business. I mean, I hate it when people ask me how much of what . . . you know."

With the excitement of his incipient publication, Mailer tried to compare his own cohort to the writers of the 1920s: "*If* my generation is a lost generation it is lost in harder basically more cynical terms which it will take my generation of writers to define. I don't know if any good books will come out of this period, but . . . there seem to be more young people wanting to write now than I can ever remember in my short career."[32] The aspiring American writers who'd come to Paris, unlike the 1920s generation, "felt the army owed them a year in Paris," Mailer wrote in the *Paris Review*'s jubilee issue. The French were proud of their culture and resisted the sizable new American presence. "One of the reasons we Americans hung together and didn't like the French is that they didn't like us," Mailer said.

The Linenthals were sympathetic to French socialists and to the campaign of Henry Wallace, the progressive candidate for US president. In Paris Stanley and Eileen Geist introduced the Linenthals and Mailers to the noncommunist leftist writer Jean Malaquais, a Polish-born Jew who wrote in French but had become an American citizen during the war. As a boy in the Warsaw ghetto Malaquais became "forever suspicious of all authority" when he saw Russian mounted police beheading people with their sabers. His novel *Les Javanais* portrayed stateless, homeless lead and silver miners in Provence whose expressive multilingual speech was the basis of Malaquais's literary style. At twenty-nine, Malaquais was a celebrated, prizewinning author. Mailer was enchanted by Malaquais, who influenced his political thinking and became the translator of *The Naked and the Dead* into French.

Before they left Paris, the Mailers treated the Linenthals to a celebratory dinner at La Tour d'Argent. "That was a gas," Mark recalled. "It's way up high and had a great view." The menus listed no prices. Mark ordered a mushroom dish that prompted the waiter to write "on a piece of paper how much it was to warn me off of it . . . it was astronomical, so I didn't order it." After trips to Spain and Italy, Norman and Bea Mailer returned to New York. *The Naked and the Dead* was a bestseller. Barbara Mailer and Barbara Probst stayed longer in Europe, using the Peugeot to drive two escaping Spanish prisoners to the French border.[33]

Zelda Fitzgerald, icon of the flapper era and modern Southern femininity, died in a fire in a mental asylum in North Carolina in March 1948. In Paris, Mark Linenthal received his certificate from the Sorbonne and wondered what to do next. The ghetto of impoverished intellectuals and American soldiers in St.-Germain-des-Prés was rapidly disappearing. Three thousand Americans arrived to administer the Marshall Plan, bringing with them what seemed ostentatious riches in the form of leather shoes and large cars and cash to rent the city's best apartments. American writers from James Baldwin and Richard Wright to Saul Bellow and George Plimpton, Blair Fuller, and Max Steele came too, beginning an echo-renaissance of the 1920s that led to the founding of the *Paris Review*. The return of tourists brought "pre-war floodlighting on monuments for a summer Grande Nuit de Paris" while St.-Germain-des-Prés became "a campus for the American collegiate set," Janet Flanner reported in the *New Yorker*. "The Café de Flore serves as a drugstore for pretty upstate girls in unbecoming blue denim pants and their Middle Western dates, most of whom are growing hasty Beaux-Arts beards. Members of the tourist intelligentsia patronize the Rue de Bac's Pont-Royal Bar, which used to be full of French Existentialists and is now full only of themselves, often arguing about Existentialism."[34]

One of the new arrivals in Paris was Kenneth Lynn's fiancée, a recent Wellesley graduate from Pittsburgh named Valerie Roemer. That couple soon returned to Harvard, where he embarked on a notable career as a scholar of American literature. Mark Linenthal applied to the program for writers at Stanford University, now directed by the novelist Wallace

Stegner, whom Mark had met earlier at Harvard. The prose sample he submitted did not win him one of six places in the 1948 class, but Stegner's letter of regret included a personal invitation to apply to Stanford's literature program. "Palo Alto is almost as nice as Paris," Stegner promised. "It turned out that Stegner had never been to Paris at that time," Adams wryly commented later. "And so, ill-advisedly, that is what we did."[35]

This move did not seem ill-advised at the time. They were returning home to begin their married adult lives. Mark would continue to receive GI Bill benefits at Stanford. From there he could launch his career as a teacher. Before leaving France, the Linenthals bought etchings from the small Galerie Michel near Quai des Grands Augustins: a Rouault female nude, two heads of Charles Baudelaire by Edouard Manet, and a music sheet cover of "Zamboula-Polka" with a lithograph by Toulouse-Lautrec—all still treasured by their son. And they bought records by Claude Luter, whom they'd heard playing jazz in the caves of St.-Germain. Those records "sounded terrible" when they played them later. But, looking back, Alice missed Paris: "I could have stayed on in that misshapen Welcome room, alone or with some nice man I'd met at the Mephisto, or the Tabou. Spending my mornings on a better novel, and my afternoons exploring the city."[36]

Were it not for "The Impersonators" and "Winter Rain" and *Superior Women*, the year Alice Adams was twenty-one in Paris would be opaque to us. These fictions convey a longing and eagerness for sensory experience and love that defined their author more than her marriage did. They reveal Adams as a young writer with acute observational skills, an accomplished and ambitious prose style, and a deep sense of her inadequacy for the experience she was having. Becoming a wife was a startling change for an only child like Alice. No longer the inventor of the stories of her dolls, she had become an adjunct to her husband, a doll in the dollhouse of Paris and Mark and his friends. If she was unhappy with this, she turned to writing rather than depression. Working quietly at her novel while Mark went to the Sorbonne and Mailer fulfilled his ambition to write the first notable novel about World War II, Alice scrutinized herself through the character of Nic (for Nicolette) in "The Impersonators."

Nic, strangely enough, was Alice's father's nickname; in choosing that name, Adams takes on the question of her identity and gender. Is she a difficult, romantic person like her father or a difficult, intellectual person like her mother? Naturally, Nic Weller's parents are divorced—the mother struggles as an artist in Greenwich Village, the father as a painter and alcoholic in Cagnes-sur-Mer. The father brings nineteen-year-old Nic to Paris, finds her a room on the rue de Seine, and sets her loose among the ex-soldiers and starving French artists of St.-Germain-des-Prés. It's his idea of what's best for her, but in almost every way he fails to offer her the support she needs. Nic is surrounded by men who do not understand her, mainly gay French artists and Americans still recovering from the war.

The fictions Adams wrote about the forties in Paris are war stories, just as Adams's marriage was a war marriage. "Women come to writing, I believe, simultaneously with self-creation," feminist critic Carolyn Heilbrun writes.[37] The legacy that Alice Adams the writer took home from Paris is folded into her later work and life. Writing of some American women who came to Paris after World War II, Yale professor Alice Kaplan notes, "They may have looked demure and regimented, but the experience was life altering to them. Their *oeuvre* consists of their diaries, their letters home, their snapshots . . . their stories have not had a place in the great American tradition of expatriate literature."[38]

The Linenthals sailed home on the SS *America*, a vessel that had carried 350,000 troops during naval service throughout the war. Alice was still twenty-one, still unpublished, but far more experienced when she "took the huge and final boat for New York" (as she puts it in "Winter Rain") than the girl who had sailed east the year before.

CHAPTER TEN

Frustrated Ambitions

— 1948–1950 —

I don't think anyone who knew her had any idea what [my mother] was like, least of all my father.

—Alice Adams to Beatrice and
Norman Mailer, April 1, 1950

Alice had lived away from home since she went to boarding school in Virginia at age fifteen. She saw her parents rarely, mostly on summer visits to Maine. They'd supported her financially and encouraged her education but kept, or were kept, at a distance emotionally. Thus she had a false sense of independence that can develop without strong roots of self-knowledge, and her adolescent rebellion against her mother extended into her twenties. As Alice became a sexually active postwar woman, her mother seemed to her like a Victorian relic. The daughter reacted to her mother's moral valor and intellectual earnestness with guilt: "She arrives like Judgment Day only it's worse because she's so quiet, it's worse to be judged so genteelly," Adams wrote of the mother figure who appears in one of her early stories.[1]

Now in her midfifties, Agatha Adams wore tailored clothing and sensible shoes, and pinned her white hair up in a knot. Her stride was brisk and she held her small, plump body erect with a forward thrust of her chin. If she was matronly—that hated term so often used to dismiss women of a certain age—she was also substantial, prolific, respected by some, and feared by others. She was a leader in a mission to "change southern America through libraries." Within the all-white, male-dominated University of North Carolina, the Library School had the only female dean and promoted feminist and progressive ideas.

Yet Alice seems to have been blind to her mother's accomplishments. She sometimes referred to her as "a failed writer." An explanation for this discrepancy is suggested by English critic Lorna Sage's theory that ambitious women (in the last century) define themselves in opposition to their mothers: "Mother is the key. The women who really nailed patriarchy weren't on the whole the ones with authoritarian fathers but the ones with troubled, contradictory mothers: you aim your feminism less at men than at the picture of woman you don't want to be, the enemy within."[2] The mother Alice feared becoming was the one she knew in her childhood. She'd heard her crying behind closed doors and felt her stifled anger at the dinner table; she'd seen her working on her husband's books or doing homework for undergraduate classes when she was in her forties. She'd seen her mother pretend not to notice Nic Adams's flirtations with other women.

Alice was young and smart and beautiful, but marriage to Mark Linenthal, for better or worse, and writing were all she saw in her future. Returned from Europe in the summer of 1948, the two of them waited for Mark's acceptance to Stanford, staying first in a sublet in Cambridge and then spending August at the Adams cabin at Lake Sebago. Alice's relationship with the elder Linenthals was "better than before but wearing." Mark's father was kind but his mother, Anna, seemed so "abysmally stupid" that Alice said, "One tends to resort to her own banalities so that she will understand."[3] At Sebago she and Mark swam, played badminton, and enjoyed warm weather and plentiful food. Celebrating her twenty-second birthday in the place she'd spent childhood summers, Alice sounds content. Her uncle Beverley Boyd, an Episcopal priest, visited and won her approval by being a "real fighting liberal and very nice." The Mailers visited Lake Sebago too, just as fame was overtaking their lives. *The Naked and the Dead* had sold two hundred thousand copies in the three months since its publication and would remain on the *New York Times* bestseller list for another year.

Also making a visit to Sebago were Kenneth Lynn and Valerie Roemer, for whom Nic Adams baked a fabulous Sally Lunn cake. They thought Alice was fond and proud of her father even as she disdained what she considered his pretensions. "He insisted on speaking Spanish with a Castilian accent even when pronouncing names of places in California!"

Roemer remembered. Nic Adams had even more opportunities to speak of San Fran*thi*sco and other California places when Mark learned that he'd been admitted to the graduate program in English at Stanford University. Alice wrote Ken Lynn that she was "extremely happy" about their next move. "We are going west to make our fortunes."[4]

In the long-nosed, ten-year-old black Buick they bought, they stopped in New York and Chapel Hill before crossing the continent to Palo Alto. They moved into a "small, cheap house, without a phone or a mailbox or an address," seven miles west of campus on Page Mill Road, not far from the hilltop where the Stegners were building a house in a remote area of the Los Altos Hills. Alice thought the California hills were the most beautiful this side of Fiesole: "There are sweeps of fields with lovely single trees and wonderful woods and ravines; I continue to be moved every time we drive up or down." The apartment was really just a room, with the kitchen at one end and the bed in the middle, but they were making it "arty" with burlap curtains and a Lautrec poster mounted on plywood.[5]

The writing fellows at Stanford were "not the gilded group we imagined in Paris," Alice decided after meeting them at the Stegners'. This crowd was more like "Gibbesville, Pa.," than Cambridge, she bitingly observed, referring to (and misspelling!) the town in John O'Hara's stories. They were too "Americana"—the category in which she placed Wallace Stegner himself—by which she meant tall, large men from the West and Midwest who dressed in white T-shirts and jeans. Their overriding message, Adams thought, was "We're writers, but we're not queer, God knows we're not."

But the new writer friend Alice fell in love with on first meeting did not fit that mold. He was William Miller Abrahams, "a small, very lively, bright-blue-eyed man instantly amusing and amused." She and Mark both felt "an immediate rapport" with him. Abrahams—Billy to his friends—was a middle-class Jew from Newton Centre, Massachusetts, who had roomed with poet Howard Nemerov at Harvard and published two novels, *Interval in Carolina* and *By the Beautiful Sea*, rendered from his stateside army experiences. "Billy had a wonderful voice, deep and resonant, and his laugh was marvelously responsive," Adams wrote in a memoir. "He was extremely funny and made you feel that you were too." He laughed when Alice pointed out that Henry James's books were at the unreachable top of the Stegners' two-story bookcase. Alice later remembered a "somewhat drunken argument with Wally about who was the better writer, Jack London or Henry James."

Their snideness was unfair to Stegner, who taught James's novels and probably defended London as part of his program to bring more attention to Western writers. And it was ironic since Alice Adams, Mark Linenthal, and Abrahams would each become part of the story of Western American literature. But for that moment, in the bright, exposing sunlight and open spaces of California, the three felt safer talking together about their Cambridge professors and friends. Billy's accent was "purest Harvard" and "Harvard was the standard by which [Alice and Mark] judged California and Californians."

With Billy Abrahams, Adams felt herself "to be a charming and gifted woman, not a nutty girl in her early twenties who wanted to write but needed a job, any job. Who secretly did not much like her husband." Another writing fellow, Russian-born novelist Boris Ilyin, walked past the laughing trio of Alice, Mark, and Billy several times before he inquired, "Just what do you three people have in common?" They laughed more, considering outrageous answers to Ilyin's question.[6] "The stereotype of the woman being mildly stupid in order to get ahead in the world never touched Alice," Abrahams said when he looked back at those first meetings. "And that didn't always make her especially loved—except by those of us who so dearly loved her. I'm tempted to say Alice was a kind of feminist before her time."[7]

Abrahams was gay and "out" by the standards of the day. He'd written about straight relationships in his published novels and served in the army without difficulty, but his sexual orientation was known to friends. To someone who later praised his bravery in the matter, he replied, "What choice did I have?" Adams elaborated, "It is hard to imagine Billy in the macho pose that most of those [Stanford] Fellows adopted." Both Linenthals indulged in suspicion of the other writers' Western-macho attitude. They watched carefully, "especially when everyone was drunk; then, [they] thought, their 'true natures' might emerge." Such attention was rewarded when a "happily married" man approached Mark Linenthal: "As he put it, 'None of this fairy stuff. I just really like you,' while heavily attempting an embrace . . . rich fodder indeed." That, of course, was long before it had become common for American men to hug one another.[8]

In the November presidential election, the Linenthals supported Henry Wallace's campaign as nominee of the Progressive Party. Wallace had been vice president during Roosevelt's third term but was replaced by Harry Truman in 1944, thus missing the chance to be Roosevelt's successor by just eighty-two days. As a candidate Wallace opposed Truman's foreign policies, declaring that attempting to contain communism would lead to a "century of fear." He also favored universal health care and full racial integration. In the South he campaigned alongside African-American candidates and refused to eat or lodge in segregated facilities.

Norman Mailer made over thirty speeches for Wallace in New York and Hollywood. To the surprise of Mickey Knox and others who heard him at a fund-raiser for the defense of the Hollywood Ten (entertainment industry professionals who had refused to testify to the House Un-American Activities Committee), Mailer launched into an anti-Soviet tirade that shocked many of the communists and fellow travelers in attendance. "That speech was a turning point," Knox told Peter Manso. From then on Mailer delivered "the Trotskyist line, Malaquais's notion that East and West were cold warriors and that the Soviets were as bad as the West." In the end, Wallace came in fourth in the popular vote—outstripped not just by Truman but also by Republican Thomas Dewey and Dixiecrat Strom Thurmond. Disappointed by the Wallace campaign, Norman Mailer didn't vote again for twelve years.[9]

These political episodes affected Alice too. All her life she continued to deplore and analyze the racism she'd witnessed as a child. That and the liberal education she'd received at Harvard led her to idealize people she'd met in Europe who were deeply, sometimes radically, committed to political change. Both she and Linenthal remained firmly progressive as anticommunism became a right-wing cause in the United States and discord in Korea threatened a new war. But she was impatient when she read political theory and always more interested in individuals. She sensed that political idealists were as corruptible as anyone else, and she understood political commitment as an offshoot of background and personality. At the same time, she understood, long before second-wave feminism concentrated on the issue, that money and political power manifested in personal relationships: the political was personal.

After a Christmas dinner some jazz-loving neighbors named Smith surprised Alice and Mark by confiding they were "perpetual marijuana smokers" who had been high every time they'd met. That, Alice said, hadn't been on their "list of speculations about people," which included homosexuality and anti-Semitism. That night they too smoked marijuana, got very sick, and quarrelled with the Smiths, "who think," Alice told the Mailers, "that anyone who doesn't smoke isn't living right and can't see the world as it is. Ah California."[10]

That winter the beautiful apartment in the hills seemed less lovely. In March, the Linenthals rented a two-story house not far from campus. For the next five years they would move to a different house almost every year. The availability of small rental houses with yards was one of their favorite things about life in California—the other being cheap wine. In their suburban neighborhoods they became friendly with other married couples. She flirted with some of the husbands, but told the Mailers that she was resigned to finding the people around Palo Alto "occasionally pleasant—no more."

Working toward his doctorate, Mark Linenthal abandoned his wish to be a novelist. He was most engaged by poetry and criticism courses taught by the legendary Yvor Winters, a proponent of metrical verse and rational poetic structure. According to Herbert Blau, an NYU engineering grad who'd grown up among gangs on the streets of Brownsville in Brooklyn and now studied drama at Stanford, Mark enjoyed arguments with and about Winters. Mark became a model for Blau, a measure of his "capacity to be literate." He admired and imitated Mark's Harvard background and style—impeccable jackets and ties. After Blau stood up to Winters in class one day, Mark stopped by the cottage by a creek where he lived with his wife, actress Beatrice Manley. Blau felt he'd "sort of made it at Stanford to have Mark's approval at that time." In those days Blau thought Alice shy and aloof. She barely talked when the two couples went to a "whoop-it-up kind of place" on a wharf in San Francisco, and Blau had the feeling that she "wondered why we were wasting our time."

Alice's letters from Palo Alto display frustration and boredom clashing with her attempt to sound like a happy wife. The ills of her marriage that were manifest in Paris go unmentioned, though she talked about them with Abrahams. For some weeks after arriving at Stanford, Alice worked at a leather factory job where she suffered punctures in her fingers and "loss of faith." Nonetheless, that venture into working-class life provided her with background for Megan Green's family in *Superior Women.* Later Alice found more agreeable jobs on campus, at the college bookstore and in Stanford's purchasing department. The tasks were tedious, but she liked her coworkers, including a Japanese woman with whom she discussed "intermarriage" and other relationships across what then seemed a racial divide. She complained that Californians are naively lacking in psychological information, but a weekend in Carmel with Nancy and Bill Webb, friends from Harvard who were both in analysis, made her frantic because "every slip of the tongue becomes fraught with subconscious hostility." She considered going into analysis herself. Meanwhile she and Mark talked about "having kids," but she said, "It seems impractical at the moment so we don't do anything about it, or rather we do."[11]

Alice didn't connect her own discontent with being a wife who lacked status in her husband's world. There was as yet no name for her problem. In 1960, Phyllis Levin published an article headlined "Road from Sophocles to Spock Is Often a Bumpy One" about the anxiety, frustration, and claustrophobia of the educated housewife. Levin noted that "the modern woman" was only forty years old, and lamented her descent from the ivory tower of academia to "push-button kitchens, supermarkets and finished basements."*[12] In letters to friends, Alice described herself as an ardent cook who baked bread and made fancy wine sauces but downplayed her literary pursuits. She said she'd reread all the books she'd "hastily read earlier and been unwisely talking about ever since," and decided "that less talk and more information would be a Good Thing for me."

To Alice, Palo Alto was a "lotus land" where "time goes by uncounted,

---

* In *The Feminine Mystique* in 1963, Betty Friedan asks: "Are [married women] putting into their insatiable sexual search the aggressive energies which the feminine mystique forbids them to use for larger human purposes? . . . Is that feeling of personal identity, of fulfillment, they seek in sex something that sex alone cannot give?"

probably because nothing happens to count by." Both she and Mark preferred San Francisco, where they could go to jazz clubs and ballet performances and fine restaurants, but those entertainments were expensive. They could not afford to travel east for a summer vacation in 1949 and planned to go camping in Yosemite instead.

Abrahams became Alice's literary mentor after she showed him pages of her novel—"still the same fucking novel" ("The Impersonators"). His response was both kind and intelligently constructive, and—most important of all, she said—"from then on he talked and behaved as though I were a writer." When Abrahams learned that she'd never read Proust, he exclaimed, "Oh, how I envy you! A first reading, and you're just the right age—so young. Start tomorrow." Alice did, and loved it. Indeed, she said, "Reading Proust was rather like talking to Billy: Swann and Mme. de Guermantes, the Verdurins and Charlus, were now included in our conversation." In this way, Adams later declared, Abrahams saved her sanity during her first year as a wife in Palo Alto.[13]

Frank Granat, a Stanford undergrad housemate of Abrahams's, saw nothing of the moody, detached housewife that Blau recalled. The scion of the legendary Granat Bros. jewelers in San Francisco, Granat thought Alice was a "beautiful exotic" who embodied chic and sophistication. "She was older than me, much more worldly," he recalled. Alice seemed tall to him (as an adult she was five foot six) and he praised her legs and big bosom, noticed that her teeth weren't aligned perfectly but found that overbite part of her natural attractiveness. "She had a way about her that was unique and I hate to use the word *delicious*, but she was." Alice introduced Granat to martinis and French cooking, either at L'Omelette ("Lommies"), a French restaurant on El Camino Real beyond the university's alcohol-free zone, or at home when the Linenthals invited him and Abrahams to dinner. "Mark always wanted to talk about old English writers I'd vaguely heard of—Alice was the fun! Sometimes when Mark was away it was just the three of us, Alice, Billy, and myself. We'd talk about France right after the war," he remembered. "Sometimes Alice talked about her sex life but in a very very funny way. Had nothing to do with reality. She was just very funny about it in a way I just can't really describe. It wasn't gossip or anything like that."

Granat believed that Alice and Mark got along, but his observations also suggest reasons for her discontent. "Mark talked a great deal but he was not a conversationalist—two different things!" Granat thought Mark "was very full of himself—there was no spark. There might have been a literary spark, but there was nothing that would make me want to get together with him and just talk about things. Alice I would have seen every week if I could."

Granat helped support Abrahams while he completed his third novel, *Imperial Waltz*, which he dedicated to Granat. In this historical novel about Princess Elisabeth of Bavaria, Abrahams told the story of a girl leaving an idyllic youth to become an adolescent and woman bound by social conventions. Abrahams's Elisabeth could be a psychological profile of Alice Linenthal: A rebellious, carefree girl roams the woods and write poems. She craves an approving father, but he—a free spirit himself—is too lackadaisical to fill that role. Her mother, having lost her own freedom to marriage, is concerned only for her daughter's social success. A forced separation from a watchmaker's son—a version of Trummy Young or Bruno Trentin?—leaves the princess forever dreamy, erratically passive. Her husband, the Emperor Franz Joseph, cherishes her but lives by his mother's command; he cannot nourish Elisabeth's soul.

In January of 1949, Alice began keeping a journal, which she described as "really a fictionalized version of what happens, or what I think happens."[14] The next summer she began psychoanalysis with a San Francisco Freudian, Dr. Joseph Biernoff. Biernoff was regarded as an expert on psychosomatic illnesses, but there's no record of Alice's complaints. Or rather, what record there probably was disappeared when she or someone else tore thirty pages from her journal. Her decision to undertake analysis was complicated given her sexual history with her father's psychiatrist, but it was not an unusual choice for a young intellectual of that era when Freudian ego-centered talk therapy was popular in the United States.

With Mark now teaching two courses at Stanford, Alice quit her full-time job, and they borrowed money from Mark's parents to afford her analysis. Each time she saw Biernoff, Alice spent part of a day en route to and from San Francisco—perhaps therapeutic in itself. Once she spotted Vida Ginsberg on the street as she boarded a bus. The woman they'd known in Salzburg had married a doctor named Quentin Deming and lived in a city apartment that reminded Alice of Greenwich Village: "High ceilings and small rooms brightly painted, a pleasant clutter of books and pictures, fruit and wine."[15] San Francisco, she was realizing, offered the historic and artistic charm that she missed in suburban houses farther down the Peninsula.

Hired by Sam Goldwyn to write a screenplay, Mailer had returned to Southern California in 1949. He and Bea lived in a modern "movie star" house in the Hollywood Hills. Alice was so "shaken up" and "self-involved" after her initial sessions with Dr. Biernoff that she considered herself "even less perceptive than usual" when she and Mark visited the Mailers in Hollywood in August. The ménage there included a "huge black maid" (as Alice described her later); Bea was huge too, seven months pregnant with a baby nurse already employed. Alice was touched that Norman threw a party for them and introduced them to Dorothy Parker, as well as John Howard Lawson, Albert Maltz, and others of the Hollywood Ten, but both Linenthals thought Bea seemed "a little overwhelmed" by Norman's overnight fame and financial success.

Mailer's new life fascinated Mark Linenthal: "I was full of Norman, drunk on Norman." He cited Norman as an authority so often that someone finally asked him, "But what do you think?" Norman urged the Linenthals to read George Orwell's *1984*, just published, for its chastening effect on their liberalism. It showed "the world in which socialism had arrived at its horrible end." Mailer now believed that anyone serious about writing must become an intellectual, "and yet nothing is harder. Intellectuality vitiates the attempt at large, serious works because you are unable to suspend the critical faculties even at the times when you should."[16] Mailer urged Alice to study original texts by Marx and Engels ("at least *Capital*") and Mark remembered, "He wanted to sit around and have formal dialectical discussion . . . And Alice and I thought, oh, fuck this, it's dreadful."

Apparently Mailer liked his wife's pregnancy better than its aftermath. When Susan Mailer was born, her father felt displaced, complaining to a friend, "[Bea] acts infinitely superior to me now."[17]

In September Norman came alone to Palo Alto for the first-ever Harvard-Stanford football game, in which the Indians drubbed the Ivy League visitors 44–0 and Alice, Mark, and Norman formed "a lonely and unloved rooting section." The two teams have not played each other since. Alice and Mark threw a "huge" party for Mailer, inviting all of Mark's graduate student colleagues. Alice said the party was "a little bit of thumbing our nose at the academic Establishment, particularly Wally Stegner," who was probably the only faculty member they invited. Mailer was an impressive visitor in the eyes of the Linenthals' circle. He made himself "pleasant and available" at the party—particularly to graduate student Lois Mayfield Wilson. She had fallen for him when she read *The Naked and the Dead*, and she attended the party without her husband. She and Mailer disappeared for a long while during the evening—and remained close for sixty years. Alice said she really liked Wilson, an attractive blond from Kentucky known sotto voce as Miss Maysex, and was glad to give her and Norman the pleasure of meeting.*

Alice's dislike of Stegner's writing program hardened when it rejected her application for a fellowship. She'd applied with six revised chapters of "The Impersonators" and Billy Abraham's blessing.[18] Decades later, when she taught a writing seminar at Stanford, she still recalled the "enraged envy" with which she'd regarded the creative writers when she was working to support her husband as "nice young wives did in those bad old days."[19]

When the Modern Language Association held its convention at Stanford in September 1949, both Agatha and Nic Adams stayed with Alice and Mark for a week. "We had a shitty time of it too," Alice wrote. "I was sick the whole time, much vomiting . . . so obviously psycho-somatic as to be quite embarrassing." After long believing her own neurosis kept her from appreciating her parents, she now "decided that they, particularly [her] father, [were] not nice at all and that [she was]

---

* The two Southern women did not remain friendly. Lois Wilson believed that Alice had an affair with her husband, Graham Wilson—which Adams denied. Alice made Wilson's affair with Mailer public in 1983 when she mentioned that postgame party for Peter Manso's oral biography of Mailer. The story did not fully emerge until Wilson talked on record about Mailer to her daughter, screenwriter Erin Cressida Wilson. That version appears—poignantly—in Michael Lennon's authorized biography *Norman Mailer: A Double Life*.

not so neurotic as one would think." Nic Adams's personality made his daughter frantic—he demanded sherry in lunchrooms and introduced himself loudly before anyone else could get his name out." Alice declined to specify her more serious reasons for not liking her father: "I'm bored by the subject."[20] She said even less about her mother.

Earlier in the year, Alice had mailed eighty pages of "The Impersonators" to William Raney, Mailer's editor at Rinehart who'd liked her earlier stories. Mailer put in a word for her, the pages circulated to several editors, but in the end Raney sent "soft words" and no contract. Still, Alice determined to write three pages a day till the book was finished. She was "more pleased than not" by what she'd written. Mark liked it too, she told the Lynns.[21] Abrahams remained Alice's closest confidant. In those days he was drawn to straight men "who were not even especially bright or interesting" and did not reciprocate his undeclared desires. Alice had a similar problem: "a string of crushes on young men of [their] graduate-student circle, men who, married or single, did not want the responsibility of an affair with a nutty married woman who wanted to write. There was quite a bit of kissing in cars, on ostensible trips out for ice or more booze—not exactly satisfactory, and hardly romantic." About such matters Alice and Billy gave each other comfort with discussions marked by "extreme discretion."[22] All of it was fodder for their friendship and—eventually—for her fiction. When she found no publisher for her novel, Abrahams urged her to write more short stories. She produced more than a dozen during the late 1940s and early 1950s. All remain unpublished, but the occasional encouraging word buried in a rejection letter from an editor was enough. "It doesn't take much to keep a writer going," she reminisced to an interviewer years later.[23]

By spring of 1950 Alice was nearly finished with "The Impersonators" and felt that "a lot depend[ed] on what happen[ed]" with that novel. She continued her sessions with Dr. Biernoff, though Mark's father no longer paid for them. Instead she wrote Norman Mailer with a request to borrow $500. The loan would bring her to the point of being "through or nearly so" with her analysis, which now took place three days a week instead of five—"a saving and somewhat less difficult." She earned $50 a month with a part-time job in the Guidance Center at Stanford and planned to devote those earnings to repaying Mailer. "Please don't regard this as a desperate demand, because it isn't," she added, "but if you could it would be wonderful." He sent a check right away.[24]

On Friday, March 17, 1950, Alice received news that her mother had died in Chapel Hill. Agatha Erskine Boyd Adams was fifty-seven. Her cause of death is reported as a heart attack. "No one knew she had a bad heart and it was a terrible shock," Alice wrote to the Mailers.[25]

Verlie Jones found Agatha's body in bed when she arrived for work at about ten. Nic Adams was "sick at the time with another depression," as Alice put it, and staying at Dr. Kemp's sanitarium in Pinebluff. Two doctors from the UNC medical school came to the house and confirmed that Agatha had been dead several hours.

It was probably Alice's uncle Beverley who phoned or telegrammed Alice, and it was certainly he who informed the coroner of his sister's death and made arrangements for the funeral held just two days later in the Episcopal chapel. There was little time for Alice to make travel arrangements and she chose not to do so. "It seemed best for me not to go home," she explained to the Mailers. That curt "seemed best for me not to go" may have been the result of discussions with her husband and her uncle. She wished, it seems, to avoid seeing her father.* Agatha was buried in the Old Chapel Hill Cemetery next to the grave of her infant son and Alice's brother, Joel Willard.

A contrast between Agatha Adams's private and public lives marks the obituaries and memorials published after her death. Nine trustees and officers of Randolph-Macon Woman's College drove from Lynchburg, Virginia, to join the large gathering for her Sunday-afternoon funeral, and newspapers across North Carolina regretted that Mrs. Adams would be unable to follow her booklet on Thomas Wolfe with a complete biography of the novelist. A scholarship fund was established in her name at Randolph-Macon; the University of North Carolina gathered one hundred volumes for an Adams Memorial Collection, including a rare edition of Nic's favorite book, *Don Quixote de la Mancha*. Agatha's

---

* Another version of not-going-to-the-funeral occurs in Adams's novel *Families and Survivors*: When her mother dies, Louisa (based on Alice) stays home because of a flare-up of colitis and because she has learned that her father tried to contest her mother's will. In the novel, that will left everything to Louisa. Outside of fiction, there's no record that Agatha wrote a will.

eulogists list her own accomplishments alongside those of her brothers, husband, daughter ("Radcliffe graduate"), and son-in-law ("a graduate student at Stanford"); the Chapel Hill paper praises her as "a hard worker" who "could be the merriest and most warm-hearted of companions."[26]

Agatha had suffered considerably in her marriage to the brilliant, charismatic, and volatile Nic Adams, but in recent years she had rendered herself independent. Her talk at Randolph-Macon in June 1949, titled "Jobs for the Helen Hokinson Crowd"—referencing the popular *New Yorker* cartoonist—recounted her return to college for her library degree.* She spoke of the necessity for "women over forty-five or over fifty" to work. "It's fun to have a job," she told her sister alums. She also noted the sense of "independence and security" that a job brings, along with "the blessed sustaining quality of routine."

Between her lines one easily sees Nic Adams's manic and depressive phases, his flirtations and his hospitalizations. Also there, more visibly to Alice, are Agatha's ambivalence about motherhood and her resentment of lost years. Trips to college meetings in Virginia gave Agatha an opportunity to rekindle friendships with unmarried friends who had successful careers in education and other fields open to women. A paragraph Agatha quotes from novelist Laura Krey, who became a successful novelist after her children left home, sums up her theme:

> For a woman's life had two parts, one when she must transmit, like stored honey, all that she has to give. Then, unlike the queen bee, she did not die, her work done; but out of the inexhaustible core of her deepest personality, started in again to weave for herself a soul, a being strong enough to face the rigors of eternity. That is, she did if she was wise. She had another choice; she could wither, turning dustier and duller every year, content to have served her biological function and to die.[27]

"Jobs for the Helen Hokinson Crowd," which was reprinted in the American Association of University Women's magazine the summer

---

* Hokinson (1893–1949) died in an Eastern Airlines midair collision just months after Agatha Adams delivered her talk. The "Hokinson Women" in her drawings were plump, earnest society ladies. When she died, Hokinson was on a crusade to defend her characters from people she felt were unfairly ridiculing them. (Carey Gibbons, "A Hokinson Woman," www.cooperhewitt.org/2018/04/10/hokinson/.)

after Agatha died, is so remarkable and moving that it seems utterly sad that her daughter did not treasure a copy of it or have a good word to say about her mother's accomplishments in any surviving letters. We cannot even be sure she ever read this essay.

Agatha Erskine Boyd Adams

To Alice her mother's death seemed "very unreal." She said the long letters she received telling her about the obsequies she'd missed made it "more remote since I kept thinking how silly Mother would have thought all the fuss. One woman even sent me a flower which she had apparently snatched from the grave." Charles Rush, director of the UNC library, found all the papers in Agatha's desk "in perfect assortment, with notations on next steps to be taken" toward a biography of Thomas Wolfe. To Rush, this orderliness proved that Agatha "felt the end for her would come quickly."[28]

Agatha died without writing a will. Nic was appointed to administer her estate, which he itemized as real estate in Maine ($1,200) and personal property ($250). In an unpublished novel she called "Mothering," Alice imagined a mother who fears she will die young, distrusts her husband, and sets aside money to leave directly to her daughter. That was a fantasy of Alice's that Agatha did not fulfill.

"I don't think anyone who knew her had any idea what she was like, least of all my father," Alice wrote the Mailers.[29] Agatha's death marked the beginning of her daughter's effort to know who she had been. For her the private Agatha would be of greater interest than the community-minded public intellectual. Alice went about her quest most strikingly through her fiction. For the rest of her life she would revise and revise again her girlhood preference for her father. In her stories and novels, her father remained something of a caricature while her mother evolved and transformed into a complex character.

"The Wake" is the first story that transforms Agatha into Jessica Taylor, a primary figure in the dollhouse of her imagination. She speaks from the point of view of "everyone" who attends Jessica's funeral on a springtime afternoon in North Carolina. Jessica dies exactly as Agatha did, the first to go in her circle of townspeople. They are shocked by the realization of their own mortality. They wonder if Agatha had been warned of a heart problem. One man fatuously declares that this could not happen to him because he has an annual physical at Johns Hopkins.

The Adams family is represented by Jessica's husband, Ran(dolph), and her son, Devlin, who "had oddly chosen to go to Harvard" instead of the University of Virginia. There is a missing child too: "Martha, the daughter and her father's early favorite, had quarreled with everyone years ago and then married an unlikely older man and gone to live in New Mexico; no one would have expected her to be there." With these siblings, Adams represents both herself and her brother who died. The sight of Ran and Devlin together reminds the mourners "that the Taylors were a family; one had tended to think of them as a set of private lives, joined, as by accident, under a mutual roof."

The climax of "The Wake" occurs when Leslie Rhett, "a giant of a woman with mad red hair and always a square-cut grey flannel suit" (based on writer Jessie Rehder, a Randolph-Macon alumna and the first woman tenured by the UNC English Department), tells the gathering: "You didn't know her a bit and never tried, but she knew all of you . . . She hated you, all of you, you women. We used to laugh at you all the time, with your cokes in the morning and shopping trips to New York and herb gardens." After Leslie is ushered out, the others feel Jessica's presence among them: "difficult, an unwelcome shade." They feel guilty for her death, "for their own un-love."[30]

In 1989, in the first of a cycle of stories about Lila Lewisohn, Adams again studied her mother in the character of Lila's mother, Henrietta Macoby. In "The Grape Arbor" we learn that Henrietta was "an exceptionally confusing parent" who always seemed to be "shopping around for some perfect daughter." She obsessively compared Lila to other girls and women her age. "I'm sure that's one of the reasons I became a psychiatrist," Lila believes. But she remembers one great day: "The time I told her I couldn't stand *Little Women*. I remember being a little scared, saying that. I was afraid you were supposed to like it. But Henrietta was absolutely delighted. 'Oh, you're right, those dreadful self righteous girls and that horrible old martyr, Marmee.' She positively chortled. . . . She was so terrifically pleased with me!"[31]

"The loss of the mother to the daughter, the daughter to the mother, is the essential female tragedy," writes Adrienne Rich in *Of Woman Born*. "There is presently no enduring recognition of mother-daughter passion and rapture," she argues. "The power of our mothers, whatever their love for us and their struggles on our behalf, is too restricted. And it is the mother through whom the patriarchy early teaches the small female her proper expectations."[32]

Against those expectations both Agatha and Alice Adams had rebelled in ways that put them at odds with one another. With her mother's sudden and early death, Alice lost forever the opportunity to form a mature relationship with the complicated and remarkable woman who brought her into the world.

CHAPTER ELEVEN

Family of Three

— 1950–1954 —

Stories suggested a possibility of illumination; writing them, one might at least understand what had happened, what people meant by their puzzling, infinitely ambiguous words (and wills).

—Alice Adams,
"The Making of a Writer"[1]

"In the tawny hills that surround the Stanford campus the dark green heavy live oaks barely move; along Palm Drive the asphalt is melting. High up in those palm trees the green-gray fronds are hard, dusty, and dry, they rattle in the slightest breeze, like snakes," Adams wrote of her first California summers.[2] Through the summer after her mother's death, Alice worked at her part-time job in the Guidance Center, finished writing and typing "The Impersonators," and went to cool, foggy San Francisco for her analysis sessions.

During this time, Alice felt "hysterical about bombs and the army." Since the end of World War II, American confidence had soured into anticommunist fervor. The Soviet Union dominated eastern Europe. Mao Tse-tung's Communist Party had taken over China in 1949, and Russia had detonated an atomic bomb. Soon the United States was developing the hydrogen bomb, about which Albert Einstein warned a television audience, "Radioactive poisoning of the atmosphere, and hence, annihilation of any life on earth, has been brought within the range of possibilities."

The Linenthals' optimistic postwar liberalism took a personal blow with the suicide of Professor Matthiessen, who had written enthusiastically of his hopes for socialist democracy in Czechoslovakia. Matthiessen had been attacked by Irving Howe, Philip Rahv, and Alfred Kazin for "good intentions" that made him a "dupe" of Stalinism. Two weeks after Agatha Adams died, forty-eight-year-old Matthiessen jumped from a hotel window in Boston. In choosing to defenestrate himself in the symbolically Czech manner, he paid homage to the idealistic friends in Prague that he'd met in Salzburg. "I am depressed over world conditions," his suicide note read. "I am a Christian and a Socialist. I am against any order which interferes with that objective."[3]

The next war was one most Americans weren't expecting. North Korean troops invaded South Korea in June 1950, prompting the United Nations to retaliate in what was called a "police action." Most of the UN troops, commanded by US general Douglas MacArthur, were American. It was supposed to be a quick war, but after the North Korean army retreated above the Thirty-Eighth Parallel, Chinese soldiers arrived in force. World War II veterans were recalled to service, and like millions of others, Mark Linenthal feared a summons.

Before she and Mark departed on a summer trip east, Alice mailed a complete manuscript of "The Impersonators" to William Raney, now an editor at Henry Holt & Co. During a wearing stay with Mark's parents in Cambridge and visits with other Boston friends, Alice wondered what the man who had published Mailer's *The Naked and the Dead* would say about her novel. When she got to New York she went downtown to meet Raney in the office where she'd worked so briefly in 1946. She thought he was "terribly nice," especially when he said he "loved" the novel and wanted to give her a contract. Thrilled, Alice told the Lynns, "He seems to want the same revisions that I do." But, since Raney's say wasn't final, Alice was "afraid to be too optimistic"—which made her drag her heels on the revisions.[4]

While she was at the Holt offices, the editor of Nic Adams's Spanish textbooks pulled Alice aside to ask what she thought could be done about her father. Nic had been expected to meet Alice and Mark in New York, but a manic spree of "fine food and liquor and trips" since Agatha's death had made him unpredictable. He didn't show up until after they departed. "He thinks he's fine and writes insane letters about how well he is, really insane," Alice said.[5] Ralph and Eve Bates, with whom Alice and Mark stayed in New York, thought Nic's condition was the result of shock treatments and assured Alice that he "did used to be fairly bright." But much of the conversation with the Bateses was political. In 1950 Ralph refused to testify to HUAC and published what would be his last book, though he lived until 2000. "His disillusion with the political scene was complete," his wife, Eve, told the *New York Times* when he died.[6]

Back in Palo Alto and still waiting on a contract from Raney, Alice discovered she was several months pregnant. She complained of "ill-fitting maternity bras" but felt terrifically strong and healthy throughout her pregnancy and announced her intention to breastfeed the baby and to try "this new natural method" of childbirth. She had doubts that "neurotic women can suddenly relax to that extent," but the baby doctor scoffed at her Freudian views. "My analyst as usual says nothing," she reported. For Alice, anticipation of a child displaced marriage problems and grief and confusion over her mother's death. She was exuberantly proud of her condition. She wrote a "sexy story about an obstetrician who hates pelvic exams" and joked that Billy Abrahams saw "very little market for this sort of thing." Mark also looked forward to parenthood and stepped up both his teaching schedule and his preparations for doctoral exams, which he planned to take before the baby was due in March.

Things that had worried Alice before didn't faze her now. After she listened to a speech given by President Truman on October 17 in San Francisco, her fears of bombs and the Korean War diminished. Truman asserted that American strength derived from a belief in human freedom and political equality. These were revolutionary values, he said, that would inspire the newly formed United Nations to resist the reactionary international communist movement. "Truman last night said annoyingly little," she wrote, "but it does seem somehow more possible to plan for the next few years. I've decided that it would be a good idea to have two children within the next couple of years." She credited her new attitude to a "state of animal content" and "generally more cheerful frame of mind" rather than to "anything that has happened."[7]

For Christmas, Mark gave Alice a "marvelous purple velvet coat . . . which buttons to look like a dress, and I think I look quite baroque and splendid. The baby's ass is quite a firm and recognizable lump near the middle of my stomach, and he kicks wildly most of the time. We really don't care which it is—I'd just like a large healthy baby."[8]

In the end, Raney could not get his editor in chief, Ted Amussen, to sign on to "The Impersonators," but he sent the manuscript over to Harold Strauss at Knopf with a note suggesting that Adams could "develop into a damned good slick, popular writer." Strauss scratched his contrary opinion on the back of a manuscript evaluation form: "I think [Raney's] nuts. This flaccid stuff lacks insight, style and structure. Reject fast. —HS." Mercifully, Adams never saw Strauss's comments, which lie with thousands of similar rejection records (labeled "Rags") in the Knopf archive at the University of Texas's Harry Ransom Center.

Adams reacted to the rejection with a sort of shrugging passivity and shape-shifting that one suspects might be a typically female and fifties way of stepping aside from her ambitions: "I can't care very much about the book. I've been working on some stories from time to time, and I like them but magazines don't. I sometimes wish that writing wasn't what I wanted to do, or really that I had both more drive and more talent. I have just enough of both to make me uncomfortable."[9]

Their friend Norman Mailer found it difficult to write novels in the early fifties. *Barbary Shore*, which the Linenthals "found bad enough" when they read an early draft, was declared a failure (*Time* cited the author's "sophomoric fatalism"). Both Alice and Mark were staggered when they read it in published form: "Incroyable . . . I think he has gone off his rocker," she said. Mailer told the *New York Times* early in 1951: "To be a novelist today is absolutely a bonecracker. . . . In the past, a novelist could create a world view, a whole thing in itself. It is different today because knowledge is broken down, departmentalized." By summer the Linenthals heard that Bea had fled to Mexico with her daughter and a Mexican lover.[10] Norman was living with Adele Morales in New York and his close friendship with the Linenthals had dwindled. Bea Silverman married Salvador Sanchez, became a doctor, and practiced psychiatry in both Mexico and Florida.

With the baby's due date approaching, the Linenthals moved to a three-bedroom house with a room for the baby and a study for Mark. Alice doesn't mention where she will write. Her father, as Alice "more or less expected," was depressed again and "back with Malcolm, his crazy doctor." Nic spent another seven months in Pinebluff, making himself welcome at the Kemps' home but refusing to follow Dr. Kemp's orders or pay his bill.[11]

About this time Alice resumed her friendship with Judith Clark, who had moved to San Francisco after she graduated from George Washington University and become the assistant advertising manager for the Joseph Magnin Company, then renowned for high-style clothing and sophisticated ads. She married *Chronicle* reporter Timothy Adams, son of the popular satirical columnist and *Information Please* radio show panelist Franklin Pierce Adams. Timothy Adams had been called up for the Korean War and was editing *Stars and Stripes* in Japan when he met an AP reporter from Chapel Hill, Sam Summerlin. The gossip they exchanged somehow put the two old friends—now Judith Adams and Alice Linenthal—back in touch. Soon Judith took the train to Palo Alto for dinner with the Linenthals: "I wore a light grey fitted wool coat with, of course, white gloves, small grey hat with veil—oh, those were so becoming—and a sensational black leather purse I wish I had right this minute."

Judith Adams remembered what she wore because Alice Adams reprised a lot of that evening in her 1974 novel *Families and Survivors*. There she portrayed herself as "pregnant, stoop-shouldered, and rather shabby" Louisa in contrast to "erect and stylish" Kate, who works for an elegant department store.

Looking at *Families and Survivors* alongside Alice's letters from the early 1950s reminds us that her fiction, despite inventions, excavates her own conflicting emotions. It's impossible to say if unhappy Louisa in the novel is more accurate than the cheerful writer of the letters. Over dinner, Kate criticizes Louisa's husband, Michael, for asking talented Louisa to work in a dull clerical job while he studies. "Louisa's femaleness makes me feel more male. You don't believe in sexual polarity?" Michael asks Kate. She retorts, "I believe in a man and a woman living together, being friends. I don't think it matters who does what . . . who does dishes or stays at home with kids." Louisa remembers that her husband once thought of her as a bulwark against his mother, so she is thrilled to defend him again in this scene. Nonetheless, Kate's view expresses her own discontent as a submissive wife.

*   *   *

Peter Adams Linenthal was born in the morning on March 20, 1951. Alice thought he was "terrific" and "bigger and healthier than most babies," and she and Mark were both "tired but euphoric." All that she squeezed on a postcard to the Lynns on the afternoon of Peter's birth.[12]

The birth occurred at Sequoia Hospital in Redwood City, and Alice found labor "considerably less than no fun" despite some dulling of the pain with Demerol and cyclopropane.* Otherwise the birth was entirely normal. Having expected her neuroses to interfere with her ability to give birth, Alice was proud of herself for this uncomplicated performance. Peter weighed seven pounds, fifteen ounces, measured twenty and a half inches, and took well to breastfeeding, though he also received bottles at the hospital. He and his mother went home after four days.

Alice said the baby looked like Mark, but photos show a high Adams forehead. They also show extremely doting parents who like each other enough to produce a full album of happy snapshots of themselves with their baby. Peter was, Alice wrote, "really a terrific baby—Mark and I are quite entranced, even at 3 am. He *is* handsome—all this stuff about babies being universally ugly is for the birds. We spend hours watching him."[13]

Peter was a month old and learning to smile when he began vomiting persistently and explosively. X-rays revealed an "acute hypertrophic pyloric stenosis," or obstruction of the passage from his stomach to his small intestine. Under a general anesthetic, a surgeon made a three-inch incision in the ten-pound infant's abdomen. A day later, the obstruction removed, his deep wound sutured with catgut and nylon and steel wire, he could drink sterile water. Soon Alice was able to hold and breastfeed him at the hospital, and he was sent home a few days later. It had been all been "a pretty terrifying experience, but now he's fine," Alice wrote.

With that first crisis of motherhood behind her, Alice reflected on her fitness for the job. "Knowing as much and as little as I do about depth psychology [the unconscious] does occasionally make me nervous— bringing up a child does seem such an enormous responsibility if you want to do it well, but I usually decide that he won't be very crazy—at

---

* In *Listening to Billie*, Catherine tells Eliza that the 1950s version of "natural childbirth" didn't work because it was "just a guilt trip that some English guy laid on women"—a reference to Grantly Dick-Read's pioneering *Childbirth Without Fear*, which suggested that modern women's neuroses and ignorance prevented them from giving birth without pain relievers or medical intervention.

least less so than me and I do manage." For good reason, fear of mental illness continued to haunt Alice. Her father was in his "padded cell" at Kemp's sanitarium, and she believed him "so mad at [her] for having a child that he won't write." For her part, she disliked him so much that "it [was] hard to feel sorry for him except in a rather abstract way."[14]

Not long after Peter's birth, Alice mailed a note and photo to Dr. Biernoff, who had advised her to stay married and stop writing. "Not that I'm jealous, but it does sound as if having a baby is better therapy than psychoanalysis. You sound like the 'after' picture of a testimonial," he replied. Indeed, it seemed to be true. Peter seems to have been a perfect baby and Alice perfectly happy to stay at home with him. "He sleeps outside in his carriage all day and goes for rides. We're all getting quite brown," she wrote. By summer, Peter was sleeping through the night and "quite lively during most of the day." Alice said, "He laughs and smiles a great deal, pisses in his bath, and tries to crawl. We find him completely fascinating. Also my friends with male children tell me that he has the largest genitalia extant in one so young."[15]

Alice continued to read her "usual quota of Freud and related books" and shared her opinions with the Lynns, in part because Valerie was becoming a psychotherapist. She praised Ferenczi's *Sex in Psychoanalysis* and a lecture she and Mark had attended by Siegfried Bernfeld, both of which reflect a determination to cure herself of some sexual insecurity or aberration and avoid afflicting Peter with the "craziness" that she and Mark saw in their families of origin. She read William Styron's first novel, *Lie Down in Darkness*, when it came out in the fall, aware that Styron was little older than herself, had grown up in Virginia, and had studied at Duke University. The novel's portrait of depressed and alcoholic Milton Loftis; his angry and vindictive wife, Helen; and their beautiful, selfish, alcoholic daughter, Peyton, disturbed and inspired Alice. For all that the Loftis marriage resembled Nic and Agatha's, Alice could only hope that she was not another Peyton, who is chronically unfaithful to her Jewish husband before she jumps to her death in Greenwich Village.*

* Of her parents' 1920s Lost Generation, Peyton tells a boyfriend: "They didn't lose themselves, they lost us—you and me. Look at Daddy, I love him so. But he lost me and he doesn't even know it. . . . I think we've got a Freudian attachment. The dear. He's such an ass. If it just hadn't been Mother he married, we all might have made out all right. She was too much for him. So we're lost . . ." (William Styron, *Lie Down in Darkness* [New York: Vintage, 1951], 235.)

Earlier, Alice had joked about choosing to spend money on a cure for her neuroses over surgery to reduce the size of her breasts; she told the Lynns about a friend who's had her breasts lifted and looks terrific: "The operation sounds quite gruesome—moving nipples around and that sort of thing—but she's beautiful and delighted. It cost her about 14 hundred bucks, so I'm not considering it, but I am in a way envious. I suppose analysis is a better investment, but it would be nice to be lovely *and* unneurotic."[16]

In pictures Alice looks quite lovely enough as a young mother. Those troublesome breasts make her belted waist look as slender as Scarlett O'Hara's. Her dark eyebrows and the glossy hair sweeping across her brow emphasize bright, happy eyes. If there's a note of disparity in these little black-and-white snapshots of picnics and birthday parties, it's the contrast of husbands wearing business shirts and jackets, even ties, and wives in housedresses or dungarees. Alice seems to prefer skirts and shorts—with her long legs often in the eye of the camera.

When Reed College in Portland, Oregon, offered Mark a teaching position, the family moved for the year. Reed, Alice thought, was the opposite of Stanford, "the best small college [she knew] anything about." Mark taught a humanities survey, Greeks through eighteenth century, keeping one step ahead of his students and "working his balls off," not finding enough time to finish his thesis. That Athenian life at Reed nearly ended when the army air corps called Mark for active duty "and something grimly known as 'processing' " (Alice wrote) in preparation for combat in Korea. Luckily, a back ailment rendered him unfit for service. "It was a nasty scare, but what a relief. This still seems to be a very good war not to be in."[17]

Portland was conservative, dreary, and of course rainy, "a determinedly dowdy city of homeowners, sans sin, or bright lights, or sun." Alice found the faculty wives an especially dull lot, "resigned to bad marriages, neurotic children, and dead ambitions." Jane Spencer Fussner, a Radcliffe grad married to Mark's "bright and quite sweet" colleague Frank Fussner, struck Alice as "a real dumbunny." Ironically, Alice and Mark missed those California friends they'd complained about for the past three years.[18]

Peter was the bright spot, turning out to have "a real comic gift" and "independent spirit." He became the common ground in the Linenthal marriage, adored by both parents, who could appreciate each other through him. Unlike the stereotypical distant, workaholic father of the 1950s, Mark enjoyed his child. Peter was about a year old when Mark wrote archly of him: "He says da-da very clearly, plays the piano, and rubs cottage cheese and broccoli into his hair. He has a Harvard tee shirt."[19]

When Norman Granz's eleventh national Jazz at the Philharmonic tour stopped in Portland, Alice and Mark went together to hear Ella Fitzgerald, Oscar Peterson, Lester Young, Gene Krupa, and Illinois Jacquet. They ran into Granz in the lobby and gave him their shared opinion that Jacquet's honking rhythm-and-blues style was "vulgar." Such high-minded moments were part of the brittle glue of their marriage.[20]

Another visitor to Portland that year was Saul Bellow. The novelist had recently returned from two years living in Europe and lecturing at the Salzburg Seminars, so he brought welcome gossip about people the Linenthals knew. Bellow's trip was, Alice said, "one of those terrible exploitive junkets for writers," but Bellow was on the run from his first marriage.[21] Bellow was then thirty-five, the author of two short novels and still discovering the "scholar-gangster" voice (as Edward Mendelson calls it) that narrated *The Adventures of Augie March* and eventually served to win him the Nobel Prize. Alice and Mark met him at the college events. On Saturday night Mark stayed with Peter while Alice went to hear the novelist she admired. As it turned out, she spent the evening with Bellow in what he described to her later as "that drunken night when you told me that I came on compulsively as a *heymish* type."[22]

It was the first infidelity of Alice's that Mark suspected. He overlooked it, perhaps understanding that her attraction was as much to the novelist as to the man. Curiously enough, Bellow, whose ancestors were Lithuanian Jews, then resembled Mark Linenthal, with prominent dark eyes, a receding hairline, a Semitic profile, and brooding good looks. Perhaps Mark found a way to be flattered.*

Bellow wrote Alice the next week to apologize for not calling her on the morning after. Bellow was a tireless philanderer known to have

---

* None of that came up when Alice wrote the Lynns about Bellow at Reed: "He was so strained and/or plastered while here that it was hard to get much of an impression. But we think we liked him. Something like Norman, only brighter, more talented. But the same vigor, and lack of humor about self."

lovers in many places. But he continued exchanging letters with Alice over the next thirty years. In 1958, he wrote her, "You have very special standing with me. I guess I have with you, too. You won my heart when you called me a *heimisch* compulsive.* That was sheer genius."[23]

Bellow had barely left Portland when Alice was hit by a flurry of letters and long-distance phone calls regarding her father that upset and depressed her. Since the previous summer, Nic had been on a manic spree of spending on "refrigerators, Spanish dancers, and chartered airplanes" and even had plans to remarry—bride unknown to history, but certainly not Dotsie Wilson, who had married someone else in the interim since her divorce in the late 1940s. According to her son, Dotsie still cared for Nic Adams but did not resume their romance after Agatha died because Nic was then in treatment for depression and alcoholism. Instead she moved to San Francisco, worked at the Hotel Commodore, and married her ex-husband's gay brother's friend David Cunningham Doster, who was several years younger than she and probably bisexual.

When Nic's spree ended, he crashed so badly that he could barely meet his classes. "In his despair," novelist Noel Houston wrote to Nic's cousin Frank Jervey, "he could only pace his living room floor and see State Hospital or death as alternatives." Chapel Hill friends had taken Nic to Kemp's sanitarium for a weekend, but Nic refused to take medication or have further shock treatments. He would lose his position at the university if he entered the state hospital. After Jervey located Alice in Portland, she considered flying to Chapel Hill, with a stopover in New York, where she thought to meet up with Bellow. In the end she decided not to make the trip or take over her father's finances or send him to a new hospital. Nic returned home but could not teach.[24]

In May Alice received a painfully stern letter from Eve and Ralph Bates in New York, who were in touch with Nic's Chapel Hill friends:

> This is one of those things in life, Alice, that whether we like to face it or not, or whether we asked for it or not, cannot be shirked. The situation can only be a highly disturbing one to you, especially since your relationship with your parents was so abnormal, but you have

---

* *Heymish* is Yiddish for "homey" or "domestic"; Bellow's spelling of it varied.

no alternative but to face it. I gather Nic was never a very satisfactory
father to you; you have certainly not been a satisfactory daughter to
him. But he is in deep trouble and you are his only surviving close
relative.

Eve Bates goes on to warn Alice that she must respond to this crisis in
order to "measure up as a woman" before ending her letter, "I'm very,
very fond of you and so have the temerity to speak out."[25]

Alice complained to the Lynns, "His friends are writing me letters
about being a bad daughter. It has occurred to some of [Nic's friends]
that he was perhaps not the best of fathers but no connection has been
made. If I sound bitter it's because I am. I have decided that everyone
is insane but me."[26] When a daughter is asked to look after her father
as her mother has done, he can no longer be the prince who reigned
over her childhood.

Time passed and Nic neither lost his job nor killed himself. Perhaps
Alice's nonintervention had been the right course. Certainly she saw
that Agatha had been correct to pursue her own satisfactions in life.

Probably with the influence of Dr. Benjamin Spock's popular *Common
Sense Book of Baby and Child Care* (1946), Alice and Mark were relaxed
parents. Peter first walked at fourteen months, later than average, but
no one worried: "Yesterday we were reading on the floor of his room,
book about some ducks," Alice wrote the Lynns, "and he all of a
sudden got up and walked out, fell down on the bathroom floor and
laughed. Has been walking ever since . . . he gets merrier and wittier
all the time."[27]

Despite the satisfactions of motherhood, Alice wanted to go back
into analysis with Dr. Biernoff. Mark had planned to teach another
year at Reed so he would not have a one-year job on his résumé, but
he deferred to Alice and accepted courses at Stanford instead. Meeting
Bellow and the turmoil over Nic had shaken her, while having a child
exacerbated the unspoken conflict she felt between her writing ambitions
and being a wife. When Mark's parents visited them in California for
a week, her analysis was kept secret ("They think that silliness is over,"
Mark wrote) and Peter charmed them.[28] No amount of analysis could
repair a cold marriage. The Linenthals did not have a second child.

Again, *Families and Survivors* gives a dark view of their situation: "When did they enjoy love together? Louisa can hardly remember, but with an effort she recalls lunches urgently pushed aside in a rush toward bed . . . More recently (and more clearly) she sees herself reaching, touching his warm soft flesh, and she hears his sympathetic voice: "Do you feel very sexy, honey?" And the frantic doomed attempts they make. Michael thinks that he is impotent; she thinks that she is frigid. At this stage neither blames the other.""

Back in the Bay Area, Alice and Mark were glad to see Billy Abrahams, who was working as a secretary for the exclusive Bohemian Club in San Francisco, and Judith and Timothy Adams, now parents of Bailey and Peter, who lived in an apartment on Union Street with a view of the Golden Gate Bridge, three other bedrooms, a roof deck, and a darkroom for $185 a month. They also kept in touch with Vida Ginsberg, and she introduced them to her former lover and now sister-in-law Barbara (Bobbie) Deming. This extension of friendships into the city was a welcome variation from their Stanford suburban world.

That fall, Illinois governor Adlai Stevenson ran for president against General Dwight David Eisenhower and his running mate, Richard Nixon. Peter had a toy donkey named Adlai, but the landlord objected when his parents put an altered poster on their house reading "Nix on Ike." After a summer sublet with swimming pool and Hawaiian-style bar shack in the backyard, the Linenthals settled into a pleasant house on Leland Avenue close to the Stanford Golf Course. They joined a neighborhood group of couples whom Adams would use as models for characters in her novel *Families and Survivors*. Their former neighbor Cynthia Scott (now Francisco) recalled, "My first husband and I were very young and naïve—married at 20 and babies right away. There was a lot of electricity in the air and we all were sexually attracted to one another but in the Fifties we didn't jump into bed quite as quickly as they do today—no pill and it was the Eisenhower years right after the War—such a different time."

Families and Survivors exhibits the sexual attractions among the young Palo Alto couples that Scott mentioned. Most of these couples later divorced. Several of the spouses—John Murray, Pauline Abbe, and Don Hall—became Alice's friends again later.

Alice was so attractive that the other wives thought of her as a "man-eater." Scott felt that she "knew Mark better than Alice—we were sort of the stay-at-home moms together" because Mark often took care of Peter. She recalled that "Mark talked about being shot down over Germany and about his brother who was gay—in those days nobody talked about that. He made light of his brother—telling about him picking up sailors. It was quite shocking and titillating to me." Indeed, Scott was so intrigued by Mark Linenthal that she signed up for a Great Books course he taught at the local high school. Her daughters played with Peter Linenthal, and she thought he was a difficult child: "I think Alice was overwhelmed by Peter! He was an only child and I think she leaned over backward never to say no to him." Peter's parents told him later that they would drive him in the car to get him to sleep or calm him with a pacifier dipped in whiskey. And he remembered *not* being punished when, as a four-year-old, he was caught peeing under a rug in the living room.

Saul Bellow, then living in New York or Princeton, wrote Alice often. He said he loved her face "with freckles, shy teeth, chin and most beautiful eyes." She had told him, "When we see each other we will be wonderful," and he agreed. They exchanged limericks. Mostly he wrote her about his own state of mind and the difficulties of finishing *The Adventures of Augie March*: "I don't like anything now. Except poetry and music. Everything else is a burden. I don't read novels, even. I don't see how I can ever ask anyone to read mine. I know this letter will disturb you . . ."

Bellow sent his letters to Alice's home address, where Mark was likely to see them. They are tender and affectionate but not love letters. Bellow tells her she "is one of the people [he] count[s] on." Though her letters to him have not surfaced, they seem to have been confiding. Returning from a "harrowing" junket to Greensboro, North Carolina, he wrote that he understood "why [she] had put N.C. behind [her] with perfect sympathy," saying, "I have never seen the likes of it. I'd sooner live under sawdust, in an ice-house. Why is the massacre of desire more terrible in the South? The more little flowers there are the more heavy the armament?"[29]

Even before it appeared in September of 1953, *Augie March* was a success, with a sale to the Book of the Month Club. It went on to win the National Book Award. Thirty-eight-year-old Bellow was famous and financially solvent. He remained friends with Alice, but their correspondence dwindled. To the Lynns, she confessed that she didn't like *Augie March* "on the whole," but she didn't say why. She'd been reading and praising big novels by Stendhal, Balzac, Melville, and Tolstoy, so perhaps she held her friend's ambitious book to their standard. Late in 1955 Bellow wrote Adams again from Reno, Nevada, where he was filing for divorce, asking if she was "miffed" with him since she'd owed him a letter for three years. She brought Peter along when they met for a drink at the Top of the Mark bar and dinner in a Chinese restaurant in November, leaving Mark a note on the back of an envelope: "Saul is here. I'm at the Mark (Top of) avec. Home by 5 or so—A—."

"I was pleased with your little boy. I like you, too, Alice," he wrote her afterward. A prolific correspondent (biographer James Atlas calls his subject's letter writing "a kind of literary profligacy"), Bellow responded to Alice by letter several times in the years ahead.

As Mark Linenthal tried to finish his doctorate at Stanford and the Korean War ground to a stalemate, Alice was a full-time mother and homemaker.

The years of the midtwenties that were considered critical in a man's career had been fallow for Alice. The men around her—Mailer, Bellow, Billy Abrahams, Kenneth Lynn, and Mark Linenthal—had made progress toward some artistic or career goal. She remained unpublished and stymied within her emotional landscape, even as she wrote a great deal and sent work to magazines and book publishers, as evidenced by the dozens of completed story manuscripts and pieces of correspondence she saved.

As a girl, Alice had written poems to please her parents and told stories about her dolls to create her separate world. After she lost her mother to heart failure and her father to depression and found her husband unable to give her all she required, she channeled her energy into motherhood and self-analysis. It was not proving to be enough. She needed to tell stories that would please others. The literary partnership she'd once imagined with Mark Linenthal was barren. Although she told friends his thesis was "extremely good," she associated critical writing with her parents. Interviewed late in life, Mark complained that Alice had never read his dissertation on Robert Penn Warren and the Southern Agrarians because she disapproved of the academy: "She thought criticism got in the way of writing," he said, "because critics commented on work but produced nothing [original] themselves."* Asked in the same interview if he had read Alice's stories, Mark said, "No. That's a hard question. I'm not sure why I didn't read them."

---

* In *Careless Love*, Jane says dismissively of a man who's interested in Renaissance history: "You mean that Southern agrarian bit? All those literary sharecroppers? Miss Daisy, come on." ("Of course not. The Italian," retorts Daisy.)

CHAPTER TWELVE

Feeling Free in San Francisco

— (1954-1957) —

In those days, women did not say negative things about their husbands, even to their closest friends. Which made many of us very lonely.

—Alice Adams, "Young Couple With Class,"
Redbook, September 1967

As was then the custom, Mark Linenthal began looking for a professorship before he completed his PhD thesis. When no good offers came from the East Coast, he joined the English Department at San Francisco State College (now University) in the fall of 1954. At last, the Linenthals would leave the Peninsula. Alice described the flat they found in Presidio Heights, at 3587 Clay Street: "[A] marvelous place, elegant, immense. 4 bedrooms, dining room, plus foyers, halls, even a maid's bathroom, if only we had a maid, and a butlerless butler's panty." There was a roof deck perfect for private sunbathing, and a tall person standing on tiptoe could see the Golden Gate Bridge from the living room. "After that box in Menlo Park we feel very free," Alice wrote Bobbie Deming, who had returned east to live with painter Mary Meigs.[1]

San Francisco is a city of fourteen hills almost surrounded by water, and each of its neighborhoods has a particular weather, a microclimate. In Presidio Heights, Adams recalled in a late story, the air "smelled of salt and eucalyptus and lemon, the blue sky, green leaves, glimpses of the soaring red bridge above the billowing, encroaching fog." She and Mark spent months shopping for used furniture, painting rooms, and waxing floors. Alice complained to Don and Kirby Hall that it was "awful to become thing-ish" but found the neighborhood pleasant, though "rigidly upper middle class."[2] Julius Kahn Playground was just over a stone wall on the grounds of the Presidio, still then a military base. Alice took Peter there for picnics, of which he remembered "big old trees, sandy ground, an outdoor cathedral—a private wonderfulness to it." He continued to be a self-sufficient child whose favorite book was *Mister Dog: The Dog Who Belonged to Himself.**

In a story rooted in those days, "Young Couple With Class," Adams analyzed her love for the prosperous neighborhood: "Anne valued substance. Conflict came because she was a rather intellectual girl; her other values were opposed to the pursuit of wealth. Her intellectual values had led her to her choice of Jim, the future poor professor." As she observed neighbors who were stockbrokers, surgeons, and psychiatrists, and their wives, who were without profession, Adams was finding material for the novels she would write about the interior lives of San Franciscans. "In those days," the story says, "women did not say negative things about their husbands, even to their closest friends. Which made many of us very lonely. We each sustained the other in our efforts to pass as happy, intelligent young women, not very questioning of our roles." That isolation also served her art.

San Francisco was "the best city for a writer, a painter, but I romanticize," Alice told Bobbie Deming after a year there.[3] The city in the 1950s was a sanctuary, "a place where the conservatism and conformity of the McCarthy era weren't so stifling, a tolerant, cosmopolitan city," writes Rebecca Solnit, "in many ways like a European city of the past with its Italian cafes, its small, pedestrian scale, its charming Victorian architecture."[4]

Most days Alice drove Peter across the city to Rhoda Kellogg's Golden Gate preschool on Potrero Hill; Kellogg, a psychologist who studied and collected children's art, analyzed two hundred of Peter's drawings of ghosts, whales, and totem poles and concluded he was "a genius," which scared Alice even though she considered him altogether an "extraordinary" and "incredibly delightful little boy."[5]

In San Francisco Alice began to recognize that she wanted to divorce

---

* In *Families and Survivors*, Adams adapted some of Peter's childhood for the girl named Maude, who was "a startling child" whose favorite book is the misremembered title *Crispin's Crispian* ("Crispin was a dog who belonged to himself").

Mark. To make some get-away money, she "wasted" some months collaborating on a murder mystery with John Deaver, a teacher at Peter's school. They had hopes of making "riches quickly" but it was "more difficult than one would have thought," she told Deming.[6] That was only part of the story. Deaver also became Alice's lover for a time. Peter didn't know that, but he did recall Deaver as his favorite teacher. He and his mom shared little jokes about his name: "Here we are at Mr. Deaver," they'd say when they passed Beaver Street.

To ready herself for single life, Alice had the surgery to reduce her breasts that she'd long wanted. A story draft in her notebook explains: "her breasts were gigantic & fallen. She felt them flap against her chest with lovers of the time—1st Jewish colleagues of her husband's, then stray crazy southern poets—she insisted on remaining fully clothed—or nearly . . . One of her greatest accusations against her husband was that he liked her breasts. (He loved them!) & a year before leaving him she went to a plastic surgeon who neatly molded them to a semblance of Hollywood youth."[7] Alice also began bleaching her dark brunette hair because it was graying early, as her mother's had done.

After a year in the city, Adams was writing "marvelous unpublished short stories," she told Deming.* One of these, "Winter Rain," came to her when she was so chilled from a severe case of the flu that she started thinking about the very cold winter she'd spent in Paris with Mark on rue de Courcelles. The story told about a finished love affair, which gave it "a certain form," she said. Usually she struggled to figure out how a story would end; this time she "knew where the story was going before [she] began it."[8]

Alice had a new lover too, Blanton Miller, who worked at the Drisco Hotel in Pacific Heights. "Blanton was a devastatingly attractive man," Judith Adams recalled. "He was a writer, and he could quote pages of Thomas Wolfe. Alice was enchanted. I remember I was kind of shocked because she was still married to Mark. I didn't realize that as a married woman she would carry on with other men. I didn't blame her except that she was married." Miller was from Horse Creek, North Carolina, a 1949 UNC graduate who might well have known Agatha or Nic Adams there. Alice's son remembered him as an animated man who knew how

---

* But in 1978 she told *People* magazine that she wrote "in a spasmodic, discouraged way" during the years of her marriage and Peter's early childhood.

to talk to children, but (again) did not realize he was Alice's paramour. For a while, Miller's Southern charm and brooding appealed to Alice's nostalgia for the South. From the University of Minnesota, where he went next to study with Allen Tate, Miller wrote Alice:

> My poor fantasy-ridden mind . . . Couldn't we see each other in some simple way? Today I've been wondering what you could have meant when you said you were tempted to say something irresponsible. I should have let you say it. I hope I get this Yaddo invitation. Not since you broke loose have I had much chance to reason things out . . . I could tramp in the woods and get all this pain and anxiety changed into sorrow. But I know when need is changed to grief, the one needed is gone.

In a postscript, Miller asked: "Is all your hair silver? Your legs brown?" Miller did spend a winter at Yaddo, where John Cheever commented on his request for an extension, "While it is always difficult to guess what is going on between a man and his typewriter he seems to be absorbed in his work and industrious." Despite interest from Atlantic Monthly Press, Miller's promising novel never appeared. He left unpaid phone and doctor bills when he departed Yaddo for a residency at the MacDowell Colony.[9]

Meanwhile, inventing freely, Adams wrote "The Fog in the Streets," a story about an older woman who comes to stay at a hotel in "the lovely unreal city" of San Francisco where her grandson has just been born. Flu prevents her from visiting the new baby, and she forms a connection with a handsome, charming bellboy named Burne from her hometown in the South. Burne is based on Blanton Miller, but the subject of Adams's deeper exploration is her mother. Putting herself in the older woman's place, she thinks, "She had wanted everything for [her son], of him, and with her wanting spoiled it all, continually." With remarkable empathy and compassion, Adams realizes that Agatha's critical intelligence and anger may have masked more tender feelings. "It's impossible to be a mother or a wife or both," Mrs. Blair in the story tells Burne. "Any closeness comes to grief."

When Mrs. Blair recovers from her flu, she goes to meet her grandson laden with inappropriate gifts, only to be told by her daughter-in-law that her presence upsets her son. As Mrs. Blair departs: "her mind ran hard pounded circles." She tells Burne the story of her visit, trying to make it comic, but he cuts in to admonish her: "You want your life to make sense, and then you want to do something about it. You even want the truth . . . There's not anything true . . . Soon as you know that you'll really know something, and you can start out to live."[10]

Adams was rarely philosophical. But Burne's dialogue delivers a strong dose of postwar existential toughness, exactly the tone Alice was trying to adopt for herself in the mid-1950s. With lovers like John Deaver and Blanton Miller, she looked outside of marriage and found no one who could sustain her, in part because she was attracted to unavailable men. One of these was Trummy Young, who joined Louis Armstrong and His All-Stars in 1952. Replacing Armstrong's all-time favorite musical accomplice, Jack Teagarden, Young played with a "loud, roaring, all swing" style. He became the backbone of the All-Stars and Armstrong's closest friend in the band. The All-Stars often played in Northern California, including gigs at the 1958 and 1962 Monterey Jazz Festivals and on New Year's Eve at the Downbeat in 1954.[11] Where and how during those twelve years Alice might again have seen the man who was in many ways her favorite lover is unknown—but the hints in her notebooks, her son's memory of meeting a tall brown musician in their Clay Street apartment, and her portrayal of him in *Superior Women* make it conceivable that some meetings occurred.

Louis Armstrong's swing jazz was considered old-fashioned in the years Trummy Young played with him. But when Arkansas governor Orville Faubus used National Guard troops to block nine black children from attending Little Rock Central High School in September 1957, Armstrong stepped boldly into the controversy. President Eisenhower had stalled for two weeks when Armstrong told a reporter Eisenhower had "no guts" and threatened to cancel his State Department goodwill tour of the Soviet Union. "The way they are treating my people in the South, the government can go to hell," he said. "The people over there ask me what's wrong with my country. What am I supposed to say?" When Eisenhower sent soldiers from the 101st Airborne to escort the children to school, Armstrong wired him: "DADDY IF AND WHEN YOU DECIDE TO TAKE THOSE LITTLE NEGRO CHILDREN PERSONALLY

INTO CENTRAL HIGH SCHOOL ALONG WITH YOUR MARVELOUS
TROOPS PLEASE TAKE ME ALONG . . . MAY GOD BLESS YOU."[12]

As the pall of the 1950s began to lift, San Francisco State was a new and expanding star in the constellation of California's four-year public colleges. Herbert Blau turned down job offers from Princeton and Yale to stay there, while also founding the Actor's Workshop theater in downtown San Francisco. Mark Linenthal got involved in the Poetry Center, which sponsored readings by Kenneth Rexroth, Karl Shapiro, Muriel Rukeyser, Allen Ginsberg, and dozens of others. Mark is a "marvelous critic of poetry," Alice wrote Deming. "I wish I didn't write prose."* As an unpublished faculty wife, Alice got little respect. Later, in a review of Joyce Carol Oates's *Unholy Loves*, she wrote that faculty wives "have even less control over their lives, no choice as to location, than do the wives of corporate executives, and God knows much less money."[13]

The artistic heart of San Francisco in the 1950s was in North Beach, lower Telegraph Hill, and the Fillmore District. Allen Ginsberg's first reading from *Howl* at the Six Gallery, mythologized in Jack Kerouac's *The Dharma Bums*, is considered the beginning of the Beat or San Francisco Renaissance movement. On that night the little gallery on Fillmore was filled to the rafters. Ginsberg was just one of five poets who read. Kerouac drank from a gallon of Burgundy and repeated lines after Ginsberg. Mark and Alice weren't there that night, but Mark was drawn to the scene and two weeks later heard Ginsberg read an expurgated version of *Howl* at the Poetry Center. Ginsberg substituted the word "censored" for the poem's transgressive words. Thus "who let themselves be fucked in the ass by saintly motorcyclists and screamed with joy" became "who let themselves be censored in the censored by saintly . . ." etc.[14]

Lawrence Ferlinghetti and Peter D. Martin (a San Francisco State sociology professor who rented a room from the Linenthals for a while)

* Adams may have been avoiding her husband's critical gaze. In portraits the prominent photographer John Brook took of them during a 1950s visit to Boston, Alice and Mark stare dramatically in different directions. But, caveat, Brook stated that his art aimed to transmit "the essential loneliness of the human spirit as it is manifest in facial expressions during unguarded moments."

had begun the all-paperback City Lights bookstore in North Beach. In 1957 bookseller Shigeyoshi Murao sold a copy of *Howl and Other Poems* (published by City Lights) to undercover police officers for seventy-five cents and was arrested, along with Ferlinghetti, for disseminating obscene literature. Mark Linenthal was one of the nine experts called to speak for the defense at a trial that drew national attention. "*Howl* seems to me a tremendously powerful indictment of a number of elements in the modern world, violence, greed, wastefulness, and it is cast not in the form of a modern prose indictment but in the form of a howl," Linenthal told the court. "The only way in which he feels in this situation it can be expressed is in language which, shall we say, exceeds the bounds of gentility." Judge Clayton Horn found the defendants not guilty, thus saving San Francisco's reputation as an open city and paving the way for other trials that permitted publication of *Tropic of Cancer* and *Lady Chatterley's Lover* in the United States.

Despite her bohemian leanings and love of jazz, Adams felt little solidarity with the Beats who were enlivening her city. Those "starving hysterical naked . . . angelheaded hipsters" Ginsberg howled about were men, and a lot of them were gay. The few women who identified with the Beat movement were poets or artists or musicians. Their wives and girlfriends, as the reports of Carolyn Cassady, Joyce Johnson, and others testify, rarely enjoyed the independence claimed by their male peers. Yet the Beats' celebration of individual freedom probably touched Alice. These artists' "sole interest is in creating," Henry Miller noted. "Indifferent to reward, fame, success . . . these young men . . . are roaming about in our midst like anonymous messengers from another planet. When the smashup comes, as now seems inevitable, they will know how to get along without cars, without refrigerators, without vacuum cleaners, electric razors . . ."[15]

Miller's "smashup" refers to the anticipated nuclear war that would wipe out civilization as they knew it. As a mother, Adams worried about nukes, but not with that apocalyptic fervor bordering on desire the Beats cherished. The smashup that concerned her was closer to home: the end of her marriage to Mark, which she regarded as inevitable—and impossible. In those days, as she observed later, "divorce was very much not the thing to do . . . being unhappily married was an indication of poor moral character."[16] More practically, Alice worried about how a divorce would affect Peter and about how she could support herself. Like most unhappily married mothers of young children in the 1950s, Alice did not see a way out of her marriage and made the best of it—hoping Mark would change or some other man would rescue her, or that she could sell her work.

Since Agatha had died, Nic Adams had been in and out of mental hospitals for his alcoholism and depression, financially strapped and barely hanging on to his position at the University of North Carolina. Then, in December 1955, he married Dorothy Stearns Wilson—Dotsie—the woman he'd fallen in love with twenty years earlier at Lake Sebago. Her second husband had walked out on her a year earlier, and Nic located her in California with the help of mutual friends. Alice, Mark, and Peter attended the wedding in a small church in the Marin County town of Mill Valley. Nic baked their wedding cake, a pound cake with bourbon frosting, as four-year-old Peter well remembered because he got a bit drunk on the frosting. The honeymoon trip Nic planned was beset with obstacles but Nic's manic energy carried them forward. After they missed the departure of the *City of San Francisco*, Nic chartered a plane to catch up with the train in Reno. That plane was delayed in Stockton by a heavy snowstorm in the Sierras, but their train plowed on ahead. The newlyweds finally caught up with their train in Omaha.

Nic's remarriage was a relief to Alice: "His wife is marvelous, & he seems saner, happier than ever in his life—after all this time we speak," Alice wrote.[17] In the summer she and Mark flew to Boston for a brief visit to Mark's parents before spending three weeks in Maine with Nic and Dotsie. Despite a poor lobster season, they enjoyed swimming and hiking. Dotsie greeted Peter as her grandson and sewed shirts for him with little tags that read, "Made especially for you by Dotsie."

The repressed flirtations of Nic Adams's youth had come to this, a marriage to a woman who adored him. The example was not lost on Alice. "My father moves me so," she wrote to Deming. "We are so like that he breaks my heart, and I can't look at him."[18]

As Peter completed first grade, Mark Linenthal completed his PhD from Stanford. He would stay at San Francisco State College for a long career as a beloved professor and the Poetry Center director. For most of those years he was the critic who team-taught poetry workshops with one of the poets. "I was a spectacular teacher," he reflected in retirement, "because I had a captive audience and I turned them all into members of my community—that's how you teach poetry—you act out your relation to the poem and teach them their own relation to the poem—by using yourself as a kind of intellectual shill."

Since kindergarten Peter had attended Town School for Boys. He'd resisted going there at first because the school had no girls but he received a scholarship and his parents overruled him. The private school in Pacific Heights was considered the best in the city. Again, he excelled in art. To his mother he was "tall, thin, blond, incredibly articulate." Also, she added thankfully, he was "more controlled" than before.

The Linenthals celebrated Mark's PhD with a trip to Mexico, in a new Chevrolet convertible. It was a jazzy car, aqua and white with vinyl upholstery. En route they swam in the "embracing, clear green water" and "subsisted mostly on shrimp and beer" at Guaymas and shopped for (as Peter recalled) "inexpensive cool stuff in the marketplaces—puppets, hats, shirts."[19] In the old silver city of Alamos, in Sonora, they stayed in a colonial-era hotel by the cathedral. This was Adams's first visit to a country she came to love. Her unpublished story "Coin of the Realm" portrays Nina, a woman in search of herself, who is driving with her husband across northern Mexico from California to Boston. She worries neurotically about money. In a town like Alamos, they meet an old, crazy American woman who hires workers to search the old mines and greedily hopes for a lost hoard of silver. The episode so upsets Nina that in the end she tells her husband she is turning their travel budget over to him.

In the elegant hotel room, resting on an "almost baroque" bed, Nina is sure that her marriage is "incredibly *right*." Later, watching the orderly procession of girls and boys around the town square, Nina is overcome by an even more definite feeling: "She sensed the verge of discovery, of learning something important. It was for this that she continually hoped: the discovered solution, the answer which, like diamonds or a vein of gold, or silver, would change her life. It was in this hope that she intensely studied, read, observed, questioned, and, finally, traveled."

And so it was that Alice Adams too, despite moments of contentment and celebration with her family, continued on a quest for an answer to a question she hadn't yet fully posed to herself.

PART III

INDEPENDENCE

CHAPTER THIRTEEN

A Return Trip

— 1958 —

Once a pair of twin black cats came toward us out of the darkness, the country night—two cats thin and sleek and moving as one, long legs interwoven with each other, sometimes almost tripping. At that we laughed and stopped walking and laughed and laughed, both wondering (I suppose) if that was how we looked, although we were so upright.

—Alice Adams, "Home Is Where,"
Beautiful Girl

"My problems were more serious than I could cope with or even think about," Adams wrote about the summer of 1958, in her story "Home Is Where." These problems were "a husband, a lover and a landlady, all of whom [she] was terrified of, and a son for whose future, in those conditions, [she] greatly feared. And so, instead, [she] thought about hot river smells, jasmine and hyacinth and gardenias, caves of honeysuckle and live oaks festooned with Spanish moss."

Adams wrote and rewrote the story of that summer at least seven times. In each version, she changed everything except herself. Always she is a depressed woman who flees San Francisco's spring—"a season of grayness, cold and wind"—to stay with her young son in her parents' house in a small Southern town and pass some weeks in love with another visitor. That much is true.

Alice had realized that she and Mark were "making each other very unhappy" but she could not afford to leave the marriage.* Then a neighbor of Nic Adams's visited Alice in San Francisco while attending a psychoanalytic conference. Lucie Jessner, then sixty-two, was a German-born psychoanalyst with "enormous intelligence and vast charm" and a "beautifully accented voice" who specialized in child psychology at UNC's medical school.[1] Jessner knew that Nic and Dotsie planned to spend the entire summer at Lake Sebago and, sensing Alice's unhappiness, suggested that a stay within her girlhood landscape would help Alice reorient herself in the world.

Dreaming of hot weather and the swimming pool in the woods, perhaps a summer love affair, Alice packed summer clothes—including the new sundress splashed with pink dots—and her typewriter. Mark gave his blessing. Their finances were already strained, so he rented out two rooms of the apartment at 308 Locust Street where they'd moved recently to escape the difficult landlady. Alice flew east with Peter in early June. They didn't call this a separation, but both she and Mark understood that some changes were necessary. In one story that summer inspired, Adams writes, "My husband took Simon and me out for a pleasant, noncritical parting dinner, at a good Italian restaurant. He only said, 'You won't be eating food like this for a while,' and I said that I supposed not. Perhaps I did not have to go home after all? But by then I was committed. Letters written, tickets bought. And those clothes."

Here, as in much of Adams's work, clothes serve as a trope for female desire and ambition in an era when both operated covertly. She loved clothes, but they also represented self-expression and freedom. She resented, for instance, Mark's mother's efforts to dress her in bargains from Filene's Basement. Later, in the unusually hot Carolina summer of 1958, Adams went to the Little Shop in Chapel Hill, where a lady she'd known all her life offered her an off-white-and-pale-yellow cotton dress marked down to $15: "I had a pleased sense of being, now, in my

---

* About this time Adams wrote "Former Friends," a story that suggests what was wrong: "I was not at all in love with Gary, my then-husband. In fact I disliked him quite a lot, which I had not as yet admitted to myself—too dangerous . . . What I minded most about Gary, really, was that he never made love to me—he never wanted to at all. What he most minded, I think, was my unhappy untidiness."

own small hometown, a grown-up at last, a woman among women."
She could not feel that kind of autonomy as a professor's wife on a
shoestring budget in San Francisco.

Alice hadn't set foot in Chapel Hill in ten years. When she and Peter got
off their plane in Raleigh-Durham, her father was waiting at the one-
story clapboard airport. Nic Adams still drank—a lot—but apparently
he did so in Dotsie's company without psychological collapse. Dinner
was never served that night but Peter happily compiled his own sandwich from the refrigerator. On another night Dotsie was shocked when
"Peter was allowed to eat his entire spaghetti dinner with his hands!"
After a couple of liquid evenings during which tempers flared and
neighbors and old friends came to inspect Alice, the prodigal daughter,
Nic and Dotsie left for Maine. Then, Adams wrote, "everything in my
life improved astoundingly."[2]

Alice and Peter occupied the old wing of her childhood home, the
part previously rented to a bachelor named Bill. The apartment was in
disrepair—holes in walls, floorboards missing, furniture broken—but
Lucie's garden supplied roses for every room. Alice set up her typewriter
on the dining table, enrolled Peter in the YMCA day camp, and worked
on her novel, which was set in Chapel Hill and was going to be titled
either *Green Creek* or *Weather in the Town*. In the afternoons, Lucie
Jessner, tired from her clinical duties, came over to swim, and she and
Alice grew attached: "If only my crazy father had married you," Alice
thought of the "small, rather bent-over woman (she had scholarly bad
posture)" who shyly arrived in a terry-cloth robe.[3] Alice's wish came
half-true: Jessner took up the role of fairy godmother to her. She adored
Peter as well and invited both of them to join her for a beach weekend
in South Carolina. Her friend Max Steele had a house at Windy Hill
and would welcome them all.

Henry Maxwell Steele had come to finish college in Chapel Hill
after the war, most of which he'd spent as a meteorologist on the island
of Trinidad, endangered only by the anger of combat soldiers returning
from Europe to learn, while laid over in the Caribbean, that they were
being sent to fight in the Pacific. As a UNC student, Steele had been
part of what author Daphne Athas describes as a "GI Bill inundation

Lucie Jessner

and rapid increase of population" that filled the town with "intellectually serious veterans, real men, older than the beer-frat types before the war." In the late forties, Athas, Steele, and other friends had been finishing novels as they waited for one thing—enough income to get themselves to Europe. They lived in unheated houses and wrote in offices lent by churches. Athas published *The Weather of the Heart* in 1947, and Steele's *Debby* came out in 1950. *Debby* won the Harper Novel Prize for the best novel by an "unnoticed" writer.[4]

So Steele went to Paris, where he consulted a Hungarian woman psychoanalyst. He wrote and hung out at Café Tournon by the Luxembourg Gardens, along with George Plimpton, Peter Matthiessen, Mary Lee Settle, William Styron, and Evan S. Connell, and became an advisory editor of the first issue of the *Paris Review*. The Tournon was also a gathering place for black Americans, including James Baldwin, Ellen and Richard Wright, and Ralph Ellison; Duke Ellington gave his first Paris concert there. A bit later Ellen Wright represented Simone de Beauvoir, Nelson Algren, and Max Steele as their literary agent. For some white American Southerners, as for African Americans, the diminished race and class distinctions of expatriate life were liberating. The photo of himself in Paris that Steele preferred shows him seated at a café table—bearded, dressed in a top hat and other flea market finds, grinning widely.[5]

From Paris, Steele returned to Chapel Hill to teach creative writing in the program directed by Jessie Rehder, who was Agatha and Nic Adams's friend and neighbor. So Alice Adams and Max Steele had heard about each other before they met. She'd read *Debby* and his short stories, prestigiously published in *Harper's*, *Collier's Weekly*, and other magazines. "He was marvelous, I thought, an extraordinary writer," she said. That much was prologue.

Adams remembered the moment she met Steele, whom she called by his first name in her memoir: "I got out and looked up at Henry, a tall man with a sad witty kind face; we shook hands and fell in love . . . Since there were a lot of people around . . . all that attraction was manifest only in a great deal of talk, much laughing at nothing . . . we knew quite a lot of people in common, from a wide range of places, and we made a great deal of that."[6]

Steele had grown up in the "up-country" part of South Carolina, the son of a real estate speculator and a woman whose "manners and courage" had brought his family through the financial reverses of the Great Depression. As a senior at Furman University before the war, Steele was voted the "Wittiest Boy" in his class. The yearbook said he "wielded the sharpest and most acidulous pen" and viewed the world with "joyous and cynical detachment."

During the return trip to Chapel Hill, Alice and Lucie Jessner speculated about Steele's relationship with a French girl who'd been with him at the beach. "She is very nice, but I think Max requires a more difficult, more demanding woman," Jessner said.[7]

"If I could relive any four or five days in my life," Adams wrote later, "I might choose those, and not because I want to change a thing; I don't—they were perfect. Or why not relive the whole summer while I'm at it?"

That "whole summer" comprised about four weeks in Chapel Hill. Steele invited Alice to a party and she wore one of those summer dresses. Still tan from the beach, she was "thin, confident, and optimistic." She and Max danced on a darkened porch. Max began appearing at the

Adams home several times a day. He told her, "I can't believe this is happening to me. I have to keep leaving and coming back to check." According to Alice, they "almost never used the dangerous 'L' word, just acted it out."[8]

Their both being writers is one reason their brief love affair stands out in their lives. Adams wrote two memoir essays and five short stories rooted in that summer. Steele wrote one too. Those narratives cast light back on the summer, fogging the line between fact and fiction more than usual.* Together these writings illuminate the feelings that changed Alice's relationship to herself, her husband, and her hometown forever.[9]

If the "L" word and serious talk were dangerous, these lovers compensated with laughter. Steele described her laughter in "Another Love Story": "She was laughing as if she couldn't stop, a startling sight, as if a statue had suddenly laughed and gone on laughing, refusing to be a statue again. Until that moment she looked frighteningly sophisticated, the sort of woman he couldn't deal with . . . but then she'd laughed and all her Radcliffe, Rome, and San Francisco poise had gone and she looked ten years younger and, for the first time, he allowed himself to stare at her magnificent legs."[10]

Travel had given them both an ironic distance from their Southern culture and they took verbal aim at it together. Max especially loved puns and wordplay, and they made fun of themselves and their ambitions. Alice recalled, "I was working on a novel that summer, but it was so hot. And I was distracted. One day I wrote, 'Waves of longing came over her like waves.' On another, just one sentence: 'Nobody had mentioned Herbert.' Max thought they were both great, especially the Herbert one. 'It tells you a lot about Herbert, right off,' he said. We laughed and laughed, which tells you something about the level of our humor."

For these two humor was catalytic. Steele was at a crisis in his writing career and life. He sensed that "the life of a teacher was far more rewarding than the highly public life of a writer or the totally absorbing life of

---

* Years had elapsed before Adams wrote her short stories about the summer; even more years elapsed before she wrote two pieces she called memoirs. In one of those she notes that the writing of fiction shapes the writer's memory of an event: "Once I wrote a story about such a walk, and I am now unsure whether I am remembering the story or the actual walk." (Adams, "Summer, Clothes & Love: A Memoir.")

an editor."[11] His love of teaching frightened him. Living in the South, he no longer heard the nostalgic "song of Carolina" that had inspired his early work or the voice that had written stories about Americans while he was in Paris. He worried that his talent was exhausted. Alice gave him a vacation from himself. As she put it in "Home Is Where," "We laughed, as all summer we were to laugh, at both the gravest and the most inconsequential matters. We laughed between our wildest encounters of love, and we talked almost not at all—and that, for that summer, for both of us was perfect."

Max liked Peter, told him terrible jokes and riddles, taught him to catch fireflies, and became his lifelong friend. But some afternoons while Peter was at camp, Max and Alice had time alone for an hour of love or a drink in a cool, quiet, dark bar. In the evenings Alice cooked dinner for the three of them and sometimes for Lucie Jessner. Adams's unpublished story "Night Fears" tells a story of Max's feeling for Peter from the man's point of view, with the character Clay standing in for Max. To him, the boy is "tall and pale and shy, too close to what Clay had been himself." After the boy was asleep the lovers swam in the pool in the woods. One night the boy awoke with a scream and his mother sprinted barefoot across rocks and branches to his bed. To the man's ears, that scream echoes his own needs and fears: "Her love was so headlong and entire, she might have been trying to destroy herself in love. And he was cautious, cautious." When the child is calm, the man says he must go home. He's understood something more about motherly love—and he feels "like a guilty intruder."

Alice and Max made no plans for the future. Max was thirty-eight and had already met the woman he would marry two years later. He had recently decided to rededicate himself to writing. For the present he had very little money. Alice was more intent on escaping her past than on looking ahead.

She'd told Mark Linenthal that she was unhappy before she left San Francisco. He too was unhappy and frightened—of change, of his mother, of the future. He had embraced a non–Ivy League career, but now childhood and financial insecurities resurfaced. During the summer he mailed a dress to Alice and pajamas and socks to Peter and made arrangements for Peter's return to Town School. Two letters he wrote to Alice that summer tell more about the breakup of their marriage than any bitter recollections they harbored later. He sounds puzzled but sincere. "Being alone this way, facing parents, getting money matters straighter, has been tough, but enormously valuable," he wrote. "I feel very different, a lot closer to being the sort of person I could enjoy being." When his parents visited, they agreed to give him $2,400 for the next year, with the possibility of an additional loan and a "hunk of dough for a downpayment on a house."[12]

Friends of Mark's have felt that Adams was cruel in her portrayals of his mother in her fiction. But Mark's own take on Anna Linenthal in his July 1958 letter is more damning than anything Adams published. He prides himself on maintaining his identity during his parents' visit "firmly enough so that [his] father had the guts to chime in on [his] behalf," observing, "But he needs my lead—he's pitifully weak and dependent on her and masochistically willing to take her abuse. His bullying: since he can't play the man with her, he takes it out on his children. It all seems so much clearer to me than it ever did before."[13]

Late in the Chapel Hill summer, Judith Adams came down from her parents' in Washington, DC, to visit Alice. Having given birth to her fourth child the previous winter, Judith was "totally worn out." She found the Adams house comfortingly shabby and in every way reminiscent of 1938. Of course their bodies have changed, "and in opposite directions," Adams writes when she describes them as Kate (Judith) and Louisa (Alice) in *Families and Survivors*: "Kate's is fuller, softer, whereas Louisa's has hardened; she is bony, perhaps too thin." Their friendship was an island of calm for Alice as she tried to explain recent events in her life.

"Alice had a manuscript spread out on the table," Judith recalled, "and several men were buzzing around. She was sought-after. I babysat Peter so she could spend a whole night with Max. By then I understood that she was unhappy with Mark." Back with her children for the foggiest San Francisco summer in forty-four years, Judith wrote, "Chapel Hill is going to haunt you, Alice. In moments of stress, and there are those in quantity, I close my eyes and dream I'm on my back again looking up at the sky seen through those beautiful trees, cooled deliciously by the green water."[14]

Confiding in Judith and having a night with Max helped Alice decide to start over. This summer out of time, of letting go of her worries, gave her courage for the postponed endeavor of changing her life. She sent

Mark a letter that was painful to him, though we don't know exactly what it said. He replied, "I've had some pretty rough moments getting my life liveable" but "I also think that the stronger, freer, more capable of joy and spontaneity I become, the greater the chances of our loving each other. I seem to see more clearly than I ever have before why things got so bad between us; this ought to help. Maybe it can't enough." He believes his financial relationship with his parents is at the root of his difficulties:

> I just wrote a letter to my father about money—not really about money, but about the only emotional context in which I could accept the money I asked for—a blunter letter than I've ever written him—in which I said that I would not take the "explaining" role again. I feel that I can no longer afford to allow myself to be called to account. And with this comes some sense of how I cruelly called you to account, or, equally cruelly, "tolerated." That an autonomous identity gives everything in life its value seems a truth I hadn't accepted. As a result of all this I think that the chances of our getting together happily are greater than they ever were. And that if we can't, that possibility would be more tolerable than I had thought it.[15]

Alice had that remarkable letter from her husband to ponder as she left her childhood home. As it turned out, she would never enter it again. She also had to say goodbye to Max. In several versions of the story of her last night in Chapel Hill, including nonfiction essays, Alice confesses, "In passion, I declared that I would always love Henry (this has turned out to be true, though not in the sense I meant it at the time), along with other statements in that vein. And Henry, while not exactly responding in kind, received what I said with love and great gentleness, thus delicately sparing me possible later shame."[16] In *his* fictional version, Max retroactively spared her that humiliation:

> "Darling," she said as they reached the grass beach, turning him toward her, "there's something I want to ask you. . . ."
> Now would come the outpouring. All the things unsaid that would demand answers and unsatisfactory explanations from him. . . .
> "What?" he asked.
> "Did you know. . . ." she started to confess but then her voice

brightened, "there's a grasshopper on your ear?" It was not what she'd meant to say, but once said it took the place of all seriousness. He had seen her realize that that was all she would say . . . "Do you mind," she asked, reaching toward the grasshopper, "if I take it off?" And then they laughed until they were lying down laughing.[17]

The interwoven themes of sex and romance and love would occupy Adams throughout her fiction. Women in her novels often want more love than they can have, declare more than is prudent, confuse sex with love, and long for some humorous understanding that will relieve these conflicts. Having found that kind of understanding in Max Steele, Adams began to know him as a friend. He would be the third person, along with Judith Clark Adams and Billy Abrahams, she wrote about late in her life as someone she fell in love with at first sight and liked continuously thereafter. He was the only one of the three who had also been her lover, but all were clear advocates of her fiction, to which she now turned her attention as she faced the end of her marriage and the need to earn a living. "I think you're going to take a while getting used to being happy," Caleb tells Claire in "Home Is Where." For Adams, a new optimism, born of "being happy," would be powerful.

Whatever was or wasn't said that night in August 1958, Max soon wrote Alice to say—in a roundabout way—that no one could understand "what it's like after being happy to be so suddenly alone."[18] Further confirming that Alice's feeling for Max was not a private romantic fantasy, Jessner wrote Alice for her thirty-second birthday: "This is to wish you the great happiness you seem so able to experience! Analysts are not supposed to believe in the magic of wishes—but residues remain. So I go on wishing that this veil of sadness you had, attractive as it is, might lift and that the hardships of the near future should not be too heavy."[19]

Alice and Peter departed for Maine. Lucie Jessner had already fled the heavy Carolina summer heat and was completing a book with a colleague in New Hampshire. Max Steele was leaving Chapel Hill with no fixed destination. Determined to be a productive writer, he worried that his three years of teaching at the university had been a detour. A month later, he was in Tampa, writing to Alice in San Francisco that "the West seems too far" and he feels "incapable of decisions."[20]

At Lake Sebago, in her mother's old lake cabin, now occupied and transformed by Dotsie, Alice revisited her grief for Agatha. She dramatized her emotions later in the story "Alternatives" with a confrontation between Avery (Alice), her father (Jack), and Dotsie (Babs). When Avery announces her decision to divorce, Jack confesses "an old-fashioned prejudice against divorce." Avery retorts, "Christ, is that why you stayed married to mother and made her as miserable as you could? Christ, I have a prejudice against misery!" Turning to Babs for support, she asks, "Don't you ever wish you'd got married before you did? What a waste those years were." Babs is startled, as Dotsie might have been, because she "never allowed herself to think in these terms, imaginatively to revise her life." She replies primly that she's grateful for the years she has with Jack.

But the father, enraged by Avery's accusation that he made his first wife's life miserable, insists, "I think I might be in a better position than you to be the judge of that." At this Avery reveals something she has heard from the housemaid: "You think she [Mother] just plain died of a heart attack, don't you? Well, her room was full of empty sherry bottles. All over. Everywhere those drab brown empty bottles, smelling sweet. Julia told me, when she cleaned it out." It may be that during her summer of return to Chapel Hill Alice had a conversation with Verlie Jones or her daughter and heard that Agatha, in the lonely last years of her marriage, had become a secret drinker. It was, at least, an explanation that Alice embraced for reasons of her own.*

Earlier in the year, Adams asked Saul Bellow to write letters in support of the novel she was working on. "Anything I've got is at your disposal . . . the more sex and Negroes the better," he replied, before telling her about the "African" book he was finishing, *Henderson the Rain King*. Perhaps he helped her sign on with literary agent Marie Fried Rodell. She sent 114 pages of "Weather in the Town" and an outline

---

* Alice and Dotsie ended the summer on a sour note. Dotsie said that Swiss renters (friends of Jessner's) who came after Alice left found the apartment so "filthy dirty" that they refused to move in, forcing Dotsie to hire people to "clean the place up." Alice said she'd left the apartment as she found it. (Undated note found among personal papers of Dorothy Stearns Adams, Peter Adams Linenthal collection.)

to Rodell in July, who submitted it to publishers. En route to Maine, Adams stopped in Manhattan to meet Rodell.

The news was a letdown. Judith Jones (Knopf editor for John Updike, Julia Child, Elizabeth Bowen, and William Maxwell) thought her pages "an aimless sort of novel about the well-to-do married set in their middle years living in a Virginia town." Most damning and illuminating is Jones's remark that Adams has insights about the nuances of her characters but is "too often hinting at things that are disappointing when they finally evolve."[21] In her life as well as her fiction Adams preferred silence to drama, which seems in keeping with the unhappy passivity that kept her married to Mark.

Nonetheless, 1958 marks a year of progress for Adams. Rodell was an important agent. She and her business partner, Joan Daves, also represented marine biologist Rachel Carson, author of the recent bestseller *The Sea Around Us*, and Martin Luther King Jr., whose *Stride Toward Freedom* was soon to be published. She was herself a mystery writer and author of *Mystery Fiction: Theory and Technique*. Adams had given her a dozen short stories to submit to slick magazines and prestigious journals that paid.

One day after driving a rough mountain road to visit Lucie Jessner in New Hampshire, Alice learned that Rodell had sold one of her stories. *Charm: The Magazine for Women Who Work* paid her $350 for "Winter Rain," her story about living in Paris after the war. *Charm* promised a December publication, anticipating an issue about European travel for its audience of "business girls." Alice telegrammed the news to Max. In years to come she would make fun of herself for believing that her agent's sale of this one story indicated that everything she wrote in the future would sell easily. She knew better even then.[22]

Nevertheless, Alice's pride in this sale made it a major event for her, part of the summer when she began her life over in Chapel Hill, from which she "derived the courage to divorce" Mark.[23]

Freedom

— 1958–1961 —

He took her hand. "You are so brave a woman. You are a true
woman."
In this unspecific, uncommitted way it was decided that Daisy
was to have an abortion. Pablo had not had to say the word.

—Alice Adams, *Careless Love*

To get a divorce in California in 1958, one had to make an accusation against one's spouse, appear in court, and wait a year for the Superior Court's interlocutory (temporary) judgment to become automatically a decree of divorce. The drawn-out process was intended to encourage reconciliation.

Alice went to court with her attorney, Ruth Jacobs, in early October, about a month after her return from the East Coast, to charge Mark Linenthal Jr. with "extreme cruelty," a stock phrase of the era. Although Mark's parents were prosperous, she did not demand a financial settlement, and she counted on Mark to remain a good father to Peter. The judge granted her custody of Peter and monthly alimony payments of $250. For Peter's support she received an additional $150 a month.* Mark received "reasonable rights of visitation" and the "right to have said minor child with him for at least a period of one month during the time said minor child is on summer vacation."

Peter vividly remembered the weekend when his mother told him about the impending divorce. As the two of them drove south on then

---

* The alimony would be worth about $2,000 a month in 2019 dollars. The senior Linenthals probably paid Peter's tuition at Town School.

two-lane Highway 101 to the Southern California beach city of Santa Barbara, Peter, seven years old, sensed they were doing this unusual trip for a reason. They stayed at the Ming Tree Motor Hotel, a casual but luxurious place for its day. "My mom told me in a not-very-dramatic way," Peter said. "Something like, your dad and I have decided we are not going to live together, we are getting a divorce. I was upset—I wanted immediately to know, well whose idea was this? Because she had said it with great equanimity and I wanted somebody to get angry at, and she said, no, this was a mutual decision."

The weekend was supposed to feel like a vacation. They toured San Ysidro Ranch, where John and Jackie Kennedy had honeymooned, and "an old boyfriend" of Alice's met them for lunch. Both Alice and Peter worked on suntans by the beach and the motel's two swimming pools. But a friend named Zoe Kernick Draper, whose history included marriage to the son of designer Dorothy Draper and modeling for Salvador Dalí, gave them bad suntanning advice: using baby oil mixed with iodine as skin lotion, Peter got a severe burn.

Mark Linenthal had been sleeping in his study in the Locust Street apartment. While Peter and Alice were in Santa Barbara, he moved onto a boat anchored at the marina in Sausalito. The German schooner, called the *Wander Bird*, had come around Cape Horn in the 1930s. Now deteriorating, it had been converted into apartments. Upstairs in the captain's cabin lived Frank Werber, a Nazi concentration camp survivor and "swinging hipster" who'd discovered and managed the Kingston Trio.[1] Peter loved exploring the boat. He visited his father there on weekends, often bringing friends along for the adventure of sleeping in curtained bunks and fishing from the docks.

Adams's novel *Families and Survivors* gives a crisp, dramatic version of Alice's and Mark's decision to divorce. In it, Michael approaches Louisa to make love after a long hiatus. She pulls back from his overture and tells him they should get a divorce. He backs out of the bedroom. The novel's narrator stays with him: "The next day . . . is bright enough to make the previous night unreal, and all that day Michael tries to tell himself (amazing, how nearly he succeeds in believing) that the night before did not, in fact, occur. Louisa did not say what, in the midst of the midnight storm, he thought he heard her say."

In this chapter of the novel, Adams maintains an icy, omniscient point of view that gives the husband's perspective. Louisa gets a job but continues to serve Michael a good dinner every evening. He believes nothing will change. Finally Louisa and their child take a brief vacation to Lake Tahoe (with Kate, the stand-in character for Judith Adams). She returns, emboldened:

> She clears her throat. "Michael, we have to see about getting a divorce."
>
> "But—" But there is nothing for him to say. He looks at her stupidly, quite aware that that is what he is doing. Then he says what is at least half true. "I thought you'd changed your mind."
>
> "Michael! How could we go on living together? How could we? There isn't anything—nothing—." Almost unconsciously, because he has opened it and it is there, they are sipping their wine.
>
> He says, "Couldn't we just—go on?"
>
> "Go on where? With no sex? I've been—unfaithful to you. Often. And I hate being like that."
>
> His face has become very hot. "I don't believe you." (But, like most pieces of sexual information, this one has always been somewhere within him, a submerged knowledge.) "What do you mean, unfaithful?"
>
> "Just that. Screwing other people. All kinds." Her voice runs out of power, trails off. She has made a great effort to say what she is saying. Or perhaps she is lying?
>
> "I don't believe you," Michael says again.
>
> With her hands she makes a small despairing gesture. "Okay, don't. But what's terrible is how little you notice. Anything."
>
> He hesitates, knowing that whatever he says will somehow be used against him. He says, "I don't know what you mean."
>
> "Exactly." She sighs, with an infinite and terrible weariness. It is clear that she is most of all tired of Michael.

That scene is too condensed, too neat to be accurate. But it's true Alice was "most of all tired" of Mark Linenthal, probably true that she hated the way she'd been sleeping around. We can't be sure if she had a mean, frightening lover like King in *Families and Survivors*, who fills Louisa with "terrified anxiety," but certainly Alice knew she was courting danger if she continued to have secret lovers. Facing the middle years of her life, she felt that marriage and the weight of the conservative 1950s were blocking her way toward fresh experiences and success as a writer.*

The divorce was not easy on Peter. He knew of just one other child with divorced parents in his class at Town School. In a survey of her Smith College classmates in 1957, fifteen years after their graduation, Betty Friedan discovered that only 3 percent had been divorced—though almost all had married.[2] The inauthentic calm with which both Alice and Mark discussed the situation confused Peter: "I know now that they thought it was very important not to have me be in the middle of it, not to make accusations. But I thought, if this is such a happy decision, why are you getting a divorce?" Adams herself put it more starkly when she described the child Maude's feelings in *Families and Survivors*: "I was too young to have seen many other people, I did not recognize my parents' marriage as being 'bad.' It is only when I remember their faces, how they looked at each other, that I see her unhappiness and his passive but total confusion." At the time, of course, Peter knew of nothing else: "In pictures from that period I look sort of out of focus to myself. I know psychologists say that children of divorce always think it's their fault. That doesn't quite ring true. It was more like there's something wrong here, something uneasy about this whole thing."

"Alice was very very bitter," Peter's friend Stephen Brown thought. "Here's my estimation of that situation: she completely regretted marrying Mark. She thought it took her on a wrong path that she really didn't want to take at that age. She resented him for her decision. She spoke of being in Europe after the war—swimming in the canals of Venice—but she left Mark out of those stories. As Peter and I got older we did wonder if her bitterness would ever end—and it never did."

Alice dramatized herself as a newly separated, soon-to-be-divorced woman in the character of Daisy Duke Fabbri in *Careless Love*: Daisy

---

* *Families and Survivors* wasn't published until 1975, though Adams had been working on its material in her notebook for years. In 1955, Norman Mailer told an interviewer that his own new novel *The Deer Park* was about sex, "the last remaining frontier of the novel which has not been exhausted by the nineteenth and early twentieth century novelists." Women's sexual experience, described by women, remained out of bounds.

was "on stage among various groups in San Francisco; to know her was to be summoned to the phone at odd hours, to grip the black receiver as Daisy's beautiful southern voice told the newest chapter. As Jane, her best friend, once said, 'If you know Daisy you don't need a TV set.'"

Exaggeration to be sure, but Alice Adams saw herself as a "bachelorette" on the lip of a brilliant writing career. San Francisco was then a small city—even a small town. Seeking a more sophisticated social set than she'd enjoyed during her marriage, Alice made forays into several wealthy and artistic groups. Among these new acquaintances was Frederick A. Breier, a stout Viennese-born economics professor, then a bachelor, who consulted for international corporations and was well connected in cultural and diplomatic circles. Probably through Breier, Alice met descendants of the German-Jewish Lilienthal and Haas and Walter families, who, like blue-jeans maker Levi Strauss, shaped San Francisco's economic and cultural life after the gold rush. Those immigrant merchants established the dry goods, grocery, and liquor businesses that serviced the "instant cities" of the Bay Area. Rapid population growth and lack of an Anglo power structure gave them unprecedented social mobility and influence. With Reform and nonreligious Jews in the majority, by 1880 San Francisco had become the second-largest Jewish center in the United States.[3] A favorite friend of Alice's in this group of descendants was the abstract expressionist painter Nell Walter Sinton, who was both a society matron and an ambitious artist. "My mother coveted friends who were smart, witty, artistic, and *not boring*," Sinton's daughter recalled, "and Alice was one of these."

Max Steele continued to write Alice from the French Quarter in New Orleans, where he moved in November. He said he might make another leap westward if he sold a story. "I sound like a constipated frog," he joked. But stories did not sell and his next move would be to Mexico, where he thought he could live on $100 a month. At one point he asked Alice to send him the classified ads from a San Francisco paper so he could calculate the cost of living there. When Alice apologized for not writing, he replied, "You kept me going in Tampa when I really needed to hear from you, and looking back it seems that you saved me from a real despair last summer and certainly made it a happy, delightful time; and I like us and the way we've been, with no demands, no expectations, and it's a real joy to me just to know you exist."[4]

Alice saved dozens of letters and postcards from Max. (She seems to have written him equally often, but little of her side of their early correspondence survived his many moves.) He told long, funny stories about himself, asked about Peter, and arranged for her to meet his good friend Evan Connell Jr., author of *Mrs. Bridge*, because he'd "discovered the more people two people know in common the longer the two people know each other. N'est-Café?" Often he advised her to keep turning out stories so she'd have a deep drawer of them ready when requests poured in after her first one came out in *Charm*.

That day was postponed. For months Alice and her friends surreptitiously paged through new issues of *Charm* on the newsstand and failed to find Adams in the table of contents. During this waiting period Max amused Alice with letters about his quest to find the magazine. His epistolary style—not to mention some homophobia and anxiety—is richly displayed in this episode from New Orleans:

> I stop in twice a day at the big newsstand and the boy there who wears pants suspiciously too tight around his little hips and waist which are suspiciously too trim is beginning to think: "Well!" Yesterday when I asked him was the new "Charm" in he said no but that the new Vogue was and that it was featuring some really "kicky" hats. I wanted to tell him if he used that expression again he'd have a kicky bottom. So he said he thought just surely it would be in this morning at the very very latest. So I trotted down this morning and it isn't. He said, "If you don't mind would you tell me why you are so anxious to see it." Well, he's not the person I'd want to talk to about your story because I know I'll want to roll it up under my arm and walk close to the buildings as though it may be taken from me, back home, and fix a cup of coffee and read it and think and not talk. So I said, no I didn't mind telling him: "My wife's picture is going to be on the cover." Now, Alice, why did I do that? You know what's going to happen: they'll have a picture of Van Johnson saying he sleeps in nothing but a cashmere sweater . . . I agree: it is terrible to be a writer. It's worse knowing writers and waiting for their stories to appear.[5]

*   *   *

The issue of *Charm: For the Exciting Woman with a Job* (a revised sub-title) with Adams's story finally appeared in July 1959. In her author photograph by Pirkle Jones (assistant to Ansel Adams and collaborator with Dorothea Lange), Alice looks thin, sexy, and mentally intense. She wears that summer dress she bought in Chapel Hill. It's slipped off of one shoulder; the cords of her neck, wrapped in three strands of pearls, stand out because of the way she is posed. Compared to the "softly controlled" hairdos and alluring smiles of the models on *Charm*'s pages, Alice looked all too real and a bit nervous. Perhaps readers of this magazine could identify with the feeling she projected—it was not easy to be an "exciting woman with a job" and with the required mix of sex appeal, domestic competence, and intelligence.

Creating that image also required money, not just for paying bills but for dressing in style. From the large apartment she'd shared with Mark, Alice wrote Max Steele that she was "broke in gold brocade with an expensive view." He urged her to move to a new apartment when her lease expired: "*Make up your mind within the next ten hours*," he urged. "Last summer I saw that indecision is as bad for you as it is for me and that once you knew what you were going to do you were totally capable of doing it."[6] She moved three blocks west to 3904 Clay Street. The downstairs flat in a substantial, south-facing duplex had a distinctive bay window facing the street, two bedrooms, and just one bathroom. Peter's friend Stephen Brown recalled, "Alice had a desk in the living room near the bay window, and when I came home from school with Peter, I saw her at that desk writing. That is my childhood image of her. When we were little boys, that was it. She kept this huge fern that covered an entire table in the bay window—four feet wide at least."

Max Steele found his copy of *Charm* with "Winter Rain" on a news-stand in Cuernavaca, Mexico, where he'd moved after Easter in 1959. He and Alice had made no serious efforts to get together again, but their long-distance friendship deepened and he became a sincere fan of her writing. After reading "Winter Rain" in print, he wrote, "I was jolted out of the story because I could see you so clearly and hear you so clearly. At other times I was jolted out by the words so surprisingly right and unexpect[ed] nevertheless: 'that huge and final boat for New York' . . . 'I wanted to hear of no other love' . . . 'too realistic and too economical for any emotional waste.'" He noticed too how Adams's scenes "keep adding up so that one doesn't get the true sum until the very last paragraph."

After reading the story, Jessie Rehder, Alice's parents' and Max's friend who taught writing at UNC but could not get her new novel published, asked Steele, "What if Alice turns out to be the genius?"[7]

Steele compared Adams's fiction to that of the French novelist Colette (Sidonie-Gabrielle Colette, famed as the author of *Gigi*): "I kept thinking of Colette because the story is so intensely feminine (stopping without stopping but racing really) telling what dress one had on which of course . . ."[8] One day Adams would be celebrated as "America's Colette." For now, she was an American woman writing stories for other women. Such writers sometimes sold but were never taken seriously by the literary establishment that she had been educated to respect. It was a quandary she could not sort out on her own.*

Postdivorce, Alice was entering the world described by Helen Gurley Brown in her 1962 book, *Sex and the Single Girl*—with one important difference. In 1958 the birth control pill had not yet been released in the United States. The most reliable contraceptive method was a diaphragm. (Peter thought Alice's was a shower cap for a doll when he came across it in their bathroom.) Nonetheless, Brown's book, following upon Alfred Kinsey's 1953 book, *Sexual Behavior in the Human Female*, publicized changes in attitudes about women's sexuality that began in the 1920s, increased following World War II, and proliferated widely during and after the 1960s. As Brown summarized when her book was republished four decades later, "Sex is enjoyed by single women who participate not to please a man as might have been the case in olden times but to please *themselves*."[9]

Not that it has ever been that simple. Like Daisy in *Careless Love*, Alice became "tired of screwing; she wanted to make love." And she wanted to fall passionately in love. She wanted to fall in love because she wanted to be loved in all the ways she believed she had not been loved by her parents. She wanted, as she wrote in her journal, "to be out of breath at a voice heard over the phone, at a face—to give all her breath to her love, to say it."

---

* *Charm* ceased publication in November 1959, when its publisher, Street & Smith Publications, known for pulp fiction and dime novels, could no longer compete with television. Condé Nast bought the company and folded *Charm* into *Glamour*.

*   *   *

That voice and face appeared to Alice in May of her first year of single life when she met Vasco Luís Caldeira Coelho Futscher Pereira, the Portuguese consul general in San Francisco. "All of his character was in his walk," Adams wrote of the stocky, bespectacled, dark-haired man who turned her life upside down. Pereira was not conventionally good-looking, but he "seemed to her extraordinarily quick . . . intelligence and sexuality were linked. . . . [She could be] seduced by a vigorous mind, by *style* . . . he was in all ways an extraordinarily vigorous man."

Alice probably met Pereira at a reception celebrating Portuguese wine that she attended with Fred Breier in the spring of 1959, or perhaps at the Grete Williams Gallery on Union Street, where she began working part-time in May. She and Pereira had a literary conversation and Alice, most likely, mentioned her story forthcoming in *Charm*. He departed without saying goodbye and called the next day to apologize for that. In her story "The Edge of the Water," she writes that "the Consul" later confessed that the departure had been intentional, a way to create an excuse to telephone her. This complex, self-conscious Latin gallantry charmed Alice. In *Careless Love*, where Adams has transformed Vasco Pereira into Pablo Valdespina, the Spanish consul (reversing his initials), the seducer is a man "extraordinarily attractive to women, though clearly in no stereotypical American way . . . He had the authority of a king, or a pirate. Or an actor." Alice was, perhaps, a latter-day Isabel Archer meeting her Gilbert Osmond.

Vasco Pereira; his wife, Margarida; his mother; and their children resided in the hulking consulate on Washington Avenue in Pacific Heights. His youngest child, Bernardo, was born in San Francisco in February 1959 shortly before Pereira met Alice. His two daughters, Vera and Cristina, attended a French-language Catholic school in Chinatown. For the entire family, but especially for the father, San Francisco was a revelation. Here, as his daughter Vera Futscher Pereira writes, Vasco and Margarida were "absorbed by a busy social life that never ceased to surprise them . . . meeting women who were more independent and daring than most European women."[10]

Pereira had come to San Francisco in 1956 after assignments in Morocco and the Belgian Congo. Two years earlier, while overseeing his government's building of a new consulate in Leopoldville, Pereira sent a letter to his superiors about independence movements in Central

Africa, specifically in Congo and in the neighboring Portuguese province of Angola. He proposed that his government should change its policies and offered to travel and learn more about the situation. They transferred him to San Francisco instead.

As newlyweds in Portugal, a country whose authoritarian regime was officially neutral in World War II, the strikingly handsome Futscher Pereiras had shared an interest in theater, art, and literature. She was a practicing Catholic, he an agnostic. She had a passionate interest and a master's degree in literature, for which she'd written her thesis on Bloomsbury-era English novelist Rosamond Lehmann—an unusual choice for a devout young woman. After the war, the couple lived in Rome for two years, coincidentally overlapping Alice and Mark Linenthal's briefer stay there. As Margarida Navarro, she wrote about Italy for Lisbon's *Diário Popular*. One essay celebrates the poetic love and collaboration of Elizabeth and Robert Browning.

Unlike that famous English couple, Margarida and Vasco soon found themselves beginning a family. According to Vera Futscher Pereira, her mother's happiness declined as her father's prospects rose. Suffering with postpartum depression after the birth of her first daughter in Rome, she returned to Lisbon. Vasco began a career with the Portuguese diplomatic service and was soon promoted to consul general in the Belgian Congo. Here Margarida gave birth to her second daughter, Vera, who grew up to be a translator, writer, and family archivist. The years in Leopoldville were happier for the young family. They entertained lavishly in the elegant new consulate with a staff of African servants.

By the time Alice met Vasco Pereira, his marriage had changed—or so he led Alice to believe. He and Margarida had both aged, certainly—she into a society matron and mother with domestic responsibilities, he into a charming middle-aged European man-about-town whose movements were assisted by Vice Consul Antonio Bettencourt.

Pereira dominated Alice's life for more than two years. Afterward, her friend Eleanor Haas told her, "You were not yourself when you were with Vasco."[11] Her feelings for him pushed other people aside. In her apartment she waited for his fugitive phone calls and visits (he had a key) or for notes left at her door by Bettencourt. Sometimes—in deference to Bettencourt's "delicacy"—she stayed away from her own front door in fear of encountering Vasco's emissary. Nonetheless, the affair was no secret from Peter or from Alice's close friends.

Judith Adams met Vasco more than once, never intentionally. "Once I came by about five one afternoon," Judith recalled. "Alice came to the door, her face very flushed, and she said 'I have guests.' And that was Vasco. She had on earrings and a velvet robe in a claret color and her eyes were just huge. She looked gorgeous, but I thought, 'Oh, my god, where is Peter?' I hoped he was at Mark's."

No doubt Peter was with his father on that afternoon, but he holds other confusing memories from these years. "My room was not far from my mom's. Only a narrow closet with doors at each end separated us. As a child I heard sounds that were scary to me. It sounded like hurting more than pleasure, and I was just sort of figuring it out." His mother spent a lot of time on the telephone too, walking the long hall of their apartment with the receiver in one hand and the big old black phone in the other, the long twisty cord trailing behind her. "She'd shoot me a glance that meant, this is a boring person to talk to—but sometimes the problem was that I was there and she wasn't talking freely."

Alice wrote to Vasco often, mailing her billets-doux to him at the consulate with special delivery postage.[12] "I am so filled—entirely—with love for you—this makes the world another color—I need new words," she declared after an early assignation. His letters to her, often in French, which they used as their private language, are equally ecstatic. Alice has talked to Vasco about her parents, her marriage, Max Steele, and her writing ambitions. When she tries to write, she complains, she can think only of letters to him: "Once I wanted to say to you furiously—how can I be a great writer when I think of nothing but you? But now I am not furious. I will write, finally better because of you, because at least what I feel for you has greatness."

Alice and Vasco participated together in the glorification of their love affair. That he was married, that they both had children, did not seem, in the early months, to be an impediment. In Adams's story "Sintra," the Portuguese lover Luiz warns Arden, "I think that you have fallen in love with my love for you." Such was the case for Alice with Vasco. She was probably thinking of herself when she sketched this character in her notebook: "Not Mme. Bovary—no vanity involved, an impassioned need to be loved, & a generous wish for everyone to be warm & well-fed, well-loved." On another day, writing to him on the gallery's letterhead as she expects him to walk into the shop any minute, she asks, "Do you remember that very dangerous thing you said to me?—that if you were sure I would always love you you would give up everything?"

Madly in love, perhaps for the first time, Alice felt the irrationality and vulnerability of her position and noted in her journal, "The fine line between infantilism & greatness—I'm on the side of the lovers who say I can't live without you, & mean it."[13] With a fervor that D. H. Lawrence would have applauded, Alice believed that sex with Vasco transformed her. "She told me," Judith Adams remembered, "that she thought his penis had 'imprinted' her. I think that was the verb, meaning he owned her in a way."

Judith Adams believes that Vasco was equally besotted with Alice, and other scraps of evidence confirm her impression. He requested and received an extension of his posting in San Francisco. One of Alice's letters mentions that Vasco has spoken with Alice's mentor, her parents' old friend Ralph Bates in New York—the same Ralph Bates who had warned Alice in 1946 not to marry precipitously. Turning to *Careless Love* for clues, we find Pablo Valdespina promising Daisy that in their future together they will spend summers on the beaches of Portugal. Also in the novel, Pablo seeks an international banking position that will allow him to leave the diplomatic corps and live in Paris with Daisy. This dream of starting over in a new country tantalized both of them. Even Peter believed they would be moving to Paris.

Separation made both Vasco and Alice frantic. He sent long love letters. She cabled her love to him at the Ministério dos Negócios Estrangeiros when he went to Lisbon for a few weeks. On her coffee table she kept a book of black-and-white photographs of Portugal that fascinated Peter with its picture of the Capela dos Ossos chapel, mosaiced with the bones of five thousand corpses. She mentioned Portugal so often in letters to Max Steele that he queried from Mexico, "[Why] all this talk of Portugal when you haven't even seen Cuernavaca?"

When Vasco was seriously ill late in 1959 with a kidney ailment and couldn't call or visit her, Alice besieged him with worried letters. Perhaps he objected, prompting her to reply: "You were right that I'm terribly concentrated in my own troubled mind—and I hate that too—I'm sorry—really sorry . . ." Nonetheless, he wrote her from his sickbed

Nicholson Barney Adams and Agatha Boyd, both scholars of languages, married in Virginia in 1920, after Nic returned from World War I. Their daughter, Alice Boyd Adams, born August 14, 1926, grew up in their farmhouse on a hilltop south of the University of North Carolina in Chapel Hill, where Nic was a professor of Spanish. Unwelcome to teach at the all-male university, Agatha became Nic's research assistant but simmered with frustrated ambitions.

In "My First and Only House," Adams wrote that her parents chose this old house with a lovely view over "the convenience of a smaller lot, a tidier house in town." Here young Alice plays with her grandmother beneath the pink and white climbing roses she celebrated in her story "Roses, Rhododendron."

4

Even before she graduated from Radcliffe College at nineteen, Alice was drawn to the tiny, smoke-filled jazz clubs on Fifty-Second Street in New York. There she heard Billie Holiday and other great musicians of the era and met and loved trombonist Trummy Young, who would become her model for the character of Jackson Clay in her bestselling novel *Superior Women*.

Alice met Mark Linenthal during her final year of college after he was released from a German prisoner-of-war camp. They married precipitously in November 1946 with Alice resplendent in a gold lamé dress. Both sets of parents attended (*left to right*): Mark Linenthal Sr., Agatha Adams, Mark and Alice, Anna Linenthal, and Nic Adams standing in front of a portrait of Agatha's ancestor.

5

6

Peter Linenthal was born in California in 1951. By the time the family of three moved to San Francisco in 1955, where Mark became a college professor, Alice—still an unpublished writer—was deeply unhappy with the marriage.

7

Alice had a love affair with the writer Max Steele when she separated from Mark to spend the summer of 1958 in her childhood home in Chapel Hill. Max became a lifelong friend who urged Adams forward in her writing career. He struck a professorial pose when he returned to Chapel Hill with his family a few years later to head the University of North Carolina's writing faculty.

8

9

Before Alice returned to San Francisco in 1958, she and Peter vacationed with her father and his second wife at his summer cabin on the shore of Lake Sebago in Maine. Adams received news of her first short-story sale at the end of that summer and made up her mind to divorce Mark Linenthal.

Beloved professor and Hispanophile Nic Adams and his second wife, Dotsie, dressed for a costume party in Chapel Hill. Alice's conflicted relationships with her father and stepmother became subjects of some of her best fiction.

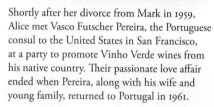

Shortly after her divorce from Mark in 1959, Alice met Vasco Futscher Pereira, the Portuguese consul to the United States in San Francisco, at a party to promote Vinho Verde wines from his native country. Their passionate love affair ended when Pereira, along with his wife and young family, returned to Portugal in 1961.

Alice, in her early thirties, posed for Vasco Pereira on a weekend trip to Yosemite. Her first published novel, *Careless Love*, was about her doomed love for a diplomat who was flawed but "nevertheless the most attractive man in the world" to her at the time.

With the handsome style of a forties movie idol, creative, self-made Robert (Bob) McNie was a charismatic, self-taught interior designer in San Francisco. He and Alice began living together in 1966. His station wagon, Old Black, was always loaded with items he'd salvaged or purchased for his clients.

By 1977, when she and Robert McNie posed for a dual portrait, Alice was a successful literary writer whose short stories often appeared in the *New Yorker* and whose novels were published by Knopf. After her third novel, *Listening to Billie*, came out, Alice told *People* magazine that she and Bob were engaged in a "long-term illicit affair."

Alice, Robert McNie, Peter Linenthal, Morissa McNie, Robert McNie Jr., and Morissa's young son were a loose, sometimes chaotic family unit for almost twenty years.

Almost every January, Alice and Bob spent two weeks at a small resort hotel above a long white beach and shining ocean bay near Zihuatanejo. She described a typical day in a story: "They swim far out into the cove together, in the clear warm green water. . . . At lunch they drink the excellent Mexican beer, and eat fresh garlicky seafood. They shower and sleep, they make love. They swim again, and shower again, and head up to the bar, which is cantilevered out into the open, starry, flowery night; they drink margaritas, toasting each other and the lovely, perfect place."

16

At the Community of Writers at Squaw Valley, in 1974, students, accustomed to hearing literary "stars" showcase their bravado, praised Adams's quieter style of teaching (*left to right*): songwriter Joe Henry; Alice's editor at Knopf, Victoria Wilson; San Francisco bookseller Edwina Evers Leggett (*in back*); Alice Adams; and Max Steele.

Adams judged the PEN/ Faulkner Award for Fiction for 1986. At the awards ceremony at the Folger Shakespeare Library in Washington, DC, she was seated with (*left to right*) Grace Paley and Beverly Lowry. "I sensed she was beautiful down to her skin," Lowry said of the way Alice looked in her crocheted dress over a silk slip. "It was all perfect. Glorious."

17

18

Ella Leffland, then working on *Rumors of Peace*, along with Diane Johnson (who'd just published *The Shadow Knows*), Sheila Ballantyne (then completing her feminist classic *Norma Jean the Termite Queen*), and Alice, began a lunch group for women writers. "It's nice to know other women out of true mutual interests, rather than because one's husbands are in the same business or graduate school—or children are of the same age, etc.," Adams said.

19

After Alice Adams and Robert McNie separated in 1987, she traveled often to Mexico with friends and wrote a travel memoir about that country. Novelist Alison Lurie, whom she'd known since college at Radcliffe, took this photo of sixty-two-year-old Alice when they toured Mayan ruins at Palenque. "Southern girls learn how to look cool and fresh even when the temperature is over 90," Lurie said. "There must be tricks to it that we Northerners haven't learned."

20

21

"I'm sorry, I have such a terrible headache," Alice (*left*) told her friends Mary Ross Taylor and Beverly Lowry (pictured), Judith Rascoe, and Carolyn See, who gathered to celebrate Lowry's latest book (*Crossed Over: A Murder, A Memoir*) and Alice's sixty-sixth birthday. If her beauty or her brains or her emotional intensity frightened men, she balanced that by maintaining many enduring friendships with women.

Daniel Simon, a medical doctor who lived in Berkeley, was one of the widowers Alice dated in the early 1990s; he became the strong-minded advocate she needed when she was diagnosed with a rare sinus cancer. She survived the cancer but satirized doctors and excoriated the medical establishment in her 1997 novel *Medicine Men*.

Like the women in her stories, Alice Adams was resilient. She had innumerable love affairs but spent what was to be the last evening of her life in the company of her only child, Peter Linenthal. Here they attend a party in San Francisco to celebrate the publication of the first book for children that Peter illustrated. An enlarged picture from the book hangs behind them.

and listened for her to drive by and "hoot" her car horn. Later Adams diagnosed her condition in *Careless Love*: "She was committed, all the way, to melodrama and to pain. She had yet to find out that these emotions are not necessarily love, or that love is possible without them."

During Vasco's illness, Alice and Peter celebrated Christmas with her father, Dotsie, and her relatives in Santa Rosa. In Alice's abbreviated report to Vasco, Nic Adams "shouted all night in Italian to [Dotsie's son's wife's] relatives who couldn't understand him," while Peter was great because "he expects grandparents to be crazy & is never thrown by them." Four years after her father's remarriage she describes Dotsie as "a bitch lacking self-awareness." It seems Alice had told her family about Vasco and they viewed him as her future spouse.

Peter met most of the men Alice dated but some were friendlier to him than others. He recalls, "One time a man was leaving and she ran to the door and yelled, 'No, no, don't go!' I felt bad for her. My mother *never* called me 'her little man' or anything like that but I felt protective of her," Peter reflected. "I think I am a good listener, and some of that must have come from this period. I'd tell her if I didn't like somebody."

One of the people Peter came to dislike was Vasco Pereira. The Portuguese consulate was near Peter's school. Always a friendly child, he once knocked at the door of the impressive building when he was walking home with a friend. Alerted, Vasco appeared and gave the boys a handful of coins and shooed them off to buy candy.

Throughout 1960—as a new decade dawned in the United States with John Kennedy's defeat of Richard Nixon in the presidential election— Alice kept Vasco Pereira at the center of her life. He switched from French to English in his letters, sometimes mentioning writing of hers that he'd read or been told about, including a novel about "Avery" and her father and Golden Gate suicides. Along with frequent love letters, Alice gave Vasco a list of American books he should read. At its head were novels by men she'd loved, Saul Bellow and Max Steele. Next came novels by Robert Penn Warren, Katherine Anne Porter, Carson McCullers, Mary McCarthy, Ralph Ellison, James Agee, John O'Hara, and William Styron, along with *The Collected Poems of Wallace Stevens*.[14] Not only does this list tell us which writers then mattered to Adams, it also reveals how much she wished for Vasco to imagine her in the company of this ménage of contemporary writers.

Vasco found excuses to leave home for weekends with Alice in Carmel and Yosemite and they talked about their plans for the future. In the snapshots he saved, Alice's hair is blond and she is thin as a model except for her voluptuous and now uplifted bosom. She brandishes a cigarette and looks like a parody of a free woman.

Expecting Vasco to divorce his wife and marry her, Alice sent his picture to Lucie Jessner, who offered that he looked "intelligent and alive and controlled—passionate."* Later Lucie notes that Alice expects to join Vasco when he becomes ambassador to Chile—"I can imagine you as ambassadresse [sic] of grand style."15 In Adams's story called "The Edge of the Water," based on a weekend she and Vasco spent at the Mission Ranch Hotel in Carmel, the consul tells her, "Of all the women I have ever known, I feel most for you." But the woman in that story also notices that her lover looks "entirely alien and enclosed." Remembering the pictures of his daughters, "little girls with great dark eyes, like his," she realizes that she is not part of his real life.16

Romantic weekends and high hopes were spanned by days of desperation. At least once Alice ended the relationship, explaining, "Always waiting for you & not being sure you could come I was so lonely." Alice declared her devotion in extreme language. "If you were suddenly to tell me that you were free to go with me, how gladly I would go, anywhere," Daisy tells her lover in *Careless Love*. But when Pablo replies, "this is the most marvelous thing of my life," Daisy understands that it is terrible. "She had said that she would leave her whole life . . . he had said nothing of the sort. Wantonly she had yielded up all her power, and her sovereignty."

The inevitable crushing of Alice's hopes came early in 1961. Vasco could not fulfill the promise she wanted from him, that someday they would live together. In *Careless Love* the breakup occurs when Daisy realizes that she is pregnant by Pablo. His reaction to this news circles through false pride and ends in cowardly horror. He will not claim the child as his own, nor will he discuss the abortion to which he tacitly consents:

---

* Jessner reserved her greater appreciation for Adams's "true and delicate and so perfectly told new story," "Truth or Consequences" (which would not be published until 1979). For this experienced psychiatrist, work mattered more than romantic love.

He took her hand. "You are so brave a woman. You are a true woman."

In this unspecific, uncommitted way it was decided that Daisy was to have an abortion. Pablo had not had to say the word.

He left, after gulping coffee. "Of all days there is much business in my office."

After considering melodramatic (but not uncommon) options—"to refuse to have the abortion (to have the child in Mexico), to blackmail him into marriage by telling a gossip columnist or the police. Or to die of dirty instruments"—Daisy talks to a doctor who connects her with an abortionist. In a remarkable section of *Careless Love*, Daisy's father makes an unexpected appearance in San Francisco and flies to Tijuana with her for the procedure, which is accomplished by a kindly Mexican obstetrician and his nurse/wife. At one point the doctor mistakes Daisy's father for the father of the child, and the mistake is hurriedly corrected in broken English and Spanish. It's doubtful that Nic Adams—whose Spanish was fluent—accompanied Alice to Tijuana. But the novel's daughter-father episode provides Daisy with something Adams craved: a loving father who accepts her as she is and sets aside his own ego in order to help her.

Years later, when Alice and a good friend compared notes on their reproductive histories, they discovered that they both remembered the same kind Mexican.[17] Also years later while in Seattle, Alice noted "Vasco—abortion" among her memories of that city. Whether she went to Seattle or Tijuana, it is almost certain that Alice aborted a child during the final days of their affair. Before he left San Francisco, Vasco wrote Alice notes promising checks for $1,200 and $800. Her letters (which he saved) begging him for the money he's promised show that she waited six weeks for the second check.[18]

Alice's breakup with Vasco left a searing pain that she felt for years afterward. Beyond the loss, she felt humiliated. Alice had told her father that Vasco was "the strongest & most honorable man [she] had known" and hated to say she'd been wrong. "I must give up this fantasy of love & protection from anyone," she wrote in her notebook. Lucie Jessner, agreeing with an interpretation Alice had offered, wrote back, "I am sad. You are so right, that for Latin people marriage and love are something quite separate. And in a way, marriage more often than not is the beginning of the end for love—but females just won't believe it." Ruth Gebhart, an illustrator who'd worked at the Joseph Magnin store with Judith Adams and lived near Alice, stopped by often during this mourning period. "We'd drink and talk—she was wonderful to talk to. We were very close friends then and we confided in each other. She told me Vasco had a stray forelock."[19]

Portugal was in the headlines as Alice's affair with Vasco ended. Henrique Galvão, an activist against the dictatorship of António Salazar in Portugal, hijacked a Portuguese ship with the intention of setting up an opposition government in Angola and declaring the independence of the Portuguese colonies in Africa. The action, which began a twelve-year war for independence in the former colonies, put Pereira in a specious position. Alice watched him on television as he defended the colonialist, right-wing (many said fascist) Portuguese Estado Novo regime against Galvão's charges. "I didn't like what you said," she wrote him afterward, "but I suppose you didn't either. What a bad job for you to have . . . You look older. It isn't good to be a diplomat, not for you."

After that Pereira finally wrote her a letter explaining the reasons he could not marry her: "We would have been happy . . . but always as two desperate human beings who know that in some way they have stolen everything they have." She responded, "If you had written that letter a year—or more—ago, I would have grieved terribly, but also I would have admired your strength & courage, your *decision.* You would have remained for me a responsible man who knew himself & who was whole—"[20]

Three weeks later, Vasco Pereira and his family left San Francisco. In the newspaper Alice saw photographs of the large farewell party held for him and Margarida at the Fairmont Hotel. "I can't imagine your marriage or life now," Alice told him in a final letter, suggesting—as *Careless Love* does—that Vasco had broached the subject of leaving his marriage and learned that neither his wife nor his mother would countenance the idea. " 'I told my wife, and she said that I could never again see the children,' " Pablo tells Daisy. " 'She made such a scene—it was horrible.' He drew out the 'r's—'horrrrrrible.' "

The Pereiras' marriage was virtually over. For three years after their departure from San Francisco, Margarida suffered from depression that hospitalized her or confined her to her room. When her vitality returned, she published two collections of her poems, but mental illness and medications had weakened her. In the final lines of her 1974 book, *Bens Adquiridos*, she addresses poet and anthropologist Ruy Cinatti, who was her close friend, to say that she will die with a sorrow and a mute secret ("*E que morro com pena e um segredo mudo*").

Pereira was assigned to embassies in Karachi, Madrid, Malawi, and Bonn; his wife stayed in Lisbon with their children and her parents. In Pakistan he began a ten-year relationship with Graziela Lima Leitão that his children accepted. After the so-called Carnation Revolution that overthrew the Estado Novo regime in 1974, Pereira played a prominent role as ambassador to Brazil, where many Portuguese businesspeople fled. He formed a new relationship with a Brazilian beauty named Maria Lúcia Pedroza ("Malu"). He went on to serve as Portuguese ambassador to the United Nations, president of the United Nations Security Council, and Portugal's ambassador to the United States. In 1980, Judith Adams came across a photograph in *Architectural Digest* magazine of Vasco and Malu Pereira in their New York apartment. "What struck me," she said, was how much his second wife resembled Alice when her hair was dark. I never mentioned it to Alice."[21] But of course Alice knew of Pereira's later career. In her story "Sintra," she describes "the marvellous confidence" of her former lover's stride and "that singular, energetic motion of his body, its course through the world, without her."

When Alice wrote Saul Bellow about the end of her relationship with Pereira, he sent his condolences with the proviso, "I always have more to say about life when it's myself that's in trouble." But he praised her vitality—he found her "a woman evidently built to make it." What puzzled him, he said, was "this feminine belief that one makes it in love, only in love, and that love is a kind of salvation. And then women, and sometimes men too, demand of each other everything—everything! And isn't it obvious by now that no human being has the power to give what we require from one another."[22] His criticism went to the heart of Adams's work.* She had told Vasco that she would be a better writer

---

* Bellow doesn't seem to have learned his own lesson, as he sought what he required from five wives and several serious liaisons. His difficulties with love began with the death of his mother when he was in his late teens, according to biographer James Atlas. As the youngest brother, he sat by her bedside every afternoon, struggling against his desire to be elsewhere. (Atlas, *Bellow: A Biography*, 35.)

because of the great love she felt for him; as it turned out, she would be a better writer because of the great loss she endured because of him.

Meanwhile, in late November 1960 Alice's other famous multimarried friend, Norman Mailer, culminated an ongoing crack-up by stabbing his second wife, Adele Morales, in the chest with a penknife. It seems beyond ironic that Adams admired and sought approval from Bellow and Mailer, two writers who were so incapable of engaging her work. Mailer's essay "Evaluation—Quick and Expensive Comments on the Talent in the Room," collected that same year in *Advertisements for Myself*, stated: "I have nothing to say about any of the talented women who write today. Out of what is no doubt a fault in me, I do not seem able to read them. Indeed I doubt if there will be a really exciting woman writer until the first whore becomes a call girl and tells her tale."

Getting over Vasco Pereira was a long process for Alice. She wrote him a letter to read later filled with the questions that tormented her: "Why? Why? *Did* we love each other? Nothing is real any more. Who *were* you? Did I always love someone else? *Please* tell me if you are alive still—"

Alice returned to her analyst, Dr. Biernoff, for counsel. The doctor's shock that she'd been in love with "a representative of a fascist country" probably made her become more critical of Vasco.[23] Rereading Vasco's letters late in 1962, Alice decided they were more full of excuses than of love. Soon she was making entries in her notebook about the character named Pablo Valdespina and the woman named Daisy who falls terribly in love with him.[24]

While the novelized Pablo Valdespina retains some of the charm that Vasco Pereira held for Alice Adams, the book is also suffused with irony and humor—and bitter oversimplification. On the one hand she labeled him a fascist, on the other she retained nostalgic passion for him. Adams generalized her new awareness of that contradiction in an unpublished short story: "My new life had made me increasingly aware of the craziness, the total inexplicability of sex, of sexual attractions."[25] For Peter too, his mother's breakup with Vasco was confusing. He hadn't liked Vasco or the moods he evoked in his mother, but he saw her misery. Peter "kept asking when we were going to Paris," Alice wrote in the letter she sent Vasco to read later. She continued, "I just said we had meant to marry but couldn't &

that's why I felt badly & why not Paris. He was very nice. Only said 'Where else could we go?' "[26]

Peter's confusion was compounded by a new event in his father's life. Mark Linenthal met Frances Jaffer Pain when she took his poetry class at San Francisco State. She was immediately attracted to her charismatic professor. They married the day after Mark's divorce from Alice was final, on October 5, 1959.

Frances Linenthal was the same age as her new husband. Her father had founded Structural Steel Inc., a manufacturer of I-beams, and she received income from stock she owned in the company.[27] As an undergraduate at Stanford, Frances had been an Anglophile and in 1942 married a Scottish-born medieval-history student named Rodney Pain, who was descended from the English naval hero Lord Rodney. Marriage to charming but philandering Pain cured Frances of her Anglophilia. In later years Pain became a dentist and local celebrity known for offering free dental treatment to artists and poor people and for playing bagpipes to entertain his patients while he waited for the anesthetic to take effect.[28]

Frances had been divorced five years when she met Mark. Her three sons, Lincoln, Duncan, and Louis, thought Mark Linenthal was a godsend. "Our mom had been dating men that none of the kids liked," Lincoln, who'd been thirteen at the time, recalled. "Then she started dating this cool, exciting guy who lived on a houseboat and actually liked kids."

Mark joined Frances and her sons in her tall, half-timbered house at 33 Jordan Avenue, a few blocks away from Alice's apartment on Clay Street. Frances welcomed Peter into their household and helped him create his own space on the top floor. Louis, about a year younger than Peter, remembered, "That whole top floor had been an architect's studio—incredible—with large, mysterious things like a closet for blueprints. And curved corkboard walls. Once we created a house of horrors up there with papier-mâché bodies. Later we made it psychedelic with Fillmore Auditorium posters."

"At first I couldn't believe that Mark would marry so ugly a woman," Alice told her friend Blair Fuller in the early 1960s. Alice was unfair—it was "as though she took it personally, that no husband of hers ought to marry a homely woman," Fuller commented. While blond, petite Frances was unusual looking—a botched nose job that her mother had insisted upon to make her appear less Jewish had turned up the tip of her nose in a curious way and a receding chin marred her profile—she was also smart, charming, vivacious, Jewish, maternal, and determined to please Mark. She confided to her mother that she was made desperate by "how complicated and difficult it is for us to manage the ins and outs of our four children and their needs and commitments." She and Alice got along by phone when they made arrangements for Peter to shuttle between their two homes. Nonetheless, Frances saw herself as the stable arbiter who had to deal with both her ex-husband and Mark's ex-wife.[29]

The novelist Alice Adams was also unkind to the character she put in Frances's role in *Families and Survivors*. In the novel, Louisa nastily tells her clueless husband to marry "rich fat" Persephone after he's divorced—and so he does. Then Persephone devotes her time and money to cooking and her husband soon becomes as fat as she. The blatant symbolism of making her husband's new wife an unattractive, smothering, manipulative woman seems to come from Alice's wounded pride. What Frances lacked in beauty, she made up for in her devotion to Mark. At first she accepted a role as his hostess for Poetry Center receptions: "She was inviting, really all-embracing," poet Linda Chown recalled. "She wanted to know everything about one, would engage guests in conversation, all her guests. She liked meeting students as well as Mark's colleagues and the visiting poet who was always the guest of honor, and she had a talent for wry remarks and levity that kept conversations from collapsing into intensity."

Peter became close to his three stepbrothers and moved easily between his father's and mother's residences. To him, during the five years following his parents' divorce, his mother seemed like "sort of an abandoned person" while his father was part of a happy, busy household just two blocks away.

What he could not then understand was that Alice, like many another lonely woman writer in those years, could not help choosing the life that would eventually serve her work. "I spent my 30s having love affairs to make up for lost time and writing as a sort of sideline," Adams told *People* magazine in 1978. Through those love affairs, Adams was becoming the mature woman and writer who could find form for the problems that engaged her.

She would soon be making up for lost time again—at her typewriter.

CHAPTER FIFTEEN

Alone

— 1961–1963 —

I had a number of love affairs, most of them serious—in fact I was always serious, I think.

—Alice Adams, "Why I Left
Home: Partial Truths"

After Vasco Pereira's departure from San Francisco, Alice realized she had dangerously invested her prospects for happiness in one man. With time and writing, she understood too that she risked becoming, as she put it in a story idea later, "the sort of woman who perhaps is going out of style, whose life is love affairs."[1] Worse, none of the men she met after Vasco could give her the thrill she sought. As she approached forty, Alice knew she should devote herself to "the boring rhythm of honest self examination."

In her notebook in 1963, Alice made two lists that outlined her difficulty as a woman and perhaps also a writer:

REAL:	IRRATIONAL:
I am 36	old & ugly
Between beaux is lonely	lonely (?) is forever
I cope fairly well	living alone is more & more impossible

Since her divorce in 1958, Alice had been suspended between those two versions of herself. Like most of her generation she was a woman who identified with men, but during these years she became skeptical of what men could do for her and more confident of what she could do for herself. She was taking on the question of how to be an independent woman in midcentury America when such women were considered an aberration. Even though the birth control pill and writers like Helen Gurley Brown promoted sexual freedom for women, it was not until Betty Friedan published *The Feminine Mystique* in 1963 that public analysis of the unhappiness of women focused on identity and economic autonomy rather than sexual behavior.

On her own, Alice began to reinvent and esteem herself by turning the story of her love affair with Vasco into her novel *Careless Love*. Adams wanted to call the novel *Nevertheless* because, she explained, this affair had been "melodramatic, 'neurotic,' a con," but "nevertheless a *love* affair." By transforming her story into that of her protagonist Daisy Duke, she could see admirable strength and wry humor in her suffering and, as she explained, examine "the lack of clear social or conventional rules for divorced or otherwise unmarried people beyond their twenties. What mores there are have to be guessed at, trial-and-error tested."[2]

While Alice was occupied with Vasco, her correspondence with Max Steele had dwindled. On New Year's Eve 1960 he married his former student Diana Whittinghill, whom he'd known several years. "When I was 21 and not his student anymore, Max deflowered me," she reminisced. "He was 13 years older than me and I did whatever he suggested. A glass of sherry was involved. Maybe two very small ones." After they married, the Steeles drove to San Francisco in a VW bus. Diana became a statistician for the California Department of Employment while Max wrote little himself and taught writing at several colleges. "Mostly we were carpenters," Diana said. They bought and renovated a house in San Francisco's Western Addition neighborhood, "where [they] were the first hetero white couple," then did the same with a three-unit building near Golden Gate Park (offering to rent a floor of it to Alice, who declined), and finally took on a big Victorian at 1366 Guerrero in the lower Mission District.

The Steeles made literary friendships in the Bay Area and invited Alice to their parties. Diana, with her offbeat sense of humor, took her husband's friendship with his former lover in stride while Alice addressed the younger woman with slightly patronizing archness as "Miss Diana." Through the Steeles, Alice met Blair Fuller, a novelist and early *Paris Review* contributor who had been George Plimpton's roommate at Harvard. After too much drink at a party, Fuller recalled,

"Alice and I fell into bed together and had an exciting time but I never wanted to do it again. I felt she was stronger than I was—I feared she would be running the show, and that's not what I wanted." They didn't see each other again immediately, but "then did and were instantly friends." Indeed, Fuller was one of the handful of people to whom Alice confided that she had been seduced by her father's psychoanalyst: "She was 15, she said. I think I wondered at the time because of the way she said it, I wondered is she adding a year? Maybe she was 14! She said it very matter-of-factly. She said it as if she had told other people the story. I'm absolutely sure that she said it to me."

Perhaps their common Harvard history led Alice to talk candidly to Fuller about her marriage to Mark Linenthal: "Linenthal seemed like a figure out of the distant past. She talked tough about him. I said something about his teaching poetry at San Francisco State, and she said, 'You call him a poet?' Cruel. Once I asked her, 'Did the Linenthals have money?' She said, 'Oh, yes, of course, of course.' I'm not making up the 'of course.'" Fuller took Alice's remark to mean that "he would have had to have had money for her to have decided to marry him." She was also indicating that this was what women of her class and education routinely did if they had no money of their own.

The men Alice dated and the women who were her friends and coworkers in the early 1960s became the warp of the fictions she was weaving and trying to sell. She was actively rewriting her history, transforming herself into someone tougher than she'd been in the past. "I had a number of love affairs, most of them serious—in fact I was always serious, I think," she wrote in her essay "Why I Left Home: Partial Truths." The men about whom she was briefly serious included artist Jack Boynton, book rep and reviewer Luther Nichols, literary critic Irving Howe, linguist Franz Sommerfeld, and architect Felix Rosenthal. All of them indirectly contributed to her fiction by telling her about their experiences in the male worlds of war and politics. Another new confidant for Alice in 1961 was the scholar and critic Richard Poirier, a friend of Billy Abrahams's who spent the summer of 1961 in San Francisco while teaching at Stanford. Poirier was then editor of *The O. Henry Prize Stories*. Alice's lifelong friendship with him was rooted in her admiration for his literary intelligence and his for her fiction—as well as in their shared relish for gossip about mutual friends.

*   *   *

Alice probably met Franz René Sommerfeld through Fred Breier, who first knew him when both were students living at the International House in Berkeley during the forties. At the I-House, one resident from those years writes, there were "Americans, Japanese, Germans, Europeans, Asians, Africans, students whose homelands were on both sides of the war—literally and figuratively holding hands in friendship."[3] Born in Berlin in 1921, Sommerfeld left Germany for Belgium and France, and came to Berkeley in 1940 to complete his BA in German literature. At Columbia University he wrote a master's thesis on *Der Ackermann aus Böhmen*, a late medieval manuscript considered a precursor of humanism.

Friends saw Sommerfeld as superintellectual, "quite intimidating, almost a caricature of the refined German man of letters." His enlarged heart gave him pain and worry and excused him from military service. He lived monkishly in hotels and wore strong eyeglasses that obscured his light blue eyes and emphasized his pale face and dark curly hair. He took an academic position at the University of Washington in 1948, but his "demand for perfection paralyzed him and made it impossible for him to publish his research." His department chair, W. H. Rey, described him as "paradoxically the most talented and most hopeless man in the department."[4] While teaching in Seattle, he often visited friends in the Bay Area. When Alice's artist friend Ruth Gebhart married an architect named John Belmeur at the Swedenborgian Church, Alice and Franz hosted a champagne reception for them in Alice's apartment. When Ruth had a miscarriage and was unable to conceive again, Alice complained to Judith that John was "very harsh" with Ruth, adding, "Girls who underrate themselves get into such troubles, don't we?"[5]

Late in 1961, Sommerfeld sent Alice money to fly to Seattle and have her hair dressed in an elaborate beehive-chignon style so she could attend a faculty Christmas party with him. She wore a gold Dior coat that he bought for her. This was an expansive time in Franz's life: With an inheritance from his parents he'd moved into a house near the university. After years of working as an instructor, he'd finally been promoted to the professoriate even though he still hadn't completed his PhD. Alice was the arm candy he brought along to celebrate. Afterward, she wrote him: "Every night I listen to Schubert and cry. What a pity you aren't here to see this—you'd be so cheered." In these intimately playful letters she gave details about how her hair remained "high as a haystack" after she took the pins out and told him she'd bought "some great new stockings that go all the way up to panties to which they're attached"—the newly marketed panty hose that soon made miniskirts possible and popular.

Alice urges Franz to burn her letters after a hasty reading: "We don't want posterity to know that such a perverse girl was ever in love with you."[6]

Was Alice in love? Peter thought Sommerfeld seemed like "a more serious connection than Vasco," in part because both he and his mother called Franz by the affectionate "Franzl" and because he sent Peter a Lionel science experiment kit for Christmas. In February of 1962, the wife of one of Franz's colleagues called Alice to tell her that Franz was at Providence Hospital. Franz soon sent a letter explaining that the problem was simply an arrhythmia of "no prognostic significance." She replied with a stream of chatty, flirtatious, self-deprecating letters. She's worried about money and writing stories but confident of Franz's recovery: "In a way I like to think of your being safely in a nice warm hospital . . . It's so bloody cold and unsafe anywhere else. What are you reading?"

Franz Sommerfeld never answered those letters. He was lying in a coma. Rey visited him in the hospital and watched as the unconscious man with long wires attached to both arms struck himself. "It seemed as if the wires were chains from which he wanted to free himself. The nurse tried to console me by pointing out that he, in his unconscious state, could not feel anything. But I was not convinced of that."

Sommerfeld died on March 3, 1962, survived only by cousins in Australia.[7] He serves as a model for characters in two of Adams's best stories: Richard Washington in "The Swastika on Our Door" (who has a defective heart and is given to "isolated, hopeless love affairs, generally with crazy girls") and the young lover named Paul who dies of his congenital heart condition in "Return Trips." When Alice reread *The Portrait of a Lady* years later she realized that Isabel Archer's beloved cousin, Ralph Touchett, was "so very much like" Franz; she called Franz, "one of my greatest, most truly loved friends—a man who taught in Seattle and died young."[8]

*   *   *

Peter was a little surprised when he eventually figured out that his parents' divorce had been his mother's idea. "Her life seemed more tenuous, she was alone sometimes. But I can remember her sitting and writing. And I remember her laughing and drinking and having a great time. She liked cooking and entertaining and sometimes we would have dinner, the two of us with the guy she would be dating. It wasn't a totally unhappy thing."

But by the time Peter was eleven or twelve, he began to feel awkward when Alice had men over. Often he spent weekends at his father's house and returned to his mother's on Sunday evening. For his stepmother, Frances Linenthal, this meant feeding and caring for four boys, two of whom were surly teenagers. In letters to her own mother she complained that Alice was unreliable: "Peter has a stomach ache so we kept him here over night because his God Damn Mother is never home Sunday night when we bring him home," she wrote at the end of one weekend. "She does this every week and Mark is just going to have to speak to her about it. But this is a difficult thing to do, because her reactions when angry are so unpredictable and likely to be extreme and unconscious and make our relations over Peter less good . . . and she refuses to have this stomach thing checked by a doctor, thinking him too hypochondriac, which he is a little but not to an extreme, and he's had this mild stomach ache for four days now. We called our doctor last night. It's tough on Mark."[9]

Perhaps Felix Rosenthal stepped into Alice's life to comfort her after the death of their mutual friend Franz, or perhaps he had been there all along. A friend and neighbor of Alice's, metal artist Imogene "Tex" Gieling, remembered Felix for spur-of-the-moment outings in his old Triumph roadster with a rumble seat. Felix came from a wealthy, multilingual assimilated Jewish family whose antiquarian bookstore in Munich faced a park where Hitler held rallies; he once shook Hitler's hand when his German nanny brought him along to a Nazi meeting. By 1935 his family had relocated to Florence, where Felix attended public school and was required to join the fascist youth organization Avanguardisti Sciatori—which purported to emphasize skiing. He was attending the University of Milan in 1938 when Mussolini's party forbade foreign Jews to attend Italian schools. He next studied engineering in Paris before emigrating to Chile and then joining his brother, Bernard, at UC Berkeley. Both brothers were classified as "enemy aliens" and lived with nightly curfews and travel restrictions until they were drafted into the US Army and were awarded American citizenship.

Near the end of the war, Master Sergeant Felix Rosenthal interrogated German prisoners of war and became known as "the Third Army's Hitler scholar." Recognized as the only member of Patton's G-2 unit who had personally met and spoken with Hitler, Rosenthal became obsessed with "probing the deranged mind of Adolf Hitler and the Nazi mindset." That fascination served him well when, with Berkeley art historian and first lieutenant Walter Horn, he was assigned to Eisenhower's MFAA (Monuments, Fine Arts, and Archives) team charged with finding the missing imperial crown, globe, scepter, and swords of the Holy Roman Empire. They interviewed high-level Nazis imprisoned at Nuremberg and were given access to secret files.

Felix Rosenthal was the imaginative theorist of a team that sought to probe "the roots of Hitler's psychosis not in Germany but in Vienna, when he was an itinerant art student, hating Jews and romanticizing his personal destiny," according to author Sidney D. Kirkpatrick, who writes in *Hitler's Holy Relics* that Rosenthal thought "Hitler and Himmler were laying the groundwork to make Germanic Christianity the new national religion of Germany" by manipulating the New Testament to suggest "that Jesus was making a holy war against the Jews and that Jesus' inner circle were not Jews but Gentiles." Relics from the Holy Roman Empire were part of a scheme wherein Hitler would crown himself emperor. In quest of the relics—they were eventually found underground in Nuremberg—Rosenthal and Horn were granted extraordinary privileges in postwar Germany.[10]

Discharged in 1946, Rosenthal returned to Berkeley, where his parents now lived, and completed an architecture degree under the renowned modernist Erich Mendelsohn, the designer of Maimonides Hospital (now Mount Zion) and the Russell House (for Madeleine Haas Russell) in San Francisco. Felix became Mendelsohn's right-hand man at UC Berkeley; but in 1950 Felix refused to sign the university's controversial anticommunist loyalty oath and was dismissed.

Then Felix moved to the Italian neighborhood on a steep slope of Telegraph Hill, where his Florentine accent was much admired. His apartment at the top of a rickety house above the Vallejo Street Stairway had a rooftop terrace with a view. It was, according to his brother, Bernard, the kind of bachelor pad that gave "every married man who entered it a touch of melancholy or nostalgia." Felix made his own vinegar and cooked passionately in his big kitchen with hanging pots and pans and a solid-core door for a table. He was friendly with all the North Beach shopkeepers and picked up bargains everywhere. In his brother's view, Felix "had an eye for the commercially disastrous. He was always designing and dreaming of all the money he would make. A paper airplane for cereal boxes! He picked the cheapest printer—a disaster." Nonetheless, Felix completed one of his most beautiful projects while he was dating Alice. That commission came to him by way of the serendipity Felix (and Alice) so much enjoyed.

When Felix had surgery for gallstones, Alice, perhaps still alarmed by the sudden death of Sommerfeld, held his hand all night in the hospital. When he was discharged, Ruth Haas Lilienthal, who had become a second mother to him, took him in her Cadillac to recover at her estate near San Mateo. Her recently divorced son, Philip III, soon arrived. Hoping her two fragile guests would get along, Ruth Lilienthal asked them to organize her wine cellar, which had been neglected since her husband's death. During a day spent tasting antique wines and whiskeys, Phil asked Felix to design a pavilion to honor his father's memory at a Boy Scout camp in the Sierra foothills.

When the shelter was done, Felix took Alice and Peter to see it. Peter remembered "an interesting origami-pleated copper-clad roof on rustic stone columns" and was amused to learn that Felix and a sculptor friend, Jacques Overhoff, had peed on the roof to initiate its verdigris. In *Careless Love*, which she was writing throughout the early sixties, Adams describes a knotty-pine-paneled motel in the Sierra foothills where she and Felix stayed but omits the architectural job itself. The narrow focus of that novel on the love affairs of Daisy Duke turns the Felix character, Jack Peterson, into a minor and somewhat laughable man Daisy dates in her first year as a divorcée.

Another portrait of Felix emerges in Adams's unpublished story "A Bachelor's Fate." Investigating single life from a man's point of view, Adams shows an egotistical bachelor who is so wary of emotional women looking for husbands that he fails to be curious about their lives. Nonetheless, this bachelor stays in long-term affairs because he dislikes "the expenditure of energy involved in beginning a new one." Realizing he may lose this girl that he likes, he asks her to marry him. "I can't do that. I'd starve," she replies, before explaining, "Partly you like to be loved, but I always had a feeling that I was giving you a present you didn't know what to do with."

When Norman Mailer; his pregnant girlfriend, Beverly Bentley; and their big black poodle, Tibo, came to San Francisco in the summer of 1963, Alice borrowed Felix's apartment for them while Felix stayed with her. Mailer was "in the first flush of being in love with Beverly, and he was his terrific old self," Alice thought, tapered down from his violent craziness during the past decade (during which she hadn't seen him). To Mark Linenthal on this visit, Mailer offered a "*mea culpa* evaluation . . . something like 'I've been so crazy' . . . but that's not the way it's gonna be in the future."[11] Alice was relieved to find Mailer intensely curious about everything. Knowing Rosenthal was an architect, he geared his conversation to topics that he might care about.

Bentley, a talented actor who had previously been the lover of Miles Davis, also impressed Alice: "I thought she was incredibly pretty, very funny. I was sure she was lying about her age." One day Alice found Beverly at the ironing board in Felix's apartment, doing Norman's shirts and scarves—"practicing to be a good wife," she thought. Meanwhile, Norman tested his mettle by walking narrow ledges on Telegraph Hill. As a foursome they spent a glorious day picnicking under tall oak trees at an abandoned winery Felix knew of in Napa Valley. Back in New York after meeting Beverly's family in Georgia, Mailer wrote a thank-you letter addressed "Dear Alice, Dear Felix" complaining about how hard it was to be back in the city. He invited Alice to come east for a visit and she was already making plans to do so.[12]

Felix was a persistent suitor in Alice's life for about three years. He never married. Tex Gieling said, "He was serious about Alice, he really was. I think it sort of spoiled him for anything else." Alice explained her ambivalence about Felix in a letter to Judith Adams, who was still happily married to Tim and awaiting the birth of her fifth child in Washington, DC: "Sometimes I think he isn't crazy enough to interest me strongly, other times I think he just isn't interesting enough. At best it seems a pleasant relationship of which not too much should be made."[13]

Other men passed through Alice's life while she was debating the merits of Felix. Trummy Young continued to perform in the Bay Area until January of 1964, when he retired from the All-Stars and moved to Oahu.* Others were one-night stands, just names on her roster of lovers: Who are Art, Noel, Larry S, Al N, and Lucas M? John A, Ed D, Mosely, and Zulli? Other encounters turned into long friendships—or long social embarrassments. Judging by the notes and letters that Alice saved, it seems that she was looking for interesting, independent men who might validate her work and her ambitions.

One of these was James "Jack" Boynton, an abstract painter from Texas who arrived in San Francisco in 1960 looking like a young Elvis Presley with longish, thick black hair and blue eyes. Jack taught at the California School of Fine Arts (now the San Francisco Art Institute), where he mixed with California figurative painters David Park, Elmer Bischoff, and Richard Diebenkorn. His work was showing in New York—in the Whitney Museum Annual and in "Younger American Painters" at the Guggenheim, and he was preparing a one-man show for the Staempfli Gallery. Boynton's incipient success was coming on the heels of severe difficulties. His wife, Texas artist Ann Williams Boynton, had suffered a stroke on their honeymoon. After the couple had two daughters, she became severely depressed and was repeatedly hospitalized.

Boynton was still married and very short of money when Alice met him. He enjoyed her intelligence and wry sense of humor. He gave her a small painting and welcomed her and Peter to his brick-walled studio in the old produce district where the Embarcadero Center stands now—"the first loft I ever visited," Peter recalled. Writer Donald Barthelme, Boynton's close friend in Houston, kiddingly called the painter an "illiterate bastard," so perhaps Boynton never noticed himself in the character of Luke Taylor in the final pages of *Careless Love*. Cheerful, handsome Luke provides Daisy with a catharsis as she recovers from her obsession with Pablo: "Daisy, true to form, made declarations. Luke didn't; he called her by no endearment other than what his voice made of her name. Daisy thought she had never felt more loved." Daisy learned to appreciate Luke's separateness: "He seemed then very separate, and

---

* No sooner had Young resettled in Hawaii than "Hello, Dolly!," one of his last recordings with the All-Stars, spent a week at number 1 on the Billboard Hot 100, displacing the Beatles and making Armstrong the oldest artist ever to occupy the number 1 spot. Alice probably heard Trummy whenever she turned on a radio.

their being together seemed an accident, a collision. She knew that he
was essentially a loner. After San Francisco he would go to New York.
Or Paris. He cared about painting. With people, even with her, he was
finally elusive."

In the end, Boynton went back to Houston to raise his daughters.
His wife committed suicide in the spring of 1963.[14] Alice corresponded
with Jack for the rest of her life. Boynton's second wife, Sharon, came
to admire Alice for her "wonderful gift of remaining friends with former lovers," and noted, "I wasn't jealous at all, and Jack wasn't about
my previous boyfriends. He really loved being around women, talking
to women." When Sharon needed surgery for breast cancer, Boynton
soothed her fears of mutilation by recalling that the beautiful Alice
Adams had surgical scars on her breasts.

Irving Howe, the founding editor of *Dissent* magazine and a leading
New York intellectual and scholar of Yiddish literature, also met Alice
Adams in the early 1960s. He'd come west at the end of his second
marriage with hope that his new love, Edja Weisberg, would join him.
She didn't. His "unwavering and desperate" attempt to persuade her
to change her mind led to nothing but huge phone bills. Howe complained about California's intellectually bland "second-rate culture"
where everything shut down by nine p.m. He'd fled Palo Alto for an
apartment on the north slope of Telegraph Hill, which should have
been cramped and urban enough to remind him of New York, but he
still felt "unmoored."[15]

Throughout two years of misery in California, Howe always appeared
"in the company of attractive women," his biographer writes.[16] Alice
became one of these in the spring of 1963. The San Francisco political
activist Paul Jacobs, married to Alice's divorce lawyer, urged Howe to call
Alice. Certainly Alice knew Howe's literary criticism and shared many
of his political views, though they disagreed about the radical youth
then emerging through the civil rights movement and students' rights
groups in Berkeley. Arriving at her apartment, Howe made a faux pas
that Alice never forgot. "You'd be beautiful if it weren't for your teeth,"
he told her. If her story "A California Trip"—in which the teeth become
a nose—can be trusted, she had a comeback: "God, thanks. Have you
ever taken a good long look at yours?"[17]

Howe confided to Alice that he was in terrible shape and recounted
his "total, shattering" affair with Edja. She told him about Vasco Pereira

and the death of Franz Sommerfeld. When Alice took Howe to a party at the home of friends Eleanor and Albert Haas in Marin County, he realized that none of the guests knew of him or his work, but was flattered to hear that Eleanor thought him "sexy."[18]

After Howe returned east to teach at Hunter College, he and Alice corresponded and spoke of future meetings. "We knew each other a mere 10 days," he reflected, "but it feels like a great deal more, and when I think back to them there is a happy sense of crowding and richness. We had much pleasure together." He asked her how she managed to recover so quickly from the loss of Franz Sommerfeld. "Is it just that you're better than me at putting up a front, or that in the tradition you were born to there is a greater stress than in mine on public restraint? And I wonder how you manage to keep up such a surface, or is it a reality, of good cheer."[19]

This view of Adams seems to have appealed to her. When she wrote stories about both Howe and Rosenthal narrated from the man's point of view, she portrayed herself as a not-very-literary, blond, healthy, good-humored woman who turns down offers of marriage from men who are needier than she. Such exercises (both stories went unpublished) suggest she was finally healing the long split between femininity and independence.

CHAPTER SIXTEEN

Careless Love

— 1963–1966 —

*It seemed to me the point of the book was precisely that: his lack
of orthodox attractiveness. This is one of the reasons that I originally wanted to call the book NEVERTHELESS—fat [but]
nevertheless the most attractive man in the world.*

—Alice Adams to David Segal, 1965

In the fall of 1963 Adams had completed at least half of her novel about
a divorcée and her married Spanish lover. After seeing Mailer and meeting Howe, she planned a trip to New York City. Her goal was to find a
new agent who could get her an advance for her novel in progress. Her
former agent, Marie Rodell, had sold only the one story.

Alice also expected to see old friends—and Howe. He made her
a hotel reservation but then found himself too busy to offer to pick
her up at the airport. Instead Norman Mailer welcomed her with "an
extremely high-powered literary party" attended by famous people she
had been anxious to meet when she was twenty-five, including Lionel
Trilling and Norman Podhoretz. Feeling ill from jet lag, Alice had hoped
for a quiet dinner. When she turned down drinks at the party, Mailer
"beat her up."[1] Later she explained to her son that Mailer had used a
judo move on her.[2]

More parties organized by Mailer filled the weekend; after one of
them Alice reported in a letter to Boynton that Howe had "raped" her.
There's no determining if Howe used force to have sex with Alice or
if she felt compromised by him in some other way. Six months later,
Adams asked him to write in support of her fellowship application to the
Ingram Merrill Foundation. He replied, "I've already written the letter

praising you enthusiastically and expatiating on many of, but not all, your talents." By then Howe was involved with Arien Mack, and Alice joked snidely that he had found his "Aryan," though in fact Mack, then a graduate student and later an esteemed professor of social psychology, was Jewish. Mack recalled (after their divorce) that Howe had courted her by sending her reprints of articles he'd written.[3] Howe's redeeming virtue, almost everyone eventually agreed, was his undeviating devotion to anti-Stalinist democratic socialism. Screenwriter Jeremy Larner, who was friends with both Howe and Adams, said, "Irving was the kind of guy who was very brilliant but missed a lot of things about people—and he didn't know it. I think he must have underrated Alice in some way that stuck with her. I could tell by her tone of voice."

A heat wave hit New York that October, which made Alice miserable in her "terrific new dark red wool suit" bought for the trip: "I lost 10 pounds, I remember, mostly perspiration."[4] That heat drove Norman Mailer and Beverly Bentley to Vermont, so Alice moved into their house in Brooklyn Heights.[5] During her stay she saw Jacqueline Miller Rice, an old friend from her Stanford days, who lived in the Village with her new husband, Dan Rice, a painter who'd played trumpet with Benny Goodman and Tommy Dorsey before beginning to paint and collaborate with the poets, dancers, and musicians at Black Mountain College. One of Jackie Rice's closest friends was novelist Dawn Powell, who made Rice her literary executor when she died in 1965. Alice also renewed her friendship with Vida Ginsberg Deming and her husband, Dr. Quentin Deming.* Alice found that she liked both Jackie Rice and Vida Deming better than ever and was encouraged that "their already good marriages had improved."[6] Perhaps unpropitiously, she failed to telephone Jack Boynton's friend Donald Barthelme, then living in the Village and years from becoming, as Lorrie Moore would dub him, commander in chief of the American short story.[7]

Overall the trip to New York was "fantastically strenuous" and made Alice sorry to return to San Francisco.[8] To Beverly Bentley and Norman Mailer, she complained, "One picks up so much in NY simply through

---

* Quentin's sister, Barbara Deming, had stopped writing fiction and become an activist for peace and racial justice. Her *Prison Notes* (1966) chronicles two months she spent on a hunger strike in an Albany, Georgia, jail after being arrested on a walk for peace. She visited Cuba and North Vietnam to protest US policies and wrote extensively about the philosophy of nonviolent protest.

osmosis, while here all you pick up is weather."[9] She was impatient with San Francisco, she told Dick Poirier, because "the local image is so swollen; reading the local papers one might think we had the best theatre, writers, entertainment in the country. When all we have is scenery and restaurants."[10]

Alice accomplished the purpose of her trip, signing with a new agent, John Dodds, the son of a California cattle rancher who then worked at McIntosh, McKee & Dodds and was married to actress Vivian Vance, known for her role as Ethel Mertz in *I Love Lucy*.[11] Alice gave Dodds pages of her novel-in-progress. When President Kennedy was assassinated shortly after her return from New York, Alice immediately wrote a short story in response to the event and sent it off to Dodds. He turned it down flat—too "current and so hooked on an event"—and Adams discarded it.[12]

If Alice had gone to New York with any notion of moving there, she abandoned that. It was enough to have an agent to whom she could mail her work. The rented flat on Clay Street, shared with her son and two cats (named Max and Diana), was home. "Peter is the only interesting person in San Francisco," she boasted to Vida Deming.[13]

Peter was at this time "headlong into adolescence," according to his stepmother, and doing poorly in grammar and math. In letters to her own mother, Frances called Alice "a pretty scared person" who "won't see Peter clearly."[14] At nearly thirteen, Peter became the focus of what Alice called an "awful crisis." He was tall, slender, and awkward, and feared that he looked odd—unlike his handsome parents. Frances and Mark Linenthal decided Peter needed to see a psychoanalyst. When Alice broached the idea to him, he "was hurt that they thought there was something wrong with [him], which magnified [his] own feelings that there was something wrong." After a few sessions with Dr. Shapiro, the father of a boy he knew at school, Peter hadn't found much to say. Alice realized she felt ambivalent about analysis for children and resisted Frances Linenthal's wish that Peter continue.* "The only good effect of all this so far," Alice wrote Lucie Jessner, "is that he's working much harder, the bad of course is that he sees psychiatry as punishment

---

* According to Peter, "Frances was very pro-psychiatry. If you wanted to be mean"— which of course he did not—"you could call it *psychobabble*—ideas about this came freely from her. Like many of that generation, she was a true believer."

(evidently I do too)." Then she made a more practical assessment of Peter's situation: "He thinks he's Picasso and so why memorize dull things? Also, with so much charm he is something of a con man. But I think he somehow will have a good life."[15]

Frances was mollified after Alice spent a day with both Peter and his youngest stepbrother, Louis: "Alice . . . called to tell me she thinks Louis is a 'fantastic' child, 'brilliant,' and a 'brilliant conversationalist,' 'utterly original,' etc. This will be useful, because up till now I think she didn't realize how valuable the friendship of both step-brothers is to the other. I think, for some reason, that all these children are quite remarkable."[16]

Alice's jobs, writing, and social life absorbed her, so she did no volunteer work at Town School beyond bringing cookies to the annual track meet in Golden Gate Park. For his part, nonathletic Peter saved face by winning the sack race—"being tall, I could jump"—and excelling at art. He received the school's Art Award for the third time at his eighth-grade commencement. His visual precocity extended to encouraging Alice to wear a dress he liked for the occasion: "It had big pink polka dots on it, fitted and flared." (It was the very dress that inspired Alice to go to Chapel Hill for the summer five years earlier.)

"This unmarried life is only possible if one is either very rich or has a very absorbing and successful career . . . this novel I'm hurrying through doesn't seem like any sort of solution, all this writing seems a great mistake," Alice wrote Barbara Mailer early in 1964.[17] She had staked a lot on the pages of the untitled, half-written novel that she'd given to Dodds. He told her it was "sprightly and gossipy" and she immediately worried that "sprightly" implied old age: "an alarming word—(she was 80 but quite sprightly)." John Leggett at Harper & Row liked it but didn't think it had a strong enough plot going yet to merit a contract. With the kind of assiduous effort that young writers think will help them succeed, Adams sat right down to read Leggett's own first novel (*Wilder Stone*, 1960) and found it "so *dreary*."[18]

In the spring of 1963 Alice had stopped working part-time at the art gallery and taken a new job as a typist at the Child Guidance Clinic of Children's Hospital in San Francisco. She had interesting friends in the office, including Jim Lamm, a psychiatrist who'd trained in Chapel Hill, and social worker Til Brunswick, who had grown up in Vienna, where her mother, Ruth Mack Brunswick, one of the few Americans in analysis with Freud, was a pioneer in analytic research. After a youth buffeted by psychoanalytic theory, world politics, her mother's early death due to morphine addiction, and some semesters at Reed and Black Mountain colleges. Til had married at nineteen and moved to California. After divorcing her husband, who'd been sent to San Quentin for unarmed robbery, she completed a degree in social work at Berkeley. She devoted herself to the practical aspects of helping people with problems and turned herself into an adult.

In her first job Til found that the work came naturally to her. "I was interested in what made people tick," she said. When Alice Adams came to work at the Child Guidance Center, she was hidden in a tiny office; rumor has it she sometimes lifted details for her fiction from the case histories she typed. When Til invited Alice to a party at her house, Alice told her she was "impressed because she'd never heard of another single woman inviting an attractive single woman to a party," Til remembered. "That started our long friendship."

Til Brunswick lived in a cottage on Russian Hill that she'd acquired with help from her grandmother's life insurance policy. Here she kept the Greek antiquities given her mother and herself by Freud, along with her family's eighteenth-century Salzburg armoire. Alice later took her friend's cottage as the model for Eliza's house in *Listening to Billie*: "On the eastern slope of Russian Hill . . . the total effect of the house was generous and comfortable, if a bit disheveled. It overflowed, literally, with books and records and magazines, usually with music and flowers and good smells of food."

Til noticed that Alice never went to lunch with coworkers—she was always writing. Despite the social and economic barriers she'd faced as a writer and wife, Alice did not call herself a feminist. "I don't find being a woman all that difficult, it's being human that's hard," she wrote Billy Abrahams after reading *The Golden Notebook* by Doris Lessing.[19] She was too devoted to love affairs, and too resistant to being like her mother to identify with the nascent women's movement. Yet, as her reaction to Til's invitation indicates, she was impatient with stereotypical rivalries between women (though not immune to them, of course). "Alice was just a free spirit," Til said. "She hadn't thought about 'feminism' yet and she had this aristocratic Southern background. Politically she was a socialist. I think her mother was similar—kind of a snob in some ways,

in other ways a complete radical." But Til was typical of Alice's women
friends in having an unusual, privileged childhood and challenging,
independent adult life.

One of Alice's Radcliffe friends had also come back into her life.
Ginny Berry, who had stood as maid of honor in Alice's wedding,
came to San Francisco in the 1950s to live with two aunts on Stanyan
Street and work as an economist at the Federal Reserve Bank. She had
a master's from New York University and next earned a law degree
from the University of San Francisco, a Jesuit institution, but worried
that she was unmarried at the advanced age of twenty-five. A bit later,
Alice learned that Ginny was "tremendously involved" with a man
she could not introduce to friends. Alice assumed the beloved was
married. "I would have wanted a more complete relationship for her,
of course," she wrote. "By that time I knew about the disadvantages
of the illicit myself." When Ginny became pregnant, Alice suggested
an abortion, but Ginny had her babies—twin boys—at a Catholic
home in another city. They were adopted and Ginny became an assistant professor in USF's school of business. Troubled by her friend's
evident loneliness, Alice challenged her for an explanation. Finally,
Ginny confided to Alice that her lover, the twins' father, was a priest.
Alice was outraged when she met the priest at a party and he (not
knowing that Alice knew he was Ginny's lover) proposed that Alice
help Ginny find someone to marry. Alice passed the priest's remark to
Ginny; after that, "some terrible drift apart began" and their friendship
went dormant.[20]

Judith Clark Adams and her five children visited San Francisco early
in 1966, en route to join Timothy Adams in Bangkok, where he had
become the regional director for the Peace Corps.[21] At a farewell party
given for Judith in Mill Valley, Judith saw that both Alice and the
attractive man at her side—his name was Bob McNie—"were drinking
heavily, more than others at the party." Alice's hair had gone prematurely
gray, she smoked, and "she was not svelte. She was beginning to look
like Agatha."

Alice's gig at Child Guidance was the first of several part-time jobs
she held at the medical institutions on the north side of the city that
proved financial lifesavers. If she'd lived in New York she might have
worked in editorial offices, but San Francisco was not a major publishing
center. Medical jobs proved easier to get—and easier to leave. Peter's

schoolmate Stephen Brown often saw Alice walking down Clay Street en route to work. "It seemed solitary and sad to me," Brown recollected. "I don't know if she felt that way. But to me it seemed unusual. I don't remember ever being in a car with Alice. She took the bus or walked. She was unlike the other Town School mothers—pedigreed and educated way more than they were but she was not one of them! They were society and she was not."

Alice never hesitated to quit office work in favor of writing. In early 1964 she left Child Guidance and began a lucrative freelance job for psychiatrist Meyer Zeligs. Zeligs had a two-thousand-page manuscript analyzing the personalities of accused communist Alger Hiss and his accuser, Whittaker Chambers. Alice found working for Zeligs "extremely interesting" until she had a dream in which Hiss confessed to her! She then decided Zeligs's project was "preposterous"—which also seems to have been the critics' view when it was published in 1967.[22]

Literary agent John Dodds kept the partial manuscript for Adams's novel moving in a frustrating comedy of errors. At Atlantic Monthly Press in Boston, the pages fell into the slush pile and were rejected outright until editor Peter Davison frantically called Dodds in New York to apologize that he hadn't read the manuscript. Back to Boston it went, where Davison requested more chapters and an outline. Adams already had five new chapters and banged out an outline within a week. This time, Atlantic responded with an offer of $250 for a right of first refusal on the book. Her editor would be her old friend from her Palo Alto days Billy Abrahams. But she was immediately frustrated by Abrahams's plan to spend the summer incommunicado in Maine working on his own book with his partner and coauthor Peter Stansky.

With hope of publication, Adams quit editing for Zeligs and applied to the Ingram Merrill Foundation for a fellowship. The letter Max Steele wrote in support of her application stands as the first coherent appreciation of Adams's fiction. He begins by admitting he found her work "too intensely feminine" when he was an editor at the *Paris Review*. But that feminine quality, he finds now, is a unique voice for writing truthful and distinguished fiction "about the physical and instinctual love of a mature woman." Adams's gift, he continues, is of "sounding light and frivolous and of being extremely readable while dealing with a bold honesty [with] the situations which envelop so much of the thought and feeling of modern woman."[23]

Adams described her novel in her notebook: "This novel is an on-the-whole amused look at San Francisco—specifically, at an enormous blonde divorcée, Daisy Duke Fabbrini, & her year in the sexual jungle. In the background are the city's incredible divorce & suicide rate, & rather kitsch social mores—and aberrant weather."[24] By the end of summer, Alice had titled her book *The Fall of Daisy Duke* and finished a first draft. Dodds thought it was marvelous, and everybody at Atlantic Monthly "adored" it.[25]

The euphoria ended when Abrahams and Davison submitted the book to senior editors at Little, Brown, publisher for all Atlantic Monthly books, who were "unrestrained in their dislike." Alice kept her long-spent advance and Davison, who became her friend during a visit to San Francisco, assured her that she'd be better off with a "more commercial" publisher; to his credit he also tried to help her find one.[26] For the next six months, *The Fall of Daisy Duke* made the rounds in New York, garnering rejections from Robert Gottlieb at Simon and Schuster, who called it "intelligent and pleasant" but "just didn't believe it"; Lee Wright at Random House; and other esteemed editors.[27]

On May 6, 1965, Alice and Peter met Diana and Max Steele for dinner at a Chinese restaurant. Alice told them about a depressing interview she'd had at a job agency and Max had a feeling "which comes when you can look at a person against everything that has ever happened to them or is likely to, when the film, which you've seen before, holds still and you can see the fear and isolation under the mascara, the bitterness which lipstick does not quite conceal—anyway it was that with her. The film had stopped. On the way home [he] kept wondering what could save her from becoming a bitter woman. The immediate answer was, of course, a sense of humor, but sometimes that's the first thing to turn bitter; and all in all it was depressing if you believe that bitterness is the real and maybe worst sin against the gift of life."[28]

The very next morning Alice received a jubilant call from her agent. David I. Segal, a thirty-seven-year-old editor at New American Library, was purchasing her novel for $2,000. Alice called the Steeles, who threw a celebratory party for her that very evening. Still, Alice worried that the phone call might have been a practical joke by Max, who boasted that he could impersonate Dodds's voice. Within days she had better evidence in a three-page critique from Segal that opened with these welcome words: "I would like to say, first of all, how pleased we all are that we will be publishing your book . . . it is cool, funny, and touching, and I think furthermore that you have a voice of your own which is original and accurate."[29]

Segal's interest in the novel was now equal to Adams's own. After a honeymoon of mutual praise and good humor, editor and author got down to the business of completing the book. Naturally, arguments ensued, most of which were resolved by means of some thirty mostly good-humored letters air-mailed between coasts. They particularly disagreed about what Daisy was "like" and whether Pablo was or should be "likable."

Segal insisted that he'd known some Daisy Dukes and that they were "characterized by a combination of hysteria and hopelessness generated by their sense of emptiness in their lives." Quickly Adams rose to her character's defense: "I know what you mean, but I thought Daisy was less hopeless, empty etc than those girls. She certainly isn't tragic like Mr. Styron's Peyton [in *Lie Down in Darkness*]. I wanted to emphasize her capacity for survival, what I like about her is a kind of life force quality, more action than introspection (she'd never do anything so neurotic as write a book) . . . I really mean to show that she could survive anything—up-and-down Daisy."

If Daisy isn't a Peyton Loftis, Segal proposed, perhaps she is more like Sally Bowles in Christopher Isherwood's *Goodbye to Berlin*. Not at all, Alice replied, her Daisy is not "epicene" like Bowles. Perhaps Alice went on, she is "a sophisticated Molly Bloom, a witty Emma Bovary—but all these references go very wrong for me. There is something in Mailer's new girl, Cherry [in *An American Dream*], but still not."

Regarding Pablo, Segal noted that Adams made it "overly clear that he is a bit of a poseur, a bit of a rake, and more than a little bit dishonest." He wanted Pablo to be attractive so he could believe in Daisy's love for him. Startled, Adams protested, "It seemed to me the point of the book was precisely that: his lack of orthodox attractiveness. This is one of the reasons that I originally wanted to call the book NEVERTHELESS— fat [but] nevertheless the most attractive man in the world." But Adams was a reasonable author, if not a sensible lover, and she admitted she'd "overdone the underplaying of his charm" and didn't want Daisy to look like an idiot.[30]

For all the resemblances that Daisy bears to her author, she remains an imaginary construct of her author's hopes and fears. Daisy is tall and large boned with no children; she is neither intellectual nor artistic nor self-reliant. She lives for love alone and the novel's story is one of resilience despite the damage love has done to her.

Segal accepted Adams's revised manuscript in September, but the novel still lacked a title. Adams sent dozens of suggestions. He turned hers down and sent back others. She turned his down. The one she hated most was "Love and Anxiety," which Peter Linenthal said sounded like a musical that just flopped. She held out for *The Fall of Daisy Duke*, the title under which the book would appear in England. But Segal preferred *Careless Love* and she learned to like it, surprised that no one had used the popular jazz-standard song title before. In a 1925 blues version by Bessie Smith, it's love itself that "brought the wrong man into this life of [hers]." Helen Merrill released her version of the song in 1965, but Adams was probably more familiar with W. C. Handy's "Loveless Love" lyrics sung to the same tune by Billie Holiday.

Other decisions quickly followed. Alice dedicated the novel to Diana and Max Steele. She went to Imogen Cunningham—whom she described as "an extremely good local photographer," though Cunningham had a national reputation—for her author photo, and hated the result: "[She] tends to take pictures of one's soul and mine was in bad shape just then."[31] Page proofs reached Alice on Christmas Eve.[32]

Once while teaching a writing class, Saul Bellow had blurted out to writer Bette Howland that he couldn't stand women writers who "wore their ovaries on their sleeves."[33] When he received proofs of *Careless Love*, Bellow said that he felt that personal contact disqualified him as a critic because he assumed that Daisy was Alice. "But I suppose that's proof of quality, since you came forward very clearly as a very charming woman, no nonsense, level-headed . . . It's an excellent portrait within its limits." The limits: "Women like your heroine do seem to live completely in relationships and think of very little apart from their own feminine happiness." The problem with that was that men were just as unreliable as in "poor Emma Bovary's time." He urged Alice to write "the last book in Bovary series. The woman who does that will be gratefully remembered."[34]

Norman Mailer read the book straight through when he got the proofs, then dallied over his response, then praised Alice for bravely overcoming her natural discretion to write about personal, painful events—"exposing the story must have opened at the same instant the desire to anesthetize the wound." But he complained that she'd failed to give any sense of whether Pablo was "a shit or a tragic man." Next, he told her, she must "start something which will enable you to explore into your biting sense of what is socially comic and maybe get it far enough away from yourself so that you don't have to hold back. You're a lady, dear prune-face, and lady writers were not meant to hold back their knowledge, because they don't know that much to begin with."*

With such friends, Alice needed her comic sense, and she used it to find flattery in Mailer's criticism: "What you're asking me to do, old friend, is either what James did or what no one else but you is doing now. As a matter of fact I don't agree with you as much about the lack of social milieu as I do about the depth—you're right, not probed, nowhere near final levels." Indeed, she said, it had not been painful to write the book: "As a matter of fact [it was] easy, which may explain deficiencies, so I don't even get points for courage." Her new novel would be "much more exacerbated" and more to Mailer's liking, she insisted.

Warning Adams about first-novel jitters, David Segal wrote a letter that belongs in the creative writing textbooks:

> There has probably never been a human being who has perpetrated a book and not in his or her secret heart been absolutely convinced it would get a front-page review in *The New York Times* Book Review section. Please repeat over and over to yourself every day until the

---

* Alice had seen Mailer when *Esquire* sent him to San Francisco in 1964 to cover the Republican Party convention that nominated Barry Goldwater for president, and again on May 21, 1965, when he was a keynote speaker at Berkeley's Vietnam Day Committee teach-in. Nothing Adams wrote would have satisfied Mailer, for whom, as Richard Poirier notes, war "determines the aspects of experience that are to be recorded and therefore the form of his books and of his career." (Poirier, *Mailer* [New York: Viking, 1972], 21.)

book is published, "I have produced a product for which there is no demand," which is, of course, the case. Nobody ever wakes up in the morning and says "Gee, I want to buy a book today." Of course what is going to happen almost immediately is that our relationship will change drastically. Up until now you considered me bright, sensitive, acute, even lovable. After all, I took the book. But in a few months you will notice there are no dirigibles flying over San Francisco skies writing CARELESS LOVE. Ed Sullivan is not inviting you to do a strip tease on his show; *The New Yorker* is not profiling you; in fact, almost nothing is happening. But let me tell you about the worst day. The worst day will be when the book is published—there will be no parades, people will not be breaking bottles of champagne over your head, Johnson will not be holding a press conference in your honor. There will be a tiny notice in *The New York Times* of books published today and perhaps one or two of your close friends will call up and say "Gee, your book is published today."

However, having painted the bleak picture I must say we do what we can. If you know anybody with a reputation who might be bludgeoned into saying something nice about the book, let me know and I will get galleys to them. They really should be either novelists, poets, or critics.[35]

Thus it was that galleys had gone out to Saul Bellow, Norman Mailer, and Irving Howe. No one was bludgeoned and no one offered a blurb. The book's white jacket had nothing on the back but Cunningham's photo of the author looking a bit frightened and matronly.* On publication day, Segal sent Alice a telegram and an advance copy of a paragraph in Martin Levin's omnibus "Reader's Report" column in the *New York Times Book Review*. Levin called *Careless Love* "fetching" and "wry" and "witty" and Daisy "emancipated but sentimental."[36] Other than that, the reviews were local: in the *San Francisco Chronicle* Maitland Zane called *Careless Love* the "best written of the rash of novels about this particular milieu" and then gratuitously mentioned that the author was

---

* The hardcover dust jacket was tasteful, with a small red heart standing in for the *V* in *Love*. But Alice was appalled by a sleazy 1967 Signet paperback that said "A Novel of Musical Beds" on the front. Agent Matson called that one "crass" and apologized but it sold over ninety-seven thousand copies. A 1989 Fawcett pocketbook reprint used the tagline "On the Cusp of Love" instead.

"the ex-wife of Professor Mark Linenthal of San Francisco State" and opined that "Daisy's anguished affair with a married Spanish banker sounds all-too-believable." But could Alice have expected more of a newspaper that captioned a picture of Governor Pat Brown and Cesar Chavez "Gripes among the grapes"? Elsewhere in the same paper a full-page picture of Jefferson Airplane celebrating the first appearance of a rock band at the Berkeley Folk Music Festival reminds us that the counterculture was then transforming San Francisco.[37]

In Chapel Hill's newspaper, retired journalism professor Walter Spearman issued a review that called Daisy "warm and vivid, a bit silly, romantic, eager to embrace life but not quite certain what life was except that it must contain a man." Spearman had an observation about the author photo that probably made Alice cringe: "The picture on the jacket of the book makes her look amazingly like her mother, Agatha Adams." He noted too that the novel was dedicated to Chapel Hillians Max and Diana Steele.

The Steeles, who with their baby Oliver Whittinghill Steele returned to Chapel Hill in the fall of 1966 when Max became the university's writer in residence, sent Alice the funniest response to her novel. Her parents' friend Dougald Macmillan had stopped by, Max wrote, to say that Alice's book had caused "a great deal of interest and talk around campus." Max's report to Alice continued,

> I said I can imagine and he gave a wicked smile and said yes indeed and of course there is talk that it may be autobiographical which makes it especially interesting here and I said you should be in S. F. where it is more interesting and causing more talk and he said he could imagine and I said I didn't think he could and he laughed nicely and said he would like to be able to imagine.

"He does have a wicked smile," Alice gamely replied.

From Chapel Hill Max again became a congenial correspondent. The Steeles' San Francisco house had been filled "with such anger," Alice confided to Lucie Jessner. "It's nice to be out of target range, which doesn't mean that I don't like and in many ways admire them."[38] Max resumed his role as Alice's conduit for news from Chapel Hill; the letters they exchanged for years to come remind us that gossip as a means of speculation is central to the making of novels of social comedy. Without gossip, as Cynthia Ozick writes, there are no stories and novels, no probing of motive and character, no interiority: "The gossiper strives to fathom the difference between appearance and reality, and to expose the gap between the false and the genuine."[39]

After reading *Careless Love*, Alice's son told her, "If I wrote your story it would be a comedy, but you would think it was a tragedy."[40]

As Alice approached her fortieth birthday, Peter was a sophomore at Lick-Wilmerding High School, a private, tuition-free boys' school on Ocean Avenue. She was proud to see that her fifteen-year-old son was "in some kind of creative explosion, paints all the time, enormous gorgeous things, a perpetual experiment." He took the streetcar across the city to school and, many afternoons, hitchhiked home by way of the Haight-Ashbury neighborhood. By 1966, the previously Irish and Russian immigrant area between Golden Gate and Buena Vista parks was home to a diverse mixture of bohemian, gay, and black residents and San Francisco State students. Activists had killed a redevelopment plan to run a freeway through the Golden Gate Park panhandle. Now the neighborhood included the Psychedelic Shop (head shop), the Straight Theater (concert hall), and the Diggers Free Store.

"You could buy the *Mojo-Navigator Rock & Roll News*, a mimeographed paper about the music scene," Peter said. "There was this feeling that something amazing is happening." *Rolling Stone* later estimated that there were about five hundred rock groups playing in the city during the late sixties.[41] With his stepbrothers Duncan and Louis Pain, Peter attended the first Bill Graham–produced concert in San Francisco. During these early days of San Francisco rock happenings, Peter helped a friend named Peter Kitchell put on light shows. Kitchell called his enterprise Lights by God! "We used an overhead projector and the faces from two clocks with oil and water between the pieces of glass to create that pulsating amoeba effect. We did it for high school parties." At Lick-Wilmerding their group called SFS—Students for Students—agitated for student power. Chet Helms (the music promoter and so-called father of the Summer of Love) gave the group a fund-raising dance at the Avalon Ballroom with Big Brother and the Holding Company and Quicksilver Messenger Service.

Peter designed a big poster for that dance and helped silkscreen it at a Sacramento Street gallery operated by a gay couple, Raymond Lew and Jim Kelly. "I hadn't seen a gay couple closely before, and I wondered how that worked," he said. Raising money for the school, Peter's friend Phillip Galgiani recalled, "was a way of getting involved in some real world activity, and finding a way to connect with all that neat stuff—the psychedelic shop, light shows, and dope—that was getting into full gear then."

Alice apologized to friends for Peter's appearance during what she hoped was just a "Haight-Ashbury hippie phase." He was six feet one inch or more and "terribly long-haired, ragged, hippy" but so "extraordinarily nice, talented, extremely funny" that she tried not to complain about his appearance. He was also "very politically involved, peace meetings. Like that. And pot."[42]

Alice Adams celebrated her fortieth birthday with Bob McNie, a man she'd known for two years—a tempestuous passage that requires its own chapter, which comes next. They hadn't been getting along well, and the situation wasn't helped when he took her on a tour of topless bars in North Beach on her birthday—"not the best possible introduction to being forty," she stated wryly in her essay "On Turning Fifty" some years later.

There was plenty to celebrate in 1966. At last she had published a first novel. On the day before her birthday she learned that Constable would publish it in Britain, using the title she liked, *The Fall of Daisy Duke*. Her new literary agent, Peter Matson, was bold about submitting her short stories to paying magazines. While many people in San Francisco felt threatened by the surge of counterculture in the Bay Area, Alice was politically sympathetic with the young people and confident of her son's ability to maintain the qualities she admired in him amid the cultural turmoil. Because her mother had been so harshly judgmental, she was determined not to criticize Peter. She sent pictures of his work to friends like Lucie Jessner and the Steeles.

A few weeks into her fifth decade, Alice had an emergency hysterectomy at Mount Zion Hospital and they took out her appendix as a bonus. "That's sort of like you take your child to the shoe store and they also give you a balloon," Fred Breier told Alice in his Viennese accent that so charmed her. Records show that Alice underwent a then-common removal of both fallopian tubes and ovaries, which causes a sudden depletion of hormones, or "surgical menopause." Alice never wrote about this change, and we don't know if she immediately took one of the newly available hormone replacement therapies.[43]

However she got through the changes, it appears Alice flourished in menopause. Nic Adams came to take care of his daughter when she got home from the hospital. "We oddly enough . . . had an absolutely marvelous time," she reported to the Steeles. "He is a most elegant old man, I must say—most attractive male nurse I've ever had."[44] While he was there, Nic purchased a big new refrigerator for her, primarily, she said, because he thought she needed an automatic icemaker. Perhaps that's also when Alice mentioned her mother's anger to Nic and he replied, "Don't you imagine that I got a lot of that too?" In her mind she responded, "Yes, but you deserved it—having affairs, drinking so much, just being so attractive, but I was just a child." Alice did not say that to her father then or ever.[45]

After the surgery, Alice bragged to the Steeles that she'd lost fifteen pounds and permanently given up her three-pack-a- day cigarette habit. In *Listening to Billie* she would describe months of feeling "lost, deprived" without cigarette in hand, followed by learning to write again.[46]

Nic's visit had gone so well that Alice agreed to visit him and Dotsie in Tucson, where he was a visiting professor at the University of Arizona. A newspaper columnist there reported that Professor Adams had hosted a party for friends to meet "his favorite author." When another Arizona paper interviewed Alice, she joked that she'd finished the book because her friends Diana and Max Steele had "threatened to publish [her] air mail postcards unless [she] wrote a book."[47]

"I think I am probably a good example of life begins at 40," Adams told the *San Francisco Examiner* in 1975. "Since then—I'm 48—they have all been an improvement. I began to come together after a long period of floundering."[48]

CHAPTER SEVENTEEN

Robert Kendall McNie

— 1964–1967 —

*It looked like its pictures only more beautiful. The shingles just
turning silver, the leaves of a wild rosebush beside the steps just
yellowing. Cynthia felt her face smile automatically, and at the
same time she felt a queasy excitement, in some unspecified place.*

—Alice Adams, "The Break-In,"
To See You Again

"I loved your hope for me that I have someone to be in love with,"
Alice replied in a letter to Lucie Jessner at the close of 1964. "I do,
but I'm not sure how 'appropriate' it is." *It?* After that witty grammatical
slippage, Alice explains that her love affair is with "an extremely handsome interior decorator, of all things, very sensitive and intense, but—of
course—troubled, just ending a 20-year marriage, unbusinesslike, etc. I
have an awful tendency to take on the role of therapist as well."[1]

The man in question was Robert Kendall McNie. They'd met in June
1964 at a party or on a blind date—which is unclear—drunk together,
come home together. They saw each other often—Alice brought Bob
to that farewell party when Judith Adams left for Thailand; he took
her to North Beach on her fortieth birthday. The relationship seemed
complicated. Alice considered, analyzed, revised. She dramatized their
first night together in a notebook entry:

> "Shall we fall wildly in love?" he asked, coming back into the room
> with what must have been their fifth drinks.
>   She was startled, but it was so much what she wanted—she was
> dying to be in love—that she forgot she didn't like him & said "Yes."[2]

Alice had doubts about Bob when she wrote those notes a year later on a page labeled "Stories." But had she really not liked him at first? Much of Adams's fiction explores the irrationality of sexual attraction. Especially after her divorce and after Vasco Pereira, she interrogated her actual and fictional relationships with a "fine satiric eye softened by tenderness toward human desire and frailty," as poet Susan Wood writes in her review of Adams's stories.[3] So it's no surprise that her feelings for Bob McNie mixed tenderness with cautious skepticism.

Nevertheless, she was hooked on Bob from the first night. He was tall, strikingly good-looking in a classic Anglo-Saxon manner, flamboyant, entertaining, creative. He had quit smoking in 1957 (well ahead of the surgeon general's 1964 report) and encouraged Alice to give up cigarettes too. Like her he carried a load of anxiety, and he understood the difficulties of turning imaginative endeavor into income. "Love without liking is anxious because empty . . . all unreal: similar gaps to be filled," Alice wrote in her notebook shortly after she met Bob.[4] Behind this worry about liking and gaps lurks the always seductive trope that lovers fulfill one another, forming together a Platonic whole. Alice played therapist to Bob in his "restive semi-married state"; later she faulted herself for not asking for what she needed of him: "I often give an impression of needing—demanding less than I actually do. An old trick of mine. I suppose from fear—don't ask." She learned that "old trick" from a childhood of shunned emotional demands.[5] What Adams did not say, but surely understood, was that an intuitive man like Bob McNie would have resisted explicit requests—as she did herself.

Alice dropped her architect lover Felix Rosenthal "like a stone" when she met Bob, though she saw other men from time to time.[6] McNie engaged her romantic energy and shared her bed during the months she was submitting, revising, and publishing *Careless Love*. Her professional success and apparent self-sufficiency appealed to him. Unlike most of the men Alice had known, McNie had no family connections or money or college education to ease or direct him in life. At the time they met, he was separated from his wife, Deen, who was also his business partner, and their three teenage children. He planned to divorce Deen but their finances were in disarray; their house in the Outer Sunset could not be sold because of a contractor's lien on it.

"I don't really like anything that's going on in my life right now," Alice complained as 1964 ended. "Bob at his best is marvelous," she said, "but too often drinks too much, too often away for weekends with kids, too unresolved in his own life. It's draining, you know." Her usual holiday gloom didn't help. The Steeles who were then still in San Francisco had given "the worst Xmas Eve party [she'd] ever been to, really ghastly . . . inadequate dinner, freaks sitting around on those kindergarten chairs."[7]

Bob shared his $200-a-month apartment in a Victorian on the edge of expensive Pacific Heights with his two older children, and Alice had fourteen-year-old Peter at home. On a typical weeknight, Bob would be nearly asleep with fatigue and drink when he came to see Alice. He seemed to her "an alcoholic of a somewhat original sort: apparently sober, at a given moment which became earlier & earlier in the evening, he would fall asleep—or do something in the area between falling asleep and passing out." For a while Alice was tolerant, "would somehow get him to bed, busy herself with the dinner dishes & go to bed herself. After a few hours he would wake & wake her. Then there would be intervals of love, of some talk—all of which later seemed unreal (esp if she had taken sleeping pills)."[8]

Bob warned Alice, "You're wasting your time with me . . . eventually I'll hurt you." Nonetheless, Alice felt "addicted" to him. "Bob and I seem better and better and better—I don't know. Sometimes I panic, can't bear being happy, or something," she wrote. She was aware of her tendency to wrap "rather simple unneurotic men in infinitely complicated emotions."[9] If he didn't answer all her needs, he at least held her attention. She wished he would be less flamboyant but found him entertaining, and they looked good together. By spring Alice had picked up Bob's joke of calling himself an "interior desecrator." He was, she realized, "the sort of very bright illiterate who learns by osmosis rather than by reading books—terribly aware of currents, fashion . . ."[10] She accompanied him on a photo shoot at the Sea Ranch residential development on the rugged Sonoma County coast, where he was designing furniture for Joseph Esherick's demonstration houses. Her story "Sea Gulls Are Happier Here" (in which a midthirties socialite meets and marries a younger man) takes its setting from that trip; a spread in the *San Francisco Examiner* showcased Bob's designs.[11]

During the months after Bob entered her life, while she was frustrated by his failure to complete his divorce, Alice thought she wanted "the kind of continuity which is probably only possible in marriage, maybe in an affair with more total rapport."[12] Such continuity was hardly possible in their situation, but Bob's very unavailability had another benefit. Alice had moments of real clarity: "A possible view: since I don't want to marry him (which *au fond* I'm sure is true) his situation helps me; ie. with his children we see each other less, I develop more of another life. I think this is the sanest position. Also, I will be the one to leave, which is important."[13]

By late summer of 1965, Alice had determined to break up with Bob but lacked the willpower to do it. As usual, she experimented with the idea in notes for a story: "She sometimes wished he would tell her that he was, after all, going back to his wife. She knew exactly what she'd say: 'Why don't you all hold hands and jump off the bridge instead?' Also, she would start smoking again."[14]

She didn't say that when Bob left her in November as the year was "plunging down to dark rain."[15] Alice felt he wanted her to suffer and beg for him the way Deen was doing. "He uses Deen against me," she said, "telling me of her misery as though I have caused it; also saying, 'You see? Everyone wants me, such a prize I am.' "[16] He didn't return to Deen and before long he and Alice were seeing each other again. She didn't resume smoking. "Preconception—an affair that ends in pain rather than marriage is a failure," she wrote in her notebook.[17] With writing and self-analysis she seemed to be developing a life less dependent on love affairs. Her understanding of how Bob might be playing her against Deen was also, perhaps, the dawning of a feminist consciousness.

When she was critical of Bob, Alice wondered if she "subscribed to a form of the Protestant ethic: sin which you don't enjoy was less sinful." She tried to work it out in her notebook as some kind of fictional algebra: "the gymnastics which were X's notion of making love were not love, not fun, had nothing to do with Y." Be that as it may, when they were apart she missed him sexually ("that long smooth strong marvelous curve").[18]

Bob McNie's divorce was finalized in September 1966, soon after the publication of *Careless Love* and about the same time Alice had her hysterectomy. A few months later Bob moved into Alice's flat on Clay

Street. Bob treated Peter Linenthal as a friend, took his art seriously, and brought him gifts of art supplies.

Before he was divorced, Bob had been sensitive about keeping up appearances as a father and discreet about his relationship with Alice. Now he introduced his children to her. Morissa and Robbie were on their own, receiving little financial support from their father, while Joch (Winky) stayed with his mother. Robbie remembered meeting Alice when he was about sixteen: "She was an interesting looking woman, handsome in all regards. She wasn't beautiful, her teeth weren't perfect, but she had a lot of character. And she was rather statuesque, large busted, voluptuous, in a sophisticated slinky black knit dress with pearls, very elegant. She was sedate but she was a Leo and there was a kind of lionesque quality about her." Morissa believed that Alice did not have "an exciting life. She sequestered herself in the mornings to write and then went to a doctor's office and greeted people. She was shy and dressed very frumpily."

Bob began to decorate the apartment soon after he moved in with Alice, adding finds from Cost Plus at Fisherman's Wharf, which was like a huge exotic marketplace: Chinese ceramics, Indian embroideries. And he recommended beautiful, simple, elegant clothes for Alice. From a tailor, she ordered dresses made "exactly like shirts": "a long sleeveless grey flannel, short long sleeve grey flannel, short offwhite silk pongee, short blue & white polka dot—all shirts," she wrote Max Steele, recommending that "Miss D." (Diana Steele) would be "smashing in a yellow satin shirt, very narrow with button down collar."[19] Bob's Pygmalion effect on Alice was balanced by the transformation that took place within her when *Careless Love* was published.

Even though the initial response to *Careless Love* had been exactly as quiet as David Segal had led her to expect, becoming a published author rather than an aspiring writer made a huge difference to Alice. Around that accomplishment, the rest of her life began to fall into place, with Robert McNie as partner in this change. He was "a show in and of himself—ascots, big sweeping statements, he loved entertaining . . . he was ahead of his time in ideas and color combinations," their young friend Deborah Sparks remarked. "Dinner with Bob and Alice was always elegant, with a silver candelabra on the circular table. Wine and conversation flowed." And photographer Fred Lyon recalled, "We all urgently need to laugh. Alice could make fun of herself. I can still hear her voice and her laugh." To Lucie Jessner, Alice wrote, "We seem to get along best when playing house. In fact we get along increasingly well. If, as an astute friend of mine remarked, we only don't louse it all up by getting married."[20] Luckily marriage was an endeavor and a formality that neither Alice nor Bob wished to repeat.

An only child born in Long Beach in 1925, Robert McNie was raised by his divorced, Scottish-immigrant mother, Helen Kyle, in Santa Barbara and San Luis Obispo. He served in the US Merchant Marine before the end of World War II, then returned to San Luis Obispo to marry his high school sweetheart, Davideen Ball (her father wanted a boy), who was now a beauty queen at the nearby state agricultural college known as Cal Poly. Both eager to leave the small town behind, the McNies arrived in San Francisco in 1945. The city was then full of young people, especially ex-navy and merchant marine personnel beginning their postwar lives. Bob first sold encyclopedias for a New York firm, then furniture at the Union Furniture Company. Architect Mario Gardano noticed Bob's taste and suggested he open his own business. He called his tiny shop downtown Studio Contemporary. Deen worked as a telephone operator, kept the books for Bob's business, and did upholstery work for his clients. Julio Gallo, a founder of the Gallo Winery, and his wife, Aileen, hired Bob to furnish their new home next to a vineyard in Modesto. The Gallos "kind of put him on the map," Morissa McNie said, but "they would call him at eleven at night to do something like drive two hours to Modesto the next day and help them decide about an ashtray. It wasn't easy." When he worked with architects and clients to design interior spaces, Bob's quick, detailed ink drawings and watercolor renderings would sell a scheme quickly. "He knew what he wanted on every level and it was all independent—he would have things made—so his drawings were really loved by the workmen who had to carry out his plans, from ironworkers to seamstresses."

Bob and Deen dressed elegantly and attended events such as the Opera Ball, where Bob met future clients. His severe profile became more handsome as he aged; Deen lightened her hair and her dramatic features began to look haunted. They took up skiing and she designed a line of skiwear, DEEN San Francisco. "Bob had such energy," photographer Fred Lyon said of those days. "He was one of the prettiest skiers I've ever seen—that was more important to him than being an accomplished skier." After the winter Olympics in Squaw Valley in 1960, they purchased five acres and a rustic early-century house near Lake Tahoe. Built with the timbers of an old logging flume, the house sat on the edge of the Truckee River, surrounded by meadow and forest. From this base, McNie continued his social climbing and expanded his business, becoming known as the "only heterosexual decorator in San Francisco."*

While Bob's business flourished, Deen was increasingly at home with her sewing machine and the duller tasks of making ends meet and looking after their three children—Morissa (Missy), born 1947; Robert Kyle II, 1950; and Joch Allin (Winky), 1951. Deen's isolation was magnified by the winning, flirtatious personality by which her husband engaged his clients. As Bob was appearing in newspaper photos in company with San Francisco society women, Deen made the mistake of falling in love with one of their husbands and telling the man so. Rebuffed, she became despondent. She made black curtains for their house—which was already draped in fog most days—because she wanted it dark inside.

During the time Bob was pursuing a divorce, Deen threatened suicide and asked Bob to come back to her. He was "very torn at the time," Alice recalled. But in his divorce settlement, Bob kept their mountain house and Deen received only $25 a month in alimony. "I think the judge didn't like that woman," Alice commented.[21] Later Deen had a mental breakdown and received a diagnosis of schizophrenia. Her daughter, Morissa, and her friend the therapist Deborah Sparks later theorized that Deen had not been schizophrenic or otherwise mentally ill "but rather that she was a frustrated housewife of the fifties who became increasingly controlling."

Curiously, Adams barely mentioned Bob McNie in her notebooks after he moved into her apartment. Almost every entry pertains to a novel (called "Mothering") or stories in progress. Such notes as there are suggest contentment, even happiness and pleasure: "Bob—that gently sensual motion of his wrist."[22]

---

* "Can't imagine that you found a heterosexual decorator in S.F. Maybe that's why he's alcoholic. Used to be a heterosexual decorator in Houston but he went broke," Jack Boynton wrote Alice on January 14, 1965.

"*Every* time we met for lunch," Sandy Boucher recalled, "Alice *had* to tell me how handsome he was. Her message was I am so lucky because I am homely and he is this beautiful creature." Alice recognized Bob's flaws but excused them because "if you fall in love with inferior men you can't then blame them for being inferior."[23] His dandyism, self-involvement, and habit of nodding off at the dinner table were hard to miss. In one line she summed up his vanity: "I've a surprise for you—himself in a new suit." Not the least of Bob's vanities was pride in his genital endowment, noted by Alice as "their shared adoration of his sex."[24]

Bob shuttled about the city, down the Peninsula, and across the bridges in a big black Ford station wagon that he named Black. It was crammed with materials he had scavenged, bought, and stored for projects. His studio, a former butcher's storefront on Powell near Washington Square Park with a bedroom and office in the back, also overflowed with finds. Jane Kristiansen had her graphic design studio next door, and Alice was jealous of Bob's closeness to Kristiansen until he invited her to dinner. Then they all bonded over Alice's cats, especially Fergus—Ferg—a haughty Manx. When Kristiansen met her life partner, Patty O'Grady, they celebrated with another dinner. After a lot of wine, Alice began to giggle when she learned that she and Patty and Jane went to the same dentist. When this dentist leaned over his patients "his private parts would be right there, almost in your face," Jane recalled. "It turned out we'd all three had the same vision of just grabbing him by the balls! So we were all rolling on the floor laughing, but Bob was stone-faced—that was not funny to him." Patty said, "Alice was a shy snob, but it was different after she got to like us."

Bob was extremely proud of his house on the Truckee River, which he'd decorated in the roughhewn style that was his trademark. Though it was poorly insulated and had difficult-to-access upstairs sleeping rooms, the house had a massive stone fireplace, a large hand-painted dining table, and a kitchen facing the stream.[25] Alice shared Bob's pride: "This weekend we are going up with some of the children to his house in the mountains; it's really the most beautiful house I've ever seen. Completely simple, completely elegant." As her story "The Break-In" illustrates, Alice worried that loving this house so much would require her to become "more concerned with owning and taking care of things, better at cleaning up." In fact, she was taking bulbs to plant around the house. "I think it's terribly funny that at 41 I suddenly find that I just want a lot of children [meaning the teenagers] and a garden—a far cry from any notions I had at 20."[26]

A far cry too from the frustrations of the past twenty years. "My new conclusion is that unmarried living together is the best of all possible worlds—everyone feels more free (although in actuality is probably more bound)," Alice told Lucie Jessner.[27]

Had she found it at last, that rare thing for a woman artist, a relationship with a man that nourished her self and her art? In her notebook for 1967, she wrote, "They lay together as close as 2 spoons, her breasts mashed against his back, his buttocks against her lower belly. This was incredibly fulfilling to Avery; his body against her thus atoned for all loss, his strength became hers." Alice's childhood longing for "bodily family warmth was fulfilled."[28]

CHAPTER EIGHTEEN

The A B D C E Formula

— (1966–1969) —

"I took a writing course one summer vacation, at home in Chapel Hill, from Phillips Russell. He said that most short stories could be divided into three, or sometimes five sections, or acts. He wrote outlines for both methods on the blackboard."

—Alice Adams, "Why I Write"

I f domestic comfort gave Alice strength in her writing career, she certainly needed it. The month after *Careless Love* appeared, she sent David Segal a revised section of a new novel. He declined it. "The new book appears to be your effort to rear back and throw the high-hard one or, if you don't follow baseball, write a big, serious and important novel. It just doesn't appear as though this is your metier." This manuscript has not survived. Adams's notebooks suggest that with titles such as "Mother's Will" or "The Witch Is Dead," it was about a family based on Nic and Agatha that appears again in the Todd stories in *Beautiful Girl*. Segal wondered if Adams was frightened of this new material because he sensed "strain and lack of confidence in the writing." His observations were likely correct, but his prescription that she give up that book and return to her forte of "the wry look at contemporary manners and morals," may have been wrongheaded.[1] Alice reacted to Segal's letter with relief, "something like: thank God, now I won't have to write that bloody book."[2]

Notwithstanding, Alice did need to write about this family mate-rial and she continued working on it. A year later Segal, now at Harper & Row, responded to a revised version called "Mothering" with the devastating comment that Adams might have been "a highly intelligent and gifted amateur who managed to pull off a successful book once." More specifically, Segal complained—insightfully—that Adams seemed "rather bored and bitter about intellectual life in SF and that this feeling permeates and deadens" her book. He missed the "light touch" of *Careless Love*.[3]

Thus instructed, Adams rewrote the novel as "A Spell in San Francisco," but Matson did not show it again to Segal.* Peter Kemeny at Viking turned down the San Francisco novel two years later with extended regret and detailed suggestions for making its older woman narrator more "acerbic, wise, cantankerous" as a way to deepen the novel's view of fashionable San Francisco.[4] Another year passed as Adams revised and changed titles again, this time with help from Billy Abrahams, who had moved to Palo Alto with his partner, historian and now Stanford professor Peter Stansky, to be Atlantic Monthly Press's West Coast editor. Matson was satisfied with the new version and reported, in January 1971, that Stein & Day were about to buy it. They did not. The manuscript has not survived.

As she came to loathe writing that novel, Adams much preferred writing stories. And, because she was now a published novelist, Peter Matson had some luck selling those stories to the women's magazines that then carried several pieces of fiction per issue. In *Cosmopolitan*, Helen Gurley Brown's reconfigured magazine aimed at single women, "Sea Gulls Are Happier Here" appeared alongside a story by Iris Murdoch. "Henry and the Pale-Faced Indian," a spoof of a Jewish man who pretends to be Native American or Negro to impress liberal Californians, also found a berth in *Cosmo*, while "Young Couple With Class," the story about her prosperous neighborhood, garnered $1,000 (with which Alice bought "a pretty little brown Austin" sports car)[5] and a full spread and author photo in *Redbook*. Those sales brought nice checks, but Alice considered the stories negligible and never collected them in books. Worse, her agent typecast her as a writer who appealed just to "the ladies," as women's magazines were known.

The popular magazine editors rejected many stories but wrote notes to try to explain their decisions—hence, Adams saw them described as

---

* Just before Christmas 1970, David I. Segal, who by then had moved to Knopf, died of a heart attack at age forty-two.

"repulsive," "ugly," "slight," "unlikable," "perverse," "disagreeable," "too sophisticated," and otherwise unappealing to their readers. She saved a dreary file folder full of such letters that Matson passed along to her. From a *Saturday Evening Post* editor she learned that the majority of *Post* readers "would feel that any kid that smoked pot deserved to be miserable," while Leonhard Dowty at *Good Housekeeping* remarked that Adams's work belonged at *Cosmopolitan*: "Eve's approach for landing a man (spending a weekend with him right after she has met him for the first time)," he explained, "just isn't our idea of boy-meets-girl." About a near-miss at the *Ladies' Home Journal*, Phyllis Levy hazarded: "I guess the vote went against on acc't of the old prejudice against divorced women finding Happiness."[6]

Once in a while Adams heard an encouraging word. While buying "Young Couple with Class," Bud Hart of *Redbook* asked Matson, "Is the author new? . . . [S]he reminds me of the *good* John Cheever of a few years ago." Adams worried that stories tailored or edited to fit the women's magazines were dishonest because they "glossed over what [she knew] to be horrible" in people's motivations and behavior. She urged Matson to try her work at the *New Yorker*, *Esquire*, or *Playboy*, suggesting that it might help to use a male pseudonym.[7]

Matson argued that every magazine favored stories that met its formula, noting that the *Saturday Evening Post* had just published a story by Margaret Drabble that the *New Yorker* had rejected as too erotic. "People don't often go to bed together in the pages of *The New Yorker*, at least not with pleasure; and, to the literary magazines a well plotted story is looked upon with suspicion," he explained. Nonetheless, Matson agreed that Adams's newest story was not for a women's magazine. He sent "Remember the Night They Drew the Swastika on Our Door?" to the *New Yorker*.[8]

The reply was swift and marvelous. Bob Hemenway, a part-time fiction editor at the magazine, liked the story and pushed it through the unpredictable and enigmatic comment process that culminated in approval by editor William Shawn. This was, Adams later said, the first story she'd written that really pleased her, that she "knew to be good."[9] The germ of it came from a quarrel between two of her European friends, Fred Breier and Franz Sommerfeld. "Moved and disturbed" by the quarrel between the two men, who had been close since their days in Berkeley, Adams shaped her distress over the broken friendship into an insightful story. She changed European-Jewish Fred and Franz into Southern brothers named Washington who were history majors at Harvard in the summer of 1943, the year that Adams arrived at Radcliffe. The two brothers, fat Roger and thin, heart-unhealthy Richard, share a room in the Adams House and become isolated eccentrics who speak in the "Polite Southern" dialect Alice so disliked. "It was as though I could not learn to write until I learned to master what was, after all, my earliest language." Taking the class in postwar problems that Adams herself took in 1944, the brothers opine that "the chief postwar problem is what to do with the black people." The Washingtons' sick, semi-ironic jokes win them no friends. Someone chalks a swastika on their door and calls them Southern fascists. The incident justifies, for Richard, "all his sense of the monstrosity of the outside world." That moment becomes, in Richard's life and in the story, an emblem of the private world he shares with no one but his brother. It also signifies the moment where their lives diverge. After the night of the swastika, Roger changes his major to economics so he can become rich; Richard switches to Greek and expects to remain "land poor."

"The Swastika on Our Door" uses the five-act formula Adams learned in Phillips Russell's writing class in North Carolina: Action, Background, Development, Climax, Ending. The structure served her well for a long story that covers several decades and four central characters. In the opening action, Roger's wife of some years, Karen Washington, discovers a photograph of her husband with his brother and a "long-necked beautiful dark girl" whose eyes are "very narrow and long, like fish." She is Ellen, who was Richard's girlfriend when he died shortly before Karen married Roger. Tellingly, Roger has never spoken to Karen about Ellen.

Even though the conflict that drives this story is between the two brothers, Adams's characterization of Karen and Ellen is critical. For Karen, she probably drew upon her friend Virginia Silverman Breier, who had married Fred Breier in 1960. Virginia Breier was English—"handsome, regular features, sunlighted streaks in her hair, resembled Vanessa Redgrave," according to Peter, so Adams disguised her life model by making Karen Erdman Washington a "big, dark, handsome" German Jew from an old San Francisco family. Ellen must be the story's version of Alice Adams; she dates Roger first, and he advises her that with her lovely eyes and legs she could marry a rich man. She resents that reckoning of her exchange value and is instead drawn to the wild intensity and loneliness of Richard: "Ellen experienced with Richard a reduction of the panic in which she normally lived." Richard has remained an outsider, a teacher of Greek who lives in a hotel, has few friends, and devotes himself to scholarship and music. But he is jealous of Roger's life with "San Francisco's very solid merchant upper class: German-Jewish families who had had a great deal of money for a long time." He cherishes his days at Harvard with his brother, when he and his brother were outcasts—together. At Roger and Karen's engagement party he makes a scene by asking loudly, wildly, "Say, Roger, remember the night they put the swastika on our door?"

The story climaxes in Richard's sudden (though not unexpected) heart attack and death. Ellen reacts with equanimity at first, "holding her hands tightly together in her lap, as though they [contain] her mind." Later, seemingly on Richard's behalf, Ellen phones Roger to excoriate him: "Horrible fat ugly murdering pig, you killed him with your never time to see him . . . Richard was all Greek to you and you never tried to learn him, how lovely he was and suffering and you found him not socially acceptable . . . you and your blubber neck and your compound interest." Roger offers money to Ellen. Further outraged, she hangs up. A few weeks later she has a nervous breakdown.

Adams ends her story in the day and place where it begins, Karen and Roger Washington's comfortable but "unwieldy" Pacific Heights home, where the two talk calmly about poor dead Richard and his "mad" (unstable) girlfriend, Ellen. Roger has by now convinced himself that Ellen wanted money because, Adams's omniscient narrator suggests, he believes "that other people's motives [are] basically identical to his own." Karen, the good wife, accepts that explanation and offers her husband more coffee: "Poor darling, you look as though you need it."

Adams leaves her readers to wonder what Ellen really meant to say to Roger and who, among Ellen, Roger, and Karen, is the more mad. That essential artist's question had particular weight for Alice Adams because she lived within the margins of the social class where Karen and Roger thrived. Virginia Breier and Alice exchanged letters when the Breiers spent a year in Europe and relied on Alice to care for their cat while regaling her with anecdotes from their travels. Alice admired and perhaps envied the Breiers and was fascinated by many upper-class San Franciscans. But in not glossing over the "horrible" family secrets that compromised a "happy ending"—and in selling this story to the

New Yorker—she moved from the "ladies' magazine" genre into complicated short fiction.

Adams's success in this transition was aided by Robert McNie. She read stories aloud to him and credited his "total aesthetic sense" with helping her find the best order for the elements of a story. He said "large, helpful things" about "Swastika": "I knew it was better than anything I'd written before, and Bob said 'Why is that there?' The sections of the story were in a quite different order, and I changed it considerably." His interest, combined with the ABDCE five-act structure, was a great boon for a writer who cared more about character than she did about plot.*[10]

Novelist Rosellen Brown, reviewing Adams's stories collected in *Beautiful Girl* (1979), noted that in "The Swastika on Our Door," Adams boldly adopts what Brown called a "novelist's prerogative" of giving her characters "all the time in the world: they did not hinge on the decisive move, the irretrievable statement. These are aerial views: the author sweeps in to overhear intimate conversation, then withdraws again." Adams had been working on such stories for a long time, but "Swastika" confirms her genius for giving the "sense of an entire life compressed and summarized" in a short story. Adams's Canadian contemporary Alice Munro has been credited for revolutionizing "the architecture of short stories, often beginning a story in an unexpected place then moving backward or forward in time." Interestingly, both Alices began publishing widely at about the same time, and both eventually won serious attention for short stories with long time frames.[11]

In Bob McNie, Alice had a partner who embraced but did not crush her identity as an artist. Under Bob's tutelage, with short, silver-gray hair and a more sophisticated wardrobe, Alice looked entirely chic. Her Southern flirtatiousness grew into mature charm, while her voice, with its Bostonian accent and traces of patrician Virginia, set her apart

---

* It's unlikely that Adams read every story she wrote aloud to McNie, but she knew the value of giving him some credit for her success. She also told Max Steele that his story "Where She Brushed Her Hair" helped by reminding her to get "everything out of a scene."

in the West. She and Bob together were known as a stylish, talented couple in the city. Alice's animus against San Francisco's provincialism and self-congratulatory tendencies faded. Asked why she didn't live in New York, she said it would be culturally "overwhelming," but of course she'd remained in San Francisco so Peter could be near his father and friends. After 1966, she also stayed because Bob McNie had his business in Northern California. Nonetheless, Alice continued to lambast San Francisco as "exquisitely beautiful but culturally deprived," with an affluent class devoted to "vacuous, self-indulgent values . . . an appalling place to live if you're not busy and happy."[12]

She was both. Like Eliza Quarles at the end of her novel *Listening to Billie*, Alice now found her work "a source of steady happiness." And San Francisco, despite its failings, offered a new laboratory for studying the human scene: a counterculture whose epicenter was about a mile from the apartment she shared with her son and Bob McNie.

Peter Linenthal was a high school sophomore—almost sixteen—when he attended the Human Be-In in January 1967. "I remember the sea of people suddenly visible as I came through the entrance tunnel onto the Polo Fields in Golden Gate Park. I think everyone was a bit shocked there were so many of *us*. This was where Town School held those annual track meets—and now it was filled with all kinds of people in interesting odd clothes, long hair. There was lots of pot smoking, some dancing, alone and in couples." Peter wandered along the edge of the crowd "just taking it in."

The Be-In's organizers wanted to unite hippies and the antiwar activists in a "children's crusade that would save America and the world from the ravages of war, and the inner anger that brings it forth, and materialism," radio host Elizabeth Gips explained. Gandhi and Martin Luther King were their heroes. With the belief that American culture was a dead end, they studied Asian mysticism and metaphysics along with pre-Christian mythologies. At the polo field that day Timothy Leary protested the recent criminalization of LSD and urged listeners to "turn on, tune in, drop out." Other men on the speaker's platform included Richard Alpert (Baba Ram Dass), Jerry Rubin, and Buddhist leader Suzuki Roshi. At some point, someone cut the electricity, so there were "no speeches, no music. Only the murmur of 25,000 people, most of them on LSD, grooving with each other, with the sunshine which had come in the midst of a rainy month, and with the manifest presence of Spirit."[13]

The Be-In initiated the movement that eventually brought a hundred thousand young people to San Francisco for the Summer of Love. For Alice's son, the tidal wave of cultural change was irresistible—and yet he surfed it with excitement rather than rebellion. He came from families where leftist politics and opposition to the war in Vietnam were a given. Allen Ginsberg, warbling East Indian chants and playing his concertina onstage at the Be-In, was the poet his father had defended in court a decade earlier. His mother had lunch with Norman Mailer on the day he delivered his famous "Hot Damn, Vietnam!" tirade against President Lyndon Johnson to a crowd of twenty thousand on a Berkeley soccer field. "The President's mind," Mailer said then, "has become a consortium of monstrous disproportions," torn asunder by the realization that American capitalism "cannot survive without an economy geared to war."[14]

For his junior and senior years of high school, Peter Linenthal transferred to Washington High School, a public school on the north side of Golden Gate Park. "It was the feeling of the sixties," Peter said of his decision. "I wanted something bigger. I'd lived in this isolated group of boys. At Washington, there were girls and it was racially mixed. I liked it. The black kids mostly stayed with each other but we were all in that school. Sometimes friends and I skipped school altogether and hitchhiked to Mt. Tamalpais for the day."

Early in 1968, when the Tet Offensive showed the US war effort to be chaotic and possibly doomed, President Johnson declined to run for reelection. "With rather little enthusiasm," Alice voted for the antiwar candidate Eugene McCarthy in the 1968 California Democratic primary, hoping, she said, that "he and Bobby [Kennedy] can somehow combine against that lobotomized prostitute (HHH, in case one wonders which one)."[15] On the night of the primary, Robert Kennedy was assassinated in Los Angeles. Hubert H. Humphrey won the party's nomination and lost the November presidential election to Richard Nixon. Perhaps thinking he'd be safer outside of the country, Peter's parents let him go to Europe with a Eurail pass for the summer. He flew Icelandic Airlines (a turboprop-plane bargain that took some fifteen hours to cross the Atlantic) to join Stephen Brown in London. "I'll never understand why our parents let us travel by ourselves," Brown recalled. "I was sixteen and Peter was seventeen! My mother knew that Peter was a responsible influence. I was wilder." In London they found a copy of *The Fall of Daisy Duke*, just published there with a Barbie Doll–ish blonde on its cover, and delivered a portfolio of Peter's drawings to the Slade School of Fine Art, where he planned to apply. While students rioted in Paris and Czechs challenged the Russian occupation in Prague, Peter and Stephen did the 1960s version of a grand tour—Wales, Scotland, Italy, Austria, France. They carried big green Kelty frame packs—"we looked like we were carrying kitchen cabinets on our backs," Brown said—and smoked hashish in Paris. Peter nearly blacked out after taking "German No-Doz" that a Vietnam veteran gave him on a train. Still, Brown remembered the trip "as an artistic opening for me—we did go to museums. It has affected my whole life. I think Alice and Mark saw Peter's artistic talent and wanted him to have this experience." At a B&B in Fishguard, Wales, Peter heard Otis Redding's new song about San Francisco Bay. "That made us homesick."

Dramatic changes awaited them. San Francisco State College students went on strike for five months in support of demands by the Black Students Union and the Third World Liberation Front and against the policies of college president S. I. Hayakawa and Governor Ronald Reagan. The Poetry Center became an organizing office, and Mark Linenthal was one of fifty professors who joined the picket line in support of students. That was "a moment of moral decision for Mark," according to poet Linda Chown, who worked at the center then.

After Bob McNie moved into Alice and Peter's apartment, his three children also entered Alice's world. Morissa, who was artistic and working, she considered her "adopted" daughter. Robbie, who had dropped out of high school, was less to her liking. He wore his thick, wavy brown hair to his shoulders and was, Peter then thought, "self-confident and dazzlingly good-looking."

Six teenage boys belonged to the associated Linenthal-Pain-Adams-McNie families, so the military draft was a worry to these parents who believed the war in Vietnam was wrong. "Peter will be some form of objector, but we don't know how or where," Alice wrote a friend as her son's seventeenth birthday neared.[16] He met with Quaker counselors to establish his conscientious objection, then with a psychiatrist, Dr. Norman Gottreich, who declared him unsuitable for military service.* After high school, he enrolled as a full-time student at the San Francisco Art Institute. The draft lottery took the pressure off of him in mid-1970, when he was assigned the number 170. Induction orders for his eligibility year, 1971, stopped at 125.

Led by Lincoln Pain, who worked actively against the war and counseled men about ways to avoid the draft, all three of Frances Linenthal's sons avoided induction. Winky McNie had psychotic symptoms that disqualified him, while his older brother, Robbie, took a more dramatic route. He received a notice to appear for a physical shortly after he turned eighteen in 1968. Having already decided that "the war seemed an error—[he] wasn't concerned about being killed," he set out to prove his unsuitability by performing a classic San Francisco caper: climbing the Golden Gate Bridge—and making sure he got caught. A friend dropped him off and headed to a pay phone to report sighting a climber; Robbie ascended through the fog on the nonskid surface of the main cable toward the north tower. As he told the tale:

> The fog cleared when I was above the last crosshatch on the tower. I saw the traffic lane blocked off and news media arriving. Two painters came out of the tower elevator and started down the cable toward me. I stepped outside the handrail, but I got a tremor in my legs. The painters were saying things like, "Don't jump, come on over for spaghetti tonight." If I'd been suicidal, they would have influenced me not to jump. But now we're at a standstill. I'm looking down four hundred feet at the water and the news media are fighting each other for the best angle.
>
> Two older jarhead cops came up. I feared they might try to grab me. I stepped back in. The painters snapped a safety belt on me and we all walked down the cable with them in control of my line to a Highway Patrol car. The guy in shotgun was talking about me in third person—do you think he's on PCP? I didn't speak a word for three and a half days to anyone about anything.

---

* "He wrote a letter that would get me out and I assumed it said I was gay but I don't think I ever saw the letter," Peter said. "I'm so lucky I was in a world where alternatives existed. At the Art Institute I knew guys who'd gone [to war] and had a terrible time, but had no idea they could figure out a way not to go."

I arrived at the County General Psych Ward as the local evening news was coming on and I was the lead story. They called me a young carpenter—well, I'm imposing that, the Christ thing, but I'd hit the nail right on top of the head, absolutely perfect. The psychiatric staff had no clue after they checked my blood for amphetamines. A young volunteer from Pacific Heights said to me, "Did you do this to get out of the draft?" I almost dropped my teeth but kept my composure. I wanted to tell her yes because she, the weakest link in the whole psychology team, was the only one with enough perception to see that.

After seven days Robbie McNie was released. When he next received a notice from his draft board, he sent it back marked "LAST KNOWN ADDRESS COUNTY GENERAL PSYCHIATRIC WARD." He also went to see a well-known pacifist psychiatrist:

I told this psychiatrist my story, and he said, "I could kiss you, man!" He got my records from County General and wrote a cover letter that basically said, "I dare you to take him. This guy has a problem with authority. And he'll turn at some point. You want him, you can have him." I got a 1-Y, meaning they might call me up in a national emergency or if borders were attacked.[17]

To support himself Robbie sold marijuana in the Haight, as much as two kilos a night at ten dollars an ounce. He and a partner "would pay $60 for a kilo and take in $340 in retail sales," he said. They also rolled joints by the hundred that they served to friends from an old Chinese box. Robbie hung out with Peter and the Pain brothers in the attic room of the Linenthals' house on Jordan Avenue—"a bunch of people all kind of lived upstairs in the big attic. Anybody that came over got their own joint." Neither of Peter's parents, having used it themselves, objected to marijuana but they tried to set limits. One morning, Alice saw Peter and Stephen Brown smoking on the front porch as she left for work. She shook a finger at them, as if to say, "Come on, Peter, wise up—don't smoke on your way to school."

Adams encapsulated her keen sense of the 1960s generational and cultural divide in "Gift of Grass," which appeared in the *New Yorker* in 1969.* Her sympathy is clearly with her teenage protagonist, Cathy, who lacks interest in school, money, and marriage. Cathy is far more observant than the adults give her credit for, but she's most herself when relaxing in the park, smoking a joint and watching the clouds: "Cathy concentrated on their changes, their slow and formal shifts in shape and pattern." Back home, Cathy watches her mother and stepfather managing a fragile marriage with tired repartee and a lot of alcohol. At the end of the evening, Bill, the stepfather, cracks a bit and tells Cathy about the confusion and difficulty he feels. He confides his opinion that the psychiatrist that Cathy's mother has insisted she see is a jackass. Before she goes to bed, Cathy leaves two pristine joints on Bill's desk.

Bill tries to analyze Cathy's gesture: "Nothing rational came to his mind. Or, rather, reasonable explanations approached but then as quickly dissolved, like clouds or shadows. Instead, salty and unmasculine tears stung at his eyes, and then he fell asleep in his chair, having just decided not to think at all." The story ends with a surrender of reason and responsibility to the "clouds" of associative feeling that marijuana represents. In this quiet story, Adams put herself on the side of the Children's Crusade against materialism and war. "I was very excited in the Sixties by genuine hope for our society and by the prospect of a personal connection to a country and culture I could be proud of," Adams told an interviewer.

The "anti-affluence" of the sixties reminded Alice of the "idealism of the postwar Forties."[18] But rather than retreating into nostalgia for the experiences of the Greatest Generation, she allowed her idealism to pique her interest in the culture emerging around her. Facing the future in this way opened new directions for her work as she became middle-aged but remained young at heart.

* The *New Yorker* purchased "Gift of Grass" after "The Swastika on Our Door" but published it sooner, making "Gift of Grass" Adams's first appearance in the magazine.

CHAPTER NINETEEN

Disinherited

— 1969–1973 —

The deaths of parents, dreadful and sad as they are, to an extent free writers.

—Alice Adams, comment on
"Roses, Rhododendron"[1]

Nic Adams, the original source of his daughter's fascination and difficulty with men, had been much on the move since his retirement and remarriage to Dotsie Wilson. He summered in Maine, traveled in Europe, and worked as a visiting professor in Chicago, Arizona, and Kentucky. But since returning home to Chapel Hill in 1969, Nic had frustrated Alice by not answering any of her letters. He was seventy-two.

In August of that year, Max Steele wrote from Chapel Hill that a local doctor thought Nic was in "bad looking shape" and that Dotsie was "denying all," but there was "general agreement about his not being in pain."[2] Denial, it seems, was a necessary pillar of Nic and Dotsie's fifteen-year marriage. Both drank heavily and insisted upon their happiness, an approach that generally worked out better for both of them than Agatha's attempts to manage Nic's behavior had done earlier in his life.

Alice kept her distance. For her the South remained fraught territory. She and Bob vacationed annually in Mexico, and they made their first trip to Europe together that fall. For news of Nic, she relied on reports from Steele and Lucie Jessner (who lived in Washington, DC, but kept up her Chapel Hill connections). Thus Alice learned that her father had felt "a little better" during a visit with his sister, Virginia Adams Dare, before Dotsie drove him to Lake Sebago for the summer of 1970. The first week in Maine was "grim" but when friends came to stay Nic "cooked spontaneously, brought wood in, all apparently in good spirits"—which led Lucie to declare, "It is not as deep as some of his former depressions have been."[3]

Alice responded by wondering if marijuana might be used to treat depression. She and Bob used it privately, as a Sunday-morning scene in her later novel about older people, *Second Chances*, suggests: Sam and Dudley Venable "laughing, in their tousled, floral-sheeted bed, now redolent of sea smells, stained with love." Two empty champagne glasses and the ends of two joints are the residue of Dudley's "happy stoned morning with Sam, whom today she truly loves." The sixties were over, but Alice was fascinated by the resulting changes in American culture and read avidly such books as *The Making of a Counter Culture* by Theodore Roszak and *The Greening of America* by Charles Reich.

Peter Linenthal remained Alice's personal window on the culture of the young. He'd grown what his mother called "a handsome beard" and lived with friends in a three-bedroom house on Van Ness near Lombard while he attended classes at the San Francisco Art Institute. "He loves the whole thing and in my head I do too but otherwise I hate his not living with us," Alice said. "The bathroom stays tidier now but unfortunately I find that no compensation at all."[4] Peter's close friend Phillip Galgiani and Bob McNie's sons Winky and Robbie were sometimes part of the fluid Van Ness ménage. Stephen Brown's mother refused to let him move in because she thought the group was too wild. The women, Nancy Oakes (later a James Beard Foundation Award–winning chef and restaurateur) and Joy Holbrook (whose baby lived there too), oversaw a kitchen that turned out copious meals to a changing cast of residents and friends. Parents were sometimes invited to dinner. To one of these meals, Alice brought beef bourguignon and sour cream pie to serve fourteen.

Peter's room in the attic held a "noisy cage of finches" and a plethora of art projects. During these years he was experimenting with drugs (mostly marijuana, plus LSD acquired from Robbie McNie, "just twice—it was too much") and sexuality. He saw Dr. Gottreich again, who assured him that confusion about sexual identity was part of growing up.

"Peter really hasn't decided on his sexuality," Alice told a writer friend named Sandy Boucher. "He's just exploring so he has some girlfriends but he also has some attractions to men." A sexual experience with a man he met in a Pacific Heights park had shown him that his attraction to men was undeniable. Yet he was also reluctant to declare himself bisexual: "Bisexuality? What does that mean? Theoretically it increases your options, but in everyday life—how is this going to work? In the sixties there was a lot of 'Oh, we're not possessive,' but I saw it didn't work out that well." Meanwhile, he enjoyed great freedom in the house on Van Ness: "I think it was healthy to experiment within reason. I sympathize with my mom having affairs. In more recent decades things have become so scary and moralistic for some kids."

Peter's somewhat communal house became the setting for the final chapter of Adams's novel *Families and Survivors*, which she'd been working on under various titles since 1965: "The great rooms with distant dusky ceilings and narrow mullioned windows are somewhat overwhelming, resistant to change. But the kids have done their best. A shawl draped here, another there—posters, driftwood sculpture. And for their party they have made a great effort at tidying up." She scrambles the identities of the young people who live there: her alter ego Louisa's child is a girl named Maude—but there are boys with aspects of Peter too: "a tall somewhat frail-looking boy" and "a dark sturdy bearded boy." On New Year's Eve, the adults are "spectators at the party. They stand together, apart from the rest, in a tentative position near the door . . . smile in an appreciative way, but they do not have a lot to say to most of 'the children' . . . with Maude or with others of her age, Louisa has begun to feel that she overdoes what she is saying, that her style is over emphatic. They say so little, these children. They so steadfastly refuse effusion."

Nic Adams may have risen from bed to cook for guests in Maine, but he deteriorated rapidly when they left. Jaundiced and bedridden, he was flown on a stretcher to North Carolina in early July, accompanied by Dotsie and a nurse. "Of course you are right, that it sounds hopeless," Jessner wrote Alice, "but the diagnosis may have been wrong." Surgery the next week revealed cancer of the left lung and of the pancreas. Hopeless indeed.

Still, Alice stayed home. "Cancer grows slowly in old age," Jessner offered. Cobalt treatments would prolong his life. After a long conversation with Dotsie on September 23, Alice wrote Jessner, "Poor lady, what an unimaginably bad time she's had. . . . Nic sounds ghastly. How cruel for him to go like this. . . . Dotsie wanted to know what to do with him, and I said I didn't know and that anything she decided was right, also to ask you. This prolongation seems horrifying."

Nicholson Barney Adams died October 2, 1970. Dotsie chose to have him buried in the Old Chapel Hill Cemetery alongside Agatha and baby Joel. Alice did not attend the graveside service conducted by the retired Community Church minister Charles Miles Jones.* Max sent her a description: "It all had a rather silent film quality to it like parts of *Blow-Up*. Maybe because I could see from where I stood the tennis courts and through the scrim-lined fences to marvelous players and they hit such perfect rhythm during the service and prayer: the ball bounced with the rhythm of a heartbeat and then was silent and that was the saddest part of the whole service."[5]

Nic Adams persisted as a nightmare of unrequited love in Alice's unconscious mind and in her writing. She could not see him as the beloved professor and respected scholar that others admired. In her fiction, Adams caricatures Southern men of Nic's generation. Louisa's father in *Families and Survivors* is a bigot who owns "vast acres of tobacco fields, who drinks too much and makes loud awful jokes about Jews and Negroes and Yankees."

Nic's association with the integrationist minister Jones suggests he was not a bigot or outright racist, but he did appear distinctly Southern and old-fashioned, and he strongly disapproved of Alice's living arrangement with Robert McNie. Once when he came alone to San Francisco, Alice invited all three McNie children to meet him, apparently to display herself en famille. Morissa never forgot this "amazing apparition": "He wore a light linen suit to dinner at Alice's, and was the picture of the Southern professor from 1860. I didn't know that this kind of propriety or arrogance still existed. His relationship to Alice was not exactly warm, like shaking hands practically."

* Charles M. Jones was a Presbyterian minister when he married Alice and Mark Linenthal in 1946 but resigned from that denomination after he was accused of heresy for hosting racially integrated spaghetti suppers at the church and for advocating that Jesus was fully human. His supporters founded the independent Community Church of Chapel Hill "for people who cannot adhere to the old time dogmas" in 1953.

Friends saw Nic as a "connoisseur of good food, poetry, and Spanish wines . . . an expert on Spanish dances, given to limericks, many of which he composed himself." A younger colleague recalled watching him "put his pipe into his coat pocket, still lit, while placing his martini glass, half-filled, in the other pocket." Before he retired from UNC, colleagues collected *Hispanic Studies in Honor of Nicholson B. Adams*. In an introduction, John Esten Keller praised Dorothy Adams (Dotsie) for her "immense capacity for life and mirth, for culture and gentility, for homemaking and companionship, and for deep, true, humanity of spirit [that] joined together to make the latter years of his career happy ones indeed."[6]

Alice suspected that her growing success as a writer had irritated her father. He had a "curious inability to find any magazine in which I was published," she said.[7] Morissa McNie also noticed, "There was something odd about his attitude toward Alice becoming a writer— whether he didn't think she could be one or what, I'm not sure." In her notebook three years before her father died, Alice wrote, "Nic always slapped me down like an irritable, self-absorbed brat." Another scrap of manuscript notes that a father's habit of telling his family "Do what you want" is really a passive-aggressive patriarchal assertion that means "he would do what he wanted to and everyone else would maneuver around his whims."[8]

When Nic Adams died, Alice was still at work on the novel that became *Families and Survivors*. In it, her alter ego Louisa describes her father as a man whose "ill-understood and violent emotions often seem hurled at his head from space, rather than arriving from within." Upset because her father must undergo shock treatment, Louisa "wonders if it is an idea, the idea called Father, that moves her to tears."*

Bob McNie was "the most incredible kind support" to Alice when she was upset about Nic's death.[9] She and her stepmother, Dotsie, tried to comfort each other by letter, though Dotsie's phrasing—"the Agony is

---

* Adams wrote Lucie Jessner in 1971 that the *Partisan Review* had accepted her short story titled "Shock Treatment." She'd rather be published there than in the *New Yorker*, she told Max Steele, but, sadly, the story never appeared in any magazine. It became chapter two of *Families and Survivors*.

more agonizing than the Ecstasy was ecstatic," for instance—put Alice off. Nevertheless she took the role of a good daughter, invited Dotsie to visit, and offered to help answer correspondence pertaining to Nic. In reply, Dotsie complained that the lawyer was very slow in filing necessary papers.

While the lawyer dallied, Dotsie mailed Alice a suitcase packed full of her mother's silver. She explained that Alice should have had all Agatha's things years ago but Nic would not let her send them. Now her Christmas gift to Alice was "a full day's work on same: polishing, packing, postage." It seemed to Alice that all Dotsie's gifts came with one of her "velvet barbs."* And was it true that her father hadn't wanted Alice to have her mother's things?

Just before Christmas, Alice received a copy of the will. Nic had left everything to his wife with no bequests to Alice other than "certain articles of furniture and silver."[10] While she understood that Dotsie would remain in the Chapel Hill house, Alice had expected that she would inherit it after her stepmother's death. She regarded Nic's failure to designate it for her in his will as a "disinheritance."

On the day Alice read Nic's will, she and Bob were to dine at the home of new friends Elaine and John Badgley. Artist Elaine and architect John had recently spent a pleasant weekend with Bob and Alice in Truckee, so Elaine optimistically included them in her plans to entertain a French friend who was a renowned chef. Elaine elaborately planned her menu and dress for the evening. "Bob and Alice were late, and when they did come my stomach dropped. Alice was drunk. She couldn't really look at anybody, and Bob said that her father had cut her out of his will," Elaine remembered of the "wonderfully terrible" meal.

"She was totally smashed. Bob was not nearly as far gone. He was one of the best-looking men that ever walked the planet. He led her to a chair, and she sat next to my husband, John. When John started to talk, Alice said, 'John Badgley, you are the most boring man I have

---

* Adams associated the "velvet barb" with Southern women. One of her favorite examples came from Lucie Jessner: "I always thought this was the special way of Southern ladies to express their feelings—their hostility in the embrace. . . . Dollie Summerlin once said to me at a party, 'What a beautiful skirt—I was so sorry when they went out of fashion six years ago.'" (LJ to AA, April 16, 1970.)

ever met in my life!' That was before dinner. And John just deflated. She struck him in the balls, which she really could do very well." At the table, Bob passed out and Alice "sat running her fingers through her very short hair. She had a fake, forced smile through this episode—she had a lovely smile when it was real. Bob awoke after they'd finished a main course of sweetbreads and oysters in puff pastry and said, 'Alice, we should go.' Alice was weaving back and forth with this strange hair and strange smile and they both staggered off down the stairs."

When Alice called Elaine the next day to say what might have been a routine thank-you, Elaine quoted to her from Malcolm Lowry's *Under the Volcano*, which they were all reading at the time: "*¿Le gusta este jardín? ¿Que es suyo?*" Elaine intended to remind Alice that she had trampled her garden, but Alice repeated her criticism of Elaine's husband. They didn't see each other again for ten years. "Alcohol did do that," Elaine said, "but Alice had fire within, this anger that was there almost all the time."

With Dotsie, Alice was more direct: "I told Dotsie I was quite hurt by Nic's will, but haven't heard from her since, so I assume she's working out one of her distortions," she wrote Jessner, who had dared to suggest that Nic felt Alice could stand on her own feet and Dotsie could not. Alice felt hate in her father's decision, even after learning that a separate written agreement stated Nic and Dotsie's intention to bequeath to her what remained of Agatha's Lake Sebago camp. That Dotsie had been her father's wife and mistress of the Chapel Hill house for fifteen years did not count with Alice. In a reply to Jessner she said, "[Nic] always saw me as a threat to his supplies, as someone who might get things he needed—attention, friends, intellectual prestige—he always had to fight me off. That was how I always felt him—it's liberating to . . . have this confirmed."[11]

Alice took another step toward releasing herself from her past when her father's cousin Frank Jervey and his wife visited from South Carolina in March. Invited to dinner, they spent part of the evening telling Bob how mean six-year-old Alice had been to their daughter, Mary—she whom Frank had asked to spell "cat" when he demanded "Constantinople" of little Alice. Thus Alice realized that "like most guilty neurotics, I grew up believing that the others in my surroundings were nice; in fact they were a bunch of crazy shits." Almost the next day Alice began "A Southern Spelling Bee," which investigates the abandonment and loneliness she felt during the weeks she stayed with the Jerveys as a child. She felt now that Frank Jervey, whom she once thought "the most marvelous, glamorous man alive," was a rude, bigoted hypocrite.[12]

Some years later, Adams told an interviewer: "My father died and I was disinherited. I was wretchedly deeply hurt and I wrote a great many stories about being disinherited. It sounds simple-minded but that was my way of coping with it."[13] By writing these stories, Adams learned that she did not actually want the house but was grieving for what it represented to her. "Berkeley House" locates the drama in the Bay Area but offers two revelations: one, that the house is the site of her mother's pain in marriage that she could never ease; and two, that she had hoped to inherit money from her father: "The realization that something as concrete as money figured in her pain was comforting; it made her feel less blackly doomed—less crazy."

"The deaths of parents, dreadful and sad as they are, to an extent free writers," Adams came to understand.[14] Men besides Nic who had influenced—and constrained—Alice also moved out of her firmament in the early seventies. Peter Matson, her literary agent, broke with her in April 1971. Her revised manuscript of the novel called "Mothering" had been rejected several times, and her correspondence with Matson devolved into quibbles about whether characters must be "likable" in order to be interesting.[15] Matson, Adams told Max Steele, "really has no idea what to do with anything that won't sell to *Redbook*."[16] She had insisted on sending stories to the *New Yorker* and now had a direct relationship with Bob Hemenway there.*

Then there was Norman Mailer. Through four wives Alice had been his friend, loyal fan, and defender—at least he was never boring, she said. That all ended when Mailer came through San Francisco in January 1971 to promote *Of a Fire on the Moon*. Alice was first on Mailer's invitation list for what she dubbed a "sheer ambition" party at the home of socialite Grace Kennan Warnecke and her then-husband, renowned architect John Carl Warnecke. As the party ended, with Alice at one end of the room and Norman and Bob chatting with an attractive woman at the other, Norman suddenly turned on Bob and picked him up and threw

---

* A drunken male writer once belligerently muttered something to Adams about her *New Yorker* connections. "I wonder how he thinks I got *New Yorker* connections—selling cookies on 43rd Street?" she asked when she told the story later. (Sandy Boucher, "Alice Adams—a San Francisco novelist who is into her third book," *San Francisco* [October 1978], 131.)

him on the floor. Host Warnecke prevented Bob ("who's been known to break jaws," Alice bragged) from retaliating and Alice called Mailer "an impotent prick." The scene over, Bob and Norman shook hands and they all went to dinner at the Mandarin in Ghirardelli Square.

Chronicle gossip columnist Frances Moffat drew ire from Adams by reporting that McNie had provoked the altercation and that Mailer had whirled—or was it twirled?—McNie over his head three times, a detail provided by novelist Don Carpenter. In a letter to Peter, Alice called Moffat "that dumb bitch." Then she told Herb Caen for his gossip column: "I thought Norman behaved quite swinishly. This makes the third physical attack by Norman on either Bob or me—three more than enough despite 23 years of friendship. Who needs geniuses?"* Alice's friendship with Mailer was never restored. Bob McNie saved all the clippings in a scrapbook. "I used to think I wanted to be a famous writer and all that but now I'm not so sure," Alice concluded in a letter describing the episode to her son.[17]

Except that was not the conclusion. From Frances Linenthal Alice heard about a dinner with a lot of psychoanalysts, "at which Mark stated that Norman had lost all curiosity, and all the shrinks figured out that he is incurious because if he were curious he would discover his own homosexuality. This kind of jargon reductiveness absolutely infuriates me—for one thing Norman is perhaps the most curious person I've ever known (I'm sure he was simply bored by Mark); for another he's been writing and speculating about his own possible homosexuality for 20 years. Anyway, I ended up again admiring if not entirely fond of Norm, and once more furious at Mark."[18] Twelve years later, Alice still regretted the "trashy demise to a what was a long good friendship." When pressed by Mailer biographer Peter Manso to explain what the fight had been about, Alice recalled that Norman that night looked "tired, old, and seedy" in a dirty, stained dark blue blazer while Bob, in an immaculate dark blue blazer, "was really looking terrific."[19]

Oddly absent from the public brouhaha was any suggestion that jealousy over Alice might have been at the heart of the situation. But

---

* The second attack occurred when Mailer first met McNie, when he was covering the Goldwater convention in 1964. As Robbie McNie heard it from his father, Norman socked Bob in the stomach and Bob answered, "Gee, Norman, for a minute I thought you were going to hit me."

Alice sensed exactly that. She wrote Lucie Jessner that Mailer "picked up Bob and threw him on the floor—I suppose to discredit him with me."[20]

Later that spring Mailer took part in a highly publicized dialogue on women's liberation at New York's Town Hall, where Germaine Greer and other feminists attempted to put him in his place. Greer expressed feelings Adams would have seconded when she said that in Mailer she was confronting "one of the most powerful figures in my own imagination, namely the male elitist society, the masculine artist, the pinnacle of the masculine elite. Most of my life has been most powerfully influenced by the culture for which he stands."[21]

In California, Alice immersed herself in reading the "women's lib books" and thought Greer's *The Female Eunuch* the best of the lot, saying, "In fact, I think she's terrific."[22] Adams felt Greer's call for a feminism that did not shun men: "Those miserable women who blame the men who let them down for their misery and isolation enact every day the initial mistake of sacrificing their personal responsibility for themselves."[23] Alice told a reporter she'd always felt "at odds with the female roles being foisted upon [her]" and welcomed feminism because it "served as clarification and support for what [she] felt all [her] life."[24]

Simply by growing up, Peter Linenthal was also moving out of Alice's daily life. No longer threatened by the military draft, he took time off from the Art Institute; performed in a Halloween show with the Cockettes, a gender-bending psychedelic theater group, in North Beach (mentioned in the last chapter of *Families and Survivors*); and then flew to Europe. He was in Spain when Alice received the disturbing news about Nic's will. Judging by the letters and drawings he sent home, Peter was a frugal and perceptive nineteen-year-old traveler. From Cadaqués, he described his fifty-cent-a-night room above an olive press: "*best-ever* omelette and salad, 60 cents, hot milk and coffee, 10 cents." He noted that the hippies he met were "spaced-out," decided not to go to the drug mecca of Morocco, and observed that an Australian nurse he'd met "sounded like one of the sisters out of *Howards End*." After some months on the road, Peter found a flat in the World's End neighborhood of London, gave up drugs and meat, took up Transcendental Meditation, and enrolled in a lithography class at the Slade School.[25]

Then a British postal strike prevented Peter from writing home for seven weeks. Alice so much missed conversation with young people that she invited Peter's housemates to dinner. The baby loved Alice's sour cream pie,* she wrote Peter afterward, and Phillip Galgiani told them about cleaning birds after a recent oil spill in San Francisco Bay. Having decided that classes at the Slade were no better than those at the San Francisco Art Institute, Peter arrived home in mid-March. "He looks marvelous and seems most pleased with himself and with his life," Alice told Jessner. She was especially pleased that he read "an incredible amount" and had moved on from Hermann Hesse to Thomas Mann. Perpetually critical of the city herself, Alice saw native San Franciscans' "mania for their city . . . as a sort of trap; they [were] caught and bound in civic affection." Yet Peter Linenthal was destined to be such a San Franciscan—which gave his mother another reason to remain in the city herself.

Though some people, including his stepbrothers, had assumed Peter was gay long before he'd had any sexual relationships, Peter took longer to settle the question for himself. When he returned home from London, he met with each of his parents to tell them he thought he was gay. He recalled, "I hadn't always known this. The sixties were so amorphous. It was possible to be gay but I didn't really know, and I thought I might not be. It seemed like things would be easier if I weren't." The life of his uncle, Michael Linenthal, especially made Peter reluctant to come out. "Michael seemed like a very sad case. He was funny, intelligent, with the sort of elevated aristocratic airs some gay people have—theatrical. He played the Old Woman in *The Chairs* by Ionesco and was excellent as a sort of nervous Jewish mother, his own mother in a certain way I think."†

Mark Linenthal accepted his son's declaration without drama, saying

---

* Phyllis Mufson saved Alice's handwritten recipe: "Cream two 8 oz packages of cream cheese with 1 c. sugar; beat in 3 eggs till smooth (not in blender); pour into graham cracker crust; bake at 350 degrees ½ hour, cool; pour on 1 pint sour cream mixed with 1 tsp sugar; put back in oven five minutes; cool, then chill a few hours."

† Peter Carnahan described Michael as "middle-aged and gay with an aura of sadness and vulnerability that hung on him like a poncho. Rotund, bald, beak-nosed, it was clearly only his sophistication and money that could attract the sylph-like young things he romantically desired, and he seemed to live in a constant state of heartbrokenness." (Carnahan, *Opposable Lives* [Bloomington, IN: Xlibris, 2009].)

quickly, "My concern is that you be happy." Peter mentioned that his uncle Michael wasn't his idea of a role model. "My father understood that," Peter said. "As a teacher, that's just the kind of guy my dad was."

As Peter feared, speaking to Alice was more complicated. She had close friends who were gay and she associated gay life with unhappiness. "Gay = melancholy," she noted once.[26] Peter told her that his current involvement was with his best friend from school, Phillip Galgiani. His mom particularly liked Galgiani, and he hoped that would make it easier for her. "She sort of sank further into the sofa, not looking happy. She had a kind of steadiness to her gaze, just straightforward without any guile or anything. This time her gaze was on the negative side." Alice asked Peter if a girl he had also been dating, a law student who seemed "a little difficult," could be the problem. "I told her, 'It's more than that.' I think the conversation ended uncomfortably, uncertainly. This was a disappointment and she took disappointments hard."

Even after coming out to his parents about his attraction to men, Peter wondered if he might yet meet a woman partner. "I did Jewish dating and folk-dancing, and dated a nice woman who went to the Art Institute. But at some point you ask yourself, what's going to last? Who can I have a future with? It took a long time, and it wasn't without agonizing, but it was a sensible decision. Luckily I was in San Francisco."

At this time Alice worked as a part-time clerk in the Cardiac Data Processing and Patient Follow-up department of the Pacific Medical Center, directed by Dr. Frank L. Gerbode, a pioneer of open heart surgery on the West Coast. For about three years, she spent long, dull hours with four coworkers, Sheliah Renée Wilbert, Maureen Looney, Sandy Boucher, and Alyce Denier. Like the doctors, they wore starched white lab coats over their regular clothes—which for the women were short skirts, hose, and heels. Occasionally they watched open heart surgeries, including a transplant, from which Alice took the lesson "stay thin and run a lot."[27] "Alice always worked with a little side of humor or sarcasm about what we were doing," Denier remembered.

Though Alice would not begin her third novel, *Listening to Billie*, for several years, it's rooted in this particular office job and her struggle to become an independent writer. Alice, like Eliza in that novel, "in a furtive way . . . liked doctors, was excited by medicine." The cast of intelligent, underchallenged women and busy, competitive male doctors in the medical center caused Alice to consider the way women spend their lives: "An important fact about that office was that almost nothing was actually done in it," she writes. The novel tells the story of Eliza Quarles, a poet who begins to sell her work and stops having to take "stupid" jobs. The book's early working titles were "Work and Friends" and "Getting to Work."[28] Adams believed her novel's theme was about women finding work to sustain them. She was inspired by a comment she attributed to Elizabeth Hardwick, "most women tend to write about women who are much less interesting than they." Eliza, Adams claimed, was more interesting than herself.[29] With second-wave feminism emerging and her own life stabilized by living with McNie, Adams paid close attention to the younger women, but Denier noticed, "Alice was incredibly approachable but she was stand-offish too. I think she participated in the banter that went on just to make the job tolerable for her."

Sheliah Wilbert was a black woman of about twenty who lived in public housing in the Fillmore District, the former "Harlem of the West" that had been torn up by a redevelopment agency to make room for the Geary Street expressway and the housing project. "After the middle-class home owners and business operators were forced out, all that was left was a crime-ridden ghetto," historian David Talbot writes.[30]

Alice liked Wilbert very much and feared that her life would end tragically. In *Listening to Billie*, Sheliah became Miriam, a character who serves as a contemporary foil for the Billie Holiday of the title. Eliza befriends Miriam but is disappointed to realize that Miriam admires her in return for dressing well and living in a nice apartment—for being "rich" in Miriam's eyes. She's uninterested in Eliza's talk about civil rights and black power: Miriam's "ambition was to be a Secretary, not a File Clerk. She had never heard of Billie Holiday. She was crazy about Elvis Presley." While Alice and Looney sometimes went to lunchtime rallies in support of the Black Panthers, Wilbert was "avid for outfits and boots and coats and velvet sofas and bedroom sets."[31]

Over time, Alice learned more about Sheliah Wilbert's life. A random shooting had killed her first boyfriend right before her eyes when she was sixteen and pregnant. She lost the baby. In the novel, the shooting is not random: a white friend playing with a gun accidentally shoots Miriam's boyfriend, and Eliza is frustrated by Miriam's passivity:

This was the sort of thing that could happen, any time. At any moment the friend you love could get blown up right in front of you. Miriam even seemed anxious not to make too much of it.

"I felt real bad for a long time after that," she said. "I don't know—"

"*Christ*, Miriam, of course you did."

In *Listening to Billie*, the white boy who shot the gun is acquitted. Both Miriam and Eliza understand what would have happened if Miriam's black boyfriend had been the shooter and his white friend the victim.

The emotional attraction that Alice felt toward black women was rooted in her upbringing in Jim Crow North Carolina and particularly in the fact that she had been most lovingly cared for by Verlie Jones. "When I was young and even more foolish I wanted to be Billie Holiday," Alice confided once.[32] Her notebook and letters describe Sheliah Wilbert as a young woman trying to survive in a dangerous urban racial environment with few marketable skills.

In the novel, Miriam lives with her light-skinned mother, who derides her for being black and mean like her father. Adams takes Miriam's point of view: "Quarreling with her mother, in those small crowded rooms, with her brothers and sisters watching, filled Miriam with need. She needed to scream and hit and cry, and she wildly wanted everything in the world that was not her mother, not the Project." For Miriam, as for Sheliah, there were temptations to escape that world. A man stopped her on the street with promises of fine clothes if she would model for him. Others offered drugs.

Other stories Wilbert told Alice also informed the novel. To Peter in Europe, Adams wrote:

Sheliah has been telling me about the funeral of a pimp that she went to last week: He used to have a green Cadillac with pale tan leather lining, and in his casket he was wearing a green knit suit with pale tan leather collar and cuffs, and all his whores were there in green outfits with tan leather boots and belts. She said the whole church was full of pimps and whores and the pimp's parents, and the preacher preached a sermon about how children should obey their parents. You probably think I made that up but I really couldn't, although I may use it somewhere.

Use it she did, actually distancing it from the funeral Wilbert attended by making it one that Miriam in *Listening to Billie* just hears about:

> One time, she had heard about the funeral of a pimp, and she had to laugh, it was so funny. Jimmy, the pimp, used to have this green Caddy with pale brown leather inside, and at the funeral there were all his whores, three black and two blond white girls, all wearing these green outfits, with pale brown leather trim. Still, Jimmy was dead, shot dead by the brother of a girl he'd pulled, one of his whores.

Alice and Sheliah Wilbert continued their friendship with occasional phone calls after they'd both left their medical jobs, though Sheliah was "usually high so conversations didn't make much sense." Alice worried about her. She was not surprised to receive a call from Sheliah's brother in 1985 informing her that Sheliah had died of a drug overdose.

Maureen Looney also ended up in *Listening to Billie*, part of the composite character of Kathleen Mooney, who also embodied aspects of Sandy Boucher. Looney, a supervisor to both Miriam and Alice in the office, was a "good Catholic girl" in her early thirties. When she became pregnant by the musician she dated, she decided to raise the boy alone. Alice took Looney under her wing: "I often went to dinner at her house. I have a picture of my son crawling around the alarmingly large Boston fern that filled her round alcove window." Looney knew Bob McNie, his kids, and Peter. Alice told her stories about North Carolina, Boston, and Paris. On lunch hours they drove in Alice's "old beater" car to shop at Macy's and "she had a positive effect on my clothing choices," Looney remembered. Through Alice, Looney became good friends with Ruth Belmeur, whose son became a playmate of both Looney's son and Sheliah Wilbert's niece and nephew.

Looney celebrated with Adams when "Gift of Grass" appeared in the *New Yorker*. When Alice was writing "Ripped Off," which turned out to be her second story published by the *New Yorker*, she asked Looney to name a song "that would be alarming if an insecure girl heard her boyfriend singing it." Looney recalled, "I didn't have to think at all—'It Ain't Me, Babe' by Dylan. I had that exact experience with my son's father." When Looney read the story later in the magazine, she "realized that Alice had taken more than the song title from me. My father was killed on Iwo Jima when I was three years old, and Alice had told me what she thought the effects of his death had been on me." In her story, Adams put the comment in the mouth of a psychiatrist, who tells the girl, "At three, you would have viewed this as a desertion—a deliberate one."

When Alice bought her brown Austin with earnings from stories, Looney helped her pick out a huge black straw hat to go with it. They shared left-wing political sympathies and attended rallies together. "We had our fists in the air shouting 'Free Bobby [Seale]! Fuck the pigs!' when Alice leaned over to say in my ear, 'I hope we don't end up on the evening news. Dr. Gerbode might not be pleased.'" When Black Panther leader Eldridge Cleaver went into hiding after his arrest on an attempted murder charge in connection with an ambush of Oakland police officers, Alice confided to Looney that she knew Cleaver was in the basement of her friends Ruth and Paul Jacobs, who had helped him raise the bail he forfeited when he fled to Cuba and Algeria.[33]

Alice and Looney clashed in their attitudes about men. "I always felt like Alice was a very sexual person, in a particular way," Looney said. "She was always gauging her pull, while I assumed I had none." After Looney and her son's father broke up, Alice tried to send her a new lover. "A man she knew came to my house one night. I hadn't asked to be set up, and I didn't like him at all. He acted as though I was just frightened and began pawing me all over. I was horrified! Alice just laughed when I confronted her the next day. She had been sexually active in her youth, and I had been brought up conservatively. I think I was a kind of challenge to her! It was the swinging sixties after all."

When Maureen Looney was offended by a doctor who called to ask her out, Alice asked, "Don't you consider it a compliment that he is interested in you?' She thought I was too much a prude. And, to Alice's credit, I did have two affairs with young doctors while Alice and I were friends. One was brief but pleasant. She and Bob were determined that I should have a settled situation—and a sex life. They even loaned his house at Truckee to me so I could spend a week with an intern that Alice called 'a Jewish Huck Finn.'"

Sandy Boucher, a writer who'd then published one short story in *Antioch Review*, also met Alice when she got a temporary job at the medical office. In about 1970, Boucher left her husband, came out as a lesbian, and plunged into the women's liberation movement. She lived in a collective in Bernal Heights with three other women, two children, and a man, and spent her free time organizing, demonstrating, helping to raise children, and publishing a broadsheet called *Motherlode*. Their friendship continued after Boucher left that job, driven by common interest in writing and Alice's curiosity. "What we experienced together was limited, our lives were so different," Boucher said. To Alice, Boucher's household seemed a "chaos of posters books pamphlets cats dogs girls—big Sandy, tart Geri, pretty Joan—children."[34] The adults asked the children to call them by their first names and regard them all equally as their parents. Boucher was surprised when she found a description of her collective in *Listening to Billie*. "I was philosophical about that and never confronted her with it. It seemed she saw what she characterized as our financial poverty and the austerity of our lifestyle, while my experience of those commune years was of tremendous richness and internal growth." When the novel came out, Sandy Boucher profiled Adams for a city magazine.

While working at Pacific Medical Center, Adams attended team meetings where cardiologists argued to keep patients on medication while surgeons promoted their newer surgical interventions. Adams wrote and rewrote a story called "An Opened Heart." Bob Hemenway at the *New Yorker* said, "We rarely publish stories as clinical as this, or ones that present their characters this coldly. It's a good story, and I hope another magazine buys it." No one did. Peter Matson thought the story "heart-rending" but could think of nowhere to send it because it was "oh so down . . ."[35] Adams scrapped it.

When Peter Matson dropped Adams as his client, she took over submitting stories to magazines herself. "As usual, I went into a sort of transition neurosis, but now it all looks much better. I was appalled to find how little he (agent) was doing," she said. When her job (which had been funded by a grant) ended in mid-1971, she was eligible for a few months of unemployment insurance—another experience that found its way into *Listening to Billie* as Eliza takes "bus trips to a frightening part of town, Third and Bryant, standing in line with discouraged, tired people . . . being terrified." Feeling nervous and guilty, Alice worked hard and productively all summer on her unruly second novel and more short stories, envisioning a collection, but found she couldn't sleep well.

Picking up her unemployment checks fanned her resentments against Nic: "Lack of money = unloved = unworthy of love."[36] She began to look forward to a new job in the fall: "I really prefer having some sort of job—just writing can get very unstructured and lonely," she wrote Lucie Jessner.[37]

She feared loneliness but in the event she was too busy to be lonely—1971 became a turning point in her writing life. "The Swastika on Our Door" finally appeared in the *New Yorker* on September 11, 1971, two years after it had been accepted. Jessner, who had just celebrated her seventy-fifth birthday, thought it was Alice's best story yet, praising places where "the *mot juste* gave the essence of these people, eg. that Richard 'lazily or perversely' held on to his land or 'if Roger, for example, had had a bad heart, he would undoubtedly have had it continually in the midst of a crowd.' "[38] Max Steele apologized that he couldn't judge the story because he "kept trying to reconstruct it and to imagine the reaction of Freddy and Virginia . . . Yiddish to Southern is a mad disguise."[39] Despite the disguise, Virginia Breier recognized her husband and herself in the story's Karen and Roger Washington and didn't like it one bit. "Luckily Fred never saw it, but it bothered me. I distanced myself from Alice a little after that."* Nonetheless, after Fred Breier died in 1975, Virginia traveled to Mexico with Alice and Bob.

"Gift of Grass" won third prize in *Prize Stories 1971: The O. Henry Awards*, edited by none other than Adams's longtime friend and supporter William Abrahams, who took over this task from Richard Poirier in 1967. Included in that volume were Abrahams's protégée Joyce Carol Oates, esteemed Southerners Eleanor Ross Taylor and Reynolds Price, Black Panther Eldridge Cleaver, and, from Berkeley, Leonard Michaels. In his introduction to the volume, Abrahams regretted the "passion for fact" that dominated magazines and shrank the markets for fiction. He aimed particular scorn at so-called women's service magazines: "Here, I suggest, is a prime target for the Women's Liberation movement, for these magazines would seem alike in their conviction that while women are qualified to read excellent recipes . . . the only stories they

---

* Breier's unease had merit. Adams later said the story was "about heavy-handed capitalist values as opposed to socialist poetic ones . . . I find I don't really like very rich people but I keep getting thrown in with them. If they only knew." (Mickey Friedman, "Alice Adams: Rewriting life into fiction," *San Francisco Examiner*, February 5, 1979, 22.)

are qualified to read are those that trivialize, sentimentalize, and falsify the aspects of life with which they pretend to deal." Having moved from fantasy to contemporary subjects, these magazines have "grown up into a kind of bogus knowingness and sophistication" that reveals their implicit contempt for women readers. Paradoxically, Abrahams continued, many of the writers who write stories "at the level of art" are women, including Alice Adams and the other five in his selection.[40]

Almost every year thereafter, Abrahams selected an Adams story for the O. Henry Awards collection. When "Swastika" was included in 1973, Adams found herself in company with first-timers Raymond Carver, James Alan McPherson, and Diane Johnson; with already recognized writers such as Bernard Malamud and John Cheever; and with writers who never achieved enduring national recognition—Curt Johnson, Patricia Zelver, Judith Rascoe. Always Abrahams included a generous selection of stories from small literary magazines and stories by female authors. And he selected more West Coast writers now that he lived in the Bay Area and associated with the Stanford writers.

Paying venues for short stories continued to disappear throughout the seventies, leading Abrahams to observe in his 1974 O. Henry collection that the short-story form "thrives in its apparent neglect, perhaps even because of it," because writers are "freed from any preconceptions and expectations but their own as they begin to write." Certainly the Adams story he chose that year, "Alternatives," is a good example of such freedom. Her story spans decades, changes its focus from one character to another partway through, and holds together primarily through language and theme rather than plot.

Not only did Abrahams promote Adams's work, he also sent her freelance jobs, including a gig as a screener for editorial submissions he received and one as "novelizer" for the script of Two People, a movie written by his former student Richard DeRoy and directed by Robert Wise, starring Lindsay Wagner, Peter Fonda, and Estelle Parsons. The latter was "a bloody ghastly rotten stifling Hollywood job—I would really rather have had a waitress job," Adams complained. Working on it, she said, kept her from her own work: "I began to feel as though there was a sponge on my brain."[41]

But the pay was enough to cover a share of a six-week trip to Italy with Bob in May and June of 1972. They traveled together happily. Bob proved to be agile at driving foreign roads; they stayed in comfortable, unusual hotels—a sixth-century abbey in Orvieto, a nineteenth-century tower in Naples. Both Bob and Alice found travel stimulating for their work, as he accumulated visual ideas and she filled her notebook with character sketches and story concepts. In Rome, Alice met prominent psychiatrists Renata and Eugenio Gaddini, who were friends of Lucie Jessner's, and had an "absolutely fascinating" conversation with Eugenio about psychoanalysis and creativity.[42] Alice also became friends with Ann Cornelisen, one of "Billy's girls," as some called the women whose books Abrahams published. She was a Vassar graduate from Rome, Georgia, whose work with Save the Children led her to write about the lives of poor women in the Abruzzi region. At first, Cornelisen thought Alice was "an odd person . . . terribly unsure of herself, yet not of her writing. Big and rather brash at times, yet timid." She said, "As you can tell I haven't straightened out her complexes yet." But when Cornelisen heard how unhappy Alice had been with Matson as her agent, she recommended her to Cyrilly Abels, a former *Mademoiselle* managing editor (for whom Sylvia Plath famously worked as a summer intern).[43]

Back from Italy, Alice felt "culture shock" exacerbated by a presidential campaign that pitted President Richard Nixon, now reviled for his invasion of Cambodia and bombing of North Vietnam, against Senator George McGovern. Immediately she had to rewrite her novelization of *Two People*, trying to meet editor Peggy Roth's wish that it feel "as though it were [her] book."[44] It wasn't her book, and her "beautiful writing" and "tremendous style" (as Roth praised them) weren't enough to vivify the story of Evan Bonner, an army deserter hiding out in Marrakesh who falls in love with a model as he travels back to New York to turn himself in. Neither the movie nor Adams's highly readable translation of it into a mass-market novel makes these characters convincing, but her evocations of Marrakesh, where she'd never been, and of Paris, where she had, are sensual and accurate.

Dick DeRoy thought Adams did a classy job on *Two People*, and they became friends when she attended a sneak preview of the movie in San Jose in the fall. The Dell paperback came out under the name Alice Boyd in 1973, just ahead of the movie, which "turned out to be terrible and bombed big time, terrific script though it was," according to the screenwriter's wife, Jewel DeRoy. Movie producer Harry Argent in *Listening to Billie* is partially based on Dick DeRoy, though the affair of Eliza Quarles with Argent is pure invention. Eliza and Harry's relationship "is idealized," Adams told an interviewer. "There's less dependence in that relationship than I've ever seen."[45]

During her year of not working at a job and not having a literary agent, Adams made progress on a novel about the drama of the generations that she now witnessed squarely from the middle. She had time for lunches with her friend Billy Abrahams and frequent correspondence with Max Steele and Lucie Jessner. With Nic Adams dead, Peter Linenthal across town, and Bob McNie sharing her life, she had finally attained something like the perfect writing situation. Jane Kristiansen, the graphic designer whom Bob considered his "little sister," saw that Bob was proud of Alice and applauded him for that because she'd seen that "some men absolutely cannot take the success of a female partner."

Bob McNie's brand of eccentric decorating and being the "only not-gay" decorator in town was bringing him more lucrative jobs.* His clients included department store magnate Cyril Magnin (brother to Joseph), both Ernest and Julio Gallo, trial lawyer Robert Barbagelata, and developer Angelo Sangiacomo. When Bob and Alice returned from Italy in 1972 he took a job decorating a suite of offices in the new pyramidal Transamerica building. "It's interesting how much better and better at our work we rather simultaneously become," Alice wrote. On weekends they put their cats in the car and drove across the Sacramento Valley to Bob's mountain house, the scene evoked in "A Pale and Perfectly Oval Moon," "The Break-in," "Snow," and "Favors." In "The Break-In" Adams's protagonist decides not to marry Roger, the owner of a beautiful house near Lake Tahoe, after the tensions surrounding a burglary there reveal class and political differences between them; Cynthia fears that Roger cares more about his house than he does about any of the women to whom he's been married (all of whose names begin with C). She also fears that *she* cares more about the house than she does about Roger.

* Sometimes Bob said things that concerned Alice. In her notebook she recorded a conversation and her reaction: "B[ob]: 'I fell madly in love with this boy in the Safeway tonight. He was just standing there, so out of it, so miserable . . . His mouth—I wanted to give him anything—take in—protect . . . My reaction was very homosexual.' Really? Why tell me?" Alice wondered if that boy reminded Bob of his sons, or if he spoke out of "self-protection" or was "testing (or trying to emulate?) my sophistication." (Alice Adams notebook, September 26, 1972.)

In real life, Alice was thrilled to show Max Steele "Bob's incredibly beautiful house" and spend a day with him when he taught a summer workshop at the Community of Writers at Squaw Valley conference, directed by Blair Fuller. Always strong in her judgments of friends and foes, Alice shunned the conference and its lead novelist, Herb Gold, but adored Steele: he looked "terribly well, a little fat but sort of jolly." She worried that he'd written little fiction since becoming a professor in Chapel Hill. "He really has the greatest face, doesn't he?" she wrote Jessner. One of Max's gestures especially amused her: "He leans back and narrows his eyes, as though very wise, and speaks from the side of his mouth, giving terrible advice—about real estate or something that he knows nothing about."[46] Max said his wife, Diana, was sometimes jealous of Alice. Years later, having survived them both, Diana said, "Alice could be utterly stupid about love, but I think she was wise in the distinctions she made about friends and lovers, really not discarding anyone except the few she had totally finished with, like Mark Linenthal."

Disposable income and grown-up children allowed Alice and Bob to travel, and many places they visited appear in her fiction. They went somewhere tropical every January, and to Europe if they could get away in the spring or fall. Stories that take place in Hawaii, Dubrovnik, coastal Mexico, Venice, and Rome were one result. They visited the Northwest in the fall, admiring scarlet maple trees and the dark, wooded San Juan Islands. They saw Morissa McNie in Seattle and rode the ferry to Victoria, British Columbia, for high tea at the Empress Hotel, from which Adams constructed a scene in *Families and Survivors*. Winter found them happily resting at a "rather shabby and very private" resort on Kauai, followed by less perfect days at a hotel on Maui. En route home, Alice thought Waikiki was "less horrible" than she had imagined because they found a "good museum, good Chinese food, and good swimming."[47] She doesn't mention that her old flame Trummy Young then led a quartet that played the Hanohano Room atop the new Sheraton Waikiki.[48] So perhaps it's pure imagining that the heroine of *Superior Women*, Megan Greene, goes alone to Hawaii and calls her old flame Jackson Clay, who spends a few days in bed with her in a hotel in Lahaina on Maui. After all, Alice was traveling with Bob, and Young was married to Sally. Not only that, Young was by then a practicing Seventh-Day Adventist and teetotaler, certainly not the Jackson Clay who smokes dope and pops

mysterious green pills and plays in a ghastly club in Lahaina. Whatever
Adams imagined for Megan, it seems possible that Alice did witness
and feel some of what she writes in *Superior Women*:

> But up there on the stage is Jackson, with his horn . . . *playing*: his
> fantastic powerful always new sounds! his wild inventions, lovely lyric
> sweetness, his pure sounds of sex. Suddenly sane, Megan thinks, as
> she listens, I'm really all right, then. In some ways Jackson is okay,
> and so am I. Her eyes fill, at her awareness that he is playing for her;
> his horn slides toward her, his wide dark brown eyes on her, he is
> talking to her, saying everything. And that is the moment that her
> trip was all about, she is later, slowly, to realize. She came there to
> hear Jackson play.

During the summer of 1972, following Ann Cornelisen's recommen-
dation, Adams showed five of her strongest stories to Cyrilly Abels.
Abels represented a sterling client list of important female writers:
Katherine Anne Porter, Carson McCullers, Flannery O'Connor, Chris-
tina Stead, and Hortense Calisher. Not only that, but Abels had been
bold in her support for controversial writers: James Baldwin, Warren
Hinckle (editor of *Ramparts* magazine and an early editor of Hunter S.
Thompson), and Eldridge Cleaver. With Paul Jacobs, Norman Mailer,
Joseph Heller, Grace Paley, Elizabeth Hardwick, Barbara Deming, and
Gloria Steinem, Abels had been active in protesting violence against
the Black Panthers by the Oakland Police Department and in raising
bail money for Cleaver.

Abels seemed immediately to understand what Adams needed emotionally and professionally. "I can't tell you what a magic person she's
been in my life, and such a graceful, bright, kind, and efficient woman,"
Adams said.[49] Of approximately the same generation as Agatha Adams,
Abels filled a place that had long been vacant in Alice's life: a demanding
but kind motherly figure who was in a position to advance her writing
career. Adams had been writing a second novel for years. Though she
didn't save the rough drafts of "Mothering" or "A Spell in San Francisco"
or any of its other iterations, the rejections and comments that survive
show a discouraging process. Abels changed all that. About the time

Gloria Steinem and her coeditors were launching *Ms.* magazine, Alice
Adams also found the nerve to try another novel.

This time she called the story *Families and Survivors*, taking her cue
from a conversation she'd had with Renata Gaddini in Italy the summer
before: "She said that our parents, the parents of our generation, had
tried to kill us, but that we had survived."[50] The novel is about two
young women who resemble Alice Adams and Judith Clark Adams. It
begins with stunning, quiet drama as naked fourteen-year-old virgins
Louisa and Kate talk about "sex appeal" by the side of Louisa's parents'
swimming pool. Abels sold the chapter as a short story to *Redbook* for
"a lot of money" and Adams just kept writing twelve more chapters that
leapfrog through Louisa's life over the next thirty years—an affair with
her father's psychiatrist; marriage to a graduate student in Palo Alto; the
birth of her daughter; lovers and divorce; remarriage and a New Year's
party at the communal house where her daughter lives—all threaded
by enduring friendship with Kate. Adams wrote the dated sections as
if each were a short story.

This progress did not mean that she *liked* writing a novel. "Someone
(perhaps you) should really stop me when I even mention novels—they
make me miserable: working on them, waiting for them to be sold,
etc—especially doing both," she told Max Steele.[51]

That misery was soon over. In the summer of 1973 Abels submitted
Families and Survivors to Robert Gottlieb, editor in chief at Knopf. He
passed it along to a young editor who decided she could help Alice revise
her manuscript into a successful novel. Victoria Wilson was twenty-three
years old, having been hired by Gottlieb after she'd attended Goddard
College and worked a year at Simon and Schuster. Here is the first
paragraph of the review of the manuscript that Wilson sent to the other
editors, including Gottlieb:

> I think Alice Adams is an extremely strong writer. There is no question
> that this is an effective, quite moving novel. Her characters, for the
> most part, are real and she is able to get at the most subtle feelings in
> an amazingly short time. But the fact that she is such an excellent short
> story writer gets in her way. There is almost an impatience with her
> characters and the movement of the book . . . she begins something
> with all the tightness that is needed when writing a story, and with

the same tightness needed to develop and complete a short story, she moves her characters in the novel just as quickly.[52]

Wilson did not stop with diagnosing a problem. Her five-page, elite-typed, single-spaced offer to accept the novel, dated July 11, 1973, gave excruciatingly detailed suggestions for the rewrite she would require, though an eager reader could find praise there as well.

Alice Adams was that eager reader. On August 3, Adams responded that she was excited and "really turned on" by Wilson's letter: "I could not be more pleased at the prospect of working on that book with you. And I've looked forward to writing you"—while waiting for Abels to complete negotiations that led to a $5,000 advance—"as I've looked forward to seeing someone with whom I could talk."

Thus began a conversation destined to last for the rest of Adams's writing life.

PART IV

SUCCESS

CHAPTER TWENTY

Editors and Friends

*Suddenly aroused, Ardis raises her head and stares at Walpole. "I
am a beautiful girl," she rasps out, furiously.*

—Alice Adams, "Beautiful Girl,"
Beautiful Girl

"I really said it all in *Families*—Christ that was 30 years of my life,"
Adams told Max Steele after the book was published.[1] The creative
and editorial process that enabled Adams to put three decades into 211
pages that told a coherent story owed much to Victoria Wilson. The
"extremely bright" young editor explained that Adams's tendency toward
tight structure and character precision hurt a novel: "I think you have
to decide who the important characters are, how they fit in with one
another . . . and how they build the novel."[2] Wilson told Adams to
leave the manuscript of *Families and Survivors* home on her fall 1973
trip to Europe. Rather, she urged her, "let it enter your dreams . . . you
can be sure your mind is typing away even if your fingers aren't." Just
finishing her first year as a book editor, Wilson found herself working
with a mature author who was, nonetheless, willing to be heavily edited
even as she sometimes opposed Wilson's suggestions. Both women typed
out their thoughts in lengthy letters, a polite, laborious process that led
to exceptional clarity. Thus *Families and Survivors* became the honeymoon book for a sometimes difficult but ultimately enduring editorial
marriage.

After returning from Europe in October, Alice rewrote many chapters, eliminated and combined characters, and got it all back to Wilson
in December. The result, Wilson found, was "at the stage where instead

of reading it with the purpose of trying to suggest changes, I just found myself soaking it in . . . it is simply fun to read." After that, author and editor spoke on the phone for the first time, beginning a personal friendship that complicated and strengthened their work together. In the end, Adams credited Wilson with an "extraordinarily perceptive understanding of what I'm trying to do." The cover Wilson planned confirmed that. Greenwich Village artist Joan Hall's assemblage of time-pieces and wedding rings surrounds an image of a couple: "How very odd," Alice said, "that that girl looks like me at 14 or 18 or something."[3] *Families and Survivors* was scheduled for publication the following fall.

While *Families and Survivors* was in production, Adams turned out a stream of new short stories and began a new novel. In a trilogy called *The Todds*—"Verlie I Say Unto You," "Are You in Love?," and "Alternatives"—she boldly explored her memories of Verlie Jones, her parents, and Dotsie. But lest anyone take these stories as pure auto-biography, she called herself Avery Todd, gave Avery a living brother named Devlin, and invented characters like the poet Linton in "Are You in Love?" (based on Billy Abrahams) as she needed them. The *Atlantic Monthly* bought both "Verlie" and "Alternatives." Alice worried about how these stories would be received in Chapel Hill, even though her stories call the town Hilton—after the place near which the troubled house named Howards End stands in E. M. Forster's novel.

Both Lucie Jessner and Max Steele assured Alice that Dotsie could not possibly object to "Alternatives"—"a good deal of tenderness in that story," Jessner said—but in the end Dotsie felt "hurt" by it and told Jessner so. Alice received such information secondhand. It was probably the character of Tom Todd in "Alternatives" that most upset Alice's stepmother: Nic, as Alice admitted to Max, came out as a "ghastly old prick." In Chapel Hill, one person told Max the story showed how "bitterly" Alice regarded her father, while another thought it showed that she regarded him with "so much love." With smiling irony, Max insisted, "It would be hard to say what your feelings are since artists are, behind the great revelations, reticent people."[4]

For Adams these stories were part of "a curious rethinking" of her mother that began after Nic died.[5] A "very moving" letter from Judith Clark Adams after Nic's death inspired Alice to write her most celebrated story. The letter (lost, unfortunately) made Alice think about what the Adamses had meant to Judith: "It occurred to me to try to write a story about us from her point of view. And, with radical changes of course, that is how this story came about."[6] Looking at her family as an outsider proved "interesting and instructive." In "Roses, Rhododendron," Jane Kilgore moves from Boston to a North Carolina town with her "big brassy bleached blonde" mother. Once there, Jane becomes the medium for telling the story of a family, their house, and their countryside:

> The house I fell in love with was about a mile out of town, on top of a hill. A small stone bank that was all overgrown with tangled roses led up to its yard, and pink and white roses climbed up a trellis to the roof of the front porch . . . the lawn sloped down to some flowering shrubs. There was a yellow rosebush, rhododendron, a plum tree, and beyond were woods—pines, and oak and cedar trees. The effect was rich and careless, generous and somewhat mysterious. I was deeply stirred.

Adams tells the story in this swirly, associative manner throughout. There's seemingly no pattern to the revelations about house, family, and countryside that Jane loves, yet Adams's now well-established ABDCE format is there, its climax coming when Jane sees "the genteel and opaque surface of that family shattered" by voices raised and words going out of control, exposing a "depth of terrible emotions" that Jane does not comprehend until later.

Imagining her story from another's—Judith's—perspective allows Adams to witness herself as Harriet. Here is her own childhood, seen primarily through love rather than fear. As the youthful friendship once did, "Roses, Rhododendron" enacts a peaceful separation from home:

> I thought Harriet was an extraordinary person—more intelligent, more poised and prettier than any girl of my age I had ever known. I felt that she could become anything at all—a writer, an actress, a foreign correspondent (I went to a lot of movies). And I was not entirely wrong; she eventually became a sometimes-published poet.

In this roundabout way, Adams could praise herself as never before—though she had already outpaced "sometimes-published" Harriet Farr.

The *New Yorker* turned down "Roses, Rhododendron" in 1973 but accepted a revision at the end of the next year. A young fiction editor, Frances Kiernan, did the editing. It appeared in the magazine early in 1975 and was included in *Prize Stories 1976: The O. Henry Awards* (with third prize) and in *Best American Short Stories 1976*. It brought fifty fan letters ("a practically perfect story," according to old acquaintance and professor Bill Webb in Cambridge).[7] Alice answered every one.

Other reactions were more complicated. Alice intended "Roses, Rhododendron" as "a sort of Valentine," she told Judith in advance of its appearance in the *New Yorker*, but said, "I know it will be hard for you to read." Indeed, Judith was not "crazy wild" about the story. Alice's parents had been idols to her, and she said to Alice, "I really don't want these idols made human although my caring for you does make me want to see it from your eyes." Judith was also troubled by the raunchiness of "her" mother, the story's Margot. Alice replied immediately: "I invented raunchy Margot . . . in no way like [Judith's mother] Dorothy." For the story, she explained the mothers needed to be so different that they would avoid meeting. "But it's terrible—one makes these distortions, and then one's favorite friend thinks: God, did she see Dorothy as raunchy? I do see the enormous difficulties in reading something by an old close friend. Bob has something of the same trouble," Alice concluded.[8] Judith understood and her friendship with Alice thrived.

Another letter came from Willie T. Weathers, a retired Latin professor at Randolph-Macon Woman's College who described herself as one of Agatha Adams's best friends. She congratulated Alice on her literary success and on fulfilling Agatha's "frustrated ambition," but scolded her for portraying her mother as a "sad and passive figure" in her stories. Agatha, she argued, "combined brains, personal magnetism, a delightful sense of humor, and talents in many fields." She hoped that sometime Alice would "try to paint her in the round."[9]

That, of course, was the project Adams was undertaking in her continual revisiting of her house and family in Chapel Hill. Weathers seems not to have registered the entirely new—invented, certainly not passive—narrative with which "Roses, Rhododendron" endows Harriet's mother. Emily Farr, we learn through epistolary gossip, left her husband "without so much as a by-your-leave" and went to work at the Folger Shakespeare Library in Washington. The narrator imagines the Farrs "happier apart" and approves Emily's valiant decision. Alas, when Lawrence Farr falls ill, Emily returns as his final caretaker and dies shortly after him. So much for the liberation of Agatha.

Adams does make "Roses, Rhododendron" a Valentine to Judith by ending the story with a letter *to* the narrator *from* Harriet (herself). In it, Harriet recalls the two girls on their bikes at the top of the hill: "Going somewhere. And at first I thought that picture simply symbolized something irretrievable, the lost and irrecoverable past, as Lawrence and Emily would be lost." But through story and through Judith, Adams *has* recovered that past. With both her parents dead and the house in her stepmother's possession, the storyteller has revivified her friendship with Judith. With a neat gambit, Adams wraps it up by having Jane's husband read Harriet's letter and say, "She sounds so much like you."

"I really have no imagination at all, just a terrific memory," Adams once claimed.[10] Certainly it was true, and sometimes a liability, that her imagination worked tirelessly upon the materials that memory and friends presented to her. Max Steele, who praised "the ease with which [she went] back and forth through time where time is all one plane and where the past is part of and as important as the present," credited this ease to Alice's "astounding memory." He added a not-unreasonable suggestion: "Sometimes I suspect you make up things and convince the rest of us that it really happened to us and we've simply forgot."[11] Be that as it may, Adams had a tremendous recombinant imagination.

This is nowhere more the case than in the stories Adams wrote about the love she'd felt in the house in Chapel Hill. Another of these, "Home Is Where," revisits the summer of 1958, when she stayed there and met Steele. Told in the first person by Claire, the story transforms deeply Southern Max into a proper Bostonian psychiatrist with the middle name of Saltonstall. As Claire heads back to San Francisco and divorce, she writes Caleb, "I think you saved my life last summer, I will really always love you." Under the title of "Learning to Be Happy," a shortened version of the story appeared in *Redbook* in September 1976. Max told Alice he loved it but would say no more because he was writing his reaction in his own story.

Steele's "reaction" became "Another Love Story" about the same Claire and Caleb, retold from Caleb's point of view. In a funny, complicated, self-deprecating way, Steele speculates that "Claire" wasn't really in love with "Caleb" so much as with the landscape of the Piedmont South where she grew up. "Home Is Where" says that Claire and Caleb laughed all through their summer together but doesn't tell what they laughed about. In Max's story, Caleb knows "exactly what they . . . laughed about . . . not just family jokes about his car but also about Roscoe and the Troll, and grasshoppers and the sensational hiccoughs." The Troll is a busybody neighbor named Louise Kroll—a familiar type from Adams's own Southern-town stories—who tries to revenge her thwarted passion for Caleb by spreading a rumor that he is homosexual. Claire champions Caleb against the destructive Mrs. Kroll by letting her know that she is Caleb's lover.* And Roscoe is a "black athlete and singer" who comes to town to give a concert at the university. As Claire and Roscoe discuss mutual friends, Caleb realizes they have been lovers. After a laughable interlude with the Troll, Roscoe departs to visit his parents in Atlanta. Steele's account references Alice's relationship with Trummy Young—whether Alice told Max about that or Young came through North Carolina that summer. Despite a whimper of jealousy, Steele gives a flattering picture of Roscoe, as does almost everyone who knew him: he possesses "the deepest, most beautifully modulated voice in the world" and exhibits "tremendous poise" in the face of Mrs. Kroll's gaucheries.† Max's remarkable fiction serves as a bit of shared intimate information between himself and Alice.

Max sent "Another Love Story" to Alice, wondering if he could publish it and if he should change the names. "If it works," he joked, "I'm going to answer all stories I read and become more prolific than Joyce Carol Oates: Max Steele's 'The Birth of Ivan Ilyich,' 'The Fourth of the Three Sisters' and so on."[12] Alice "adored" Max's story and urged her editor at *Redbook*, Anne Mollegen Smith, to buy it.[13] It appeared (titled "About Love and Grasshoppers") in the May 1977 issue, accompanied by

---

* Rumors that Steele was gay circulated in later years but no one I spoke to believed them. The notion seems to stem from the fact he never remarried and became somewhat reclusive in Chapel Hill except for his friendships with younger writers.

† Trummy Young played at UNC Memorial Hall in 1954 and appeared in the movies *The Glenn Miller Story* and *High Society*, so Steele might have seen Young before hearing about him from Alice. (But Young did not have a deep voice.)

a picture of Alice and Max sitting near each other (but hardly together) in Squaw Valley and an explanation that the "fictional fiction writer named Claire Hamilton" in Adams's recent story "is also a character in Max Steele's story." Let the speculation begin.*[14]

Adams began what would be her third novel, *Listening to Billie*, in 1974. As the title suggests, it is threaded with Billie Holiday's voice and brokenhearted songs. When Billie "died, killed herself, or was killed— one could take any view" in 1959, Adams's heroine reacts to the death "in a violent, personal way."

Racial and economic differences would have made it pretentious for Adams to claim the identity she felt with Billie Holiday. Nonetheless she understood that for herself, as for Eleanora Fagan (Billie's birth name), the aspiration to elegance and loveliness and ladylikeness had been a trap. Beauty attracted men who made promises. Disappointment followed. Indeed, Adams's face has a beauty comparable to Holiday's in its large expressive mouth, less-than-perfect teeth, high forehead, prominent eyebrows, large eyes, and Roman nose. In the 1950s Alice sometimes wore her hair pulled back from her forehead just as Billie often wore hers. Only a lovely face can bear so much light.

Holiday's song "God Bless the Child" articulates a lesson Alice was mastering in the 1970s. Writing income and living with Bob McNie freed Alice from part-time jobs. She was reluctant to identify with the movement then called "women's lib" but it had a deep effect upon her. The liberation movement, Gloria Steinem believes, "happened not so much by organization as contagion."[15] Exposure to feminist ideas prompted Alice to realize the prejudices that had held her back. Having a woman agent and woman editor changed the entire landscape of publishing for her.

* Writer Randall Kenan, who first met Alice Adams when he was a student of Steele's, recalled: "For a couple of months [in the late 1980s] I worked as the receptionist at Knopf. One day Alice Adams stepped off the elevator. I introduced myself and she was very friendly. I mentioned that I had recently read the two stories in *Redbook*, and she gazed off into the distance and said, 'Yes, Max still thinks that's funny, doesn't he?'" About the same time, Alice sent a copy of Max's story to Bryant Mangum with a note asking him what he made of it, thus hoping he would see the connection between the two stories.

And that success shook up her friendships. Some friends she'd made in San Francisco over the years were ambivalent about her success as a writer. A few glimpsed themselves in her fictional characters while others simply envied her. Patricia Zelver, an Abrahams protégée whose stories were appearing in *Esquire* and the *Atlantic*, refused to understand that *Families and Survivors* had been purchased by Knopf; she kept saying, "*If* you sell your novel . . . ," when she spoke to Alice.[16]

Not that Alice was easy to please. Zelver's husband recalled, "You were always afraid you'd say something and then she'd say she thought you were a shit"; he believed that Alice had dropped Patricia without reason, whereas Alice reported, "The Zelvers have totally dropped us."[17] When a commercial artist gave Alice a gift of stationery with ALICE ADAMS embossed across the top in the *New Yorker*'s signature typeface, she thought it was too ostentatious—but used it anyway. As a writer in San Francisco she felt lonely: "I seem to have very little in my mind but writing. And I really wish you were around to talk about it," she wrote Max.[18]

Shortly after President Nixon resigned in August 1974, both Max Steele and Victoria Wilson came west for the writers' conference in Squaw Valley, where Alice and Max were leading a workshop. Wilson stayed with Alice in Truckee and was dazzled by Bob and his house. Alice thought her editor was "very gentle delicate brilliant." Vicky Wilson was still mourning her father, physicist and novelist Mitchell Wilson, who'd died not long before. Mitchell's decision not to join Enrico Fermi and I. I. Rabi to do atomic research in Los Alamos because he "knew full well what the bomb would be used for" had led him to become a popular science writer instead, so Vicky grew up around writers and publishers. Max Steele described Wilson afterward as "that nasty little snip from Knopf" (was he jealous?) but Alice saw her new editor as a godsend of whom she felt both protective and possessive. When a sudden squall delayed Wilson's return from a hike with conference instructors Anne and David Perlman, Alice arrived at the Perlmans' in a "towering rage." She accused them of trying to cozy up to Wilson and ended her friendship with them. Alice was terribly nervous about facing the workshop audience, but students praised her as a star and requested more women on the faculty. Wilson thought Alice was "the only serious writer there."[19]

Literary success made San Francisco more appealing in a particular way: it enabled Alice to find new friends. While *Families and Survivors* was in production, she and four other literary writers, Sheila Ballantyne, Margery Finn Brown, Diane Johnson, and Ella Leffland, formed the nucleus of a group of "lady writers" who met for lunch at the Washington Square Bar and Grill.* They pointedly avoided Enrico's, the "too macho" North Beach bar frequented by Richard Brautigan, Don Carpenter, Jeremy Larner, Evan S. Connell, Herb Gold, and Herb Caen. Alice held "a half-baked theory that women writers are less ego-bound than men."[20] Asked by *Publishers Weekly* to name writers she most admired, Alice loyally mentioned her four lunchmates as well as fiction writer and *Gourmet* columnist Laurie Colwin, who lived in New York and was edited by Wilson. "I see a movement among all writers, male or female, away from the conventional 'male stud novel' toward something far more diversified and exploratory, Alice said."[21]

"One pleasant aspect of women writers getting together," Alice said, "is that it's nice to know other women out of true mutual interests, rather than because one's husbands are in the same business or graduate school—or children of the same age, etc."[22] These lunch group writers wrote books that were subversive in their evocation of women's lives and characters. Ballantyne's maudlin, brilliant 1975 novel *Norma Jean the Termite Queen* was an instant classic in the mad-housewife genre. Like Adams's heroines, Norma Jean finds salvation by doing significant creative work. Brown, who was older and married to a retired military man, was publishing short stories in women's magazines and working toward a story collection.[23] Leffland's *Mrs. Munck* is about a woman taking revenge on the man who seduced and impregnated her years before; her more recent *Love Out of Season* chronicles a woman painter's sexual obsession during the late 1960s. When their lunch meetings began, Leffland was writing her most-read novel, *Rumors of Peace*; Ballantyne was finishing *Imaginary Crimes*; and Johnson was in the midst of *Lying Low*.

Unlike most of Alice's friends, Leffland was a native Californian, educated at San Jose State College. She lived alone because marriage terrified her: "I thought it would interfere too much with what I wanted to do, which was to paint and write." She protected herself by choosing already-married or "not marriage material" lovers. Alice described Ella

---

* When their meetings began to draw notice from *Chronicle* gossip columnists, they began meeting at each other's homes.

as "serious, dedicated, intense, rather shy, sly sense of humor, quite beautiful."[24] They were amused to discover that they'd both had affairs with Doubleday's West Coast editor, Luther Nichols. "Neither of us knew he was the biggest skirt-chaser in San Francisco at the time! I don't think anyone knew because you wouldn't think it of Luther that way, there was that quality to him. That's what both Alice and I saw in him."[25] Alice and Ella also confided in each other that they'd had abortions—by the same Tijuana doctor, as Leffland recalled. Alice talked about affairs easily, with a sort of "collegiate flip" in her attitude, Leffland said.

Johnson was also published by Knopf, where Robert Gottlieb was her editor. Johnson's husband, pulmonologist John Murray, recalled Alice from twenty years earlier when he and his first wife, Sally, attended summer barbecues with the Linenthals and other Menlo Park friends. When Johnson read *Families and Survivors*, she was amused to recognize names and personalities from her husband's family. Perhaps only another fiction writer could accept the strangeness of that coincidence.

By the time *Families and Survivors* was published, those first marriages had ended. John Murray and Diane Johnson met later at UCLA, where he was on the medical faculty and she had completed a PhD in nineteenth-century literature and divorced the father of her four children. When she and Murray moved to the Bay Area, she had published two novels and *The True History of the First Mrs. Meredith and Other Lesser Lives*, her groundbreaking biography of the extraordinary Victorian sexual transgressor Mary Ellen Peacock. "A lesser life does not seem lesser to the person who leads one," Johnson wrote of the argumentative, beautiful, scandal-marked wife of the famous novelist George Meredith. Not long after she met Johnson, Alice Adams read *Lesser Lives* and sent her a note of admiration.

Alice and Bob and Diane and John went out together and clicked easily in social situations. Despite the great difference in the men's vocations, they were united by interest in food, travel, houses, and politics. Pauline and Richard Abbe, old friends of John's, became close to Alice and Bob. They got together at the Johnson-Murray home in Berkeley, at Lake Tahoe, and at beach houses. When the Johnson-Murray cat had kittens, Alice and Bob took two and named them Black and Brown. As a professor of literature at UC Davis with teenage children at home, Johnson managed an ambitious schedule. Her newest novel, *The Shadow Knows*, about a divorced woman with four children threatened by real and imagined dangers, was forthcoming at about the same time as *Families and Survivors*. After reading that novel, Adams praised her friend's ability to write about depths of neuroticism and fear that she wouldn't attempt herself. As Adams saw it, you had to be "a very sane, okay person" to write Johnson's books; "I wouldn't touch it," she said. Alice loved the novel but thought Johnson deserved an award for "least satisfactory ending . . . Christ I have no idea what happened and I wonder if she did."[*][26]

Their group was "nothing like a writing group," according to Leffland. It was a "mixture of talk—gossip—by bright people who were interesting to be with." An experiment with group critiques of works in progress failed. The writers in this group, later including Judith Rascoe, Millicent Dillon, and Susan Sward, usually completed a work before showing it to others. During an era when many women were participating in "consciousness-raising" sessions to discuss their lives from a feminist perspective, Alice's lunch group filled a niche: these writers had been raising their consciousnesses all their lives and now valued one another as published writers who understood the peculiarities of their vocation.

Through Johnson, Alice became friends with Alison Lurie, who had been the other woman in Albert J. Guerard's writing seminar at Harvard in 1945–46. "She's a lot warmer and more real than I'd remembered or perhaps has changed: God knows, I'm nicer than I was at 18, not to mention happier," Alice said.[27] Lurie (then Alison Bishop) and Johnson had met as unhappy wives at UCLA in the mid-1960s. Lurie's fifth novel, *The War Between the Tates*, garnered acclaim in 1974 when she was a part-time lecturer at Cornell University, where her estranged husband, Jonathan Bishop, was a full professor. On a visit to the Bay Area, Lurie was the guest of honor for dinner at the Johnson-Murrays' in Berkeley. That evening Lurie asked Alice how she liked Bob's new

---

* Robert Towers, reviewing for the *New York Times*, shared this opinion: "But for all its brilliance of insight and characterization, *The Shadow Knows* is significantly flawed by a basic irresolution, by the failure of the author to track down a sufficiency of the hares she has let loose." ("Four Days of Four Lives," *New York Times*, November 19, 1978.)

mustache. When Alice admitted that really she didn't care for it, Lurie challenged Bob: "How would you like it if Alice came to bed with a small toothbrush attached to her upper lip?" Alice thought the remark was hilarious and retold it often.[28] Undeterred, Bob wore a mustache for the rest of his days.

As her star rose, Alice sensed complex reactions from other women. She associated these with Agatha Adams: "I am the successful rival of my mother! Anger-fear: Margery, Anne F—Anne P, Connie C, Pat Z, Gail, Ruth B, Mig," she wrote in her notebook. Success meant getting paid for her work—her next entry in the same notebook is a toting up of recent earnings.[29] She was as generous to writers she admired as she was dismissive of those who lost her favor. When Gina Berriault, author of exquisite short stories who lived in San Francisco with Leonard Gardner (revered author of a single novel, *Fat City*), needed an agent, Alice referred her to Cyrilly Abels. "I think this will enormously improve her life," Alice told Max Steele after Abels agreed to represent Berriault.[30] Likewise, Alice urged Sandy Boucher, her former coworker whom Alice called a "women's libber," to send work to Victoria Wilson. By then Boucher had come out as a lesbian and published a collection of stories with a small press. "Alice was open to new ideas," Boucher felt. "Wedded to her lifestyle, not going to toss that and try something else. But she wanted to know what others were doing, thinking." They remained friends when Boucher moved to Oakland and became a Buddhist. "Alice asked questions about Buddhism—does-it-help-you-get-through-life? kind of thing." During this time, Boucher published well-received nonfiction books about feminism and Buddhism—about "American women in that patriarchal religion."

Publication of *Families and Survivors* caused tremors in Alice's psyche. "You possibly don't think of me as Jewish but I am," she told Victoria Wilson as she described her condition with a favorite Yiddish proverb: "'A Jew's joy is not without panic'—things seem to be going so well, I am besieged by cancer phobias, fear of flying etc."[31] On the day *Families and Survivors* came out, Alice was in Mexico, at the Catalina Hotel in the resort village of Zihuatanejo, which would become her favorite winter retreat and a frequent setting for her short stories. Bob read the novel there and said, "Oh, so that's what you do!" (He'd "liked it a lot," he added later.) Others back home were more critical, especially of her characterization of the Wasserman family in her novel. The Wassermans, like Mark Linenthal's family, on whom they are based, are Jewish. Alice's lead character, Louisa Calloway, marries into this family with mixed feelings about her future husband: "Her instincts impossibly war; she wants to hit Michael in the face, to run away by herself and cry; she wants to be loved by and married to Michael, and accepted as a Jew by all Jews." When marriage makes her unhappy, Louisa blames Michael's domineering mother.

In the novel's third chapter, Louisa and a woman named Barbara attend an awkward Sunday dinner at the Wasserman home in Cambridge. Mrs. Wasserman makes anti-Catholic remarks about her Irish maid, describes a nervous young man as "kikey," and quips tactlessly about her older son's homosexuality. Louisa and Barbara are appalled by the family dynamic they witness. Later, Barbara remarks that "the first Jews she ever met were horrible ('unfortunately')" and is reminded by "more thoughtful friends that the awfulness of the Wassermans has little if anything to do with their being Jewish."

Adams had no patience for anyone who suggested she was anti-Semitic. The object of her venom was her former mother-in-law. Nonetheless, because Adams had divorced Mark Linenthal and made no secret of her dislike for him, the novel caused a stir in the English Department—people joked that Mark should call a lawyer, and his friends shunned Alice. The description of Mrs. Wasserman's nose, for instance, set off alarms: "Her ugliness accuses everyone: her big bulbous nose and small stingy mouth, her pigeon-fat body, her impossible thinning gray hair." Nor did the damage stop with the Linenthals. "To tell the truth, the anti Jewish things were hard to take," Lucie Jessner wrote Alice. "I had not thought I was so touchy, but with a wave of such feelings getting stronger here all the time, it did hurt me."[32]

Upset by Jessner's hurt, Alice quickly replied: "I guess you mean horrible Mrs. Wasserman—but is it really anti-Jewish to describe a horrible person who is Jewish? And one of the most horrible things about her, I thought I said, was her anti-Semitism, her use of that dreadful word, the word I am unable to say. Also, the 2 other most unpleasant people, Jack Calloway and King, are also described as being specifically anti-Semitic. I would have thought it an anti-anti-Semite book . . . the 'Wassermans' were so truly horrible, and so intent on doing me in—that I could not *not* write about them. And I did hold off until they were dead."[33]

Over at the Linenthal household no one talked about the novel much but it was understood that Alice had been exorcising the ghosts of her first marriage in this autobiographical fiction. When Peter Linenthal told his mother he thought she'd been "a little hard on Daddy," she talked to him about "people changing, some people being poison to live with for certain other people."[34] When he also asked his mother why she had made the second Mrs. Wasserman very fat (unlike his stepmother, Frances), Alice shrugged that it was "just fiction." As for the caricature of his grandparents, Peter understood that his mother was "very pro-Jewish, liked Jewish people, maybe even wished she were Jewish." "But," he went on, "she really disliked Anna Linenthal and I can see why. Anna was small-minded, clingy, complaining, guilt-inducing, a stereotypical Jewish mother you could say. My mom didn't like the control Anna had over my dad, and neither did he."

The Linenthal family underwent changes in the 1970s. Radicalized and disabused of some of his Harvard elitism by late-1960s political events at San Francisco State, Mark Linenthal saw a psychoanalyst. About the same time, Frances Linenthal criticized a friend of her son's named Judith Freeman for being obsessed with women's rights. Freeman responded that feminism was worth being fanatical about; she cited Marge Piercy's essay "The Grand Coolie Damn" for its exposé of sexism in leftist organizations and families in which men got attention and glory while women did the unpaid daily "shitwork."[35] "This was so shocking to my mother that she decided to study it," Lincoln Pain said. "It started her on a road to feminism."

Frances had once been serious about poetry. But she was stymied by a male teacher's criticism and stopped writing for twenty years. She'd become "Queen of the Dips"—as she styled her hostess role—rather than a poet. At fifty-three, she changed. "She said, 'I didn't want to go to sleep in the middle of my life,'" recalled the younger poet Rachel Blau DuPlessis. "She was a native intellectual—she had the usual good or decent education and opportunities for travel of her class, but it was as if suddenly everything fell into place. It was, I think, a conversion experience of the kind many women were having at this time. . . . She wanted 'ideas going into action' (to cite Pound). Frances's intellectual and poetic verve—her sense that it mattered—were a great gift." *HOW(ever)*, the journal Frances founded with several other poets, nurtured several generations of women artists.[36]

Mark Linenthal "was perplexed and not used to being screamed at all the time," Lincoln Pain said of his stepfather's struggle with the changes that feminism brought into his life. "It was difficult to be a man of the 'greatest generation' suddenly confronted with this new anti-patriarchy. Those guys believed the patriarchy had just saved the world." But Frances Jaffer, emboldened with feminist theory and her rediscovered creative energy, insisted on discussion and change. She also defended men, Lincoln remembered, and told friends that criticizing men was "a distraction from what is important about feminism, and, besides, they should raise a few [men] before speaking about it."

Nonetheless—*however*—raising three boys and living with Mark, who was known for his enthusiastic domination of conversations, had silenced Frances long enough. In a radio talk and reading when she was sixty, she explained her idea of female aesthetics: "Since form has inevitable connection with content and since our lives are different and our bodies are different, there may be some formal differences." After Frances was diagnosed with rheumatoid arthritis, she and Mark moved to a smaller house on Twin Peaks where she designated a room as her study. When he was younger, Peter Linenthal remembered, Frances had "listened intensely and stood up for anyone at the dinner table who wasn't being heard (often by my dad)." When discussions of feminist issues dominated the table, he "was not a guy to stick his feet in the cement—he took things seriously and came around." He took over much of the cooking after the boys were out on their own and became a supporter of his wife's work.[37]

Though Mark learned to appreciate feminist poetry and tolerate feminist ideas, he apparently never stretched his appreciation to include his former wife's accomplishments during the same era. Living in the small, sometimes chilly literary world of San Francisco, Alice and Mark had few kind words for each other. Money may have been one subtext. A brief exchange of letters between lawyers occurred when Peter moved out of Alice's house and Mark withdrew child support payments. After Mark Linenthal's father died in 1976, he and his sister inherited their parents' estate.

For Michael Linenthal, who had stopped practicing law and moved to San Francisco to pursue his interest in theater, the moral and financial freedom his parents' deaths might have provided came too late. He had become paralyzed by a polio virus he contracted in Mexico during the summer of 1973, where he had been enjoying one of his few long-term relationships with a lover. The treatments he needed were extreme, including a sort of corset to assist his breathing. In January 1974 he died. Alice thought his death might have been a suicide: "Very sad all around, and I don't know why I'm telling you this," she wrote Max Steele, "except Peter and I were just talking about it on the phone. Poor Peter had to telephone Mark, who with his customary tact was in Mexico himself, and Mark's father."[38]

Though Peter had long viewed his uncle Michael as a terrifying example of gay life, they'd established a more comfortable relationship in recent years when Michael owned a house on Baker Street and Peter had an affair with a man who lived downstairs in that house.

With what seems a late-game act of self-assertion against his family, Michael Linenthal passed over his siblings and other nieces and nephews and left his house to Peter, who was supporting himself as a teacher and artist. Peter decided to sell his uncle's house and seek more for his money in the working-class and artistic Potrero Hill neighborhood. In the meantime, he invited Morissa McNie, who was pregnant, to live in the Baker Street house until her baby was born. Alice gloated with amusement over the whole arrangement: "Missy will be living there, among furniture from the elder Linenthals' house in Cambridge . . . wonderfully ironic because those old shits always said that you should buy furniture for grandchildren, and this afternoon I'm putting all this into a new story; may not even change any names."*[39]

Bob's daughter's pregnancy amused and fascinated Alice. "We're going to be sort of doubly illegitimate grandparents," she wrote Lucie Jessner, meaning that she and Bob were not married and neither was the mother-to-be. The father was Stephen Webster, son of Alice's friend and literary fan Ellis Webster; Morissa had no interest in marrying.

---

* Two stories, actually: "You Are What You Own: A Notebook" in *Return Trips;* "The Furniture: A True Story."

Alice and Bob were "neither entirely pleased nor the reverse—of course one is struck by the unreality of young girls who've never taken care of babies, not to mention young children." Twenty-seven-year-old Morissa planned to take the baby to work with her at City Lights bookstore.

Morissa's embrace of motherhood is behind the character of complacent Catherine in *Listening to Billie*. As Eliza worries over her daughter's pregnancy, "Catherine continue[s] with the platitudes of her generation as, silently and uncontrollably, Eliza did with those of hers." The young woman declines birth control, abortion, and marriage. While migrating between friends from Mendocino to Big Sur, she gestates a dark-haired boy she names Dylan. After Dylan's birth, Eliza finds herself taken by unexpected joy. Alone, she drinks a bottle of champagne, plays records by her favorite female singers (Billie, Lena Horne, Bessie Smith), and does "a very private swaying little dance." The story continues, "And she thought I am dancing a Grandmother Dance. Thought, Have I finally gone mad? But of course she had not; what she felt was wonderful—happiness, relief."

The birth of Morissa's baby—"a big fat boy named Jesse"—was another adjustment to new-age social arrangements for Alice. A year later, she declared: "Our grandchild is terrific—what is strange is that he looks a little like me—only much better. Missy is wonderful with him, I think probably better than if she were married." By then Morissa and baby Jesse Kyle McNie had followed Peter to his building on Potrero Hill.

The four-story bay-windowed structure had languished on the market because its seller wanted a large down payment. With cash from the sale of his uncle's house, Peter bought it for $55,000. Morissa, Jesse, and the thrift and recycling business she began occupied the downstairs. Above, rental apartments gave Peter some income; he converted the third floor and a large attic into living and studio space for himself. His kitchen window had a view across the city to Twin Peaks and beyond. "Peter has an interesting quality of knowing and finding and getting what he wants," Alice said. "I suppose really good instincts. Anyway, he is crazy about his house, his new garden, his views."[40] After Morissa and Jesse moved on and the neighborhood became gentrified, Christopher's Books moved into the first floor. Forty-some years later, Peter still lives and works there with Alice Adams's library alphabetically shelved in the attic and the Potrero Hill Archives Project in his basement.[41]

During the 1970s, both Alice and Peter were susceptible to the charms of the McNies. Bob was sophisticated and social and, because of his extreme good looks, appealing to both men and women. "I was probably attracted to him," Peter said later, though he didn't consider it that way at the time. His elder children, Robbie and Morissa, were also charismatic and "dazzlingly good-looking." Robbie made his own sheepskin coats and talked about living in the woods; Morissa had her love child, her artwork, her freedom. Alice contrasted her stepdaughter's sexual freedom with her own generation's: "Sex: the mistake of seeing it as an absolute, as final as death—whereas, Missy (probably) would see it as something that happens, an interchange between 2 people, more or less pleasurable, or not; having nothing to do with anyone else. The former attitude leads to jealous agonies—Missy's, not."[42]

In the case of Bob's youngest son, Joch Allin, known as Winky, nonconformity had a dark side. A year younger than Robbie and displaced by his parents' divorce and moves, Winky dropped out of high school. He moved to Pacific Grove with his mother, and he talked about being a marine biologist but made no educational plans. Given barbiturates for anxiety, he began to have paranoid episodes. "When he stayed with me when he was seventeen," Robbie recalled, "I found him at the mirror with a steak knife in his ear all bloodied trying to get the voices out." He was institutionalized several times and diagnosed with schizophrenia. After accompanying Bob on a visit to Winky at a facility in Napa in 1972, Alice noted, "Once his eyes were vacant. Now [they are] narrowed, confiding meanness. His malice, an awful echo of one's own."

Joch Allis McNie hanged himself on January 16, 1976, a full-moon night during a winter of severe drought. His mother, Deen McNie, found him, his feet only inches from the floor, in the doorway of a garage behind her house near Agate Beach in Pacific Grove. He was twenty-four.

Bob and Alice were at Bob's house in the mountains when they learned about Winky's suicide. They expected Diane Johnson for dinner and decided not to tell her, but then did. "Curiously, Bob has taken it better than I would have thought, and me worse," Alice told Max Steele. The young man had been "a miserable kid, hating himself and everyone else, and [they] knew this would happen," she continued. Whether that was so, whether Bob really wasn't upset, remains impossible to know.

Alice reacted with fear and fascination. "Wink, suicides. The *manner* of doing it: is hanging more hostile than shooting? Jumping off the Bridge seems least so: no one has to see something terrible—a mess," she wrote in her journal. A couple of weeks later she dreamed that Vasco Pereira had returned and was taking her to services for Winky. She recognized that she wasn't grieving for Winky: "I guess I'm so suicide-prone myself that I can't stand it when anyone does."[43]

Winky's mother organized a memorial for him. Seven people gathered in the dunes and a Universal Life minister read selections from Robinson Jeffers, who was, they noted, also a suicide. Morissa and Robbie took their brother's ashes up in a light plane and scattered them over Monterey Bay. Migrating gray whales spouted below them. Bob McNie chose not to be there.[44]

A few days later, Alice and Bob invited Robbie and Morissa and her toddler son to dinner. Robbie met silence when he tried to speak about his brother's death: "They just sat there, frozen, iceberg expression. And then Alice piped in and said, 'Robbie, this is not appropriate. We've dealt with this,' or maybe she said '*he's* dealt with this and shared with me privately.'" The evening devolved further when Morissa started a food fight with her brother. Winky's death hit her hard too. She began to drink heavily, moved to Seattle, and fell into a relationship with a man who abused Jesse. Later she moved east and made a new start. When she asked her father to visit her there without Alice so they could get to know each other, he replied that Alice had reacted angrily, then with tears. Morissa only half believed that, confiding to a friend that her "request that he share some of the process of his life" had frightened her father. "Emotional repression was what he taught me, and my confession of love in the letter was a breach of the contract with him . . . I wanted to relate to him. No go."[45]

After that dinner, Robbie distanced himself from Alice. "I wanted to cut her throat," he said. "I mean, if he's not going to be expressive about my brother's death—a suicide at that, and I express some feeling of myself . . . and I meet with HER retort, which was duplicated by him. That just fried me. Fucking fried me." But Alice had her own observation: "Robbie: the swollen presence of murder," she wrote in her journal.[46]

* · * · *

Other deaths also shadowed Alice during this decade. Her adored literary agent, Cyrilly Abels, died of cancer late in 1975. The success Abels had brought Adams was certified only weeks later when the National Book Critics Circle nominated *Families and Survivors* for the best fiction award. Authors of the other nominated books—all men—included her old friend Saul Bellow (*Humboldt's Gift*), Larry Woiwode (*Beyond the Bedroom Wall*), William Kotzwinkle (*The Fan Man*), and the winner, E. L. Doctorow (for *Ragtime*). The NBCC award, a new award that year (easily confused with the National Book Award), garnered little publicity. In fact, Alice later had to ask Victoria Wilson who'd won. With a referral from Wilson, Adams soon secured representation from Lynn Nesbit, then a principal at International Creative Management. Wilson's sister, Erica Spellman, worked there and took care of magazine submissions.

Ginny Berry, Alice's Radcliffe friend who taught at the University of San Francisco, was just forty-nine when she died of cancer early in 1976. Her death prompted Alice to write "What Should I Have Done?," a story she insisted came straight from Berry's life, as did some aspects of Cathy's character in *Superior Women*. Both versions tell of a passionate woman whose long love affair with a priest results in a pregnancy and in either a red-haired daughter (in the story) or a son (in the novel) or twins (as Alice wrote in a letter to Wilson) given up for adoption. After Berry's death Alice felt "grief—rage—anguish . . . and some guilt at never having called her" and wondered, "Just when did that start, that malevolent process of her cells?"

"Maybe I wrote that story out of too-strong feelings. You know that whole thing actually happened including the twin sons . . . and if I ever see that fucking priest again . . ."[47] The story's forbidden subject and harsh attitude made it difficult to publish until Alison Lurie, who had become an editor for Cornell University's *Epoch*, accepted it for that journal.

Another of Alice's friends, who is unnamed here at the request of her children, became the centerpiece of her story "Beautiful Girl." In the 1950s this witty, sharp-tongued widow from a southern city had been a featured debutante in a *Life* magazine spread on the custom of presenting "eligible daughters to polite society." She moved to Alice's San

Francisco neighborhood after her husband's suicide. She was a good writer who was discouraged by rejection notices but, with help from Alice, published an essay in the *Virginia Quarterly Review*. She and Alice shared a sense of humor and an understanding of growing up in the South and the expectations of women there; like Alice, she spoke of having a handsome black lover—"It was part of making a statement," one of her daughters thought. Alice and Bob became good friends with her daughter and Alice's most cherished of many cats was a little Manx given to her by this friend.

By 1976, Alice was deeply worried about her friend; she had changed "from an acerbic, amusing sometime-drunk [into] a rich mean alcoholic, barely ambulatory." To Staige Blackford, the *VQR* editor who'd published the essay, Alice confided that her friend's alcoholism was now so acute that you couldn't have a conversation with her after eleven in the morning. "I know a lot about heavy drinkers, having grown up among them, but this is something else," Alice told Blackford as she realized her friend should be hospitalized.[48] Perhaps Alice hoped that publishing "Beautiful Girl"—it came out in the *New Yorker* in 1977—would convince her friend to accept help. But her friend, whom Alice didn't alert in advance of the publication, was devastated that Alice would hurt her in this way. She never spoke to Alice again after "Beautiful Girl" appeared.

Adams replaced details about her friend's life with Chapel Hill settings when she created her character "Ardis Bascombe, the tobacco heiress, who twenty years ago was a North Carolina beauty queen" and now sat "in the kitchen of her San Francisco house, getting drunk" at four thirty in the afternoon. The plot concerns a visit to Ardis by Walpole Green, a man who hated Ardis for her popularity in college—until she gave him one drunken kiss. From then on, "he watched her as a lover would." In San Francisco, Green plans to take Ardis out to dinner but she's too drunk to go. Instead he concocts a plan to "save" her by taking her to a drying-out facility in Connecticut that caters to senators' wives. That outcome seems unlikely, but the possibility reveals Adams's concern about Bob—who, like Ardis, sleeps or passes out at the table—and her dawning recognition of her own risks and involvement.

In "Beautiful Girl," Adams also sends a message to her friend's daughter, who sometimes took refuge at Alice and Bob's apartment: she "will be more beautiful than Ardis ever was. She will be an exceptional beauty, a beautiful woman, whereas Ardis was just a beautiful girl."

The encroachments of age and alcoholism were much on Adams's mind throughout this decade of personal losses and professional successes. Reviewing Richard Yates's novel *The Easter Parade*, Adams notes, "Yates is especially strong on the non-pleasure of too much booze; some pages literally seem to smell of sweet cocktails."[49]

Diane Johnson noticed that "Alice disapproved of Bob's drinking—he could be loud and obnoxious when he got drunk, which was often, but she also drank and abetted him in other ways." In writing and publishing "Beautiful Girl" as the story of a woman sinking into alcoholism, Adams does more than appropriate her friend's story. She recognizes that it may be futile to try to change an alcoholic and makes a pact with herself that she will not be trapped in such a story herself.

CHAPTER TWENTY-ONE

Very Colette

— 1976–1979 —

Fate, as I should have recognized by now, tends to reward happiness rather than virtue . . .

—Alice Adams, "Lost Luggage,"
To See You Again

The charms and excesses of Bob McNie were fully on display for Alice's fiftieth birthday on August 14, 1976. For the occasion, the "mad person" Alice lived with presented her with fifty presents, each wrapped elegantly in brown tissue paper with darker brown ribbons.[1] "The fifty presents were not all diamonds—it is hard to think of anything I would like less than fifty diamonds," Adams said in her essay "On Turning Fifty" for *Vogue*. "There were a lot of cotton bandanas, all colors, a wonderful spectrum, but also some silk shirts, sweaters, books," and a Billie Holiday T-shirt. Opening this bounty "took several days (and think of the time it took R. to wrap them all)," she wrote, "with time out for Champagne and pasta feasts and a trip to a jazz place to hear Horace Silver, my favorite pianist." Even though she enjoyed this birthday more than she did her fortieth, being in her fifties also meant that she thought "about death much more than [she] did at thirty or forty . . ."[2]

Thinking about death at fifty meant wondering whether she or Bob would die first and "which was worse." Alice learned she had high blood pressure—but she said of the doctor who told her, "[He was] so handsome that I think that is what raised my pressure"—and tried both meditation and biofeedback to lower it.[3] She fielded phone calls from old friends with serious illnesses and weighed those against the story of a newer friend, Lavina Calvin, whom she came to know on

321

her now-annual January trips to Zihuatanejo. Lavina and her husband, Henry, were both in their seventies. Alice admired Lavina, who was a survivor of pancreatic cancer, for her determination, intelligence, and taut beauty. The couple's company, Henry Calvin Fabrics in Jackson Square, imported Belgian linen and other fine upholstery and drapery materials that formed the basis of Bob's decorating style.*

Adams celebrated the Calvins in stories. They can be traced in Carlotta and Travis Farquhar in the Zihuatanejo stories "At the Beach" and "The Haunted Beach." The portrait that most conveys Adams's admiration for this couple, and for Lavina in particular, is "The Girl Across the Room." Here Lavina is Yvonne Soulas, a cancer survivor whose strength Adams attributes to her husband's need of her: "She saw Matthew, so gaunt and stricken that she knew she had to live. It was that simple: dying was something she could not do to Matthew." That's the heart of a story that is enveloped by another episode in which Yvonne holds her husband in their marriage when he has fallen in love with a younger woman: ("*Je tiens à Matthew*," she thinks in her native French. "Tenir à. I hold to Matthew . . ."). She does this by treating Matthew "like someone with a serious disease . . . as though his illness were something that she didn't want to catch."

Alice and Bob liked both Calvins very much and the feeling was reciprocated. When Lavina read of herself in Adams's stories, it seemed to Alice that Lavina "became the person I had somewhat invented." The example of Lavina's quiet strength in her relationship with her husband, an artistically inclined entrepreneur like Bob McNie, may have given Alice hope for a similar rebalancing of power in her second decade of living with Bob. "With Carlotta and Travis Farquhar," Adams wrote in "The Haunted Beach," "Charles [a stand-in for Bob] tamed down, drank less, and shouted not at all; he was, in fact, his best, most imaginative, entertaining, generous, and sensitive self."

Adams had her next novel, *Listening to Billie*, under way before *Families and Survivors* came out, and excerpts from it appeared in magazines

---

* Adams virtually advertises the shop in *Rich Rewards*: "The Henry Calvin building, then, contained more beautiful linen samples than I could have imagined . . . Even the company's nice brick building had an old-world quality of excellence, of care."

before Adams submitted the whole manuscript to Victoria Wilson. If her previous novel was "social history," this one, Adams said, was "mostly about writing."[4] When she finished it early in 1976, feeling that it had been "horrible to write for some dark reason," she asked friends to read the manuscript before sending it to Nesbit and Wilson.[5] Knopf advanced her $10,000 this time, double what she received for *Families and Survivors.* Nonetheless, the editing process proved arduous. Wilson's first reading proposed difficult changes in the tone, structure, style, and focus of the book. "I have a hunch this isn't the book you want to write," she asserted. "I think you want to be inside of your characters so that we see each of these women as they see themselves . . ." Wilson felt that the book she wanted to read would sound more like the recently published "Roses, Rhododendron," which she adored. She thought Adams had instead brought the faster pace and exterior perspectives that worked in *Families and Survivors* to a story that needed to be "slow and rich in detail."[6]

This was a critical moment in an editorial relationship, analogous to the third year of a marriage. In May, Adams welcomed Wilson's detailed suggestions and spent the summer revising. In July, for instance, while working on chapter 6, she told Wilson, "[I] suddenly saw what you meant about re-writing from the inside out. That's what I'm doing." But after a phone call in September during which Wilson told her to cut her chapter about working in a medical office, Adams said, "[I felt] we were talking about different books. I didn't want to write a mother-daughter book (I think you're much more interested in that area than I am at this point) . . . What interested me about Eliza—and actually everyone else in the book—is WORK—and friends." Wilson answered these objections with a long letter and annotations on the revised manuscript, insisting she did not want to change the novel's "work" theme but that it had to be realized through the story of Eliza and her mother and half sister.[7]

Adams's outrage crested in the letter she wrote back: "All the time we were working on F&S, I had the most terrific feeling that . . . you understood what I was doing better than I did. Now I have exactly the opposite feeling, and I cannot tell you how unhappy, upset this has made me. I feel as though a horse had galloped over me . . . as though someone had wadded up my novel and thrown it back to me as a spitball . . . it now looks like one of my third grade spelling papers."

With that and more off her chest, Alice felt better: "I've often thought I needed assertiveness training, and this may be it." She would think about the novel while in England for the next three weeks. She even ended this letter with a joke: "Just so there'll be no confusion as to intent, from the start, my new novel is about circumcision fellatio and communism."[8]

The specifics of this editorial debate show two women intensely committed to their own positions. Wilson contended that Eliza could not be just a poet, she needed also to be an essayist "a la Diane Johnson." Adams protested, "Eliza *is a poet*, that is what this book is about. Diane is one of the most brilliantly rational, sanest people I know, not given to flukey intuitions. She would never write poetry, Eliza would never write essays." Then she added a sarcastic proposal: "(Oh well, what the hell, let's make her a ceramicist—something I really know about)."* Wilson's criticism of Eliza's vocation had merit. Eliza is unconvincing as a poet, probably because the reader is told about her poems but never given one to read, or because most readers know that poetry is not a way to earn a living. (As poet Howard Nemerov observed, poets are sometimes paid to talk about poetry but rarely to write it.) But for Adams, the point was not arguable. In the published novel Eliza *is* a poet.

Adams also accused Wilson of "trying to impose a very linear structure on a rather discursive book" and noted that feminist theorists "call a linear structure 'phallic'"—referring, probably, to the metaphor of the pen as a penis. Language, in this formulation adopted from French feminist critics, represents patriarchal law, while imagination represents chaotic bodily instincts. Virginia Woolf's novels, for instance, were nonlinear in their attempt to portray female protagonists such as Clarissa Dalloway in *Mrs. Dalloway* and Mrs. Ramsey in *To the Lighthouse*. As a poetic protagonist, Eliza asserts her history as a female body. Her story begins in pregnancy, followed by marriage to a gay man who commits suicide, years of raising her daughter alone, affairs with men who prove unsatisfactory or unattainable, and satisfying moments such as the Grandmother Dance she performs for herself alone. We can only

---

* "I had become so bored about pretending to write about a painter when I really know nothing about painting and a great deal about writing," Adams said in 1980. "I see an affinity between poetry and the short story and thought I could cope with Eliza's writing poetry." (Interview with Neil Feineman.)

assume that Eliza's poems are—as Adrienne Rich writes in "When We Dead Awaken"—"like dreams: in them you put what you don't know you know."

Alice's assertive letter stunned Wilson. An edited draft of her reply, preserved in Knopf's editorial files at the Harry Ransom Center, reads: "In the end you must write the book as you see it and if my changes or suggestions are helpful then so much the better."[9]

Adams reconsidered: "What upset me most was my feeling that if brilliant terrific Vicky thinks this book is so terrible as to need so much change—obviously she is right. . . . I have what I'm afraid is called a deficient ego." She apologized if she'd agreed to suggestions by phone that she later chose not to make. "I do not react well on my feet," she explained. "PLEASE do call, I love it—but just don't expect intelligent response to serious questions."

After consulting with Lynn Nesbit and Diane Johnson, walking, thinking, and rereading "the bloody ms. AGAIN," Alice agreed to rework it, though she actually made few concessions, saying, "In general, I agree with where you have fingered something being wrong but less often with your solutions." What Adams needed—and received—was time to see it anew.

Wilson had converted much of the novel from present to past tense, and Adams let that stand except in chapters about Eliza's half sister, Daria. Wilson noticed that Eliza's character was cued off of her mother's and urged Adams to offer more details about the mother, Josephine, who is a biographer. "When I contemplate the work of a biography," Adams inserted, "hours in libraries and museums (my cold feet in the British Museum, pneumonia in Yorkshire: Charlotte Brontë), the correspondence with uncooperative sources—when I think of all that, poetry seems an almost silly exercise, a childish toying with words." We can sense Alice's own mother, the librarian and biographer, as the ideal reader of that empathetic detail.

In the end, Alice revised quickly, despite days out for jury duty during which she realized she missed public contact ("the sheer solitude of writing often gets to me") and convinced her fellow jurors to award money to a black person injured on a bus. The day after Christmas, as Alice was packing for Zihuatanejo, she heard from Wilson: "You have now put in what you had written to me you wanted the book to be more of—more of a sense of her work life, those friendships, those people who allow you to move and agree to follow you through and those who just can't. The book is exciting now, and in its own way daring."[10]

Listening to Billie was a successful compromise, a collaboration. The "Office Work" chapter, which Adams insisted was the heart of her novel, remained. She had declined to change the ending of the chapter in which Eliza seduces the heart surgeon who is her boss; he is unable to get an erection and fires Eliza when she refuses to give him a second chance. It was and still is a bold scene—written long before the topic of sexual harassment in the workplace became daily news. Adams stood her ground about the character of Miriam, who is based on her friend Sheliah Wilbert. Wilson objected that Miriam was "an old time darky" who wants to be white and not a believable black character in the civil rights era. To senior editor Robert Gottlieb, Wilson confided that Adams was "loaded with pre–Civil War Southern care" and found it "rather amazing how unconscious Alice is about all the attitudes that she still seems to have toward blacks and Jews."[11] At one point Adams promised Wilson she would give Miriam a good job in the novel, but in the final revision she left Miriam as she had written her. She believed that lack of money and self-confidence (due to her racist surroundings) endangered Sheliah. She refused to turn her into a liberal success story.

In the end, Alice dedicated *Listening to Billie* "to Victoria Wilson with love." Wilson visited San Francisco in January 1977 and "all went well." Wilson "is one of those 30-year-old geniuses," she told interviewer Wayne Warga. "I don't like editing and we've had some rough times, but we've worked it through. I feel somehow she's rescued me and stayed by me."[12] Privately—to Lucie Jessner—Alice explained, "There is a certain problem with her youth (27); and personality type—she finds giving affection and praise extremely difficult, whereas I am really the opposite, terrible trouble with even legitimate anger."[13]

The correspondence between Adams and Wilson provides a remarkable record of arduous, fruitful editorial work. Wilson's accomplishment becomes more impressive if compared with the method used by her colleague Gordon Lish, who moved to Knopf in 1977 and, like Wilson, worked under Robert Gottlieb. Both editors had firm visions of the books they wanted their authors to produce but Wilson explained why she wanted changes whereas Lish made his changes in ink, directly on manuscripts. Still, it's interesting that both Adams and the author of the first book Lish edited, Raymond Carver, viewed themselves as spineless and even suppliant in relation to their editors. But Adams, unlike Carver, acknowledged her fears of having her book reshaped to friends (Max Steele, Diane Johnson, and Lucie Jessner) before speaking with her editor, thus preparing to stand her ground.[14]

Listening to Billie is also Adams's meditation on—and rejection of—suicide. As Cara Chell writes, "Adams underscores the question of Eliza's own survival, not the survival of her personality within a family group (as with Louisa and Kate), but her own fight against depression and suicide."[15] Three men commit suicide in the novel: Eliza's father, Caleb Hamilton; her husband, Evan Quarles; and her lover, Reed Ashford, formerly a student of Evan's whose beauty made Evan wonder if he was queer. After Reed's suicide, the sorrow and despair once felt by those men "poured through [Eliza's] veins like some dark dye, staining her blood and thickening in her heart. Their blind deathward surge became her own. Suicide had caught up with her. Death. Impossible to work. What she felt was all black and destructive. It was not grief for Reed that she felt; it was sheer fear of death, her own private terror of suicide."

In the end, it's work, the work of poetry—as Adams insisted—that unifies the novel. Eliza, who has been unhappy in all her relationships, finds joy in vacations with Harry, a filmmaker who is as devoted to his work as she is to hers. As the novel ends, they are both eager to get home and back to work: "For a moment against those thoughts she closed her eyes, and in the dark space behind her vision she saw, or suddenly felt, an urgency of words, a kaleidoscope that stopped to form a pattern. Words, her own work. But stronger, somehow enlarged."

During the fall of 1977, while *Listening to Billie* was in production, Alice and Bob spent a few days in New York before flying on for a vacation in Paris and the Dordogne. "I plan finally to brave New York after too many cowardly California years," Alice confided to her *New Yorker* editor, Frances Kiernan.[16] Sally Arteseros, a Doubleday editor who worked with Billy Abrahams on the O. Henry Prize volumes, hosted a luncheon at La Petite Marmite to introduce Alice to Kiernan, and to

Anne Mollegen Smith, the fiction editor at *Redbook* who'd edited Alice's stories in that magazine.* "Bob was handsome and charming and seemed to enjoy being the sole man among four women, three of whom he'd just met," Kiernan recalled. After lunch Alice and Fran walked to the *New Yorker*'s offices. "My office was across from that of Senior Fiction Editor Roger Angell's, and I am pretty sure I introduced Alice to Roger, who admired her story 'The Girl Across the Room' that the magazine published that very week."

Kiernan then invited Alice and Bob to spend the coming Sunday with her and her husband, orthopedic surgeon Howard Kiernan. Bob and Alice spent an afternoon with the Kiernans at their rented cottage in Sneden's Landing overlooking the Hudson River. After the Kiernans drove Alice and Bob back to the Westbury Hotel on East Sixty-Ninth, they had nightcaps at the hotel's Polo Lounge. The Kiernans' Himalayan cat, Selima, came too, conveyed in a "very smart looking wicker cage," thus providing the two cat-loving couples with an anecdotal beginning for their friendship. Both Kiernans liked Alice, but Bob made Fran feel uneasy—"a bit too self-consciously masculine for my taste," she said. Later in the same season when Howard attended a medical convention in San Francisco, Fran came to Alice's house for her monthly "lady writers' lunch" and met Diane Johnson and the others.

With a sweep of white-streaked wavy hair, bright blue eyes, and a lively expression, Kiernan was a generation younger than Alice. She was half-Jewish and considered herself "half-Southern" because she'd spent summers of her youth in her mother's hometown, Leitchfield, Kentucky, but came of age in New York City. After starting at the *New Yorker* as a receptionist, Kiernan became secretary to fiction editors William Maxwell and Roger Angell, and eventually a fiction editor herself. She edited, among others, Cynthia Ozick, Peter Taylor, Edna O'Brien, Lore Segal, and Shirley Hazzard. Kiernan's background helped her understand Alice, whom she thought "quintessentially Southern.

---

* At a San Francisco party Alice learned that Vasco Pereira had become Portugal's perma-nent representative to the United Nations: "Can you believe it? That effing swindler—I thought he would be in jail, rotting with other fascists. With my luck I'll probably run into him in NY." (Alice Adams to Judith Clark Adams, September 8, 1977.) It cannot have been lost on Alice that La Petite Marmite, called "the kind of place that gives New York its culinary ballast in these trendy and turbulent times" by the *New York Times*, was a favorite rendezvous of the United Nations community.

Indirect. Very complicated. Much stronger than she might appear to be at times."

Frances Kiernan

Listening to Billie, published in January 1978, enlarged Adams's reputation. The redoubtable John Leonard of the *New York Times* praised it as "a little engine that could. It pulls its freight cars—full of people and calamities and disappointments and imponderables—up to the top of the hill, where there's some fresh air," and noted that Eliza "*thinks* her way into a new life." Anne Tyler wrote about the novel twice, once in the *Detroit News* to discuss how "mothers hang over their daughters" and how Adams reveals that "both fragile and unbreakable" relationship, and later in *Quest/78* to praise Adams's arrangement of "brief and apparently random moments" to create "real life" in the form of "magnificent" characters like Miriam and Eliza herself. Another writer whose career was just beginning, Lynne Sharon Schwartz, wrote in the *San Francisco Review of Books*, "It is difficult today to pull off a 'happy' ending . . . Adams succeeds for two reasons . . . she is not afraid of exploiting the quotidian and seemingly banal [and] she spares us none of the intermediate states of Eliza's indecision, false moves, and failures."[17]

Alice herself especially liked her friend Grover Sales's review in the *Los Angeles Times*: he called her the "Boswell of our neurotic intelligentsia" and praised her "delicious humor and gift for self-mockery." But she probably also liked—loved?—Max Steele's review in the *Charlotte Observer*; he compared her book's kaleidoscopic structure to drawings by young children with no horizon line: "the horizon (in fiction, time is the horizon) of before and after is often dim, sometimes lost . . . the bright design that charms and states the message: all time is now, all love is this love."[18]

A review by Barbara Grizzuti Harrison in Gloria Steinem's *Ms.* magazine reinforced Alice's emerging feminism. Harrison argues that women like Eliza Quarles survive because "Adams believes that people who feel in their souls primarily the suffering of others choose bravely to live" while those who are "infatuated with their own suffering" embrace death. Women are the strong survivors in this novel. Harrison found *Listening to Billie* "disturbing and energizing" as she was "jolted by recognition" again and again. "Recognition" was a buzzword in second-wave feminism, a name for the "click" moments when puzzling indignities revealed themselves as political effects of patriarchal, sexist systems. As if to confirm Adams's place in the new feminist discourse, the review was sandwiched between one about Frida Kahlo (with Kahlo's art reproduced) and one of a book called *Menopause: A Positive Approach* reviewed by activist and short-story writer Grace Paley.[19]

All in all, the number and variety of reviews gave Adams courage. Some praised aspects of the novel that Wilson had wanted to cut. Almost all recognized a serious literary artist with a unique voice and way of telling a story. To poet Helen Chasin, writing in the *Village Voice*, Eliza Quarles is a rare, admirable thing—a poet who "is by no means the ambitious, driven, isolated, disturbing genius that Plath was . . . laid-back and steady are her way of making the distance."

Chasin might have said that of Alice Adams herself. From now on Alice would be steadfast in her own intuitions. The book Wilson produced, with Richard Diebenkorn's painting *Woman with Hat and Gloves* on the jacket, gave the novel the polish it deserved.* It was selected as an alternate by the Book of the Month Club and issued by Pocket Books as a mass-market paperback. Soon thereafter a reissued paperback of *Careless Love* sold thirty thousand copies. The Guggenheim Foundation, which had turned Adams down before, gave her a

---

* Alice shopped for a blue silk suit to go with the rich blues of the cover.

fellowship. And the *New Yorker* offered Adams a "first-look" contract, which paid her a small fee to submit her stories there before they went to other magazines.

And then there was the *People* profile. A two-page spread celebrated the sophisticated author of *Listening to Billie* with no shortage of biographical drama. Here Adams confides her affair with "a married, Catholic, Fascist diplomat" during her thirties when she was "having love affairs to make up for lost time and writing as a sort of sideline." She talks about her divorce—"very much not the thing to do in the early 1950s"—and her "long-term illicit affair" with Robert McNie, who's photographed kissing Alice as he leaves for work toting a classy leather briefcase. Alice told *People* of their first meeting, "We hated each other from the start. I don't like good-looking men. It's a common prejudice—one thinks they are going to be extremely dumb. You can imagine how he felt about lady writers. His intelligence has been a sheer joy."[20]

Having revealed all that, Adams also explains, ironically, that she and McNie have not married because they "are rather private people who feel our relationship is not the business of the state." After the *People* crew departed, Adams worried that the article would be "tackier than tacky."[21] In the event Alice regretted only that "you can't see the gorgeous face of Robert."[22] For Bob, publicity as a good-looking, intelligent interior designer was icing on the cake of Alice's success.

Alice looked great herself in these profiles, attired in the clothes Bob had helped her choose. From Paris, which had been so poor and crippled by shortages when she lived there thirty years before, she wrote to Frances Kiernan, "Paris is cool & terrific—prosperous looking, great clothes all over." In San Francisco she patronized shops where the salespeople knew her and bought good things in fine fabrics; she wore cowl-necked sweaters and dramatic scarves and bold necklaces. The classic styles of the 1978 fall season especially appealed to her and she went to great lengths to order a particular red Ralph Lauren blazer.

Periodical editors often asked Adams to write reviews, and Wilson sent her books she was publishing. Writing about one of these for *Harper's*, Adams found Lisa Alther's *Kinflicks* "continuously *funny*" and went on to say more about women's fiction. She confesses that she used to read

The Golden Notebook during unhappy love affairs and Jane Austen during depressions. But Adams and many women of her generation wanted to compete in the wider, supposedly ungendered but mostly male literary world. She objects to the "silly form of put-down" implied by the term "women's novel" because "surely literary preferences are not sexually determined." She thinks Erica Jong's *Fear of Flying* (the celebrated novel about the "zipless fuck") "boring and unconvincing," its heroine, Isadora Wing, an unrealistic "super-stud."

Adams much preferred "the humaneness" of Alther's approach to sex, including the portrayal of Ginny Babcock's discovery of sexual satisfaction in a relationship with a woman: "This is no more a 'lesbian novel' than it is a 'woman's novel,'" Adams insists. Alther's true and winning message about sex is "we're all in trouble . . . and no prizes are given out, no blame attached . . . when it comes to sex we're all amateurs."[23]

When Adams saw proofs of *The Easter Parade* by Richard Yates at Billy Abrahams's, she thought, "If I love it I'll ask to review it, and then maybe I'll hear from terrific Richard Yates." Adams considered Yates's *Revolutionary Road* one of the best novels she'd ever read. She also knew, as Richard Ford later wrote, that invoking that novel "enacts a sort of cultural-literary handshake among its devotees."[24] Adams wanted Yates to know she was a devotee and hoped he would read and admire her fiction. In her review for the Sunday paper, Adams promoted her belief—or hope?—that literary skill is gender-neutral: Yates's "insight into these three women is so powerful and so sympathetic that too much could be made (and probably will be) of the fact that he is a man, writing about women. More to the point is his being a first-rate writer sensitive to women, and to men—and to the many particulars of life in the Thirties and the early Seventies."

Yates was pleased: "Of all the reviews I've seen so far, yours is the one I'd most like to have reproduced in some pocket-sized, laminated-plastic format, like a credit card, for use in helping me out of scrapes with frowning authorities," he told her. "You seem to have understood the book better than anyone, which leads me to believe that you must be very nice." He hoped they could meet for a drink when he was next in San Francisco.

The ensuing correspondence was deliciously flirtatious. Alice reminded Yates that they'd met ten years earlier at Max Steele's house just as *Careless Love* was coming out. Yates remembered "about eight lovely girls there" but allowed that he'd been drunk and did not recall that one of them was novelist Alice Adams. "My loss as usual," he said. He would get Adams's novels from the library so that, he promised, "In my very next letter I'll be able to tell you what a wonderful writer you are. In the meantime, it's abundantly clear that you are the nicest, kindest girl on the whole West Coast. Oh, Alice Adams, please take care of yourself, and eat your vegetables and brush your hair a hundred strokes a night, and stay away from terrible guys of all kinds."

Not to be outdone in charm, Alice replied, "I think it's wonderful that you remember me as eight lovely girls." Then she told Yates about the dueling stories she and Max were publishing in *Redbook*, virtually announcing that they'd been lovers, and described the gorgeous Mexican beach town where she was headed for winter vacation—without mentioning that she'd be going there with Bob McNie. "You're absolutely right—I should always have stayed away from terrible guys; but then what would I write about? Or what would I do at night after I've finished brushing my hair."[25]

Good as his word, Yates telephoned Alice before he came west in March 1977. By then she'd heard more about him. He "does sound creepy," she wrote Victoria Wilson.[26] Worse, on the phone, he said that he could never understand why Billie Holiday "distorts music the way she does with that whining voice." Even though Yates offered to extend his trip to accommodate Alice's schedule, she demurred and they never had that drink. That was probably just as well. "Yates didn't think women were cut out to be serious artists," his biographer Blake Bailey writes, "since such a difficult business interfered with their main function as caregivers—in short, as the persons who *support* serious artists . . . he regarded a handful of female writers as first-rate—Jane Austen, George Eliot, Alice Munro, Gina Berriault, perhaps one or two others . . ."[*][27]

Opinionated Adams pulled no punches when she reviewed books she didn't like. In fact, she sometimes sought those books out. She reviewed *The Widow's Children* by Paula Fox because her old friend Irving Howe

---

* It doesn't seem that Yates ever wrote to Adams about her books. Despite that, she called his next book, *Liars in Love*, "first-rate stories, by a superior writer." (Alice Adams, "Seven Brilliant and Grim Tales," *San Francisco Chronicle*, November 8, 1981.)

gave it advance praise: "One of the best novels written in America these past twenty or thirty years," he said. Adams countered that it was so "incomparably unpleasant" and that she could think of "no other novel that had left [her] so bored, uneasy and irritated." Her long review for the weekly *Bay Guardian* is thorough—she's found another novel by Fox, *The Western Coast*, that better meets her standards. It's hard to decide, finally, if Adams is more disturbed by Fox's fiction or by Howe's praise.

Adams also worked a slow takedown of C. D. B. Bryan's *Beautiful Women, Ugly Scenes*; regarding the narrator's description of a desirable woman who has nipples like the "noses of small puppies," Adams wonders "if a couple of nice live puppies might have done him just as well. He is a very confused little boy, and this is a very confused, long book."[28]

More to Adams's liking was *Slow Days, Fast Company: The World, the Flesh, and LA* by Eve Babitz, who'd become known for posing nude while playing chess with Marcel Duchamp, being Igor Stravinsky's goddaughter, and sleeping with Jim Morrison, Paul Ruscha, Stephen Stills, and Harrison Ford, among others. Now Babitz was a writer published by Victoria Wilson. Adams compares Babitz to two male-fantasy characters, Sally Bowles (Isherwood's *Cabaret*) and Holly Golightly (Capote's *Breakfast at Tiffany's*). Unlike them, "Babitz is very real indeed—real and infinitely more alive than Didion's trendily alienated heroines." Adams quotes Babitz: "I had a collection of lovers to keep me warm and my friendships with women, who always fascinated me by their wit, bravery and resourcefulness . . . I had a third collection of associates who were men but not lovers." Adams understood—perhaps envied—the ease with which Babitz sorted her people. Babitz thanked Adams for the review in long, bubbly letters full of funny innuendos: "Erica [Spellman, Eve's agent] says you are the living end in wonderfulness and even Vicky [Wilson] says so and she never says anything like that, as you may know." Babitz says she's in the sky now with everything going so well for her: "The only fly in the sky is my horrible past when I used to be a piece of ass (or piece of Cheese as Linda Ronstadt so darlingly put it for Time's cover story interview)."[29]

Adams understood that worry all too well as she superseded her past as a "bachelorette" in San Francisco. "She would say rather harsh things about certain men," Diane Johnson remembered. "Or she would say, oh, no, I can't go to that because what would I wear and [X] would be there with his beautiful wife. She went out with a lot of people in that phase before I knew her."

When Johnson's *Lying Low* came out, Adams gave it "a rather simple-minded rave" in the *Chicago Sun-Times* because she was "truly and absolutely crazy about the book." She admired Johnson's whole motley set of dignified, quirky, complex characters who live in a Victorian boardinghouse in a California college town. One of them, political fugitive Marybeth, represents a last gasp of sixties political fervor as the seventies unwind into random violence. Adams particularly endorsed this statement by Theo, the aging ballet dancer who owns the house: "Men are generally more law-abiding than women. Women have a feeling that since they didn't make the rules, the rules have nothing to do with them. I have this feeling myself. Men, on the other hand, care about rules and forms."[30]

There's a critical analysis of Adams's poetics of fiction and her evolving professional demeanor waiting to be written out of the forty-eight book reviews she published between 1976 and 1984. Mostly she wrote for Chicago and Bay Area papers—often, in those pre-Internet days, the same review in two papers. She exhibits fierce and justified loyalty to friends who are good writers: Ella Leffland, Evan S. Connell, Laurie Colwin, Alison Lurie, Mark Schorer, John L'Heureux, and Carolyn See. Upon reading a negative review of one of See's novels, Alice immediately called her friend long-distance to "issue a stunning string of curses about the other reviewer." Adams also felt curiosity and enthusiasm for younger writers like Bobbie Ann Mason who brought news of people and places, especially "mid-new Southerners" not heard from before, and strong sympathy for non-trendy literary writers like Lynne Sharon Schwartz, who "spells out rather than signals her effects" in novels of "old-fashioned density."

The war between the sexes doesn't dictate Adams's opinions. Reviewing a second novel by Marilyn French, whose *The Women's Room* was a bestseller, Adams writes, "French is simply too angry to write well or to think clearly . . . her politics are superior to her fiction." Her characters fail to "enact rather than talk about the troubles between men and women, as well as the troubles between men-and-women and the world." When other reviewers came down hard on Berkeley short-story writer Leonard Michaels for his comedic novel *The Men's Club*, Adams defended it as "a small masterpiece" that says, "unforgettably, new things about how men and women do and do not get along with each other." In the club of the title, the men share "stories of male bafflement and failure, of frustrated needs for love," while also drinking, smoking, breaking things, getting into fights, and eating all the food that the host's wife had prepared for *her* women's group meeting the next day. Alice maintained a friendship with Michaels for years to come.[31]

Through her heartfelt, demanding reviews Alice met on paper authors she eventually came to know, including Scott Spencer (another of Wilson's authors), Alice Walker, Joyce Carol Oates, and Margaret Atwood. After Adams reviewed Spencer's *Endless Love*, he wrote her, "You are the perfect reader. Truly, had I been able to imagine your reading my novel with such sympathy and perception, I would have been able to write a better book. . . . [L]ack of a full and interesting critical response is, I think, the loneliest part of writing fiction." Alice offered her bound galleys of Spencer's novel to Max Steele with a note that *Endless Love* made her "more envious than any book since [Styron's] *Lie Down in Darkness*.[32]

CHAPTER TWENTY-TWO

Beautiful Girl

– (1979) –

*Sometimes a male reviewer will choose to review what he takes
to be the moral character of the woman writer as evinced by the
sexual behavior of her heroines. . . . What I'm saying is that con-
versely that doesn't happen to men. You don't hear men writers
being criticized for sleeping around or leaving women.*

—Alice Adams,
interview with Don Swaim

For decades Adams had wanted to publish a collection of her short
stories. After writing almost a hundred stories, publishing a handful
in the *New Yorker* and dozens elsewhere, and winning eight O. Henry
Awards and several mentions in *Best American Short Stories*, her goal was
in sight. She and Wilson began putting the collection together while *Listening to Billie* was in production. About half of the sixteen stories they
chose are Southern, the rest Californian. Each story was reedited to catch
repetitions of phrases from story to story. Wilson suggested grouping
the Todd family stories at the beginning of the book, and Alice lobbied
to include the not-previously-published "What Should I Have Done?"
(printed by *Playgirl* before the book came out), "Attrition," and "A Pale
and Perfectly Oval Moon." The advance was a mere $3,500, "the stingiest
advance I ever heard of," Alice told Lynn Nesbit. Alice loved the short-
story form and didn't seem to be aware of the publishing commonplace
that story collections don't sell. Even though the late seventies and eighties
would sometimes be called a short-story renaissance, few authors saw large
advances for their collections. Ann Beattie, Raymond Carver, Tobias Wolff,
and Donald Barthelme earned a living by teaching or writing novels.

Alice took Wilson's suggestion to make "Beautiful Girl" her title story, despite the fact that she no longer associated with the woman who'd inspired it. The elegant sienna and beige cover of *Beautiful Girl* signaled the importance of this volume while Henry Fong's dreamy portrait of Adams in a cowl-necked sweater caught her arch intelligence and wide-eyed, full-lipped beauty. "One reason I've always wanted to publish a book of short stories," Adams confided to Ann Cornelisen, "is that I want to dedicate it to Billy (this is a secret)."[1] The dedication of *Beautiful Girl* read, "For William Abrahams and Peter Stansky."

Alice spent the first two weeks of 1979 with Bob in Zihuatanejo, intentionally being out of the country on the publication day of *Beautiful Girl*. Before they left, she already knew that *Newsweek* ("as stirring as the best work of [Katherine] Mansfield") and *Vogue* ("a heroine among today's women writers: personal, but never self-absorbed") had given the book thumbs-up.

The rest could wait while she and Bob celebrated the Calvins' forty-ninth anniversary, swam, sunned, lounged, drank, ate garlicky seafood at beachside grills, and enjoyed each other. Alice's friend Edwina Evers (later Leggett) noticed, "Bob wasn't up to Alice intellectually at all, but I think it was a very sexy relationship. When they'd come back from Mexico every winter they just looked besotted with sex—just beautifully calm together." That aspect was marred on the 1979 trip, at least for Alice, by a bachelor friend—Alice assumed he was gay—who kept close company with Bob and her at the resort. He was architect Dmitri Vedensky, who had worked with Bob on projects at Sea Ranch and in the city. "I know you would not allow yourself to be bored for so long," she told Jessner, "and yet you would never be as rude [to him] as I really wanted to be."[2] Shortly after their return, Alice sent Vedensky a note of non-apology for being cross with him: Bob and I "give an impression of being much more gregarious than in fact we are," she wrote. "We have enormous needs for privacy, for simply being alone—which was one of the initial reasons we went to Mexico. Having the same needs, the Calvins work out perfectly." She told Vedensky she hoped he would never again make Zihuatanejo reservations for weeks she and Bob would be there.[3]

The airline lost Alice's suitcase on the way home. That small incident prompted "Lost Luggage," a first-person account by a recent widow whose circumstances differ in almost every detail from Alice's own. Yet the story conveys Alice's newly felt optimism and independence: "I knew myself to be a strong woman: surely I could turn my life around?" the widow thinks as she ponders her lack of income and the loss of the notebook she kept after her husband died. "I was not really dependent on a middle-class support system, on certain styles of dress and entertaining, on 'safe' neighborhoods. I could even, I imagined, find a big house to share with some other working women . . . Such prospects excited and to a degree sustained me." In a new, smaller notebook, this widow chooses not to re-create the memories of her late husband but instead to move "farther back, much farther, to some childhood colors" and says, "I finished that notebook and I bought another small one, and probably I will keep on buying them. And, without really noticing it as something remarkable, I began to feel a great deal better." It was writing, she realized, the act of writing and not the work thus created, that made her happy.

Mexicana Airlines did eventually find and return Alice's suitcase and notebook. By then a suntanned Alice was enjoying the reviews of *Beautiful Girl*.[4]

Those reviews praised Adams's stories for their delicacy, wit, grace, style; a few noted serious themes such as the "mutual loneliness" created by racism, or the "mysteries of little girlhood." Laurie Stone, writing in the *Village Voice*, pointed out that for Adams "beauty—or the lack of it—is a fundamental matter" that shapes character, often in unpredictable ways. While Stone complained that Adams's narrators "tend to get sappy" with nostalgia and romance, Susan Wood in the *Washington Post* noticed that Adams more than any other recent writer extended F. Scott Fitzgerald's Romantic idealism of the self: "Although the times may not call for characters on the scale of a Jay Gatsby or a Dick Diver, the search for love, for the self in others, goes on, and the characters in *Beautiful Girl* have not given up the search." Wood also noted that Adams had "a fine satiric eye softened by a tenderness toward human desire and frailty."[5]

Nothing better illustrates the intricate dance of Romanticism and satire in Adams's life than her friendship with Max Steele. To friends she criticized him—"I do wish he could get back to writing, and stop taking care of so many people"—and to his face she urged him, "Shove other things and people aside, JUST WRITE." She knew he was depressed and consumed with teaching, mentoring, and his uneasy marriage. Her letters asked him to visit her and hinted that her recently divorced friend Edwina Evers was looking fantastic, would be glad to see him, and had a fine house that he'd like. Deflecting, Max replied that he loved "leafing through the *New Yorker* and being startled by [Alice's] picture looking out from the ad."[6]

In the spring of 1978 Steele wrote Alice that his wife, Diana, "is better looking at 43 than she's ever been in her life: dark hair in a rather Gibson girl hairdo, very thin, much more relaxed. I just wish I liked her." Alice told Jessner, "I honestly don't think that marriage has been at all good for him—in fact very likely none would have, don't you think? His expectations of marriage are so—quaint, really—and then he is drawn to such neurotic women." Jessner agreed. Then Alice elaborated: "*Most* people are unsuited [for marriage], just as certainly most people should not have children, and I think I would put myself in both groups. Especially marriage as we have all been brought up to regard it, the total solution."[7]

By June the Steeles were legally separated. Max didn't tell Alice until August and then he expended most of his words to defend their living arrangement: "Chapel Hill real estate is worse in price than S.F. and the only way we can maintain our standards of living (and it is a beautiful house) is to divide it into 2 condominiums." Their two sons' rooms would be in the middle. This split-house arrangement disturbed Alice: "I would think separation more important than an expensive life style," she told Lucie. But Max was sure it would work. "I feel 20 years younger," he wrote. On the phone, Alice and Max discussed their "shared slowness to catch on" that it was time to leave a relationship:

ALICE: What if we had gotten married that marvelous summer?
    MAX: We would probably still be married.
ALICE: Oh, darling Max, don't be depressing. You know I can't bear
        it when you're depressed.

Adams said that she could not remember who'd said which line. The main thing was that they "had the great good sense to stay close friends."[8]

The Steeles divorced after two more years. Writing Alice, Max compared his emotional pain to having "your foot or arm go so completely to sleep it feels missing, non-existent and then hurts like hell before it begins tingling pleasantly and [becomes] bearable. I'm now to the tingling stage but hope I won't fall in love like a fool." Alice encouraged him to work on the novel he'd jokingly titled "I Married a Witch" and invited him to San Francisco: "We could have lunch and laugh all day."[9] In Chapel Hill, where he remained a beloved professor of writing at UNC, Max had daily "hours" at a café where students and friends stopped by to talk with him, his son Oliver Steele recalled. He was close to his colleagues Doris Betts and Daphne Athas. Neither he nor Diana married again.

In reality, Alice saw Max infrequently. Though she remained committed to living unmarried with Bob, her letters indicate a flirtatious element in many of her friendships. Women noticed that Alice felt a certain claim on any man she'd ever loved no matter how many years had passed since the conquest. Was it possessiveness or simply intimacy turned to friendship? Perhaps both.

"Old beaux," Alice told Lucie Jessner after her thrice-married eighty-year-old friend laughingly confessed to wondering what to wear when a man she'd once been in love with came to visit, are "something I have thought about a lot." A couple of years earlier, Alice elaborated, she had read in a political column that a man she had been in love with in 1947 was now a leading Italian Communist, and admitted, "I have certainly had a lot of fantasies about him." The man, of course, was Bruno Trentin, now the leader of the Italian General Confederation of Labor (CGIL) and member of the Italian parliament. "If you are in Rome," she wrote Diane Johnson after seeing the column, "and see that name or the name of that union in a phone book—but then what would I do with it? When I knew him he was a fabulous boy."[10] This news of Trentin inspired the romantic plot of Adams's next novel, *Rich Rewards*.

Alice had not been to Chapel Hill since 1958 but she relished the hometown gossip she received in letters from Max, Lucie Jessner, and Dollie Summerlin (who had once been Judith Adams's mother's best friend and was now a friend of Max's). Thus she learned about Dotsie Adams's beau named Herbert Cannon who sent oranges from Florida and had good handwriting. Dotsie took Herbert to Maine, which Alice found ironic: "probably because I still regard it as my mother's property, which of course it was," she said. The irony, apparently, was that Nic was being posthumously cuckolded by Dotsie in the same house—Agatha's house—where he'd broken Agatha's heart by falling inappropriately in love with Dotsie.*

Herbert and Dotsie wanted to live together, but the old Adams house was too large to manage. His plan to buy a one-story house in Chapel Hill lapsed when he suffered a stroke. Dotsie exhausted herself caring for Herbert until his sons insisted on moving him to a care facility in Florida. Jessner worried that "money play[ed] a decisive role in their caretaking" and Dotsie was "*very* unhappy."

In the spring of 1979 Dotsie sent Alice a cryptic postcard about moving to a smaller house without mentioning her plans for the Adams house. Thus she revived Alice's "old trauma of Nic's will" and "root-like attachment to the house itself." Jessner, trying to mediate between her two friends even as she struggled with severe emphysema, understood: "I promised myself, on leaving Germany, never to hang my heart on possessions; with houses I do feel different, they are almost people."[11]

The house saga lasted months. Almost everything Dotsie said about the house contradicted what Alice's father had promised her: "Nic told me always that eventually I was to have the house, and that if Dotsie had to sell it she would share whatever with me 'of course.'" Now Dotsie claimed in a late-night, possibly drunken phone call that Nic had wanted her son, Tom Wilson Jr., to have the house and that she had no legal obligation to give Alice anything. Alice viewed that as an "obvious, absolute arrant lie . . . in the first place Nic didn't like Tommy, often said how boring and stingy he is; in the second, Nic was not duplicitous; he would not have told Dotise [*sic*] that and me such an entirely other version." Alice was so upset by the call that she put Bob on the phone to end it: "She seems to want to go to any lengths to convince me that Nic cared nothing about me at all, which of course is not difficult."[12]

---

* Five years earlier, Alice had consoled Dotsie because "Mr. Canon" [*sic*] had returned to his wife: "I certainly can't imagine living with a man who wanted to be somewhere else . . . I'm certainly lucky that Vasco's wife won out (I'm sure he would have found several dozen young girls by now)." (AA to DSA, August 13, 1974.)

Alice remembered a letter (apparently not preserved) that her mother had written her during the last winter of her life: "A terrible letter from Agatha, not long before she died, that awful winter when Dotsie was happily off with second young husband, David, Nic in a depression at Malcolm Kemp's—anyway, Agatha wrote me that the two most 'piercing' events of her life had been the death of her baby son and her husband's 'continuing attraction' to Dotsie. So for Dotsie now to claim it—Jesus—"[13]

Dotsie also claimed that she was spending "night and day" trying to separate out things Alice might want from other possessions. "I would be locked up having shock treatment by now if not for you and Lucie," Alice told Max as the saga wound down.

At that point Peter volunteered to go to Chapel Hill and help Dotsie with the sorting. He thought he'd get a free vacation, and Alice thought he was doing her a favor. Peter stayed with Max (they got along terrifically) and helped Dotsie pack a cardboard drum for his mother. The items in it, Alice said when they arrived, "looked like they came from a garage sale in a not-good neighborhood." A nice Victorian sofa Alice liked was promised to Nic's sister, and a valuable Gustave Doré–illustrated edition of *The Divine Comedy* that Alice loved was sold to a book dealer. "That woman [Dotsie] is as shrewd as she is stupid," Max told Alice on the phone. "She knows the value of everything in that house and she is not about to let you get anything good." Max reported that Dotsie had given Peter a broken chair, all the while saying she was generous to give him and Alice anything at all. "I'm trying to think it's funny," Alice wrote Lucie.[14]

Before she sent *Rich Rewards* to New York in August, Alice asked Diane Johnson to read it and found that "the most terrific help. Really another writer is so much better than an arrogant editor. She thinks it's going to be wonderful—very Colette, she says. I thought it was political—oh well."[15] That "very Colette" comment recalls Max Steele's earlier comparison of Adams to the French writer.[16]

Gaining confidence from Johnson's approval, Alice told her agent, Lynn Nesbit, "I really want a lot of money for this one." Nesbit thought she could get a higher offer on the book from another publisher, and Alice wondered how much the prestige of being published by Knopf was worth to her. She'd become good friends with Victoria Wilson but was sometimes frightened of her in her editorial role. It was all complicated by their age difference. Alice wondered if an impersonal editorial relationship would be better. For instance, she didn't "in a personal way" like Nesbit, but knew she was terrific at her job. Likewise, she then had "a totally uninteresting cleaning person, as a result of which the house is extremely clean. With old black cleaning ladies I always confused them with Verlie, and wanted to hear about their lives and make coffee for them."[17]

Victoria Wilson

Negotiations dragged on with Alice—in her own words—"rather unnecessarily insisting in advance that [she wouldn't] make changes." She began to wonder "if [she] really want[ed] the experience of being edited by Vicky again," saying, "She is just so difficult, and our neuroses do not work out well—my dependencies, her overbearing arrogance, tightness—plus being 20 years younger." The unsettledness of the situation was "beginning to get [her] down," she confided to a friend. In the end she accepted a "small" advance ($17,000) for *Rich Rewards* from Knopf.*[18] That resolved, Wilson read the manuscript for the second

---

* A note in the Knopf files at the Harry Ransom Center suggests that Robert Gottlieb, who called the novel "extended romantic wetdreaming," resisted a higher advance for *Rich Rewards*. (HRC, Knopf Addition.)

time and wrote: "I am really amazed by the difference in the voice; there is an assurance here, and an ease which I don't think came through in the early books, but which struck me instantly when I read 'Lost Luggage' . . ."[19] With this fourth book in seven years, Alice learned to fully trust her editor.

In mid-September 1979 Alice and Bob flew to New York City for a whirl of lunches and dinners to celebrate her signing of the contract for *Rich Rewards* before they continued to Italy. As it happened, Pope John Paul II was making the reverse journey, speaking to enormous crowds and disrupting traffic in New York. Alice got a glimpse of the popular pope in his limousine but was disturbed by his message. He urged the poor not to despair and to shun violence but refused to address the problem of overpopulation. "I am obsessed, who is not? with millions of starving children," she wrote editor Alice Quinn, whom she'd met through Wilson, "so to hear someone talking about birth control and moral laxity is—difficult. The most wonderful teacher I ever had, F. O. Matthiessen at Harvard, used to explain his positions by saying, 'I am a Christian and a Socialist,' which I sometimes feel like saying—who'd care though." To Diane Johnson, who was spending a sabbatical year in Paris, she fulminated about friends who admired the pope: "Did he do something wonderful that I missed? Just caused traffic jams, I thought."[20]

New York exhausted Alice and Bob before they arrived in Milan to begin a three-week drive through Northern Italy with stops at Lake Como, Verona, Bergamo, and Florence. No doubt they looked at statues and paintings and cathedrals but the moments Alice preserved in writing were personal and often funny. When a pink silk nightgown in a shop window in Florence caught her eye, Bob looked at the price tag and calculated forty dollars. It was a "perfectly okay gown but more the thought of souvenir" that led her to pull out her credit card as Bob admired a "sensational slipper satin grey robe, lined in brown silk," priced at 249,000 lire. Over lunch she studied the Mastercard receipt. It showed too many zeros, and besides, $40 seemed too cheap for pure silk: "Bob said obviously a mistake, we'll go back. At last shop reopened, and person said no mistake, $400. pink silk gown . . . MC slip already taken to bank but happy to exchange. And that is why I have a really gorgeous heavy grey silk robe—and a blue linen gown that takes half an hour to iron. I plan to wear the robe Christmas morning, in fact every Christmas morning—all my life."[21]

Alice carried Bruno Trentin's Rome office address with her but didn't contact him while she was in Italy.[22] Nonetheless, she was inspired to write a story about a sexually aggressive woman that combines details from her trip with episodes she had discussed with the writer Frances Gendlin, a close friend of Saul Bellow's who then lived in San Francisco. With unusual candor, Alice asked Gendlin if she'd mind if she borrowed some of the things they'd discussed about women who "liked the chase of men." In "The Chase," which appeared in *Cosmopolitan* in August 1981, a mathematician named Pamela (a near-beauty with a "bold, strong-boned, handsome face") attends a conference at Villa d'Este on Lake Como with her fiancé, a physicist. (A conference sponsored by *Scientific American* had taken place at that luxurious hotel while Alice and Bob were there.) Pamela has been a "sort of sexual forager, a pirate, choosing and inviting whomever she felt she would enjoy." Nonetheless, Pamela has trouble rejecting men who want to marry her. "The Chase" ends in a museum in the Villa Giulia in Rome, where Pamela has gone alone because her fiancé is ill. An attractive man makes a pass at her as they both stare at the famous Etruscan *Sarcophagus of the Spouses*. The symbolism of the terra-cotta couple that has survived more than two millennia is not lost on Pamela, who feels "a certain alarm at this juxtaposition, or opposition: marriage versus an attractive, chancily come-upon man." The man asks her to call him in New York. Back at her hotel, she tells the physicist she cannot marry him. "*How odd*, she thinks, *women are supposed to be the ones who always want to marry*."

For twenty years, Lucie Jessner had been the mother figure who faithfully encouraged Alice in both love and work. She'd consoled Alice as Dotsie sold the Adams family house. By early December Lucie's emphysema had worsened. Alice and Bob went to visit her at home in Washington, DC, for a last time: "Lucie is in very bad shape," Alice wrote Diane Johnson, "but in the three days we were there she seemed to pick up, and talking to her was wonderful . . . so incredibly graceful and generous, so interested in everyone but herself. She is being taken care of by an adorable handsome grandson and a marvelous black lady, Thomasina—an ideal combination, when you think of it."[23]

Alice and Bob stayed with Judith and Tim Adams in Washington, giving Alice and Judith a chance to renew the mutual admiration and friendship that had survived on letters for many years. En route to DC, they'd visited Charleston, South Carolina—"so fucking pretty [she] could hardly stand it." Nor could she stand the people. Their Southernness brought back "all that childhood panic and rage." When their flight between Washington and Atlanta unexpectedly made an unscheduled landing at Raleigh-Durham, Alice burst into tears over the irretrievableness of the past. That event became the germ of her story "An Unscheduled Stop."*[24] A stopover in New Orleans was not much better. Alice thought the vaunted food seemed like it all came smothered with the same béchamel sauce from a giant vat beneath the city. Her favorite thing on her first return to the South in more than twenty years was a traditional New Orleans jazz concert at Preservation Hall. Otherwise, she couldn't wait to leave: "I used to think that everyone I knew there was stupid and a racial bigot and I found out I was at least half right."[25]

Lucie Johanna Ney Jessner died December 18, 1979. "How perfectly in character, how exquisitely polite of her to wait for death (for which she must have longed, she was so miserably uncomfortable) until after I had come and gone," Alice wrote of her later in a story she called "Elizabeth." In a eulogy she sent to be read at a memorial service held at Georgetown University, she said she often reread letters from Lucie as she did "certain favorite books, certain poetry. For, as in all writing of the highest order, Lucie's letters have the unique and beautiful sound of her own voice." Lucie's letters, Alice said, had additional magic because "on days when a letter arrived from Lucie, there would always be, along with that considerable pleasure, some piece of remarkably good news."[26]

Though eulogies can be an occasion for exaggeration, Alice Adams believed in the magic of Lucie Jessner's influence. Through this friend she'd met Max Steele and found the courage to divorce. She'd learned of the sale of her first short story after spending a day with Lucie later the same summer. Over the years, she insisted, her best news—winning a Guggenheim fellowship in 1978, for instance—arrived in tandem with a letter from Lucie Jessner. In "Elizabeth," Adams wrote: "With her I was

* The story's protagonist, Claire, returns home to Hilton and has a summer affair with a doctor, which makes it somewhat of a sequel to "Home Is Where." Claire is dispossessed of the house where she grew up because her mother wills it to a religious order.

less trivial and mean, and much more intelligent, more finely observant than usual, and if not elegant at least restrained." That Max Steele felt the same way about Lucie made him something like a brother; Adams included a stand-in for Max named Judson in "Elizabeth"—even as she transformed the setting from Washington, DC, to a small coastal village in Mexico.

The losses of the past year, reminders of mortality, prompted Alice to criticize herself. As a new decade approached, she wrote in her notebook, "Twenty years ago I was broke & underweight, often lonely & often suffering from some anguished love. Now I am 5 pounds overweight & have plenty of money. I worry about what to buy, worry that I could be missing some available treat in clothes, or trips, or food, something to buy. I worry about investments, I give more thought to my digestion than to love . . ."

She caught herself "looking at poor people, people not making it, like the person I used to be, with a sort of contempt."[27]

Alice didn't like the successful, self-involved woman she felt herself becoming. She sensed that shaping her personality to complement Bob and his alcoholism (the proverbial elephant in the room) had corrupted her. Once she'd made a choice to be a serious writer rather than a woman whose life is love affairs." Was she now living for "lifestyle" (the kind of trendy nonword she hated) in a city devoted to conspicuous consumption, in a state and country that had just elected Ronald Reagan, a Republican movie actor, to be president?

As Alice moved into the latter part of her century, the 1980s, she mourned the passing of Lucie Jessner—"that impossibility, a perfect person." Lucie had been an unselfish defender of her work, a conscientious soul who influenced and inspired Alice without trying to alter her. How, she now asked herself, could she pursue financial and personal independence while at the same time maintaining the purity and playfulness of her artistic vocation?

CHAPTER TWENTY-THREE

Rewards

Missing one bus accident is no sure sign that a person's life will always come up rosy, because nobody's does, not for long.

—Alice Adams, "Alaska,"
To See You Again

During her meditation upon the loss of the house in Chapel Hill, Alice reached a "valuable insight": "My anguish, tortured labyrinth of pain [is] actually worth more than any house, or furniture; that *is* my capital."[1] After Dotsie sold the house for $84,000 in January 1980, Alice saw the episode as a traumatic confrontation with her father that left her feeling that neither she nor her mother had ever owned the house. The working title of one story she wrote about the sale was "Disinheritance." She began it after Margery Finn Brown told her that she'd also been upset about losing a family house, but then realized she'd been really miserable in that house. "That would certainly apply in my case too," Alice said. "Those years with Agatha and Nic were awful. In any case since she said that I feel more detached from the house." In the story a young woman "has not one but three mean, avaricious and stupid stepmothers, three in succession, I mean." Alice read the story to Bob before she sent it out; he assured her that "it certainly did not sound at all like [her] situation with Dotsie." It appeared in the *New Yorker* with the title "Berkeley House" in the spring of 1980.[2]

In "My First and Only House," an essay published in *Geo* magazine in 1984, Adams described how she had been "imprinted" by that house beside Pittsboro Road and wondered why, living as she did in "real-estate-crazed California," she had never been the owner of a house. "Circumstances aside," she speculated, "is it possible that I have never bought or seriously thought of buying another house because of the strength of that imprinting . . ." The circumstances that caused Alice to live in houses owned by others were clear enough. When Bob McNie divorced, he kept his showcase vacation home in Truckee and moved into Alice's large flat at 3904 Clay Street, where the rent remained affordable at $400 a month in 1979. After smoke and water damage from a fire in the apartment upstairs, Bob updated their flat with refinished floors, cushions for the circular window seat and a teal-blue linen velvet couch for the living room, butcher-block counters and tomato-red walls in the kitchen. They felt no motivation to purchase a house in San Francisco.

And yet, Adams frequently considered how a woman makes a mental home for herself in the material world. She characterizes Northern Californians by their particular houses and communities. They live in Victorian or redwood-beamed or sea-sprayed houses or apartments with views of the bay or the hills; they travel along the Pacific coast from Carmel to Stinson to Mendocino, from the Marin County enclaves of Ross and Belvedere down the Peninsula to Stanford and east into the Berkeley Hills, Sacramento, and Lake Tahoe. While readers who don't know Northern California may need a map to follow her, they can sense how Adams makes distinctions among cities and towns, hillsides, mountains, and beaches to delineate her characters, viewing houses and towns, as Max Steele wrote of her, "with the eye of an artist, never that of an auctioneer."[3] Nowhere are these domestic and geographic details sharper than in *Rich Rewards*, the novel she completed in 1979 and saw published in 1980.

The comic tone and unlikely coincidences Adams devised for this novel echo E. M. Forster's *Howards End*—which also concerns itself with houses. Her first-person narrator, Daphne Matthiessen (named, we can speculate, for Adams's Harvard professor, the late F. O. Matthiessen), is neither rich nor a homeowner. Her life so far has been defined by "a series of love affairs that were much more of an occupation than [her] work." In this she embodies what Lee Upton labels "women's sense of homelessness and cultural displacement."[4] This novel also celebrates, as Laurie Stone argues, "lust and fleshly joy." Stone notes, "Adams's women are every bit as curious and reverent as men are about anatomical won-ders, just as delighted sometimes to place the whole person behind his parts . . . like men, they think about sex—remember it, want it, resist it—most of their waking and sleeping hours."[5] *Rich Rewards* begins when Daphne comes to the "spoiled and lovely city" of San Francisco because she is "running away from a bad love affair in Boston." But Daphne is hard on herself. Like Bob McNie, she is a self-trained home decorator who likes to think about houses and how to make them suitable—and livable—for their occupants. Her old school friend Agatha Marshall has summoned her to San Francisco to renovate the house that she purchased with money inherited from her father, the General. Agatha is an unmarried, civic-minded San Francisco pediatrician who still lives in a messy downtown apartment furnished "like a disguise, and maybe that is just what she was doing, hiding herself there among all that blond Danish modern."

Introduced to Agatha's friends, Daphne becomes a witness to violent events in the post-Vietnam, posthippie, post-Watergate city, where gay activist and city supervisor Harvey Milk and Mayor George Moscone were assassinated in their offices at city hall in November 1978 just days after the mass suicide in Guyana of nine hundred followers of local cult leader Jim Jones. She settles temporarily into Agatha's house and begins to hate and become addicted to the "extreme localness" of the daily newspapers. From the *Chronicle* and *Examiner* she learned about random shootings and other crimes in a city that lived in fear of "Manhattanization," though she "gathered that the term referred to high-rise buildings, not to murder." *Rich Rewards'* love plot develops when Daphne sees an old beau's name in the *Chronicle*, just as Alice once saw Bruno Trentin's there. Adams used Trentin as her model for Jean-Paul, a distinguished French socialist writer whom Daphne loved "permanently" when she was young in Paris. At the end of *Rich Rewards* she's met him again and plans to move to Paris with him. To some reviewers this would seem a "tacked-on" happy ending. Laurie Stone located the problem not in Adams's imagination but in "the myth it's hooked into." Jean-Pauls are "as false as the angel/whore myth of women" and "ideals of manly splendor are mucking up women's minds, not to mention their books."[6] But Adams insisted, "If Daphne is redeemed in the end it is through ideas and politics, not love."[7]

Certainly Alice's memories of Bruno Trentin were idealized, but Jean-Paul in *Rich Rewards* is less than perfect. Ella Leffland thought the ending "quiet, totally valid, & horrible": horrible because the romantic lover of Daphne's youth with whom she looks forward to living with "exhilaration and apprehension" is now ill with emphysema.[8] What if, Daphne asks herself, they move into Jean-Paul's tiny Parisian flat only to discover that "in a long-run day-to-day way, we just [don't] get along too well?" Or what if, as Leffland implied, Daphne reunited with her old love only to mourn his death?

Adams told a reviewer that she'd found *Rich Rewards* "easier to write than any of the others."[9] Richard Poirier, to whom she dedicated it along with Diane Johnson and John Murray, told her he thought the novel "at every point *interesting*, and that, as Henry James tells us, is first and last the essential thing . . . what is made interesting by your writing and your perfect sense of timing, are sights, sounds, odors that together constitute a nearly sacred combination for adults, an opening of the locks of feeling. You only seem to care more for your characters than for the things that surround them . . . It's, at last, a book that makes me feel good about my age."[10]

"Adams forecast the Yuppie era" in *Rich Rewards*, Karen Evans wrote in a profile of Adams in 1987.[11] Daphne is alarmed by consumerism, although her profession represents "a sort of epitome of crazy spending" because it is dependent on other people's excess income. Unfairness and corruption in the economic and political systems also figure in *Rich Rewards*. Adams crafted the dark-money plot that organizes this novel from allegations of CIA schemes to assassinate foreign leaders first published in the *New Yorker* by Seymour Hersh and later investigated by Frank Church's committee in the US Senate. In Adams's novel, Agatha's inheritance from her father, the General, turns out to be much larger than his military salary would explain. That and a suspicious car accident that befalls a woman who challenges the General's will make Agatha fear that her father was "involved in the murder of Allende, in Chile, or involved in Korean bribery; having been an influence in the sale of arms to some big oil country."

Nor were Alice's politics restricted to the pen. Proposals to build a nuclear power plant over an earthquake fault in Diablo Canyon near San Luis Obispo, California, had roused her to activism. She dressed in her best clothes to look like "a middle-aged straight lady" and had "a marvelous time" handing out leaflets to "rude businessmen" outside of the Pacific Gas & Electric headquarters. After that she promised "to stop being a closet radical and come out."[12] But when Peter and other friends planned to participate in the Abalone Alliance's blockade of the plant site, she analyzed the pros and cons of participating—"For: virtue, notice; Against: shyness, time, discomfort sleeping out in bags"—and decided not to go.

Alice talked about her political views in an interview with Sandy Boucher. "I'm an inactive socialist," Adams told her. "I feel strongly about poverty, unemployment, women's rights. I don't think there should be nuclear plants or nuclear testing. I don't even think most people need to drive cars." She cited Friedrich Engels's belief that "a writer's function is to present an ideal society" to explain her effort to "create a sort of myth" in which some characters are idealized. Adams admired writers like Grace Paley and Barbara Deming who were more directly engaged but said, "What always stops me is that political activity usually begins in going to a meeting and meetings drive me to some sort of claustrophobic frenzy . . . but I'm very good at marches. I love marching."[13]

Asked if she could separate "Alice Adams, the person, from Alice Adams the writer," Alice told an interviewer, "Less and less. I am, I would say, extremely motivated." She carried her confidence into the classroom when she agreed to teach a creative writing class as Diane Johnson's sabbatical replacement at the University of California's Davis campus in the spring of 1980. She had trepidations about facing a class but a salary and professional respect appealed to her. With her parents deceased, her son content in his own life, and her relationship with Bob going smoothly, Alice had liberated herself into work. During her sixth decade, in the conservative environment of the Reagan-era 1980s, Alice became more independent even as she continued to live with Bob McNie. When *Rich Rewards* came out, she asked Knopf to mail a book to Bruno Trentin. She heard nothing in return and "really didn't expect to," she told Cornelisen. "He must be a terribly dignified middle-aged Communist by now, not thinking a lot about youthful escapades."[14]

That escapade mattered less to Alice by then too. Nostalgia had served her artistic purpose, and perhaps a personal one as well. Adams's dispossessed female characters, Upton argues, "turn to their memories as their most volatile, and promising, possessions. These women rechart their lives, actually returning—imaginatively and more often than not, physically—to past landscapes." The function of such nostalgia is not a conventional escape but rather self-recovery, "a form of imaginative housekeeping" that serves their maturity.[15] By reimagining Trentin in *Rich Rewards* as an aging intellectual with emphysema, Adams reaffirmed the choices of her own maturity.

Adams was at work on a new, big novel she would call *Superior Women*. She hoped to make more money with it than she had with her previous books. As a result of her successful move into full-time author-ship, the fiction she produced almost overshadows the biographical facts of her life in the early 1980s. Her writing days were simple. Most writers complain about chores that impede them in the morning, but Alice said those odds and ends helped her ease into the day. "I work every day for several hours in the morning, a stop for lunch, then I try to work all afternoon." Her most productive hours often began at about two in the afternoon.[16] She wrote first drafts in bold longhand that marched steadily across unlined pages with few corrections. Usu-ally she typed these up herself, though she sometimes gave corrected typescripts to a typist to make fresh, final versions. Of course she made exceptions to that all-day schedule, but even on vacations she always worked on notes and first drafts, copyediting, or whatever she needed to do. She brought a portable typewriter when she and Bob went to the house in Truckee.

Alice said her January trip to Mexico in 1980 was the best ever, partly because she arrived sick, tired, and depressed about the Chapel Hill house and the death of Lucie Jessner. She felt "thousands of times better" when she and Bob woke in Zihuatanejo on the morning of the Calvins' fiftieth anniversary, which they celebrated with champagne and a fire-works show on the beach arranged by Henry Calvin. The older couple, with whom they had "rather formal relations," made Alice and Bob feel "extremely young."[17] In the spring, Adams wrote another admiring story about them and what she regarded as their very old age—"probably somewhere in their eighties." In "At the Beach" they appear at the same hour every day "in trim dark bathing suits, over which they both wear white shirts . . . advancing on their ancient legs, they are as elegant as tropical birds—and a striking contrast to everyone else on the beach, many of whom wear bright colors." Their nearness to death, Adams implies, makes them "seem highly conscious of each moment."

At the beach that year Alice met Doris Dörrie, a young German filmmaker who was traveling with her then-boyfriend, a dentist whose first name was Wulf. To Doris, Alice seemed like a free spirit: "I never would have struck a friendship with a woman of her age in Germany because they were far more conventional." She admired Alice because she "seemed so completely independent and determined to write. Great discipline. Even on her holidays she'd sit in the shade and write." On that trip, with Alice as her role model, Dörrie wrote a screenplay about a dentist that became her first feature film, *Straight Through the Heart*. When Doris and Wulf read in the local paper that a fifteen-year-old boy named Eugenio* had been arrested for the murder of the wealthy owner of a coconut plantation, they decided to visit the boy in jail. Reports indicated that Eugenio had "witnessed the murder of his father by this rich owner, a reputed drunk," Adams wrote. Accompanied by Wulf as their translator, Doris and Alice visited Eugenio in the town jail. Their idea was that two gringas taking an interest might improve the boy's chance of receiving justice. Wulf introduced Alice as an American journalist and Doris as a German filmmaker, and thus they conveyed "a sense that . . . anything that happened to Ernesto was being watched, internationally."[18]

Eugenio, a thin, pale boy who had lost a lot of blood when the owner's guards shot him, was sitting on the dirt floor with other prisoners. He asked for comic books. They visited several times, bringing candy and clothing as well as comics. Once a cousin of Eugenio's, a law student, confronted them: "He was afraid we were spies for the man who had been killed. We learned from him that there was a contract out on the boy," Alice recalled. Back at the hotel they took up a small collection from other guests to help Eugenio's mother, "a small, dark, fearful looking

---

* The boy's name was Eugenio, according to Dörrie's letters to Adams. Adams changes his name to Ernesto in *Mexico* and to Felipe in "Teresa." Several of Adams's letters state that Eugenio was fifteen, but he's older in her travel book and story.

woman" who came by bus from her village to visit her son. Before Alice
and Doris left Mexico, they urged other tourists to visit Eugenio. "We all
kept writing letters to the local jail after returning home," Dörrie said.
"Somehow we helped get him sent to a juvenile facility, and I know he
graduated from school." At one point Dörrie hoped to bring Eugenio to
Germany or convince Alice and Bob to try to bring him to California.

Adams wrote about this episode twice, as nonfiction in her travel
memoir, *Mexico*, and as fiction in "Teresa," included in her collection
To See You Again. It is one of two stories from that collection that she
was unable to sell to a magazine, ostensibly because it was too unlike
her earlier work. With the tone of a legend or fairy tale ("At that time,
in that small town, there was a young girl named Teresa, about sixteen"),
it recounts the life of a woman from a village near Zihuatanejo. She
marries Ernesto, who stepped forward to protect her when, as a fearful
young girl, she was ogled by the predatory blond plantation owner, Señor
Krupp. In an almost wordless marriage, Teresa raises a son and three
daughters. Her husband and her son, who both work on Krupp's plantation, are "dark and mysterious" and "distant." After a friend of Ernesto's
is found murdered, Ernesto challenges Krupp about working conditions
and is himself killed. Teresa's son, Felipe, is allowed to assume the father's
job. Teresa finds "him increasingly disturbing, with his silences and
angry eyes," and pays less attention to him. Felipe acquires a gun and
kills Señor Krupp on the first anniversary of Ernesto's death.

At this point "Teresa" intersects with Alice's visit to the Zihuatanejo
jail in January 1980, but she never brings herself or the Germans into
the story:

> In the middle of that room, on the floor, sat a very old man with
> no legs, on a tattered blanket; he grinned and stared at Teresa in an
> evil way, so that she shuddered and held to the arm of [her cousin]
> Aurelia. And the room was so crowded with persons, mostly men,
> but also some young women, one of them holding a baby, that at
> first Teresa and Aurelia could not find Felipe. Also it was so dark, no
> windows at all and one single light bulb, very dim, that hung from
> the ceiling. They found him in a small room just off the main one.
> He had been sitting on the floor, but he got up as they came in—still
> really a boy, not very tall. He embraced his mother, who despite herself
> was crying, and then his cousin, who also wept.

Adams's dark tale again diverges from the known events. "A boy with no money, the son of a plantation worker, could not kill a rich and powerful man, and live," she writes; eventually the authorities tell the grieving Teresa that Felipe has been killed in a prison fight. After that, Teresa, who "had withstood more than was possible for her," suffers terrible grief until "in another part of her mind new words [began] to form, new ideas and sentences; she began to think, Now I have no more to fear; now everything has befallen me that possibly could, and for the rest of my days I am safe. I can go to sleep without fear, I could even walk among North Americans, fearing nothing."

The way Adams developed a story about a Mexican woman she met only once suggests the intensity of her interest in the existential elements of women's lives. No longer tied by her husband or son to the unknowable world of men or to the traditions of plantation life, Teresa will move away from the "coconut palms that rattle so fiercely on windy nights" and live in a beach hut with her daughters, where she feels she will "grow old and be safe forever."

"Legends," another short story Adams could not sell to a magazine during this time, also breaks the mold of her previous stories. It is "dense and ambitious and old-fashioned," Victoria Wilson said. "If the New Yorker were really smart as a magazine and at all watchful of the people they publish," she continued, "they would see that this story is particularly interesting just because it is so different from what you've written and that the richness of it—its old-fashionedness—makes it something important." Novelist Alice Walker told Adams that these two unpublishables "contain knowledge that women are not supposed to write about," and we can guess that Walker was talking about the loss of self that may silently occur as a consequence of devotion to a man.[19] "Legends" in that way is more cerebral than "Teresa" because it adopts the point of view of Jane Phelps, whose relationship to a famous, deceased composer has become a romantic legend—a legend that Jane herself feels is false.* Inspired in part by the story of Lillian Hellman

* Like Alice's father, the composer Randolph (Ran) Caldwell has an impenetrable accent. As Jane recalls in the story, "Half the time I hadn't the slightest idea what he was talking about, but I was excited by his voice, as I was by everything about him, his hair and his sad dark eyes, his cigarettes; his hunting shirts, his shabby tweeds, his snappy car. At worst, you could call it a crush." Also like Nic Adams, Ran is "a small-town, Southern white Protestant, [with] a Presbyterian conscience."

(who was close to Alice's friend Billy Abrahams) and Dashiell Hammett (of whom Diane Johnson was writing a biography), Adams hangs her story on the twin dangers of envy and alcoholism. Jane recognizes herself in the unattractive Candida Heffelfinger, who comes to interview her: "Ugly women as lovers are fantastic," Jane thinks, because "a beautiful woman would expect to be made love to, we expect to make love." Then Candida asks Jane a question she's avoided for many years—about another lover of the famous composer's: "I began to cough, passionately, as though I were trying to cough up my heart, that sudden cold stone in my chest."

Jane sends Candida away, which leaves the middle of the story open to accommodate an account of Jane's feelings for the composer: "I was obsessed with him in an ugly, violent way that seemed to preclude other softer, gentler feelings." Jane and Ran fight often and bitterly during the ten years of an affair that lasts until Ran dies of emphysema (the disease that took Lucie Jessner, and Jean-Paul in *Rich Rewards*). After a night of self-scrutiny during which Jane realizes she suffers from "unshakable, implacable self-dislike," she invites Candida to return. Quickly they sum up and set aside the topic of Ran. Then—with great relief and joy—they turn to a new subject: all morning and into the afternoon they talk about Jane Phelps's own successful work as a sculptor.

"What really happened" while Jane Phelps was involved with Ran was a breakthrough in her work. "I had just begun to work in a serious way; I worked furiously, excited about what I was producing . . . I was just moving from small carved wooden sculptures to larger figures, and in my mind were even larger constructions, the sort of shapes that I eventually achieved." Likewise for Alice Adams, "what really happened" during the late 1970s and early 1980s—in addition to her involvement with Bob McNie and his busy, alcoholic life, despite much travel and teaching and public success—was a remarkable increase in her writing output. Adams's larger constructions were longer novels and whole books of short stories.

Alice and Bob entertained family or friends for dinner in the city and for lunch or dinner or whole weekends in the mountains. The fact that Bob often passed out during an evening meal did not prevent them from setting a beautiful table—lots of candlelight and silver. Alice often cooked throughout the day to make a long-simmered stew or baked dessert, but after guests arrived she and Bob seemed to have "worked out some magic combination of who does what, which at the time seems no one is doing anything—until on comes a sumptuous feast," as Ann Cornelisen remembered after a visit to San Francisco.[20] At Bob's house in the mountains they kept it simpler, but meals were enhanced by the beauty of the house and the dining room's bay window overlooking the Truckee River.*

For the most part their cooking was European influenced, simple and hearty, and accompanied by plenty of drink. Anne Lamott, whose first novel *Hard Laughter* prompted a fan letter "of affection and respect" from Alice, remembered her first visit to Alice and Bob's apartment in late 1980: "It was like a museum of a still-active literary great, elegant and immaculately organized bookshelves, manuscripts and bound galleys everywhere, lying around on furniture like cats. She and Bob and I got very drunk. She loved gossip, and seemed to hate two out of three writers, agents, etc. and was very funny and brilliant and Southern in her hatred. We were friends forever after that."

Lamott, looking back at those years after decades of sobriety, recalled, "Bob was a huge drinker, definitely alcoholic. I was very fond of him but the disease got the best of him." In Lamott's view, Alice looked forward to drinks with people but remained in control of her drinking: "She was very disciplined in everything she did—writing, swimming, but of course if she'd had the disease in her, all the discipline in the world couldn't have saved her . . . [so] I don't think she was a drunk." Nevertheless as Alice aged and the demands of her writing career escalated, she made resolutions like this one in her notebook for 1982: "Resolves—exercise, 2 glasses wine (none at lunch)—(oh, how bleak)."

Alice's determination to limit her drinking coincided with a severe depression that consumed Bob. As his son recalled, Bob's problems were precipitated by the collapse of the interior design cooperative that had provided him and other designers with a financial umbrella. "My father's whole security base was pulled out from under him about the

---

* Alice sent her "Easiest Chicken for a lot of People" recipe to Judith Adams: "Grind or roll out into fine crumbs some seasoned stuffing, add chopped garlic, Parmesan, and chopped parsley. Roll chicken parts (legs and thighs, breasts, less successful with wings) in melted butter, then in the Parmesan etc mixture. Bake for about an hour in 350 oven, turn off—serve whenever." (AA to JCA, April 9, 1984.)

same time Alice was becoming so successful. Then he lost his North Beach studio, not really a surprise, but he was around 60 and he was losing all this stuff—BANG BANG BANG."

Having Bob moping around home during the day interfered with Alice's work and the depression became "contagious." It took him months to find a new studio that suited him. Nothing Alice attempted cheered him up. She brought him with her to Alaska for a writer's conference, adding on a weekend of touring before the meetings in Fairbanks. They viewed wildlife from an Outdoor World Ltd. bus in Mount McKinley (now Denali) State Park, excited to see moose, caribou, and Dall sheep as Alice struggled with acrophobia on the narrow gravel road cut through a steep landscape. Alice was billed as a star at the Midnight Sun writers' conference in Fairbanks. Host Dave Stark carried a copy of *Rich Rewards* when he met her and Bob at the airport. "Oh, you have my book," Alice said, to which Stark quickly riposted, "I carry it everywhere." But she and Bob were disappointed to find themselves lodged in a crowded student apartment during a heat wave. The hot, brilliant sunshine at four a.m. was "enough to make you crazy as well as exhausted," a situation made worse for Alice by "a huge bicycle right next to my side of the bed, so that I was entangled in handlebars as well as hot and sleepless." Soon after the conference began, a tour bus rolled down a cliff from the very road where Alice and Bob had been. Alice's fear was justified: "Our bus. The very next day. I don't know what to make of that." The newspaper reported three killed, twenty-nine hospitalized.

For Bob the ten-day conference in Alaska seemed endless, and Alice was "almost sorry" she'd talked him into coming along to Fairbanks—"probably the Stockton of Alaska, totally dull." Increasingly comfortable as a workshop teacher, Alice told her students how the ABDCE pattern had helped her tighten up the rather scattered material of her stories and made them easier to publish. She liked the other writers, including the "marvelous" poet Galway Kinnell and a couple of very good students. Early on the last morning a handsome young man approached her in the coffee room. "I really like the unusual occupations of your heroines," he told Alice, who accepted the compliment. "I especially like the one about the turkey-sorter," he continued. Alice was so exhausted that she thought she might have written such a story and again said thank you. It came to her later. The story in question was "The Turkey Season"—by *that other Alice*, Canadian author Alice Munro, whose stories had begun appearing in many of the same magazines as Alice Adams's stories.[21]

Adams worked the bus accident into "Alaska," a story of two house cleaners, young, white Gloria and older, part-black Mrs. Lawson, who work for a wealthy woman in San Francisco. Gloria, who is obsessively worried about a small lump on her calf, visits her sister in Fairbanks, where she takes the wildlife bus tour and finds the midnight sun coming through foil-covered windows in student housing more panic-inducing than the "thick dark fogs that come into San Francisco in the summer." Back home, Gloria tells Mrs. Lawson about the headlines in the Fairbanks paper: " 'They said, BUS TOPPLES FROM MOUNTAIN, EIGHT KILLED, 42 INJURED. Can you imagine? Our same bus, the very next day. What do you think that means?' This question too has been rhetorical; voicing it, Gloria smiles in a satisfied, knowing way."

A very polite woman, Mrs. Lawson smiles gently too. "It means you spared. You like to live fifty, sixty years more." Gloria thinks that too, especially because the lump on her leg that has been worrying her for weeks disappeared on the day of the bus accident. Mrs. Lawson, who could have told Gloria that the lump was a knot of muscle if only she'd asked her, now thinks—but does not say aloud—"The truth is, Gloria could perfectly well get killed by a bus in San Francisco, this very afternoon, or shot by some sniper . . . Or Gloria could find another lump, some place else, somewhere dangerous. Missing one bus accident is no sure sign that a person's life will always come up rosy, because nobody's does, not for long."

The *New Yorker* turned down "Alaska" with the explanation that the author seemed "too distanced" from her characters.[22] After the story appeared in *Shenandoah* and was anthologized in a collection from that quarterly, short-story writer Daniel Stern praised it for its difference from Adams's *New Yorker* stories: "The author hones a sharp style and uses it elegantly and with passion to create an Alaska of the spirit that comes to stand for both hope and fate. It is, somehow, to the point that although I have read Alice Adams's stories in *The New Yorker*, this is the one I have found the most enjoyable and most fully realized."[23] Joyce Carol Oates chose "Alaska" for *The Oxford Book of American Short Stories*, calling Adams a "superb social observer" like Edith Wharton, John Cheever, and John Updike. "Alaska" is typical of Adams's "exquisitely wrought fiction, in which dialogue is preeminent, recorded with a flawless ear," Oates writes, but less typical in its protagonist, "the cleaning lady of a wealthy woman."[24]

Oates was not alone in recognizing Adams as a preeminent short-story artist whose appeal reached beyond the particular tastes of that era's *New Yorker* readers. Her longtime friend William Abrahams considered her a leading short-story writer of her era. She'd already been included in the O. Henry Awards volume ten times when Abrahams selected her for the Special Award for Continuing Achievement, which he'd previously awarded to Joyce Carol Oates in 1970 and John Updike in 1976.* *Prize Stories 1982: The O. Henry Awards* announced Adams's receipt of the Special Award and included two stories she'd written out of her term at UC Davis: "To See You Again," about the attraction felt by a professor for her "brilliant, beautiful" young student during a time when her husband is severely depressed, and "Greyhound People," about the people on the bus by which Alice commuted to teach at UC Davis. The latter, Abrahams writes, "beautifully conveys [Adams's] virtues: her clear, sometimes poignant, sometimes ironic, but always deeply sympathetic view of the complexities of contemporary life."

Taking aim at postmodern and metafiction writers like John Barth and Donald Barthelme and minimalists such as Ann Beattie and Raymond Carver (as edited by Gordon Lish) in his preface to the volume, Abrahams notes that Adams "is a writer whose achievement is particularly to be valued at a time when spectacular 'effects' are too often exploited for their own sake." He praises Adams for her "art that conceals itself in a deceptive effortlessness—secure alike in what she does and in what she chooses not to do. (One finds it hard to imagine her writing an unintelligible sentence.)"

The vitality of the short story, Abrahams believed, depends on writers like Adams "who continue to write, year after year, not always achieving the standard of excellence they have set for themselves in their best work, but even in their lesser work unmistakably revealing themselves to be dedicated writers for whom the task is, in the precise sense of the word, a vocation."[25]

---

* Alice Munro became the fourth (and so far last) writer to receive the O. Henry Special Award for Continuing Achievement in 2000.

CHAPTER TWENTY-FOUR

A Fateful Age

— 1981–1983 —

50 reasons not to write . . . screws up relationships.

—Alice Adams, notebook,
November 16, 1983

When sunshine returned to San Francisco in September, Alice was so tired of Bob's melancholy that she thought about renting an office for herself as a sanctuary where she could write. Instead Bob located a former warehouse space at 63 Bluxome in a reviving area south of Market Street. His prospects continued to improve when I. Magnin invited him to model a double-breasted, white wool sport coat in a newspaper ad for their "totally new Man's Store." He sounds like a new man himself as he boasts, "I wear a tie about three days a week, I wear boots most of the time . . . on weekends I always wear a bandana at the neck. In Tahoe I ski in jeans."[1]

While Bob set up his studio, Alice headed to New York for a few days to meet with Victoria Wilson. Initially apprehensive about traveling alone, she stayed with the Kiernans' cats in their Park Place apartment while they were away and had a wonderful time. She "walked to the museums, ate and drank a lot, and walked farther." She dined with Dick Poirier and attended a "horrible" literary party given by her agent, Lynn Nesbit, afterward reporting that she was frozen with "boredom and disbelief" as she listened to a distinguished editor praise Ayn Rand's *Fountainhead*; on that same occasion she met author Harold Brodkey, whose long-anticipated, reputedly four-thousand-page novel had recently been purchased by Knopf. Back home, she was still feeling "a sort of New York excitement," and said, "In fact it's hard to calm down." She chewed

over the current New York literary scene with Billy Abrahams. When he
suggested Brodkey was a "closet queen" she told him "of course" but later
called both Brodkey and an unnamed publisher "closet castrati"—"the
total lack of sexuality in both those people is quite sinister—which is
how I feel about Nixon, come to think."[2] Alice's impressions of Nesbit's
party found their way into *Superior Women*, where Megan Greene endures
a similar party in an "overheated, overcrowded room, so full of violent
conflicting odors: perfume and the sweat of anxiety, liquors, aromatic
foods, plus all the smoke from cigarettes, pipes, cigars."

Bob remained "astoundingly cheerful" through the holidays and their
winter trip to Mexico. As happened every few years, in 1982 they gave in
to an impulse to explore some part of the country beyond their beloved
Zihuatanejo. With Pauline and Richard Abbe they went to the colonial
city of Oaxaca, where they stayed in an old convent turned hotel and
visited the Zapotec archaeological sites. Everywhere, Adams wrote later,
she heard the voices of people who had inhabited that valley for eleven
thousand years. In the tombs of Mitla she felt dark premonitions. On
the ride back from Mitla their taxi slowed for an accident: "We could
all too easily see, stretched there on the highway, two blanket-covered
bodies, one large, adult-sized; the other very small, a child. And feet:
four feet stuck out from those blankets. A woman's shabby black shoes,
a child's sandals." Alice was upset, and Bob told her (she recalled later),
"You make too much of things. Two people. It happens every minute.
Somewhere every second. New York. Bangladesh."

"I know," Alice replied. "But those two—the feet." She couldn't quite
explain why she was so upset, but the episode stayed in her mind to
become a new story, "Mexican Dust." There it's Miriam, a small, dark
woman traveling with her three large "blond, full-fleshed" California
in-laws, who harbors the "weird science-fiction thought . . . that all the
dust particles in Mexico could be silicon chips, programmed for some
violence." From Oaxaca, Bob and Alice and the Abbes, like the four
people in the story, flew to Puerto Escondido, a popular surfing spot,
where their hotel was consumed by a noisy New Year's Eve celebration
that no one cleaned up after the next day. They planned to drive to
Zihuatanejo but there were no cars to be rented, so they boarded a
second-class bus. They missed connections repeatedly as their one-day
drive stretched into two days. Adams recounted the miserable trip more
than once; what's interesting in these accounts is that both Alice and the

character she identifies with, Miriam, feel like outsiders in the company of other gringo tourists who are relentlessly in pursuit of luxury and willfully ignorant about the Mexican people. "If any of them spoke Spanish it would all have been different, Miriam thinks. They would have understood what was being said in the station about the buses, and even, maybe have grasped a little more about the terrible accident on the road."[3]

Alice persistently tried to learn Spanish, which she found difficult because she associated it with her father. But with cassette player and study she made some progress. Ten years later, when she traveled to the Yucatán Peninsula with women friends, they relied on Alice to manage things. "Her Spanish was fluent enough to hire a car, negotiate with the hotel, and change our tickets if something went wrong. She talked to people in the shops and restaurants," Alison Lurie recalled.

Because Alice's new novel was taking longer to write than planned, Victoria Wilson had agreed to publish a story collection in the interim. For the most part reviewers applauded *To See You Again* as they labored to classify and summarize its nineteen stories, nine of which had appeared in the *New Yorker*. Norbert Blei in the *Chicago Sun-Times* said these stories placed Adams "at the forefront of American writing with exquisitely rendered stories that explore the tenuous times and conflicts of women," and Paul Gray in *Time* noted characters who refuse "to enlist in the war between the sexes" because they sense that both sides "are fighting on different fronts against common enemies—aging, disillusionment, what one character calls 'the sheer fatigue of living.'" In the *Richmond News Leader* Judi Goldenberg noticed that Adams included more "ordinary people" in these stories—she points to the bus riders in "Greyhound People" and the young waitress in "By the Sea" as examples.* Diana Ketcham, in the *Oakland Tribune*, mentioned some similarity of subject between Adams's stories and soap operas but found the stories redeemed by Adams's "skeptical view of conventional success."[4]

---

* Robbie McNie came across "Greyhound People" and wrote Alice a mean note: "I didn't like your article . . . I thought it was a small piece, unworthy of my time. I hope you will take the bus to real experience. Your shyness is keeping you from feeling. Why don't you write for a magazine that talks to blacks, like Jet. . . . Better luck next time." (Undated, signed "Bob.")

One review made Alice "laugh with sheer pleasure." Carolyn See, the Los Angeles novelist who later became her good friend, skewered the conventions that reigned in reviews of women's fiction. Noticing that the book jacket compared Adams to Flannery O'Connor and Katherine Mansfield, See quipped that all Adams had in common with those two was that she was a woman who wrote short stories. Why not compare her to Walter Cronkite, "because you can believe what she says," or to Norman Mailer, "because she'd knock him out in the first round." See observed that Adams's stories ask an essential question: "Whom are we attracted to, and why, and how does that, how should that, affect our lives?"[5]

Jacob Stockinger, a reviewer in the *Capital Times* in Madison, Wisconsin, also offered a comparison: Colette. Adams sees "events and characters as inner events and beings that unfold through the external world. Insight is the great drama and love is the supreme insight."[6] Stockinger, who'd just completed a doctorate in French literature, could not have come up with a comparison that would better please Adams. Though she'd shrugged when Diane Johnson called *Rich Rewards* "very Colette," Alice admired that Colette was "a real woman" who surpassed "her own heroines in courage and energy" and in "unlimited capacities both for work and for love." In a review of Colette's letters Adams had praised Colette's professionalism: her "ability to keep on with one's work no matter what"—the *what* including poverty and deprivation, a career in theater, love affairs, divorces, two world wars, her most beloved husband's incarceration by Nazis, and painful illnesses.[7]

For the publication week, Knopf brought Alice to New York, meaning they paid her expenses and scheduled her to give four readings and several interviews. She stayed at the Wyndham Hotel on West Fifty-Eighth Street—"both cheap and swell." Again Bob stayed home because he was "still so far behind from all that time wasted looking for a new studio, moving," and Alice thought, "It sure will be odd to spend 10 days by myself. Maybe good for my character although I think it's too late for improvement."[8] Improving of character or not, her ten days were filled by celebrations of which she was the star. She and Diane Johnson shared the stage at the Three Lives & Company bookstore in the West Village; then she joined Johnson at a dinner given by *New*

York Review of Books editors Barbara and Jason Epstein. The guest list, snidely observed Richard Poirier, who bowed out to dine with New York City Ballet director Lincoln Kirstein, sounded "about as much fun as the guest list for Jean Harris's Christmas party in her cell," referring to the then-infamous murderer of a Scarsdale doctor. At least in the version of it Poirier wrote down after hearing about it from Alice, the party was a disaster: "fag hags and sexless gays except for Kempton and Lizzy [Hardwick]," dominated by Sontag's "talking about herself for three hours" and gossip about Lillian Hellman, "who'd made a big thing about not being invited."*

Alice loved gossip, but such brushes with New York's literary scene reminded her that she truly preferred living in San Francisco where, she said, there was "no literary community. There are a few writers. I see a great deal of Diane Johnson . . . you can sustain yourself if you live with someone you like and have work that you like."[9] In short, New York made her feel rushed and bitchy. As Eve Babitz put it, "There are no spaces between the words" there. "Certain things don't have to be thought about carefully because you're always being pushed from behind."[10] Next on Alice's itinerary was Washington, DC, for a visit with Judith and Timothy Adams as well as Judith's intrepid elderly mother, Dorothy Funk Clark, "just sitting there full of observations, and wit." Alice thought Judith looked beautiful and together they saw a marvelous Rodin exhibit.[11] This was in many ways a perfect life. Old friends and new, east and west, united in praise of the talented one for whom they'd held high hopes—hopes that were now coming true.

Alice returned home to freezing rain and hail in San Francisco, which drove her and Bob to the mountains for a weekend, where they found too much snow for cross-country skiing. On Monday she began teaching a graduate seminar at Stanford at the invitation of John L'Heureux, who then directed the writing program. As Mark Linenthal's wife, Alice had regarded Stanford's Creative Writers (she scornfully capitalized the words) "with a sort of enraged envy." She said Wallace Stegner and Richard Scowcroft "would barely speak to her" when she became more successful in the 1970s. "I do still get awful vibrations from that place,"

---

* Guests included Arthur Gold, Robert Fizdale, David Kalstone, Elizabeth Hardwick, Susan Sontag, and Murray Kempton. (Richard Poirier, notes to himself dated March 11, 1982, Columbia University Rare Book and Manuscript Library.)

she recalled after lunching with L'Heureux and meeting her students. Nonetheless, she admired L'Heureux and enjoyed her status as a Stanford faculty member with special relish. She befriended several of the students, including Harriet Doerr and Dennis McFarland. Of Alice's teaching, McFarland recalled, "She was so completely an intuitive writer, almost like a musician who plays only by ear, she was not especially articulate about craft. Still, she was very good at spotting the strong and weak moments in a given story, and that, I think, is generally the most important feedback a writer can get from a workshop. She was kind and allowed the students to do most of the talking; she wasn't the sort of leader who ever tore anybody's work apart."

Harriet Huntington Doerr had been a Stegner fellow and continued attending seminars with L'Heureux while she worked on the stories that became her novel *Stones for Ibarra*, published when she was seventy-four. L'Heureux urged her to participate in Adams's workshop but she found the volume and diversity of comments she heard there overwhelming. She took her dilemma to Adams, who told her, "Listen to Dennis McFarland." Doerr conveyed the compliment when she met with McFarland. "That was the sort of thing that really boosted my ego at a time when I was beginning to see my contemporaries bring out their first books and I was yet so far from having one," he recalled.[12] Adams continued to mentor both writers after her term at Stanford ended. She gave a party for Doerr when *Stories from Ibarra* appeared in 1984 and a reading with her in New York in 1990. When McFarland and his wife, poet Michelle Blake, moved to San Francisco, a friendship blossomed between them and Alice and Bob (who seemed "a very polished lout, who wore ascots and loved her cats"). She introduced them to Anne Lamott and to Fran Kiernan, who eventually acquired McFarland's first novel, *The Music Room*, for Houghton Mifflin. "You could feel a strong sense of choice in her friendship," McFarland said, "and it made you feel very chosen. You had the feeling that there was you and Alice and your other friends, and then there was the rest of the world, who didn't quite come up to snuff."[13]

By now Adams had discovered a teaching method that worked for her. Marjorie Leet (later Ford), one of a handful of women who took a UC extension course from Adams in 1981, recalled: "She had an unusual method of presenting our stories: each would be read aloud not by the author but by another member of the class . . . Hearing a stranger read your story gave you a sense of how the words flowed, of whether the humor came through, or the tension or the tender parts." Adams also told the class that "writing was one of the only careers she could think of where it paid to get older. She felt she had a tremendous advantage, being over fifty. Writing, she said, was one field where an accumulation of years made you richer, more and more capable."[14]

All spring Alice toured to promote *To See You Again*. Her dizzying itinerary began with a talk at Boise State University in Idaho, of which she was so scared that she tried to persuade Max Steele to meet her there. When she saw a marquee on campus that said "Welcome Alice Adams" she didn't realize it was about her until her host explained.[15] Scheduled around her teaching days at Stanford were trips to Madison, Dallas, Austin, and Los Angeles. Her story "On the Road" evokes the strangeness of a lecture tour—confusion and exhaustion; endless, often intrusive questions; fantasies of going to bed with someone just met; and fears of simply ordering a much-needed drink alone in a bar. Despite these complaints, she was eager to travel more and asked Steele, "What do you mean Annie Dillard was there [in Chapel Hill] for 2 weeks? Why not me?"[16]

Alice's discontent persisted. Success was separating her from Bob while his difficulties were driving him deeper into alcoholism, which magnified their troubles. They had terrible quarrels; a fight could flare suddenly, "as though all the space around & between them were coated with kerosene."[17] One such fight was going on as they packed to fly to Santa Fe in early July 1982. They were "whispering vileness to each other" all through a performance of *The Marriage of Figaro* under the stars.[18] Alice asked Bob to move out when they got back to San Francisco, but she didn't really want him to do that because "living alone would be terribly lonely." A few weeks later Alice confided to Max Steele, "Things are a lot better, Bob drinking a great deal less—but it all seems rather frail, I don't think I could take any more eruptions like that—on the other hand they may not happen; he sure knew I was serious about his moving out."[19]

That fall Alice and Bob were having dinner with Carolyn See and John Espy at the Belle-Vue restaurant in Santa Monica. Bob was driving a car borrowed from Alice's old friend Dick DeRoy, which he'd left with a valet to park and wash. "The four of us sat at a corner booth and Bob, as always, was in a piss-poor mood and Alice was apologetic and smiling," See remembered. As they were finishing a meal already made awkward by Bob's mood—it was hard to know if he'd had too much to drink or needed more—the parking attendant came in and told Bob that somebody had run into the car while he was washing it. "Bob had a tantrum," See said. "He just screamed and hollered and carried on. The poor guy couldn't do anything, had to stand there and take it in front of all the customers. Of course Bob didn't want to return a damaged car, but he just didn't rise to the occasion. He was terrible, and again Alice was apologetic, nervous, smiling in an embarrassed way."[20]

Alice fought her own discouragement and anxiety over Bob's behavior with work and exercise and a surprisingly robust correspondence with new acquaintances and old friends. One of these was her "most beautiful student" from UC Davis, Scott Crawford.[21] Crawford held the sort of charm for her that Seth held for the woman professor in "To See You Again." The fictional professor manages her attraction to Seth by domesticating her "unruly feelings" for him—she imagines his visiting her house and seeing her "sad fat husband, a distinguished architect—and [her] most precariously balanced, laboriously achieved 'good life.'"[22] "To See You Again" ends with a muted optimism that is typical of Adams's midlife work. Even though the professor has just taken her severely depressed husband to the hospital, she thinks hopefully of a future when he "will be completely well, the cycle flat, no more sequences of pain. And maybe thin again. And interested, and content. It's almost worth waiting for."

Alice corresponded with Crawford for a year or so after the story he had inspired appeared in the *New Yorker*. He wrote a review of *Rich Rewards* for the student paper; she sent him upbeat reports on her life and wrote him recommendations for graduate school. To Diane Johnson, who had also been his writing teacher, she worried that he would become a "perpetual student."

Jeanne Harris became another epistolary confidante for Alice. Harris had been a young mother from Ohio "sitting out the depression" in a rented house on Pittsboro Road in Chapel Hill in 1937 when she first knew "a ten-year-old little girl with glossy hair and bangs" named

Alice Adams. She wrote after seeing Adams's stories with North Carolina settings in the *New Yorker*. Soon they were exchanging anecdotes
about Chapel Hill people as well as about their present lives. Harris
wondered why Alice's father stopped to talk whenever he saw her
outside even though they didn't find much to say. Alice replied that
Nic Adams "was always a terrible flirt" and she was a pretty red-head.
In another letter Harris recalled seeing Verlie Jones with her car stuck
in the mud for the longest time until two black men came to help.
"Do you have to be colored to help colored down here?" Harris had
wondered at the time.

Fan letters from strangers also sometimes led to friendships. For
instance, a young man named Richard Carr wrote, "I'm a jazz musician
who works by night and reads magazines in hotel lobbies, often far away
from home, by day." Carr came across "Verlie I Say unto You" in an
old *Atlantic Monthly* in the lobby of the Château Frontenac in Quebec
City. He admired the story's simple, honest compassion and told Alice,
"You're really kind of a hot shit." More specifically he praised her for
knowing—as a good jazz musician does—"what to leave in and what
to leave out."

Carr had written to authors before, and his life on the road made him
grateful for any replies that landed in his mailbox in Solon, Maine. He
hit a jackpot with Alice, who sent a package of books and encouraged
him to write to her again. Then he sent her a cassette tape that she and
Bob listened to on the way to Truckee: "There we were driving in the
bright equinoctial dark, listening to you." The correspondence went on
until 1987. Alice told Carr she'd "much rather be a jazz musician than
write . . . writing is an awful thing to do. Lonely, regarded by most
people with deep suspicion—and you don't ever know if what you're
working on is any good. No instant applause . . . I especially hate writing
novels, and if I were more sensible I would not; you get so bored, they
go on forever."[23]

In fact, Adams was still far from finishing *Superior Women* when she
wrote that. She'd slowed her progress to teach and to write dozens of
book reviews and short stories and then to promote *To See You Again*.
Nor was it just boredom that impeded her. *Superior Women* was a much
bigger project than any she'd undertaken before. She first wrote the title

"Superior Women" in her notebook in November 1977. The novel's
four leading characters are white women who become friends at their
Ivy League College—Radcliffe—during World War II. A fifth woman,
Janet, remains outside of their group because she is Jewish, yet her story
is central to Adams's panorama of their generation. *Superior Women*
covers forty years in the lives of these women with many branch stories
of their lovers, spouses, and colleagues. The ambitious novel quickly
evolved from its roots in Adams's college classmates and took on its
own life as "an unofficial history of the years I know about." Although
she meant to write a plot outline for it, Adams soon returned to her
character-driven method of composition: "I simply acquainted myself
with the women, and began to know them so well that I could easily
imagine the rest of their lives."

A few statistics about these women: three of five marry, two of those
three divorce, four have children; one comes out as a lesbian; one has a
love affair (and child) with a priest; two have professional careers. Megan
Greene, the daughter of a carhop on the Bayshore Highway in East Palo
Alto, is the character who is psychologically closest to Adams. "So much
has been done on Easterners who come West," Adams said. "I thought
it would be interesting to approach it from the other way."[24] With that
light scrambling of geography Adams freshened her perspective on the
other four Radcliffe women and endowed Megan with a naïve openness
about class, sex, religion, and even race that had not been available to
a young Southerner of her generation.

Adams at last mailed off her "monstrous" 5-pound, 537-page, 80,000-
word manuscript to Lynn Nesbit in April of 1983. Joe Kanon, then at
E. P. Dutton, wanted it and promised to make it the lead novel for his
spring list but couldn't top Knopf's offer of $80,000 for the hardcover
edition. Alice thought it a "huge fortune" and soon found a financial
advisor who set her up in an annuity fund. For the first time in her
life she had savings and investments—and was enabled "to meet the
requirements of [her] imagination" as James wished for Isabel in *The
Portrait of a Lady*.

Wilson thought *Superior Women* "a great leap forward," and both
she and Robert Gottlieb thought the book had a "real chance" to
break out into bigger popularity and sales. She praised all the major

characters—"so interestingly distinguished from each other"—as well as "how strong and right your sense of place is." Wilson's and Gottlieb's criticisms were minor, mainly to do with Adams's penchant for coincidences, and she set about working on these "soft spots" with real enthusiasm. They offered little complaint about the epilogue, in which several characters converge to celebrate Megan's mother's birthday at an old tobacco farm where they provide shelter for homeless women from nearby cities. Some reviewers didn't believe this utopian ending but it fits perfectly in the arc of Adams's biography.

The novel's farmhouse, purchased by Peg Sinclair, one of the original Radcliffe friends, mirrors the one where Alice grew up. It "sits on a hilltop, in a grove of oak and pine, overlooking a valley of green cornfields, in the summer, and a brighter green thick border of a creek," and features "a long, broad porch, with a sloping green-shingled roof, now overgrown with thick wisteria vines—and just now, in midsummer, overhung with lavender blossoms, hanging heavily, falling finally to the drying grass below." To this house in *Superior Women*, Adams brings characters from different episodes of the novel: Peg and her lover, Vera, and Peg's drug-damaged daughter; Megan Greene and her mother; two of Megan's lovers, Henry Stuyvesant and Jackson Clay; and her gay editor friend, Biff. When a workman at the house tells them he's worried about his sister who is to be released from prison, Peg and Megan take her in. Soon they are hosting other homeless women. The unlikelihood of all these people's coming together is mitigated by Adams's utopian vision for her characters and the simple kindness of their effort. In embracing their ideals in the hills of North Georgia, these characters reject the values of Ronald Reagan's America and strive to save their own souls.

Poet Carolyn Kizer wrote of *Superior Women*, "All our lives we have been presented with books that explore the initiation rites that introduce young men to maturity. Now we are hearing the women's side. The strain of nostalgia, even pathos, in Adams' book arises from her sensitive awareness of how grown up we have to be before we grow up."[25]

After finishing *Superior Women* in the summer of 1983, Adams had "grown up" enough to resolve some of the long-shunned issues of her childhood and youth. On August 14 she would reach the fateful age—fifty-seven—at which Agatha Adams had died. Approaching that date, Alice wrote in her notebook, "My mother died long before the long, scarring war between us was in any way resolved, and not quite by accident I chose the year in which I became as old as she was at the time of her death to return to the scene of our darkest, most corrosive hours."[26]

It was also probably not an accident that Alice chose to visit Chapel Hill as she was on the cusp of financial success. After a writers' conference at Georgetown University, she booked a roomette for her "ceremonial" train journey to North Carolina. Max Steele met her at the station, organized her visit, and gave her a yellow summer dress ("the most exciting color," she said) that he'd purchased for her in Egypt. Conveniently, Dotsie Adams was out of town. They drove by her parents' house, now sold. It was painted a new color, and huge trees blocked the view. Six months later, she confessed: "But that freshly painted, viewless house is non-existent in my mind; it is not where I live. I live in a huge, mad house with the loveliest view. With everything in bloom."[27]

While in Chapel Hill Alice saw her childhood friend Josephine MacMillan, now suffering from alcoholism, and wrote her afterward that she "had to get off the sauce." Adams's stories "Child's Play" and "Tide Pools" were probably inspired by that encounter. So much had changed in Chapel Hill that Max suggested touring the Old Cemetery at the edge of the campus. He said he knew more people there than he knew downtown. They remarked on the gravestones of the families she'd known and—of course, how could she have missed them?—the granite stones that marked Agatha's and Nic's graves. Adams replicated her walk in that cemetery with Max in another story based on that trip. In "The Visit" an actress named Grace tells her old friend, "Well, they won't get me in there. Not with them."

A year earlier, Alice had written Max: "I do not think we should live together you and I. (I am always afraid that you will think I think that.) I want you my friend for life and then let's do get a plot together."[28] Eventually, as he was recovering from a long period of depression, Max purchased a gravesite well apart from the Adamses: "It's like getting into Westminster Abbey," he said of the process. He planted pink and white azaleas and a dogwood tree near it. "Going there everyday digging and planting and fertilizing and watering and walking around gave me a real feeling of peace and proportion," he wrote Alice. Naming their future cemetery neighbors, he added, "Now it is beginning to be amusing."[29]

From back in San Francisco Alice wrote Max, "How I loved seeing you, how kind and generous you were," and added (tongue in cheek), "If only you would ever, just once, say something funny, you'd be perfect." So it seems that the laughter that Alice and Max had shared in the summer of 1958 continued to unite them. For his part, Max wrote, "Your visit was as exciting and as traumatic as I knew it would be." He followed up with several phone calls.[30]

Soon after this emotional return to Chapel Hill, Alice received a letter that drew her further into reminiscence about her Southern roots. Bryant Mangum, a young professor who was teaching a class about the *New Yorker* at Virginia Commonwealth University in Richmond, Virginia, wrote that he'd fallen in love with Adams's work and especially her woman narrators after reading "An Unscheduled Stop" and other stories in *To See You Again*. As it turned out, Mangum was a South Carolinian who'd attended the University of North Carolina before completing doctoral studies on F. Scott Fitzgerald back in South Carolina and becoming a professor at VCU. He closed his letter by inviting Alice to have a beer with him. She quickly wrote back that "funnily enough" she'd just passed through Virginia on her wonderful train trip to Chapel Hill. The correspondence that flourished between them gave her needed ballast as she approached her fateful birthday.

Adams was then writing her story called "Return Trip." On August 10, she told Steele that she was "stuck in the middle" of it; on August 16 she wrote Mangum that she "was quite lost in a new story—about going back to Hilton, which may be too soon to write."* At the heart of "Return Trip" is the narrator's changing relationship to her mother, who, like Agatha Adams, died years earlier: "I thought of my mother with increasing sympathy. This is another simplification, but that is what it came to. She did her best under very difficult, sometimes painful circumstances is one way of putting it."

And that is exactly what Alice was also trying to do as she entered her fifty-eighth year. Her birthday passed without an entry in her daybook. Her stepmother had sent her a battery-lit compact—"so useful for midnight make-up," she snarkily told Max. She and Bob were still having trouble getting along: he "is *very* cross with me a lot of the time," she wrote Judith. "Or maybe [its] my ghastly hypersensitivity—or both.

---

* Hilton was the fictional name Adams often used for Chapel Hill. The story became plural—"Return Trips"—when it was collected in the volume of that title.

I do think men age much less well than women . . . They get so mean & nutty."[31]

Alice did not stop working on *Superior Women* until the week she returned the manuscript to Wilson; her daybook shows she was still developing her characters—changing their names and histories, thinking about Megan Greene as an innocent comparable to Isabel Archer in *Portrait of a Lady* or Henry Stuyvesant as a man who likes women for their complexity.[32] In October she flew east with the finished pages in hand. Wilson took her to the Four Seasons, a posh power-lunch restaurant, to celebrate, but the occasion was ruined by the presence of Henry Kissinger at the next table: "Yuck—that horrible vibrator voice, really awful." From there Alice made a "strange, rushed" trip to Charlottesville to see her wonderful old, blind uncle Munny Boyd and his wife. It was "all too depressing and sad, in really awful shape, and not much can be done—I mean unless you moved in and took charge."[33]

Shortly after she returned from Charlottesville, Alice and Bob flew to Spain and Portugal. In Barcelona her handbag was snatched in exactly the way she told the story in "Barcelona." In Lisbon, she noticed that the Ritz Hotel had been built in 1959, the year she met Vasco Pereira, and she imagined meeting one of his later lovers who turned out to be "quite like herself." Climbing to the "wild ruins" of Castelo de São Jorge and seeing *his* city, she felt Pereira's presence everywhere, experiencing "some exceptional, acute alertness; as though layers of skin had peeled away, all her senses [were] opened wide," as she describes the feeling in "Sintra."

Alice probably knew that Pereira had returned to Lisbon to be minister of foreign affairs after finishing his term as ambassador to the United States in Washington. As minister, he had negotiated for the independence of East Timor in its struggle against Indonesia. Married to Malu after Margarida's death, he spent weekends painting in the country. To Alice, Vasco was emblematic of Portugal, and of course Bob knew about Vasco's inevitable presence in Alice's memory.

In her notebook Alice mentions "the force of never mentioning a name, which the other person repeats, repeats—an excoriating ritual." Rather than say the forbidden name, Bob joked, "Do you want to call anyone, like Prince Albert?"—referring to the prince of Monaco who made a second home on the "Coast of Kings" at Estoril.

The weather in Portugal proved to be as variable as Northern California's, prompting Alice to note that Vasco's "violently charming, quite unstable" personality must have been due to the weather in Portugal.[34] One afternoon Bob rented a car to drive them out to the coastal resorts of Cascais and Estoril, but a "black flood" of rain rerouted them to the town of Sintra, where Pereira then had a home. That detour marked a turning point in her relationship with Bob, though Alice wouldn't fully realize this until she wrote it into a story she'd call "Sintra."

When she got home from Portugal that fall, Alice added "screws up relationships" to a list of "50 Reasons Not to Write" she was keeping in her notebook.[35] She was thinking about personal freedom and planned to get a new driver's license so she'd be less dependent on Bob. Still working to control her high blood pressure and knowing that her mother had died of a heart problem, she cut back her alcohol consumption and began swimming two miles a week at the Rossi Pool a few blocks from her flat. "Swimming makes you look thinner, really stretches you out," she told friends, "[and] has immensely improved my disposition, it's so calming for tense types like me—also my blood pressure has shot down to normal, which is cheering."[36]

After mythic journeys to Chapel Hill and Portugal, both repositories of her past, Alice was making herself anew body and soul.

CHAPTER TWENTY-FIVE

Superior Women

— 1984–1986 —

Are some men put off by extremes of intelligence or even attractive-
ness in women—put off by superior women?

—Alice Adams, *Superior Women*

The sale of the right to publish *Superior Women* in paperback profoundly changed Alice's life. Knopf auctioned these rights in June
of 1984, three months in advance of the novel's hardcover publication
day. With the stunning offer of $635,000, publisher Leona Nevler at
Fawcett Crest won the prize. "I'M RICH!!!!!!!!!!!!!!!!!!!!" Alice wrote Max
Steele that very afternoon. "So funny, you sit down and write a silly
novel about what happened to you and your friends and people pay
crazy money for it—why aren't you here to help me celebrate?"[1]

Bob McNie was more than ready to celebrate. Signing himself
"Mr. Anonymous" but writing on his business letterhead, Bob sent
news of the sale to Herb Caen at the *Chronicle*. Caen duly reported
in his column that Adams "was in the big chips" with a "more than
healthy" six-figure sale. Good news kept rolling in as *Superior Women*
was chosen as a main selection by the Literary Guild and sold to
publishers in England and Scandinavia. Forecasting the big novels
for the fall season, the *Chicago Sun-Times* featured Adams alongside
Norman Mailer, Richard Yates, Joseph Heller, Stephen King, Belva
Plain, Helen MacInnes, Arthur Hailey, and her Radcliffe friend Alison Lurie.

Thus Victoria Wilson shepherded *Superior Women* into the marketplace as a breakthrough book, potentially a bestseller. Alice's reaction was
mixed. Thrilled and proud, she told Bryant Mangum she was waking

up early "with crazy fantasies about taking the Concorde to Paris." In the meantime, she was engulfed by the "endless and appalling chore" of judging dozens of applications for National Endowment for the Arts fellowships in fiction—the first of many such duties she accepted as a midlist author. "My idea of heaven at the moment is some free time in which to start a new story."[2]

Following their publication of "My First and Only House," *Geo* magazine offered to pay Alice's expenses to write a travel piece and she immediately thought of a late spring return to Portugal, where she'd been with Bob the previous autumn and where, she'd recently learned, Vasco Pereira was dying of a brain tumor. She began a story about him in her notebook before she and Bob arrived, remembering their visit to Sintra the previous fall and trying to imagine Vasco elderly, dying: "Impossible to picture thinned hair, eyes dulled, perhaps afraid—once so brilliant & bold, if always melancholy—my elegant one—incontinent?"[3] She wondered if she should contact him while she was there. Ultimately she did not, but Vasco's presence in her mind shaped the trip.

Beginning in Lisbon, Bob and Alice stopped in medieval Estremoz, then drove south to the Algarve coast, and finally flew to Madeira for a stay at the Reid's Palace hotel. The commissioned piece that paid for the trip, "The Wild Coasts of Portugal," gave Adams trouble—"In stories I know what to leave out (I think) but in this I don't know where I am."[4] The result was as much travel essay as journalism.* "The strands of impulse, mingled desire and indecision, that lead one to travel at last to a particular place have struck me as odd," she began before confessing, albeit obliquely, to her own impulse: "Many years back a poet friend of mine had a disastrous romantic collision with a Portuguese diplomat. In the wake of that I heard a lot about Portugal." Adams herself was that poet, and the freshness and emotion the country still held for her makes bittersweet her descriptions of traveling with her "best friend, R . . . an exceptional driver."

---

* Never discarding good material, Adams turned her leftover notes into "Crossing Madeira: Enchanting Vistas of the Wild North Coast: Notes on a Drive from Funchal to Porto Moniz." (*San Francisco Examiner*, December 17, 1989, T8–T9.)

Finding half-built condos blighting the Algarve coast, Adams wonders, "Which would be worse, the eventual decay and rot of all those
buildings and their return at last to burial in the soil or their eventual
completion and occupation by vacation-hungry humans . . ." Then,
just as she so often does in her fiction, Adams gazes beyond the petty
human scene with a historical and geographical perspective: "Long green
fingers of land spread out into the sea . . . You imagine the conquering
Moorish sailors who came in from the sea and scaled those cliffs some
1,000 years ago—conquerors who saw something commensurate with
their capacity for wonder."[5]

Those last seven words, borrowed from *The Great Gatsby*, indicate
the romantic drama in Alice's mind as she immersed herself in Vasco
Pereira's country. She approached that theme directly in her short story
"Sintra," which drew as much on her recent trips to Portugal as upon
the story of her affair with Pereira. In that story a writer named Arden,
who is traveling with her current partner, Gregor, "experiences a sudden
rush of happiness, as clear and pure as the sunshine that warms the small
flowers near her feet," as she stands in a garden above the city of Lisbon.
Her joy emerges during a "demented instant" in which she thinks of
telling her former lover (here called Luiz) how much she likes his city,
a "memory lapse," because she has forgotten that he's dying. Her speculations wander as she fills in the background of an affair in which she
once felt "the wildest reaches of joy, but never the daily, sunny warmth
of happiness." During the trip, Arden quarrels with Gregor, who feels
excluded as Arden thinks about Luiz. Gregor accuses Arden of using
him as a travel companion while cutting him off emotionally. While in
Portugal Arden shields herself from her usual "worrying preoccupation"
with Gregor and his "lens-like observations [that] make her nervous;
they make her feel unattractive, and unloved." Back home, suspecting
that he sees other women—"looking for her replacement"—she is content to let him do so.

Vasco Pereira was alive while Alice was in Portugal. On July 4, the
sixty-two-year-old retired diplomat and amateur painter needed a wheel-
chair to attend an exhibition of his art entitled *Sunday Paintings* at a
museum in Lisbon. He died on August 20. A week later Judith Adams
mailed Alice a two-inch newspaper clipping headlined "Deaths Elsewhere." The clipping appears almost verbatim in "Sintra," including the
detail that Pereira "was the first Portuguese ambassador to voice strong,

public support for the armed forces coup in April 1974 that ended half a century of right-wing dictatorship."[6]

To complete "Sintra," Adams places Arden alone in a Washington, DC, restaurant to contemplate her former lover's death. The news that Pereira took an antifascist stance in 1974 becomes a grace note in Adams's story. Maybe, Arden thinks, the man was genuine. Maybe the man she'd hated for years for being a fascist and for his deception of her was (as he claimed) an antifascist, and maybe—by extension—he had truly loved her.

And so, in this instance, as we read of Arden transfixed by a "sudden nameless pain. Nameless, but linked to loss: loss of Luiz, even, imminently, of Gregor. Perhaps of love itself," we can see just how Adams made fiction out of her life, how events were factual and yet transformed to serve her emotional needs and the requirements of the short-story form. "Odd: working on the story is for me a way of not thinking about him. I guess we call that esthetic distance," she told Judith Adams.[7]

When Vasco Pereira's children sorted his papers they found a fat folder of carbon copies of works by Alice Adams—stories and chapters of a novel about women named Arden or Avery, along with two poems Alice addressed to Vasco after their final parting. Saved too were snapshots, notes, and letters that Alice sent Vasco during the months of their affair, folded and packed tightly in a white envelope labeled with her name in his handwriting.[8]

Bob threw a party at his new studio to celebrate the publication of *Superior Women* in September. Balloons in pink and teal matched the color blocks on the novel's modernist graphic cover. Old and new friends who came to celebrate included Anne Lamott; Jack Leggett, the former Harper & Row editor who once turned down *Careless Love* and director of the Iowa Writers' Workshop, now married to Edwina Evers; and seventy-four-year-old artist Nell Sinton, now divorced and enjoying her life as a traveling artist and teacher. Peter Linenthal, wearing a full dark beard, was there too.

Alice headed east for promotional events and parties in Boston and New York that were now de rigueur for authors. In Boston, she met her jazz-musician fan-turned-friend Richard Carr. The young man, still in his twenties, wondered how much his older pen pal would be able to walk! As it turned out they covered at least five miles during an afternoon in the Public Garden and ducked into a coffee shop on Newbury Street. "She gave every panhandler five dollars—her book was doing well and she was feeling the liberation of being able to do that."

"The trouble with a book coming out," she wrote Carr afterward, is "you are impaled on it . . . it's hard to get on with anything else. I'm still going around doing readings, all that stuff. And I'm not a performer, for Christ's sake, just a writer."[9] As this whirlwind commenced, Alice noted, "V[asco] dead—a cluster of death, & money—freedom—but not—still bound."[10]

This "cluster" of death included her admired older friend Lavina Calvin, with whom she and Bob had become close in Zihuatanejo. After the death of Henry Calvin, eighty-three-year-old Lavina had begun dating a "much younger man, blond, alcoholic, bisexual," also named Henry, whom Alice intensely disliked. They bickered when Alice and Bob refused invitations to get-togethers that included that man. "I understand about being lonely, the necessity for having a man around," Alice told Lavina. "However if something should happen to Bob, and I became involved with someone (as I surely would, as soon as possible, I am like you in this) if you didn't like him, rather disapproved— I would be very sorry but I would not . . . expect to see you in his company." Lavina died in July when her pancreatic cancer returned after a fifteen-year remission. "It seemed (to me) a willed death," Adams wrote. "(I may have only felt that because I so loved her and wanted her to live forever.) But I think she was tired of being old and alone, although she was beautiful still and lived in a beautiful house." Lavina Calvin left the entire contents of her house to Alice and Bob.[11]

Death took another person dear to Alice on September 10. Trummy Young, then seventy-two, suffered a cerebral hemorrhage in San Jose, while visiting his daughter on his way back to Hawaii after playing Gibson's Jazz Party in Denver. Gary Giddins, who met and heard Young there, recalled it was "a relief to hear him playing so strongly after he'd virtually disappeared from jazz, and a tonic to discover that he was the kind of man his music led you to believe he might be. Very relaxed, comfortable in his own skin, quiet spoken, easy to be around. [His wife,] Sally, as tiny as he was tall, was unbelievably sweet. The first time he brought his daughter Arlene to Gibson's Party, the joke among musicians was: no wonder he's hiding away in Hawaii, to keep her under wraps. She had his color and her mother's Hawaiian features, a total knockout."*

Alice Adams hadn't seen Young for many years, but she felt the loss deeply. She had resisted Victoria Wilson's suggestion to cut the Jackson Clay character, who was inspired by Trummy, from *Superior Women's* utopian epilogue. In a next-to-final draft of the novel, Megan and Jackson enjoy occasional secret afternoons at a hotel in Atlanta where they "exhaust each other's bodies and imaginations." Wilson objected that Jackson's presence in Georgia was not believable; Adams kept Jackson in Georgia but rewrote the secret afternoons as a "recurring fantasy" of Megan's. Young's death in the very week of the novel's publication had eerily turned her happy memory into a eulogy. "Did I tell you my black lover the trombonist also died," she wrote Judith Adams as her novel found its place on the bestseller list. "It's too much."[12]

Superior Women got predictably mixed reviews during this era when books about women's independence and sexuality often came in for bashings by moralizers and highbrow critics, but it sold well. It rose to twelfth place on the *New York Times* bestseller list in October and hovered there for the rest of the year.

Novels about women friends during their schooldays and after, Barbara Quart writes in *Ms.*, are a version of *The Naked and the Dead*—a framework for stories of the battleground women must traverse before finding out "what life after all is going to let [them] have." Quart felt Adams had not filled out her framework enough to make it deeply engaging because of her preference for quick, revealing sketches and present-tense narrative that suited short stories and slim novels. Nonetheless she achieved something *Ms.* approved: the diminution of East Coast Lavinia, "the thinnest and blondest of elite dream girls," and the elevation of sturdy, sensual Megan Greene from working-class Palo Alto is "a redefinition over time of what, socially and morally, constitutes a 'superior woman.'"[13]

---

* Arlene Young told Giddins a story from her father's days with Louis Armstrong and His All-Stars: "Trummy had taken her on the road when she was a little girl, and Lucille Armstrong made an unexpected visit to a city where they were working. Arlene was playing in the hotel corridor when Lucille arrived. Arlene told Mrs. Armstrong that Pops was with one of his secretaries: 'Pops sure has a lot of secretaries,' Arlene added. Well, Pops had a fit and told Trummy no more kids on the road."

The novel's title set some people on edge. A few couldn't resist an impulse to call a novel about superior women *inferior*. The title is uttered first by Megan, as a question: "Are some men put off by extremes of intelligence or even attractiveness in women—put off by superior women? This is a new thought, highly puzzling, unwelcome, and difficult to digest. And it is true; she is quite sure of that." Adam Marr, the character Adams based on Norman Mailer, answers that question in a hostile confession later in the novel: "You superior women have a real problem for yourselves, don't you. Just any old guy won't do. You wouldn't like him, and even if you did your strength would scare him, even make him mad. You know, that's actually one reason I had to dump Janet, though I can't say I knew it at the time. I began to have some black suspicion that she was stronger than I was."*

Michiko Kakutani at the *New York Times* thought Adams had "chosen to exercise neither her ability to delineate a character's inner life nor her ability to conjure a precise social world." Jonathan Yardley in the *Washington Post* deemed it "an inert lump of a book" in his opening sentence and then kept his insults rolling for many paragraphs. Such words probably stung but did not shock Alice. Trent Duffy, an editor who admired Adams's short stories, recalled that Billy Abrahams asked him what he thought of *Superior Women*. Duffy answered cautiously that he found it slick and commercial compared to her short stories. And Billy replied, "That was the point!" He meant, Duffy assumed, that Alice "deliberately wrote something that might be less literary and more sell-able."

Lois Gould discerned more: ". . . the author with a fine, wry logic will make us see that disappointment, bitterness, waste, all come with this territory. Is it the terrible cost of being superior—or wanting to be? But she is at pains to tell us these women don't feel strong, don't want to scare away their men, their happiness: it just works out that way." Finally, Gould wrote, Adams's book is a Jamesian study of "the severity of America's class system and the futility of outsiders' dreams." Even in 1984, after a decade of second-wave feminism (of which many men had surely tired), "rich, poor, fat, thin—even, perhaps especially, superior—women are outsiders."[14]

---

* The conversation quoted above from *Superior Women* so matches Norman Mailer's attitude about his first wife and Alice's friend, Beatrice Silverman, that one suspects Alice heard the line from him. Mailer's letters to Silverman, recently placed at the Harry Ransom Center, have a similar tone.

Poet Carolyn Kizer also saw the novel's larger significance. Dismissing the idea that *Superior Women* is a roman à clef comparable to Mary McCarthy's *The Group*, she writes: "Megan is the 'New Woman' that girls of my generation barely dared to dream of becoming." For Kizer the other lead women function as "*anima* figures . . . aspects of women [we] were afraid of being. . . ." American women, she concludes, "have such amorphous identities when we are young! We barely know who we are . . . life—as Adams so bravely and wittily demonstrates in this novel—cruelly teaches us to become ourselves."[15]

John Updike also credited the novel's strengths in a long review for the *New Yorker*. He noticed that "superficially antithetical" Megan and Lavinia, like the two girls in "Roses, Rhododendron," become, "somehow, one." That's a true biographical insight. Self-centered, manipulative Lavinia and open-minded, sexy Megan both represent aspects of Alice Adams, and the author has designed her plot to allow Megan and her values to triumph over Lavinia's.[16]

But Updike is troubled by Adams's critique of empty WASP values. He argues that Adams denies Lavinia "a fair shake" by making her snobbish, feral, narcissistic, qualities that symbolize "the sterility of the haves." He notices that "the Wasps are the heavies, with their ghastly clubbiness and haughty prejudices . . . whereas the blacks are beautiful people: Jackson Clay a great musician, if a little stoned in his later, Hawaiian phase, and Cornelia so loyal and gentle that just a perfunctory sprinkling of money turns her from a cook into a schoolteacher, and Vera, who is Mexican and only *looks* black, . . . the Jews, too, are beyond reproach." And so on. Updike has put his finger on some of the novel's underpinnings and he doesn't like them one bit.

Tellingly, in his memoir "On Not Being a Dove," Updike acknowledges that he disliked the sixties because the peace movement interfered with his comfortable success: "I had left heavily trafficked literary turfs to others and stayed in my corner of New England to give its domestic news. Now along came this movement wanting to gouge us all out of our corners, to force us into the open and make us stare at our bloody hands and confront the rapacious motives underneath the tricolor slogans and question our favored-nation status under God." Updike cites *Superior Women* as one example of how women writers of his generation recall the sixties as "a wonderful time" and he sees why: "Fists uplifted, women enter history. The clitoral at last rebels against the phallic. . . . I must have felt challenged."[17]

Exactly. Social comedy and concern with women's lives in Adams's novel are undergirded by awareness of WASP privilege and government corruption. One of Lavinia's lovers, a rich, crippled man, has deep connections to the Nixon administration; he brags, "'It's exciting how few people we've managed to get it down to, just a very few, in total control. There's not much spreading around these days, baby doll, in terms of real power,' and he laughs, excitingly." When Nixon was elected, Megan and her almost-husband put off their plans to marry because "they are both so depressed by Nixon that they are stunned into a sort of immobility." Updike finds that "one of the strangest moments in romantic fiction," because, having avoided political commitment during the Vietnam era, he simply does not know how the hopes and disappointments of those years affected others.*

Adams did know. And she also grasps the notion of white privilege, showing just how various and ubiquitous it can be through her ideal alter ego Megan, who distances herself from her family in order to attend the WASP citadel of Radcliffe. Her experience there and in New York City teaches her that the world is bigger than Radcliffe. In the end she brings her mother back into her life, and joins with recovering WASPs like Henry Stuyvesant and Peg Sinclair to try to live in a new social contract at their Georgia farmhouse. The ending of the novel, Adams told Lois Gould, "is almost too unreal. It is a longed-for condition."

In *Superior Women*'s forty-year time span reviewer Roberta Smoodin saw the influence of Henry James and Marcel Proust: "[Adams is,] thematically, the most Proustian writer working today. I can think of no one so concerned with the effect of time on character, of duration on relationships, of subtle shadings of personality because of events. Proust's main concern in his fiction was the combination of time and personality that revolutionized modern fiction; he used memory as his vehicle for examining these phenomena. Adams, since her earliest work, has played with time, but in the reverse way—she is much more interested in the future than in the past (her own basic optimism as opposed to Proust's hypochondriacal pessimism?) and uses parenthetical leaps

---

* Updike's calling *Superior Women* a romantic novel sounds patronizing, but, as his biographer Adam Begley asserts, Updike "needed to dress up garden-variety infidelity as the inescapable consequence of some grand passion . . . he was in love with love." Perhaps Updike disliked Adams's jaundiced take on romance in her novel. (Adam Begley, *Updike* [New York: Harper, 2014], 258.)

of time to clue us in to what the future holds." For Smoodin, reading the novel was "thrilling . . . akin to hearing really wonderful gossip or having a dream with obviously good portents."[18]

While some wondered if this book was a sellout, Alice learned to bask in invitations to give readings, attend conferences, and judge contests—and travel on someone else's buck. She absorbed it all, reporting in letters to friends on the surprising beauty of Cincinnati or the ostentatious wealth of Rodeo Drive ("all those *clothes*—makes you want to try sackcloth and sainthood"). While judging the NEA fiction awards she met writers she admired, such as Walker Percy and Tim O'Brien ("a really dear kid"). At the Toronto International Festival of Authors, she and Alison Lurie swam laps together and became closer friends while enjoying "terrific" hospitality to writers in Canada, "a country that isn't so nuke-impoverished . . . not to mention all free doctors, and no handguns."

Success also gave Alice energy to become more active politically. The progressive views she embraced in her youth remained strong. In 1985, she signed the Pledge of Resistance sponsored by the Emergency Response Network (ERN). During the early months of 1985, the ERN expected an increase in US military activity in Central America, where the CIA was already involved in supporting the government of El Salvador and Contra guerrilla troops opposed to the Sandinista government in Nicaragua. President Reagan and Secretary of Defense Alexander Haig pushed to increase military aid to the Contras, but Congress was reluctant. Meanwhile ERN staged actions to publicize the violence already taking place in Central America. Signers committed to making a "strong non-violent response" immediately after any incursion by the US military into the ongoing wars in Nicaragua and El Salvador. Members of the group took a six-hour nonviolence training course so they'd be prepared to take direct action in the street.[19]

Alice became acquainted with Marie Pastrick and Ken Butigan, who coordinated ERN activities in San Francisco, and they recruited her, along with Jessica Mitford and Valerie Miner, to organize the Writers' Protest at the Phillip Burton Federal Building in San Francisco. She held a planning meeting at her apartment and oversaw the printing of orange postcard invitations that went out to writers she knew. She contacted magistrate judges and ascertained that the usual penalty for the kind of civil disobedience the writers planned was five days in jail or some hours of community service.

Butigan and Pastrick hoped that involving writers would raise the profile of the actions they'd been holding. Both were awaiting trial for participating in a "blood pouring" at the federal building a month earlier: they'd splashed their own blood out of baby bottles onto photographs of people killed by Contras. Later in May, when the Reagan administration imposed a trade embargo on Nicaragua, three thousand people demonstrated at the federal building and six hundred were arrested.

At the Writers' Protest on May 30, participants identified themselves and spoke briefly about the reasons for their protest; they passed out lists naming the participants, including Peter Stansky, Deirdre English, Blair Fuller, and Carolyn Kizer, who'd just won the Pulitzer Prize for Poetry. "They wanted to get arrested," Butigan recalled, "but the police were too smart for us; I think when they realized there were people of some celebrity, they wouldn't touch it."

The writers were likewise too polite to cause much disturbance. After they sat in a circle in the lobby for a while, Butigan urged them into "a situation where [they] would be in the way—that really helps." Mitford and three others stood in front of the IRS's door; they told those who wanted to pass through that they were "trying to block the doorway" and then stepped aside! The *Chronicle* reported the event with the headline "Jessica Mitford's Very Civil Disobedience: Police Decline to Arrest Writers."[20]

Having failed to get arrested herself—according to the *Chronicle*, most of the writers remained "outside the glass doors looking in and smiling"—Adams developed strong curiosity about the prison experience of Pastrick, who was sentenced to forty-five days in a federal women's prison near Pleasanton, California, for her part in the blood-pouring. Pastrick impressed Alice with her Christian commitment to justice; for Pastrick, pouring her own blood had been a rite of passage, an irrevocable commitment to world peace. Alice sent her books in prison and Pastrick promised to tell her stories from "inside": "Poignant is too small a term to apply to some of these women's lives. There's terrific material in here, trust me."[21]

Alice took detailed notes when she met with Pastrick and hoped to write an article for *Mother Jones* or another magazine.[22] Pastrick described meeting Rita Lavelle, a "bright, sharp" Republican who said she'd been screwed by EPA administrator Anne Gorsuch Burford (mother of Supreme Court justice Neil Gorsuch) in the so-called Garbagegate scandal over misuse of Superfund money, and "psycho" Sara Jane Moore, convicted of shooting President Gerald Ford. A year later the Iran-Contra scandal revealed that the ERN had been correct about the American military's plans for Central America. Ken Butigan, now professor of Peace, Justice and Conflict Studies at DePaul University, believes that his group's efforts to draw public attention to the situation dissuaded the Reagan administration from taking more direct military action.

Adams used the material she acquired from Pastrick in her short story "Favors." She turns Pastrick, then in her thirties, into Maria Tresca, an elderly activist just released from prison who comes to rest at her mountain home. Her visit invades the honeymoon privacy of her son's friend. The irritation he and his new wife feel seems to be the main subject of the story. But then, after an awkward few days and a frightening thunderstorm, Maria explains:

> "The thing about prison . . . is that they do everything to wreck your mind. 'Mind-fuck,' some of the younger women called it." A faint, tight smile. "But they do. Rushing you all the time. Starting you in to do something, and then right away it's over. Even eating, even that horrible food I never got to finish. And they mix up everyone's mail so you think it must be on purpose. And the noise. Radios. And people smoking."

"Favors" combines Pastrick's experience with Adams's thoughts about changes in social relations due to sexual fluidity—in this case, her son's relationship with a good friend who had once been his lover but was now married to a woman.[23] In the story Phoebe (the new wife) wonders at "the strength of the two men's affection for each other; so rare, in her experience, such open fondness between men. She has even briefly wondered if they could have been lovers, ever, and concluded that they were not." In resolving the question, "Favors" chooses simplicity. Phoebe forms a bond with Maria (her husband's friend's mother) and the question of old sexual histories is muted as they celebrate Maria's release from prison.

"Favors" also raises the activists' classic debate over whether it is "better to go to jail, or to stay out and do whatever your work is and send money to your cause." After Marie Pastrick's experiences, it became clearer to Alice that she should act upon her convictions on the outside. She also continued to weave her political views into the fabric of her stories and novels.

Late in 1985, Alice had plastic surgery on her eyelids. "Already I look *much* younger (I think)," she told Lurie a few days afterward. "Healing seems to be something I do well—compensation for deplorable skin, I guess."[24] When she'd fully recovered, Bob gave a little party, as if unveiling Alice's new face. "She was the first person I knew who had any form of cosmetic surgery, so I was surprised and curious," *Mother Jones* editor Deirdre English said. "I thought, good for you for having it done. And for being really open about it."

Also that fall Bob and Alice's landlady at 3904 Clay had her property reappraised and learned that the rent was severely under market. (Had she read about Alice's new fortune in Herb Caen's column?) She raised the rent to $725 a month—and warned that she would keep increasing it until it caught up to the market rate. After a tax advisor showed them the deductions they were missing out on, they began looking for a house in bad shape that Bob could fix up. Nothing suited until Alice's friend Sydney Goldstein, founder of the City Arts & Lectures series, and her husband, attorney Charles Breyer, mentioned that they needed more space for their growing family. Even though the Goldstein-Breyers's house was already in good shape, Alice and Bob bought the moderate (thirteen-hundred-square-foot) brown-shingled Italianate Victorian on the south edge of Alta Plaza. Alice provided most of the cash for a down payment, and Bob planned to make it a showplace for his work. Ownership would be in both their names, and thus their "long-term illicit" and recently troubled affair moved toward commitment.

They celebrated with their annual respite at the Catalina Beach Resort in Zihuatanejo. From the balcony of the small, jerry-built, and familiar hotel Alice watched "slow, laced circular surges of foam in the black satin sea. Above, like thrown diamonds, [were] stars, a brilliant cascade—."[25]

Ripe with hopes that this new house would soothe and center their lives, Alice looked toward a future as bright and unknowable as that cascade of stars.

CHAPTER TWENTY-SIX

Fame and Fortune

— 1986–1987 —

*What does it mean to love an animal, a pet, in my case a cat, in
the fierce, entire, and unambivalent way that some of us do? . . .
Does the cat (did the cat) represent some person, a parent, or a
child? some part of one's self? I don't think so—"*

—Alice Adams, "The Islands,"
After You've Gone

Alice and Bob accomplished the twelve-block move early in February
1986. Moving was traumatic. Unlike many people, Alice felt that
disruption pushed her to write: "Writing so many stories to regain balance, really," she noted, feeling the loss of the apartment "containing
so much (esp. V.)," where she'd lived longest, twenty-six years.[1] She
mourned the years of Peter's boyhood and her young womanhood, and
her love affair with Vasco Pereira conducted in secrecy there.[2] Later,
though, she told an interviewer that the new house instantly felt right:
"I like it so much I can hardly believe it. I never want to move from
this house." Her three cats, Ferg, Black, and Brown, also liked the new
house: "They have stairs. They're like elderly people who've been advised
to get more exercise," Alice said. "They have a more interesting life here.
There are more birds to watch, more patches of sunshine."[3]

The house at 2661 Clay Street faced north toward the terraced slope
of Alta Plaza—a sight reminiscent of a Mayan temple. From the back of
the house French doors opened to a deck that Bob and Alice filled with
potted plants; below that was a lovely, small formal garden designed
by Thomas Church with boxwood hedges and a large mirror inset in

the foliage against the back fence. They planted a magnolia tree in one corner: it flowered profusely and reminded Alice of the South.

Bob's studio on Bluxome was "cold enough to hang meat with no spoilage" that winter, so Bob spent most days at home altering the house, which needed few improvements. The narrow Victorian, one of a row of six in a development by the Real Estate Associates in the 1870s, had the false front and small connected rooms with high ceilings typical of that style.[4] Bob glued large mirrors to the parlor walls above couches that faced each other. "You saw yourself in the mirrors behind the couch," Judith Rascoe remembered, "but you learned to avert your eyes and ignore them and it did produce that infinite mirror thing."

When Bob finished his transformation, the downstairs rooms had dark hardwood floors. The foyer was painted chocolate brown and featured one English riding boot gleaming with oxblood polish by the marble hearth; a brass chandelier adorned with rams' horns didn't throw much light on the scene, but it added to a faux–*Wuthering Heights* aura. He painted the dining room walls a glossy mahogany red and filled every available space with lovely wood furniture and art, including large paintings by Theophilus Brown and Peter Linenthal. The overall effect, Sydney Goldstein thought, resembled a "dark, glossy opera set."

The pièce de résistance of Bob's redecoration of the house was a mostly black downstairs powder room: black lacquered walls, black tile, black toilet, black curtains. Aluminum buckets converted to light fixtures and a shiny stainless-steel sink bowl finished the look. Some called the effect astonishing and elegant; others sensed something odd and frightening about it.

The second floor was a realm of light compared to the downstairs. In the master bedroom pale walls and a white tile floor, quilts from Alice's family, and a bed facing a bay window overlooking the garden and city created "a marvelous place to sleep," recalled Trent Duffy, who once cat-sat for Alice. Bob added two revolving storage units for his own large wardrobe. Overnight guests were accommodated in a smaller bedroom or a lower-level garden suite.

Alice's study stretched across the front of the house on the second floor. From here, "far too often," Alice watched the walkers and runners and dogs in Alta Plaza. On her long, wide desk—a door on two filing cabinets—she kept a beautiful hand-colored picture of Agatha as a girl, photographs of friends, and a row of her own books to remind her, she said, "when faith fails, that this is indeed what I do, have done, will presumably do again." She wrote on a "big, fancy typewriter" next to the desk. A framed quilt made by her grandmother Boyd that had lain across Alice's bed when she was a child, a small carved desk inherited from Lavina Calvin "still crammed with mementoes from her life," and a wall of bookshelves completed the room. "There is remarkable harmony between the patterns of book jackets and spines, and the pattern of the quilt," Alice noticed.[5]

In this study—she called it "America's Room, and Mine" in honor of the Guatemalan nanny who'd lived there with the Goldstein-Breyers—Adams would work through her most prolific writing years, producing six novels, two story collections, and a travel memoir about Mexico.

These triumphant years were not without difficulty and sorrow. As Alice's renown and income were rising, Bob McNie struggled to maintain his mental and financial equilibrium. For years Alice had known that Bob drank too much. She also understood that her success might disturb him—that, after all, is a theme that preoccupies Megan in *Superior Women*. Alice probably hoped that buying a house with Bob (providing much of the money for the house in exchange for his physical management of it) would satisfy his ego and balance the scales.

Bob touted Alice's success in public, but privately his discontent simmered and sometimes erupted. On February 18, 1986, among pages of notes about dreams and outlines for stories, she wrote: "The worst fight: violent threats—scared but planning: Chuck, AW—move to condo."

Chuck refers to Chuck Breyer, the attorney from whom they had purchased their house and someone in whom Alice confided. AW is Allen Wheelis, the psychiatrist Alice had been seeing once a month in recent years. Her clinical relationship with Wheelis was complicated by the fact the doctor was also a published writer whose books reveal his personal history and predilections. Author Daphne Merkin praises him for "the seeming ease with which he divulges his own unrequited needs, implacable fears and unacceptable impulses in the name of illuminating his patients' and readers' neurotic quandaries."[6] Wheelis, a man raised in Texas who struggled to overcome cruel treatment by his father, was considered a maverick among analysts because of his willingness to try unorthodox methods of treatment. He "operated more in an authentic

psychoanalytic spirit than did the psychoanalytic establishment; and
the establishment, sadly, never realized it," according to his friend and
fellow analyst Owen Renik. Known for his existential despair, Wheelis
was, nonetheless, an inspirational force who could "inspire hope in a
hopeless patient or courage in a fearful one," Renik said.*[7]

Alice's connection to Wheelis was intense, at least on her side. Her
notebooks show that she consulted Wheelis for several years, kept notes
on dreams to tell him about (some of which involved him), owned
and read his books, and pondered his advice. She noted that she had
to resist a "wish to instruct him literarily" and asked herself if that
desire was generous or controlling or perhaps a "means of extending"
their connection;[8] later she noted, "I was *very* attracted to him, is the
truth. I guess I wanted him for my dad—a totally unavailable person."[9]
(When Til Stewart, who was also seeing Wheelis at this time, confided
to Alice that she found it difficult to quit Wheelis, Alice felt jealous of
Til.)[10] Sessions with Wheelis and readings from the Al-Anon program
for codependents gave Alice courage to change her relationship with
Bob McNie. She probably also attended Al-Anon meetings, as this note
from March 1986 suggests: "Panic—rage at R. But—friendly dream,
helpful Bob re: Peter. Al-Anon: fear—rage—control."[11]

Alice's reinvolvement with an analyst influenced her to produce
her series of stories about two psychiatrists, Lila Lewinsohn and Julian
Brownfield. These two have been lovers since medical school and through
several problematic marriages but never fully available to each other.
Now late middle aged, they continue to see and need each other even
as they avoid further commitment. Tall, intelligent Lila is "a seriously
disturbed walking wounded person who is good at her work—a depressive," and her lover, based on Wheelis, is "courtly, graceful, depressed."[12]

Peter Linenthal was also on the threshold of a new life. Even after Peter
told his mother about his relationship with Phillip Galgiani, he brought
the occasional girl to meet her. In 1974, Alice had written Lucie Jessner,

---

* Wheelis inscribed one of his books to Alice: "We live in a desert, / We are choking on
bread. / Where may we find the wind of the spirit? / Where seek for that exultation, /
that divine intoxication of which we have so slight a memory?" In another inscription,
he quoted Czesław Miłosz's Nobel Lecture: ". . . leaving behind books as if they were
dry snake skins, in a constant escape forward from what has been done in the past . . ."

"Peter has a NEW GIRLFRIEND who in an odd way reminds me of myself; some jarring combination of shy and bold."[13]

In the spring of 1979 when Adams was writing her story "Snow," about a father's dawning acceptance of his daughter's lesbian orientation, Peter was involved with a man named Ethan whom he brought to meet his mother and Bob. When Alice "at last" told Peter that she and Bob thought Ethan was really nice, she reported to Diane Johnson, "P. tells me that he thinks being gay is 'unnatural,' he is terribly interested in a beautiful girl named Barbara, who is blonde and shy. Honestly—why do we even listen to our children when they say alarming things?"[14]

By the 1980s though, during a time when gay men were coming to San Francisco's Castro District from all over the country, Peter was certain that he would live his life as an openly gay man. The election of Harvey Milk to the board of supervisors in 1977 culminated a decade of gay rights activism and led to the passage of the nation's first ordinance outlawing discrimination based on sexual orientation. Richard Rodriguez writes of the first Gay Freedom Day parade that he saw: "There were marching bands. There were floats . . . from the foot of Market Street they marched, east to west, following the mythic American path toward optimism."[15]

Peter patronized the gay bathhouses that flourished then. "Those were not just for bathing," he explained. "They were like a health club except there were private rooms you could go into." In the bathhouses he encountered former teachers as well as gay runaways; he met a guy named Louise "who looked like a woman, or rather like Fred Flintstone dressed like a woman." He appreciated that he'd never had to leave his home city to express his sexuality: "My parents were part of San Francisco, they were part of this new world." When Supervisor Milk and Mayor George Moscone were assassinated, Alice mourned the death of Milk as "the greatest loss" because he was "a true original." She attended his public funeral and found it "most affecting."[16]

But by 1984, the AIDS epidemic had become widely evident in San Francisco. "You saw a lot of people in the Castro District walking around with big sores. It was awful," Peter recalled. His former partner Ethan, who had married a woman and fathered a child, was diagnosed with the disease. Much of the gay community and some of the city's straight population came together to care for those who were dying. Alice helped Project Open Hand prepare and deliver meals to homebound AIDS patients. People talked about losing two-thirds of their friends within a few years. When a Catholic church in the Castro honored members of its AIDS support group, gay, straight, male, female, young, and old people stood shyly before the congregation: "AIDS was a disease of the entire city," Rodriguez writes. "Its victims were often black, Hispanic, straight. Neither were Charity and Mercy only white, only male, only gay."[17]

In the midst of this plague, Peter lost only a few people that he knew well. He felt "odd, lucky, and guilty." He also knew that he wanted a more settled life. In January 1983, he placed a classified ad in the *Bay Guardian*:

GM, 32, artist, teacher, liberal, tall, swimmer, intellectual. Would like to meet a man about my age also involved in work he finds rewarding, who considers monogamy a possibility, likes to have a good time, and not particularly into gay scene. Tell me about yourself.

A "big pile" of replies arrived in his mailbox at the weekly paper. "I divided them up into 'no way,' 'hard to tell,' and 'interesting,'" Peter said. He met seven or eight men for coffee or at his house but soon realized that "if they come to your house they know a whole lot more about you than you know about them. What if they are creepy or you never want to see them again?"

One reply stood out. "I am an architect who enjoys his work . . . and has hopes of greater accomplishments in his field," Philip Anasovich wrote. "I suppose the person who said 'The art of living is to live with art' (Andre Malraux?) expresses my feelings." Anasovich said he enjoyed painting and photographing, singing and cooking, as well as opera, ballet, symphony, theater, cinema, reading, dining out, and travel. "If we were to meet on the street you would find a tall (6'1") and slender man of 33 years, with brown hair and beard (very small) and green/brown eyes."

He continued, "There is much I do not understand about gay life and about myself. I'm not into the 'gay scene' as you call it. I must be me." He added that he thought Peter's ad was brave and requested that Peter write him a letter about himself. "You can tell so much about a person from the way they write a letter," he said later.

Peter and Philip exchanged several letters, using their home addresses, and Peter drove by Philip's apartment on Bay Street. Then Peter broke his rule and invited Philip to his place on Potrero Hill. "So," Peter remembered, "we did meet here the very first time. Phil was on his way to a voice lesson, I showed him art I was working on, I could tell he was a genuinely interested and intelligent person and I'd like to see him again."

The search was over.

Philip Anasovich grew up in a small town in Connecticut. His mother, Violette Micheline Graux Mayo, born in Compiègne, France, just after the First World War, married William Anasovich, an American soldier of Russian descent, shortly after the Second World War. He was a chemist assigned to investigate chemical weapons in Germany; she, a secretary for Francolor (a Swiss dye company), served as his translator. He brought Violette home to Seymour, Connecticut, a small town where he had many cousins among the numerous other Belarusian families; she later earned a master's degree in French literature at Wesleyan University. After Phil finished high school, he attended the University of Southern California and earned a master's degree in architecture. He'd been living and working in San Francisco for three years when he met Peter.

The next year Phil gave up his pleasant apartment and wonderful bay view and walkable commute to move in with Peter on Potrero Hill. Their two cats, Phil's Cassandra and Peter's Snapper (named for the cat's favorite fish), got along, and Phil remodeled the kitchen and helped Peter find places for the collection of steel sculptures he'd been building in his living room. Phil's first meeting with Alice Adams stayed in his memory: "Two shyer people meeting could hardly be imagined," Phil said. "She was kind, beautiful, and gracious. I brought her some flowers. It seemed as though we had barely met, but things seemed hopeful." Their friendship deepened as they discovered they shared a love of French culture and were both deeply read in French literature. "As a teenager, I read all the nineteenth-century classic novels," Phil recalled, "to learn about life and my mother's heritage."

"My mom really liked Phil from the beginning," Peter said. "That was obvious. They both have a sort of precision about them that I'm not sure I have. My mom was pretty specific and had a very sharp memory about things. And Phil is also exact and has great knowledge about history. He's read a lot and he's judicious." At first Phil "envied the kind concern and support Peter received from his mother." But soon, he said, "I found myself, as most of Peter's friends did, an object of that kind concern." Phil also came to appreciate the way Alice could just toss off an opinion or swear to emphasize a point. "I won't forget the sound of her speaking voice. She'd say, 'Christ!' or 'Jesus!' or 'He's an asshole.' I've never heard anyone swear as elegantly."

In public, Alice usually referred to Phil as Peter's "friend"—this being years ahead of the now-ubiquitous "partner" description—but her fiction bore witness to her deepening acceptance of her son's sexual orientation. Her novels and stories from *Rich Rewards* through *After the War* include gay or lesbian characters, as do a number of her later stories. She was happy that Peter and Phil could live openly, without the closeted identities that had made life difficult and frightening for the gay people of her generation. Indeed, Peter and Phil as a couple were exactly the kind of intelligent, handsome, cultivated people she most enjoyed. They allowed her to overcome her assumption that gay people often lead unhappy lives.

Peter Linenthal and Philip Anasovich

On the heels of *Superior Women*, interest in Adams's short stories surged. Of her third collection, *Return Trips*, in the fall of 1985, Michiko Kakutani in the *New York Times* noted that these stories are about "the emotional consequences of dislocation" for characters on the move "from home to home, relationship to relationship, with all the improvisatory skill of veterans of the 60's." A sour note came from *Chronicle* books editor Patricia Holt, who observed (in an otherwise glowing review) Adams's repetition of modifiers in these stories: "Characters are, for example, 'violently alarmed' or 'violently disapprove' or smell 'violently of gardenia perfume' or have 'violent feelings,' walk through a 'violent green jungle' . . . The word 'funnily' is used at least three times, and Adams' penchant for turning present participles into adverbs—'compellingly,' 'caressingly,' 'blindingly,' 'record-breakingly'— is clumsy and amateurish."[18] That closing judgment hurt, so much so that Alice did not speak to Holt again for years. It's doubtful that any editor could have persuaded Adams to give up the adverb constructions she loved, but why hadn't a copy editor squelched those repetitions when the stories were collected?

The Texas writer Beverly Lowry spent days crafting the first sentence of her review of *Return Trips* for the *New York Times Book Review*: "Nobody writes better about falling in love than Alice Adams." The women in Adams's stories, Lowry continues, know "full well that the man in question might be inappropriate . . . they do know better. That is the glory of an Adams heroine, she is that smart and still goes on: 'Ah,' she says to herself, sighing, 'this again: *love*.' "[19]

Alice and Lowry met later in 1985 when they both served as judges for the PEN/Faulkner Awards. They and a third panelist, Richard Bausch, read and reread dozens of books and shared lists before they convened in Austin. Alice and Lowry and her husband, Glenn, became friends instantly; Alice thought Glenn, a stockbroker, was "old-fashioned and very solid," and he became her informal financial advisor. Just as immediately, Beverly remembered, Alice took a dislike to Bausch—"She could be very cranky—it was quite wonderful." Why? Lowry didn't question Alice ("She was powerful and I was a little cowed, not about to ask her things") but guessed that Bausch appeared to fit a type of extremely nice Southerner whose niceness Alice just didn't trust. For the award the panel selected a book that had not been on any of their first-cut lists, Peter Taylor's *The Old Forest and Other Stories*.* It can't have hurt that Alice had met Taylor at the Toronto International Festival of Authors and found him to be "terrific fun."[20]

The PEN awards ceremony at the Folger Shakespeare Library in Washington, DC, in May was a splendid occasion, made more so by the moss-green open-lacework dress Alice wore. "You could see a beautiful

---

* Adams favored some books that did not make the final nominations: *Solstice* by Joyce Carol Oates; *Where She Was* by Anderson Ferrell; *Honeymoon* by Merrill Joan Gerber; and *Through the Safety Net* by Charles Baxter. (AA to Lowry and Bausch, December 21, 1985.)

slip under it and I sensed she was beautiful down to her skin," Lowry said. "It was all perfect. Glorious." A photograph from that evening shows Alice with a glowing smile as she takes her seat while Lowry, Grace Paley, and others applaud. From the admiring look on nominee Grace Paley's face, we can guess that Adams spoke in praise of short stories and those who write them.

In the guest room of her new house Alice filled two wide shelves with O. Henry Award volumes, and fiction by her favorites, Iris Murdoch and Joyce Carol Oates. She'd been reading Oates since her friend Nancy Webb first recommended her in 1968. "I literally get high reading her . . . her productivity . . . it's literally as though she were possessed by some demons," Adams told Lucie Jessner when she sent her *Marriages and Infidelities* in 1972. Ten years later, reviewing *A Bloodsmoor Romance*, Adams wrote, "I do not believe Oates is generally envied, even, by other writers; she is out of the question, out of range, as is the beauty of Greta Garbo, say, even for the most beautiful people." Adams compares Oates to Trollope, whose forty-seven books, "much as one may love them, all sound somewhat alike. Whereas Joyce Carol Oates sounds like no one else who has ever written, nor does she sound, from book to book, much like herself—whoever that self may be."

Alice remained baffled about who Oates was even after they met. "When you sit next to her talking at a meal, as I did twice, it's pretty tough going; she is nice—but you don't feel much real warmth, or intimacy. But then, she gets up on the lecture platform and sounds like your dearest friend over the phone. She can evidently only be intimate with a large audience." Alice noticed too that Oates was "phobic about grease" and that her husband, Raymond Smith, "sneak[ed] French fries."[21] Nonetheless, a friendship founded on admiration evolved. "I love the adroit and seemingly artless braiding of detail in your stories—and know how much work goes into that smooth-flowing surface," Oates wrote Adams.[22] They also shared a love of cats. The *Ontario Review*, edited by Oates and Smith, published two pet-centered stories that Adams had not been able to publish elsewhere: "Molly's Dog" and "The Islands." Both these stories, apparently sentimental but actually angling in deeper waters, deal with a question Adams poses in "The Islands": "What does it mean to love an animal, a pet, in my case a cat, in the fierce, entire, and unambivalent way that some of us do? . . . Does the cat (did the cat) represent some person, a parent, or a child?" some part of one's self? I don't think so."

Self. Parts of one's self. The topic comes up often in Adams's mid-1980s work (with and without reference to animals). Her new novel, *Second Chances*, was well under way before *Superior Women* appeared in paperback. She wrote this group novel out of her realization that aging brings another identity crisis.* Celeste is based on Lavina Calvin, whom Adams memorialized in her travel memoir *Mexico*. There too she named her Celeste and named her late husband Charles. In the opening chapter of *Second Chances* Dudley Venable and Edward Crane discuss their recently widowed friend: "Celeste who—at her age, and with Charles just dead!—has taken on, apparently, a suitor, a beau." Fussy, critical Edward, who is actually quite worried about his own relationship with a younger man, thinks Celeste's behavior is silly. More generously, Dudley suggests, "Or is it a question of finding new parts for herself?"

But of course aging was not just about new opportunities—the "second chances" of the title. "Death, dying, fear" were major themes of this novel about "old folks."[23] The recent deaths of friends and former lovers urged Adams toward the subject, and she tested similar material in a story called "Waiting for Stella," about a memorial lunch for the first person to die among a group of friends. In that story, one guest thinks, "rancorously, uncontrollably . . . of youth, of obviously taken-for-granted health and sensuality. The condition of youth now seems to Baxter a club from which he has abruptly and most unfairly been excluded."

Then, in May 1986, Alice underwent surgery for removal of a malignant polyp in her colon. Dr. Peter Volpe recalled Alice's "fortitude" in facing the diagnosis.[24] She mentioned the episode obliquely to friends, telling Bryant Mangum, for instance, that her new bedroom "has an

---

* Mary Catherine Bateson in *Composing a Further Life: The Age of Active Wisdom*: "It was confusing in adolescence to be flooded with hormones, and it is confusing again as they dwindle; confusing in adolescence to discover zits on one's face and confusing again to deal with wrinkles; confusing to become an object of sexual desire and confusing again to be invisible." (New York: Knopf, 2010, 79.)

endless city view, including a lot of sky—I had to spend some weeks there in May—and I did think I couldn't have been in a better place." Adams assigned some of her recent medical experience to the character of Celeste, who can barely bring herself to describe her symptoms to a doctor. After a colonoscopy, she thinks "she is much too old and too fragile, really, to have withstood such treatment—nevertheless, withstand it she did, and the bed in which she lies is her own. Her own bed, own room, own beautiful and familiar home. Though her entrails— everything inside her was mauled and pummeled; she feels battered and bruised." A bowl of consommé that a younger friend served her "cools on her nightstand—impossible even to sip."

The popularity of *Superior Women* came with a price tag. The covers of the mass-market Fawcett Crest editions could not have been tackier. A metallic gold cover with metallic fuchsia type and illustrations of overcoiffed women with only slight resemblance to the women in the novel adorned the book. (Where are black Jackson Clay and Jewish Janet Cohen? one wonders.) Promotional folders in the same color scheme included a bumper sticker: "Stay up all night with SUPERIOR WOMEN." When novelist Gish Jen addressed a Radcliffe alumnae panel on the subject of gendered book covers in 2014, she chose that *Superior Women* cover as one example. By using "stereotypically feminine signifiers—a lipstick tube, a woman's naked back"—to seek wider sales, Jen said, a cover "can inadvertently disqualify a novel from the world of serious literature."*[25] The success of *Superior Women* emboldened Fawcett Crest to publish mass-market editions of several other Adams books, all glinting with flesh and flowers on their covers.

Happily, a thirty-something editor at Penguin named Gerald Howard read *Rich Rewards* and invited Alice to lunch on her next visit to New York: "She struck me as an older women who had *style*, and she carried herself like somebody who had always been beautiful and knew it. Not that she swanned around but she was confident in her allure

---

* For comparison, see Fawcett Crest's paperback of John Updike's *Couples* (1968), also hot pink, also slathered with juicy quotes, but reprinting the gracefully seductive image of William Blake's watercolor *Adam and Eve Sleeping* from Knopf's hardcover edition that emphasizes the artfulness of Updike's explicitly sexual novel.

to men. I felt it. You couldn't help having a crush on her. It was one of my earliest author lunches, and I was a reprint publisher who actually cared." Howard's great triumph was to pair Adams's fiction ("her sophisticated, swanky, attractive people") with paintings of women's faces by pop artist Alex Katz. Katz's paintings "look easy, the way Fred Astaire made dancing look easy and Cole Porter made words and music sound easy, but don't be fooled," John Russell observes.[26] Like Adams's fiction, Katz's technique is so "confident" and "crisply articulated" that it "makes us see the world the way he sees it . . . with all but the most essential details pared away" (in Calvin Tompkins's words).[27] "They really looked good," Howard said of his covers, "and it was my cheap thrill to go into bookstores and admire these Penguin Contemporary volumes on the front tables. Alice said she liked those covers a lot too."

From conversations with Alice, Howard formed the impression that she'd had "flings and more" with most of the New York intellectuals. "A name would come up, like Irving Howe or Norman Mailer, and she'd say 'Oh, Irving' or 'Oh, Norman'—I heard a whole world of implication in her tone. I was too polite to inquire, but it seemed as if she'd come down from Radcliffe and been a shiksa among all the sharpies—that they condescended to her and she took it all in and gave it back in her way in a literary sense." Howard met Alice again at a party in New York with Bob McNie: "I thought of him as the last straight man in San Francisco. He was an aging matinee idol type, very distinguished, gray hair, rocking a blue blazer. They made a handsome couple."

Deirdre English, coauthor with Barbara Ehrenreich of *For Her Own Good: 150 Years of the Experts' Advice to Women* (now reissued as *Two Centuries* of said advice) and editor of the San Francisco–based magazine *Mother Jones*, remembered meeting Alice around town (meaning the Bay Area): "I think of seeing her in over-the-knee boots she was sporting, [which] most people her age wouldn't wear. Pretty bold statement." Alice and English formed a friendship that included English's husband, Don Terner, president of a nonprofit corporation that developed affordable housing. Alice invited the couple to a dinner party to celebrate a special occasion. "I believe it was Alice's birthday," English recalled. "I can't imagine a more glamorous party in San Francisco. There were about a dozen people there. Bob put a tremendous amount of effort into the incredible food and décor—black tablecloth, candelabra with lots of candles, very baroque. We felt like stars ourselves because we'd been invited. Like something in *Vanity Fair*—this was the top of something." But any self-flattery English and Terner felt at the beginning of the evening was shattered later as McNie became very drunk. "He became domineering, overly talkative, and bullying; and Alice began to look miserable. She was completely oversensitive to what was happening. You could see in her face that she was embarrassed, humiliated." To English, Bob seemed "like a child saying 'I built this castle so I can destroy it.'" Both English and Terner felt crestfallen when they sensed that, despite his grand gestures, Bob had some psychological hostility to Alice. "I realized I'd rather have a ham sandwich with somebody than have a fancy dinner party with someone who was jealous of me, who wanted to undermine me or felt threatened by me. Don and I really pondered that, talking about it afterwards. A life lesson for us."

Bob and Alice's fights found their way into the marriage of Dudley and ex-drinker, over-the-hill artist Sam Venable in *Second Chances*: In their pacified senior years, Sam is haunted by memories of "god-awful" scenes of "big shouting, schoolboy words thrown out like garbage. Not hitting anyone, at least I never hit, but a lot of ugly noise, and then lurching out . . . Blind crazy drunk." Dudley and Sam's love has been addictive, filled with hate and resentment as well as love.

The day was coming when Alice would have to choose between her hard-earned independence and the comfort and pride of having Bob McNie at her side. Through Al-Anon she was learning that her own sensitivities, her patterns of fear and rage that were rooted in being the child of an alcoholic, contributed to the difficulties she blamed on Bob's heavy drinking. The permutations of her childhood need to be fed—"unless someone is feeding me I am impoverished," she wrote in the notebook—and her adult need for love were complex, endless. She should, Dr. Wheelis suggested, think about autonomy, think of herself as "an okay, self-sufficient person." She was distorting herself by feeling "hurt" or otherwise subject to the emotional roller coaster of an alcoholic: "'Hurt'—a not-true concept—one is not actually hurt by anyone else. HURT—a non-word," was one of many similar notes she wrote to herself.[28]

As Alice's life widened, it seems that Bob's narrowed and his resentments grew. When *Mother Jones* magazine purchased Alice's story "A

Public Pool," Deirdre English suggested that putting Alice Adams's picture on the cover would increase newsstand sales. Rock-and-roll photographer Norman Seeff, known for his pictures of Joni Mitchell, caught Adams looking triumphant—scintillating, really—against a nighttime city. Only her imperfect teeth, working hands, and unvarnished nails reveal that this person is not a movie star.* Inside the magazine, "A Public Pool" offers an entirely different persona in its first-person narration by a large, overweight, shy, unemployed nursing-home worker named Maxine who lives with her mother but discovers an alternative self in her daily swims at Rossi Pool. As the story opens, Maxine says, "Reaching, pulling, gliding through the warm blue chlorinated water, I am strong and lithe: I am not oversized, not six feet tall, weighing one eighty-five. I am not myself, not Maxine."

Mother Jones's fact-checker called to ask Adams if Maxine was based on anyone recognizable who might sue them; Adams declared with a laugh: "Of *course* not. It's me!" When English next saw Alice, she told her, "You're much too thin and self-confident to identify with *this* character." But Alice disagreed: "Not in my heart I'm not. I don't know about men, but women do tend to have notions of ugliness and deformity about themselves."

"A Public Pool" is the sort of story that other magazines told Adams they couldn't publish because it "didn't sound like her" or would damage her image. "It's enraging," Adams told another interviewer. "If there is a perceived story that is mine, I would choose to surpass it."[29]

Like Maxine in the story, Alice was swimming to feel "possessed of powerful, deep energy" that would carry her into an uncertain future.

---

* Alice rejected the art director's wish to photograph her by a swimming pool.

PART FIVE

NOT MIDDLE AGE

CHAPTER TWENTY-SEVEN

Things Fall Apart

— 1987–1989 —

*I was getting toward being 60 myself . . . it struck me that 60 is
not middle-age. I do not know a lot of people who are 120. So I
began to think in a conscious way about what I hope will be the
last third of my life . . . and I began looking at people who are
10 to 15 years older.*

—Alice Adams, speaking about
Second Chances[1]

In January 1987, the owner of the *New Yorker* forced seventy-nine-year-
old William Shawn to step down as the magazine's editor in chief. His
replacement would be Robert Gottlieb.

Alice was in Zihuatanejo when someone in New York called to tell
her. "She came running out of the water toward me just as the sun was
setting and told me, 'Mr. Shawn is gone,'" Jay Schaefer recalled. Schaefer, the San Francisco–based founder and editor of *Fiction Network* who
was also vacationing in Zihuatanejo that week, realized Alice was eager
"to tell somebody who would know what this meant."[2]

No one really knew what Shawn's exit would mean for the magazine and its writers. Alice, along with most of the *New Yorker*'s several
hundred staff members, was shocked by the decision to hire someone
from outside of the magazine. While Gottlieb had backed Victoria
Wilson's publication of Adams's previous seven books, Alice lacked
confidence that the *New Yorker* would buy her stories under his reign.
At the magazine's offices on West Forty-Third Street, the question of
a successor to Mr. Shawn (as he was always called) had been roiling
for several years as Shawn considered and declined internal aspirants.

In the end publisher S. I. Newhouse hired Gottlieb and most of the staff stayed.[3] A few months later, when Frances Kiernan left to take an editorial position at Houghton-Mifflin, Alice had more reason to worry. "The Drinking Club," which appeared in August, was Adams's last appearance in the *New Yorker* during the 1980s.

Despite the news from New York, being in Zihuatanejo aroused Alice's imagination. She made pages of notes on cats who'd been accidentally poisoned at the resort one previous year, dogs "more innocent than cats, funnier, frisking after new friends or waves," black butterflies and amber bougainvillea, all of it "too beautiful to leave—the sea so *bright*." She outlined "The End of the World"—a story about two married women characters who contemplate changes in their lives in the "unreal warmth" of the Mexican beach and under the distorting influence of a ferocious tropical rainstorm that attacks the roof "like bullets." This was Alice and Bob's thirteenth trip to their beloved Zihuatanejo. They still missed the dignified Calvins; cruise ships disgorged boatloads of tourists in gaudy clothes who despoiled their quiet cove with raucous volleyball games; and yet they tried "to live in the sensually perfect present—which is in fact imperfect."[4]

Things were far less perfect back in San Francisco. For about a month after their return Bob suffered from alarming digestive tract symptoms. A colonoscopy showed a mass in his intestine. In late February a surgeon removed a section of his colon. It was the same surgery Alice had undergone in 1986. In Bob's case, the inflammation proved not to be cancer but rather chronic amoebiasis caused by a parasite he'd picked up in Mexico. He was prescribed a one-month course of Flagyl (metronidazole) to cure the infection. When doctors warned him not to drink alcohol while taking Flagyl, he abruptly gave up his two bottles of wine a day.[5]

A severe change in Bob's mental state ensued, as a side effect of either abrupt alcohol withdrawal or of Flagyl. He was so depressed and agitated that he could not go to his studio or complete projects for which he'd taken advance payments. "The shift was dramatic," Peter Linenthal said. "He went from life-of-the-party to staring-at-the-floor. The change cannot be exaggerated." He sank into debt. Alice had understood that the things Bob brought in to redecorate 2661 Clay were bargains he'd had lying around his studio or found about town. Now he informed her that he'd spent his savings to beautify their home. She loaned him money—$40,000 to $60,000, reportedly—but he was still unable to get back to work.

By midspring Bob had lost forty pounds. Suffering from insomnia, decreased appetite, and chronic bowel complaints, he began seeing a psychiatrist in May 1987.

Many a woman—many a woman writer in particular—would have been paralyzed by these setbacks plaguing a loved one in her household. Alice, though, remained optimistic. When Beverly Lowry told her that she didn't think Bob was suited for the role of "the Patient," Alice replied: "Robert has done really well. He looks great (when does he not, so unfair) does everything, just gets sort of tired." Nonetheless, she continued, "The Patient has to go. For one thing it is so damn exhausting for the one who is not. Who is doing all that cooking, etc—hospital duty. And then there's the overdose of togetherness when they're home. We actually weathered that better than I would have thought."[6]

During that winter—as always—Alice found both escape and satisfaction in her work. "I think my being at least half concentrated on my novel helped a lot. A whole other element."[7] While Bob recovered from surgery, she finished writing *Second Chances* and dedicated the book to Judith Clark Adams, Judith's husband, and Judith's mother. She sent the novel to Knopf in March of 1987. Wilson called to say she loved it. Alice told Lowry, "[She went] on and on about how wonderful—but I don't know what she has in mind in terms of dollars . . . we're talking big bunches. Bundles I guess I mean."[8] Alice felt anxious while her agent, Lynn Nesbit, and Wilson negotiated a contract. "The differences between projected sums are so huge: 300,000–500,000 or 750,000," Adams noted. "It's those differences causing my anxiety."[9] Alice also worried that the negotiations would damage her relationship with Knopf and Wilson. With Robert Gottlieb already moved to his new post at the *New Yorker*, the decision of how much Adams would receive for *Second Chances* fell to Knopf's incoming editor in chief Sonny Mehta, who was moving to New York after a brilliant publishing career at Picador in London.

In April Knopf offered Alice $1 million for *Second Chances* and a yet-untitled second novel, to be paid out over several years as the books were published in hardcover and paper editions. This was an unusually high amount for literary novels—over $2 million in 2019 dollars.* For Alice it renewed the ticket to freedom she'd gained with the paperback sale of *Superior Women*: she could support herself. Even with Bob not working, they might afford their new house. Bob was thrilled too. He sent off another one of his ridiculous not-anonymous notes to inform Herb Caen at the *Chronicle* that Alice had accepted a "low seven-figure contract for her next novel" (omitting mention of its other conditions). He enclosed a photo of Alice celebrating with Diane Johnson, whose new novel *Persian Nights*, dedicated to Alice Adams and Barbara Epstein, had just come out.[10]

Because of *Superior Women*, in the words of Carolyn See, being an Alice Adams fan was no longer "an elitist thrill, a *frisson* of knowing that you and only a few others were initiated, knew that this writer existed." For both the author and her publishers, the success of *Superior Women* set an expectation that her next book would also be a commercial success. No doubt that expectation influenced Adams to fill several of her succeeding novels with people whose lives have been intertwined for years. What these novels gained in scope, they lost in intensity.

Throughout Bob's recovery from surgery, his depression, and his ongoing battle with intestinal discomforts, Alice tried to manage her own nerves, fatigue, and irritation while keeping up a heavy schedule of professional obligations such as interviews with Kay Bonetti for the American Audio Prose Library and with Karen Evans for a profile in the *Examiner*'s Sunday magazine; for the latter, she steered the conversation toward talk about her cats. She'd agreed to go to the University of Utah as a visiting writer because she thought Bob would enjoy skiing at Park City. Now she had "to go to the goddam place" alone. She hated the university's writer's apartment with its "baskets of stiff dull-colored artificial flowers—small pillows all over, always in the way, fake oil

---

* Writing and revising *Second Chances* took Adams about three years and her next novel took another four, so the large advance averaged out to an annual salary of about $150,000, less her agent's commission. In addition Adams received some income from royalties on previous books, sales of articles and stories, and visiting-writer jobs.

lamps, their switches concealed" but no food except a can of garbanzo beans. She also hated the forced conversations with other faculty. Even the students—the group Alice often enjoyed most—were disappointing: "Someone demanded to know if I was aware that not one of my fictional heroines was morally pure, and I had to say that I was not," Alice fumed later.[11]

Alice was "rescued" from the kitschy apartment when poet Mark Strand and cookbook author Julie Strand invited her to stay with them. She thought the poet, then in his midfifties, "so handsome that he [was] hard to look at." He found Alice lovely for her "stylishness in clothing and manner" and recalled, "She was a very tasteful dresser, very easy socially, she seemed like a grown-up to me, who had been used to frumpy, messily and tastelessly clad academic women." A friendship ensued and the poet stayed in Alice's garden-level guest room on future visits to San Francisco. When she sent him *Second Chances*, he felt "unbelievably moved by it . . . [he] felt eighteen when [he] began the novel, then just as old as Celeste, Dudley, Edward, by novel's end," and found it "so smart about what we choose to disclose and what keep secret."[12]

In May Bob, apparently drinking again, accompanied Alice to a teaching gig at Bates College in Maine. Together they visited the site of her childhood summers at Lake Sebago. Alice's stepmother, Dotsie Adams, now suffering from an alcohol-precipitated neurological condition called Korsakoff's syndrome and living in a nursing home in California, was keeping her promise to give Alice the property that had once belonged to Agatha. Alice hoped that the cottage would become a project for Bob, but they found it a shambles: "Even if you didn't know Nic and Dotsie, you'd know crazy people had been living there," she wrote Max Steele. Bob had no interest. But the lakefront property was valuable, so Alice gratefully paid the back taxes and completed the transfer. She had at last inherited a house from her parents.

A visit to Judith and Timothy Adams at his family's "ravishing" place on Bailey Island was the best part of this trip to Maine for Alice.[13] But Alice's dear old friend was alarmed by Bob: "He came with practically a case of wine—and they were going to be with us for two or three days? And I said, 'Bob, that's a lot of wine!' And he said, 'Oh we'll drink it, we'll drink it!' Well, Timothy and I are not huge drinkers and I thought, 'Uh-oh, that's a lot of drinking.' But he was a bon vivant, a very dramatic man. He was charming about the fact that Alice had introduced him to a different world. He said he'd been to Europe fifteen times with Alice—that Alice had introduced him to this wonderful sophisticated life and how much he loved it and he fit right in. He was fun! I think he adored Alice and he gave her a glamorous persona."

Fun or not, Bob got worse, his condition moving "from severe to acute"—"a suicide watch"—when they got home, Alice told Max and Judith in back-to-back letters. Finally, reading an article in *Newsweek* persuaded Bob to try a combination of talk and drug therapy. After seeing Dr. Richard Shore, he made a few phone calls to clients to explain why he hadn't met with them. "Work seems to be the largest block, worst area, whatever, though of course also years of booze, which I'm sure was to mask depression," Alice wrote.[14]

Bob's depression caused Alice to question her own accomplishments, as if she were starting out again. As the 1987 commencement speaker for the Berkeley English Department, she reminisced that she'd been "in no sense in charge" of her life when she arrived in California in 1948. As a broke, unpublished, unhappily married writer moored in bland, suburban Palo Alto, she'd longed for the complexity, free speech, and subversiveness of Berkeley. That environment, she said, made a good training ground for writers. She urged the graduates to "read enormously" and think subversively: "I have come to believe that people are drawn to writing by an at least unconscious perception of fiction as the place where the unsayable may be said."[15]

For Alice, in 1987, there was still an unsayable: her fear that Bob didn't love—or had never loved—her and that the vitality of their lives together was depleted. Was she to be, as her mother had been, perpetually tied to a man who was emotionally unavailable to her, either drunk or manically engaged with others or buried under his own despair? Her notes on her dreams and her sessions with Dr. Wheelis say she felt a regressive pull toward her childhood, specifically to the feeling of being unloved. "R. [is] a constant reminder of the distorted failure of my life," she wrote in late June.[16]

That very same week she accepted an invitation to serve on the 1988 Pulitzer Prize for Fiction jury—a job not offered to failures. True, she hadn't won that prize herself, but being on the judging panel with Julian Moynahan (a professor at Rutgers) and Richard Eder (an esteemed book reviewer) was an honor. How much recognition would it take for her to overcome the undertow of her lonely childhood?

* * *

In July, Bob was admitted to Mount Zion Hospital with worsening agitation, weight loss, and depression. It seems that he'd disappeared for days at a time during the preceding weeks. He stayed at Mount Zion until September, trying several different medications that failed to alleviate his problems.

Adams's story "What to Wear" gives a glimpse of these months as she felt them. The story abbreviates and simplifies what had been an extremely difficult year for both her and Bob. Her character, Sheila, can't decide what to wear to visit her lover in the psychiatric ward because she "has never known what might please him, might make him laugh, might interest or infuriate him, and the effort of trying has worn her out, or nearly." Wanting to show the man how important he is to her, Sheila dresses in a new silk shirt, then changes her mind because it might look too conspicuous in the psych ward. Her choice is wrong. He mocks her gray sweater with a tone "so brutally familiar—always, he has bludgeoned her with this heavy irony—that, reeling, Sheila thinks, But he's really just the same. Has he always been mad?"

Alice's notebooks tell us she was mourning her life with Bob: "Mourning: loss, 23 yrs of emotion. Sentiments over childhood." She was often on the phone with Dr. Shore, who reported that Bob refused his pills. With techniques from the Al-Anon twelve-step program she tried to learn how to break her "total concentration on R" and wrote, "I must detach, he is not my barometer." She talked often with her younger friend Anne Lamott about her experience of alcoholism and recovery: "Her father's mental illness was obviously the defining aspect of her childhood," Lamott said. "It was why she needed to achieve so much, and run so far away from the South. When Bob started coming apart noticeably, it was very familiar, and excruciating, not to be able to save the latest Dad stand-in." Trying to carry on with her social life, Alice felt "lonely in a world of couples." She remembered feeling the same way when she was a six-year-old among married adults. "Everyone likes someone better than me," she had told her aunt then.

At the Galería de la Raza and the Mexican Museum in San Francisco's Mission District, Alice saw an extraordinary exhibit of paintings by

Frida Kahlo: "The overall effect was cumulative, brilliantly powerful, almost overwhelming . . . only consummate skill could have produced such meticulous images of pain, and love, and loneliness." She became fascinated by Kahlo and pursued her interest by contracting to write a piece about her for *Art & Antiques* magazine. The next year she went to see Kahlo's and Rivera's houses in Mexico City with two younger friends, Mary Ross Taylor, a Texas art critic then living in San Francisco, and Beverly Lowry. She hadn't traveled out of the US without Bob at her side for many years, and every practical aspect of this trip challenged her. Lowry remembered that Alice was afraid to call "this witch of a woman who had control over many of Kahlo's paintings. She sat there looking at the phone and saying, 'She's probably not there. It's three o'clock. I'm sure she's taking a nap.' And I said, 'Alice, don't write nonfiction!' "

In the essay about Kahlo she would eventually finish, Adams sees an affinity between Kahlo and Billie Holiday, who "shared a tendency toward extremes—of talent and personal beauty (Kahlo in photographs is more beautiful than the self she painted), as well as addictiveness"— to drugs, alcohol, and love. Both women's faces, she thinks, combine "almost conventional prettiness & harsh 'masculine strength.' " Why, Adams asks, did Frida adore "a man who was continuously, compulsively unfaithful to her, and who was for long periods of time conspicuously off and away with other, often famous, women?" She offers two answers. First, "Diego entirely supported Frida's work; he considered her "one of the greatest living painters," understood the "intensely female, anguished complexity of her work," and "compared his own painting unfavorably to hers." He also built a wonderful studio for her—Adams felt she could "forgive Diego a great deal for having built this space for Frida's work." Second, "Frida was absolutely addicted to Diego; she could be said to have been impaled on her mania for Diego, as she had been literally impaled in the horrifying streetcar accident that, when she was 18, so painfully, horribly transformed her life. She herself referred to the 'two accidents' in her life, the streetcar crash and Diego."[17]

Alice saw Bob McNie as her Diego Rivera.*[18] For most of the twenty years they'd lived together he had been busy with his own work—and so not interfering with hers; he'd paid his share and more of their household expenses, and he'd been a handsome, usually charming com-

* Or perhaps her second Diego: in another note Adams wrote: "Diego—Vasco."

panion. Also from the beginning, Alice had recognized and accepted the element of addiction in her love for Bob. "Alice loved to have a flurry in her life. It wasn't the men, it was the flurry that was addictive to her," Frances Gendlin thought. Bob provided flurry. In the words spoken by Celeste in *Second Chances*: "I think that all my life I've been falling in love with men as a kind of substitute for something else." The something else: her father's love, withdrawn from her at age six when Nic Adams was hospitalized for severe depression after the death of her baby brother.

With Bob's alcoholism cresting and his ability to make her feel loved diminished, Alice understood that her devotion—her addiction—was a danger to herself. Alice confided these things only to friends who were not part of their San Francisco social circle. "She told me Bob threatened her," Judith Adams said. "He had a breakdown, from the alcoholism probably, and he told Alice he was going to *bring her down with him*. And she told me, 'I have to break the relationship.' This is verbatim.

"She probably told me on the phone, or maybe when she came east that year. I think she interpreted it as a threat almost on her life, that she was frightened and she had to be rid of him. He had to be out of her life," Judith continued. "Her livelihood depended on her ability to write and she could not write with this kind of distraction and threat. I was very sympathetic to that. She was saying I come first. Her sanity and her health came before trying to mend him. I think she felt that he was broken. I also felt that—this is my own feeling now—that she was not capable of taking care of him."

Near the end of August Bob came to lunch with Alice a couple of times. "Your mother doesn't want me back," he afterward told Peter, who was still friendly with the man who had become a stepfather to him.[19]

Dr. Shore saw a "twenty percent improvement" in Bob's depression on desipramine and released him from Mount Zion in September. Records are unclear about where he then lived and Alice's personal notebooks are also silent on the subject. He probably spent some time with Alice and some at his house in Truckee. His and Alice's attorney, Charles Breyer, began to manage his financial affairs. His medical record says he did poorly as an outpatient, refusing food and drink.

Trying to decide what to do about Bob, Alice considered the love she felt for him and others. On October 6, she made notes and a list toward a future novel:

Title MUCH LOVE (?)

love—okay to love R.—does not mean wanting to live with, or sex— means wishing well, actually—Christian?

Love—	Like—
RKM [McNie]	Din [Diane Johnson]
Peter [Linenthal]	Syd [Goldstein]
Dick [Poirier]	Til [Stewart]
Billy [William Abrahams]	Gigi [Geraldine Green]
Vic [Victoria Wilson]	Bill B. [Theophilus Brown]
Frannie [Kiernan]	
Allen [Wheelis]	
Judith [Clark Adams]	
Max [Steele]	

The next day, Alice had made a decision. She and Bob would not go on together. She wrote to Bob's daughter, Morissa, now forty, who lived and worked at Camphill Village, a school for mentally disabled people in Pennsylvania. Neither Bob nor Alice had replied when Morissa sent them news of her recent marriage and new baby daughter. Then Morissa received this letter from Alice:

I'm very sorry to break such a very long silence with not good, not at all good news, which is that Bob is very, very severely depressed, has been really since his surgery. Needless to say this is why you haven't heard from him which I'm sure has been upsetting. Physically he's okay, except for extreme weight loss, and at the moment a prostate problem. But, totally depressed. Negative. Hopeless. He's been seeing a psychiatrist, in whom I do not have great faith but he won't go to another, although he hates this one. You see?

What caused this—God knows. Literally. My feeling, or one of them is that it's undoubtedly been coming on for years, all that drinking was a way of staving it off. Bob hadn't been drinking at all since the surgery, so one of his current problems is that of being what AA calls a dry drunk.* Also, as you know, he's never really faced or talked about inner turmoil.

Alice enclosed a gift check for Morissa's six-month-old, Serena. "I love the name, lately I've spent a lot of time with the Serenity Prayer in Al-Anon, which may be saving my remaining sanity." Alice was preparing to hand Bob over to his daughter.[20]

Bob was readmitted to Mount Zion, where he had minor surgery to remove a benign tumor in his prostate on October 12. After five days he came home for one night but was too ill to stay. Alice returned him to Mount Zion, agreeing to pay the $600-a-day cost. Robert Jr. (Robbie), then living with his wife and two small sons in Portland, used frequent-flyer points gifted him by a friend to visit his father. He found Bob "in very bad shape—physically suffering from medical problems unaddressed, a dreadful prison-ward set up, and the WRONG anti-depressant which had him climbing the walls."[21]

Alice bought Morissa a ticket to San Francisco. With Serena, she arrived in late October, spoke briefly with Alice when she picked up the keys to Bob's cars, and took charge. She and her brother moved Bob to the Langley Porter Psychiatric Institute at UC San Francisco on Parnassus Street on November 3.

His admissions interview there reports that Bob said "his girlfriend has left him and says she desires no further contact with him. He is not welcome at her house." His new doctors diagnosed "Bipolar Affective Disorder Mixed with Mention of Psychotic Features." His ability to function was assessed at 38 out of 100. In the past year Morissa had recognized an "archetypically alcoholic pattern" in her father's attitudes toward her. She thought "his fear of his weakness" led him to be dishonest with people who cared about him. She was angry and spoke forthrightly to him.[22] She told Peter Linenthal, "I'm just surprised that it happened so soon; that entertaining facade eventually had to crack with all the pain he's had."[23]

* Alice's statement contradicts Judith Adams's precise memory that Bob was drinking wine when he and Alice visited her at Bailey Island, Maine, earlier in the year.

Over the next five weeks, Bob improved significantly. Another course of Flagyl cleared up his bowel complaints and he was treated for a urinary tract infection due to his prostate surgery. Taking lithium and clonazepam, he gained fourteen pounds, his depression "greatly improved," and he became "bright, jovial, and joking." He told Morissa that his relationship with Alice was "worn out" because they were "leading different lives, and [he was] such a clam-up." Morissa accused her father of "systematically casting out his children" and said she thought it was curious that Bob and Alice had never married. He replied that Alice had been frightened by Robbie McNie. He also said that he could no longer do his work because "it's for the young—it's competitive" and because he'd "ruined his credit." He told her he'd "wanted out for some time but [couldn't] do anything else."[24]

As Bob got better, he called Alice to tell her he wished he could move back into their house. She felt some sympathy but answered that this was impossible. He was now well enough to "be irritating—all surface." He asked her to take some of his clothes to the dry cleaner. As she went through them, she lost patience again: "So *many*, unused, all wadded up." She was further disturbed when Bob called her friend Nell Sinton and asked her to urge Alice to see him: "His successful manipulation of her, doing what he wanted."[25] Alone at midnight on Christmas Eve, she had another insight: "A shaft into my chest—*R* is the beautiful object of love, who will always turn me down, find me deficient—"

Bob declined to discuss plans for his release from UCSF. He refused to go to Pennsylvania with Morissa and insisted that he would live independently. Charles Breyer served as a mediator. Alice agreed to provide Bob with $2,000–$2,500 monthly against his share of the house as part of their separation agreement. Breyer found an apartment Bob could afford at 2714 Webster Street in San Francisco and put his house near Truckee (of which Alice was *not* a co-owner) on the market, priced at $400,000 for sale "as is." It needed maintenance. Bob's house was "falling apart, looking terrific—like him," Alice noted sarcastically.[26]

Bob was discharged from UCSF on December 10 with prescriptions to continue his medications (lithium, phenelzine, and clonazepam) and referrals for outpatient care. "However," the final report by Dr. Victor Reus and Dr. Kavitha Rao read, "the patient appeared to be ambivalent about outpatient psychotherapy as well as the need for continued medication." They considered Bob's prognosis "guarded." Within days of moving into his apartment a few blocks downhill from what had now become Alice's house on Alta Plaza, Bob stopped taking his meds. According to Morissa McNie and others, his severe depression continued for another five years.

At first Alice felt relieved to put the great "accident" of Bob and his problems behind her. She began a new notebook to mark the change. It had been "a good 'Colette' day," she wrote after a long walk and dinner with artist friends Bill Brown and Paul Wohner on November 15, perhaps wishing to emulate the freewheeling life of the French writer to whom her work had been compared.[27]

In early March Alice hopped a plane to Southern California for a weekend at the Santa Anita racetrack with Mary Ross Taylor and the Lowrys, who owned a racehorse at the time—"Fun—though I don't see the tracks as a permanent part of my life," Alice said—and found there the setting for her Lila Lewisohn story called "At the Races."[28] By the summer of 1988, Alice realized, "What I mourn is actually dead. His craziness—*concealed* in a curious way in booze, drunk he [was] most himself—angry, promiscuous, entirely irrational."

Entries about Bob punctuate Alice's notebook for months. As she grieved, she analyzed the roots of her need for him and admitted to herself that she'd stayed with Bob much longer than she should have and that she'd known he had affairs while they were together: "Years of total dedication, riveted attention to Bob . . . even when he had affairs, deeply painful. You could say I was addicted to him, and I was—"*

Alice's anomalous situation—"a non-husband gone mad, and gone"[29]—was socially awkward. Not everyone was sympathetic. Pride had prevented her from complaining about Bob to friends in San Francisco, so few knew about his dark side. "In a way," Diane Johnson recalled, "it was wonderful for a writer to have this caretaker person, but

---

* Her reference to Bob's affairs indicates she'd known Bob was unfaithful, but she may not have admitted it to herself or talked to anyone about it. When Bob emerged from his long depression and began a relationship with Elaine Badgley Arnoux, he confided to her that he'd had affairs with other women while he lived with Alice: "He kept a little studio down in North Beach and it had a bedroom where he brought them," Badgley Arnoux recalled. "He was loyal to those women . . . the woman that he was with when he died was someone he had been seeing for years. And yet he loved Alice."

there was a price. It was slightly infantilizing." To these friends, Alice's decision to break with Bob appeared sudden and cruel. "We thought Alice sort of turned on Bob in a rather baffling way. She couldn't handle his illness—so maybe it was a time for resentments that had been building up to come out? It was a strange thing that a lot of people were not quite in agreement with," Johnson said. "Even if they ended up being friends with Alice, there was this tiny reservation."

Trying to resume her social life, Alice went to a dinner party with a cardiologist named Ray Rosenman who did research on type A personalities. Seated on the other side of her was Robert Flynn Johnson, a curator at the Fine Arts Museums of San Francisco. "At a certain point," Johnson recalled, "Rosenman was pontificating about something and Alice leaned toward me conspiratorially, 'Can you get me out of here?'" They made excuses and Johnson drove Alice home. "She opened an extremely cold bottle of chardonnay and we drank the whole bottle and talked." Johnson, who was some twenty years younger than Alice, became a close platonic friend. "We entered into each other's social circles," he said. "She was highly opinionated, wonderful sense of humor, a self-deprecating but highly original individual. I did worry that I might end up in one of her short stories."

When a mutual friend suggested to Alice that her recently divorced doctor, David Rabin, was interested in her, she invited him to dinner. After one evening, she knew they had no chemistry together. Yet, she romanticized Rabin for a few weeks, wanting of him "fun, talk, and kissing" but finding the idea of sex too scary. He was just her "current name for loneliness," she soon realized. When they spoke again, she had the flu, so their next meeting was a professional "house call" rather than a date. Within days, Adams began "Your Doctor Loves You," a story in which she braids the pain of separating from a man while still living in a house he'd furnished with the awkwardness of beginning to date again. The story ends when the protagonist's doctor and love interest sends her a bill for his house call. That really happened. Unlike Holly in the story, Alice objected, and she saved Rabin's handwritten apology.[30]

It would take Alice much longer to work her way toward a fictional treatment of the life she'd shared with Robert Kendall McNie. Her notebooks are rich in feelings but often cryptic. She was plagued by "ancient longings" and "nameless yearning" for men.[31] She dreamed about Malcolm Kemp, her father's psychiatrist who had seduced her when she was still a teenager. Her attachment to her current psychiatrist, Dr. Wheelis, she realized, was "a bought relationship, like that with a masseur, that would end when she stopped writing him checks." She mourned lovers who'd died recently—Trummy Young and Vasco Pereira. She looked up "sentimental" in the dictionary and copied out: "addicted to indulgence in sentiments of a superficial nature" and "nostalgia for what never existed, or—was false (Fitzgerald)." Had the loves that had so much shaped her life been sentimental indulgences? As she learned to think of Bob "without tears" she wondered if she still had "too much anger" toward him.

When recommendations for the 1988 Pulitzer Prize for Fiction were due, Adams convinced at least one fellow juror, Julian Moynahan, to support *Beloved* by Toni Morrison. "I take it all back about Toni M.," he wrote Adams. "I just finished *Beloved* and it's high up there—with Faulkner, Hawthorne—a masterpiece—four and twenty blackbirds baked in a pie (all the way through)." The panel's decision came on the heels of the controversial awarding of the National Book Award to Larry Heinemann's first novel, *Paco's Story*, a choice that had disappointed both supporters of *Beloved* and those of Philip Roth's *The Counterlife*.[32] The jurors' committee of Adams, Moynahan, and Richard Eder submitted their list of finalists and statements to the Pulitzer Prize Board on December 26, 1987. Their finalists were *Persian Nights* by Diane Johnson, for which Adams wrote the statement;* *That Night* by Alice McDermott, for which Eder wrote; and *Beloved*, for which Moynahan wrote. Adams had loyally supported her friend Johnson's novel but also played a decisive role in securing the prize for Morrison.

Before the Pulitzer board announced the winner in April, forty-eight black writers signed a letter published in the *New York Times Book Review* in January deploring the fact that neither James Baldwin (who died in 1987) nor Morrison had won a National Book Award or Pulitzer Prize.

---

* Johnson's "consummate novelistic skill, including a genius for social comedy," Adams wrote, "has produced a novel of extreme moral and historical complexity—the classic Americans-abroad situation with many differences, and some new and startling excellences."

John Edgar Wideman, one of the letter's signers, told reporters that his group did not intend to influence the Pulitzer committee, which didn't prevent many people from assuming that was exactly their intention. In that context, it's important to know that Adams and Moynahan and Eder had turned in their selections, including Moynahan's strong argument for *Beloved*, well ahead of the published letter.[33]

During 1988 Wilson helped Adams prepare *After You've Gone*, her fourth collection of short stories. The title story takes the form of a letter from a lawyer to her former lover, a poet. He's gone, but the younger woman he left with, Sally Ann, sends the narrator letters of complaint about how he treats her. The witty ironies of "After You've Gone" suggest that Alice had reached a similar point of bemusement in her recovery from Bob. The story explains the ownership of 2661 Clay: "*The house. I know that it was and is not yours, despite that reckless moment at the Trident (too many margaritas, too palely glimmering a view of our city, San Francisco) when I offered to put it in both our names, as joint tenants, which I literally saw us as, even though it was I who made payments. However, your two-year occupancy and your incredibly skillful house-husbanding made it seem quite truly yours.*" Released in September 1989, with a jewel-toned dust jacket—Diebenkorn's *Seated Woman* (1967) on the front and a delectable author photo by Thomas Victor of Adams with a longer, more feminine haircut—*After You've Gone* was ignored by the *New York Times* but got good reviews elsewhere. These stories, playwright and social historian Elaine Kendall noticed, have a "feminist undertow" because their admirable women are "hopelessly involved with unworthy men."[34]

Composing her seventh novel, *Caroline's Daughters*, occupied Alice during the tortuous months following her breakup with Bob McNie. She escaped the turmoil of her own feelings by cramming this novel with news and scraps of gossip and pithy observations like "Men are not really mad for complexity in women, or big intensity." Of all her novels, this one has the most extravagant plot—and for all its fun and energy, *Caroline's Daughters* picks up the apocalyptic mood that Alice felt. Maybe it was in self-defense that Adams told Penelope Rowlands that *Caroline's Daughters* was her "most fictional book ever."[35] Caroline Carter, the novel's matriarch, who is part Alice Adams and part Judith Clark Adams, returns to San Francisco after five years in Lisbon to her house on Alta Plaza (it's Alice's house exactly) with fresh eyes for a changing city and the lives of her five daughters. The novel is a six-ring circus organized around Caroline and her daughters, each of whom takes the lead in six chapters—hence a total of thirty-six chapters. Readers witness a semi-incestuous attraction, high-end prostitution, and a political lawyer who sleeps with two half sisters and pursues their mother; there's also a mafioso-style murder, domestic abuse and rape, a homeless former doctor's wife, a stock-market crash, and a restaurant teetering toward bankruptcy. Caroline and her daughters display increasing comprehension of what it means to compete as a woman in the eighties: "Now women are supposed to have a great husband and children and run several corporations; be good at Leveraged Buy-Outs or design marvelous post-modern houses. Or run for public office. Or maybe all of those somehow at once. Not to mention being very thin and aerobically fit, a memorable cook-hostess-decorator. And fabulous in bed, multi-orgasmic and tender and demanding, all at once."

Despite its density of message, *Caroline's Daughters* is a page-turner. With apparent glee, Adams drops cameos of friends and enemies into her story: her former *New Yorker* editor's husband, Dr. Kiernan, "the best orthopedist at New York Presbyterian," takes care of Sage's broken arm; a barely disguised Herb Gold, a "so-called writer" named David Argent, "never misses a chance to appear in print." With two exceptions—Caroline's third husband, Ralph Carter, a retired labor leader on the model of San Francisco's longshoreman-writer Eric Hoffer, and Stevie, the manager of Fiona's restaurant who keeps things running and eventually marries Sage—the men in this novel are an unworthy crew. There's Noel, a carpenter who's uneducated, untrustworthy, unwise, and selfish but beautiful to look at (shades of Bob McNie or his son Robbie), and Roland Gallo, a Latin seducer and lawyer whose plans to run for mayor collapse when he's connected to a prostitution ring. Adams took Gallo's last name from Bob McNie's winemaking clients, his seductive personality from Vasco Pereira, and his political ambition and downfall from reports about San Francisco city administrator Roger Boas, who stood trial in 1988 for his involvement in a prostitution ring involving underage Asian girls and police corruption.[36]

Through these stories, Adams attacks the materialism and corruption of values in American life during the presidency of Ronald Reagan, whom she'd disliked since he'd been governor of California from 1967 to 1975. In Adams's eighties morality play, the kind, honest people end up better off than the envious and greedy ones. She targets power imbalances between men and women in a money-driven culture dominated by traditional male values. The most ambitious, least likable daughters, Fiona and Jill, fight by men's rules—earning money and using the power and prestige they've acquired to do, well, almost anything they want to do. The more vulnerable, less ambitious daughters, Sage and Portia, resist macho values and are (after some floundering) rewarded with artistic success, kind lovers, good friends, and beauty in their lives. Throughout, *Caroline's Daughters* is salted with comments that indicate Adams now sees through feminist eyes: after Sage's husband, Noel, takes over a dinner planned by Portia to celebrate Sage's representation by a New York gallery, Portia thinks, "If two men were scheduled to have dinner together, a woman married to one of those men would not automatically assume that both men were really dying to spend the evening with her."

Adams's richest insights into the silent compromises that even powerful women make involve sex. When Roland forces his way into Fiona's apartment and pushes her onto her bed, Fiona understands, "This is what rape is . . . Someone you know, even someone who knows you want him. But not so quickly, so easily." Fiona tells Gallo no and twists her face away from his, but he does not stop. When he has Fiona pinned by his weight, Gallo switches to a "slow, curiously respectful motion" to complete the act. That's where, melodramatically, Adams closes her chapter.

The next morning Fiona asks her sister Jill a question that continues to plague discussions of sexual assault: "Does it count as rape if you come?" Because (like most of Adams's strong female characters) Fiona is both romantic and highly sexed. These women fall in love easily—and are slow to see that the men they are with treat them badly. They want to please men; trying to tell her husband he needs a haircut, Liza asks herself, "Why must I always be so flattering—to Saul and to all men, really? No wonder I used to be such a popular girl. Why can't I just say, Go get a haircut, you asshole? You really need one."

Like Adams, Caroline's eldest daughter, Liza, is "given to gossip" and has literary aspirations: Liza "gathers material." Liza will succeed as a writer in part because being curious gives her access to people's lives. By the end of *Caroline's Daughters*, Liza is engaged in a debate with an editor at a commercial magazine who wants to buy her work if she will radically change her story to suit their requirements; Liza hears an "other inner voice is saying they could be right, you know, they're not all dummies. They could be really improving the story. And then it all gets more confused because of the money."

Not coincidentally, having this debate with herself and challenging the magazine editor about her story gives Liza the nerve to challenge her husband about his sexual infidelity.

During those months she was writing *Caroline's Daughters*, Alice vented some of the anger about Bob that she'd long kept to herself. The writing became cathartic for her. No mention of fatigue in writing or anxiety about editing occurs in her notes for this book. It was already under contract to Knopf. She sent her typescript, then titled "The Last Lovely City," to Amanda Urban, whom she chose as her literary agent at ICM after Lynn Nesbit left to found her own agency in 1989.

Urban read it fast, over New Year's weekend, and called Alice on January 2, 1990, to say she loved it. This novel is vivid with a quality that Urban appreciated in Alice: "Of all the people I knew," Urban recalled, "Alice and Clay Felker [legendary magazine editor, founder of *New York* magazine] were the most fun to talk about other people with. They both had a lot of smart insights and observations about people."

Generosity to friends became a hallmark of Alice's single life. When she read in the paper that *San Francisco Examiner* columnist Stephanie Salter, a woman she'd met just once, had been mugged and slashed with a knife in front of her house, Alice mailed Salter an invitation. "She could only imagine that I must be very afraid now to come home and be alone, she said. If I wanted I could come live with her until my physical wounds healed and I got back my confidence."[37] Alice also stepped in to help Anne Lamott when she gave birth to her son, Samuel, by paying her rent for several months and going in with others "on a washing machine that hooked up to the kitchen faucets—it was a thing of beauty." When Sam moved from a crib to his big-boy bed Alice gave him a set of Power Ranger sheets that "filled him with courage," Lamott said.

Alice continued to give parties when she lived alone. Sandra Russell, an aspiring painter who supported herself by catering, loved working for Alice: "She kept chicken stock she'd made in the freezer; she owned good old Sabatier knives and some beautiful silver from her mother, beautiful glasses from Mexico." Russell's multicourse menus featured risottos, paellas, or seafood stews. Film critic David Thomson and photographer-writer Lucy Gray, who moved to San Francisco from Dartmouth College in 1983 and met Alice through Diane Johnson, recalled, "She gave big dinner parties, catered, for twenty people or more. Formal. Drinks first, passed by someone hired. These were serious occasions, anybody who was invited had credentials. Talent." People like the biographer Diane Middlebrook, chemist Carl Djerassi (developer of oral contraceptives), painters Bill Brown and Bob Bechtle, art historian Whitney Chadwick, and literary agent Fred Hill might be there, along with writers Caroline Drewes, Diane Johnson, Leonard Michaels, Anne Lamott, Mary Gaitskill, and guests from out of town—novelist Carolyn See, agent Amanda Urban and her husband, *New Yorker* writer Ken Auletta. "The conversation was serious and competitive, people throwing their hat in the ring."

In New York City and Sag Harbor in September 1988, Alice enjoyed seeing Victoria Wilson and other friends, but something was lacking. Previously such trips had been "an escape from R, no expectation but that." She now missed that frisson of freedom—even as she also knew she would not want him back.

Alice had a "marvelous" trip to Baton Rouge in November.[38] Soon after she wrote a story set in a diner there. "Breakfast at Louie's Café" is about an aging gay man from San Francisco who resembles Bob McNie in appearance and manner:

> Once very handsome, too handsome, almost, with his wavy hair, high fine brow and strong nose—he was frequently, often violently loved. But now most of the thick black hair is either gray or gone . . . Scotty these days lives very much alone . . . he puts a good face on things, his friends like to say . . . He is fun, or usually he is fun . . . the "face" and the fun require a certain effort: they cause a strain that at times he fears might even be visible.

On the way back to the New Orleans airport, Alice insisted on stopping for oysters. "She was *extremely* nervous about getting to the airport on time, but didn't want to miss out on oysters," Betsy Wing, her driver that day, recalled.

A year after the breakup, Alice's notebook tells us, she felt "washes of pain." But she faulted Bob for telling Sydney Goldstein that he couldn't come to her Thanksgiving dinner because the contrast with the bleakness of his life would be too painful. In that reasoning Alice saw Bob's "terrific self-pity—He could live less bleakly—He could call me—knows I'm sympathetic, available—" Maybe that was a turning point.

Sunday, November 27, 1988, found Alice enjoying a "bright better day—work—A walk . . ." A week later, she spent an afternoon with her son, Peter, and Phil Anasovich in Golden Gate Park: "the bright grass & sunshine . . . Trees—Eucalyptus, cypress, Giant tree ferns." They looked for the house near the park where Bob had lived with his family in the 1950s, and Alice thought, "I've outgrown Bob." She was able to continue the walk toward "the beach, striped mauve sky. Tea—"

Alice kicked off 1989 by giving a seventieth-birthday party for Billy Abrahams at her house. Her guests included Billy's partner Peter Stansky (in on the surprise, of course), Diane Johnson and John Murray, Millicent Dillon, Jessica Mitford, literary agent Fred Hill, Richard Poirier, and Joe Kanon. "My party for Billy was the greatest ever, he will never recover—nor I—A total surprise," Alice told Max Steele.[39]

"Is it okay to be well?" Alice asked herself in February 1989. Now she allowed herself to miss the "good Bob . . . wise, funny, even strong." She missed his "dailiness, the dumb jokes. In fact all day I've missed his ordinary (okay) voice (the sane nice Bob) coming in [saying]—'Anybody home?'"

Alice's essay "Frida Kahlo's Passion" appeared, beautifully illustrated, in *Art and Antiques* magazine in January of 1989. For the second winter since breaking with Bob, she would not begin her new year in Zihuatanejo. "Am I 'sick with longing' for Mexico?" she asked herself. As a substitute she was describing the beach resort for a book of travel essays she'd contracted to write. *Mexico: Some Travels and Some Travelers There* would also allow her to re-embrace her love of Mexico by taking trips with various friends to sites in the country that were not Pacific coast beach resorts—*not* the Zihuatanejo she'd known with Bob.

In a profile headlined "The Next Chapter: Alice Adams Embarks on New Travels, New Projects and a Life Lived Alone," Alice's neighbor and new friend Caroline Drewes emphasized beauty: "Her image, as she lifts her glass, is repeated in the mirrored walls of this cloistered room. Reflected there is a tall slender woman, quite wonderful looking with the gray-green eyes and that swing of shiny silver hair. She wears pale corduroy slacks and a loose crimson sweater and the sometimes heavy jewelry that becomes her. She is a woman who knows very well what becomes her. Silk and satin and velvet, among other things." Adams told Drewes she felt ambivalent about living alone. She can "write at odd hours and not feel silly" and "eat corn flakes for supper" but feels anxious about owning a house and traveling alone. "I've become much more independent and competent. I've had to."[40]

Even when travel went wrong, Adams made use of the material. In October 1989, shortly after the opening reception of an exhibit of Peter Linenthal's sculpture at Triangle Gallery in San Francisco, she participated for the second time in the Toronto International Festival of Authors. A reporter who interviewed her there found her "as under-stated as her fiction, with a kind of youthful openness and suggestion of wonderment in her unadorned features that belie her 63 years." Both Peter's exhibit and Alice's return from Canada were disrupted by the Loma Prieta earthquake, which violently shut down San Francisco on October 17. Alice retrieved the day with one of her richest Lila Lewisohn stories, "Earthquake Damage," in which Lila feels extreme anxiety about the safety of her lover, Julian, when she is stranded alone in Toronto after a major Bay Area earthquake. Lila has just attended a conference about contemporary single life that has shaken her; Julian is home in Marin County "harboring" his alcoholic ex-wife, Karen. "Earthquake Damage" is about the human need for "primal reassurance" and "crea-ture comfort." One last delay on the runway as Lila finally heads home leads to this metaphorical denouement: "Glancing from her [airplane] window, quite suddenly Lila sees . . . a large, lean, yellowish dog, whose gallop is purposeful, determined. He will get back to his place, but in the meantime he enjoys the run, his freedom of the forbidden field. His long nose swings up and down, his tail streams backward, a pennant, as Lila . . . begins in a quiet, controlled, and private way to laugh. 'It was just so funny,' she will say to Julian later. 'The final thing, that dog. And he looked so proud! As though instead of getting in our way he had come to our rescue.'"

Peter was less fortunate. In traumatized San Francisco, no one was thinking much about art that season. His brightly painted metal reliefs and mobiles—hand-cut organic forms held together by trailing twists of wire—were beloved by friends and family but drew no reviews and few sales; after the gallery show closed his sculptures lodged in the basement of Alice's house or his stepbrother Lincoln's yard in Berkeley.

To celebrate the end of a decade of success beyond her imagining and, at the same time, painful changes in her personal life, Alice again looked to Mexico. Researching her travel book, she met Fran and Howard Kiernan in Oaxaca City for Thanksgiving in 1989 and then spent a week alone in Cuernavaca. As she planned that trip, she recorded a curious reversal in her notebook. Instead of missing Bob as a travel companion, she was missing the thought of him at home, taking care of things: "Missing Bob on trips: there's no one home (But there is: Peter, cats)."[41]

Traveling by her side or staying home, Bob had been part of Alice's life for twenty-three years. Everything she wrote in the late 1980s, from *Second Chances* and *Caroline's Daughters* to *Mexico: Some Travels and Some Travelers There*, the stories in *After You've Gone*, and other stories and essays never collected, was imbued with the spirit of Bob and her effort to reinvent herself.

The "Book of Bob" (as she referred to it in her notebook) that would tell the story "simply, as it was," took much longer.

CHAPTER TWENTY-EIGHT

Book of Bob

— 1990–1992 —

It was as though craziness were a heavy black rubber ball (so Stella imagined it) tossed back and forth between them; thus if one of them had it, the other did not.

—Alice Adams, *Almost Perfect*

Eager to recoup the large advance paid to Adams, Knopf launched *Caroline's Daughters* with style in March 1991: a high-gloss black cover with striking graphics in yellow, teal, melon, and lavender; a full-page ad in the *New York Times Book Review*; a featured selection of the Literary Guild. The major papers gave the book rave reviews. Christopher Lehmann-Haupt in the *Times* explains how Adams manages so many people and such melodramatic plot events without sacrificing her profound interest in women's lives: "Adams achieves her best effects by juxtaposing the obvious with the subtle," he writes. "As the plot roars around off stage sweeping the reader in its path, the characters go calmly about their business, dreaming their dreams, fearing their fears, reacting to one another." Penelope Rowlands's profile of Alice and her "sexy new book" in *San Francisco Focus* bore the headline "Our Own Colette."[1]

Other novelists also responded with enthusiasm. Lynne Sharon Schwartz noticed that "like a capricious fairy godmother, Alice Adams has endowed each of Caroline's daughters with assets one or more of her sisters might covet: artistic talent, beauty, wealth, a constant husband, a pure heart" and found the novel "a roomy and tantalizing old-fashioned read. I know of no other contemporary novelist who is both so smoothly charming and so ominously intelligent. It's like sherbet laced with absinthe."[2] Carolyn See, reviewing in the *Washington Post*, called the new novel "the best book Alice Adams has ever written," praising its "history and sociology of a great American city" and tacitly reminding readers that a novel by and perhaps for women can also be a thriller: "Caroline has had her adventures the female way." See's closing comment seems prescient of the challenges ahead for the Bay Area: "This San Francisco they live in is still an earthly paradise. Worldly riches have nothing to do with this God-given glory . . . but this particular earthly Eden has been tampered with, eroded, polluted by man-made greed. And here, if I read correctly, Alice Adams gives us her version of sin. It's not adultery . . . It has to do with *greed* . . ."[3]

Caroline's Daughters showed up in the *Post*'s bestseller list after See's review but stayed there just two weeks. With competition from Danielle Steel's latest romance on the sleaze side and from a host of fine new novels by the likes of Jane Smiley, Joyce Carol Oates, and Milan Kundera on the literary side, Adams's novel never touched the *New York Times* bestseller list.

Caroline's Daughters, Adams told one interviewer, is a moralistic book: "I lived through the '80s with enormous disapproval," she said. "I hated the Reagans for starters. He seemed to say that greed is good and conspicuous consumption terrific and rich people are swell."[4]

No doubt it's ironic that Adams's Trollopian novel about greed and envy completed her million-dollar contract with Knopf. When her affairs were disentangled from Bob's, she found herself financially independent for the first time in her life. She was familiar with the lust for clothes, restaurants, and houses that drives her characters. At the same time, entering her midsixties, Alice felt pressure to produce and sell work and provide for her old age. After 1987, many of her stories were going to smaller magazines that paid almost nothing. Being solo, riding buses, swimming at a public pool, and taking long walks made her acutely aware of economic displacements and suffering in the city. This novel's harsh view of yuppies and focus on money and style—"I've often wondered, where would Eighties conversations be without food and travel?" one character asks—is complemented by some characters' earnest wishes to help homeless people and AIDS victims. Her unpublished essay "Street Woman" (sentences of which appeared in *Caroline's Daughters*) imagines several tall, strong homeless women, each of whom "was at one time almost all right, and whose life in a gradual way fell entirely apart." Alice had led a comfortable enough life, always housed and fed, but she saw how a few different events—sexual assault or accidental pregnancy or alcoholism or uninsured illness—might have put her in the street woman's predicament.

Alice's empathy went beyond most people's, Millicent Dillon thought: "Whenever we went out, she spoke with the black woman who sat in front of the Clay Theater and gave her $20. And I know she was thinking, I am that woman, part of me is that woman, and at the same time she knew she could not imagine the life of that woman." Alice joined Mark Childress, Ethan Canin, Amy Tan, Al Young, Bharati Mukherjee, and other writers who performed at benefit dinners for AIDS research and local hospices. She read her story about a gay man coming out to an old friend, "Breakfast at Louie's Café." The three-evening series raised $77,000.[5]

With *Caroline's Daughters*, Alice Adams said goodbye to the glamour represented by Bob McNie, goodbye to carefree European trips (with Bob at the wheel), goodbye to hedonistic winter trips to Zihuatanejo. She would continue to live in San Francisco, of course, and to enjoy her beautiful house, rich friendships, and occasional romances there, but the party seemed to be over. With Peter as a go-between, Bob reclaimed his personal things and some of the ornamental items he'd purchased for 2661 Clay Street. Alice kept the dark downstairs rooms with big mirrors just as Bob had decorated them. She hired Scott Massey, who had just lost his partner to AIDS, to take care of the deck and garden. Alice was usually "schlepping around in a housecoat" when Massey came to work, so he barely recognized her when he "saw her up on Nob Hill one day looking like a million bucks in a red suit, with big ring-type earrings." Massey said that Alice loved blue flowers, "one of the most difficult colors in the flower kingdom—[he] was never able to satisfy her craving for blue flowers." As they got acquainted, she told him that Bob's personality was very dark and that was why they had a black bathroom. There was also a plant, a succulent, on the deck, and Massey remembered, "It was *black*—a dark, flower-type thing on a long stem. As we were rearranging the deck, I would say 'we'll put roses here and Bob's plant here.'" After a couple of those conversations, Alice told Massey not to refer to it as Bob's plant. "It was the only time she ever got cross with me. I never said a word about it again and that plant stayed there, part of the darkness of Bob McNie."

Translating Bob into memory rather than active pain would be the goal of Adams's eighth novel. By mid-1989, as she was still composing *Caroline's Daughters*, a more intimate fiction flickered on her horizon. She outlined three aspects for this story. Her working title was "Book of Bob":

1. For about 20 years I was "madly" (ill-advisedly, mindlessly) in love with a man who does not seem to have loved me very much, & certainly not liked me—but maybe I did not like him so much either—

2. For many years I was involved with a man who drank a lot, as I did too in those days. For years almost every night the 2 of us were fairly drunk, which led us from what had begun as violent love to hideous quarrels—

3. I lived for a long time with a man who went, finally, quite mad—in retrospect the process was clear, he was always a little crazy, surely one of his attractions—but so was I & the effort of, finally, not being mad myself has been enormous—

Everything I have said so far is true—but so complicated!—I want to tell this story simply, as it was.[6]

When Adams agreed to be the guest editor for *The Best American Short Stories 1991*, the series' new editor, Katrina Kenison, gave her the choice of reading stories "blind" or with authors' names attached. Recent editors Mark Helprin and Margaret Atwood had chosen blind; Richard Ford had not and Adams followed his lead. After years of being among the "unchosen" she wished to use any influence she had.[7] The volume she assembled comprised stories by both emerging and established writers, twelve women and eight men. It included her favorites, Joyce Carol Oates and Alice Munro; her *New Yorker* rival John Updike; her former student Harriet Doerr; and two good friends, Millicent Dillon and Leonard Michaels. With refreshing candor, Adams admitted that she found it easy to choose the best stories and that "there should have been more first-rate stories from which to choose." Why had there not been? Because of "the sheer economics of short story writing," she argues. In the 1940s, "writing short stories was a plausible full-time trade" but now slick women's and men's magazines were publishing fewer serious stories than ever before, leaving the *New Yorker* as the only magazine paying well for literary fiction.

In her introduction to *BASS 1991* Adams declares that she is "deeply enamored" of short stories. "The form delights me," she writes before explaining why certain stories win her attention: "On reading these stories, I am seized with a desire to write a story of my own." Pointedly—and it seems gleefully—she disagrees with a statement by Wallace Stegner, her old Stanford nemesis, that short stories are "a young writer's form." She cites her own experience—"I *know* I am writing better stories now than I did at thirty"—and adds that the "greatest living practitioner of the form, V. S. Pritchett," is over ninety.[8]

Adams was using the pulpit of that introduction to state her commitment to short stories at a time when she earned little money from them herself. She was still bristling from a recent tangle with *Redbook*, from which she withdrew her story "Your Doctor Loves You" because she found the editor's questions and requests for cuts disrespectful and irrelevant.[9] The *New Yorker* continued to offer her a first-reading agreement each year, and fiction editor Pat Strachan read Adams's submissions with care but accepted few. Strachan's rejection letters mention such problems as "gaps in chronology" and "almost enough material here for a novel"—the kind of thing that typically distinguishes an Adams story—without the editorial suggestions Bob Hemenway and Frances Kiernan sometimes offered for turning such problems into assets. During the editorship of Gottlieb, only two stories by Adams, "Earthquake Damage" and "The Last Lovely City," graced the magazine's pages. Nonetheless, ICM and Adams doggedly kept the stories in circulation and most were published. *Crosscurrents*, a quarterly edited by Linda Michelson Brown in Southern California, published six, including four from the Lila Lewisohn series.

As commercial fiction languished, Adams learned that beauty and home magazines might pay thousands for light, personal essays by a successful novelist. During the nineties she wrote more than a half-dozen whimsical pieces that offer glimpses into her life. In "A Natural Woman" (for which *Allure* paid $5,000), she ponders the meaning of gray hair. When her dark hair began to gray while she was in her twenties, she experimented with home bleaching and professional "frosting" until a man said her gray hair looked pretty in the sunlight: "I had seen myself as blond, not gray, but on going home to my mirror I saw what he meant: What was not blond, between the streaks, was gray. I had gray hair."

From that day forward, Adams writes, "I stopped having my hair frosted, or streaked, or anything at all—and thus began a much easier, happier, and, I think, more attractive phase of my life." She argues that for some women, going gray signifies "giving up" on sexual attractiveness and leads them to forgo good haircuts, diets, and attractive clothes; for others—like herself—it signifies "growing up" to independence and strength.[10] Marjorie Leet, who first met Alice in 1981, recalled that her hair was then dark gray, "somewhere between pewter and tarnished silver, and not stylishly cut." During the eighties, her hair became "polished silver" worn in a gamine cut that Bob approved. After Bob, her hair remained bright silver, but she let it grow longer. Pictures from the early nineties show an elegant sweep of silver crossing her forehead and grazing her shoulders.[11]

Adams had contracted to write her travel memoir about Mexico for Prentice Hall's *Destinations* book series mainly for the money and the opportunity to travel.* In the end she disliked the project: "It became so Alice-in-Mexico, so embarrassing. But no other way to do it ever appeared," she confided to poet Don Hall. "Doing a book for hire, as it were, is probably a bad idea, don't you think? A stray article can be fun—but not a whole book." Reviews were scarce but the *Chronicle* catches the appeal of *Mexico: Some Travels and Some Travelers There* as a book "full of pleasant, subtly drawn surprises." It is infused with the emotional struggles of Alice's post-Bob years; the chapter on Cuernavaca, where Alice traveled alone, "is darker, the ubiquitous sharp association of place and mood even more accentuated." In a personal letter to Alice, Carolyn See responded to *Mexico*'s emotional tenor, writing that the three

---

* The short-lived series focused on off-the-beaten-path destinations: Mary Lee Settle on Turkey, Herbert Gold on Haiti, M. F. K. Fisher on Dijon, France. Each volume was introduced by Jan Morris, who called Adams's entry "a kind of retrospective journal" that reminds her of the diaries of Virginia Woolf because "the whole adds up to so much more than the sum of the parts."

chapters about Zihuatanejo with Bob "are the most beautiful evocation of lost beautiful Times I've *ever* read . . . the account of those days took me back to Mazatlán in the 60s and how much Time we had (or thought we had) . . . God! Also the later chapters are so vulnerable, so full of affection, so sad but so *controlled*—I was bowled over Alice. I really was."[12]

When Alice gave a copy of *Mexico* to her neighbor Richard Rodriguez, she told the esteemed essayist that she would be embarrassed by any comparison of her book with his recent *Days of Obligation: An Argument with My Mexican Father*. Rodriguez "took it as a kindness more than a compliment" and said, "I had demons in Mexico to contend with—my 'advantage' in writing—that she did not have. I wished at the time that Mexico could be for me, as it was for Alice, a serene and beautiful retreat for the soul. My Mexico has been a nightmare place, but also a loving and relentless mother."

As Alice regained her personal confidence after her break with Bob McNie, she discovered that there were few available men who really interested her. "I seem to be semi-involved in several Relationships," she confided to Alison Lurie. All three men were widowers. "It's very interesting about widowers, I find—or, it's true what everyone says: they are dying to reconnect in some way," she told Lurie.[13]

One widower was Frank Smith Fussner, a historian retired from Reed College whom she'd met forty years earlier when Mark Linenthal taught there. Now Fussner lived on a ranch in the Columbia River gorge. After a visit to his home in Spray, Oregon, Alice reported, "It's absolutely incredibly beautiful up there. Canyon country—small bare hills and meadows . . . all just now in marvelous fall shades. And the drive from Portland to there is really breathtaking . . . BUT: it is four hours from Portland, terribly isolated." A year later she and Fussner drove together along the Oregon coast, which provided the setting for her story "Up the Coast." One more meeting, in Seattle, proved to be the last. Adams's story "Love and Work" sums up that parting with a metaphor about how they handle their luggage: The man waits in the hotel lobby "with a surly, superior expression on his face for someone else to bring his luggage down"; the woman, in contrast, pridefully lugs her own overstuffed carry-on bag, though doing so hurts her shoulder:

"At least I didn't have to wait. And (at least, these days) I am very mobile. Free."[14]

Sidney Hedelman, a physicist from Marin County, asked Alice out weeks after the death of his wife, who had been Alice's friend too. Though Alice didn't date him for long, Hedelman named Alice Adams in his self-published *Collected Works* as "a warm, unaffected companion who laid the foundation for some of my stories."[15]

Alice had already touched on the topic of awkward later-life "dating" in *Second Chances* and she took it up more explicitly now in new short stories called "Old Love Affairs" and "The Wrong Virginia."

The idea for the latter story came from her relationship with another recent widower, Daniel Stewart Simon. Diane Johnson invited both Alice and Simon to dinner but never thought they would get together. Simon, then about seventy, had retired from his medical practice to direct the care of his wife, Alice Nison Simon, who had succumbed to cancer after a four-year ordeal. Simon, who was tall and energetic with a forceful smile and thick white hair, reminded Alice of Bob. In a wry, imaginary dialogue in her notebook, she wrote that she was still in love with Bob, "But now we're calling him Dan."[16]

Dan Simon talked so often to Alice Adams about Alice Simon that, Adams writes, "it is asking too much of me, I think—to be new love and old friend." Dan's late wife was such a presence in his mind that Alice felt as if she were "going out with someone who's married." But Dan's inhibitions about being with a new Alice increased Alice's desire to win his interest for herself—at times she was "turned on by [his] sheer lack of interest." In southern Mexico with Alison Lurie, Alice talked about Dan, waited for his phone calls to their hotels, and counted the hours till she would see him again. When Lurie asked her, "Who did you love the most?" Alice replied, "Bob, of course." That, she wrote in her journal, was "the simple answer to 23 years." Talking freely with Lurie while at breakfast or wandering through the ruins at Palenque was "happiness" for Alice. As she told Lurie about Bob's "warmth, generosity, lack of meanness, sensitivity, wit, intuition," she became settled in her intention to write her "Book of Bob."[17]

In San Francisco, Alice and Dan Simon tried to figure out how to have a relationship with each other. Dan studied pictures of Bob McNie that Alice left out in her house, asking Alice if he was still so handsome. That Alice Simon was dead and Bob was still alive made it hard for Dan to understand why Alice Adams still had strong feelings about Bob.[18] In "The Wrong Virginia," Adams put this thought into the mind of the character based on Simon: "Curiously, Fielding thought, the presence of another woman in his life, instead of stilling old longings for Virginia, seemed rather to fuel them. He dreamed of her often, of his Virginia; more than once he woke in tears." Most likely Alice felt a parallel anomaly: being with Dan made her miss Bob.

A more practical problem arose too. Dan was not used to a woman who worked, and Alice thought he was too demanding of her time. Her need to be home alone to work and her need to travel to give readings or workshops—which she did often in these years—baffled him. In "The Wrong Virginia," the new Virginia details a plan limiting their evenings to two nights a week, a glass of wine at her house and dinner at a restaurant on Fillmore. During these evenings Fielding steers conversations away from what he saw as "feminist obsessions" and "psychologizing" and "her intensely protective feelings toward all gay people" before returning to her house, where "they would or quite possibly would not go to bed together."

Peter Linenthal and Phil Anasovich found Dan Simon "slightly obnoxious with no sense of propriety at all. He did what he wanted to do and said what he wanted to say." Phil recalled, "We gave him a book on Mediterranean cooking—usually when people receive gifts they make some kind of gesture toward acceptance. Not Dan. He said, 'Why did you give me this?'—strange and embarrassing for us. And we thought he liked to cook." Peter considered him "creepy." On a hike in the Berkeley hills, Peter remembered, "Dan told us he liked my mother to be dressed in clothes that reminded him of a little girl. Maybe she was wearing knee socks and shorts? It was just odd that he would share his observation with us, whatever his fantasies were. But he was handsome, like out of an L.L.Bean catalog: thick hair and big white teeth that looked like tombstones. We saw him with my mother for a couple of years, and during that time we and her friends were all kind of trying to tell her, you can do better than this. He had no literary interests, didn't appreciate the work she did."

Nor did she appreciate his work. When she had an anaphylactic reaction accompanied by changes in her EKG after eating undercooked salmon, Simon insisted she undergo a full cardiology evaluation. He also paid attention to her breathing when she slept and referred her to a pulmonologist for sleep apnea because he noticed her snores had become louder and her breathing more rapid.[19]

Another issue that stood between Alice and Dan was his indifference to cats, of which she usually owned three. When she had to put her beloved tall-eared, tailless Ferg down a few days before she traveled with Dan to Kauai, he simply could not respond to her grief, which was enhanced by being in "such an alien place."

Again, a story told the deep emotional truth as Alice felt it. "Islands" (anthologized in the Everyman's Library Pocket Classics Series' *Cat Stories*) also speaks about Adams's love of coincidences, which she liked to see as evidence of "the mysterious ways" of God. The narrator goes to the island of Kauai, a place much loved by the woman named Zoe Pinkerton who gave her the striped, tailless cat she named Pink.* Her late husband also loved the cat, so in missing the cat she also misses him. She travels with Slater, a developer whose business plans will lead to the destruction of the island culture that Zoe cherished. The narrator and Slater encounter several cats in Kauai. Fatally for the relationship, Slater asserts that a cat they encounter, "a black cat with some yellow tortoise markings, a long thin curve of a tail," looks like Pink. "What—Pink? But her tail—Jesus, didn't you even see my cat?"

In her notebook, as she worked on the story, Alice wrote: "Men who don't like cats: bullies . . . Cats won't fawn, or be manipulated. Men who hate the female in themselves hate cats."[20] Bob, of course, had loved cats—another reason she missed the man he had once been.

Alice's relationship with Dan Simon didn't end quickly. She hoped a trip with him to Zihuatanejo in May would improve their relationship and prove to her that she was really over Bob. That trip failed in several ways, most of them included in the story "The Haunted Beach," in which Penelope arrives with expectations that "some special Mexican balm" will "make everything come right, would impart its own magic" to her affair with a new man. But she concludes, "Alas, poor Mexico, you

* Speaking of coincidences, the original beauty for Adams's story "Beautiful Girl," who gave her the Manx cat but no longer spoke to Alice, died of alcohol-related disease in 1991 as Adams was completing "Islands."

can hardly heal yourself, much less me." Afterward she tells her closest friend that she did not think about either her old lover or her new one on this trip. "But I thought a lot about Mexico . . . the trip made me feel a lot better," Penelope continues. "About everything. More free." She adds, with a laugh, "I can't think why."

Freedom was clearly what Alice craved. Dan Simon loomed as a sort of patriarchal presence, resented but also deeply necessary to Alice. "I remember a time I was up there, it was after she and Bob split up," Carolyn See said. "We were having wonderful strong coffee and croissants on the terrace that looked out on the city, and I said, 'You live so beautifully,' and she said, 'Yes, but I'm unbearably lonely.'" But she told an interviewer, "There's a lot to be said for writers living alone." Likewise she found that living in San Francisco suited her because she preferred to be "surrounded by people doing other things," whereas she believed she'd be "claustrophobic and depressed" in New York surrounded by many other writers.[21]

Some version of that happened when the American Academy and Institute of Arts and Letters, an honor society limited to 250 writers, artists, and musicians elected for life, chose Adams for an Arts and Letters Award in literature. In New York for the award ceremony in May 1992, she was seated onstage between Elizabeth Spencer and E. L. Doctorow and near Ralph Ellison. Pleased to receive the $7,500 award, she was also impressed by the company, which included: Alice Munro, Cynthia Ozick, Grace Paley, Jackie Kennedy, John Updike, and Alfred Kazin, the man who'd brought her and Mark Linenthal to the Salzburg Seminar in 1947. The pomp of the occasion combined with simply being in New York City plagued Alice with warring feelings of panic and rage. She simultaneously wished "(1) not to be there, or if there invisible (2) to rise and dominate." What would it mean to rise and dominate? Alison Lurie had been an elected member of the academy for several years; Diane Johnson then held a lucrative five-year Mildred and Harold Strauss Living award. Younger, less productive short-story writers than Alice Adams had also been elected to permanent membership. Sitting on the stage as a guest before the academy's 120 esteemed members, Alice was not sure if she'd rather be out of the fray in San Francisco or elevated to the full membership she deserved in this predominantly white, male club. It was a question she never had to answer.[22]

*　　*　　*

Adams composed her "Book of Bob" during the first two years of the 1990s. She titled it *Almost Perfect*, a phrase that seems to describe the novel's protagonist but (tellingly) is never actually applied to him in the book. When Victoria Wilson returned the edited manuscript in September 1992, she immediately declared, "It is without question your best book. I had a wonderful time reading it. It seems to me a real reach and successfully done at that."[23]

The novel is not the story of Alice and Bob. It is the story of destructive love between two people who borrow many of their characteristics. Like Alice, Stella Blake is a struggling writer at the beginning of the novel and a successful one at the end. Like Bob, Richard Fallon is a handsome, self-made, self-employed visual artist (he does advertising work but is talented at home design too) who came to San Francisco from a humdrum town. Alice tried to make herself unrecognizable in Stella, a small, dowdy, half-Mexican woman with an "overreceptive imagination" whose father, a minor novelist, knew important people in the 1920s, and whose Mexican mother was "a pal of Frida Kahlo's." As a very young woman Stella was the lover of a famous actor. Despite those disguises, the novel's financial and sexual themes are transformed versions of the joys and difficulties that Alice and Bob experienced during twenty-three years together.

Adams condensed her life with Bob into a plot that covers just two years. She drew an X-diagram showing the rising pattern of Stella's life and the downward slide of Richard's and stuck to that plan. She outlined chapters and controlled the flow of information she gave her readers (abandoning her usual loose omniscience) by alternating chapters among the viewpoints of Stella, Richard, and other friends. Stella falls in love with Richard despite her own and her friends' hunch that she is not the type of Nordic blonde he prefers. Richard drinks heavily and Stella tries to keep up. He moves her out of her own apartment while he has it renovated and redecorated—spending more than he can afford. But affection for Richard prods Stella to earn more money and think more seriously about her career. And, as Bob had done for "The Swastika on Our Door" before Alice sold it to the *New Yorker*, Richard suggests a restructuring of the first article Stella sells to a magazine called the *Gotham*.

Richard, whose first wife is mentally ill and often hysterical, is frightened by emotion: "He can hear his mother's voice, and the note that all women sound, sooner or later." He cringes from Stella's calls (answering machines figure in this novel) when her father dies, and then neglects to call back because he's in bed with Eva, a German model he's just met. But when Stella is hospitalized with pneumonia, he returns to take care of her. They live together blissfully for some months, even as his flashes of anger remind Stella "there are so many versions of Richard, and she lives with all those different men." One of these different Richards finds emotional and sexual relief with his young, gay friend Andrew Bacci. After Richard dumps his ex-wife, Marina, in an emergency room lobby and tells a passing doctor, "She's psychotic," he invites Andrew to visit him in the bedroom behind his studio. There HIV-positive Andrew makes love to Richard. Andrew wears a condom. Richard exclaims with pleasure.

Stella does not know about Richard's involvement with Eva or Andrew. Adams keeps Richard from seeming wholly monstrous by using his viewpoint to let readers understand "his insecurities and their symptomatic manifestations in bisexuality and deceit," as one reviewer wrote.[24] But as Richard's secrets multiply, his behavior becomes more erratic. Stella tries to reason away her apprehensions: "Richard is dangerous. That is a sentence sometimes whispered by that same sane (feminist) woman of Stella's imagination. However, since she knows her imagination to be fairly wild and unreliable, and also since she deals in words all day, it is no small wonder that various random sentences enter her mind."

Richard and Stella fight with intensely personal attacks. "Which one of them was crazy? That crude question, sometimes voiced, seemed central to all the conflict between Stella and Richard. 'You're crazy!' one or the other of them would desperately, furiously, drunkenly yell at the other. It was as though craziness were a heavy black rubber ball (so Stella imagined it) tossed back and forth between them; thus if one of them had it, the other did not."

Their discontent comes to a crisis at a performance of *The Marriage of Figaro* in Santa Fe, as did Alice and Bob's in 1982. After that it's downhill for Richard. A design convention in Germany is canceled, thereby killing his plan to see Eva. When his first wife, Marina, is murdered by an abusive lover shortly after she is released from the mental ward,

Richard knows he should cry but remembers "crazy jealous Marina, making scenes at a party." Instead of weeping for Marina he remembers "how he . . . hated her sometimes," while at the same time he thinks, "What a shit I am, what a total shit." After a man Richard had counted on for an important artistic commission jumps off the Golden Gate Bridge—a suicide that Richard anticipated and imagines he might have prevented—he becomes clinically depressed.

On an impulse, Richard gives away five thousand dollars he meant to leave for Stella to a beautiful boy he sees in a diner, imagining this gift from a stranger might make the boy's life better than his own has been. Then he goes to drown himself in a sea cave near Stinson Beach, thinking, "This should all be on video: a man who is reasonably young, and handsome (well, everyone says he is, and women in the street still stare, and some men). This handsome brave man walking with such resolution, walking toward his own anonymous extinction. His death march." The vanity so clearly displayed in that thought prevents Richard from diving to his death.*

For months, Richard avoids everyone, living alone in his beach house. The ending of *Almost Perfect*—pure invention—shows Stella in a relationship with a younger man who admires her while Richard has come out of his seclusion to telephone Andrew. He learns that Andrew is dying of AIDS and agrees to travel with him to Mexico for a "cure" offered at a clinic there.

Being in Mexico City stokes Richard's ego and he enters a new manic phase. He believes his handsomeness is enhanced by being among shorter, darker people. Indeed, he feels so happy, his racist narcissism full-blown, that he imagines he can return to Stella:

He loves Mexicans, all those lovely dark-eyed, dark-haired people, many with brownish skins. How blond he feels, and how tall! How they stare! I would not have liked it in Cologne, he decides; I would have looked too much like everyone else there. Eva and I looked too much alike. No wonder Stella loved me so much, he thinks.

* The sea crater resembles Minn's Cauldron on the coast of England in *The Sea, the Sea* by Iris Murdoch, one of Alice Adams's favorite novelists. A similar cave, the Little River Blowhole, exists in Mendocino County, where Bob McNie and Alice often went for a spring weekend.

He is seeing bits of Stella everywhere. Stella, in all the faces in Mexico.

I was never so beautiful as when I was with Stella, Richard thinks.

In a way that's really too bad.

Maybe someday he'll go back to Stella.

The subplot of Richard's love affair with a gay man surprised many who knew Bob and read *Almost Perfect*. Might vindictiveness against Bob or unacknowledged homophobia have led Adams to invent this aspect of Richard? Diane Johnson, who'd known Bob and Alice for years, thought making Richard actively bisexual in the novel was "so much the quality of the kind of thing Alice would make up after she became angry with Bob," and explained, "Of course, Bob had a feminine side and he was a decorator, but if he'd been French it would be okay for him to know about china and furniture, it's partly cultural. He definitely did not give off gay signals. And he had that period of mental illness that could have affected him." Indeed, most people considered Bob McNie "a flirt but basically straight" (as Margot says about Richard in the novel). As a designer in San Francisco, he associated with many gay men, including his good friend architect Dmitri Vedensky (the one Alice had instructed never again to come to Zihuatanejo when they were there), who teased him about being an interior "desecrator." Nonetheless, McNie worked hard to maintain his reputation as the "only" straight designer in San Francisco, and family, clients, and colleagues believed him.

Frances Kiernan was shocked "to learn how dark that relationship had been." She said that she and Victoria Wilson, both experienced editors, "knew that most fiction is not made up out of whole cloth. Alice had at times touched on her life with Bob in a fairly disguised fashion, but it hadn't occurred to us that some of the darkness there might actually be true. Fact is, I didn't want to believe it." Peter Linenthal was also shocked when he read *Almost Perfect*, both by the idea that Bob was bisexual and by his mother's boldness in writing about the topic. He had difficulty believing that his mother had known Bob was bisexual. "I don't believe she would have tolerated sharing a lover," he said. "She was just not that kind of person. She was too focused, too devoted—not someone I could imagine taking disloyalty lightly."

Nonetheless, we can be fairly certain that Alice did not invent the bisexual theme. After he and Alice separated, Bob lived in the Webster

Street apartment, which he'd turned into a "madman's lair packed to the ceiling with pack-ratted stuff." He'd painted the walls of the bedroom, bathroom, and kitchen gloss black, and glued dominoes on the door frames. Tiny pathways connected the rooms. He never went outside during the daytime. When, one day in the early 1990s, he felt alive again, he walked into a clothing store on Grant and told the owner, Marcus Livingston, "I've been in a catatonic depression for five years and you are the first person that I've talked to since I began coming out of that." "He was so fired up," Livingston recalled, "that you couldn't send him away. Forceful. Just rocking the whole time, like he had saved it up! Putting it all out there as fast and enthusiastically as he possibly could." They began having lunch about once a week until Livingston tired of Bob's performance and ended the friendship.

In his new manic state, Bob hoped to win Alice back. He wrote her letters and sent her one hundred yellow roses. She rejected these overtures—"kindly," one friend said. In about 1992 he began seeing the artist Elaine Badgley Arnoux. "I was in love with Bob for about fifteen minutes," she said later. But "at the beginning it was very wonderful to fall in love and he *knew how to do that*. He said to me, 'I thank God when I wake up in the morning that I found you.' That was in the blissful days of the first six months." Under the spell of that ripe intimacy, Bob confided in Elaine about his sexual history. "He didn't tell me their names, but he told me there were three or four girlfriends who came to his studio bedroom while he was with Alice and then he said he had these affairs with men." The possibility that Bob was bisexual was further confirmed to Elaine by his need to arouse himself with "a pretty men's book OR a women's lesbian book, but not a [heterosexual] couple book," when they went to bed together. "That's the only way he could perform. But that was how we managed to have some sexual interplay."

Almost Perfect was published in June 1993, when Bob had come out of his depression and was already with Elaine. Bob's daughter, Morissa, wrote about it to her best friend, therapist Deborah Sparks: "Elaine said she couldn't stomach it, but father is reading it straight through and seeing himself in a true way through Alice's partial distortion."[25]

In October 1993, Elaine Badgley Arnoux exhibited one of the most celebrated projects at the opening of San Francisco's new Center for the Arts at Yerba Buena Gardens. She installed a train of twenty shopping carts seen as covered wagons, which she decorated with assistance from homeless artists.[26] Elaine was unable to enjoy the success of her daunting project because Bob was jealous of the attention she received. A year later, while she and Bob were in Taos, New Mexico, Elaine noticed that Bob seemed distracted and frequently went off to make private phone calls. Then she discovered a letter he was composing and heard phone messages that showed he was sexually interested in a man who lived in his apartment building. She confronted him, he reacted violently and said the letter was a fantasy, and she broke with him. After that, she did read *Almost Perfect*; then, she said, "I knew it wasn't a fantasy." Even though Elaine felt that *Almost Perfect* confirmed her fears, she thought it was too harsh: "She didn't need to dice him up into so many little pieces toward the end."

Still, novels are fiction, memories are flawed, and sexual orientation is a subject beset by ambiguity. Despite society's recent openness about it (and oddly oxymoronic need to categorize it), an individual's needs and ways of satisfying them vary over time. The explosion of sexual freedoms in the late 1960s and 1970s prompted a lot of people to explore homosexuality; fear of AIDS in the 1980s caused the same people to become more conventional again. Although we can be fairly certain that Bob displayed an interest in homosexuality, we have only hearsay evidence that he was actively involved with any man. Besides what Bob confided to Elaine Badgley Arnoux, we have just this recollection from Sandy Boucher, in whom Alice sometimes confided things that she did not tell people in her social group: "After she was no longer with Bob, Alice told me he was having affairs with men the whole time he was with her." If that is correctly remembered, Alice had reason to worry about her exposure to HIV.

When Robert McNie died of cardiovascular problems in 2005, he was living with Linda Hogan, a woman he'd already been involved with during his last decade with Alice. Among Bob's things in her basement, his son and daughter found boxes of gay pornography and books by psychiatrists about homosexuality. "It was sad because they were not books that gave a healthy picture at all," Morissa McNie said. "These books emphasized deviance. It just infuriated me so much to know that my father never revealed his orientation, never let homosexuality be an open aspect of his life." At that time, Morissa called Deborah Sparks, and through their conversation they "both saw that that was the missing piece about Bob, which helped Morissa understand him better, at last."[27]

But that understanding came too late for the several women—Deen, Alice, Elaine—and children whose lives had been damaged by Bob's lack of self-knowledge, deceptions, and alcohol abuse.

When Morissa and Robbie found Bob's gay pornography, Peter Linenthal felt shocked again. "We talked about it," his friend Stephen Brown recalled, "and I said to him, 'Remember ALMOST PERFECT??!! And you wonder if she knew what was going on? Wake up!'"

Whatever part Alice played in suppressing knowledge of Bob's bisexuality, because of pride, distaste, kindness, passivity, or embarrassment, she probably found it cathartic to take on the subject in her structurally "almost perfect" novel. Those inclined to wonder what "really happened" must live with some ambiguity.

To the extent that *Almost Perfect* was cathartic for Alice, it also exhausted her. The summer she sent the manuscript to Wilson, while she was trying to bring herself to break up with Dan Simon and start a new novel that would be about Chapel Hill, Alice was troubled by headaches, general malaise, and redness on her face that she attributed to a respiratory infection or allergies. Despite giving up swimming for exercise, she lost weight. An MRI of her head showed that her sinuses were full of fluid, which neither antibiotics nor steroids relieved. On a visit to writer Mary Gaitskill in Marin County, she became "unexpectedly exhausted" after a short walk. She blamed allergies. In July, she visited the Kiernans in Sag Harbor, New York, where she luxuriated in the comfort and pleasantness of the house and told Trent Duffy that the fresh pesto sauce he made was the best she'd ever had. She spent her days floating in the pool and taking naps, explaining that she'd been troubled by migraines.

Just before her sixty-sixth birthday in 1992 Alice visited with Carolyn See in Santa Monica. They had dinner with Beverly Lowry, Mary Ross Taylor, and a newer friend, screenwriter Judith Rascoe, at a Mexican restaurant called La Serenata. "I was so enthralled," See recalled. "I thought, this is it, this is the literary life!" This group of talented, successful women was celebrating Lowry's book *Crossed Over*, just that morning on the cover of the *Los Angeles Times Book Review*, drinking and telling outrageous stories. One of Lowry's stories, See said, "was about taking the kids to nursery school and seeing the housewives dropping off their kids all perfectly dressed and made-up—because they weren't going home but out to a tryst. And Alice told about the doctor she was dating who was so protective of her that she found it irritating."

All through that evening of crazy stories and laughing and eating and drinking, Alice was pinching the bridge of her nose and saying, "I'm sorry, I have such a terrible headache."

During these late-summer weeks, Alice often called Judith Adams and her husband, who was dying of esophageal cancer. On Labor Day, the day after Tim died, Judith called to thank Alice for being a true friend. "I can't begin to tell you how much Tim loved your phone calls . . . your courtesy and manners are astounding and unusual; they make a difference in our crazy, chaotic world," she added in a following letter. "I'm strong," Judith told Alice on the phone. "I took care of him." For their generation, which had lived through a deep depression and a world war, physical and emotional strength were great virtues.

Alice resisted admitting that she was sick. Her doctor blamed allergies. She had already told Dan Simon that she wanted to break up with him, but she said okay when he called one morning offering to bring soup. "It would take more character than I have [to say no]," she wrote in her notebook.[28] She thought Dan Simon was the cause of her malaise and continued to plan trips without him. In Austin, Texas, she stayed in "the B and B from hell—terminal English-inn cute" (it became the setting for her story "A Shadow on the Brain") and dined with Tom Staley, the director of the Harry Ransom Center, who offered to acquire her papers for the center's collections. While there she had several nosebleeds. Then she went to the Grand Tetons in Wyoming with her artist friends Theophilus (Bill) Brown and Paul Wohner.

"We'd be at her house or out to dinner and a little bit of blood would start coming out of her nose," Peter remembered. "She'd notice or I'd mention it, and she'd take a hankie and start dabbing, and she'd say, 'What a drag' or 'What a pain in the ass.' It seemed like it was scaring me more than her."

By then her internist, Dr. Jerome Botkin, had referred her to an ear, nose, and throat specialist, Dr. Mark Singer. He scheduled her for an endoscopic surgery to remove polyps in her sinuses. As Alice awoke from anesthesia on the afternoon of September 22, 1992, she asked her doctors what they had found.

Dr. Botkin said, "We didn't like what we found up there." He explained that there was a tumor in her sinus. It was probably malignant.[29]

"What are my chances?" she asked.

"About 25%," Dr. Singer answered.

"You mean 75% die?" Alice asked.

"You could put it like that."

Recording that conversation in her notebook, Alice wrote that she felt "a curious calm." She remembered thinking she had "about three years to live, plenty of money for that. Sell my house, sell everything— all vague—"[30]

Peter brought his mother home from the hospital.

When Dan Simon came to visit, she said, "Well, now you have another Alice with cancer." And so, Simon reentered her life, ready to use his medical experience to save Alice Adams from the fate that had snatched Alice Simon away from him.

CHAPTER TWENTY-NINE

Sick

— 1992–1995 —

"But I still don't see why everyone has to wait so long. Everywhere."
"Everyone is busy."
"Yes, but the patients are sick."
"Oh, sick," he muttered, as though "sick" were nothing to
"busy."

—Alice Adams, *Medicine Men*

Alice had tried to break up with Dan Simon before she heard her cancer diagnosis. When she told him about it, he stepped up as the medical advisor she needed to guide her through the delicate process of determining the best treatment. Simon believed that Alice's internist had mishandled her case by treating her for sinusitis while the tumor in her nasal cavity and sinuses was threatening her optic nerve and the base of her brain.[1] Dr. Mark Singer, who discovered the tumor, has pointed out that its location and rapidly growing type made it extremely difficult to diagnose.[2]

In any event Simon just took over and brought Alice to Stanford Medical Center, where he had good connections because his wife had been treated there for four years with non-Hodgkin's lymphoma. "Alice may not return to the care of her internist, Dr. Botkin, so why don't you make me the referring doctor, so all letters and reports come to me," he wrote to one of his Stanford contacts. Simon had not been practicing medicine for several years, so his letterhead carried his home address.

Alice underwent surgery at Stanford University Hospital on October 19, 1992. To accomplish the removal of the large squamous-cell carcinoma that involved her entire nasal cavity as well as her maxillary and sphenoid sinuses, her ethmoid cavity, nasopharynx, her posterior septum, and the nasal surface of the soft palate, otolaryngologist Willard Fee Jr. and neurosurgeon Lawrence Shuer and their colleagues performed a "degloving" of her face. They used multiple incisions to move her face aside and remove the extensive tumor. An incision was also made from inside her palate.

Happily for Alice, she could not see all the work that had taken place in the interior spaces of her head and she probably never read the operation report. On the first night she had double vision and thought there were two clocks on the wall and two other patients in the room with her, one old, one young, both speaking Spanish. Hoping to sleep, she used sign language to get someone to turn off a loud TV, but soon it went on again.[3]

The removed specimens analyzed at the Stanford pathology lab were eight fragmented parts measuring as large as seven centimeters. Dr. Fee estimated that the tumor had been "two golf-ball sized." The medical team saw that the tumor had not invaded the dura mater covering the brain and found no evidence of metastasis to lymph nodes or other sites; nonetheless, they planned to recommend further treatment for microscopic disease that might have spread to Alice's neck.

Swollen and bandaged, Alice's face looked "very different, Asian in a way," to Peter when he saw her after the surgery. She was unable to speak because of tubes in her throat and her nose, and the front part of her hair was shaved. Beneath the bandages her face was covered with stapled incisions, but Peter "could see *her* in her eyes." He brought a big red cardboard heart he'd painted and told his mother how relieved he was that she was okay, and she replied that she never expected to die from this surgery. She saved the heart for the rest of her life.

Alice asked Sandra Russell, the painter from England who had catered parties for her, to visit her in the hospital: "We had become friends—she used to tell me I should charge more and be more serious about painting," Russell recalled. "She thought I would tell the truth about how she looked. And the truth was, she looked awful, all bruised. It wasn't like her. She was such a strong woman. She was scared to look in the mirror and scared that people would be shocked when they visited her. I did tell her that she just looked a little bruised and puffy—but that she looked better than some people I'd seen after a face lift! I know that I felt that she could never look ugly—she was a beautiful person inside and out."

Dan Simon became more obsessively involved in Alice's life than ever. He discussed her case with the other doctors and the nurses as they made rounds and took pride in her recovery. Adams reports one of these conversations in her novel *Medicine Men*, published in 1997. Her main character, Molly Bonner, feels dehumanized as a female patient with an all-male medical team. Her surgeon and his acolytes on their rounds "always seemed extremely happy to see her . . . because she was regarded as a triumph, living proof of their consummate skill. In a self-congratulatory way they spoke among themselves: 'Beautiful nose, no scars. You can barely see that line across her forehead. Her hair growing back already. Great job!'"

Alice came home to "a houseful of flowers and presents—and confusion." Peter visited. Dan was there almost all the time. Bob called or visited. A week later, back at Stanford, Alice was fitted with a face mask to protect her eyes and mouth while her nasal area and neck were irradiated. More than ever, she hated the indignity and reduction of being a patient. Why, she asked Dan Simon, did the patients have to spend so much time in waiting rooms? An exchange between Molly and Dr. Dave Jacobs in *Medicine Men* catches Alice's frustration:

"But I still don't see why everyone has to wait so long. Everywhere."
"Everyone is busy."
"Yes, but the patients are sick."
"Oh, sick," he muttered, as though "sick" were nothing to "busy."

Along with six weeks of radiation therapy at Stanford, Alice's oncologist started her on test doses of chemotherapy. She developed severe mouth ulcerations as a side effect of bleomycin chemotherapy, so that was discontinued and another adjuvant treatment was proposed. Dan Simon accompanied Alice to Loma Linda University Medical Center in Southern California, where she received proton-beam radiation. While there she "developed severe mucositis (inflammation of the digestive tract) which necessitated insertion of a feeding tube," followed by severe nausea that was alleviated by a prescription.[4]

As treatments continued Alice's misery and irritability increased to the point that she noticed herself thinking about people in the medical profession by categories—all of which seemed negative to her. She listed them in her notebook as "ex-football, Chinks, Irish, Black Israeli"; a woman who was slow to bring her pain medication was "a slow Mexican nurse who asks if she can watch TV here, at midnight." But her other persona, the writer, asked herself on the same page: "Why do I make so much of her being Mexican?—what is this new racism?"[5]

Along with her own outrage at what had happened to her, Alice had to cope with the invaluable help she was receiving from Simon. As Peter summarized, "That was the problem. Dan was a drag as a person but knew a lot about cancer." One reason that Simon was difficult, Alice now realized, was his "rage at the world for not being Alice."[6] His grief for the wife he had been unable to save was channeled into aggressive control of Alice Adams's medical treatment. Her feelings about her condition, the sort of anger and frustration that most cancer patients experience, infuriated him and he didn't hesitate to tell her so. Nor did Dan hesitate to let Alice know that his late wife had been a "perfect patient-wife," more passive and trusting than Alice Adams.[7]

In late January, home from Loma Linda, Alice sat in the sunshine at her house and felt "some control."[8] She thought about how to limit her interaction with Dan and began a short story to be called "Humpty Dumpty"—about a woman whose head had been taken apart and (she hoped) put together again.[9] At a follow-up visit to Stanford in mid-February, the oncologists told Alice that her treatments were finished. There would be no further chemotherapy. Immediately following that appointment, she told Dan Simon that they were finished as a couple.[10] She saw him just once more in her life, when he surprised her at a reading three years later. He'd attended, apparently, not out of literary or romantic interest but rather to assess her condition. The next day he wrote to Dr. Fee at Stanford: "You did a wonderful job on her . . . I believe she is cured."[11]

When her scars healed, Alice's face still looked very different. The bridge of her nose had collapsed, "so her nose looked smaller, as if she'd had a nose job and it had been overdone," Peter said. For months after her radiation treatments ended, she struggled to eat. She'd lost her senses of taste and smell. She suffered from lack of saliva and nausea and fatigue. THC pills relieved the nausea but she weighed just 122 pounds at her five-month checkup in June.

After a June 1993 visit to Stanford, Alice transferred back to her San Francisco internist, Dr. Jerome Botkin. When she was ready to start going out in public again, she asked a handsome man, her friend Robert

Flynn Johnson, how her face looked. "If they knew you before, they'd look closely," he answered, "but if they didn't know you, they would just assume that's who you are." Johnson later said, "It wasn't that she was vain. I think she felt that she was *maimed*. I had to reassure her that she was way overstating her situation." Film critic David Thomson thought that Alice's essential beauty—her grace—increased after the surgery. "She never lost that sort of glamour—it was her inner spirit."

Alice rarely spoke of the changes in her appearance. In part her reticence can be attributed to her Southern manners or her disinclination to hear about illnesses. Once when Frances Gendlin mentioned that she was feeling better after a bout of digestive difficulties, Alice replied, "And you've been so good about not talking about them." But Millicent Dillon, the biographer of Jane and Paul Bowles who became closer to Alice after her surgery, was astonished and impressed by Alice's acceptance of the damage to her face: "She was so beautiful and then the cancer and the surgery altered her face and marred her beauty. Yet she made no attempt to have reconstructive surgery. I don't think she was afraid of surgery. It was something else. She had this sense of herself—this presence, this elegant demeanor—that was unbroken." Still, Alice probably felt the insult when her longtime hairdresser on Sacramento Street suddenly became too busy to schedule her. The changes in Alice's face disturbed her, the hairdresser confided to another client. Alice found someone new to style her bangs to cover the scar on her forehead.[12]

"To say she wasn't a complainer is to put it mildly," Peter Linenthal said. "Imagine what it was for a person who loved flowers and perfume and food to lose the ability to taste and smell! All she would say about it was that it made the texture of food more important to her. As if that terrible loss were a gift she'd received. She especially savored oysters." Peter wondered if somehow his mother's fear of her own mother's criticism had conditioned her resilience. "Somehow she spared everybody her suffering. And she said she never forgot anything that happened to her; hard for me to imagine, but it gave her a lot of material."

After her medical ordeals, Alice found solace in working on a novel set in Chapel Hill. "I started writing *A Southern Exposure* at a time when I wasn't feeling too great and wanted to get somewhere else," she told the journalist Joan Smith.[13] Alice's cancer was a very close brush with mortality; even though she'd survived it, she needed to use whatever wisdom she'd acquired to look at her own past with a longer lens. When Peter began doing photographs and illustrations for children's books, Alice conceived a story about a cat—her Maine coon named Sam—that she hoped they could write and illustrate together. Sam sat in a window and wished he could be outside with the birds. "It was poignant," Peter said, "and it reflected her loneliness, but it didn't work as a children's story." Then she traveled to Miami ("An eccentric destination," she said, "but I've always wanted to see it—and I need some warmth") with Bill Brown, Fran and Howard Kiernan, Victoria Wilson, and Regina Tierney—they stayed at the historic Biltmore, and Alice added on a visit to Alison Lurie in Key West.

Completed before her cancer diagnosis, Adams's "Book of Bob," titled *Almost Perfect*, came out in the summer of 1993. She dedicated the book to friends she'd first met through Bob, G. G. (Geraldine) and Larry Green, and to her own dear friend Edwina Evers Leggett and her new husband, Jack Leggett, a writer and retired director of the Iowa Writers' Workshop, all people who'd stood by her during the rupture with Bob. Carol Devine Carson's stark glossy jacket and Joyce Ravid's warm, sexy portrait of pre-surgery Alice Adams introduced a book that the *Wall Street Journal* called "stylish, brittle, and engrossing." That paper's reviewer, Merle Rubin, praised the author for telling the story of a "normally sensible woman who falls for a deeply rotten man" with "intriguing suspense without resorting to lurid or cheap melodrama."

Always-perceptive Ella Leffland wrote that *Almost Perfect* was Adams's "most powerful novel," especially for its "haunting portrait" of Richard, "that essentially desolate being, awful and yet moving." Certainly Leffland knew whereof she spoke, having published her novel *The Knight, Death and the Devil*, a study of Nazi Hermann Göring, whose monstrous egotism and complexity were acted out on a larger scale than poor Richard's. Out of deference to her health, or perhaps to Bob McNie, Alice did little touring to promote *Almost Perfect*.

Quite the opposite. Alice spent part of July at a remote cabin in the Bitterroot Mountains of Montana with Derek Choate Parmenter, a New Englander by birth, recently divorced, whom she'd first met when he was a student at UNC fifty years earlier. Parmenter had come south for college during the Depression. Judith Clark and Alice met him at beer parties at St. Anthony Hall, the Delta Psi house. At that time, Parmenter said, he knew Judith "very well." More recently Alice and Bob had known him socially through his former wife, Marian Parmenter, the cofounder with Sally Lilienthal of the SFMOMA Artists Gallery, a rental gallery that supports emerging artists. Now Parmenter was retired from his business as a stockbroker with E. F. Hutton in San Francisco. He phoned Alice when he heard she was no longer with Bob and was recovering from cancer surgery.

That was in April 1993. Alice quickly recognized her vulnerability to a new man, a new romance: "Derek frenzy: a whiff, not much more, of the old addictive substance—and I'm off, really off. It's not a fun game, since I play to lose—Dan never fit the pattern—too present, too reliable."[14] Immediately their relationship was complicated. "I've known Derek Parmenter since I was fifteen," Judith said. "And I don't think Derek was particularly good at intimacy. It's not an important part of his life and it was an important part of Alice's life." In addition to native reserve, Derek, then seventy, struggled with health issues and depression. Dan had been out her life for only two months, so she found it "hard . . . going from [Dan's] continuous presence to zero." The problem, of course, was with Alice's expectations. She recognized her frustration in a haiku: "All my anxious amorous fantasies / flew like birds / to land on his uncertain shoulders."

When they first dated, Alice was debilitated by surgery and radiation treatments and not yet permitted to swim. She wanted to get stronger and Derek suggested that they go hiking together. "She was very weak. It took a year or two for her to recover," Parmenter said, "but then she became a strong hiker. She had the ideal figure." They settled into a pattern of spending part of their weekends together: "I did the planning, packed a lunch, and chose the route from a guidebook of Marin County. She was very pleased when we were walking uphill that she did so well. What I enjoyed most about her was her brain. She was very sharp. Good sense of humor and great style. Though we didn't speak about it, we probably were in love."

Whether in love or simply loving, Derek became an essential part of Alice's life. Still, Alice struggled with her "obsession"—her need for the flurry of romance that Derek did not provide. Alone with him in

Montana, she made notes about a character (herself) who studied her man's "moods, needs, whims, neuroses—vulnerabilities—as she did the sky, for the weather—and much more successfully: being intelligent & sensitive, of course she did well, better than most, only at times she wondered: is this—is *he* worth such a major effort?"[15] As Alice resigned herself to Derek's emotional quietude, she came to value him "as a true gentleman" and "loyal friend," according to Frances Kiernan.

Derek Parmenter became her escort for public occasions as well as smaller gatherings. "She had a lot of brainy pals, and from my standpoint it was fun. A well-known writer would come to town and she and the writer would have dinner and I was able to tag along. I remember having dinner with Cynthia Ozick once." Some friends wondered why Alice was with Derek. Italian-food writer Carol Field found him so "terminally boring" that she dreaded being seated with him at dinner, but her husband, architect John Field, speculated that Derek's undemanding personality might have been a relief to Alice after Bob's: "That's a phenomenon you see often, from complicated to simple, especially if the woman is ambitious." Edwina Leggett noticed Derek's anxiety at parties: "He would come with almost a list of things in his mind that he could talk about. He would fire off questions while he sat there crunching up his napkin." He was more comfortable in one-to-one conversations, Frances Kiernan thought. Once when Alice was sick, Kiernan rode with Derek to Napa County for dinner with Jack and Edwina Leggett. She said, "He was excellent company throughout. A quiet man but a surprisingly bright man. And kind."

On another visit to the Leggetts, a black dog, predominantly Lab, wandered onto the deck and attached himself to Alice, who sneaked him slices of meat she'd been served. "He was a joyful dog who belonged to the lady next door, who wanted to get rid of him," Derek recalled. "So I went up to look at him and try him out, and, you know, you never just try out a dog, you have the dog. So that was Pepper. I had him about five years." Adams wrote a story of that episode titled "A Very Nice Dog." She changed most of the human details (Napa became Sausalito, the Leggetts a gay couple rather like Billy Abrahams and Peter Stansky) but celebrated her role in finding a new home for "an aging Lab, slightly grizzled around the jaw," with "beautiful dark-brown–purple velvet eyes."

"A Very Nice Dog" gives insight into Alice's shyness. Its plot is built upon its first-person narrator's desire to get acquainted with an older

man named Justin that she encounters while walking in her neighborhood: "The appeal was not sexy; he looked to be at least ten years older
than I am, and I am too old to be turned on by older men." In a brief
friendly exchange that the narrator wants to repeat, the man confides
to her that he'd like to get a dog. She dreams up the more elaborate
plan of arranging for Justin to rescue a black dog she saw at a friend's
house. She manipulates the situation so successfully that Justin adopts
the dog without ever knowing that it was all the narrator's idea. Here
the story might end—but does not. The narrator wants credit for her
matchmaking: "The only missing element for me, and I had to admit
this to myself, was my own role . . . Better to be thought a little indis-
creet than to remain almost invisible." Thus the narrator confesses to
vulnerability and egoism of a sort considered unseemly for a woman
of a certain age. It's one of the shocking charms of Adams's later fiction
that she wrote boldly about the needs of older women for sexual companionship and recognition.

A year after her surgery, Alice made an ambitious trip east. In "old &
familiar & dirty & very beautiful" Boston she had a good visit with
her former student Dennis McFarland; his wife, Michelle Blake; and
their kids, who were her godchildren. When Dennis and Michelle had
learned their son would be born without a left hand, Alice told them:
"This is what I think (a quite clear vision)—you will have an absolutely
extraordinary, amazing child. Person."[16] In New York City, Alice walked
miles, admired the precision and skill of fifteenth-century watercolors at
the Frick Collection, spent time with Fran and Howard Kiernan, dined
with Amanda Urban, and shopped for a gift for Derek (who favored
preppy clothes), and found herself feeling like "a fake rich person."
After a few days of that she boarded a train bound for North Carolina,
grateful to hear black voices and see leaves and swamps. Derek joined
her for a stopover in Washington, DC, where they stayed with their
mutual friend Judith Adams. Still suffering fatigue from her cancer, Alice
was critical of everyone: Derek was more affectionate to Judith than to
herself, and Judith seemed too loud and opinionated.[17]
    Alice continued alone to North Carolina, where she found relief in
"laughing happy old Max" (now on friendly terms with Diana, his former wife) and long walks in "the deep old woods." Of course, nothing's

perfect. Max took Alice to see his neighbor, ninety-two-year-old Norma Berryhill, who had known Alice's parents. A resulting story, "The Visit," tells how the old lady (now Miss Dabney) flattered Grace, a famous actress who had grown up in town and returned for a visit: "Miss Dabney leaned forward. 'You know, we've always been so proud of you in this town. Just proud as proud.'" Grace is inordinately pleased by this remark. But then Miss Dabney ruins Grace's triumph by saying that the "proudest" moment was when Grace, as an "adorable little two- or three-year-old" crawled under the dining table and bit her mother right on the ankle.*

"The Visit" concludes with Grace's defiance of the rule that "Southern ladies [do] not contradict other ladies." As Miss Dabney tediously recounts the ankle incident, Grace rejoins: "I guess up to now no one ever told me so as not to make me feel small and bad. I guess they knew I'd have to get very old and really mean before I'd think that was funny." The last line of the story comes from Miles, the character based on Max Steele: "As Miles thinks, Ah, that's my girl!"

That apparently simple anecdote, which Mary Gordon selected for the fiction issue she edited for *Ploughshares* and Adams included in her collection *The Last Lovely City*, becomes an artistic short story because it encapsulates Adams's lifelong struggle to distinguish nostalgia from truth in her memories of her parents' unhappy marriage and the culture of her upbringing. Adams neatly puts down old Chapel Hill society, allies herself with her mother, and maintains her bond with Max, the former lover and dear friend who mediates between herself and Chapel Hill. In her introduction to the *Ploughshares* volume, Gordon writes, "The short story is like a wagon wheel: the spokes must be connected to the hub, or graceful movement is impossible." In Adams's Chapel Hill stories, the hub is always a lonely little girl who feels she was misplaced in the world but works diligently to redeem herself.

*   *   *

* Alice told a reporter a different version of the episode: Alice had not bitten anyone, and the woman she supposedly bit was not Agatha, just a woman no one liked. Of her visit with Mrs. Berryhill, Alice said her "feelings were quite hurt, I guess my anticipation had been aroused, that finally I am thought to be a nice person here." Afterward, Alice asked Max, "Does she even know that I write?" He replied, "Yes, but she would rather not think about that." To the reporter, Adams added, "I cannot tell you what a Southern story that is." (Joan Smith, "Ask Alice," *San Francisco Chronicle*, October 22, 1995.)

Despite her cancer fatigue, by the summer of 1994 Adams had finished the manuscript of her fourteenth book and ninth novel, *A Southern Exposure*. She'd been thinking about this book for almost four years, since she wrote, "Old Chapel Hill novel? All those people . . . like Breughel," in her notebook in mid-1990. She wrote it quickly. This revisioning of her parents' generation is set just before World War II. Much of the action in her fictional "Pinehill" revolves around the elusive figure of poet Russell Byrd, who is plainly based on Paul Green, a luminary figure in the Carolina Playmakers and winner of the Pulitzer Prize for Drama in 1927. Alice's parents knew Green and his wife; Green's sister Caro Mae was married to the writer Phillips Russell, from whom Alice learned her ABDCE plot pattern. Agatha Boyd Adams wrote a brief biography called *Paul Green of Chapel Hill*. In it she notes that in Green's work "details of landscape and folkways are sharply etched"—citing "hog-killings" as one example. Oddly enough, in *A Southern Exposure* Russell Byrd's killing of a pig in a car accident causes "an explosion of foulness, a ghastly smell. Fecal—worse than fecal"—that becomes a haunting image for Byrd, who is said to be writing a verse drama about it. The novel's Jimmy Hightower, who has moved to North Carolina from Oklahoma in hopes of apprenticing himself to Russell Byrd, is modeled on novelist Noel Houston, who similarly came to Chapel Hill to seek out Paul Green.* Then there's a psychiatrist, Clyde Drake, who irresponsibly socializes with his patients and experiments with shock therapy: clearly a retread of Alice's father's unscrupulous psychiatrist Malcolm Kemp.

While *A Southern Exposure* captures "this lovely place and golden time, just before things got so damn serious forever,"[18] as novelist Lee Smith wrote in a review for the *New York Times*, it is most interested in how a woman named Cynthia Baird becomes modern. Cynthia is a Northerner—she comes to Pinehill from Connecticut (as did Judith Clark's parents) because she and her husband can live more cheaply in the South; Cynthia also has a secret wish to know the famous Russell Byrd. By telling the story of the Bairds' movement into Pinehill society, Adams exposes the intricate rules, scandals, racism, sexism, secrets, hatreds, and loves in a small-town society stranded between

---

* Houston authored the bestselling novel *The Great Promise*, which Alice read and disliked when she was in New York in 1946.

the Depression and the coming war. As male characters pursue their ambitions and Southern women mostly cleave to their men, Cynthia evolves to meet her circumstances and opportunities. Beginning as a fashionable social climber whose "golden money seemed an endless stream" before the 1929 crash, she finishes a college degree and aspires to go to law school and work for civil rights when the war is over.

Moving her setting to the South allowed Adams to study women's lives from a new angle. As Joan Smith noted in a profile, Adams had been writing about California life so well and for so long that she'd been, in the words of Billy Abrahams, "mimicked to death" by other writers. "It seems to me that Southern women have the problems that all women have of being brought up to be subservient and amused, rather than amusing, only it's worse in the South," Adams told Lee Smith. Writing the book caused her to realize that her mother had been critical of her because she "overrated" her daughter's potential.[19] Alice also admitted that she wrote for revenge, and this novel of manners allowed space for that in her analysis of Chapel Hill's hypocritically genteel racism and narrowness.[20] Perhaps surviving a deadly illness gave Alice courage to challenge the hegemony of Chapel Hill society that she'd once run away from but hadn't escaped in her mind.

Because *A Southern Exposure* was quite different from her previous novels, her agent, Amanda Urban, to whom it was dedicated, offered it to at least one publisher in addition to Knopf in hopes of generating an auction. As Alice waited two months for responses, she worried and felt disloyal to Victoria Wilson. But Urban, whom Alice considered a "realist," reminded her that this was about getting paid for her work. She asked Alice if she would accept as little as $200,000. She would.[21] In the end Nan Talese of Doubleday declined *A Southern Exposure*, writing that "it is certainly wonderful Alice Adams and no reader will be disappointed, but in this time of high-profile marketing, one needs a 'hook' to break beyond the recognition an author has previously enjoyed." Neither Talese nor Doubleday president Stephen Rubin could find the necessary hook.[22] Wilson remained steadfast, and Alice accepted a $125,000 advance from Knopf.[23] "Dark day—hangover? (2 wine, & Halcion)," she noted. Her gloom was exacerbated when Republicans swept the midterm elections to elect their first majority in the House of

Representatives since 1946 with Newt Gingrich designated to be Speaker. The only bright spots, she thought, were Senator Dianne Feinstein's reelection in California and the defeat of Lieutenant Oliver North, architect of the Iran-Contra scandal, for a Senate seat in Virginia.

Alice weathered her disappointment (and some humiliation too, because the auction had unveiled her willingness to leave Knopf) about receiving a lower advance for *A Southern Exposure* than she'd received for her previous novels by—what else?—plowing into the composition of a new novel.

"I'm thinking hard about a doctor novel," Alice had written earlier in 1994 to poet Donald Hall whom she'd known in Palo Alto in the 1950s. Hall had survived metastasized colon cancer and his wife, poet Jane Kenyon, was then undergoing treatment for leukemia. "I'm very over-involved with doctors," Alice wrote. "They are awful, don't you think? Their language—and sensibilities. The last time I complained (mildly, really) one said to me, 'You don't know how lucky you are to be here.'" When Hall replied that his doctor experiences in New Hampshire had been far better than elsewhere, Alice answered, "I'm STILL going to write a mean novel about them."[24]

Medicine Men would be about cancer, doctors, and women's friendship. Adams dedicated it to her "always kind and often brilliant" psychiatrist, Dr. Allen Wheelis, because he'd helped her find the inner strength to survive her disease. The novel so clearly emerged from Alice's recent experience that those who knew of her illness read it as a memoir. "I found it impossible to read as fiction," Mavis Gallant told Alice. "It remained to the end the forced march, over a minefield, of someone I know. I shall have to wait to reread it until it turns into fiction in my mind."[25] Although she's only forty, Molly Bonner resembles Alice in being a once-divorced, once-widowed Southerner (Alice considered herself a kind of widow after Bob's mental defection) who lives in San Francisco, where she has worked for years as a medical secretary and formed strong opinions about "medicine men." Add to that the fact that her novel included a doctor named Dave Jacobs playing almost exactly the ex-lover/good-Samaritan role that Dan Simon played for Alice, while, less glaringly, the ENT specialist who, in the book, is slow to diagnose her sinus cancer is named Dr. Mark Stinger, just one letter off from Alice's ENT specialist, Dr. Singer. The most despicable doctor in *Medicine Men* is an abusive heart surgeon named Raleigh Sanderson who has an affair with Molly's best friend, Felicia; it's unclear to what degree Sanderson resembles the late Dr. Frank L. Gerbode, about whose sexual appetite Alice gossiped to her friend Ruth Belmeur during the time she worked in his department at the Pacific Medical Center. Less troubling but still unappealing as men are Alice's caricatures of the Stanford doctors who saved her life. For instance, her surgeon is "a large bluff man with the aggressively swaying walk of a football player—or a surgeon" who greets forty-year-old Molly with the same words every other doctor has used: "Well, young lady, what seems to be the trouble?"

Alice told an audience at UC Davis that her novel about doctors was "mean and angry" and that a lawyer warned her that she might be sued by one of the doctors when it was published. If that happened, she replied, she would just sue the doctor back for malpractice.[26] Friends of Dr. Mark Singer's did suggest he sue Adams because, as he recalled, she had barely changed his name, used something close to the name of one of his residents, named Mount Zion Hospital, and "concocted a story of malpractice." Singer said, "Alice was my patient for about three days. I made the diagnosis and she and the guy she was living with, an internist, were upset and they fired me." In the end no lawsuits were filed.[27]

When Adams was finishing *Medicine Men*, Don Terner, the husband of her good friend Deirdre English, was killed in the crash of a US government plane in Croatia. That tragic incident also found its way into the novel with the death of "wild and handsome and funny, intelligent and sexy" filmmaker Paul West, Molly's second husband, in a helicopter accident. Paul's recently purchased accident insurance makes Molly rich; her knowledge that Paul wished for a divorce when he died—"Paul did not like being married; they were both too young, he said"—makes Molly miserable with moral confusion and regret, as if she does not deserve her wealth. In that Molly resembles Alice herself, who still worried that she did not deserve and could not afford the house she had purchased partly as an investment and partly to please Bob McNie.

Although *Kirkus*, *Publishers Weekly*, and other review outlets cautiously warned that *Medicine Men* was unfair to doctors, many independent reviewers and readers responded with whoops of recognition.

The novel still has tremendous value as a critique of the indignities suffered by patients in the medical system and the mystique that doctors have acquired in American society. "Doctors in *Medicine Men* seem rather like supermen or alpha males, embodying everything that's most alien, mystifying and appealing to the women they have contact with," Francine Prose wrote.[28] In this passage, Adams portrays an archetypal cancer patient:

> An elderly man in a wheelchair. A patrician head with fine thin hair, a broad lined brow, and wide pale eyes. But dressed in the awful greenish hospital garb, and some terrible slippers. And there he was, in his wheelchair. Those old eyes avoided Molly's eyes as though from shame at his situation, certainly not of his choosing. His reduction—to this. In all the time that she spent, hours and hours in those corridors, Molly saw that same look again and again, a look of embarrassment, of wondering, What terrible thing have I done to be brought so low, to this place of punishment and pain?

It was as if Alice Adams had started a support group for sick people. Her mailbox filled with confessions and testimonials from readers. "I was a fragile child, raped in a hospital," one began. "The personal is political. This time you gave the creeps what they deserve," wrote another. Lynne Sharon Schwartz told Alice, "At last someone has done it, not just alluded briefly or indirectly to these guys . . . but really dug in. Especially the terrible procedures of making you wait half-naked in chilly rooms, dealing with the nurses, not returning calls . . . I not only enjoyed it gleefully but admired it too: it's your smoothness, but the knife is more unsheathed, even serrated."

Author Gish Jen wrote that Adams's attack on the behavior of doctors was "unfailingly on target." Cyra McFadden, author of a popular illustrated satirical novel about Marin County yuppies, *The Serial*, was intrigued by a question Adams raises: "Which came first, the ego or the doctor?" Adams turns the tables on the female patient–doctor relationship by patronizing and infantilizing the doctors in just the way her novel's doctors patronize their patients. Indeed, Molly wonders if all doctors start out as "smart little boys who liked to play doctor with little girls, who retained a lingering interest in poopoo, in the form of fecal jokes." *Vogue* called *Medicine Men* a "lean mean work," and

Millicent Dillon called it her friend's "most daring book" and praised her for taking risks on every page.[29]

The heroine of *Medicine Men* ends up on her own, feeling a year after her surgery "extremely well, healthy and strong, walking fast in that euphoric, brilliant air. She did not need to be 'involved' with anyone at all. She needed sunshine, and long fast walks in this clean fresh lively wind." Molly is a survivor, and the only relationship she counts on in the end is her friendship with Felicia.

But that image of Molly's renewal is *not* the closing movement of *Medicine Men*. Adams jettisons the kind of romantic woman-finds-man happy ending for which she'd often been criticized in favor of a different redistribution of just deserts: revenge. Diagnosed with prostate cancer, the awful sexist, racist famous heart surgeon must go to the hellish hospital in Southern California to receive proton radiation. In the novel's last chapter Sanderson realizes that radiation will not be enough to cure him. He will have to submit to the hands and scalpels of other surgeons, a surgery that will leave him impotent: "And he thought, as Molly Bonner had before him, This is the worst place I've ever been. This is hell."

The late works of distinguished artists often break a pattern set in earlier works, challenging their interpreters to place them in context with a different, earlier style. Edward Said, writing about late Beethoven, noticed that "the power of [his] late style is negative, or rather *it is negativity*: where one would expect serenity and maturity, one finds a bristling, difficult and unyielding—perhaps even inhuman—challenge."[30] With similar unyieldingness postcancer Adams insists on telling what she has seen and knows: cancer and the often futile, always painful and humiliating effort to defeat it are brutal. *Medicine Men* cannot end as a novel of manners would, with some sort of harmony. It must end as it does, with its most arrogant, godlike doctor, the one who repairs human hearts, forced to see that he is a weak human being consigned to hell on earth.

CHAPTER THIRTY

The Age Card

— 1995–1999 —

He no longer knows where he is. What place is this, what country? What rolling gray-green ocean does he walk beside? What year is this, and what is his own true age?

—Alice Adams, "The Last Lovely City,"
The Last Lovely City

In late summer 1990, before her cancer, Alice Adams attended an outdoor luncheon party in Stinson Beach, "the strange, small coastal town of rich retirees; weekenders, also rich; and a core population of former hippies, now just plain poor, middle-aged people with too many children." The meal was served by waiters on white tablecloths in gardens belonging to Barbara Lansburgh Chevalier, the ex-wife of Haakon Chevalier, a man who'd left the United States after he was investigated by the House Un-American Activities Committee for soliciting atomic secrets from J. Robert Oppenheimer. Barbara became an interior designer and maintained her parents' elegant oceanfront estate.[1]

The gathering provided the canvas for one of Adams's best stories. Among the aging fashionable guests at the luncheon were Pat Silver, the mother of a school friend of Peter's; author and editor Norman Cousins; and a portly, balding, and gray-bearded Felix Rosenthal—the man Alice quit seeing when she met Bob McNie. Encountering Rosenthal again all these years later engendered an "awfulness" of recalling that she'd once liked "these sleazy people—was flattered by them . . . underneath all the kisses and the darlings, money lurks and at some time later begins to smell."[2] Rosenthal saved photos of the occasion in an envelope on which he wrote, "Alice Adams, present and seen for the first time since, wrote this party into a short story that promptly appeared in the 'New Yorker'!"[3]

The story Rosenthal refers to encapsulates a feeling Alice had often in the 1990s: that her extremely good memory teemed with images from her full life. In her notebook she wrote: "Derangement—too many segments of past: where am I? how old? what year is it?" Out of that feeling she conceived the main character of "The Last Lovely City." Like many men Alice knew in the 1990s, Dr. Benito Zamora is a recent widower. The successful Stanford-trained physician, who was born in Oaxaca, Mexico, greatly misses his wife: "A problem with death, the doctor has more than once thought, is its removal of all the merciful dross of memory: he no longer remembers any petty annoyances, ever, or even moments of boredom, irritation, or sad, failed acts of love." For Zamora, who's known as Dr. Do-Good because of the clinics he founded in Chiapas, the gathering of "rich old gringos" becomes a horror. As Alice was at the Chevalier party, Zamora is disoriented "by ghosts from his past . . . he feels their looming presences, and feels their connection to some past year or years of his own life. He no longer knows where he is. What place is this, what country? What rolling gray-green ocean does he walk beside? What year is this, and what is his own true age?"

Zamora's ghosts are Dolores Gutierrez, "an old lady friend, who's run to fat," now with an Anglo married name, and Herman Tolliver, the corrupt lawyer who sold him an interest in Tenderloin-neighborhood tenement hotels where sex traffickers housed preteen Asian girls. "It seems to me now that I was pretending to myself not to know certain things that I really did know," Zamora tells Carla, the young woman who brought him to the party. Briefly he imagines that Carla will marry him and return light to his beautiful empty house. Alas, Carla is a journalist. She knows some things about that deal that helped make Zamora rich; furthermore, she's engaged to the son of the party's host.

Zamora is crushed and transformed by the evening's events: "The sun has sunk into the ocean, and Benito's heart has sunk with it, drowned. He shudders, despising himself." He will leave lovely San Francisco, now terrible to him, and move to Chiapas to comfort his mother in her old age and "work in his clinics, with his own poor."

"The Last Lovely City," published by the *New Yorker* in 1991 and selected by Robert Stone for *The Best American Short Stories 1992*, forecasts themes that recur in Adams's personal life throughout the decade

and make it the perfect title story for her final collection, which appeared
in 1999. Like Dr. Zamora, Alice often found herself encountering ghosts
from her past. When Mark Linenthal celebrated his seventy-fifth birthday in 1996, she wrote to an old college friend with what seems a hint
of fondness, "I remember him best at 25."[4]

During the late nineties, San Francisco was further reconfigured by
the economic upheaval that had begun in the eighties. As the Bay Area
became the center of a technological revolution, housing costs escalated;
even as the city celebrated the achievement of civil rights and social
freedom for its gay community, its artistic and African-American and
Latino communities were priced out. When Lucy Gray created a pho-
tography project titled *Naming the Homeless* (1998) about twenty-eight
people without fixed addresses who wanted jobs, "Alice thought it was
wonderful. She was *not* one of the people who worried about how the
homeless would spend their money or who said you should give it to an
agency instead," Gray recalled. Contrasting images showed the homeless people first in their current clothing and street setting and then in
new clothes and professional settings. Gray paid each subject $300, the
going rate for models, and exhibited the photos at Grace Cathedral at
Christmastime, including names and contact information for her subjects. Eight of them found jobs and housing as a result of Gray's show.[5]

Although many older, middle-class people she knew were protected
by rent control or limits on real estate taxes, Alice was painfully sensitive
to changes in her neighborhood. The newly rich undertook ten-million-
dollar renovations or bought up adjacent houses just to tear them down
and build new mansions. The value of Alice's house rose too but she
worried about keeping up her $2,125 monthly mortgage payments on
a house that sometimes felt—like the house she grew up in—too large.

Without a live-in companion, Alice cultivated her friendships more
than ever. "She put time and effort into her relationships," Penelope
Rowlands thought. Even so, she could be judgmental of her friends,
holding them to a standard that was difficult to meet. "I think that she
liked people of a certain caliber," Rowlands said. "Alice spoke about her
other friends all the time—even ones I didn't know—and often seemed
to be sifting, appraisingly, through aspects of their personalities."

Just as Adams sometimes dropped people who had offended her in some minor way, she actively sought out people to nourish her mental and emotional life. After she broke with Bob, she joined a reading group made up of Deirdre English, Anne Lamott, Orville Schell, Sedge Thomson, Ethan Canin, Larry Friedlander, and Adam Hochschild. When that group dwindled, Alice and Hochschild formed a smaller group with Hochschild's wife, Arlie Hochschild, and Millicent Dillon. "There was no rationale to what we were reading," Dillon said. "We read the Greeks, the nineteenth-century Russians, Trollope, Henry James. Adam [Hochschild] approached reading in terms of 'What is the world out of which this book comes and how does it relate to the world we are in now?' And I, being analytical, would look at how this work is put together. But Alice would do something else. She would respond absolutely directly to the feeling of what she was reading. It was so intense, so immediate, very direct, no intellectualizing."

When they read *Heart of Darkness* because Adam Hochschild was working on his history of the Belgian Congo, *King Leopold's Ghost*, Alice said, "I had a terrible time reading this story again. I could not stand the cruelty to the Africans." A couple of years later, Alice proposed reading *Don Quixote*. It had been a favorite of "so many terrible men" in her life, "Nic through Saul Bellow and Vasco."[6] She wanted to conquer her aversion but when the group met she was still having trouble with it. The difficulty, Dillon thought, "was that her reading was so intense and so direct and so connected to her life."

When judging a contest for the Bush Foundation in Minneapolis, Alice fell into a new friendship with a fellow juror, the essayist Phillip Lopate, who lived in Brooklyn. When they dined together Lopate's "eyes, so beautiful and intense,"[7] held Alice's attention as they exchanged stories of their lives. Lopate thought his friendship with Alice "was about one stubborn evolved self meeting another stubborn evolved self and saying no matter what they do to me, they are not going to break me down. There is a great comfort in such people meeting each other." It helped, he thought, that he was a Jewish intellectual. They enjoyed speculating about mutual friends—"we were like minor Henry James characters, amateur psychologists." Their friendship continued through later visits when Alice met his family; Lopate came to admire the way Adams's narrators are "knowers who understand the flow of time." To him Alice seemed worldly and accepting "of the pettiness, vanities, and so on" of the people she knew, and had come to terms with her "aloneness." She wanted to be seen as well-read and literary, but she wasn't preoccupied with her place in literature: "There were none of the rough edges you sometimes find in writer-writer relationships," Lopate said.

Changes in her longest friendships also reshaped Alice's life in the late 1990s. Diane Johnson and John Murray spent much of the year in Paris; beginning with *Le Divorce* in 1997, Johnson's popular French trilogy edited by Billy Abrahams brought her bestseller status. Twice Alice visited Diane and John in Paris, staying on the top floor of an old Latin Quarter hotel with no elevator and a steep spiral staircase that reminded her of the hotel where she'd lived in 1947. On these trips she became friends with the Canadian writer Mavis Gallant, whose "serious pleasantness" Alice appreciated. The two began a correspondence and Alice brought an inscribed copy of Gallant's novel *Green Water, Green Sky* home to Phil Anasovich.

Also in Paris, Alice renewed her friendship (begun in Toronto in 1989) with William Jay Smith. Smith and his wife, Sonja Haussmann, gave a cocktail party for Alice and introduced her to Odile Hellier, who then owned the English-language Village Voice bookstore. "Alice was so beautiful, lovely, intelligent, and witty," Smith said. When they took in an exhibit about Verlaine together at a small museum, Smith realized that Alice read French easily and knew a lot of French poetry. "We talked about it at lunch afterwards," he said. Since first meeting Alice in Toronto, Smith had recommended her several times for membership in the American Academy and Institute of Arts and Letters. "She didn't get in because she was living in California. It's as simple as that," said Smith. People who live in New York and go to the meetings, they're the ones who influence everything."

Another California writer, Ella Leffland, was virtually homebound for ten years while she wrote her monumental novel about Hermann Göring, *The Knight, Death and the Devil*, and cared for her invalid mother in her apartment. When most of their friends switched to email, Alice and Ella resolutely mailed letters across town to each other, sharing news of cats and men (Leffland had a long companionship with an engineer who lived upstairs from her) and praising each other's recent publications. The stories Leffland singled out for praise, Alice noticed, were usually the ones she'd had the most trouble publishing; Alice regarded that as evidence of her friend's superior taste.[8]

Alice's long working relationships with her editor at Knopf, Victoria Wilson, and with her former *New Yorker* editor Frances Kiernan had grown into rich and enduring friendships. Wilson joined Alice on occasional trips but was usually occupied by her editorial job; by renovation of her farmhouse in Sullivan County, New York; and by work on a biography of Barbara Stanwyck that she called "a cultural history of her time."[9] Kiernan, then researching her documentary biography of Mary McCarthy, and her husband met Alice in Mexico and San Francisco, and she visited them in New York. One summer Alice stayed in the Kiernans' Upper East Side apartment for two weeks while they were away. She found herself worn out by the city after ten days.

During her single years Adams befriended many younger writers. As a judge for an Avery Hopwood Award in the early 1980s, she selected short stories by Mary Gaitskill and then provided a comment—"Ferocious, terrifying stories, skillful as they are scary. Gaitskill's voice and talents are wonderfully new, as honest as rain, and as welcome in a long, dry season"—for her first collection, *Bad Behavior*. When Gaitskill moved to a cottage in Marin County in 1989, she and Alice became friends. "At the time when I came to live there," Gaitskill reminisced, "a lot of people I met, not all from the same milieu, seemed kind of crazy—neurotic, reactive, second-guessing everybody, aware of social hierarchies and ready to judge people about where they were in that hierarchy." She found Alice refreshingly beyond such concerns. "She had that ability to look at people and see who they were underneath that."

Gaitskill was drawn to Adams "partly because she seemed sane." They met for lunch or dinner every few months and talked on the phone more often. "I do think she thought I was a little crazy, but she was very tolerant, very kind. She could be critical, but I never saw her be gratuitously nasty." Gaitskill found it reassuring that a successful writer thirty years her elder "seemed very interested in dating and having relationships," noting, "She had men around her and she seemed ambivalent about that, too. She was probably looking for somebody that she could love, but I didn't have the impression she was really happy with any of the men she was with."

Alice's elegance also impressed Gaitskill. "I went to a party at her house. She must have been 70, and she was wearing leather pants and they looked really good on her! They weren't skin tight, they weren't meant to look sexy, they were sort of loose-fitting, very expensive, not black, some kind of cream-colored, and she was wearing a sweater with them. And I remember thinking *wow*." The way Alice presented herself, Gaitskill wrote later, reflected her "intense elegance, grace, and an organic mental integrity that was distinctly feminine in nature."[10]

Thaisa Frank met Alice when they were reading together at a Bay Area college and both read stories about animals. Adams invited Frank to go out to dinner with her—a thrill for the younger woman that soon turned into a challenge. "We got together about five or six times and basically just talked about our lives and people we knew. I think she was lonely and things were waning for her and she was used to being catered to," Frank reflected. "Many of the stories she told me about people were about depression or nervous breakdowns. It was dark," Frank thought. She talked about her marriage and her divorce from Mark Linenthal, Bob McNie's breakdown, and other men she'd known. "Her conversation about men was a mix of disparaging the men she'd been with and at the same time being lonely and a little needy. I think she confided things to me that she would not have confided to, say, Diane Johnson. The person she was positive about was her son. She thought he was wonderful. She was open about his being gay."

Alice encouraged Frank by being a good listener. "I was getting divorced at the time, and Alice told me to go on welfare if I had to in order to get out of the marriage where I was unhappy. I think she told me she'd been on welfare at one time." Despite that sympathy, Alice wanted to command the logistics of their friendship. She insisted on early dinners even though Frank lived in Berkeley and had a son at home. After one frustrating drive across the bridge at rush hour in rainy weather, Frank arrived to find Alice waiting impatiently: "I have a vision of her: she came down the steps wearing a black-and-white checkered suit with a buttercup-yellow top—and buttercup-yellow galoshes. Very stylish, something you'd get in France—something a teeny bopper would wear but Alice really pulled it off. She had dressed for dinner—it was an event in a lonely person's life."

*   *   *

Frances Kiernan came to San Francisco for Alice's seventieth birthday. She felt her "old reliable birthday neurosis," but Edwina Leggett hosted a small party of her close friends at her historic Craftsman house above Cole Valley, and Alice deemed it a "good birthday" with only the "smallest paranoia."[11] "You either ignore such a milestone or really splash it up, and I seem to have chosen the latter, though not all my doing," Alice said of the party. As her friends climbed the stairs to Edwina's front door, they encountered a poster-sized photo of Alice as a coed in bobby socks and short skirt. "Many people [were] wondering who that was," Alice quipped.* Peter astounded his mother by turning up in a three-piece suit rather than what she called "his usually terrible" clothes.[12]

The satisfaction Alice found in close friendships in these years failed to give her one bodily comfort she craved: a man to share her bed. "Bob was at best a genuinely affectionate person, and that's really something I miss," she complained to Judith. "It's good I have my cats, but even Sam shoves me off sometimes. Men."[13]

Alice didn't recognize Bob when she encountered him in a restaurant late in 1996. His thick, prematurely graying hair was dyed brown. The tall, thin dyed blonde with him showed evidence of a face-lift. Of course Adams fashioned the moment into a story, "The Best Revenge," published in *Boulevard*, in which she writes of Bob (here called Frank): "She remembered how it used to take all her strength not to telephone Frank, in the days and weeks she suffered most acutely, when she would have pled with him to come back. And she is moved now again to make a call, although (again) she does not. But this time she would like to say, Frank, I'm sorry your life isn't better than it is. I'm sorry I didn't know you."[14]

Alice's attempts to find a partner were often bedeviled by confusion about affection and sexuality.

Well past menopause (since her hysterectomy in 1966), Alice used a hormone replacement medication that counteracted some of the sexual limitations of aging. But there was no solution for erectile dysfunction, a problem (less discussed in these pre-Viagra years) that afflicted many

---

* The picture was taken by 1947 Harvard alum Paul Southwick, a war photographer who later worked at the White House. (AA to Betty Love White, August 16, 1996.)

of the men in her age group. "Old Love Affairs," published in the *New Yorker* on October 23, 1995, frankly discusses male impotence. This story would turn out to be Adams's last—and her twenty-seventh—in the magazine, then edited by Tina Brown, who took over from Robert Gottlieb.*
In "Old Love Affairs," "sheer sexual starvation" leads the "almost old but lively" narrator, Lucretia, to go to bed with a widowed man named Burt whom she does not really like: "After several long, futile minutes of strenuous efforts on his part, and some effort on hers, Burt said, 'I'm sorry. I had this prostate surgery, and I was afraid, but I had hoped—'" Determined to please Lucretia, Burt moves "heavily, laboriously down her body, positioning himself," as she thinks, "This is not something he usually does . . . Oral sex was not on the regular menu with Laura, the wife."

Lucretia pretends "more pleasure than she actually [feels]" in order to make him stop his cunnilingual attention. Why couldn't Lucretia simply tell Burt that she didn't want to see him? Because she does not want to hurt a man's feelings. Despite professional success and sexual freedom, many of Alice Adams's midcentury women find themselves confined by outdated terms of engagement in their dealings with men. Their long habit of conflating sex with affection becomes a barrier to finding the affection they need in old age. Or perhaps the century and gender roles had little to do with it. At one point in the story, Lucretia counsels herself, "Enough of sex and love. I've surely had my share, and maybe more." But then she reads an article on "geriatric sex" or encounters a man who reminds her of youthful feelings. Her "very blood would warm and flare, and she would think, Well, maybe. Even as a more sensible voice within would warn her, Oh, come on." The story has an open ending. Having invited a man she knew years before to dinner, Lucretia asks if he minds eating early:

> "Not at all. It's a terrible thing about age," he said, with his attractive, crooked smile. "I find that I'm tired a lot."
> "Oh, I am, too!" and she flashed her answering bright smile, as she thought, Oh good, I won't have to pretend anymore. And I won't even think about falling in love.
> But of course she did.

* Alice Quinn, who was mainly the poetry editor at the *New Yorker*, continued to offer Adams first-reading contracts every year.

*   *   *

No matter how vividly Adams imagined her characters, the realistic mode of her fiction invited speculations about their identities—was Lucretia Alice and, if so, who were the two men that Lucretia dated? Adams rejected such simple equivalences but sometimes told her friends when she'd borrowed from their lives. Caroline Drewes, an older journalist who was her friend and neighbor and had "large green eyes" and a driftwood-framed mirror like Lucretia's, believed that "Old Love Affairs" grew out of stories she'd told Alice about her own affairs.[15] When Alice published a story called "Great Sex" about why women stay with men who make them unhappy, she gave a copy to Penelope Rowlands. "Alice told me that the character named Alison wasn't entirely based on me, but that Alison and I had in common a certain sympathy towards men, arising from a sense that women are often unfairly hostile towards them. It seems a rather subtle, and telling, detail to have picked up on. Yet so Alice-like, too."

Derek Parmenter remained the leading man in Alice's life throughout the 1990s but she never got over the frustrations she felt with him. "I should lay off ruses to sleep together," she noted in 1996. Happening to see him with another woman in a restaurant near her house, she was "wildly jealous" and considered ending their friendship after "almost 4 years of terribleness." A couple of weeks later they've been on a beautiful hike and Derek has explained that the woman is just an old tennis partner. "I think [Derek] is rather deficient, Forster's 'undeveloped heart,'" Alice complained to Judith.[16] Nonetheless, she loved days when they hiked, listened to jazz (including an evening of Trummy Young recordings), and cooked together. On a book tour to Seattle she missed him "mildly" as she reminisced about emotional attachments to that city: "Vasco—abortion; Franzl; Bob—missing Bob."[17] Most of all, she adored Derek's dog, Pepper, and his eighteen-month-old granddaughter, Serena: "the most enchanting tiny girl whom I consider my granddaughter . . . so odd to fall in love with a baby, I don't generally like them, but she is so great: she looks at me and bends over double, laughing, the best reaction I've ever had, after a long life of trying to be funny."[18]

*   *   *

When Richard Poirier read *A Southern Exposure*, he told Alice the book merited a sequel. Adams took her friend's idea as a challenge to re-sort her thoughts about Southern culture and began *After the War* by rereading novels by William Faulkner.[19] Her intention was, of course, not imitation but inspiration and avoidance. "Nobody," as the Irish writer Frank O'Connor said when Faulkner was still alive, "wants his mule and wagon stalled on the same track the Dixie Limited is roaring down." Her own recent visits to Virginia and North Carolina also fed Adams's imagination as she demystified the society of her childhood by following the lives of its modern women and younger men; she also continued to reveal the subtle bigotry of native Southerners and the pretensions of Northerners.

In *After the War* Russell Byrd, the decadent romantic bad boy of *A Southern Exposure*, suffers a heart attack while riding on the back of a train in Texas. Standing next to him and unable to prevent his fall is a black army sergeant returning from the Pacific front with his separation pay in his wallet. His name is Ed Faulkner. Accused of causing Byrd's death and stealing his money, Faulkner undergoes a darkly comic journey through postwar America. American communists, eager to have a black hero, break him out of jail. Eventually he survives both Southern racism and the leftists' misguided adulation to enroll at the University of Wisconsin. Adams brings other black characters to the fore in this novel too, including the maid Odessa and her family, and the janitor's son, football player Ben Davis, who graduates from Harvard and seems likely to marry Byrd's daughter Melanctha. On the whole Adams's postwar world conveys little of the entrapment Alice felt after the war. Rather it's a novel of retrospect, reconciliation, and hope, a late-stage comedy ending with a wedding, couples reunited, and a warning from Harry Baird that people are going to miss the war: "The heroic certainty of it all. The moral clarity. Hitler was bad, we're good. And we'll miss the excitement, the fervor. Wars are sexy—"

As Alice Adams had done for much of her life, in her last novel she ponders the complexity of sexuality. Harassment about her large breasts drives Melanctha Byrd to leave Radcliffe, while her gay half brother, Graham, finds contentment with a (necessarily) secret lover. Abby Baird finds such complete pleasure in making love to Joseph Marcus that she plans in medical school to "study this enormous and misunderstood difference in orgasms. Freud, she thought, had oversimplified. Clitoral versus vaginal, that was not the issue. Unless, and she smiled to herself, unless what she experienced with Joseph was both at once." Meanwhile Abby's mother struggles to understand her own infidelities and her husband's coming-home impotence.

Adams worked on *After the War* from 1995 until the fall of 1998, years in which she also wrote dozens of short stories and personal essays. Even though commercial markets were drying up, magazines from *Agni* to *Redbook*, from the *Paris Review* to *Gentleman's Quarterly*, eagerly solicited and accepted work from an established author whose style and form now ranged well beyond the patterns she had honed with the *New Yorker* in mind. On a notebook page next to the one where she listed men she'd loved, Adams noted every magazine acceptance: altogether sixteen essays and one hundred twenty short stories appeared in thirty-nine different periodicals during her forty-year writing career.

Alice Adams had graduated Radcliffe early with a mediocre transcript and great eagerness to get out into the wider world. She had no plans to attend her fiftieth class reunion until organizers selected her for an Alumnae Recognition Award and invited her to speak at a symposium. For the reunion souvenir book she wrote:

> At this point my life on the whole seems good and most fortunate. I love my pretty San Francisco postcard house, my cats and my garden, and especially my son and my friends.
>
> I certainly wish that I were a better writer although small successes here and there have pleased me. Some things that I've written seem all right and I'm still working at it.
>
> And I desperately, sometimes despairingly wish that the world were a better place—kinder, fairer, more peaceful.

Both Peter and Phil, along with Dennis McFarland and Michelle Blake, attended the symposium, where Alice shared the stage with actor Anna Deavere Smith and other younger alumnae. Adams's award citation declared that readers appreciate her wit, her keen eye for social situations, and her "inimitable style at once brilliant and lyrical."

Pulling out big reading glasses and confiding that "the speech and the essay [were] intimidatingly unfamiliar forms" to her, Adams addressed the assigned theme of "The 21st Century: Defining the Challenges" by remembering the optimism expressed in the Harvard class she'd taken in 1945 on the subject of the postwar world. In contrast, she felt no joy at the idea of a new century. To prepare something to say to the symposium about "the future of writing" Alice queried Amanda Urban, who predicted that a generation of readers used to sound bites would require brevity but that creativity would survive. Victoria Wilson—"of a darker turn of mind," Alice said—believed that "what was published would be increasingly determined by the needs (for needs read greed, I think) of the increasingly gigantic corporations that own the publishing houses." When Alice asked Wilson about the discrepancy between advances given to "best-selling trash" and those given to good poets and novelists, Wilson frowned and said, "In the future there may be no advances."

After passing on more gloomy forecasts about publishing, Alice reminded her audience that writers face the same challenge everyone does, "to confront and make even the smallest effort to change the terrible and increasing gap between the overfed and the starving, between any person here and any person in Rwanda or the Congo. We have, somehow, to cope with the greedy spoilage of our planet."

Undissuaded by his mother's predictions about the future of publishing, Peter went on to New York City to meet with editors. He had taken a year off from teaching and was working full-time on illustrations for children's books. As for herself, after weeks of standing up to read "mean and funny" passages from *Medicine Men* on a book tour and trying to forecast the twenty-first century at Radcliffe, Alice concluded, "I'm not a performer or a sales person. I can't wait to get home to write."[20]

Over the past decade Alice had come to regard Philip Anasovich as her son's permanent partner and her own close friend. She was deeply worried in the summer of 1998 when alarming symptoms suggested that Phil might have a brain tumor. Happily the neurology team at UCSF was able to determine that he actually suffered from an arteriovenous malformation that was successfully treated with gamma knife radiosurgery early in 1999.[21]

When Phil became ill, Alice was already reeling from the loss of seventy-nine-year-old William Abrahams, who died of congestive heart failure on June 2, 1998. "Billy Abrahams seems suddenly very old, but still quite great, happy with Peter Stansky," Alice had written a mutual friend a year earlier.[22] Her life had been entwined with Billy's for fifty years. When he lived in California they talked on the phone several times a week. Though never her book editor, Billy was often her first reader, both "brilliantly intelligent" and "exceptionally tactful." He and Stansky had often visited with Alice and Bob McNie in Truckee, and Bob decorated two residences for them. Alice was recovering from a long, severe bout of pneumonia when Billy died. Feeling too ill to attend the private memorial service that Stansky held at their hillside home in Hillsborough, Alice asked Millicent Dillon to read a section about Billy from an essay she'd just finished about him and Judith and Max— friends she'd loved at first sight.[23] Afterward, when Dillon described the day to Alice and said she was sorry she couldn't have been there, Alice responded fiercely, "Oh, no, I didn't want to be there. I want to think of him as still being alive and that's what I'm going to do."

Billy Abrahams

Nineteen ninety-eight was arduous for Alice Adams in other ways. As she wore herself out with professional travel, she also packed in emotional visits with old friends. Lavishly accommodated at the Houstonian

Hotel in "a pretty room, pink sunset like Venice," in February, Alice saw her former lover Jack Boynton and his wife, Sharon; her financial advisor, Glenn Lowry; and Mary Ross Taylor, the art critic who'd been her confidante during some of the rough weeks after her breakup with Bob. In April, upon arriving in Chapel Hill for a literary festival, Alice discovered that a mix-up in the reservation dates made it necessary for her to stay at Max Steele's condo for two nights before she could move to the Carolina Inn. She loved seeing Max but slept poorly in his spare bedroom: "Birds woke me early, and something about the house itself made me restless. Max collects *things*, every space is crowded with *objects*, so that I longed for the anonymous peace of a bare hotel room." The poor sleep was also due to "boozy dinner parties" with Max's friend from his *Paris Review* days, George Plimpton, also in town for the festival.

During a week already packed with nostalgic visits, Alice dined with the "always marvelous" Alison Lurie and met Lurie's younger husband, writer Edward Hower, whom she called "such an attractive smart kind funny man, what one would wish for a friend."[24] Introduced to novelist Elizabeth Spencer at Diana Steele's house, which had tiny chairs because it was also her nursery school classroom, Alice picked up a couple of big cushions and plopped them in the corner. The two of them, who'd both published in the *New Yorker* extensively, "just chatted like Southern women do," Spencer recalled.

At the literary festival Alice also relished the discovery that the writer Daphne Athas, an acquaintance from Chapel Hill High School who'd then been "the most out of the out crowd," was now "infinitely better than those God-awful ins, who were now Republicans with paunches." Oddly enough, some of those "God-awful ins" from Alice's school days turned up for the literary festival, prompted by her correspondence with Robert Macmillan (the one she'd knocked over as a toddler who later showed her his penis, and, later still, dated her friend Judith). Despite Macmillan's "huge paunch and weighty, somewhat cross expression" and self-confessed "politics to the right of Jesse Helms," and the presence of Macmillan's long-suffering wife, Alice felt "a sort of warm current" between herself and him. "Sex, I guess, and we all know how mysterious and intellectually unreliable that can be."[25]

The reunion was a flop. One woman brought a photo album with pictures of their parents "plastered and smoking their heads off" at a costume party in the 1940s. Alice failed to recognize "a tall dark woman with an exceptionally mean, disapproving face." But someone else identified her as Agatha Adams in a black wig, shot from an angle that made her look tall. Seventy-two-year-old Alice was startled: "I had not recognized my own mother? But of course in a sense I had; I recognized a mean spirit, and passed by it as quickly as I could—just as, years back, I had left home as soon as possible, for good."

Alice's correspondence with Robert Macmillan ended with the festival. Perhaps, she realized later, the rapport she'd felt with him had been based on the fear of Agatha that both of them felt as children. With all the Southern subtlety that she claimed to despise, Alice "took a slap at Robert" by writing his twin brother to say "how great [it was] to see him so thin and elegant . . . No mention of R. at all."[26] She also wrote an essay called "Why I Left Home: Partial Truths" about the whole incident (with some fictional enhancements that further insulted Robert) and sent a copy to Judith Adams.

Already feeling wiped out by Chapel Hill, Alice flew to Oaxaca to spend Easter week with Peter and Phil. She complained about ninety-eight-degree days, the bathroom in their $20-a-night hotel, and the men's tireless shopping, but she told Alison Lurie, "I think I got a good-sport award from Peter," The zocalo was beautiful, jacaranda trees were in purple profusion, the coffee was fantastic—but it would be her last trip to Mexico, which to her seemed "too hot, poor, dusty—slightly unreal—Indians, the unknown, possibly dangerous."[27]

Again Alice found San Francisco wonderful to come home to, despite the usual summer fog, and she stayed put for the next few months. Frances Kiernan flew in for her seventy-second birthday weekend. They celebrated with a small dinner party at Peter and Phil's kitchen table on Potrero Hill. Alice wore a stylish close-fitting sweater with her signature chunky jewelry. Derek Parmenter, in a checked sport coat, attended, and Carolyn See sent a "tower of flowers." Alice declared it "all very nice, especially for an old birthday phobe."[28] But Kiernan noticed that Alice was napping often and wasn't able to walk in the city as they'd done in the past.

Alice came to New York City in late September 1998. She'd hired someone to word-process a typescript of *After the War* and looked forward to discussing the book with Wilson. She directed the driver of her taxi from the airport toward her usual hotel, the Wyndham, but found Fifty-Eighth Street cordoned off because Israeli prime minister

Benjamin Netanyahu, in town for negotiations with Madeleine Albright and Yasser Arafat, was staying at the Plaza. As Amanda Urban recalled, Alice got out at the blockade and dragged her suitcase the rest of the way, injuring her knee and exhausting herself. "Alice could be so stubborn and independent," Urban said. "People lost patience with her because she wasn't taking care of herself on occasions like that. She could be ornery." But Urban had good news for Alice. Wilson was reading the manuscript of *After the War.* Though she thought there were too many characters in the opening scene, she had agreed to purchase it.

Before year's end Alice had patched up her mostly epistolary friendship with Donald Hall, which had suffered a break when Hall told Alice about his "twenty-hour date" with a gorgeous young woman who was "fantastic in bed." In a first reply, Alice teased Hall that his happy confession had "a very Herb Gold sound" and said, "I hope your prose is not affected." A week later, she explained that it was hard "to make the leap from sympathizing with a man in total mourning to cheering on a boyish sexual reincarnation. Also, I don't have any other friends who speak in that way of their intimate lives (Herb Gold and I don't speak)."[29] Given that she published stories far more explicit than his letter, Hall may have been surprised to hear that he'd offended Alice. She discussed the matter with Alison Lurie, who replied, "We have to remember that the genes of most men, even at a relatively advanced age, are always urging them to seek out stupid young females and knock them up. . . . We are lucky because our genes only suggest that we cultivate our houses and gardens and be kind to whatever helpless creatures such as cats, students, and grandchildren." Eventually Alice understood that Hall had had a manic episode, part of his "total derangement at Jane's death," and felt "rather insensitive and stupid: I certainly should know about manic-depression, both my father and Bob . . . Also over and over again I've seen people in mourning go into 'inappropriate' love affairs as part of the process; I did the same thing myself."[30]

Nor was Alice content, as Lurie had posited, with domestic pursuits. Late in 1998, as the House of Representatives moved toward impeachment of President Clinton, Alice's friend Susan Sward introduced her to Agar Jaicks, a recent widower and Democratic Party leader. Alice thought Jaicks was both nice and sexy—an expert flirt—and thus he held her attention for several weeks. That ended after it turned out that he was highly allergic to cats; they wished each other well and agreed that neither of them, in his words, "felt whole in the relationship."[31] In her notebook she wrote, "Men our age are scared of us—it's not (just) that we look old & ugly—they think we have something on them—and we do." She called her dates with Jaicks her "latest romantic disaster," but a few months later when she saw him ceremoniously embracing Nancy Pelosi on television, "spruce and dapper—oozing sincerity—warmth"— she felt "reactivated fantasies—I did like his voice."[32]

Alice reminded herself: "So much complicated attention to single broken inferior men—*write their stories*." In no time, she was at work on two new ones about widowers, "First Date" and "Her Unmentionables."[33]

Adams's fifth collection of short stories, *The Last Lovely City*, came out in January, about the time the Senate voted to acquit Clinton. A review in the Sunday Book Review section of the *New York Times* on February 14 was no Valentine. Susan Bolotin disliked the characters of Adams's "densely populated and lonely" world because they "let life lead them by the hand. Things happen to people. The people, too tired or too drunk to fight back, go along for the ride. Chance is destiny." Their main flaw, as Adams understood the review, was age.

What Bolotin saw as passivity seemed like artful realism to seasoned readers who realized their smallness in the face of human frailties, including the emotional force of one's own history. "These people may be high achievers in the socioeconomic realm, but when it comes to love they're no more in control than teen-agers," Alison Baker wrote in the *Oregonian*. Indeed, there's ironic self-awareness in characters like the lovers Lila and Julian in the Lila Lewisohn stories, who watch their lives from the sidelines in the four final stories of the book. For them, finding a way to be together after years when other obligations made that difficult is a minor triumph.

Sallie Bingham reminded readers of the *Santa Fe New Mexican* that getting old is not a passive activity: "In a world with no tomorrow, a magnificently accoutered world that is, in the end, a hall of mirrors, surviving is an act of courage." In the *Southern Review* Randall Curb noticed that "like Colette, Adams tends to focus on women beyond the first bloom of youth . . . yet despite heartbreak and disaffection, they never get enough of love." Other reviewers thought Adams's stories continued to "exemplify the kind of perfection that theorists and critics extol . . . the deftly limned but fully realized character, the complication quickly described, and the denouement which offers insight or a catch in the throat." And such artfulness was enough to offset any malaise that readers might absorb from Adams's characters, Carol Lake argued in the *Austin American-Statesman*: "You laugh and in laughing you feel rescued from a similar malaise. You can feel Adams' strong voice as she sorts out incidents to create a structure, to give form and meaning."[34]

Despite the many good reviews, Alice complained to friends that she'd been attacked for writing about old people. Mary Gordon responded with an ad hominem attack on Bolotin. From Paris, Mavis Gallant reminded Alice: "Shakespeare played the age card with 'King Lear.' Verdi and Shakespeare did it with 'Falstaff.' Balzac played it with 'Pere Goriot,' Hemingway with 'The Old Man and the Sea,' Brecht with 'Mother Courage.' Nothing stings so much as the dumb remark, particularly when it is anonymous or made by someone one has no use for. Every work of art has a card to play. The real difficulty is when one is up against people who have no idea how fiction is written."[35]

"I thought I gave a rather attractive view of old age," Alice wrote to Diane Johnson. She was looking forward to arthroscopic surgery on her left knee, hoping to regain her mobility after several months of hobbling about on a cane. She felt "ready for the ice floe" after a recent accident at home had left her with a cracked rib too. Of course, checking herself into a hospital again was troubling. "Are you certain your doctors have not read *Medicine Men*?" Donald Hall asked her.[36]

Alice's surgery went smoothly and she recovered happily, saying, "I love lying in my beautiful room with a bed full of cats and books." Peter was "the greatest help" and stayed over several nights. She drafted a story called "Sending Love," which she described to Dick Poirier as "a very affectionate one about Bob. High time, I think. He really was in most ways so marvelous."[37] Thirteen pages (two typed, the rest in her semicursive printing) survive among Adams's papers. By so much condensing the long relationship, Adams emphasized how quickly she'd fallen for Bob. In the story, "Tom" brings the narrator orange juice in bed and has "an actor's voice, all feeling so it doesn't much matter what he says." She's so desperately worried when he's hours late for their second night together—"I knew next to nothing of his life, there were no possibilities to which to anchor my fears—and so I feared everything"—and so relieved when he arrives that she whispers, "Don't explain." Thus her easy forgiveness sets a pattern. Their "entire connection is marked always by a lack of explicitness; we did not spell things out or make plans." But what terrific times they had—in bed, in the kitchen, on a trip to Madeira, he was "affectionately warm, always a lot of kissing and loving touches, and cheerfully funny." Years in, when she began to make demands—"I think you might say when you're not coming over"—the man balks. He's having business troubles, then falls into a deep depression, dons an old gray robe, and begins "to sit around in this robe all day, doing absolutely nothing."

"Sending Love" hews closer to the facts of Alice and Bob's relationship than anything else Alice wrote. If, as she intended, it's "very affectionate," it is also sadly self-diagnostic. Through this story Adams recognizes that the lapses that finally made cohabitation with Bob impossible for her were there from the beginning, part of the attraction itself. Intuitively knowing she could not change this man, she writes, "she let him believe she was "much less anxiously needful than in fact [she was]."[38]

Two weeks after her surgery, Alice was getting about on a colorful cane from Mexico. She could walk, take showers, and even get on the city bus. When Jack Leggett invited her to dinner (Edwina was away) they walked to Via Veneto on Fillmore and had a lively time discussing the importance of wealth. The best story she'd ever read, she told Leggett, was "The Rich Boy" by F. Scott Fitzgerald. When he got home, Leggett read the story and called Alice to tell her he found it "formless" and didn't understand her enthusiasm. "But, Jack," she replied, "you know I don't care for plot at all."[39]

On Thursday, May 20, 1999, while sitting at home alone, Alice felt a severe pain in her chest that radiated to her arms and jaw. Her knees buckled when she got up to call for help. Her Alabaman neighbor Colmont Hopkins immediately came to drive her to the emergency room at Mount Zion Hospital. By then the pain had subsided, but she felt weak, nauseous, and dizzy. Aspirin, nitroglycerin, and a small dose of morphine soon brought her symptoms under control, and Dr. Botkin admitted her to the hospital on the assumption that she'd had a heart attack. She canceled plans to go out for dinner with Penelope Rowlands on Saturday night. Sunday morning rapid atrial fibrillations sent her to the ICU for the weekend. On Monday morning a cardiac catheterization revealed that her arteries were healthy, though the area where her aorta joined her heart was "tortuous" (twisted) and "dilated," probably due to high blood pressure.

On Tuesday morning cardiologist Dr. Edward Cohen corrected Alice's heart rhythm with a procedure called cardioversion—two electrical shocks that returned her to normal. But Dr. Botkin still had no explanation for the attack she'd had on May 20. Its etiology was, he noted, "a puzzle." If the earlier diagnosis of non-Q-wave myocardial infarction was wrong, then perhaps Alice had a pulmonary embolism (blood clot in her lungs), perhaps because of her recent knee surgery. Botkin called in pulmonologist Thomas Addison, but his tests (ventilation and perfusion) showed only minor defects in her lungs, nothing to account for the attack. Addison's notes describe Alice as "a somewhat chronically ill appearing lady who is in no distress" and "a delightful lady." Speculating about the attack, he noted, "dissection also comes to mind, but the cardiac catheterization I would think essentially rules that out."

After six nights and five days in the hospital with no diagnosis, Alice insisted on going home. She would see Dr. Botkin the next week and have an MRI of her aortic root on June 9. In the late afternoon Peter arrived to visit and spend the night.

A reading group discussion of *The Father* by Strindberg scheduled for that evening had already been canceled. Alice rested in bed, exhausted after the ordeals at the hospital and glad to be home with her cats. Before she fell asleep she called her gardener, Scott Massey, and left him a message to apologize that she hadn't been able to let him in that morning: "I was in the hospital, I just got out today—I don't know, a heart attack or atrial fibrillation or some fucking thing . . . I'm extremely sorry if you came and didn't know I wasn't going to be here, but boy am I glad to be out of the hospital. Anyway, talk to you soon."

Peter, who'd been out on the water most of the day on a Baykeeper boat cruise with his father, read downstairs for a while and then fell asleep in Alice's childhood bed in the room next to his mother's.

In the morning he came downstairs and did a few things in the kitchen before he realized he hadn't heard his mother stirring. He went upstairs to check on her. She was lying on the bed with her eyes wide open and the cover thrown off. It was as if she'd tried to get up and then fallen back on the bed. He saw immediately that she was dead. There was no doubt. He touched her once and then covered her body with a blanket and went to the telephone to call first Phil and then 911.

The rest of the morning was a blur to Peter. Edwina Leggett, one of the first friends to arrive, said, "I'll never forget the day Alice died. Sydney Goldstein and I were both there before Derek Parmenter arrived. We were going to go up and put Alice in a pretty nightgown or something she'd be proud to be buried in and we lost our nerve. We just couldn't do it. And when Derek came in he went right upstairs to see her even though she had died. And I thought, 'That's very brave of you.' "

The emergency crew confirmed what Peter knew when he first saw Alice awkwardly collapsed on her bed. His mother was dead. They efficiently wheeled her away in a body bag on a folding gurney. Peter requested an autopsy, which would show that Alice had suffered fatal damage to her thoracic aorta. Her pericardium, the sac enclosing the heart, had filled with blood, and the blood compressed the chambers of her heart so they could no longer pump.[40]

On May 27, 1999, at the age of seventy-two, Alice Adams died of a broken heart.

Epilogue

If she had felt herself to be dying that last evening, she would not have mentioned it, not wanting to ruin Peter's visit.

—Diane Johnson, memorial for Alice Adams,
read by her son Kevin Johnson, June 27, 1999

Before his mother died, Peter Linenthal had been troubled that his beautiful, smart mother lived alone. His own relationship with Philip Anasovich was stronger than ever—they were able to marry in 2008—and he saw how much she needed companionship. As more responsibility for Alice had fallen to him, the two of them had become good friends. But he knew she would like to be with someone. Perhaps that's why, after the initial shock, Peter felt some relief when Alice died.

"If I were a self-castigating person," he said, "I could blame myself for being relieved that this difficult time had ended for her." The last years had been arduous because of her health and her loneliness. At one point she confided that maybe there comes a time when a person has lived long enough. Peter understood she was talking about herself. But understanding is not acceptance.

A doctor Peter spoke with later explained that a dissection of the aorta can be very painful but extremely quick. Peter thought he might have heard a sound from his mother's room on the night she died but he'd never be sure of that. Nor could he ever know if hearing that sound would have allowed him to ease his mother's death. At a memorial service for his mother, Peter told several hundred of her friends and admirers, "I know that I am very lucky to continue to know my mother through her writing, but I also know that I will miss her forever. I had imagined another twenty years with her."

On the morning of May 27, before the news of Alice's death was published, people kept calling to welcome her home from the hospital. "We were supposed to have dinner on the Saturday of the weekend when she went into the hospital for the last time," Penelope Rowlands remembered. "Then Peter called me and said, 'Alice is all right but she won't be seeing you tonight.' And he let me know when she came home." The next morning, Rowlands called and started to leave a lighthearted message. She was saying, "Alice, you'll do anything not to have dinner with me . . . ," when Peter picked up and told her, "I found my mother dead at eight this morning. She's upstairs." "It was devastating," Rowlands said.

Soon Sydney Goldstein and Edwina Evers took over the phones. A friend wanted to bring lunch. The hospital wanted to schedule tests for the following week. Scott Massey wanted to work in the garden. Housekeeper Alice Garrett was coming to clean. Reporters called with questions. The funeral director needed instructions, so Peter was left to guess that his mother would have chosen cremation. Then he found his mother's address books and began calling those who should hear the news from him before they could read it in a newspaper.

The *New York Times*, the *Los Angeles Times*, and the *San Francisco Chronicle* ran lengthy obituaries.[1] "She was a great romantic, with the highest expectations of life. As a writer, she was unfailingly wise," Frances Kiernan told the *New York Times*. Victoria Wilson added that Adams's writing "fused the seductive intimacy of the South, the intellectual sophistication of New England and the sense of adventure and openness to new experiences of the West." The two-column photograph of her that accompanied that obituary had been taken by the acclaimed civil rights photographer Don Hogan Charles. Nearer home, the *Chronicle*'s tribute by Sam Whiting and Susan Sward reported that John Leggett called Adams "the center of a literary community here, widely admired and regarded as one of the most distinguished writers in San Francisco." Ella Leffland mentioned Adams's "buoyant youthful spirit" and said, "I've never known a writer who was less blinded by her success than Alice." A week later, *Chronicle* books editor David Kipen proposed that a street in San Francisco be renamed for Alice Adams. It should be a street "in keeping with her refined yet risqué sensibility," one with an uphill grade to commemorate the obstacles Adams had overcome to achieve success in the publishing world. Those obstacles were "never turning her back on the short story"; writing about "the vicissitudes of romance" rather than being a romance novelist; and choosing to live in the West.[2] Alas, it turned out that street-renaming had become controversial in San Francisco, especially after Lawrence Ferlinghetti got a dozen downtown lanes and alleys near City Lights bookstore named after luminaries such as Jack Kerouac, William Saroyan, Kenneth Rexroth—and himself. To date, no street has been renamed for Alice Adams.

Over the next month Alice's friends huddled and talked together, trying to understand why they'd lost her so suddenly. Some had theories. Could pool chlorine have caused her sinus cancer? Did the radiation treatments for that cancer weaken her heart? Physicians including Diane Johnson's husband, John Murray, and Millicent Dillon's son-in-law, a cardiologist, noted that a dissection of the aorta is "very hard to catch." Still, a CT scan with contrast probably would have revealed the thoracic aneurysm. But would Alice have wanted an aggressive treatment? "She looked very pale to me there in the hospital bed that last day," Blair Fuller said. "It was clear they hadn't figured out what was wrong. She was determined to go home. And I said, 'Maybe you shouldn't do that, Alice.' And she replied, 'Shhh, don't tell a soul.'" Peter could not imagine his mother going through any more medical procedures, "she would have really really hated it. So she probably died in a way that would have been okay with her."

"I felt so empty, so awful after Alice died," Rowlands remembered. "I went out to dinner with Edwina Leggett so we could talk about Alice. And Edwina said to me, 'For someone who didn't like people, Alice sure had a lot of people.'" Most of them came to the memorial celebration Peter hosted at the Presidio of San Francisco on the afternoon of June 27, 1999, in the Golden Gate Club, overlooking the great orange bridge. They celebrated a woman who was "just the right person to have written Alice Adams's fiction," Orville Schell wittily noted. The event was, like Alice Adams herself, both private and public, announced in the newspapers and broadcast afterward on the radio by the City Arts & Lectures program. People who hadn't spoken to Adams in years attended. Peter worked closely with Sydney Goldstein to plan this afternoon. The stage was adorned with huge bouquets of blue and white flowers. A pianist performed selections from Debussy, Mozart, and Schubert. The voices of twenty-two people who spoke from a podium next to a vase of bright nasturtiums from Peter's garden offered a biography in miniature, threads for a tapestry of her life.[3] Aside from Alice Garrett, who said that Ms. Adams always gave her a hug when she arrived to clean her house, and artist Theophilus (Bill) Brown, who choked up and apologized because he hated to speak in public, most of these eulogists read composed, practiced essays that were as graceful and lively as the woman they attempted to describe. The words most used were "beautiful," "elegant," "fierce," and "generous."* Sheila Ballantyne, Anne Lamott, Leonard Michaels, and Mary Gaitskill all praised Alice as an inspiring and generous colleague. "I'd read Alice Adams's work for years before I actually met her, and I had been inspired by it primarily for the directness and elegance of the prose," Gaitskill remembered. "I was also inspired by the way she portrayed women. In my early twenties, which was when I was reading her, it was wonderful to read about women in their forties and fifties, which was ancient as far as I was concerned, who were still out there in the world, falling in love, having affairs, being really pissed, working, traveling, just doing something. . . . This was not something I saw reflected in my world." Lamott added, "Alice was the only person I ever knew who closed her voice mails with "Love, Alice" or "Much Love.""

Carolyn See described Adams as "an elegant, old-fashioned sexpot" and "a wild, a great beauty" who "drove men nuts—some of whom are in this room." Among those were Derek Parmenter, Daniel Simon, Robert McNie, Max Steele, and Mark Linenthal. Peter asked his friend Christy Rocca to sit with his father because he had a tendency to speak his mind and do so loudly. As he listened to people talk about how wonderful Alice was, Mark interjected, "What are they talking about? I did not know that person!" and Rocca struggled to get him to whisper his comments in her ear. "He just could not get over the personal affection people had for her," she said. But afterward Peter's father told him, "You know, I don't hate her anymore." Debilitated by emphysema, Mark Linenthal held a weekly salon of former students and poetry lovers at his home until his death in 2010.

Shortly before the memorial, Peter and Phil had dinner with Robert McNie, partly to gauge how he would behave at the service. At the

---

* The speakers were: Peter Adams Linenthal, Philip Anasovich, Victoria Wilson, Frances Kiernan, Alice Garrett, Theophilus (Bill) Brown, Edwina Leggett, Ella Leffland, Kevin Johnson for Diane Johnson, Orville Schell, Anne Lamott, John (Jack) Leggett, Judith Rascoe for Carolyn See, Millicent Dillon, Mary Ross Taylor, Beverly Lowry, Blair Fuller, Leonard Michaels, Sheila Ballantyne, and Max Steele.

Golden Gate Club Bob looked gaunt and intense, bearded and with dark circles under his eyes, as if he had worn himself out. He approached Mark Linenthal, whom he hadn't seen for years; shook his hand; and rather dourly gave his name. "I *know* who you are," Linenthal said with a suggestion of double entendre. Fran Kiernan introduced Bob to Dan Simon, then quickly withdrew because she knew that Bob could be as alarmingly volatile as Dan could be obtuse. Before Dan Simon left that day, he approached Peter and said, "Tell me, how did she die?"

Max Steele, who'd made the trip to San Francisco from Chapel Hill, came to the podium last. In his deep voice he told a funny, much-embellished old family yarn he'd heard from Alice's father. He began with a wealth of the delaying, made-up details that Southerners love, in this case a long, poetic description of the gracious life Nic's aunt enjoyed "before the Hitler war." Her husband was a doctor and none of his patients had money to pay him during the Depression. Then he died, Max said, leaving the aunt with nothing but debts. She learned to type sixty-five words a minute and took a government job in Washington. Alice's parents traveled to Washington "to see if they could help her find an easier way of life in a more congenial place, perhaps even in Chapel Hill.

"But," Max continued, "the aunt said, 'Agatha, I like Washington. And I like the Census Bureau. And I like most of the people who work here. But I want you to know there is one girl in this department who went down to the Mayflower Hotel last weekend and spent the night with two Marines. [Pause.] As hot as it is!' " Max's story drew a burst of laughter from his audience. "How good to end with laughter a love that began over forty years ago with laughter," Steele continued. "Laughter was our language of love and a protection against its dangerous depths."

When Peter returned to the stage, he read part of a poem he'd found in the drawer by his mother's bed. "Letter from San Francisco" speaks of "A wild bright day, splendid, sun-split," that turns summer fog from gray to white, makes the sea blue, and fills the air with scents of eucalyptus and lemon. "This day should not have come—as grief / Comes back, that should be dead. Recalled, / You pierce my cool grey days with light."[4]

And so it was that through grief, Alice's friends remembered her.

A hundred and forty people signed the guest book. Peter wasn't sure how many curious observers attended but didn't sign. Adams "breathed in the attention of men as if it were pure oxygen" and yet "gathered other beautiful women around her too . . . to encourage their talents, to teach them, and to be taught," Stephanie Salter wrote in her article about the memorial celebration for the *San Francisco Examiner*.

After the public memorial, Peter hosted a private buffet dinner at his mother's house. He invited the guests to choose something they liked from among his mother's personal things. Victoria Wilson selected a bronze rose that lay on the desk where Alice wrote the books that Vicky edited; she keeps it still in her office at Knopf. Although Edwina Leggett worried that in going through Alice's things they were like "those rapacious women in *Zorba the Greek*," friends treasured Alice's jewelry and scarves. Several wore them when they were interviewed for this biography. Peter sent a selection of photographs and one of Alice's favorite rings to Judith Clark Adams in Washington, DC. "The ring is one I've seen many times," she replied. "I put it on immediately and heard her laughing at me. Never mind. While not on such a distinguished hand, it still looks good!" Now in her nineties, Judith continues to wear it with pride.

Shortly after the memorial, Peter called Stephen Brown, his friend since his school days. "After listening to all those eulogies, he needed to talk to someone who knew his mother in another way, who knew she could be a real bitch," Brown said. "She was a tough woman. She did not suffer fools at all. She let her opinion be known and she could be pretty severe. She had a hard side. Mark Linenthal was an ever-present figure, but you did not bring up anything about him in front of Alice."

In the will she had made in 1988, Adams made bequests to Sydney Goldstein and Charles Breyer's children and left most of what she owned to Peter. She designated Breyer as executor of her estate. Since Breyer had been appointed by President Clinton as a senior United States District Court judge in 1997, Goldstein and a different attorney took care of the details. Later in the summer, when Peter was preparing his mother's house for sale, he invited Bob over to take some items that had been his. By then Bob lived with Linda Hogan in a house virtually across the street from where he'd first lived with Alice. Bob worked for hours prying the huge mirrors off the walls at Alice's; those that didn't shatter he piled on top of his station wagon. "As onerous and sad as the overall project was," Bob wrote Peter afterward, "it was quite nice to be in harness, so to speak, with you."*

Alice's papers and correspondence, a selection of her childhood books, and some of her wardrobe, including the Helga Howie green crocheted dress she wore at the PEN/Faulkner Awards ceremony in 1986, went to the Harry Ransom Center at the University of Texas. The rest of her library fills a space under the eaves in Peter and Phil's attic. In the fall Alice's house sold for $1.7 million, about three times what she'd paid for it twelve years earlier. After the mortgage and hefty estate taxes were paid, Peter still received a windfall he'd never expected. He surprised several writer and artist friends of Alice's with generous checks.

Peter buried some of his mother's cremated remains at the top of Mount Vision in Point Reyes National Seashore where she'd loved to hike. With him were Phil Anasovich, Millicent Dillon, Judith Rascoe, Derek Parmenter, and Derek's black dog, Pepper. The rest of Alice's ashes Peter placed in a handmade paper box and mailed to Max Steele for his writers' corner in the Old Chapel Hill Cemetery.

On behalf of Knopf, Victoria Wilson hosted another memorial gathering at the Kiernans' apartment in New York in December 1999. Peter attended, along with friends who hadn't come to the San Francisco service. Among these was the distinguished critic Richard Poirier, who reminisced about time spent in restaurants with Alice. For her, he said, "food wasn't the most important part of going out to dinner . . . Talk was what mattered most—gossipy, playful, bright talk." He told an anecdote about Alice's indignation at a man who was making an "utterly stupid" argument that San Francisco's restaurants were superior to those in Paris or New York. Trying to calm Alice, Poirier said the man might be right. " 'So what if he's right?' " she retorted. "In essence she was saying, 'Why ask such a question? We go to dinner with one another for joy, the fun of doing so—and that's that. Ask a stupid question, she was saying, and you get a stupid answer. It's what *Lear* is all about."[5]

* Bob lived with Hogan until he died in 2005. Peter stayed in touch with him and made efforts to help his surviving children. Morissa McNie died of lung cancer at the home of her friend Deborah Sparks on Orcas Island in 2010; Robbie died of a heart condition while living in a storage container near the San Francisco waterfront in 2014.

Alice would have hated "all the folderol" about the new millennium, Wilson commented to Peter after that gathering. Nonetheless, *After the War*, her last novel, would be published in that epoch, in December 2000. Adams hadn't polished the manuscript, so Knopf hired Trent Duffy, a friend of Alice's who had often worked with Billy Abrahams, to go over it. When Duffy turned in corrections to the novel's time scheme to Knopf's production editor, she told him she knew that Adams was a little bit careless about things like that and they usually didn't bother to fix them. For the dust jacket Wilson selected a candid photograph of Alice from "after the war" in 1948. Likewise, reviewers took the occasion to survey Adams's whole career. Randall Curb, writing in the Raleigh *News & Observer*, called her final story collection, *The Last Lovely City*, one of Adams's finest works. Her "unflagging curiosity about people's hearts has led some to call her America's Colette," he wrote. Then Curb posed a question that first arose with the commercial success of *Superior Women* and has persisted in discussions of Adams's work, particularly of her novels. Was she "a gossipy purveyor of the literary equivalent of the 'chick flick'" or an "astute, bemused anatomist of contemporary urban life—a master of the comedy of manners"?[6] Like King Lear's question to his daughters, it was the kind of question that Adams would have disdained. Gossip and romance were serious matters, not to be separated from analysis of contemporary life.

Thinking ahead, Steele had already purchased a modest upright gravestone for himself, carried it around in his car for a while, and then had it set at the head of his plot. When rumors of his death became a nuisance, he placed a smaller stone that said "HE'S NOT HERE" where his feet would have been if his body were there. When Max ordered that footstone, he also bought a flat marker that said "ALICE ADAMS WRITER" and placed that in his plot. One summer morning in 2005, Steele fell down the stairs in his town house, broke his neck, and died. His ashes were buried under his monument, just to the side of the stone he'd laid there for Alice.

I began to hear about Max Steele soon after I decided to write this biography. One of his sons met me for coffee in San Francisco and showed me a picture of an Adams letter on his phone. (Where was it now? He wasn't sure.) A few of the letters they'd exchanged were archived among Adams's papers at the Harry Ransom Center, but their number simply did not account for this long friendship between writers. On my first trip to North Carolina to see where Alice grew up, I interviewed Max's former wife, Diana Steele. The family renting Max's town house let me examine Max's shelves and furniture. Antique desks and cabinets, all with many cubbyholes for papers, were empty. No letters. Still Max's presence abided, especially on bookshelves that held his full run of the *Paris Review*, and books dedicated to him by friends, including Alice Adams. I learned that Oliver Steele's wife, Margaret Minsky, had stored some cartons in a locked closet of the condo. We emailed. There were cartons in the attic as well. Finally, in May 2011, I joined Margaret for a few days of biographical housecleaning in Chapel Hill, which seemed the best way to read any letters from Adams that Max had saved. I accepted Margaret's offer to stay in the guest room of Max's house—where Alice had slept in 1998—so I could work late into the night. I hadn't counted on the musty smells that assaulted us as we dug through boxes that had been stored in a humid climate. For three days Margaret and I talked and sorted, two women who'd just met but had this work in common—page by page, folder by folder, box by box. We found dozens of letters and postcards from Alice to Max, along with letters and other writings by Max.

In the evenings we sat outside in the warm, blossom-scented Carolina evening air that Alice Adams so loved. When Alice wrote stories and novels set in Chapel Hill, she asked Max to tell her what bloomed during a particular month so she could describe it correctly. When we finished going through the papers, a crew from the Wilson Library at the University of North Carolina collected the boxes of letters and manuscripts. But there was still a heavy package that confounded me. It sat on the top shelf in Max Steele's closet wrapped in silky brown printed cloth. I mentioned it to Margaret, who said, "Those must be Alice's ashes."

I was skeptical. Weren't the ashes buried under the granite marker that said "ALICE ADAMS WRITER" in the Old Chapel Hill Cemetery? I called Peter Linenthal and asked him how his mother's ashes had been sent to Max. He described a handmade box and a sleeve of Balinese batik fabric. I told him what we'd found. Peter was astonished, but there was no denying these were the mortal remains of Alice Adams.

I called the writer Daphne Athas, a friend and colleague of Max's, who was less surprised. "Max did not make a great separation between intentions and actions," she explained. "I imagine he *meant* to put her ashes in the cemetery." Novelist Jill McCorkle remembered, "Max told everyone proudly that he kept her ashes on his dresser. It was well known that he had a great love affair with Alice. *He* told people. There was speculation in town that Max wanted Alice's ashes mixed and buried with his own."

It was too late for that. Strange as it might have been to leave Alice in the custody of a woman who was in some way her rival for Max's affections, Diana Steele became the caretaker of the ashes while Peter thought through this problem. When Diana moved to a condo, she gamely sent Peter a picture of the wrapped urn—of Alice—at a new address: "You can Google it. Light and airy . . . She's there in the cupboard over the refrigerator in the kitchen."[7]

On the day after Mother's Day in 2013, Peter Linenthal and his husband, Philip Anasovich; Adams scholar Bryant Mangum; and I joined Diana at Max Steele's writers' corner in the Old Chapel Hill Cemetery. The five of us improvised a ceremony to complete Alice and Max's old plan "to get a plot together." Diana brought the batik sack, digging tools, and a basket of loose leaves and petals from her garden. Peter set the "ALICE ADAMS WRITER" stone aside. He dug a deep hole in the soft dirt and poured the second half of Alice's ashes into the ground. We mixed in some bright, sweet petals and leaves. We added handfuls of dirt to refill the hole and washed our hands in a basin of water that Diana had thought to bring.

Peter replaced the stone marker and set lilies and a vase of roses beside it. Bryant and I added two long-stemmed roses, one red and one white, representing our hopes to write books about the work and the life of Alice Adams. It was a beautiful blue Carolina day with high cumulus clouds, not too hot. One of Max's azaleas was in full pink bloom. The graves of Alice's parents, Agatha and Nicholson Adams, were some twenty yards away, marked by similar but widely separated upright stones. A young tree grew between them.

We read aloud from Alice's childhood poem "Radiant Ghost" and her story "Home Is Where." We closed with lines from Adams's essay called "At First Sight: Love and Liking, a Memoir" about the validity of first impressions and her three great friendships—with Judith Clark Adams, Billy Abrahams, and Max Steele—that began with instant love and liking.

In that essay, bringing the story of her life full circle, Alice describes her spring visit to Chapel Hill just a year before she died: "The old town was at its most beautiful—everywhere, white dogwood delicately spreading its branches. Max and I took our customary walk through the cemetery."

Chronology

1893   Agatha Erskine Boyd born February 20 in Roanoke, Virginia.

1895   Nicholson Barney Adams born November 6 in Fredericksburg, Virginia.

1912   James (Trummy) Young born January 12 in Savannah, Georgia.

1920   Agatha Boyd and Nicholson Adams marry on June 12 in Roanoke, Virginia.

1921   Mark Linenthal Jr. born November 12 in Boston.

1922   Vasco Futscher Pereira born in Lisbon, Portugal; Henry Maxwell Steele born in Greenville, South Carolina.

1925   F. Scott Fitzgerald publishes *The Great Gatsby*.

1925   Robert Kendall McNie born June 12 in Long Beach, California.

1925   Agatha and Nic Adams purchase farmhouse near Pittsboro Road in Chapel Hill, North Carolina, where Nicholson is an assistant professor of Spanish.

1926   Alice Boyd Adams born August 14 in Fredericksburg, Virginia; Judith Walker Clark (later Adams) born February 23 in Madison, Wisconsin.

1929   Thomas Wolfe publishes *Look Homeward, Angel*.

1931   Death of baby Joel Willard Adams on August 30 in Durham, North Carolina.

1932   Nic Adams hospitalized for a nervous breakdown.

1933   Franklin D. Roosevelt (FDR) inaugurated president; Adolf Hitler becomes chancellor of Germany.

1935   Nic Adams falls in love with Dorothy Stearns Wilson.

1936   Civil war begins in Spain.

1937   Judith Clark and her parents move to Chapel Hill.

1938   Agatha and Nic Adams travel in Cuba and Mexico while Alice spends the summer at a girls' camp in Maine. Germany annexes Czechoslovakia.

1939   Billie Holiday first performs and records "Strange Fruit"; *The Grapes of Wrath* by John Steinbeck is published. Germany invades Poland.

1940   Alice completes tenth grade at Chapel Hill High School and begins eleventh grade at Wisconsin High School in Madison, Wisconsin. FDR elected to third term as president.

1941   Alice enrolls at St. Catherine's School in Richmond, Virginia. Germany invades Russia. Japan attacks US at Pearl Harbor and US declares war on Germany and Japan.

1943   Alice graduates St. Catherine's School in May and begins first year at Radcliffe College in the summer.

1944   Mark Linenthal shot down and becomes prisoner of war in Germany.

1945   Mark Linenthal liberated from POW camp and enrolls as graduate student in English at Harvard. FDR dies; World War II ends.

1946   Alice Adams graduates from Radcliffe, moves to New York City, marries Mark Linenthal in Chapel Hill on November 30, and moves with him to Cambridge.

1947-48   Alice and Mark Linenthal sail to Europe for a year, where they become friends with Norman and Beatrice Mailer in Paris.

1948   Norman Mailer publishes *The Naked and the Dead*; Alice and Mark Linenthal move to Northern California, where he attends Stanford; Harry S. Truman elected president.

1949   *Le deuxième sexe* by Simone de Beauvoir published in France (first English translation published 1953); Alice begins psychoanalytic therapy in San Francisco.

1950   Agatha Boyd Adams dies in Chapel Hill on March 17.

1951   Peter Adams Linenthal born March 20 in Redwood City, California.

1951   Alice, Mark, and Peter move to Portland, Oregon, while Mark teaches at Reed College.

1952   Alice meets Saul Bellow; Alice, Mark, and Peter move back to California; Dwight D. Eisenhower elected president.

1954   Mark Linenthal joins faculty at San Francisco State College; Alice, Mark, and Peter move to San Francisco.

1955   Nic Adams marries Dorothy Stearns Wilson (Dotsie).

1956   Alice, Mark, and Peter vacation at Lake Sebago; Mark completes his PhD and Peter begins kindergarten at Town School for Boys in San Francisco.

1957   Alice, Mark, and Peter drive through Sonora, Mexico, on a summer trip.

1958   Alice and Peter spend summer in Chapel Hill; Alice meets Henry Maxwell Steele.

1959   "Winter Rain" published in *Charm*; Alice and Mark Linenthal divorce; Alice meets Vasco Futscher Pereira.

1960   Judith Clark Adams and family move from San Francisco to Washington, DC; John F. Kennedy elected president; *To Kill a Mockingbird* by Harper Lee published.

1961   Vasco Futscher Pereira leaves San Francisco; Max Steele and his wife, Diana, move to San Francisco.

1962   Franz Sommerfeld dies in Seattle.

1963   Alice working at Child Guidance Clinic in San Francisco; *The Feminine Mystique* by Betty Friedan published; John F. Kennedy assassinated; Lyndon Johnson becomes president.

1964   Alice meets Robert Kendall McNie.

1965   New American Library purchases Alice's novel *Careless Love*.

1966   *Careless Love* published. Alice begins living with Robert McNie. American soldiers engage in active fighting in Vietnam.

1967   Peter Linenthal attends Human Be-In in Golden Gate Park, transfers to public high school for eleventh grade; *Careless Love* published as *The Fall of Daisy Duke* in Great Britain.

1968   The *New Yorker* purchases "The Swastika on Our Door"; Alice works at Institute of Medical Science; William Abrahams moves to Northern California; Richard Nixon elected president.

1969   The *New Yorker* purchases and publishes "Gift of Grass"; Peter Linenthal begins study at San Francisco Art Institute and moves out of his parents' houses.

1970   Nicholson Adams dies in Chapel Hill on October 2; Alice learns she is not mentioned in her father's will; Peter travels in Europe; *The Female Eunuch* by Germaine Greer is published.

1971   "Gift of Grass" wins third prize in O. Henry Awards; Alice collects unemployment insurance.

1972   Cyrilly Abels, Alice's new literary agent, sells stories to the *Atlan-
        tic*, *Redbook*, *McCall's*; Alice publishes novelization of movie
        Two People under pseudonym Alice Boyd.

1973   United States military withdraws from Vietnam; Victoria Wilson,
        editor at Knopf, acquires *Families and Survivors*.

1974   *Families and Survivors* published; Alice starts women writers'
        group with Diane Johnson, Ella Leffland, and others; Richard
        Nixon resigns, and Gerald Ford becomes president.

1975   Alice and Robert McNie take their first winter trip to Zihua-
        tanejo; the *New Yorker* publishes "Roses, Rhododendron";
        Families and Survivors nominated for National Book Critics
        Circle Award; Alice's Knopf editor, Victoria Wilson, comes
        to Truckee to meet Alice; literary agent Cyrilly Abels dies and
        Adams becomes client of Lynn Nesbit at International Creative
        Management.

1976   "Roses, Rhododendron" wins third prize in O. Henry Awards and
        National Endowment for the Arts award; John Updike receives
        O. Henry Special Award for Continuing Achievement; Alice
        publishes "Learning to Be Happy" (later "Home Is Where")
        in *Redbook*; Saul Bellow wins Nobel Prize for Literature; Joch
        Allin (Winky) McNie commits suicide; Alice receives fifty gifts
        from Robert McNie on her fiftieth birthday; Jimmy Carter
        elected president.

1977   The *New Yorker* publishes "Beautiful Girl" and Alice meets her
        fiction editor there, Frances Kiernan.

1978   *Listening to Billie* published; Alice and Bob profiled in *People*
        magazine; Alice wins Guggenheim Fellowship; assassination
        of Supervisor Harvey Milk and Mayor George Moscone at
        San Francisco city hall.

1979   *Beautiful Girl* (story collection) published; Dorothy (Dotsie)
        Adams plans to sell the house where Alice grew up in Chapel
        Hill; Dr. Lucie Jessner dies.

1980   *Rich Rewards* published; Amanda Urban begins represent-
        ing Adams's short stories for ICM; Ronald Reagan elected
        president.

1981   AIDS recognized as epidemic in San Francisco.

1982   Alice receives O. Henry Continuing Achievement award after
        her twelfth consecutive appearance in the O. Henry Awards

anthology; *To See You Again* (story collection) published; John Cheever dies; *The Color Purple* by Alice Walker published.

1983 Alice visits Chapel Hill for the first time since 1958.

1984 *Superior Women* published; James "Trummy" Young dies in San Jose, California; Vasco Futscher Pereira dies in Lisbon, Portugal.

1985 *Return Trips* (story collection) published.

1986 Alice and Robert McNie purchase house at 2661 Clay Street, San Francisco; Alice has surgery for malignant tumor in her colon; Joyce Carol Oates receives O. Henry Special Award for Continuing Achievement.

1987 Robert Gottlieb replaces William Shawn as editor of the *New Yorker*; Alice Adams and Robert McNie separate.

1988 *Second Chances* published; George H. W. Bush elected president.

1989 *After You've Gone* (story collection) published; Amanda Urban of ICM becomes Adams's primary literary agent.

1990 *Mexico: Some Travels and Some Travelers There* published.

1991 *Caroline's Daughters* published.

1992 Alice has surgery for cancer in her sinuses; Alice receives Literature Award from American Academy and Institute of Arts and Letters; Alice's stepmother, Dorothy Stearns Adams, dies in Santa Rosa, California; Tina Brown becomes editor of the *New Yorker*; Bill Clinton elected president.

1993 *Almost Perfect* published.

1995 *A Southern Exposure* published.

1997 *Medicine Men* published.

1998 John Updike selects "Roses, Rhododendron" for *The Best American Short Stories of the Twentieth Century*; Alice completes manuscript of *After the War*, her eleventh published novel.

1999 *The Last Lovely City* (story collection) published; Frances Jaffer Linenthal dies, January 20, 1999; Alice Adams dies at home in San Francisco on May 27.

2000 *After the War* published posthumously.

2002 *The Stories of Alice Adams* published.

2005 Robert Kendall McNie dies in San Francisco; Max Steele dies in Chapel Hill.

2007 Norman Mailer dies in Manhattan.

2008 Peter Adams Linenthal and Philip Anasovich marry in San Francisco.
2010 Mark Linenthal dies in San Francisco.
2011 Daniel Simon dies in Berkeley.
2015 Derek Parmenter dies in Mill Valley, California.

Acknowledgments

An Alfred A. and Blanche W. Knopf Fellowship and an Andrew W. Mellon Foundation Research Fellowship from the Harry Ransom Center at the University of Texas allowed me to spend three months in close daily contact with Alice Adams's manuscripts, correspondence, travel photos, and childhood books, and even a small collection of her jewelry and clothing. Also at the marvelous Ransom Center are the papers of Diane Johnson, Millicent Dillon, Norman Mailer, and other associates of Alice Adams, as well as the editorial records of Victoria Wilson. I'm grateful to Thomas Staley, Steven Ennis, Richard B. Watson, Eric Colleary, Bridget Gayle Ground, Kate Hayes, Kathryn Millan, Gil Hartman, Selina Hastings, Joanne Ravel, Wanda Penn, Kevin Keim of the Charles Moore Foundation, and Caffé Medici for making me welcome in Austin. In addition, with help from Tim West, I found troves of valuable material at the Louis Round Wilson Special Collections Library at the University of North Carolina in Chapel Hill. Visits to the Cecil H. Green Library at Stanford University (for William Miller Abrahams papers), the Special Collections at UCLA (for Carolyn See's papers), the Environmental Design Library and the Graduate Union Theological Library at UC Berkeley, the San Francisco Public Library, and the New York Public Library (where David Smith provided extraordinary assistance) were also essential.

Many other archivists, historians, and institutions provided me with information by email, including: Arielle Orem at Randolph College; Gregory R. Kreuger of the Lynchburg Museum System in Virginia; Julia Randle at Virginia Theological Seminary; Lisa S. McCown at Washington & Lee University; Judith Chaimson at the Central Rappahannock Heritage Center; Bland Simpson at the University of North Carolina; Tyler Bird Paul at St. Catherine's School in Richmond, Virginia; David Null at the Steenbock Library, University of Wisconsin; staff at the

Houghton Library at Harvard University and the Schlesinger Library at the Radcliffe Institute; Katherine Salzmann at Texas State University in San Marcos (for Beverly Lowry's correspondence); Katrin Kokot at Deutsche Nationalbibliothek in Frankfurt (for Lucie Jessner's papers); Allan Ochs at the History Center of San Luis Obispo County, California; the Special Collections Research Center, Syracuse University (for Joyce Carol Oates's papers); the Special Collections Library at Vassar College (for Ann Cornelisen's papers); and Tim Ronk and Joel D. Drout at Houston Public Library. The Sonoma County Public Library is my home team and I owe particular thanks to the skills and patience of David Dodd and the Interlibrary Loan Department.

During the nine years I've worked on *Alice Adams: Portrait of a Writer* I've spoken with or exchanged written messages with hundreds of friends and colleagues of my subject. These conversations are acknowledged at the head of my endnotes for each chapter of the book. Here I'd like to name a few individuals who found time to give me more extensive interviews: Chester Aaron, Philip Anasovich, Daphne Athas, Elaine Badgley Arnoux, Ruth Gebhart Belmeur, Eleanor Bertino, Nancy Boas, Sandy Boucher, Virginia Breier, Stephen Brown, Theophilus Brown, Alyce Denier, Millicent Dillon, Stephen Drewes, Deirdre English, Anne Fabbri, Carol and John Field, Cynthia Scott Francisco, Thaisa Frank, Blair Fuller, Diana Fuller, Imogene Gieling, Lucy Gray and David Thomson, Adam and Arlie Hochschild, George Homsey, Diane Johnson, Robert Flynn Johnson, Frances Kiernan, Jane Kristiansen and Patty O'Grady, Jeremy Larner, Ella Leffland, Edwina Evers Leggett and Jack Leggett, Mark Linenthal, Phillip Lopate, Beverly Lowry, Judith and John Luce, Alison Lurie, Fred Lyon, Peter Manso, Scott Massey, Maureen Looney Mather, Margaret Mayer, Morissa McNie, Robert McNie Jr., Margaret Minsky, John Murray, Nancy Oakes, Phyllis Silverman Ott-Toltz, Lincoln Pain, Louis Pain, Derek Parmenter, David Reid, Christy Rocca, Richard Rodriguez, Jean Salter Roetter, Bernard Rosenthal, Penelope Rowlands, Sandra Russell, Jay Schaefer, Carolyn See, Beatrice Silverman, Deborah Sparks, Anya Spielman, Matilde Brunswick Stewart, Susan Sward, Amanda Urban, Barbara Mailer Wasserman, and Nancy and Thomas Wilson Jr.

Some of Alice's friends have been such an integral part of this project that I cannot imagine having completed it without them: Alice's dearest friend, Judith Clark Adams; Bryant Mangum, whose monograph *Understanding Alice Adams* is the first comprehensive study of Adams's work; Adams's editors Frances Kiernan and Victoria Wilson; Peter Stansky, life partner to the late Billy Abrahams; Margaret Minsky, daughter-in-law to Max Steele, and Diana Whittinghill Steele, former wife of Max Steele. Alice Adams's son, artist and historian Peter Adams Linenthal, with the cooperation of his husband, Phil Anasovich, has been a tireless co-researcher and has generously shared his curiosity about his mother's life without ever limiting my freedom to write her biography as I've seen fit.

I'm grateful to Biographers International Organization, founded in the year I began this book, for being the only organization of its kind devoted to all aspects of the art and craft of biography. Good friends of mine have encouraged me with their questions and theories and simply by becoming readers of Alice Adams and discussing her life and stories with me: Rose Balistrieri, Martha Bergland, Annette DeBernardi Brass, Flora Coker, Cathy Curtis, Kathleen Fenton, Kathryn Madonna, Robert Marshall, Beth Phillips, Laurie Prothro, Mary Anne Sobiereij, and Stephanie Ranger Turner. Others have become comadres of the book by suggesting research angles or reading drafts—especially Sarah Barrow, Anne Heller, Bryant Mangum, Deborah Denenholz Morse, Carol Polsgrove, and Deborah Robbins. At home, R. M. Ryan has been patient and loving while also asking many important questions. In myriad ways Robert Lewellin Ryan, Katherine Snoda Ryan, and Hongshen Ma have offered their perspectives on the subject of how people live and do their work. Lisen Caroline Ma and Kai-Ling Ma have provided wonderful distraction and good cheer.

Sandra Dijkstra, Elise Capron, Andrea Cavallero, and their team at Sandra Dijkstra Literary Agency have been stalwart devotees of the Alice Adams story. At Scribner, the still incomparable Colin Harrison, Nan Graham, and Susan Moldow provided unstinting encouragement from the outset of the project, and Sarah Goldberg has devoted her inexhaustible verve, patience, humor, and intelligence to its completion. Thank you also to Laura Wise, Aja Pollock, Jaya Miceli, and Kyle Kabel.

Works by Alice Adams

BOOKS

Careless Love (novel). New York: New American Library, 1966. Republished as *The Fall of Daisy Duke*. London: Constable, 1967.
Families and Survivors (novel). New York: Knopf, 1974.
Listening to Billie (novel). New York: Knopf, 1978.
Beautiful Girl (stories). New York: Knopf, 1979.
Rich Rewards (novel). New York: Knopf, 1980.
To See You Again (stories). New York: Knopf, 1982.
Superior Women (novel). New York: Knopf, 1984.
Return Trips (stories). New York: Knopf, 1985.
Second Chances (novel). New York: Knopf, 1988.
After You've Gone (stories). New York: Knopf, 1989.
Mexico: Some Travels and Some Travelers There (nonfiction). New York: Prentice Hall, 1990.
Caroline's Daughters (novel). New York: Knopf, 1991.
Almost Perfect (novel). New York: Knopf, 1993.
A Southern Exposure (novel). New York: Knopf, 1995.
Medicine Men (novel). New York: Knopf, 1997.
The Last Lovely City (stories). New York: Knopf, 1999.
After the War (novel). New York: Knopf, 2000.
The Stories of Alice Adams (stories). New York: Knopf, 2002.
The Stories of Alice Adams, with an introduction by Victoria Wilson (stories). New York: Vintage, 2019.

UNCOLLECTED WORKS CITED IN THIS BIOGRAPHY

"Arabel's List." *Ploughshares* 24, no. 2–3 (Fall 1998): 76–84.
"At First Sight: Love and Liking, a Memoir." *Southern Review* 35 (Summer 1999): 567–78.

"At the Races." *Crosscurrents: A Quarterly,* "Selections" (1989): 70–88.

"Balcony Scenes: A Portrait of the Artist as a Young Movie Romantic." *American Film* 16 (March 1991): 76.

"The Best Revenge." *Boulevard* 13, no. 3 (Spring 1998): 82–91.

"Breakfast at Louie's Café." *Key West Review* (1989).

[Comment]. In *American Voices: Best Short Fiction by Contemporary Authors with Comments by the Authors,* ed. Sally Arteseros. New York: Hyperion, 1992, 1.

"Complicities." *Michigan Quarterly Review* 34 (Summer 1995): 324–29.

"First Date." *Redbook* 193, no. 2 (August 1999).

"Frida Kahlo's Passion." *Art & Antiques* 6, no. 1 (January 1989): 58–67, 98.

"Great Sex." *Southwest Review* 83, no. 4 (1998): 512–19.

"Henry and the Pale-Faced Indian." *Cosmopolitan* 163, no. 4 (October 1967): 146–50.

"Her Unmentionables." *Yale Review* 87, no. 4 (October 1999): 44–51.

"Introduction." In *Best American Short Stories of 1991,* ed. Alice Adams. Boston: Houghton Mifflin, 1991, xiii–xvii.

"The Last Married Man," *Virginia Quarterly Review* 54, no. 2 (Spring 1978): 289–396.

The Lila Stories, in addition to four collected in *The Last Lovely City*:
   "Answering Machines." Unpublished typescript, HRC.
   "At the Races." *Crosscurrents,* "Selections" 8, no. 3 (1989): 70–85.
   "The Grape Arbor." *Crosscurrents,* "Selections" 8, no. 3 (1989): 52–69.
   "Time Alone." New Yorker (August 4, 1986): 28–36.

"Love and Work." *Southwest Review* 77, no. 4 (Autumn 1992): 466–79.

"Madeline and Me." *Life* 13 (July 1990): 103.

"A Natural Woman." *Allure* [1991 or 1992, original not located].

"The Nice Girl." *McCall's* 101, no. 11 (August 1974): 94–95, 108ff.

"On Turning Fifty." *Vogue* 173 (December 1983): 230, 235.

"Postwar Paris: Chronicles of Literary Life." *Paris Review* 150 (1998): 317–19.

"A Propitiation of Witches," *Redbook* 134, no. 4 (February 1970): 60–170, 172ff.

"Sea Gulls are Happier Here." *Cosmopolitan* 162, no. 1 (January 1967): 108–111.

"Summer, Clothes & Love," *SFE Image* (June 10, 1990): 28–31.

"The Three Bears and Little Red Riding Hood in the Coffin House," *Mirror, Mirror on the Wall: Women Writers Explore Their Favorite*

Fairy Tales, ed. Kate Bernheimer. New York: Anchor Books/Random House, 2002, 5–6.

"Up the Coast." *Gentleman's Quarterly* 62, no. 5 (May 1992): 113–16.

"What to say to friends who have just published something—anything." *Christian Science Monitor*, September 18, 1973.

"A Week in Venice," *McCall's* 102, no. 2 (November 1974): 112, 182, 184, 188.

"Why I Write." *First Person Singular: Writers on Their Craft*, compiled by Joyce Carol Oates. (Princeton, NJ: Ontario Review Press, 1983), 273–76.

"The Wild Coasts of Portugal," *Geo* 6, no. 11 (August 1984): 56–65ff.

"The Wrong Virginia." *Agni Review* 43 (1996): 193–205.

"Young Couple with Class." *Redbook* 129, no. 5 (September 1967): 72–121ff.

UNPUBLISHED WORKS CITED IN THIS BIOGRAPHY

The following typescripts are among the Alice Adams Papers at the HRC:

"America's Room, and Mine" (essay, c. 1991).

"A Bachelor's Fate" (short story, c. 1965).

"A California Trip" (short story, c. 1970).

"Coin of the Realm" (short story, c. 1958).

"Commencement Address for English Department," University of California Berkeley (May 22, 1987).

"The Cruellest Month" (short story, 1946).

"Curtains" (short story, 1946).

"The Edge of the Water" (short story, c. 1962).

"The Fog in the Streets" (short story, c. 1955).

"Former Friends" (short story, 1983).

"The Furniture: A True Story" (short story, c. 1976).

"The Green Creek" (short story, c. 1955).

"The Hills" (short story, c. 1947).

"The Impersonators" (novel, c. 1951).

"Ladies in Waiting" (short story, c. 1960).

"A Lesson" (essay, 1996).

"Letters to Cambridge" (short story, c. 1960).

"Night Fears" (short story, c. 1962).

"Out Where the Birds Are" (story for children, c. 1995).

"A Room Alone" (short story, 1946).

"School Spirit" (short story, c. 1960).

"Sending Love" (incomplete short story, 1999).

"Street Woman" (essay, c. 1989).

"The Wake" (short story, c. 1955).

"Why I Left Home: Partial Truths" (essay c. 1998, discovered in an unopened envelope by JCA in 2013).

"Wonderful" (short story, 1946).

SELECTED INTERVIEWS WITH ALICE ADAMS

Kay Bonetti, American Audio Prose Library, 1987.

Neil Feineman, "An Interview with Alice Adams," *StoryQuarterly* 11 (1980).

Marilyn Scharine, "Our Arts" Wasatch Radio, Salt Lake City, March 1987 (HRC).

Michael Silverblatt, "Bookworm" KCRW (Los Angeles), 1989 (HRC).

Don Swaim, "Interview," September 17, 1984. Audio recording, Archives and Special Collections, Ohio University, Donald L. Swaim Collection.

Notes

The Alice Adams Papers are held by the Harry Ransom Center at the University of Texas in Austin. Notebooks and unpublished materials and interviews not further identified here are held in that collection; the records of Alfred A. Knopf Inc. are also held at the Ransom Center. The Papers of Agatha Boyd Adams and those of Henry Maxwell Steele reside at the Wilson Library at the University of North Carolina in Chapel Hill.

In an effort to keep these endnotes from being endless, I have omitted notes for quotations from published works by Alice Adams that are cited within the text. Statements attributed within the text are from interviews I conducted in person or by letter, email, or telephone. At the head of each chapter's notes I have listed people who provided information for that chapter. The notes below document sources not identified in the text. I have sometimes silently corrected spelling errors in Alice Adams's notebooks or letters and silently omitted inessential words from quotations. Dates given in brackets are estimates based on contextual information.

Abbreviations used in the notes:

AA	Alice Adams
ABA	Agatha Boyd Adams
AP	*Almost Perfect*
ATW	*After the War*
AYG	*After You've Gone*
BG	*Beautiful Girl*
CD	*Caroline's Daughters*
CL	*Careless Love* or *The Fall of Daisy Duke*
CS	Carol Sklenicka
DJ	Diane Johnson

DSA   Dorothy Stearns Adams
FJL   Frances Jaffer (Pain) Linenthal
FS   *Families and Survivors*
HMS   Henry Maxwell Steele
HRC   University of Texas, Harry Ransom Center
JCA   Judith Clark Adams
LB   *Listening to Billie*
LJ   Lucie Jessner
LLC   *The Last Lonely City*
MEX   *Mexico: Some Travels and Some Travelers There*
ML   Mark Linenthal Junior
MM   *Medicine Men*
N   Notebooks of Alice Adams, Harry Ransom Center
NBA   Nicholson Barney Adams
NM   Norman Mailer
NYPL   New York Public Library, Manuscripts and Archives Division
PA   Philip Anasovich
PAL   Peter Adams Linenthal
PUL   Princeton University Library
RKM   Robert Kendall McNie
RMWC   Randolph-Macon Woman's College
RP   Richard Poirier
RR   *Rich Rewards*
RT   *Return Trips*
SC   *Second Chances*
SE   *A Southern Exposure*
SU   Green Library, Stanford University
SW   *Superior Women*
TS   typescript
TSYA   *To See You Again*
UNC   University of North Carolina
VW   Victoria Wilson
WMA   William Miller Abrahams

PROLOGUE

1 AA to Kenneth and Valerie Lynn, November 5, 1949.
2 "It's a very good year for Alice," *San Francisco Examiner*, January 31, 1975, 22.
3 AA, "Summer, Clothes & Love."

4 AA, "At First Sight: Love and Liking, a Memoir."

5 AA, "Summer, Clothes & Love."

6 AA, "At First Sight: Love and Liking, a Memoir."

7 AA, "Home Is Where," *BG.*

8 Ann Kolson, "She Writes of the Life Within," *Philadelphia Inquirer,* October 15, 1984.

9 AA, "Roses, Rhododendron" and "Alternatives," *BG.*

CHAPTER 1: SAVED BY HER DOLLS

1 AA, "Madeline and Me."

2 Ibid.

3 VW, memorial for AA, June 27, 1999. Audio recording, HRC.

4 AA, "Why I Write."

5 AA, "On Turning Fifty."

6 N, November 9, 1959.

7 Birth certificate from Mary Washington Hospital, PAL collection; ob/gyn ward logbook, Duke University Medical Center Archives.

8 Virginia Adams Dare to PAL, September 1, 1985.

9 *FS.*

10 Laura Croghan Kamonie, *Neabsco and Occoquan: The Tayloe Family Iron Plantations, 1730–1830* (Prince William, VA: Prince William Historical Commission, 2003); Laura Croghan Kamonie, *Irons in the Fire: The Business History of the Tayloe Family and Virginia's Gentry, 1700–1860* (Charlottesville: University of Virginia Press, 2007).

11 George McCue, *Octagon: Being an Account of a Famous Washington Residence: Its Great Years, Decline and Restoration* (Washington, DC: American Institute of Architects Foundation, 1976).

12 Winslow M. Watson, *In Memoriam: Benjamin Ogle Tayloe* (Washington, DC: Sherman, 1872), 78–79.

13 Anthony Trollope, *North America* (Philadelphia: Lippincott, 1863), 2:50–51.

14 Anne Montgomery, "Buena Vista—Roanoke Plantation," *Journal of the Roanoke Historical Society* 1, no. 2 (Winter 1964–65): 23–24.

15 Richard S. Dunn, "The Demographic Structure of American Slavery: Jamaica versus Virginia," *Proceedings of the American Philosophical Society* 151, no. 1 (March 2007): 43–60; Tayloe family papers are held by the Virginia Historical Society, Richmond.

16 Agatha Boyd Adams, "Jobs for the Helen Hokinson Crowd," *RMWC Alumnae Bulletin* 42, no. 4 (June 1949): 8; reprinted in "Wanted: Jobs for the Helen Hokinson Crowd," *AAUW Journal* 43, no. 4 (Summer 1950): 213–18.

17 Agatha's grandmother, Elizabeth Henrietta Tayloe, died in 1864; two years later Munford married his first wife's cousin, Emma Tayloe, who was the daughter of William Henry Tayloe of Mount Airy.

18 Pearl S. Buck, *My Several Worlds* (New York: The John Day Co., 1954), 90–93.

19 "*flouncy frocks*": Hilary Spurling, *Pearl Buck in China: Journey to "The Good Earth"* (New York: Cambridge University Press, 2010), 71–77; "*made the acquaintance*": ABA, "For the Latin Majors," *RMWC Alumnae Bulletin,* 43, no. 3 (April 1950): 13.

20 AA, "Verlie I Say Unto You," *BG*.

21 ABA, "For the Latin Majors."

22 *1915 yearbook*, RMWC; *childhood portrait*, PAL collection. The 1915 photograph, which AA kept on her desk, was taken by James Abbe, who became a renowned photographer of famous personalities including Shirley Temple, Rudolph Valentino—and Joseph Stalin. Jessica Abbe noticed her grandfather's name on the picture while she was cat-sitting for AA in the late seventies.

CHAPTER 2: AGATHA AND NIC

Interviews: PAL.

1 Virginia Adams Dare (Nic's sister) to PAL, October 12, 1987.

2 Virginia Adams Dare to AA, August 23, 1988.

3 Spencer Tucker, Paul G. Pierpaoli, and Walter E. White, *The Civil War Naval Encyclopedia* (Santa Barbara, CA: ABC-CLIO, 2011), 1:156–57.

4 Virginia Adams Dare to PAL, April 23, 1986.

5 AA, "The Green Creek," chapter 1, TS, HRC.

6 The following limerick appeared in the *Torch* yearbook at Collegiate School for Girls in 1917: "There was a young Roman named Boyd / So teaching Latin she could not avoid / But she gave up her job / When she said with a sob, / "For Adams' Express Company I've just been employed."

7 Virginia Adams Dare to AA, August 23, 1988.

8 US Census, 1920.

9 NBA, *The Heritage of Spain: An Introduction to Spanish Civilization* (1943; rev. ed., New York: Henry Holt and Co., 1959), ix.

10 Virginia marriage license, June 11, 1920.

11 Columbia University Registrar's Office, email to CS, September 7, 2011. Nic's dissertation was published as *The Romantic Drama of Garcia Gutiérrez* (New York: Instituto de las Españas, 1922).

12 Virginia Adams Dare to PAL, Christmas 1988.

13 AA, "Wonderful," unpublished TS, HRC.

14 Thomas Boyd, email to PAL, January 15, 2015; John Esten Keller and Karl-Ludwig Selig, eds., *Hispanic Studies in Honor of Nicholson B. Adams* (Chapel Hill: UNC Press, 1966), 9.

15 ABA, *Paul Green of Chapel Hill* (Chapel Hill: UNC Library, 1951), 10.

16 AA interview with Kay Bonetti, American Audio Prose Library.

17 ABA, "The Pastelero de Madrigal in Nineteenth-Century Spanish Literature," MA thesis, Department of Romance Languages, UNC, 1925. "The madcap expedition to Africa of the young Portuguese king has a romantic charm which allures the fancy even in the dry pages of history; small wonder that poets, dramatists, and balladmakers, have returned to it again and again," writes Agatha Adams. Perhaps the same species of romantic charm drew Agatha to Nic Adams and Alice to men like Vasco Pereira.

18 ABA, "Jobs for the Helen Hokinson Crowd."

19 AA, "My First and Only House," *RT*, and Orange County, North Carolina, records.

CHAPTER 3: THE FAMILY ROMANCE

Interviews: JCA, Sandy McClamroch, Avery Russell, Diana Steele, Jacqueline H. Wolf.

1 *BG*, 6.
2 "Letter to Cambridge," unpublished MS, HRC.
3 *Tar Heel*, January 26, 1925; *Tar Heel*, February 4, 1925. This paper became the *Daily Tarheel* in 1929.
4 *Tar Heel*, November 2, 1926.
5 Hazel Rowley, *Richard Wright: The Life and Times* (New York: Henry Holt, 2001), 223–24.
6 "The Green Creek," unpublished MS, HRC.
7 Record for SS *Île de France*, arriving in New York from Le Havre, July 23, 1929.
8 Keller and Selig, *Hispanic Studies*, 11–13.
9 Archives of Henry Holt and Co., PUL.
10 AA to LJ, January 25, 1979.
11 AA, "Why I Left Home: Partial Truths."
12 ABA to Mrs. J. W. Boyd (dictated by Alice Adams), November 10, 1930.
13 AA, "Child's Play," *AYG*.
14 AA, "Why I Left Home: Partial Truths."
15 AA, "The Three Bears and Little Red Riding Hood in the Coffin House."
16 NBA to Tom Wilson, August 19, 1931.
17 Virginia Adams Dare to AA, August 28, 1988. Dare wrote, "Ed and I loved you but were too involved with Gee as an infant to give you the T.L.C. you really needed."
18 Ann Dally, "Status Lymphaticus: Sudden Death in Children from 'Visitation of God' to Cot Death," *Medical History* 41 (1997): 70–85; H. B. Dodwell, MD, "Status Lymphaticus: The Growth of a Myth," *Clinical Pathology in General Practice* (January 16, 1954), 149–51.
19 The record for Joel Adams's birth does not mention anesthesia, but the records show that many other cesarean births at Duke used the layered anesthesia protocol, according to Jacqueline H. Wolf, *Deliver Me from Pain: Anesthesia and Birth in America* (Baltimore: John Hopkins University Press, 2009), 94–95, 102–3.
20 A North Carolina certificate of death and Chapel Hill Cemetery records list the burial of Joel in section 3 of the Old Chapel Hill Cemetery. Neither grave marker nor evidence of a metal casket was found near Agatha and Nic's stones in 2010.
21 The ob-gyn logbook for 1931 at Duke University Medical Center Archives raises other questions about Agatha's history, listing her with three previous full-term pregnancies, no previous abortions or miscarriages, and two living children at the time of her admission to Duke Hospital in August 1931. No record of any children besides Alice and Joel has been located.
22 AA, "My First and Only House," *RT*.

CHAPTER 4: DEPRESSIONS

Interviews: Daphne Athas, John Ball, Mary Elizabeth (Jervey) Kilbey, Avery
Russell, Tom (Tombo) Wilson Jr.

1 N, April 22, 1999.
2 Daphne Athas, *Chapel Hill in Plain Sight* (Hillsborough, NC: Eno Publishers,
   2010), 117.
3 AA, *MEX*, 95.
4 AA, "Why I Write," 273.
5 William E. Leuchenburg, *The American President from Teddy Roosevelt to Bill
   Clinton* (New York: Oxford University Press, 2015), 146.
6 Athas, *Chapel Hill in Plain Sight*, 254–73. Abernathy published Langston Hughes,
   James Joyce, and Samuel Beckett, and reported the local literary news, including
   this item: "William Faulkner while guest of *Contempo* was surprised to learn
   that the University of North Carolina library cannot afford a copy of any of his
   novels."
7 Gertrude Stein, *Everybody's Autobiography* (1937; New York: Vintage, 1973),
   251–52.
8 AA, "Why I Write," 272–73.
9 PAL to CS.
10 AGA to Tom Wilson, Holt archive, PUL.
11 AA, "At First Sight," *TSYA*.
12 Tom Wilson to AGA, Holt archive, PUL.
13 DSA (then Wilson) to NBA, postmarked December 18, 1937, Flushing, New
    York, PAL collection.
14 AA, "Truth or Consequences," *TSYA*.
15 AA to Kay Bonetti.
16 AA, "Truth or Consequences."
17 ABA to DSA (then Wilson), August 20 [1936].
18 AA, "A Southern Spelling Bee," *TSYA*.
19 AA, 1937 diary, HRC.
20 AA, "Ladies in Waiting," unpublished TS, HRC.
21 "Legacy" by Agatha Adams (from PAL collection):

(for Alice)

I cannot give you beauty
Or yet the glow of charm
But I have given you far subtler weapons
The hosts of evil to disarm.
For I have made you free of lake and mountain
The quiet of tall birches is your own . . .
Secure retreats against the assailing years
Since you will find in loveliness remembered
A sanctuary from all hurts and fears.

22 ABA to DSA (then Wilson), August 20 [1936].

23 AA, "Why I Write," 273–74.

24 AA, "Child's Play," *AYG*.

25 Interview with AA by Marilyn Scharine, 1987, HRC.

26 AA, "My First and Only House," 193.

27 AA, "Why I Left Home: Partial Truths."

CHAPTER 5: GIRLS

Interviews: JCA, Daphne Athas, Doris Dickson, Mary Elizabeth (Jervey) Kilby, PAL, Dougald Macmillan, Ford Worthy.

1 AA, "Why I Left Home."

2 *"very Bostonian manner":* AA, "Why I Left Home"; *"I thought anyone":* AA, "At First Sight: Love and Liking, a Memoir."

3 N, May 15, 1965.

4 AA, "At First Sight: Love and Liking, a Memoir."

5 JCA to AA, c. 1990.

6 Athas, *Chapel Hill in Plain Sight*, 156.

7 AA, commencement address, University of California Berkeley, May 22, 1987.

8 JCA to AA, n.d.

9 Simone de Beauvoir, *The Second Sex*, trans. Constance Borde (New York: Knopf, 2010), 374–76.

10 AA, "An Unscheduled Stop," *TSYA*.

11 *"woods as dense"* and *"We came to":* AA, "Roses, Rhododendron," *BG*.

12 De Beauvoir, *The Second Sex*, 376.

13 Mary McCarthy, *How I Grew* (San Diego: Harcourt Brace Jovanovich, 1987), 27–28.

14 AGA, "Jobs for the Helen Hokinson Crowd."

15 Mary Elizabeth (Jervey) Kilby recalled that she was urged to learn to like olives in advance of the trip, but not whether Agatha and Alice were also to be part of Nic's entourage.

16 NBA, *The Heritage of Spain* (1943; rev. ed., New York: Henry Holt, 1959), 251–67.

17 Brenda Maddox, *D. H. Lawrence: The Story of a Marriage* (New York: Simon and Schuster, 1994), 364.

18 D. H. Lawrence, *Quetzalcoatl: The Early Version of "The Plumed Serpent,"* ed. Louis L. Martz (Redding Ridge, CT: Black Swan Books, 1995), 17.

19 ABA, *A Journey to Mexico* (Chapel Hill: University of North Carolina Press, 1945), 5.

20 ABA, diary, Southern Historical Collection, Wilson Library, UNC.

21 Josephus Daniels's son, Jonathan Daniels, had just published his bestselling defense of New Deal programs, *A Southerner Discovers the South*.

22 Jennifer Ritterhouse, "Dixie Destinations: Rereading Jonathan Daniels's *A Southerner Discovers the South*," *Southern Spaces* (May 20, 2010), Emory Center for Digital Scholarship: southernspaces.org/2010/dixie-destinations-rereading-jonathan-danielss-southerner-discovers-south.

23 ABA, *A Journey to Mexico*, 5.

24 Mavis Gallant to PAL [1999].
25 AA, "Balcony Scenes."
26 Willie T. Weathers to AA, April 22, 1975. In "Balcony Scenes" and "Return Trips," AA gives her autobiographical characters parents who are divorcing.
27 N, November 11, 1954. AA later developed this sketch into her Todd-family story titled "Are You in Love?"
28 "At First Sight: Love and Liking, a Memoir"; Alice's Otis IQ test, reported on her CHHS transcript, was 133.
29 De Beauvoir, *The Second Sex*, 321.
30 Letters from camp courtesy of JCA and PAL.
31 De Beauvoir, *The Second Sex*, 372.
32 AA, "An Unscheduled Stop," *TSYA*.
33 Doris Dickson to CS, April 24, 2013.
34 University Archives, University of Wisconsin.

CHAPTER 6: NORTH AND SOUTH

Interviews: JCA, Elizabeth Robinson Buttenheim, Barbara Bates Guinee, Bryant Mangum, Tyler Paul, Jean Salter Roetter.

1 AA described her year in Madison in several sources: letters to JCA; a five-page untitled manuscript, HRC; "The Nice Girl;" "1940: Fall," *AYG*; "Balcony Scenes;" N, July 10, 1987, and August 17, 1987. Background information: Madison *Capital Times*, and Wisconsin High School records, Steenbock Library, University of Wisconsin.
2 AA to JCA, December 26, 1940.
3 Ibid., May 22, 1941.
4 Ibid., "Wednesday" [July 10, 1941].
5 Ibid., July–August 1941.
6 Ibid., December 26, 1940.
7 De Beauvoir, *The Second Sex*, 391.
8 Ibid., 397.
9 McCarthy, *How I Grew*, 75–78.
10 AA to Richard Carr, September 28, 1981.
11 Hugh Morton Collection of Photographs and Films, UNC.
12 "Allies Describe Outrages on Jews, United Nations Office Here Releases Report on Fate of 5,000,000 in Europe, Extermination Is Feared, Situation in Each Country Held by Germans Is Analyzed in Summarized Form," *New York Times*, December 20, 1942.
13 St. Catherine's School archives; Schlesinger Library, Radcliffe.
14 N, February 15, 1982.

CHAPTER 7: RUMORS OF WAR

Interviews: JCA, George Avakian, Barbara Bates Guinee, Anne Fabbri, Alison Lurie, Adeline Naiman, Phyllis Silverman Ott, Mary Bachhuber Simmons, Barbara Mailer Wasserman, Betty Love White.

1 AA to Barbara Bates Guinee, March 1, 1998.

2 Elizabeth S. Zuckerman, "A 'Very Romantic' Native of Chapel Hill Pursues the Literary Life," *Harvard Crimson*, January 2, 1997.

3 Elaine Kendall, *Peculiar Institutions: An Informal History of the Seven Sisters Colleges* (New York: G. P. Putnam, 1976), 154.

4 Alison Lurie, "Their Harvard," in Diana Dubois, ed., *My Harvard, My Yale: Memoirs of College Life by Some Notable Americans* (New York: Random House, 1982), 34.

5 AA to Laura Furman, August 11, 1981.

6 AA to Barbara Bates Guinee, November 16 [1998].

7 AA to Peter Manso, February 15, 1983, transcript, NM Papers, HRC.

8 AA, untitled MS, HRC folder 19.5.

9 Lurie, "Their Harvard," 37.

10 Douglass Shand-Tucci, *The Crimson Letter: Harvard, Homosexuality, and the Shaping of American Culture* (New York: St. Martin's, 2003), 149–55.

11 AA in Jackson R. Bryer, ed., *F. Scott Fitzgerald at 100* (Rockville, MD: Quill and Brush, 1996), unpaginated.

12 Lurie, "Their Harvard," 39.

13 ABA, "The Tradition of Women at the University of North Carolina," fall 1949, TS, UNC.

14 AA, "A Natural Woman."

15 AA, "Wonderful," unpublished TS, HRC.

16 N, 1949–72; entry for July 28, 1960: "—the first man she had ever slept with (really the second: she had been in the midst of confessing the first) had been her manic-depressive father's psychoanalyst—Malcolm—"

17 Ann Kolson, "She Writes of the Life Within," *Philadelphia Inquirer,* October 15, 1984.

18 Ibid.; AA in interview with Mildred Hamilton, *San Francisco Examiner*, January 31, 1975, 22; AA, "A Lesson"; I believe AA was referring to Kempton because of an inscription in a copy of Kempton's short-story anthology that Bill Mulder gave AA in Salt Lake in 1987: Mulder writes that AA "had a score to settle with Kempton."

19 AA to Kay Bonetti, American Audio Prose Library.

20 Randall Sandke, *Where the Dark and the Light Folks Meet: Race and the Mythology, Politics, and Business of Jazz* (Lanham, MD: Scarecrow Press, 2010), 143.

21 Jan Morris, *Manhattan '45* (New York: Oxford University Press, 1987), 198–99.

22 For details of how that happened, we have only Adams's description in *Superior Women*; for corroboration, we have her lifelong interest in Young and the name "Trummy" on her list of lovers, secondhand recollections of later meetings, and AA to JCA, October 29, 1984.

23 John Norris, "Trummy Young: An Interview with John Norris," *Coda* 11, no. 2 (July–August 1973): 8–11; Charles E. Martin, "Trummy Young: An Unfinished Story," *Second Line* 30 (Summer 1978): 30–35; Al Monroe, "Swinging the News," *Chicago Defender*, July 31, 1943, mentions that Edith Young, wife of Trummy, has accompanied her husband on tour with the Charlie Barnet band in Chicago; Don Burley, "Back Door Stuff," *New York Amsterdam News*, September 11, 1943,

March 18, 1944, and December 2, 1944; NAMM Oral History by Dan Del Fiorentino, www.namm.org/library/oral-history/trummy-young.

24 AA to Radcliffe College Alumnae, June 6, 1997.

CHAPTER 8: COCKTAIL OF DREAMS

Interviews: George Avakian, Eileen Finletter Geist, Jacob Levenson, ML, Richard Linenthal, Elizabeth White Love, Alison Lurie, Valerie Roemer Lynn, Doris McMullan, Mary Bachhuber Simmons.

1 AA to Elizabeth Love, July 21, 1996.
2 "*Most of the men*": Lurie, "Their Harvard," 41; "*sophisticated*": Millicent Dillon, "Writer Alice Adams Cuts to the Core in Her Fiction and in Her Reading," *Stanford Campus Report*, June 9, 1982; *Guerard believed*: John G. Wofford, "Creative Critic," *Harvard Crimson*, December 14, 1955.
3 "Wonderful," five-page TS, HRC.
4 AA to ABA and NBA [March 1946]; AA to Philip Mayer, June 21, 1976, HRC.
5 Millicent Dillon, interview with AA, *Stanford Campus Report*, June 9, 1982.
6 AA to NBA and ABA [March 1946]; B. V. Weinbaum's withering review of *The Great Promise* ran in the *New York Times Book Review*, April 14, 1946.
7 AA to ABA and NBA [March 1946].
8 Oral history, United States Holocaust Memorial Museum, collections.ushmm .org/search/catalog/irn512420; family archives, PAL; Richard Linenthal to CS, January 31, 2011.
9 AA to Manso, HRC.
10 AA to ABA, "Friday" [June 1946].
11 Morris, *Manhattan '45*, 240.
12 Ronald B. Elkin, MD, to Bill Fee, MD, October 15, 1992, Stanford medical records.
13 Carolyn Heilbrun, *Writing a Woman's Life* (New York: Ballantine Books, 1988), 118–19.
14 AA, "Book Beat," 1984, Donald L. Swaim Collection, Ohio University Archives and Special Collections.
15 AA to ABA and NBA, "Tuesday" [October 1946].
16 AA to Allen Tate, November 16, 1946, Archives of Henry Holt & Co., PUL.
17 AA, "Stork Club," TS, HRC; AA to ABA and NBA, "Tuesday" [November 1946].
18 AA to Allen Tate, November 16, 1946, PUL.
19 AA, "What Should I Have Done?" *BG*, 225.
20 "*curious*": Ibid.; Charles Miles Jones Papers, UNC; wedding photographs, PAL.
21 AA to Peter Manso, transcript, NM Papers, HRC.
22 In *Families and Survivors*, Maude wonders why her mother ever married her father and decides that "after a lively and perhaps tiring adolescence . . . she wanted a rest."
23 Salzburg Seminar Newsletter, May 19, 1947, archives of the Salzburg Global Seminar.
24 ML to Peter Manso, transcript, NM Papers, HRC.

25 Alfred Kazin, *A Lifetime Burning in Every Moment: From the Journals of Alfred Kazin* (New York: HarperCollins, 1996), 90.

26 Ibid., 88–90.

27 Earl G. Harrison, "Report of Earl G. Harrison," 1945, Dwight D. Eisenhower Presidential Library. https://eisenhower.archives.gov/research/online_documents /holocaust.html (accessed June 4, 2019); and Harrison's 1945 journal, United States Memorial Holocaust Museum. collections.ushmm.org/search/catalog /irn503791#?rsc=127813&cv=0&xywh=-1191%2C-165%2C4266%2C3281&c= 0&m=0&s=0 (accessed June 4, 2019).

28 AA, "Related Histories," *TSYA*.

29 Matthiessen recorded his own words as follows: "We have come from many countries and across the gulf of war. Some of you Europeans were in prison camps in my country. One of our American staff was in a prison camp near Salzburg. . . . I take it for granted also that one thing that unites us is that we are all strong anti-Fascists." (*From the Heart of Europe* [New York: Oxford UP, 1948], 13.)

30 Valerie Roemer Lynn had recently read her late husband's letters to his parents when she spoke with me. Both Lynns maintained a friendship with the Linenthals for another ten years, during which Alice sometimes confided her marital discontents to Kenneth Lynn.

31 Kazin, *A Lifetime Burning*, 93, 102.

CHAPTER 9: IMPERSONATORS

Interviews: Blair Fuller, Gerald Howard, Ella Leffland, ML, Valerie Lynn, Phyllis Silverman Ott, Beatrice Silverman, Barbara Mailer Wasserman.

1 Stanley Geist, "Memoires d'un touriste: Paris, 1947," trans. René Guyonnet, *Les temps modernes* (1948): 536–47.

2 The address on ML's French driving permit.

3 Geist, "Memoires d'un Touriste: Paris, 1947."

4 AA to Doris Dörrie, July [10,] 1981.

5 "I did live with just such a woman although unfortunately I was married at the time, no beautiful Italian lover," AA wrote Dörrie; but earlier, when editing "Winter Rain," for *Beautiful Girl*, she said, "I'll change the first [name] to Bruno (actual name and now he's a very famous Communist leader, isn't that interesting?)." (AA to VW, June 10, 1977.)

6 Anthony Beevor and Artemis Cooper, *Paris After the Libertion 1944–1949* (New York: Penguin, 2007), 185.

7 Description of Adam Marr in AA, *SW*.

8 NM to I. B. Mailer, November 1, 1947, NM Papers, HRC.

9 Peter Manso, *Mailer: His Life and Times* (New York: Simon and Schuster, 1985), 60.

10 Louise Levitas, "*The Naked* are Fanatics *and the Dead* Don't Care," *New York Star*, August 22, 1948, reprinted in J. Michael Lennon, ed., *Conversations with Norman Mailer* (Jackson: University Press of Mississippi, 1988), 8.

11 AA to Manso, transcript, NM Papers, HRC.

12 Manso, *Mailer*, 71.

13 Kenneth Lynn to Carl Rollyson, recorded interview, June 28, 1990, Carl Rollyson Collection, McFarlin Library, University of Tulsa.

14 William Raney to NM, January 20, 1948, NM Papers, HRC.

15 ML to Manso and AA to Manso, transcripts, NM Papers, HRC.

16 NM to Francis Gwaltney, October 7, 1947, quoted in Carl Rollyson, *The Lives of Norman Mailer: A Biography* (New York: Paragon House, 1991), 46.

17 AA, "Postwar Paris: Chronicles of Literary Life."

18 The undated list is at the back of N, 1991–1997 on page 158.

19 Arthur Miller, *Timebends: A Life* (New York: Grove Press, 1987), 249.

20 *Car and travel to Spain*: AA and ML to Manso, transcripts, NM Papers, HRC; NM to Raney, February 7, 1948; Barbara Probst Solomon, *Arriving Where We Started* (New York: Harper & Row, 1972); Barbara Mailer Wasserman, "Spain, 1948," *Hudson Review* 53, no. 3 (Autumn 2000): 363–84. Contrary to what J. Michael Lennon reports in *Norman Mailer: A Double Life* (New York: Simon & Schuster, 2013), 105, the Mailers and Linenthals did not travel together to Barcelona in the Mailer Peugeot.

21 Eugenio de Nora, *Pueblo cautivo* (1946; León, Spain: Diputación Provincial de León, 1997).

22 NM, "Spanish Preface," unpublished TS, NM Papers, HRC.

23 Ibid.

24 AA to Kenneth Lynn, March 19, 1949; Sandy Pearl and Bernard Goldberg, "William Hunt Diederich (1884–1953): Forging His Noble Beasts," Incollect, incollect.com/articles/william-hunt-diederich-1884-1953, accessed October 23, 2018; Michel Gaudet, *La vie du haut de Cagnes (1930–1980) la bohème ensoleillée* (Nice: Mémoire directe Demaistre, 2001), passim.

25 *Cagnes-sur-mer*: AA to Philip Mayer, September 7, 1976.

26 Kenneth Lynn to Carl Rollyson, recorded interview, June 28, 1990.

27 Michael Gorra, *Portrait of a Novel: Henry James and the Making of an American Masterpiece* (New York: Liveright, 2012), 278.

28 N, January 19, 1949.

29 ML and AA to Manso, transcripts, NM Papers, HRC.

30 AA, "Partial Truths"; AA to Manso, transcript, NM Papers, HRC.

31 Wasserman, "Spain, 1948."

32 NM to William Raney, February 25, 1948.

33 Wasserman, "Spain, 1948"; Solomon, *Arriving Where We Started*, 65–102.

34 Janet Flanner, *Paris Journal 1944–1955*, ed. William Shawn (New York: Harcourt Brace Jovanovich, 1965), 91–92.

35 AA, "Postwar Paris."

36 "*sounded terrible*": AA to Lynns, March 19, 1949; "*I could have stayed*": AA, "Postwar Paris."

37 Heilbrun, *Writing a Woman's Life*, 117.

38 Alice Kaplan, *Dreaming in French: The Paris Years of Jacqueline Bouvier Kennedy, Susan Sontag, and Angela Davis* (Chicago: University of Chicago Press, 2012), 5.

CHAPTER 10: FRUSTRATED AMBITIONS

Interviews: Herbert Blau, Frank Granat, Valerie Lynn, Peter Stansky.

1 AA, "Green Creek, Chapter I," HRC.

2 Lorna Sage, quoted by Elaine Showalter in *Inventing Herself: Claiming a Feminist Intellectual Heritage* (New York: Scribner, 2001), 18.

3 AA to Barbara, Bea, and NM, July 19, 1948, HRC.

4 AA to Kenneth Lynn, August 28, 1948.

5 AA to Kenneth and Valerie Lynn, December 5, 1948.

6 *Stanford Writers*: AA, "At First Sight: Love and Liking, a Memoir."

7 WMA quoted by Joan Smith in "Go Ask Alice," *San Francisco Examiner Magazine*, October 22, 1995, 13–15.

8 AA, "At First Sight: Love and Liking, a Memoir."

9 Manso, *Mailer: His Life and Times*, 129–31; Lennon, *Norman Mailer: A Double Life*, 110–11.

10 AA to Bea and NM, January 2, 1949, HRC.

11 Ibid., April 27, 1949, HRC.

12 Phyllis Lee Levin, "The Road from Sophocles to Spock Is Often a Bumpy One; Former Coeds Find Family Routine Is Stifling Them," *New York Times*, June 28, 1960; Betty Friedan, *The Feminine Mystique: 50 Years* (1963; New York: W. W. Norton, 2013), 365.

13 AA, "At First Sight: Love and Liking, a Memoir."

14 AA to Lynns, March 19, 1949.

15 AA to Lynns, November 5, 1949.

16 Harvey Breit, "Talk with Norman Mailer," *New York Times*, June 3, 1951; reprinted in Lennon, *Conversations*, 16.

17 Sources on the Mailers in Hollywood: Manso, *Mailer*; AA and ML to Manso, transcripts, HRC; Lennon, *Norman Mailer*; Carl Rollyson, *The Lives of Norman Mailer*.

18 AA to Lynns, March 19, 1949.

19 AA to Scott, December 19, 1981.

20 AA to Lynns, November 5, 1949.

21 AA to Bea and NM, April 27, 1949, HRC; AA to Lynns, May 20, 1949.

22 AA, "At First Sight: Love and Liking, a Memoir."

23 Susan Walker, "Adams can't avoid battle of the sexes," *Toronto Star*, October 16, 1989, C4.

24 AA to NM, March 12, 1950, HRC.

25 AA to Bea and NM, April 1, 1950, HRC.

26 *Death of ABA*: North Carolina Collection Clipping File, UNC; certificate of death, North Carolina; Old Chapel Hill Cemetery records, Town of Chapel Hill; AA to Mailers, April 1, 1950, HRC. In 1992, Adams told Dr. Ronald Elkin that her mother died of "cerebral hemorrhage"; I cannot account for this discrepancy. (Elkin to Bill Fee, MD, October 15, 1992.)

27 ABA, "Jobs for the Helen Hokinson Crowd"; ABA, "For the Latin Majors"; and Harriet Fitzgerald, "In Memoriam: Agatha Boyd Adams, 1915," *RMWC Alumnae Bulletin* 43, no. 3 (April 1950).

28 Charles E. Rush to Mabel Wolfe Wheaton, March 20, 1950, North Carolina
   Collection, UNC.
29 AA to Mailers, April 1, 1950, HRC.
30 AA, "The Wake," TS, HRC.
31 AA, "The Grape Arbor," *Crosscurrents: A Quarterly* (Spring 1989), 52–69.
32 Adrienne Rich, *Of Woman Born: Motherhood as Experience and Institution* (New
   York: Bantam Books, 1977), 240–46.

CHAPTER 11: FAMILY OF THREE

Interviews: JCA, Cynthia Scott Francisco, Diane Johnson, John Murray, Peter
Stansky.
1 AA, "The Making of a Writer," TS, HRC, a longer, probably earlier version of
   "Why I Write."
2 AA, *Superior Women*, chapter 1.
3 William E. Cain, *F. O. Matthiessen and the Politics of Criticism* (Madison: University of Wisconsin Press, 1988), 111–12; "F. O Matthiessen Plunges to Death
   from Hotel Window," *Harvard Crimson*, April 1, 1950.
4 AA to Lynns, October 18, 1950.
5 Ibid.
6 Valentine Cunningham, "Writer who kept his devotion to republican Spain alive
   in his novels," *Guardian*, December 11, 2000; Martin Douglas, "Ralph Bates,
   Novelist Who Evoked Spain and Then Fought Franco, Dies at 101," *New York
   Times*, December 4, 2000.
7 AA to Lynns, October 18, 1950.
8 Ibid., December 1950, and February 5, 1951.
9 Ibid., February 5, 1951.
10 Harvey Breit, "Talk with Norman Mailer," *New York Times*, June 3, 1951, 212.
11 AA to Lynns, October 18, 1950, and February 5, 1951.
12 Ibid., March 20, 1951.
13 Ibid., May 15, 1951.
14 Ibid., Ibid. ; medical records, Sequoia Hospital, Redwood City, CA.
15 Ibid., May 15, 1951.
16 Ibid., February 5, 1951.
17 Ibid. November 7, 1951.
18 Ibid.
19 ML to Lynns [spring 1952].
20 AA to Lynns, November 7, 1951.
21 Ibid., May 20 [1952]; James Atlas, *Bellow: A Biography* (New York: Random
   House, 2000), 172.
22 Saul Bellow to AA, February 23, 1966, HRC, reprinted in *Saul Bellow: Letters*,
   ed. Benjamin Taylor (New York: Viking, 2010), 256–57.
23 Saul Bellow to AA, February 25, 1958, HRC.
24 AA to Lynns, May 20 [1952].
25 Eve and Ralph Bates to AA, May 18 [1952].
26 AA to Lynns, May 20 [1952].

27 Ibid.
28 ML to Lynns, September 10, 1952.
29 Bellow to AA, HRC. Most of Bellow's letters are undated except by context or postmark.

CHAPTER 12: FEELING FREE IN SAN FRANCISCO

Interviews: JCA, Herbert Blau, PAL, Tom Wilson Jr.

1   AA to Barbara Deming, February 18, 1955, Papers of Barbara Deming, Schlesinger Library, Radcliffe Institute.
2   AA to Don and Kirby Hall, October 5, 1954, Donald Hall Papers, University of New Hampshire.
3   AA to Barbara Deming, July 15, 1955.
4   Solnit, "Fillmore: The Beats in the Western Addition," FoundSF.org.
5   AA to Barbara Deming, February 18, 1955.
6   Ibid., February 18, 1955.
7   N, July 28, 1960.
8   AA, "Outlining," unpublished TS, HRC.
9   Blanton Miller to AA, undated, HRC; Blanton Miller guest file, Yaddo papers, NYPL.
10 "The Fog in the Streets," unpublished TS, HRC.
11 Ricky Riccardi, *What a Wonderful World: The Magic of Louis Armstrong's Later Years* (New York: Pantheon Books, 2011), 162–65.
12 Ibid., 70.
13 AA, "A Campus Comedy of Horrors" (review of *Unholy Loves* by Joyce Carol Oates), *Chicago Tribune Book World*, September 1979.
14 James Campbell, *This Is the Beat Generation: New York, San Francisco, Paris* (Berkeley: University of California Press, 1999), 189.
15 Henry Miller, *Big Sur and the Oranges of Hieronymous Bosch* (New York: New Directions, 1957), 17–18.
16 Nancy Faber, "Out of the Pages," *People*, April 3, 1978, 48, 53.
17 AA to Barbara Deming, October 30, 1956 [dated by recipient].
18 Ibid.
19 AA, *MEX*, xvi.

CHAPTER 13: A RETURN TRIP

Interviews: JCA, PAL, Diana Steele.

1   The paper LJ read displays the commonsense intelligence that attracted Alice. It's published as "Some Observations on Children Hospitalized During Latency," *Dynamic Psychopathology in Childhood*, ed. Lucie Jessner, MD, and Eleanor Pavenstedt, MD (New York: Grune & Stratton, 1959), 257–68.
2   AA, "At First Sight: Love and Liking, a Memoir."
3   Jessner's third husband was the late actor and theater director Fritz Jessner. He acted in plays directed by Max Reinhardt and was associated with the Jewish Kulturbund Theatre Company in Berlin until it was forced to close; after a stay

in Switzerland, he emigrated to the United States and worked at the Yale School of Drama, Smith College, and Wellesley College until his death in 1946.

4 HMS, "Song of Carolina," *Furman Magazine* 39, no. 1 (Fall 1995): 32–37; Daphne Athas, "Max on the Beach," *Chapel Hill in Plain Sight* (Hillsborough, NC: Eno Publishers, 2010), 125.

5 The photo is printed in "Postwar Paris: Chronicles of Literary Life," *Paris Review* 79 (1981), 303; HMS, "Song of Carolina."

6 AA, "At First Sight: Love and Liking, a Memoir."

7 Ibid.

8 AA, "Summer, Clothes & Love: A Memoir."

9 *Narratives of summer 1958*: By AA: "Summer, Clothes & Love: A Memoir," *San Francisco Examiner/Image*, June 10, 1990, 26–31; "At First Sight: Love and Liking, a Memoir," *Southern Review* 35, no. 3 (Summer 1999): 567–79; "Ladies in Waiting," "Night Fears," and "Home Is Where," unpublished MSS, HRC; "Learning to Be Happy," *Redbook*, September 1976, 100+, reprinted as "Home Is Where" in *BG*; "An Unscheduled Stop," *New Yorker*, September 29, 1980, 41–47, reprinted in *RT*. By HMS: "About Love and Grasshoppers," *Redbook*, May 1977, 126+, reprinted as "Another Love Story" in *The Hat of My Mother* (Chapel Hill, NC: Algonquin, 1988).

10 HMS, "Another Love Story," 50.

11 HMS, "Song of Carolina," 32–37.

12 ML to AA, July 21, 1958.

13 Ibid.

14 JCA to AA, early August 1958.

15 ML to AA, August 3, 1958.

16 AA, "Summer, Clothes & Love."

17 Steele, "Another Love Story."

18 HMS to AA, August 17, 1958.

19 LJ to AA, August 13, 1958.

20 HMS to AA, September 11, 1958.

21 Knopf papers, HRC.

22 AA, interview with Don Swaim.

23 "Summer, Clothes & Love: A Memoir."

CHAPTER 14: FREEDOM

Interviews: JCA, Chester Aaron, Ruth Gebhart Belmeur, Margot Sinton Biestman, Virginia Breier, Stephen Brown, Linda Chown, Blair Fuller, Ella Leffland, PAL, Lincoln Pain, Louis Pain, Vera Futscher Pereira.

1 Peter Fimrite, "Frank Werber, charismatic music agent, entrepreneur," *San Francisco Chronicle*, June 8, 2007.

2 Betty Friedan, *The Feminine Mystique: 50 Years* (1963; New York: W. W. Norton, 2013), 432.

3 Edward Zerin, *Images of America: Jewish San Francisco* (Charleston, SC: Arcadia Publishing, 2006); Gary Kamiya, "Fleeing Repression, Jewish immigrants found success in Gold Rush SF," *San Francisco Chronicle*, August 18, 2017.

4 HMS to AA, November 27, 1958.

5 Ibid., January 25, 1959.

6 Ibid., February 2, 1959.

7 Ibid., July 13, 1959.

8 Ibid.

9 Helen Gurley Brown, *Sex and the Single Girl* (New York: Bernard Geis, 1962), xiii.

10 Vera Futscher Pereira, *Retrovisor: Um álbum de família* (Cascais, Portugal: Rui Costa Pinto Edições), 2009.

11 N, October 13, 1961.

12 Vera Futscher Pereira and Bernardo Futscher Pereira found letters and typed manuscripts by AA among their father's papers. Vera told me that her father's companion Graziela Lima Leitão told her about Adams's novel *Careless Love*, which would seem to indicate that Vasco was also familiar with it.

13 N, February 5, 1961.

14 *Alice's reading list*: Saul Bellow, *The Victim, Adventures of Augie March*; Max Steele, *Debby*; Robert Penn Warren, *All the King's Men, Brother to Dragons, World Enough and Time*; Wallace Stevens, *Collected Poems*; Katherine Anne Porter, *Pale Horse, Pale Rider*; Carson McCullers, *The Heart Is a Lonely Hunter*; Mary McCarthy, *The Company She Keeps*; Ralph Ellison, *The Invisible Man*; James Agee, *A Death in the Family*; John O'Hara, *Appointment in Samarra*; William Styron, *Lie Down in Darkness*.

15 LJ to AA, August 20, 1960; *"I can imagine you"*: LJ to AA, November 10, 1960.

16 AA, "The Edge of the Water," TS, HRC.

17 Ella Leffland to CS.

18 Vasco Pereira to AA, January 28 and March 2 [1961]; AA to Vasco Pereira, March 1 [1961].

19 LJ to AA, "Sunday night" [1961].

20 Vasco Futscher Pereira to AA, February 15, 1961, HRC; AA to Vasco Futscher Pereira, n.d., PAL.

21 Vera Futscher Pereira, *Retrovisor: Um album de família*; C. Ray Smith, "An Ambassador at Home," *Architectural Digest* 79, no. 8 (October 1980) 120–26.

22 Saul Bellow to AA [1961], HRC, reprinted in Taylor, *Saul Bellow: Letters*, 200.

23 AA to Nancy Webb, March 6, 1967.

24 N, August 7, 1962.

25 AA, "Former Friends," unpublished TS, HRC.

26 AA to Vasco Pereira, PAL collection.

27 US individual tax return of ML and FJL, 1959, PAL collection.

28 Marcy Bachman, "The Improbable Dr. Pain," *San Francisco Chronicle*, September 19, 1971.

29 FJL to her mother and stepfather, Dr. and Mrs. Leonard Greenburg, April 18, 1959, PAL collection.

CHAPTER 15: ALONE

Interviews: Ruth Gebhart Belmeur, Nancy Boas, Sharon Boynton, Virginia Breier, Blair Fuller, Imogene Gieling, PAL, Bernard Rosenthal.

1 N, July 12, 1972.

2 AA, statement about *CL* for David Segal, HRC.

3 Hal Gilliam, "International House Celebrates 70 Years," ihouse.berkeley.edu /alumni/times/timesF00/seventy.html.

4 W. H. Rey, *Du warst gut zu mir, Amerika! Roman einer gewagten Emigration* (Frankfurt am Main: Haag + Herchen, 1999), 88–90, translated by G. H. Hertling.

5 AA to JCA, August 20, 1963.

6 Letters from AA to Franz Sommerfeld, PAL collection.

7 "Prof. Franz R. Sommerfeld of U.W. Dies," *Seattle Daily Times*, March 5, 1962.

8 AA to RP, November 11, 1980.

9 FJL to Dr. and Mrs. Leonard Greenburg, January 28, 1963, and April 30, 1963, PAL collection.

10 Sidney D. Kirkpatrick, *Hitler's Holy Relics* (New York: Simon & Schuster, 2011), 172–74.

11 Manso, *Mailer*, 379–381; AA and ML to Manso, transcripts, HRC; Lennon, *Norman Mailer*, 336–37.

12 NM to AA and Felix Rosenthal, September 10, 1963.

13 AA to JCA, "Tuesday" [1963].

14 *Jack Boynton*: Correspondence of James W. Boynton, Smithsonian Archives of American Art; Boynton's correspondence with AA, HRC and private collection of Sharon Boynton; Katie Robinson Edwards, *Modern Art in Texas* (Austin: University of Texas Press, 2014); Helen Moore Barthelme, *The Genesis of a Cool Sound* (Bryan, TX: Texas A&M Press, 2001).

15 Gerald Sorin, *Irving Howe: A Life of Passionate Dissent* (New York: NYU Press, 2005), 174–78.

16 Ibid., 181–82.

17 AA, "A California Trip," TS, HRC; AA to Peter Matson, August 5, 1970, states that "A California Trip" is "about an Irving-Howe-type New Yorker in Calif."

18 Irving Howe to AA [1963]; AA, "A California Trip," TS, HRC.

19 Irving Howe to AA [1963].

CHAPTER 16: *CARELESS LOVE*

Interviews: JCA, Sharon Boynton, Phillip Galgiani, Jeremy Larner, PAL, Lore Segal, Til Brunswick Stewart, Barbara Mailer Wasserman.

1 AA to Jack Boynton [late 1963].

2 AA to PAL, February 5, 1971.

3 Sorin, *Irving Howe*, 199.

4 AA to Dolly Summerlin, October 5, 1981.

5 AA to LJ, January 6, 1964; AA to Jack Boynton [1963 or 1964].

6 Brian E. Butler, *Dan Rice at Black Mountain College: Painter Among the Poets* (Asheville, NC: Black Mountain College Museum and Art Center, 2014); Vincent Katz, ed., *Black Mountain College: Experiment in Art* (Cambridge, MA: MIT Press, 2002), 210.

7 Lorrie Moore, "How He Wrote His Songs" (review of *Hiding Man: A Biography of Donald Barthelme* by Tracy Daugherty), *New York Review of Books*, March 26, 2009.

8   AA to LJ, January 6, 1964.

9   AA to Beverly Bentley and NM, "Wednesday" [1963].

10 AA to RP, March 31 [1964].

11 Mutual friends in San Francisco, including Zoe Draper, Ruth Gebhart Belmeur, and John Belmeur, probably introduced Alice to Dodds.

12 John Dodds to AA, January 20, 1964.

13 AA to Vida Deming, Tuesday [1964].

14 FJL to Dr. and Mrs. Leonard Greenburg, February 4, 1964.

15 AA to LJ, January 6, 1964; AA to LJ, December 18, 1964.

16 FJL to Dr. and Mrs. Leonard Greenburg, April 29, 1964, PAL collection.

17 AA to Barbara Mailer (then Alson), January 23, 1964.

18 Correspondence between AA and John Dodds, 1963–65, HRC.

19 AA to WMA and Peter Davison, December 27, 1964.

20 General catalogs, University of San Francisco; AA to Max Steele, February 10, 1976; AA to LJ, March 11, 1976; Anne Fabbri, interview with R. E. Jenkins; AA to Victoria Wilson, June 18, 1977; "What Should I Have Done?," *BG*.

21 JCA to AA, February 17, 1966.

22 AA to John Dodds, March 21, 1964; AA to WMA, May 30, 1964; the book was Meyer A. Zeligs, *Friendship and Fratricide: An Analysis of Whittaker Chambers and Alger Hiss* (New York: Viking Press, 1967).

23 HMS to Merrill Foundation [1964].

24 N, June 2, 1964.

25 John Dodds to AA, November 4, 1964.

26 Correspondence between AA and Peter Davison, 1964–67, HRC.

27 Robert Gottlieb to John Dodds, November 10, 1964; Lee Wright to John Dodds, December 10, 1964. These letters are in the AA collection at HRC.

28 HMS to LJ, May 8, 1965, Jessner collection, Deutsche Nationalbibliothek.

29 Correspondence files between AA, John Dodds, and David I. Segal, HRC.

30 Correspondence of AA and Segal, May 14–June 3, 1965.

31 AA to Victoria Wilson, February 13, 1974.

32 Correspondence between AA and David Segal, 1965–66, HRC; correspondence between AA and Peter Matson, 1965–66, HRC.

33 Atlas, *Bellow*, 311.

34 Bellow to AA, February 23, 1966, HRC, reprinted in Taylor, *Saul Bellow: Letters*, 256–57.

35 David Segal to AA, October 20, 1965.

36 Martin Levin, *New York Times Book Review*, May 22, 1966, 39. Books that turned up in this long-running column were said to have been "Levinized" because they had not received stand-alone reviews ("Martin Levin, Prolific Book Reviewer, dies at 89," *New York Times*, May 30, 2008).

37 Maitland Zane, "First Novel of Action in Upper Bohemia," *San Francisco Chronicle*, July 3, 1966.

38 AA to LJ, July 9, 1969.

39 Cynthia Ozick, "The Novel's Evil Tongue," *New York Times*, December 16, 2015.

40 AA to Peter Davison, December 7, 1965.

41 David Talbot, *Season of the Witch* (New York: Free Press, 2012), 93.

42 *PAL in high school*: AA to LJ, December 18, 1965; AA to Steeles, December 1, 1966; AA to LJ, July 5, 1967; AA to Nancy Webb, March 15, 1967.

43 AA to Steeles, "Wednesday" [September 1966]; AA to LJ, July 5, 1967; UCSF autopsy report, May 28, 1999.

44 AA to Steeles, 1966 [September].

45 N, April 22, 1999.

46 UCSF medical records, September 22, 1992.

47 Dorothy Gaines, "In and About Tucson," *Arizona Daily Star*, October 6, 1966; Libby Brady, "San Francisco Author Tries Short Stories," *Tucson Daily Citizen*, October 13, 1966.

48 Mildred Hamilton, "It's a very good year for Alice," *San Francisco Examiner*, January 31, 1975.

CHAPTER 17: ROBERT KENDALL MCNIE

Interviews: Sandy Boucher, Imogene Gieling, Jane Kristiansen, PAL, Fred Lyon, Maureen Looney Mather, Morissa McNie, Robert McNie Jr., Patty O'Grady, Deborah Sparks, Peter Stansky, Til Brunswick Stewart.

1 AA to LJ, December 18 [1964].

2 N, September 24, 1965.

3 Susan Wood, "Stories of Love and Loss," *Washington Post*, January 21, 1979.

4 N, July 9, 1964.

5 N, August 15, 1964.

6 "like a stone": Imogene Gieling to CS.

7 AA to Peter Davison, December 27, 1964.

8 N, June 1, 1966.

9 "*You're wasting*": N, February 4, 1965; "*addicted*": N, August 7, 1965; "*Bob and I seem*": AA to Peter Davison, "Wednesday" [May 26, 1965]; "*rather simple*": N, August 22, 1965.

10 N, June 14, 1966.

11 Fran Renoe, "North of the City, Where Nature Holds Command," *California Living, San Francisco Examiner*, August 1, 1965; Kelsey Keith, "Paradise at the End of the World: An Oral History of Sea Ranch," February 20, 2019, www.curbed.com/2019/2/20/18231590/sea-ranch-northern-california-sonoma-county-coast-history.

12 N, March 8, 1965.

13 Ibid., May 22, 1965.

14 Ibid., August 27, 1965.

15 Ibid., November 17, 1965.

16 Ibid., June 28, 1966.

17 Ibid., December 3, 1965.

18 Ibid., June 6, 1966.

19 AA to HMS and Diana Steele, June 27, 1968.

20 AA to LJ, September 8, 1967.

21 AA to HMS and Diana Steele, September 15, 1966.

22 Ibid., February 18, 1967.

23 Ibid., November 22, 1966.

24 "*I've a surprise*": Ibid., April 5, 1967; "*their shared adoration of his sex*": Ibid., May 3, 1967.

25 Bob's house on the Truckee River was featured in Richard Von Warton's article "Lighthearted Idea from California Ski Lodges," *House & Garden* 126, no. 4 (December 1964), 162–64.

26 AA to LJ, September 8, 1967.

27 Ibid., July 9 [1969].

28 "*They lay together*": N, May 3, 1967; "*bodily family warmth*": "My First and Only House," *RT*, 193.

CHAPTER 18: THE A B D C E FORMULA

Interviews: Virginia Breier, Stephen Brown, Linda Chown, PAL, Maureen Looney Mather, Robert McNie Jr., Lincoln Pain, Louis Pain.

1   Segal to AA, September 6, 1966.

2   AA to Matson, September 9, 1966.

3   Segal to AA, September 18, 1967.

4   Kemeny to AA, November 21, 1969.

5   AA to Matson, June 11, 1968.

6   *rejections*: "Susan" at the Curtis Publishing Company to Matson, November 29, 1967; Leonhard Dowty to Matson, September 19, 1967; Phyllis Sari Levy to Matson, May 18, 1967.

7   AA to Matson, June 11, 1968.

8   Letters between AA and Peter Matson, spring 1968.

9   AA, "Why I Write," 275.

10 AA to Kay Bonetti, American Audio Prose Library, 1987.

11 "*novelist's prerogative*": Rosellen Brown, "Stories of Dreams Lost" (review of *BG*), *Chicago Sun-Times*, [1979]; "*sense of an entire life*": Bruce Cook, "Sketching life portraits in just a few pages" (review of *RR*), *Detroit News*, [1980]; "*the architecture*": Julie Bosman, "Alice Munro, Storyteller, Wins Nobel in Literature," *New York Times*, October 11, 2013.

12 Leona Sherman, "A Conversation with Alice Adams," *San Francisco Bay Guardian*, November 19–26, 1980, 14.

13 Elizabeth Gips, *Scrapbook of a Haight-Ashbury Pilgrim: Spirit, Sacraments, and Sex 1967-68:* lists.village.virginia.edu/lists_archive/sixties-l/2794.html.

14 Manso, *Mailer*, 407–8; AA to Peter Davison, May or June [26,] 1965; NM, Speech for Berkeley Teach-In, May 21, 1965, rpt. in NM, *Cannibals and Christians* (New York: Dial, 1966), 67–82.

15 AA to Nancy Webb, June 3, 1968.

16 Ibid., March 6, 1968.

17 Maureen Looney recalled hearing about Robbie's plan to "suspend himself from the Golden Gate Bridge" when she came for dinner with Alice and Bob at their apartment.

18 Sherman, "A Conversation with Alice Adams," 15.

CHAPTER 19: DISINHERITED

Interviews: Elaine Badgley Arnoux, Sandy Boucher, Virginia Breier, Stephen Brown, Alyce Denier, Jewel DeRoy, Phillip Galgiani, Jane Kristiansen, PAL, Maureen Looney Mather, Morissa McNie, Robert McNie Jr., Phyllis Mufson, Nancy Oakes, Lincoln Pain, Louis Pain, Diana Steele, Tom Wilson, VW.

1 AA, comment in *American Voices: Best Short Fiction by Contemporary Authors*, selected by Sally Arteseros (New York: Hyperion, 1992), 1.
2 HMS to AA, August 14, 1969.
3 LJ to AA, July 29, 1970.
4 AA to LJ, July 9, 1969, and August 19, 1969.
5 HMS to AA, October 7, 1970.
6 "*connoisseur of good food*": Keller and Selig, *Hispanic Studies in Honor of Nicholson B. Adams*, 12; "*put his pipe*": James Street Jr., letter to the editor, *Chapel Hill Weekly*, October 7, 1970, 3.
7 Joan Smith, "Go Ask Alice," *San Francisco Examiner Magazine*, October 22, 1995, 14–15.
8 "*Nic always slapped*": N, January 21, 1967; "*Do what you want*": "Caroline," MS, HRC.
9 AA to LJ, September 24, 1970.
10 Orange County, North Carolina, Estates Division, File and Docket 70-E-168, Film 72-8-283. The will was dated May 8, 1958.
11 "*I told Dotsie*" and "*[Nic] always saw me*": AA to LJ, January 21, 1971; *who had dared:* LJ to AA, January 14, 1971.
12 "*like most guilty*": N, March 24, 1971; "*the most marvelous*": AA to LJ, May 24, 1971.
13 AA to Kay Bonetti, American Audio Prose Library.
14 AA, comment in *American Voices: Best Short Fiction*, 1.
15 Correspondance between AA and Peter Matson, HRC.
16 AA to Max Steele, April 26, 1971.
17 *NM's attack on RKM:* AA to PAL, February 4, 1971; Frances Moffatt, "Who's Who," *San Francisco Chronicle*, February 5, 1971; Herb Cain, "Herb Cain," *San Francisco Chronicle*, February 9, 1971; AA, "A Famous Friend," incomplete story outline in N, February 6, 1971.
18 AA to LJ, March 4, 1971.
19 AA to Peter Manso, 1983, TS, HRC; Manso, *Mailer*, 557.
20 AA to LJ, March 4, 1971.
21 *Town Bloody Hall*, film by Chris Hegedus and D. A. Pennebaker, 1979: https://phfilms.com/films/town-bloody-hall/.
22 AA to LJ, May 24, 1971.
23 Germaine Greer, *The Female Eunuch* (New York: McGraw-Hill, 1971), 241.
24 Leona Sherman, "A Conversation with Alice Adams," *San Francisco Bay Guardian*, November 20, 1980, 15.
25 Postcards, PAL to ML; AA to LJ, March 12, 1971.
26 N, May 9, 1974.
27 AA to HMS, June 27, 1968.

28 AA to VW, September 15, 1976.

29 Sandy Boucher, "Alice Adams—a San Francisco novelist who is into her third book," *San Francisco*, October 1978, 130–31.

30 Talbot, *Season of the Witch*, 62.

31 N, December 28, 1970.

32 AA to Richard Carr, September 1981.

33 Paul Jacobs to NM, January 29, 1969, HRC.

34 N, May 27, 1971.

35 Robert Hemenway to AA, October 29, 1969; Peter Matson to AA, November 10, 1969.

36 N, August 4, 1971.

37 AA to LJ, May 24, 1971.

38 LJ to AA, September 19, 1971.

39 HMS to AA, September 28, 1971.

40 WMA, ed. *Prize Stories, 1971: The O. Henry Awards* (New York: Doubleday, 1971), xi–xii.

41 AA to LJ, July 2, 1972, and August 10, 1972.

42 Ibid., July 2, 1972; LJ to AA, July 30, 1972.

43 Cornelisen to Cyrilly Abels, September 13, 1972, Vassar College Special Collections.

44 AA to WMA, April 29, 1972.

45 Boucher, "Alice Adams," 131.

46 AA to LJ, November 1, 1972.

47 Ibid., February 6, 1973.

48 Charles E. Martin, "Trummy Young: An Unfinished Story," *Second Line* 30 (Summer 1978): 35.

49 AA to Ann Cornelisen, August 14, 1973.

50 AA to LJ, October 30, 1973.

51 AA to HMS, June 22, 1973.

52 VW, memo [1973], Knopf papers, HRC.

CHAPTER 20: EDITORS AND FRIENDS

Interviews: JCA, Rachel DuPlessis Blau, Sandy Boucher, Carolyn Burke, Linda Chown, Beverly Dahlen, Kathleen Fraser, Blair Fuller, DJ, Randall Kenan, Ella Leffland, Bryant Mangum, Morissa McNie, Robert McNie Jr., PAL, Lincoln Pain, Louis Pain, David Perlman, Tom Schmidt, VW, Al Zelver.

1 AA to HMS, September 5, 1975.

2 Correspondence and editorial records, AA collection and Knopf collection, HRC.

3 AA to VW, December 18, 1974.

4 LJ to AA, January 20, 1972, March 22, 1972, August 25, 1972; AA to HMS, November 5, 1971; HMS to AA, September 29, 1973.

5 AA to LJ, October 27, 1971.

6 AA in *American Voices*, 1.

7 Bill Webb to AA [February 1975].

8　AA to JCA, January 14, 1975; JCA to AA, [spring 1974] and [January 1975]; AA to JCA, February 7, 1975.

9　Willie T. Weathers to AA, April 22, 1975.

10　AA to VW, March 3, 1976.

11　HMS to AA, July 23, 1975.

12　Ibid., September 13, 1976.

13　AA to HMS, September 22, 1976.

14　HMS, "About Love and Grasshoppers," *Redbook*, May 1977, 40, 126–27, 206ff. "Another Love Story" is collected in *The Hat of My Mother: Stories by Max Steele* (Chapel Hill: Algonquin Books, 1988), 47–61.

15　Gloria Steinem, "The City Politic," *New York*, March 10, 1969.

16　AA to Margery Finn Brown, quoting Patricia Zelver, December 17, 1973. Stanford-grad Zelver lived near Palo Alto, and Alice had recently given a party in celebration of her second novel, *The Happy Family.*

17　AA to Ann Cornelisen, July 20, 1978, Vassar College Special Collections.

18　AA to HMS, June 22, 1973.

19　*Squaw Valley Writers' Conference:* Max Steele to AA, September 1, 1974; AA to Max Steele, September 10, 1974; AA to LJ, September 12, 1974; VW to AA and RKM, August 26, 1974.

20　AA to VW, December 7, 1974.

21　Patricia Holt, "PW Interviews: Alice Adams," *Publishers Weekly*, January 16, 1978, 9. *Publishers Weekly* spelled incorrectly the names of Margery Finn Brown (as Margaret) and Laurie Colwin (as Lori Coleman).

22　AA to "Helen," July 28, 1975. AA's letter refers to an interview she recently gave Helen (no last name given) for a publication called "Bookletter" that I have not found.

23　*Prize Stories 1972: The O. Henry Awards*, ed. William M. Abrahams (New York: Doubleday, 1972), 209.

24　AA to VW, December 7, 1974.

25　AA told HMS (AA to HMS, March 13, 1978) that her story "The Last Married Man" is "sort of about" Nichols, herself, and Leffland.

26　*"very sane":* AA to Michael Silverblatt, "Bookworm," KCRW (Los Angeles), 1989; *"least satisfactory":* AA to VW, November 12, 1974.

27　AA to DJ, May 19, 1975.

28　AA to VW, May 20, 1975.

29　N, June 30, 1977.

30　AA to HMS, May 6, 1974.

31　AA to VW, December 28, 1974.

32　LJ to AA, March 13, 1975.

33　AA to LJ, March 18, 1975.

34　AA to JCA, February 28, 1975.

35　Marge Piercy, "The Grand Coolie Damn," originally published 1969, now at www.feministezine.com/feminist/modern/The-Grand-Coolie-Damn.html.

36　Beverly Dahlen, "The Naming of *HOW(ever)*," unpublished MS, 2011.

37　"Frances Jaffer Reads Her Poetry," interview with Shelley Messing for WBAI radio, Pacifica Radio Archives, archive.org/details/pacifica_radio_archives-IZ1422 (recorded 1982).

38 AA to HMS, January 22, 1974.

39 Ibid., May 6, 1974.

40 AA to LJ, June 16, 1975.

41 Denise Sullivan, "History Buff Peter Linenthal Is a Potrero Hill Treasure," *San Francisco Examiner*, November 25, 2018, www.sfexaminer.com/history-buff -peter-linenthal-potrero-hill-treasure/.

42 N, December 26, 1975.

43 AA to VW, January 27, 1976; AA to HMS, February 10, 1976.

44 Typed and handwritten journal entry by Morissa McNie, n.d, collection of Serena Burman.

45 Correspondence saved by Morissa McNie, collection of Serena Burman.

46 N, January 24, 1976.

47 AA to VW, June 18, 1977.

48 AA to Staige Blackford, April 19, 1976.

49 AA, "Powerful, Vivid Novel of Two Doomed Sisters" (review of *The Easter Parade* by Richard Yates), *San Francisco Chronicle-Examiner*, October 17, 1976.

CHAPTER 21: VERY COLETTE

Interviews: Sally Arteseros, Patricia Holt, Frances Kiernan, Edwina Evers Leggett, PAL, Diane Johnson, Carolyn See, Anne Mollegen Smith, Diana Steele, Oliver Steele.

1 AA to VW, August 16, 1976.

2 AA, "On Turning Fifty."

3 Ibid.; AA to HMS, February 1, 1977.

4 AA to VW, October 2, 1974.

5 Wayne Warga, "Alice Adams," *Los Angeles Times Book Review*, November 16, 1980.

6 VW to AA, May 24, 1976.

7 Ibid., September 16, 1976.

8 AA to VW, September 24, 1976.

9 Draft of letter from VW to AA, October 20, 1976, HRC Knopf papers.

10 VW to AA, December 26, 1976.

11 VW to Robert Gottlieb [1977], Knopf papers, HRC.

12 *"all went well"*: AA to HMS, February 1, 1977; *"she is one of those 30-year-old geniuses"*: Wayne Warga, "A sophisticated author gets by with help from her friends," *Los Angeles Times*, November 16, 1980, 335.

13 AA to LJ, February 3, 1977.

14 AA to DJ, September 14, 1976; AA to Max Steele, November 16, 1976; AA to LJ, October 23 and November 18, 1976.

15 Cara Chell, "Succeeding in Their Times: Alice Adams on Women and Work," *Soundings: An Interdisciplinary Journal* 68 (Spring 1985): 62–71.

16 AA to Frances Kiernan, July 2, 1977, NYPL.

17 John Leonard, "The Poet and the Painter," *New York Times*, January 10, 1978; Anne Tyler, "Mother and Daughter and the Pain of Growing Up," *Detroit News* February 5, 1978; Tyler, "Two Women," *Quest/78* no. 2 (March–April 1978): 84–85; Lynne Sharon Schwartz, "Listening to Billie by Alice Adams," *San Francisco Review of Books* [1978], 26–27.

18 Grover Sales, "A Boswell of the Neurotic Intelligentsia," *Los Angeles Times*, January 29, 1978; HMS, "'Listening to Billie': Novel's Bright Design States Its Message," *Charlotte Observer*, January 29, 1978.

19 Barbara Grizzuti Harrison, "The Clairvoyance of Passion—Alice Adams's 'Listening to Billie,'" *Ms.* 6, no. 8 (February 1978), 31–33.

20 Nancy Faber, "Out of the Pages," *People*, March 27, 1978, 52–53.

21 AA to HMS, March 13, 1978.

22 AA to Frances Kiernan, April 3, 1978.

23 AA, "Endjokes," *Harper's*, May 1976.

24 Richard Ford, "American Beauty (Circa 1955)," *New York Times Book Review*, April 9, 2000.

25 AA, "Powerful, Vivid Novel of Two Doomed Sisters," *San Francisco Chronicle-Examiner*, April 17, 1976; correspondence between Yates and AA, November–December, 1976, HRC.

26 AA to VW, 18 March 1977.

27 Blake Bailey, *A Tragic Honesty: The Life and Work of Richard Yates* (New York: Macmillan, 2004), 482.

28 AA, "Loving Odette" (review of *Beautiful Women, Ugly Scenes* by C. D. B. Bryan), *New York Times Book Review*, August 28, 1983, 10.

29 AA, "In Love with L.A.," *San Francisco Sunday Examiner & Chronicle*, April 24, 1977, 40; Eve Babitz to AA, April 28, 1977.

30 *"rather simple-minded"*: AA to Alison Lurie, October 25, 1978; AA, "Diane Johnson, delving deep into humanity" (review of *Lying Low*), *Chicago Sun-Times*, October 29, 1978, 11.

31 Reviews and associated correspondence HRC.

32 Scott Spenser to AA, August 27, 1979; AA to HMS, August 28, 1979.

CHAPTER 22: *BEAUTIFUL GIRL*

1 AA to Ann Cornelisen, May 18, 1976.

2 AA to LJ, January 25, 1979.

3 AA to Dmitri Vedensky, February 5, 1979.

4 Mickey Friedman, "Alice Adams: Rewriting life into fiction," *San Francisco Examiner*, February 5, 1979, 22.

5 Laurie Stone: "Short Circuits," *Village Voice*, April 2, 1979, 87; Susan Wood: "Stories of Love and Loss," *Washington Post*, January 21, 1979.

6 AA to LJ, February 2, 1978; AA to HMS, March 13, 1978; HMS to AA, March 2, 1978.

7 *"[Diana] is better looking"*: HMS to AA, March 2, 1978; *"I honestly don't think"*: AA to LJ, March 23, 1978; *"Most people are unsuited"*: AA to LJ, August 28, 1978.

8 AA, "At First Sight: Love and Liking, a Memoir."

9 HMS to AA, November 16, 1979; AA to HMS, January 1, 1979.

10 *"Old beaux":* AA to LJ, March 23, 1978; *political column:* Joseph Kraft, "Italian Communism," *San Francisco Chronicle*, April 22, 1976, 35; *"If you are in Rome":* AA to DJ, May 13, 1976.

11 AA to HMS, April 23, 1979; AA to LJ, April 26, 1979; AA to LJ, April 30, 1979; LJ to AA, May 20, 1979.

12 AA to LJ, May 23, 1979; LJ to AA, May 31, 1979; AA to LJ, June 4, 1979; AA to HMS, June 6, 1979; AA to LJ, June 23, 1979; LJ to AA, July 7, 1979; LJ to PAL, July 12, 1979; AA to HMS, July 13, 1979; AA to LJ, July 19, 1979.

13 *"a terrible letter":* AA to LJ, June 9, 1979.

14 Dotsie's gifts and the phone call from HMS as described in AA to LJ, June 23, 1979.

15 AA to HMS, July 13, 1979.

16 HMS to Ingram Merrill Foundation [1964].

17 AA to LJ, September 5, 1979.

18 Ibid., September 8, 1979.

19 VW to AA [November, 1979], HRC, Knopf papers.

20 AA to Alice Quinn, October 29, 1979; AA to DJ, October 24, 1979.

21 AA to Frances Kiernan, November 2, 1979.

22 Ann Cornelisen to AA, June 14, 1979. Cornelisen sent AA Trentin's office address, adding, "His home address seems to be a state secret and he's not wrong, with kidnappings et al."

23 AA to DJ, December 18, 1979.

24 AA interview with Marilyn Scharine, 1987.

25 AA to Diane Johnson, December 18, 1979; Neil Feineman, "An Interview with Alice Adams," *StoryQuarterly* 11 (1980): 27–37.

26 "Dr. Lucie N. Jessner: Psychiatrist, Teacher Dies," *Washington Post*, December 23, 1979, B6; AA, "The Loss of Lucie Jessner," TS, enclosed in AA to HMS, January 1, 1980.

27 N, December 4, 1979.

CHAPTER 23: REWARDS

Interviews: Jean Anderson, Sandy Boucher, Doris Dörrie, Frances Gendlin, Frances Kiernan, Anne Lamott, PAL, Robert McNie Jr., Lynne Sharon Schwartz.

1 N, October 13, 1979.

2 AA to LJ, July 19, 1979, and September 8, 1979; AA interview with Marilyn Scharine.

3 To the Ingram Merrill Foundation in 1964, HMS wrote: "But the parties and the vivid picture one gets of various interiors, always by the well-chosen suggestion of an artist never the appraising eye of an auctioneer, are really only counterpoints to the chaos and devastation which is going on inside this girl who knows, in the best sense, that love is the only important thing in the world."

4 Lee Upton, "Changing the Past: Alice Adams' Revisionary Nostalgia," *Studies in Short Fiction* 26, no. 1 (Winter 1989): 33–44.

5 Laurie Stone, "Shlong Song" (review of *RR*), *Village Voice*, November 26, 1980.

6 Ibid.

7 Leona Sherman, "A Conversation with Alice Adams," *San Francisco Bay Guardian*, November 20, 1980, 13.

8 Ella Leffland to AA, June 11, 1980.

9 Wayne Warga, "A Sophisticated author gets by with help from her friends," *Los Angeles Times*, November 16, 1980.

10 RP to AA, June 19, 1980.

11 Karen Evans, "Alice Adams: An Intimate Portrait, with Cats," *San Francisco Examiner Image*, May 3, 1987, 19.

12 Mickey Friedman, "Alice Adams: Rewriting life into fiction," *San Francisco Examiner*, February 5, 1979, 22.

13 Boucher, "Alice Adams," *San Francisco*, October 1978, 132.

14 AA to Ann Cornelisen, May 26, 1981, Vassar College Special Collections.

15 Upton, "Changing the Past."

16 Wayne Warga "Alice Adams," *Los Angeles Times Book Review*, November 16, 1980; Boucher, "Alice Adams," 131.

17 AA to DJ and John Murray, January 29, 1980; AA to HMS, February 21, 1980.

18 Alice Adams, *MEX*, 27–30; correspondence, AA and Doris Dörrie, HRC; Millicent Dillon, "Writer Alice Adams cuts to the core in her fiction and in her reading," *Stanford Campus Report*, June 9, 1982, 9.

19 VW to AA [spring 1979]; *Alice Walker's comment:* AA, interview with Marilyn Scharine.

20 Ann Cornelisen to Cyrilly Abels, September 13, 1974, Vassar College Special Collections.

21 *Alaska:* AA to Doris Dörrie, July 10, 1981; AA to Dollie Summerlin, 1981.

22 AA to Frances Kiernan [1982], NYPL.

23 Daniel Stern, "Take Back Your Mainstream," *New York Times Book Review*, January 19, 1986.

24 Joyce Carol Oates, ed., *Joyce Carol Oates: The Oxford Book of American Short Stories* (New York: Oxford University Press, 1992), 571.

25 "Introduction," *Prize Stories 1982: The O. Henry Awards*, William Abrahams, ed. (Garden City, NY: Doubleday, 1982), x–xi.

CHAPTER 24: A FATEFUL AGE

Interviews: Michelle Blake, Richard Carr, John L'Heureux, Alison Lurie, Dennis McFarland, Carolyn See.

1 I. Magnin ad in *San Francisco Chronicle*, November 5, 1981, 11.

2 AA to RP, October 27, 1981.

3 AA, *MEX*, 23–27, 91–93.

4 Reviews of *TSYA*: Norbert Blei, *Chicago Sun-Times*, June 13, 1982; Paul Gray, "Balances," *Time*, April 19, 1982; Judi Goldenberg, "Two Collections Reveal Feminist-Tinged Writing," *Richmond News Leader*, June 2, 1982; Diane Ketchum, *Oakland Tribune*, August 15, 1982.

5 AA to Carolyn See, May 2, 1982; Carolyn See, "23 Stories Form Necklace of Thought," *Los Angeles Times*, April 13, 1982.

6 Jacob Stockinger, "Dr. Jake's Art & Book Takes: Alice Adams' women are mainstream, marginal," *Madison Capital Times*, June 4, 1982.

7 AA, "Colette Surpasses Even Her Own Heroines in Courage" (review of *Letters from Colette*), *San Francisco Chronicle,* November 23, 1980.

8 AA to RP, February 1, 1982; AA to HMS, February 6, 1982.

9 AA interview with Don Swaim, September 17, 1984.

10 Eve Babitz, *Eve's Hollywood* (1974; New York: New York Review Books Classic, 2015), 188.

11 AA to JCA, March 30, 1982.

12 AA to Jacqueline Rice, May 6, 1977; AA to VW, December 9, 1981; AA to Scott Crawford, December 19, 1981.

13 Dennis McFarland, memorial remarks for Alice Adams, New York, 1999, TS by Dennis McFarland.

14 Marjorie Leet Ford, "Writing a Writer," unpublished essay.

15 Robert Allen Papinchak, a scholar who wrote about Sherwood Anderson, arranged the program. AA gave presentations at the college and in the city. In addition to airfare and a room at the Imnaha Hotel, she earned a $1,200 stipend.

16 AA to HMS, April 23, 1983.

17 N, April 1982.

18 Ibid., July 8, 1982.

19 AA to HMS, July 5, 1982, and August 26, 1982.

20 Carolyn See wrote to AA on November 17, 1982, that DeRoy's daughter commented "*off-handedly* that her Dad's car had been to hell and back about 20 times already."

21 AA to RP, February 1, 1982.

22 Bryant Mangum's *Understanding Alice Adams* (Columbia: University of South Carolina Press, 2019), 61–63, offers an excellent analysis of this story.

23 AA to Richard Carr, September 28, 1981.

24 Terry Trucco, "The First 'Alice Adams Woman,'" *International Herald Tribune*, February 18, 1983, Weekend section, 7W.

25 Carolyn Kizer, "Alice Adams Explores the Women We Feared to Become," *San Jose Mercury News*, September 16, 1984, 22–23.

26 N, July 28, 1983.

27 AA, "My First and Only House," *RR*.

28 AA to HMS, July 5, 1982.

29 HMS to AA, May 22, 1987.

30 AA to HMS, July 9, 1983; HMS to AA, July 8, 1983.

31 AA to HMS, August 10, 1983; AA to JCA, September 9, [1983].

32 N, summer 1983.

33 AA to JCA, October 15, 1983.

34 Details of trip to Portugal from N; AA's passport stamps; AA to Bryant Mangum, November 28, 1983; Vera Futscher Pereira, *Retrovisor*, 170–78. Adams's story "Sintra" draws on this 1983 trip as well as on her return to Portugal in spring 1984.

35 N, "Lecture—50 Reasons," November 16, 1983.
36 AA to JCA, October 15, 1983.

CHAPTER 25: *SUPERIOR WOMEN*

Interviews: JCA, Kay Bonetti, Ken Butigan, Richard Carr, Trent Duffy, Deirdre English, Gary Giddins, PAL, Bryant Mangum, Vera Futscher Pereira.

1 AA to HMS, June 28, 1984.
2 AA to Bryant Mangum, July 5, 1984.
3 N, May 24, 1984.
4 AA to HMS, June 28, 1984.
5 AA, "The Wild Coasts of Portugal," *Geo* 6, no. 11 (August 1984): 56–65+.
6 Vera Futscher Pereira, *Retrovisor*, 180; newspaper clipping in N, July 24, 1984; JAC to AA, August 1984. N, August 31, 1980, says, "V. dead."
7 AA to JCA, November 16, 1984.
8 Vera Futscher Pereira sent these papers to me in 2011; they will join the letters from Pereira to AA at HRC. The two poems by AA that he saved are:

Letter from San Francisco

A cool grey city breathes the salt
Of summer fog; hills rise above
The spreading, sullen sea:
It is expected weather.

But one day breaks the list of days:
A wild bright day, splendid, sun-split.
Grey is white! The whole sea blinds
With blue. Our senses snatch
At air—at eucalyptus lemon scents,
Mediterranean. Unreal.
We think of unvisited Greek islands,
And Portuguese beaches.

This day should not have come—as grief
Comes back, that should be dead. Recalled,
You pierce my cool grey days with light.

Loss

Entered with wind, and mist,
Foghorns that mourn invade this blue,
This haunted room,
All night.

Your dark face haunts the dark
Behind my eyes. A tentative [attempt] at love
Subsides—to tears against the blind
Blond shoulder of a stranger.

My whole house screams with loss.

9 AA to Richard Carr, October 23, 1984.
10 N, August 31, 1984.
11 *"about being lonely . . ."*: AA to Lavina Calvin, "Friday morning" [spring, 1984]; *death of Lavina*, AA to Bryant Mangum, August 16, 1984; *"It seemed (to me) a willed death": MEX*, 39.
12 AA to JCA, October 29, 1984.
13 "A Woman's 'Naked and the Dead,'" *Ms.*, September 1984, 28.
14 "Life After Radcliff" [*sic*], *New York Times Book Review*, September 23, 1984, 9.
15 Carolyn Kizer, "The Women We Feared to Become: Alice Adams," *Picking and Choosing: Essays on Prose* (Cheney: Eastern Washington University Press, 1995), 15.
16 John Updike, "No More Mr. Knightleys," *Odd Jobs: Essays and Criticism* (New York: Alfred A. Knopf, 1991), 345–50.
17 John Updike, *Self-Consciousness* (New York: Knopf, 1989), 143–45.
18 Roberta Smoodin, "Rewards of Alice Adams," *Los Angeles Herald Examiner*, September 28, 1980, F5.
19 AA "Protest Correspondence" folder, HRC; writings and papers of Ken Butigan, Pledge of Resistance collection, Graduate Theological Union, Berkeley, California.
20 William Cooney, "Jessica Mitford's Very Civil Disobedience," *San Francisco Chronicle*, May 31, 1985, 10.
21 Marie Pastrick to AA, July 20, 1985, HRC.
22 N, 1985, HRC.
23 Ibid., June 17, 1985, and June 6, 1986.
24 AA to Alison Lurie, n.d.
25 N, January 16, 1986.

CHAPTER 26: FAME AND FORTUNE

Interviews: PA, Trent Duffy, Deirdre English, Sydney Goldstein, Patricia Holt, Gerald Howard, PAL, Beverly Lowry, Daphne Merkin, Lincoln Pain, Louis Pain, Owen Renik.

1 N, January 30–31, 1986.
2 N, January 31, 1986.
3 Karen Evans, "Alice Adams: An Intimate Portrait, with Cats," *San Francisco Examiner Image*, May 3, 1987, 25.
4 Harold Gilliam and Phil Palmer, *The Face of San Francisco* (New York: Doubleday, 1960), 79; Susan Dinkelspiel Cerny, *An Architectural Guidebook to San Francisco*

and the Bay Area (Layton, UT: Gibbs Smith, 2007), 63; Robert Olmstead and T. H. Watkins, *San Francisco's Architectural Heritage* (San Francisco: Chronicle Books, 1968).

5 AA, "America's Room, and Mine," [1991]. The essay was written for *House & Garden* but I have not been able to locate the issue in which it appeared.

6 Daphne Merkin, "A Neurotic's Neurotic," *New York Times Magazine*, December 30, 2007.

7 Owen Renik, eulogy for Allen Wheelis, 2007.

8 N, January 8, 1986.

9 Ibid., February 26, 1994.

10 Ibid., May 26, 1987.

11 Ibid., March 31, 1986.

12 Ibid., April 10 and 15, 1987.

13 AA to LJ, May 25, 1974.

14 AA to Diane Johnson, December 18, 1979.

15 Richard Rodriguez, "Sodom: Reflections on a Stereotype," *San Francisco Examiner Image*, June 10, 1990, 10–16.

16 AA to Frances Kiernan, December 1, 1978.

17 Rodriguez, "Sodom: Reflections on a Stereotype."

18 Patricia Holt, "Adams' Return," *San Francisco Chronicle*, April 8, 1985.

19 Beverly Lowry, "Women Who Do Know Better," *New York Times Book Review*, September 1, 1985.

20 AA to Lowry and Bausch, November 21, 1985; AA to Margery Finn Brown, November 5, 1985.

21 AA to Margery Finn Brown, November 5, 1985.

22 Joyce Carol Oates to AA, February 4, 1983.

23 N, February 25, 1986.

24 Email from Peter Volpe to PAL, April 6, 2011.

25 Gish Jen, "Gender and the Business of Fiction," Radcliffe Institute, www.youtube.com/watch?v=OSfskTbU6TI, 9:30 minutes; Eugenia Williamson, "Cover Girls: How lipstick, bathing suits, and naked backs discredit women's fiction," *Boston Globe*, June 28, 2014.

26 John Russell, "Alex Katz and the Art that Conceals Its Art," *New York Times*, March 14, 1986.

27 Calvin Tomkins, "Painterly Virtues: Alex Katz's life in art," *New Yorker*, August 27, 2018, 58.

28 N, October 25, 1986.

29 AA, interview with Kay Bonetti, American Audio Prose Library.

CHAPTER 27: THINGS FALL APART

Interviews: JCA, PA, Elaine Badgley Arnoux, Carol Field, John Field, Frances Gendlin, Lucy Gray, Diane Johnson, Robert Flynn Johnson, Frances Kiernan, Anne Lamott, PAL, Beverly Lowry, Morissa McNie, Robert McNie Jr., John Murray, Jay Schaefer, Deborah Sparks, Peter Stansky, Mark Strand, Mary Ross Taylor, David Thomson, Tom Wilson Jr., Betsy Wing.

1 AA quoted by Mervyn Rothstein in "On Death and the Job of Arriving There," *New York Times*, May 19, 1988, B3.

2 N, January 16, 1987.

3 Ben Yagoda, *About Town* (New York: Scribner, 2000), 412–16.

4 N, January 10, 1987.

5 UCSF medical records, obtained with permission of the McNie family.

6 AA to Beverly Lowry, March 16, 1987.

7 Ibid.

8 Ibid.

9 N, March 24–25, 1987.

10 Contract, Knopf, HRC, and Robert McNie to Herb Caen, April 8, 1987.

11 AA to Beverly Lowry, March 16, 1987; N, March 23–28, 1987.

12 Mark Strand to AA, 1988.

13 *Maine:* AA to HMS, May 27, 1987.

14 *Bob's depression:* AA to HMS, May 27, 1987; AA to JCA, May 29, 1987; UCSF medical record.

15 AA, commencement address, UC Berkeley English Department, 1987.

16 N, June 22, 1987.

17 *Essay:* AA, *MEX*, 209–14.

18 AA, N, passim.

19 *Notebooks:* N, July 18, 1987–September 1, 1987.

20 AA to Morissa McNie, October 7, 1987 (collection of Serena Burman).

21 UCSF admissions report, November 3, 1987; Morissa McNie correspondence and notes, collection of Serena Berman.

22 Morissa McNie to Deborah Sparks [December 1987], collection of D. Sparks.

23 PAL to D. Sparks (quoting Morissa McNie), October 10, 1987, collection D. Sparks.

24 UCSF medical records; notes taken by Morissa McNie, collection Serena Berman.

25 N, November 17, 1987.

26 Ibid., November 19, 1989.

27 Ibid., November 15, 1987.

28 AA to Bryant Mangum, March 15, 1988.

29 N, January 21, 1988.

30 Ibid., December 18, 1987, and January 7, 12–13, and 15–24, 1988; Dr. David Rabin to AA, "Saturday," 1988.

31 Ibid., February 5, 1988.

32 On the jury for the National Book Award were Gloria Naylor, Hilma Wolitzer, and Richard Eder. Those three jurors agreed that their deliberations would remain private, according to Wolitzer in email to CS, March 17, 2018.

33 Julian Moynahan to AA, November 10, 1987, HRC; Julian Moynahan to Pulitzer Prize Board, December 26, 1987, Pulitzer Prizes Collections, Columbia University Libraries; "Black Writers in Praise of Toni Morrison," *New York Times Book Review*, January 24, 1988. Richard Eder served on both the 1987 National Book Award jury and the 1988 Pulitzer Prize for Fiction jury.

34 Elaine Kendall, "Stories Explore the Variety of Response," *Los Angeles Times*, October 10, 1989.

35 Penelope Rowlands, "Our Own Colette," *San Francisco Focus*, March 1991, 24.

36 David Deitz and Robert Popp, "Boas Pleads Guilty in Teen Sex Case—Jail Unlikely Under Plan by Lawyers," *San Francisco Chronicle*, October 21, 1988. Boas was one of fourteen customers, including businessmen and police officers, indicted for patronizing "the decade-old brothel operation."

37 *Examiner* Staff, "Mugger Slashes Arm of Examiner Columnist," *San Francisco Examiner and Chronicle*, August 20, 1989; Stephanie Salter, "Alice Adams: Fierce, sexy, generous," *San Francisco Examiner*, July 1, 1999.

38 AA to JCA, November 12, 1989.

39 AA to HMS, January 25, 1989.

40 Caroline Drewes, "The Next Chapter: Alice Adams embarks on new travels, new projects and a life lived alone," *San Francisco Examiner*, October 25, 1989, B1–B5.

41 N, October 19, 1989.

CHAPTER 28: BOOK OF BOB

Interviews: PA, Elaine Badgley Arnoux, Stephen Brown, Millicent Dillon, Trent Duffy, Willard Fee, Mary Gaitskill, Lucy Gray, DJ, Robert Flynn Johnson, Frances Kiernan, PAL, Marcus Livingston, Beverly Lowry, Alison Lurie, Scott Massey, Morissa McNie, Robert McNie Jr., John Murray, Judith Rascoe, Richard Rodriguez, Penelope Rowlands, Carolyn See, Deborah Sparks, Mary Ross Taylor, David Thomson, Amanda Urban, Hilma Wolitzer.

1 Christopher Lehman-Haupt, "The Rising and Falling in One Family," *The New York Times*, March 21, 1991; Rowlands, "Our Own Colette," 24.

2 Lynne Sharon Schwartz to VW, April 2, 1991, Knopf papers, HRC.

3 Carolyn See, "Spoiled in Paradise," *Washington Post Book World*, March 10, 1991.

4 Carol Fowler, "New Novel Attacks Values of 1980s," *West County Times*, May 7, 1991.

5 Patricia Holt, "Literary Evenings for AIDS Research," *San Francisco Chronicle*, April 26, 1990.

6 N, August 12, 1989.

7 Sigmar Warner Wilson to AA, September 11, 1989.

8 AA, ed., *The Best American Short Stories of 1991* (Boston: Houghton Mifflin, 1991).

9 Correspondence between AA and *Redbook*, HRC.

10 N, August 13, 1991, states that she is writing a piece on gray hair for *Allure* for $5,000.

11 Marjorie Leet Ford, unpublished essay.

12 William Neuman, "Surprises South of the Border," *San Francisco Examiner and Chronicle*, October 27, 1991, 3; Carolyn See to AA, October 22, 1991.

13 AA to Alison Lurie, September 8, 1990.

14 Seattle: N, March 24, 1991.

15 Sidney Hedelman, *Collected Works* (Benfleet Hall@EntertainmentHighway.com, 2011), ii.

16 N, February 20, 1990.

17 Ibid., February 18–24, 1990.

18 Ibid., February 5–9, 1990.

19 Ronald B. Elkin, MD, to Bill Fee, MD, October 15, 1992, Stanford medical records.

20 N, September 19, 1990.

21 Penelope Rowlands, "The Adams Family," *W*, April 29–May 6, 1991, 32.

22 N, May 21, 1992; John Updike, ed. *A Century of Arts and Letters* (New York: Columbia University Press, 1998), vii-xii, 264–91.

23 VW to AA, September 20, 1992.

24 Robert Taylor, "Adams' elegant, complex 'Almost Perfect,'" *Boston Globe*, July 28, 1993.

25 Morissa McNie to Deborah Sparks, [summer] 1993, collection of Deborah Sparks.

26 Kenneth Baker, "Critics Preview Yerba Events—Surprises in first Galleries show," *San Francisco Chronicle*, October 11, 1993, E1.

27 Morissa McNie and Deborah Sparks to CS.

28 N, September 7, 1992.

29 Ibid., September 22, 1992; medical records, Mount Zion Hospital, UCSF. The medical record reports there was "a large left nasal mass that completely occluded the airway and extended in the region of the sephnoethmoid recess to the nasal pharynx. This nasal mass was polypoid in some portions but had a friable and granular texture as well. The disease of the left paranasal sinuses was more extensive. This included disease of the entire ethmoid labyrinth extending to the sphenoid. There was gross disease along the lateral nasal wall in the region of the osteomeatal complex. There was trapped mucopurulent fluid behind this mass lesion."

30 Ibid., September 22, 1992.

CHAPTER 29: SICK

Interviews: JCA, Steven Barclay, Ruth Gebhart Belmeur, Michelle Blake, Millicent Dillon, Willard Fee Jr., Carol Field, John Field, Frances Gendlin, Lucy Gray, Robert Flynn Johnson, Frances Kiernan, Edwina Evers Leggett, PAL, Dennis McFarland, Derek Parmenter, Sandra Russell, Mark Singer, Diana Steele, David Thomson, Betsy Wing.

1 Daniel Simon, MD, to Willard Fee Jr., MD, late 1995, as reported to CS by Dr. Fee by telephone, July 1, 2011.

2 Mark Singer, MD, to CS by telephone, December 2, 2010.

3 Stanford University Hospital medical records; N, [October–November] 1992.

4 Radiation oncology report by Rami Ben-Yosef, MD, Stanford records, February 11, 1993.

5 N, November 13 and January 11, 1993.

6 Ibid., December 14, 1992.

7 Ibid., November 11, 1992.

8 Ibid., January 24, 1993.

9   The story appeared as "A Shadow on the Brain" in *Allure*, September 1993, 170–73, 209. To Adams's consternation, the magazine presented the piece as nonfiction.

10 N, February 15, 1993.

11 Ibid., October 27, 1995; Daniel Simon, MD, to Willard Fee Jr., MD, late 1995, as reported to CS by Dr. Fee by telephone, July 1, 2011.

12 Edwina Evers Leggett to CS.

13 Joan Smith, "Ask Alice," *San Francisco Examiner Magazine*, October 22, 1995, 13.

14 N, April 8, 1993.

15 Ibid., "Montana," July 22, 1993.

16 Dennis McFarland, memorial remarks for Alice Adams, 1999.

17 Details of trip east in N, October 12–19, 1993.

18 Lee Smith, "Going South," *New York Times Book Review*, October 8, 1995, 19.

19 Joan Smith, "Ask Alice," *San Francisco Examiner Magazine*, October 22, 1995, 13–14.

20 Joan Smith Cramer to CS, November 29, 2016.

21 N, October 12, 1994.

22 Nan Talese to AA, October 18, 1994.

23 N, October 25, 1994.

24 AA to Donald Hall [July 11], 1994.

25 Mavis Gallant to AA [1997].

26 Elisabeth Sherwin, "Adams Gives a Reading, Encourages Others to Write," *Davis Virtual Market*, July 14, 1996.

27 Mark Singer, MD to CS by telephone, December 2, 2010.

28 Francine Prose, "Hippocratic Oafs," *Los Angeles Times*, June 8, 1997.

29 *Correspondence and reviews regarding MM*: HRC.

30 Edward Said, *On Late Style: Music and Literature Against the Grain* (New York: Pantheon Books, 2006), 12.

CHAPTER 30: THE AGE CARD

Interviews: JCA, PA, Michelle Blake, Millicent Dillon, Stephen Drewes, Deirdre English, Thaisa Frank, Mary Gaitskill, Adam Hochschild, Arlie Hochschild, Diane Johnson, Frances Kiernan, Anne Lamott, Ella Leffland, PAL, Phillip Lopate, Alison Lurie, Dennis McFarland, John Murray, Derek Parmenter, Bernard Rosenthal, Penelope Rowlands, William Jay Smith, Elizabeth Spencer, Susan Sward, Amanda Urban.

1   "The Last Lovely City," *LLC*.

2   N, August 27–28, 1990.

3   Envelope of photos taken by Barbara Chevalier and saved by Bernard Rosenthal from Felix Rosenthal's papers.

4   AA to Elizabeth Love, November 11, 1996.

5   Lucy Gray, "Naming the Homeless," artist's website, lucygrayphotography.com /photo_gallery/naming-the-homeless/.

6   AA to LJ, May 23, 1979.

7   N, February 4, 1995.

8 AA to Ella Leffland, February 24 [1999].

9 Cathleen Medwick, "Visions and Revisions: An Editor's Dream," *New York Times*, October 27, 2006, F1.

10 Mary Gaitskill, "Alice Adams," Salon.com, June 9, 1999.

11 N, August 11 and 14, 1996.

12 AA to Betty Love White, August 16, 1996.

13 AA to JCA, July 28, 1998.

14 N, November 3 and 14, 1996; AA, "The Best Revenge," *Boulevard* 13, no. 3 (Spring 1998): 82–91.

15 Stephen Drewes to CS.

16 AA to JCA, July 28, 1998.

17 Notebook entries about DP: November 10, 1995, May 1, 1996, February 26, 1997, July 28, 1998, and passim.

18 AA to Betty White Love, February 3, 1999.

19 AA to RP, September 19 [1995].

20 Video of "The Twenty-First Century: Defining the Challenges," Radcliffe College, June 6, 1997, Schlesinger Library, Radcliffe Institute for Advanced Study.

21 Philip Anasovich, memorial talk for Alice Adams, June 27, 1999.

22 AA to Adeline Naiman, April 12, 1997.

23 AA, "At First Sight: Love and Liking, a Memoir."

24 AA to Alison Lurie, "Tuesday" [April 1998]; AA to Don Hall [April 1998].

25 AA, "Why I Left Home: Partial Truths."

26 AA to JCA, July 28, 1998.

27 N, April 12, 1998; AA to Don Hall, n.d.; AA to Alison Lurie, "Tuesday" [April 1998].

28 AA to Carolyn See, August 22, 1998; photograph, PAL.

29 AA to Donald Hall, May 21 and 28, 1996, Hall papers, University of New Hampshire.

30 AA to Alison Lurie, July 30, 1996, and Alison Lurie to AA, August 22, 1996.

31 N, October–December 1998; Jaicks to AA, December 28, 1998.

32 Ibid., March 28, 1999.

33 Ibid., December 5, 1998; AA, "First Date" and "Her Unmentionables."

34 Susan Bolotin, "Semidetached Couples," *New York Times Book Review*, February 14, 1999; Alison Baker, "Collection Simmers Below Surface," *Sunday Oregonian*, February 14, 1999; Sallie Bingham, "Private Lives," *Santa Fe New Mexican*, March 21, 1999; Randall Curb, "When Is a Story More Than a Story? A Fiction Chronicle," *Southern Review* 35, no. 3 (Summer 1999): 608; Rita D. Jacobs, "The Last Lovely City," *World Literature Today* 73, no. 4 (Autumn 1999): 735; Carol Lake, "Prisoners of Passivity: Malaise Afflicts Characters in Adams' Short Stories," *Austin American-Statesman*, March 7, 1999.

35 *Mary Gordon:* N, February 9, 1999; Mavis Gallant to AA, March 11, 1999.

36 AA to DJ [April 1999]; Donald Hall to AA, May 7, 1999.

37 AA to RP, May 5, 1999, Columbia University archives.

38 AA, "Sending Love," MS and TS, AA Papers, HRC.

39 Jack Leggett, memorial for AA, June 27, 1999.

40 UCSF medical records. In an email to CS in July 2018, Dr. Thomas Addison commented, "I regret that I was wrong about the cardiac cath ruling out a dissection. A CT scan of the aorta would have been a better study which I suspect was not done. I suspect that today should the same symptom complex arise, a CT with the contrast would have been ordered to evaluate the possibility of a thoracic aneurysm dissection."

EPILOGUE

Interviews: PA, JCA, Blair Fuller, Sydney Goldstein, Diane Johnson, Frances Kiernan, Edwina Evers Leggett, PAL, Morissa McNie, Robert McNie Jr., John Murray, Judith Rascoe, David Reid, Andrea Richardson, Christy Rocca, Penelope Rowlands, Carolyn See, Amanda Urban, Victoria Wilson.

1 Peter Applebom, "Alice Adams, 72, Writer of Deft Novels," *New York Times*, May 28, 1999, B11; Elaine Woo, "Alice Adams; Novelist, Short-Story Writer," *Los Angeles Times*, May 29, 1999, B8; Susan Sward and Sam Whiting, "Alice Adams—Renowned S.F. Novelist," *San Francisco Chronicle*, May 28, 1999, D8.

2 David Kipen, "A Street Named Alice Adams," *San Francisco Chronicle*, June 3, 1999, E1, E7.

3 Memorial audio recording, June 27, 1999, HRC.

4 The entire poem appears in note 8, chapter 25.

5 Richard Poirier, "Remembering Alice Adams," unpublished TS, PAL collection.

6 Randall Curb, "Did Alice Adams lead a double life in literature?" *Raleigh News & Observer*, December 31, 2000, 4G.

7 Diana Steele to PAL, July 9, 2011.

Photo Credits

INTERIOR

5   Courtesy of Peter Adams Linenthal.
53 Copyright Dorothy Funk Clark, courtesy of Judith Clark Adams.
53 Copyright Dorothy Funk Clark, courtesy of Judith Clark Adams.
67 Courtesy of St. Catherine's School.
162 North Carolina Collections, University of North Carolina Library at Chapel Hill.
189 Courtesy of Vera Futscher Pereira.
194 Courtesy of Peter Adams Linenthal.
297 Courtesy of Peter Adams Linenthal.
329 Copyright Marion Ettlinger.
344 Copyright Joyce Ravid.
398 Copyright Irene Fertik.
407 Courtesy of Peter Adams Linenthal.
481 Copyright Christine Alicino.

INSERT

1   Courtesy of Peter Adams Linenthal.
2   Courtesy of Peter Adams Linenthal.
3   Courtesy of Peter Adams Linenthal.
4   Courtesy of LaBudde Special Collections, UMKC University Libraries.
5   Courtesy of Peter Adams Linenthal.
6   Courtesy of Peter Adams Linenthal.
7   Courtesy of Oliver Steele.
8   Courtesy of Peter Adams Linenthal.
9   Courtesy of Peter Adams Linenthal.

10 Courtesy of Vera Futscher Pereira, *Retrovisor: Um Album de Família.*
11 Courtesy of Vera Futscher Pereira.
12 Courtesy of Peter Adams Linenthal.
13 Photograph © Harry Fong.
14 Courtesy of Peter Adams Linenthal.
15 Courtesy of Peter Adams Linenthal.
16 Courtesy of Peter Adams Linenthal.
17 Courtesy of Peter Adams Linenthal.
18 Photograph © K. William Leffland, courtesy of David See.
19 Photograph © Alison Lurie.
20 Courtesy of Carolyn See.
21 Courtesy of Peter Adams Linenthal.
22 Courtesy of Peter Adams Linenthal.

Index

Note: works by Alice Adams are indicated by the title followed by type of work in parentheses; i.e., (novel); (story).

About the Author

Carol Sklenicka is the author of *Raymond Carver: A Writer's Life*, which was named of one of the ten best books of 2009 by the *New York Times Book Review*. She grew up in California in the late 1960s. She attended college in San Luis Obispo, California, and earned a PhD at Washington University in St. Louis, where she studied with Naomi Lebowitz, Stanley Elkin, and Howard Nemerov. Her stories, essays, and reviews are widely published. She lives with her husband, poet and novelist R. M. Ryan, near the Russian River in Northern California.